Gender Considerations and Influence in the Digital Media and Gaming Industry

Julie Prescott
University of Bolton, UK

Julie Elizabeth McGurren
Codemasters, UK

A volume in the Advances in Human and Social
Aspects of Technology (AHSAT) Book Series

Information Science
REFERENCE
An Imprint of IGI Global

Managing Director:	Lindsay Johnston
Production Editor:	Jennifer Yoder
Development Editor:	Austin DeMarco
Acquisitions Editor:	Kayla Wolfe
Typesetter:	Thomas Creedon
Cover Design:	Jason Mull

Published in the United States of America by
Information Science Reference (an imprint of IGI Global)
701 E. Chocolate Avenue
Hershey PA 17033
Tel: 717-533-8845
Fax: 717-533-8661
E-mail: cust@igi-global.com
Web site: http://www.igi-global.com

Library of Congress Cataloging-in-Publication Data

Library of Congress Cataloging-in-Publication Data

Gender considerations and influence in the digital media and gaming industry /
Julie Prescott and Julie Elizabeth McGurren, editors.
     pages cm
 Includes bibliographical references and index.
   ISBN 978-1-4666-6142-4 (hardcover) -- ISBN 978-1-4666-6143-1 (ebook) -- ISBN 978-1-4666-6145-5 (print & per-petual access) 1. Women in the professions. 2. Women in computer games--Case studies. 3. Women in the mass media industry--Case studies. 4. Women--Employment. I. McGurren, Julie Elizabeth, 1972-
   HD6054.G45 2014
   331.4'81302231--dc23
                            2014013828

This book is published in the IGI Global book series Advances in Human and Social Aspects of Technology (AHSAT) (ISSN: 2328-1316; eISSN: 2328-1324)

British Cataloguing in Publication Data
A Cataloguing in Publication record for this book is available from the British Library.

For electronic access to this publication, please contact: eresources@igi-global.com.

Advances in Human and Social Aspects of Technology (AHSAT) Book Series

Ashish Dwivedi
The University of Hull, UK

ISSN: 2328-1316
EISSN: 2328-1324

MISSION

In recent years, the societal impact of technology has been noted as we become increasingly more connected and are presented with more digital tools and devices. With the popularity of digital devices such as cell phones and tablets, it is crucial to consider the implications of our digital dependence and the presence of technology in our everyday lives.

The **Advances in Human and Social Aspects of Technology (AHSAT) Book Series** seeks to explore the ways in which society and human beings have been affected by technology and how the technological revolution has changed the way we conduct our lives as well as our behavior. The AHSAT book series aims to publish the most cutting-edge research on human behavior and interaction with technology and the ways in which the digital age is changing society.

COVERAGE

- Activism & ICTs
- Computer-Mediated Communication
- Cultural Influence of ICTs
- Cyber Behavior
- End-User Computing
- Gender & Technology
- Human-Computer Interaction
- Information Ethics
- Public Access to ICTs
- Technoself

IGI Global is currently accepting manuscripts for publication within this series. To submit a proposal for a volume in this series, please contact our Acquisition Editors at Acquisitions@igi-global.com or visit: http://www.igi-global.com/publish/.

Titles in this Series

For a list of additional titles in this series, please visit: www.igi-global.com

Examining Paratextual Theory and its Applications in Digital Culture
Nadine Desrochers (Université de Montréal, Canada) and Daniel Apollon (University of Bergen, Norway)
Information Science Reference • copyright 2014 • 419pp • H/C (ISBN: 9781466660021) • US $215.00 (our price)

Exchanging Terrorism Oxygen for Media Airwaves The Age of Terroredia
Mahmoud Eid (University of Ottawa, Canada)
Information Science Reference • copyright 2014 • 347pp • H/C (ISBN: 9781466657762) • US $195.00 (our price)

Women in IT in the New Social Era A Critical Evidence-Based Review of Gender Inequality and the Potential for Change
Sonja Bernhardt (ThoughtWare, Australia)
Business Science Reference • copyright 2014 • 274pp • H/C (ISBN: 9781466658608) • US $195.00 (our price)

Gamification for Human Factors Integration Social, Education, and Psychological Issues
Jonathan Bishop (Centre for Research into Online Communities and E-Learning Systems, Belgium)
Information Science Reference • copyright 2014 • 362pp • H/C (ISBN: 9781466650718) • US $175.00 (our price)

Emerging Research and Trends in Interactivity and the Human-Computer Interface
Katherine Blashki (Noroff University College, Norway) and Pedro Isaias (Portuguese Open University, Portugal)
Information Science Reference • copyright 2014 • 580pp • H/C (ISBN: 9781466646230) • US $175.00 (our price)

Creating Personal, Social, and Urban Awareness through Pervasive Computing
Bin Guo (Northwestern Polytechnical University, China) Daniele Riboni (University of Milano, Italy) and Peizhao Hu (NICTA, Australia)
Information Science Reference • copyright 2014 • 440pp • H/C (ISBN: 9781466646957) • US $175.00 (our price)

User Behavior in Ubiquitous Online Environments
Jean-Eric Pelet (KMCMS, IDRAC International School of Management, University of Nantes, France) and Panagiota Papadopoulou (University of Athens, Greece)
Information Science Reference • copyright 2014 • 325pp • H/C (ISBN: 9781466645660) • US $175.00 (our price)

Uberveillance and the Social Implications of Microchip Implants Emerging Technologies
M.G. Michael (University of Wollongong, Australia) and Katina Michael (University of Wollongong, Australia)
Information Science Reference • copyright 2014 • 509pp • H/C (ISBN: 9781466645820) • US $265.00 (our price)

IGI GLOBAL
DISSEMINATOR OF KNOWLEDGE
www.igi-global.com

701 E. Chocolate Ave., Hershey, PA 17033
Order online at www.igi-global.com or call 717-533-8845 x100
To place a standing order for titles released in this series, contact: cust@igi-global.com
Mon-Fri 8:00 am - 5:00 pm (est) or fax 24 hours a day 717-533-8661

Editorial Advisory Board

Table of Contents

Foreword xiv

Preface xvi

Acknowledgment xxx

Section 1
Education, Computers, and Gaming
Profile 1: Carrie Warwick
Profile 1: Carrie Warwick
Profile 2: Elinor Townsend
Profile 3: Anna Ljungberg
Profile 4: Jo Daly

Chapter 1
From the "Damsel in Distress" to Girls' Games and Beyond: Gender and Children's Gaming.............1
Alyson E. King, University of Ontario, Canada
Aziz Douai, University of Ontario, Canada

Chapter 2
Women and Men in Computer Science: The Role of Gaming in their Educational Goals...................18
Jill Denner, Education, Training, Research, USA
Eloy Ortiz, Education, Training, Research, USA
Linda Werner, University of California, Santa Cruz, USA

Chapter 3
The Only Girl in the Class! Female Students' Experiences of Gaming Courses and Views of the
Industry 36
Lauren Elliott, University of Bolton, UK
Julie Prescott, University of Bolton, UK

Section 2
The Experience of Women Working in the Computer Games Industry: An International
Perspective
Profile 5: Fiona Cherbak
Profile 5: Fiona Cherbak
Profile 6: Sheri Graner Ray
Profile 7: Lindsey "Lindz" Williamson Christy
Profile 8: Julie McGurren
Profile 9: Althea Deane
Profile 10: Dianne Botham
Profile 11: Joy Dey
Profile 12: Hannah Payne

Chapter 4
A Look inside the Current Climate of the Video Game Industry 82
   Vachon M.C. Pugh, Electronic Arts, USA

Chapter 5
The Experiences of Women Working in the Computer Games Industry: An In-Depth Qualitative
Study 92
   Julie Prescott, University of Bolton, UK
   Jan Bogg, University of Liverpool, UK

Chapter 6
Career Development among Japanese Female Game Developers: Perspective from Life Stories of
Creative Professionals 110
   Masahito Fujihara, Senshu University, Japan

Chapter 7
Women's Participation in the Australian Digital Content Industry 125
   Anitza Geneve, Southbank Institute of Technology, Australia

Section 3
Future Outlook
Profile 13: Sabine Hahn
Profile 13: Sabine Hahn
Profile 14: Elizabeth Richardson
Profile 15: Faye Windsor-Smith
Profile 16: Phil Goddard

Chapter 8
Professional Socialization in STEM Academia and its Gendered Impact on Creativity and
Innovation 156
   Gloria-Sophia Warmuth, Vienna University of Economics and Business, Vienna
   Edeltraud Hanappi-Egger, Vienna University of Economics and Business, Vienna

Chapter 9
Lessons from the STEM Sector 175
    Vachon M.C. Pugh, Electronic Arts, USA

Chapter 10
A Framework for Addressing Gender Imbalance in the Game Industry through Outreach 186
    Monica M. McGill, Bradley University, USA
    Adrienne Decker, Rochester Institute of Technology, USA
    Amber Settle, DePaul University, USA

Chapter 11
Female Game Workers: Career Development, and Aspirations 206
    Julie Prescott, University of Bolton, UK
    Jan Bogg, University of Liverpool, UK

Final Thoughts and Concluding Comments 223

Related References 256

Compilation of References 284

About the Contributors 306

Index 310

Detailed Table of Contents

Foreword xiv

Preface xvi

Acknowledgment xxx

Section 1
Education, Computers, and Gaming
Profile 1: Carrie Warwick
Profile 1: Carrie Warwick
Profile 2: Elinor Townsend
Profile 3: Anna Ljungberg
Profile 4: Jo Daly

Chapter 1

From the "Damsel in Distress" to Girls' Games and Beyond: Gender and Children's Gaming.............1
Alyson E. King, University of Ontario, Canada
Aziz Douai, University of Ontario, Canada

In this chapter, the authors critically assess the gendered nature of the products developed by the computer gaming industry. The chapter takes a historiographical approach to examining the nature of children's video and computer games as a type of toy that immerses children into current gender stereotypes even as they hold the potential for social change. New ways of bridging the gap between stereotypes and change is explored through a virtual world for children. In addition to an introductory section, the chapter is organized in three main sections: First, the authors place existing computer and video games into a broad and historical context. Second, the chapter takes into consideration feminist critiques of video games for adults. Third, the authors analyze the case of WebkinzWorld, a toy-based social-networking portal offering less gendered video game environments for kids. The authors argue that this mixed method analysis is important not only for computer game designers and marketers who aim to appeal to broad demographics, but also for educators, parents, and caregivers who need to understand the underlying or hidden messages of games for children.

Chapter 2

Women and Men in Computer Science: The Role of Gaming in their Educational Goals...................18
Jill Denner, Education, Training, Research, USA
Eloy Ortiz, Education, Training, Research, USA
Linda Werner, University of California, Santa Cruz, USA

Playing digital games is described as a pathway to computer science (CS) classes and majors, but not all gamers want to study CS. The goal of this chapter is to explore which gaming motivations and practices are most strongly related to an interest in studying computer science, and whether the connection between gaming and computer science is similar for men and women. The data are from 545 male and female gamers taking an introductory computer science class at one of 15 community colleges in the US. Survey responses were analyzed to provide a picture of what, how often, and why they play, and interviews from 39 of the most avid gamers were analyzed for why and how they play. The results show that, on average, men play more frequently than women, and there are gender differences in the type of games they like to play and why they play them. However, playing more frequently was not associated with greater interest in studying CS for either gender. Interest in CS was highest among men who were motivated to play in order to increase skills, be with friends, connect with the game features, and by the art or graphics. However, CS interest was highest among women who consider themselves to be more serious gamers, play racing and puzzle games, play on a game console, and are motivated by fun, relaxation and social interaction. The results can inform efforts to increase the number of women that pursue computer science. The chapter concludes with recommendations for future research on how game play and interest in CS are related.

Chapter 3
The Only Girl in the Class! Female Students' Experiences of Gaming Courses and Views of the
Industry 36
Lauren Elliott, University of Bolton, UK
Julie Prescott, University of Bolton, UK

Four female students studying a games course at one UK University took part in a qualitative study of face-to-face semi-structured interviews. Although a small sample, the study provided an interesting insight into that experiences of the females on the course as well as their views of entering (or at least potentially entering) the male dominated computer games industry. The findings related by the chapter reveal the females choose to study games because they enjoyed playing games. Despite all participants experiencing the course positively, there was some apprehension about going into the industry. Interestingly, the study suggests the male dominated working environment may be off-putting to women, even to women studying and interested in going into that area of work. The main themes that emerged in regard to the negativity associated with the industry were the long hours culture and potential sexism within the industry.

Section 2
The Experience of Women Working in the Computer Games Industry: An International Perspective
Profile 5: Fiona Cherbak
Profile 5: Fiona Cherbak
Profile 6: Sheri Graner Ray
Profile 7: Lindsey "Lindz" Williamson Christy
Profile 8: Julie McGurren
Profile 9: Althea Deane
Profile 10: Dianne Botham
Profile 11: Joy Dey
Profile 12: Hannah Payne

Chapter 4

A Look inside the Current Climate of the Video Game Industry 82
Vachon M.C. Pugh, Electronic Arts, USA

The issue of the lack of women in the video game industry has been a hot topic for quite some time. For the past twelve years, Game Developer Magazine has published their annual Game Developer Salary Survey, which not only lists the average salaries for each department; but also breaks down each department by gender. By examining the salary surveys for the past four years (2009-2012), an initial assessment can be made on the amount of women working in the game industry, and in what disciplines. The purpose of this chapter is to assess the current climate of the video game industry, and briefly discuss possible causes of the lack of women in this particular field.

Chapter 5

The Experiences of Women Working in the Computer Games Industry: An In-Depth Qualitative
Study 92
Julie Prescott, University of Bolton, UK
Jan Bogg, University of Liverpool, UK

This chapter provides a unique understanding of women working in the computer games industry. In depth interviews were undertaken with seven female game workers based in the UK. The women were interviewed as part of a larger study focusing on women in this male dominated industry. The issues detailed in this chapter focus on the industry as a viable career for women, the experience of being a woman working in games and the working environment; including work life balance issues, experiences of discrimination and experiences of sexism. The research discussed is related to attracting and retaining women in games development. The issues are of relevance to employers, professional bodies, policy makers and researchers of the games industry and the wider ICT and SET industries. Recommendations from the findings and future research directions are provided.

Chapter 6

Career Development among Japanese Female Game Developers: Perspective from Life Stories of
Creative Professionals 110
Masahito Fujihara, Senshu University, Japan

The purpose of this chapter is to clarify the process of female developers' career development and their characteristics based on the life stories of creative professionals employed in the Japanese gaming industry. This study followed a one-to-one semi-structured interview format and employed a qualitative methodology. The survey was conducted on 21 female game developers who have more than five years work experience in the Japanese gaming industry. One of the most important analytical results of the study is the behavioral characteristics of female game developers in their career development are that they support persons who have similar problems in the workplace, and they contribute to mentor game developers in the next generation. In conclusion, female game developers do not have clearly defined career goals; however, they have the ability to alter their work situation, and evaluate and manage it if needed. Therefore, it is important that female game developers have diverse role models. Further research directions are discussed.

Chapter 7
Women's Participation in the Australian Digital Content Industry 125
    Anitza Geneve, Southbank Institute of Technology, Australia

There is a need to understand the phenomenon of women's under-representation in the Australian Digital Content Industry (DCI) workforce. This chapter presents the findings from an Australian case study where both women working in the industry and industry stakeholders were interviewed for their insight into the influences on women's participation. The rich empirical data and findings from the case study are interpreted using the Acts of Agency theory—an original theory by the author of this chapter. As the chapter reveals there are five 'Acts of Agency' (containing 10 agent-driven mechanisms) identified as influencing women's participation. Agent-driven mechanisms recognise the causal effect of people themselves; that is, the role individuals play in their participation.

Section 3
Future Outlook
Profile 13: Sabine Hahn
Profile 13: Sabine Hahn
Profile 14: Elizabeth Richardson
Profile 15: Faye Windsor-Smith
Profile 16: Phil Goddard

Chapter 8
Professional Socialization in STEM Academia and its Gendered Impact on Creativity and
Innovation 156
    Gloria-Sophia Warmuth, Vienna University of Economics and Business, Vienna
    Edeltraud Hanappi-Egger, Vienna University of Economics and Business, Vienna

The chapter focuses on internal professionalization processes in STEM academia and their impact on creativity and innovation capacity. The discussion looks at how internal structures and value systems in STEM academia are used to shape the professional self-understanding of members. Exemplified by a higher education institution in the field of science, engineering, technology and math we show how gendered exclusion and inclusion is established structurally. Restrictive and rigid professional scripts and role expectations are identified as the main obstacles to greater potentials for creativity and innovation.

Chapter 9
Lessons from the STEM Sector 175
    Vachon M.C. Pugh, Electronic Arts, USA

The purpose of this chapter is to examine possible causes such as lack of interest, lack of skill/ability, and anticipated work/family conflict (WFC), in addition to analyzing successful recruitment tactics that have brought more women into various other male dominated fields in an attempt to solve this problem. Results of the literature review show that the main contributing factors for the lack of women within the sector are lack of confidence in skills and abilities, lack of female industry role models, and lack of available mentorship and community outreach programs for interested women. This chapter takes this information into consideration and makes possible suggestions for the industry on how to remedy this problem.

Chapter 10

A Framework for Addressing Gender Imbalance in the Game Industry through Outreach 186

Monica M. McGill, Bradley University, USA
Adrienne Decker, Rochester Institute of Technology, USA
Amber Settle, DePaul University, USA

Though the lack of diversity in the game industry workforce has received a great deal of attention recently, few initiatives have been implemented to address it. In particular, gender composition in the game industry workforce and among students studying games at post-secondary institutions is highly imbalanced, with an approximate 9 to 1 ratio of male to female students. This chapter considers three key aspects: 1) the current demographics of the game industry, 2) the effects of gender imbalance on the game industry and one of its current pipelines, and 3) a potential framework to address the imbalance. The proposed outreach strategy is informed by a discussion of established frameworks for initiating change in related fields. The chapter concludes with suggestions for future research to address the gender imbalance in the game industry and its pipeline.

Chapter 11

Female Game Workers: Career Development, and Aspirations 206

Julie Prescott, University of Bolton, UK
Jan Bogg, University of Liverpool, UK

Understanding the career factors that influence women's career aspirations in male-dominated occupations is important for increasing women's progression within these occupations. This chapter assesses the impact of career influencers on career aspirations of women working in the male-dominated computer games industry. An online questionnaire obtained international data from 450 women working in the computer games industry. A structural equation model was employed to investigate the influencers. Findings suggest that to increase women's career development and career aspirations within the computer games industry, self-efficacy, attitudes towards career barriers, work-life balance attitudes, person-environment fit and job satisfaction are crucial.

Final Thoughts and Concluding Comments 223

Related References 256

Compilation of References 284

About the Contributors 306

Index 310

Foreword

In 1995, in Los Angeles California, I walked up on to the stage at SIGGRAF and gave a presentation on girls and games. My talk was quite controversial, even preposterous, as it was considered common knowledge at the time that girls and women did not and would not play computer games. In fact, the idea that we should even consider women when talking about games was met with disbelief and derision.

Today, no one would dream of arguing that women don't play computer games. Study after study has shown that not only do women gamers make up nearly half of all game players but that they are a lucrative market unto themselves. The game industry is fairly falling over itself in an attempt to cater to this fast growing market segment.

With this complete turnaround in the game industry's attitude toward female game players, one would assume the same thing would have happened in the makeup of the game industry personnel. This, however, is not the case.

Traditional industry, outside the game industry, has had diversity measures in place for over 20 years. This has produced a wealth of information that has proved over and over again that diversity in the workforce is good for business. The fascinating thing about diversity is the way it improves business; not by just by improving efficiency or streamlining processes, but by increasing creativity and inspiring innovation (Forbes Insights, 2012).

Creativity and innovation - these are the two key things the game industry must have to succeed. Yet, the game industry is still primarily a monoculture.

That is why this book is so keenly important to the industry right now. Through this book, Prescott and McGurren clearly paint a picture of where women currently are in the games industry. Using empirical studies and theoretical work the book explains their situation and explores the forces at work to keep them there. The books use of individual stories to highlight the studies brings a fascinating personal note which humanizes the situation and gives it an immediacy that drives home the message.

Finally, this book not only concisely explains the current situation and provides thought provoking analysis of how and why the industry got into this shape, but it also provides ample opportunity to explore avenues for moving forward. This is the key for this industry. If we want the creativity and innovation that comes with diversity, we must understand how we got where we are and then be open to exploring how to change our situation. Works like this one are keystones in that journey.

Sheri Graner Ray
Women in Games International, USA & Zombie Cat Studios, USA

Sheri Graner Ray *is the Founder and CEO of Zombie Cat Studios, an independent game studio and consulting firm. She started in the game industry in 1989 as a writer/designer and designer and has worked with such companies as EA, Cartoon Network, the US Navy and most recently, Schell Games. Sheri co-founded Women in Games International and authored the book Gender Inclusive Game Design - Expanding the Market. In 2005 she was awarded the IGDA's Game Developers' Choice Award for her work in gender and games.*

REFERENCES

Insights, F. (2012). *Diversity & inclusion: Unlocking global potential.* Retrieved from.http://images. forbes.com/forbesinsights/StudyPDFs/global_diversity_rankings_2012.pdf

Preface

This preface describes both the need for, and purpose of this book – current work in the field of gender and the computer games industry. The book's guiding message comes from the perspective that there is a need for women to be involved in the production of computer games and all forms of technology development at all levels. We will explore the issues women face working in this relatively new industry and present some UK-based research as well as research that has recently been conducted globally in the USA, Australia, and Japan. In general, the message of our book is that females should be involved in the development of such an economically and culturally influential industry. Although the book includes women working in other digital media industries, the focus is on women working in the computer games industry.

INTRODUCTION

Women and men are segregated within the workforce, and although women are increasing in the workforce, they are segregated into certain jobs (horizontal segregation) and at lower levels (vertical segregation) within sectors and organisations. Occupational segregation is an important issue and can be detrimental to women (see Prescott & Bogg, 2012 for an overview of the issues). Women face a number of barriers which hinder their career choices and career progression, this is especially so for women working in male-dominated occupations and careers. For instance, Eagly and Carli (2003) found women in male-dominated organizations suffered from gender stereotypes more than women in more gender-neutral or female-dominated organizations. This does not appear to be the case for men working in female-dominated occupations, who often gain from working in gender-incongruent industries. Although there is some research that suggests men are penalized for not adhering to gender norms (Heilman, et al., 2004; Heilman & Okimoto, 2007), it is not to the same extent as women. With regard to the identity of women working in male-dominated work environments and occupations, it appears women have conflict due to gendered behavior expectations. Social role theory as proposed by Eagly (1987) is an important theory when discussing expectations. According to this theory, due to conflicting gendered expectations of what behavior is appropriate, both men and women experience disadvantages when they participate in gender-incongruent behavior. However, the disadvantages are particularly detrimental to women's careers, as leadership is associated with masculinity women's career progression and advancement is negatively impacted. Gender role identity is a pertinent issue for women in gender-incongruent occupations and industries, with research (i.e. Gottfredson, 1981; Cejka & Eagly, 1999; Kawakami, et al., 2000; Willemson, 2002; Oswald, 2008) suggesting women need to adopt a more masculine identity in order to fit into the male-dominated environment.

There is a need for more women in a number of male-dominated areas, especially SET (Science, Engineering, and Technology) and ICT (Information and Communication Technology). Computer games could be a potential way forward in achieving more female representation in not just the computer games industry but also other computer-related industries (Prescott & Bogg, 2014). The relatively new industry of computer games is itself highly male-dominated, with recent figures suggesting that women represent just 4% of the UK's games industries workforce (Skillset, 2009). Similarly low figures have been reported in the USA (Gourdin, 2005), Canada (Dyer-Whitheford & Sharman, 2005), and Australia (Geneve, Christie, & Nelson 2009, also in this edition). Research has found a number of reasons for the underrepresentation of women in the SET sector. These reasons are similar to those that research has found exists in the computer games industry, in particular the long hours culture and the lack of flexible working practices available (Deuze, Martin, & Allen, 2007; Prescott & Bogg, 2010, 2011, 2012; Sweetser, Wyeth, McMahon, & Johnson, 2013). Sweetser, Wyeth, McMahon, and Johnson (2013) found from their research on women working in the Australian computer games industry that, aside from the reasons for the underrepresentation of women in the SET sector more generally, the games industry has a number of additional reasons for this underrepresentation. The games industry does not attract and retain women due to the additional reasons of a lack of information on careers in the industry, the gendered perception related to the industry and computer games generally, as well as parental perceptions of the industry. These act as additional barriers to women entering the games industry, so despite a number of similarities for the underrepresentation of women in the games industry compared to the wider ICT and SET sector, the industry itself is unique.

The computer games industry could potentially benefit from attracting a more diverse workforce and be viewed as a viable career to women by increasing the appeal of games to a more diverse gaming/gamer audience (Prescott & Bogg, 2014). The industry could widen its appeal through an increased awareness of the variety of roles and skills within the industry and through highlighting the benefits and rewards of working in such a creative, competitive, and growing industry (Prescott & Bogg, 2014). Computer games are important to today's society and significant both economically and culturally. In 2010 it was estimated that worldwide the industry was a US$41.9 billion industry (Vancouver Film School, 2010). Games are a mainstream form of entertainment with many titles outselling film releases. Indeed computer games have become one of the most popular leisure activities for children and adults in Western and Asian societies (Hartmann & Klimmt, 2006). According to the Entertainment and Software Association (ESA, 2012), in 2012 72% of American households played computer games. To illustrate the increasing impact of computer games over recent years, the ESA (2011a) reports that in 1996 the American entertainment and software industry sold about US$2.6 billion in sales revenue, and in 2009 sales were US$20 billion. Despite being a relatively new industry under the umbrella of the SET and ICT sectors, the computer games industry has become an important and established industry in itself. The impact of computer games has changed the media landscape and will continue to do so. The new media landscape includes digital technologies such as Web 2.0 applications, online dating, and mobile phone technologies. The computer games industry has become one of the biggest of the digital technology industries in both economic and cultural terms. To illustrate the magnitude of the industry, in 2009 games were one of the biggest forms of entertainment in Britain, outselling films (including going to the cinema and DVD sales; Wallop, 2009). *The Prince of Persia: The Sands of Time* is currently the highest grossing movie based on a computer game. Excluding DVD sales, the movie has made US$312,583,548 worldwide (Mai, 2010). The 5th *Grand Theft Auto* game in September 2013 is currently the world's biggest selling game, earning the games developers, Rockstar, US$800 million in the first day of release, US$1 billion in the first three days of release – faster than any other entertainment launch (CVG, 2013). The game made UK£65 million in revenue in the UK alone (CVG, 2013).

Recent figures suggest the games industry in America directly and indirectly employs more than 120,000 people in 34 states (ESA, 2011b). Canada's games industry earned approximately US$2 billion in 2008, which according to the VFS (2010) is more than many parts of the entertainment sector. The games industry is made up of a number of specialism's including development, production, design, level design, audio design, art, and testing. According to 2008 figures, the UK industry supports an estimated 28,000 jobs, directly and indirectly (Oxford Economics, 2008). The estimated turnover of the UK computer games industry in 2008 was UK£625 million, having a direct contribution to UK GDP (Gross Domestic Product) of approximately UK£400 million (Oxford Economics, 2008). More recently, the Vancouver Film School (2010) suggests that in 2009 the worldwide games industries worth stood at US$41.9 billion.

The games industry itself is an interesting industry and has developed in accordance with the popular demand of games themselves. The game industry has grown over approximately four decades from a small sector, niche market into a thriving multi-billion dollar industry and a mainstream entertainment choice for millions globally. Advances in both technology and the changing gamer demographic of the last decade have been instrumental in the evolution of the industry, which seems set to grow. The relatively new computer games industry has accelerated from small firms and individuals programming in their bedrooms to an industry dominated by multinational hardware producers. Despite the games industry being a global industry with game development companies in the UK, USA, Australia, Iceland, Brazil, and South Korea, to name but a few, it appears that the industry has three distinct geographical areas: North America, Europe, and Japan. These three distinct geographical areas produce cultural products distinct to their geographical area. The greatest difference in the nature of games occurs between Japan in the East and the American and European markets of the West. This cultural difference is worth noting in this preface since one of the chapters within this edition is investigating Japanese female game developers. It is therefore important to gain an understanding of the differences and similarities between this industry compared to the Western, American, and European markets.

The Japanese games industry is based on comic books, such as Manga, with the games sold in Japan being produced by Japanese producers, whereas the other two markets (the American and European) interrelate more (Johns, 2006). According to Mia Consalvo the game industry is "a hybrid encompassing a mixture of Japanese and American businesses and (more importantly) cultures to a degree unseen in other media industries" (Consalvo, 2006, p. 117). This hybrid of cultures is interesting, and in a case study of Japanese game publisher Square Enix, Consalvo found distinctions between what the company produces for its home market and what they successfully sell abroad. For instance, Consalvo found countries give characters a more "native" look and more "native" items, such as Asian objects in the Sims game.

Through a brief look at the history of computer games, it seems the American and Japanese markets have always had a close, yet competitive relationship. The first electronic game, *Tennis for Two*, was developed in 1958 by William Higginbotham at the US Department of Nuclear Energy's Brookhaven National Laboratory (Kline, et al., 2003). In 1977, Atari released the 2600 home computer console in America, whilst Nintendo released its first console in Japan. In 2004, it was reported that North America accounts for approximately 40% of the global games market, Europe nearly the same, with the remainder divided between Japan and the rest of Asia (DFC, 2004). The top game producing countries are the USA,

Japan, Britain, Germany, and France, followed by Canada (DTI, 2002, cited in Dyer-Whitheford & Sharman, 2005). Within Europe, Britain has the highest number of game development studios (ISFE, 2004, cited in Krotoski, 2004). More recent figures suggest that the UK games industry has 9900 employees (Oxford Economics, 2008), with just over two-thirds of these people working in games development and the remainder focused on publishing, marketing, and other core business functions.

It has been suggested that 10% of games make 90% of the money (Dyer-Whitheford & Sharman, 2005). This is because major game publishers prefer clones of proven hits rather than experimentation, as indicated by the "franchises" that dominate the bestseller lists (Dyer-Whitheford & Sharman, 2005), producing what Shaw terms a "narrow vision" (Shaw, 2010). Many games are based on other media, such as blockbuster films (i.e. *Enter the Matrix*), popular books (i.e. *Harry Potter*), and television programmes (i.e. *The Simpsons Road Rage*). What gamers play is also impacted by the design teams, who make and produce the games (Gansmo, Nordli, & Sorensen, 2003). In particular, it is argued that there is a male dominance in the culture of computer games generally, and more specifically in terms of the development of the games (Prescott & Bogg, 2014). Prescott and Bogg (2014) posit that all aspects of computer games culture is gendered, with women underrepresented throughout the games industry and gaming culture generally, including the games themselves.

Women have become increasingly more visible in games culture, especially as gamers in recent years. Brathwaite (2010) views the social network site Facebook as a catalyst in which women are increasingly becoming more hard-core gamers. The issue of gender and computer games is timely and relevant. The image of the games industry, like the wider ICT and SET industries, is still very much "boys' work." However, this image could change with a more diverse workforce and an increasing number of female gamers; the industry may then begin to lose its "for-boys-only," masculine image. Findings from the research discussed within this book highlight issues that prevent women from entering the industry, as well as highlight issues that may enable the games industry to review its policies and working practices in order to facilitate women and other minority groups to enter the working environment. Instead of women "fitting in or getting out," more can be done to eradicate career barriers and discriminatory work practices in all aspects of the games industry. More research is needed in this area to continue in developing an understanding of the issues, eradicate barriers, and find and enable solutions. As with the SET and ICT sectors, a one-solution-fixes-all approach is not viable (Prescott & Bogg, 2012).

The Target Audience

In writing this book, we had a broad mix of audiences in mind. The target audience of this book will be composed of professionals and researchers working in the field of education and career development of women in male-dominated industries and occupations, in particular the computer games industry but also including those interested in the wider ICT and SET sectors. Moreover, the book will provide insights and support those concerned with attracting and retaining women in ICT disciplines, specifically computer games, where women are traditionally underrepresented. The book will also provide valuable information to executives and members of professional bodies representing computer games industry workers and those working in the digital media who wish to encourage women during their career progression. The research, which considers the experiences of women within the industry, is not restricted to the Western computer games industry; it also includes a chapter on the experiences of women working in the Japanese games industry. This range of experiences will hopefully broaden the book's appeal. In preparing this book, we hope the personal profiles from women currently working in the industry will inspire and provide hope for increasing the diversity within the industry. The book presents an overview of current research and issues, while encouraging the reader to think of future directions, both in research and in practice.

AIMS OF THIS BOOK

The overall objective of this book is to present a collection of recent empirical studies and theoretical work related to the careers of women working in the computer games industry and digital media. The book will bring together current international research investigating underrepresentation in gaming and digital media industries. In particular, the book will include research looking at the experience of workers working in this male-dominated environment, including the personal and professional barriers of working in this industry, and will include viewpoints from female industry workers. This book will represent a valuable snapshot of the current state of the field with the aim of bringing together a wide range of perspectives in the area and sparking more debates and future research questions.

Our aim is to edit a book that provides a collection of recent high-quality empirical studies related to the computer games and digital media industries. This book will provide a valuable contribution as it will add to the literature on women working in male-dominated industries, the new industries of digital media, and women's underrepresentation in the wider SET and ICT sectors. The book will provide a valuable contribution, as it will highlight the personal experiences of women who currently work in this new technological industry and male-dominated work environment.

The chapters within section two, "The Experience of Women Working in the Computer Games Industry: An International Perspective," are critical to this book, as they give the women in the industry a voice and provide readers with an insight into their lived experiences. What is particularly interesting and an important contribution of this book is that it has chapters from women in different parts of the world. As acknowledged throughout this edition, women working in the computer games industry are an understudied, under-researched area, resulting in a lack of knowledge about the experiences of females working within the industry.

ORGANISATION OF THE BOOK

In writing this book, we aim to provide the readers with recent empirical research considering the gendering of computer games, the computer games industry, and digital technology. In order to give the book structure, the book has been organised into three sections: section one, "Education, Computers, and Gaming" (chapters 1-3), section two, "The Experience of Women Working in the Computer Games Industry: An International Perspective" (chapters 4-7), and section three, "Future Outlook/Lessons from the STEM Sector" (chapters 8-11). The book also profiles the experiences of women working in the field of computer games development, the promotion of computer games, or in the education of computer games. The profiles give the reader an understanding of how and why these females made their career choices, what they do within the industry, a snapshot of their personal experiences, and what they hope for the future. The females, who were asked to submit a profile, vary in their roles, their experience, and include women from the UK, Sweden, Germany, USA, and Canada.

Section 1: Education, Computers, and Gaming

Section 1 has three chapters focusing on different aspects of education and computer games.

Profiles

Profile 1: Carrie Warwick

Carrie Warwick has been working in the UK games industry since completing her degree in Games Art at the University of Bolton in the summer of 2013. She is currently a 3D Artist at Rivet Studios, an innovative new games studio based in Manchester aiming to launch their first title.

Profile 2: Elinor Townsend

Elinor Townsend graduated in 2013 and is currently working in her first full-time position in the industry as a programmer at the games company Ninja Theory Ltd.

Profile 3: Anna Ljungberg

Anna Ljungberg is originally from Sweden and has been working in the UK games industry for 18 months, since graduating from Staffordshire University with a first in "Game Artificial Intelligence." She is currently based at Codemasters as a gameplay programmer and has one released title under her belt.

Profile 4: Jo Daly

Jo Daly has been working in the games industry since 1996 and has many years of experience in developing games as a texture artist, 3D generalist, character artist, concept artist, lead, and manager. She is currently a lecturer on the BA Games Art course at the University of Bolton and is also developing an as-yet-unannounced iPad product with her partner.

Chapters

Chapter 1: From the "Damsel in Distress" to Girls' Games and Beyond – Gender and Children's Gaming

In the opening chapter, Alyson E. King and Aziz Douai take a historiographical approach to investigate how computer games as toys socialise children into traditional gender stereotypes and roles. The chapter includes a feminist critique of computer games, discussing the impact of the "games for girls" movement as well as a discussion of the current gender divide within the industry. Gaming and gender is analysed within the chapter through the analysis of the toy-based social networking portal Webkinz World. Through the case study of Webkinz World, the authors argue that such gaming models have the potential to bridge the gendered digital divide from early childhood.

Chapter 2: Women and Men in Computer Science – The Role of Gaming in their Educational Goals

The second chapter by Jill Denner, Elroy Ortiz, and Linda Werner explores how gaming motivations and practices are related to an interest in studying computer science. The study involved a survey with 545 male and female student gamers. The study also included a number of interviews to gain a deeper understanding as to why and how avid gamers play computer games. Interestingly, the study found that frequency of play was not associated with interest in studying computer science. An interest in studying computer science was found to differ by gender and motivation for why and how the student participants played games. Female students who considered themselves more serious/hardcore gamers showed the highest interest in studying computer science. The chapter provides recommendations for future research into how game play and an interest in studying computer science are related.

Chapter 3: The Only Girl in the Class! Female Students' Experiences of Gaming Courses and Views of the Industry

In this chapter, the authors, Lauren Elliot and Julie Prescott, investigate the experiences of female undergraduate game students at a UK university. The chapter discusses the findings from four semi-structured interviews with female undergraduate gaming students studying different game-related courses, including games art and game design. Although a small sample, the study provided an interesting insight into the experiences of the females on the course as well as their views of entering (or at least potentially entering) the male-dominated computer games industry. The females choose to study games because they enjoyed playing games. Despite all experiencing the course positively, there was some apprehension about going into the industry. Interestingly, the study suggests the male-dominated working environment may be off-putting to women, even women studying and interested in going into that area of work. The main themes to emerge were the long hours, culture, and potential sexism within the industry.

Section 2: The Experience of Women Working in the Computer Games Industry – An International Perspective

Section 2 has four chapters, one from the USA, one from the UK, one from Japan, and one from Australia. This section provides the reader with an understanding of some recent research that has been conducted in the area from different worldwide perspectives.

Profiles

Profile 5: Fiona Cherbak

Fiona Cherbak has two decades of experience in entertainment business development, marketing, staffing, and strategic planning for interactive games, feature films, television, theme park shows, music production, and theatre arts. As president of marketing and media firm ThemePark Studios, she spearheads fundraising, marketing, and publicity campaigns for a cross-section of interactive, film, and tech companies and organizations. Presently, she is co-producer and promoter of the Boston Festival of Indie Games.

Profile 6: Sheri Graner Ray

Sheri Graner Ray is an award-winning game designer/developer. She is also the author of *Gender Inclusive Game Design: Expanding the Market* and is a sought-after speaker on gender and games. In the game industry since 1989, she has served in many capacities from writer/designer to Director of Product Development. She has more than 30 titles to her name and is currently the CEO and founder of Zombie Cat Studios, based in Austin, Texas.

Profile 7: Lindsay Williamson Christy

Lindsey Williamson Christy has been working in the Vancouver publishing, games, and film industries since 1997. She has over 16 years of project management experience working on several blockbuster films and AAA game titles. She is currently an instructor at the Vancouver Film School in the Entertainment Business Management program.

Profile 8: Julie McGurren

Julie McGurren has been working in the UK games industry since 1999 and has more than 14 years of experience in developing AAA racing titles as an artist, lead, and manager. She is currently an Art Producer at the games company Codemasters.

Profile 9: Althea Deane

Althea Deane has been working in the games industry since 2000 as a character animator. She has worked at a number of companies in this time and has credits on many published titles. She is 46, unmarried, and currently working as a self-employed freelance animator based in Liverpool.

Profile 10: Dianne Botham

Dianne Botham has been working in the games industry as an Environment Artist since 2002 and has created artwork for seven AAA tiles for two different game developers in the UK. She was employed by Bizarre Creations for almost nine years as an Environment and Principal Artist, until the company's closure in 2011, and she currently works as an Environment Artist at Ninja Theory.

Profile 11: Joy Dey

Joy Dey has been working in the games industry for just over five years. Following completion of a degree in Game Development, she has held roles at a number of different companies working within the QA department as a Localisation Technician and a Senior QA Tester. At the end of 2013, Joy realised a career dream and was offered a role as a designer at Headstrong Games. Originally from Sweden, she is now based in the UK.

Profile 12: Hannah Payne

Hannah Payne has been working in the games industry since 2010. With experience in both art and design roles, primarily in mobile games, she now works as a junior artist at mobile game developer Kwalee.

Chapters

Chapter 4: A Look inside the Current Climate of the Video Game Industry

The first chapter in this section, by Vachon M. C. Pugh, examines the game developers' salary survey for the years 2009-2012. This chapter discusses the underrepresentation of female game developers and further examines the roles women play within the games industry from an American context.

Chapter 5: The Experiences of Women Working in the Computer Games Industry – An In-Depth Qualitative Study

In this chapter, the authors, Julie Prescott and Jan Bogg, discuss the findings from one-to-one semi-structured interviews with seven women currently working in the UK computer games industry. This chapter provides a unique understanding of the experiences of women in the industry from a small sample of women who work in it. Discussed are issues around the viability of the industry as a career for women, the experience of being a woman in the industry, work-life balances issues, and experiences of discrimination and sexism in the workplace. The chapter discusses the issues in order to gain an understanding of attracting and retaining women in games development, while also highlighting the benefits of working in this industry and the positive experiences women working in the industry have had.

Chapter 6: Career Development among Japanese Female Game Developers – Perspective from Life Stories of Creative Professionals

This chapter by Masahito Fujihara discusses findings from one-on-one interviews with 21 female game developers with over five years of work experience in the Japanese computer games industry. The study found that Japanese female game developers display 10 characteristics regarding their careers. Although the author finds no typical career path or clearly defined career goals of female Japanese game developers, most had previously played games. Due to the lack of female game developers in the Japanese gaming industry, the women in the current study strive to become role models to increase more female participation. This is an exciting chapter since little research has been conducted on the Japanese game market for a Western audience.

Chapter 7: Women's Participation in the Australian Digital Content Industry

In this chapter, the author, Anitza Geneve, discusses the findings from 18 semi-structured interviews with women and stakeholders working in the Australian digital content industry, which includes computer games. The chapter discusses the findings of the interviews using a theoretical framework, "the acts of agency theory," underpinned by both human agency and critical realism. The chapter provides the reader with a background to the theory used and how the theory can offer insights for the underrepresentation of women with the computer games industry and other digital media industries.

Section 3: Future Outlook and Lessons from the STEM Sector

Section 3 has four chapters that consider future directions for the industry and how the computer games industry can take lessons from the underrepresentation of women in the wider STEM sector.

Profiles

Profile 13: Sabine Hahn

Sabine Hahn worked in the wireless gaming industry in both the United Kingdom and Germany for 10 years before taking a break and focusing more on the academic side of gaming.

Profile 14: Elizabeth Richardson

Elizabeth Richardson has grown up with gaming and now runs a channel on YouTube that centres around playing and reviewing video games. The channel started in January 2011 and has been growing ever since.

Profile 15: Faye Windsor-Smith

Faye Windsor-Smith joined Codemasters as a Q.A. Tester in 2011 and is currently working as a Monetisation Games Designer for their Southam Digital development team.

Profile 16: Phil Goddard

Phil Goddard is an obsessive-compulsive Creative Director with a 14-year career in digital media, casual games, and virtual worlds. Phil has designed and led projects for The Cartoon Network, EA Games, Monty Python, Nickelodeon, and the BBC, including the casual MMO game for the 2014 summer blockbuster movie *Legends of Oz: Dorothy's Return*. Phil now leads a new indie studio in Manchester focusing on a new gaming project, MMA Federation.

Chapters

Chapter 8: Professional Socialization in STEM Academia and its Gendered Impact on Creativity and Innovation

This chapter by Gloria-Sophia Warmuth and Edeltraud Hanappi-Egger introduces the topic of professional socialization and how it is gendered. The chapter examines the role of gender scripts in SET organisations through a case study of academics in an Austrian higher education institution of technology and engineering.

Chapter 9: Lessons from the STEM Sector

This chapter by Vachon M. C. Pugh considers the possible causes of the lack of women in the computer games industry through a look at the underrepresentation of women in the STEM sector. The chapter examines successful recruitment strategies from studies in STEM and non-STEM fields. From the five studies under discussion, a number of trends emerge which the author suggests could be applied to the computer games industry to increase the number of women in the industry. The four main areas for possible recruitment avenues from the study findings are recruitment programs, marketing tactics, mentoring programs, and social games. Each area is discussed within the chapter in relation to the computer games industry.

Chapter 10: A Framework for Addressing Gender Imbalance in the Game Industry through Outreach

In this chapter, the , Monica M. McGill, Adrienne Decker, and Amber Settle, address three questions. Firstly, why is the issue of gender imbalance important in the games industry? Secondly, what is the current state of gender imbalance in the games industry and its pipelines? And thirdly, what are the ways in which this issue can be addressed? The chapter discusses a number of existing frameworks for addressing gender imbalances, with initiatives in the UK and USA discussed. The chapter proposes a conceptual framework for outreach initiatives as well as a framework for future research and outreach initiatives to bring more women into the industry.

Chapter 11: Female Game Workers: Career Development and Aspirations

This study by Julie Prescott and Jan Bogg assesses the impact of career influencers on career aspirations of women working in the male-dominated computer games industry. An online questionnaire obtained international data from 450 women working in the computer games industry. A structural equation model was employed to investigate the internal and external factors that influence career aspirations. Findings suggest that to increase women's career development and career aspirations within the computer games industry a number of factors including self-efficacy, attitudes towards career barriers, work-life balance attitudes, person-environment fit, and job satisfaction are crucial. The psychological constructs included in the study are described for clarity, and future research recommendations are discussed in the aim of increasing women's participation within the industry.

A COMMON GROUND

In writing this book, we hope to highlight the need for more women working in the science, engineering, and technology industries, in particular the computer games industry. We hope this book will encourage more empirical research as to why women work and do not work within this culturally significant industry. We hope this publication stimulates both reflection and action.

Julie Prescott
University of Bolton, UK

Julie Elizabeth McGurren
Codemasters, UK

REFERENCES

Brathwaite, B. (2010, March 24). *Women in games from famine to Facebook*. Retrieved from http://www.huffingtonpost.com/brenda-brathwaite/women-in-games-from-famin_b_510928.html

Cejka, M. A., & Eagly, A. H. (1999). Gender-stereotypic images of occupations correspond to the sex segregation of employment. *Personality and Social Psychology Bulletin, 25*(4), 413–423.

Consalvo, M. (2006). Console video games & global corporations: Creating a hybrid culture. *New Media & Society, 8*(1), 117–137.

CVG. (2013) *GTA V global retail sales top $800 million in one day.* Retrieved from http://www.computerandvideogames.com/430009/gta-v-global-retail-sales-top-800-million-in-one-day/

Deuze, M., Martin, C. B., & Allen, C. (2007). The professional identity of game workers. *Convergence: The International Journal of Research into New Media Technologies, 13*(4), 335–353.

DFC. (2004). *DFC intelligence releases new market forecasts for video game industry.* Retrieved from http://www.dfcint.com/news/prsep222004.html

Dyer-Whitheford, N., & Sharman, Z. (2005). The political economy of Canada's video and computer game industry. *Canadian Journal of Communication, 20*, 187–210.

Eagly, A. H. (1987). *Sex differences in social behavior: A social role interpretations.* Hillsdale, NJ: Erlbaum.

Eagly, A. H., & Carli, L. L. (2003). The female leadership advantage: An evaluation of the evidence. *The Leadership Quarterly, 14*, 807–834.

ESA. (2011a). *Video games & the economy.* Retrieved from http://www.theesa.com/gamesindailylife/economy.pdf

ESA. (2011b). Essential facts about the computer & video game industry. *Entertainment Software Industry.* Retrieved from www.theESA.com

ESA. (2012). *Essential facts about the computer & video game industry 2012 sales, demographic & usage data.* Entertainment Software Association.

Gansmo, H. J., Nordli, H., & Sorensen, K. H. (2003). The gender game: A study of Nigerian computer game designers. In C. MacKeogh, & P. Preston (Eds.), *Strategies of inclusion: Gender & the information society: Experiences from private & voluntary sector initiatives* (pp. 139–159). Trondheim, Norway: NTNU.

Geneve, A., Christie, R. J., & Nelson, K. J. (2009). Women's participation in the Australian digital content industry: Initial case study findings. In K. Prpić, L. Oliveira, & S. Hemlin (Eds.), Women in science & technology (pp. 139-161). Zagreb, Croatia: Institute of Social Research-Zagreb Sociology of Science and Technology Network of ESA (European Sociological Association).

Gottfredson, L. S. (1981). Circumscription and compromise: A development theory of aspirations. *Journal of Counseling Psychology, 28*(6), 545–579.

Gourdin, A. (2005). *Game developers demographics: An exploration of workforce diversity.* International Game Developers Association. Retrieved from http://archives.igda.org/diversity/IGDA_DeveloperDemographics_Oct05.pdf

Hartmann, T., & Klimmt, C. (2006). Gender & computer games: Exploring females' dislikes. *Journal of Computer-Mediated Communication, 11,* 910–931.

Heilman, M. E., & Okimoto, T. G. (2007). Why are women penalized for success at male tasks? The implied communality deficit. *The Journal of Applied Psychology, 92,* 81–92. PMID:17227153

Heilman, M. E., Wallen, A. S., Fuchs, D., & Tamkins, M. M. (2004). Penalties for success: Reactions to women who succeed at male gender-typed tasks. *The Journal of Applied Psychology, 89,* 416–427. PMID:15161402

Johns, J. (2006). Video games production networks: Value capture, power relations & embeddedness. *Journal of Economic Geography, 6,* 151–180.

Kawakami, C., White, J. B., & Langer, E. J. (2000). Mindful and masculine: Freeing women leaders from the constraints of gender roles. *The Journal of Social Issues, 56*(1), 49–63.

Kline, S., Dyer-Whitheford, N., & de Peuter, G. (2003). *Digital play: The interaction of technology, culture & marketing.* Montreal, Canada: McGill-Queen's University Press.

Krotoski, A. (2004). *Chicks & joysticks: An exploration of women & gaming* (White Paper). Entertainment & Leisure Software Publishers Association.

Mai, P. (2010). *The highest & lowest grossing video game-based movies.* Retrieved from http://blogs.ocweekly.com/heardmentality/2010/07/hollywoods_lowest_grossing_vid.php

Oswald, D. L. (2008). Gender stereotypes and women's reports of liking and ability in traditionally masculine and feminine occupations. *Psychology of Women Quarterly, 32,* 196–203.

Oxford Economics. (2008). *The economic contribution of the UK games industry: Final report.* Retrieved from http://www.oef.com/FREE/PDFS/GAMESIMPACT.PDF

Prescott, J., & Bogg, J. (2010). The computer games industry: Women's experiences of work role in a male dominated environment. In A. Cater-Steel, & E. Cater (Eds.), *Women in engineering, science and technology: Education and career challenges* (pp. 138–158). Hershey, PA: IGI Global.

Prescott, J., & Bogg, J. (2011). Segregation in a male dominated industry: Women working in the computer games industry. *International Journal of Gender, Science, and Technology, 3*(1), 205–227.

Prescott, J., & Bogg, J. (2012). *Gendered occupational differences in science, engineering, and technology careers.* Hershey, PA: IGI Global.

Prescott, J., & Bogg, J. (2014). *Gender divide and the computer gaming industry.* Hershey, PA: IGI Global.

Shaw, A. (2010). What is video game culture? Cultural studies and game studies. *Games and Culture, 5*(4), 403–424.

Skillset. (2009). *2009 employment census: The results of the seventh census of the creative media industries December 2009.* The Sector Skills Council for Creative Media.

Sweetser, P., Wyeth, P., McMahon, N., & Johnson, D. (2013). Female game developers wanted: Low pay, long hours, inflexible work environments. In *Proceedings of the Games Innovation Conference (IGIC)*. IEEE. doi: 10.1109/IGIC.2013.6659142

Vancouver Film School (VFS). (2010). *The game industry now & in the future 2010: Industry facts, trends & outlook*. Vancouver Film School.

Wallop, H. (2009, Dec. 26). Video games bigger than film. *The Daily Telegraph*. Retrieved January 4, 2009 from http://www.telegraph.co.uk/technology/video-games/6852383/Video-games-bigger-than-film.html

Willemson, T. M. (2002). Gender typing of the successful manager - A stereotype reconsidered. *Sex Roles, 46*, 385–391.

Acknowledgment

The authors who contributed to this book deserve our heartfelt thanks for their contribution, patience and co-operation throughout the process of compiling this book. All the chapter contributors are listed with biographical sketches in a section of the book. To those who contributed to the publication with a profile we thank you for the very personal insight into your life, education, career choices and hopes for the future. We hope these profiles will serve as an inspiration to readers. Sincere thanks also to Sheri Graner Ray for writing the Foreword and for her valuable contribution to the field of gender and computer games.

Sincere thanks to our reviewers and members of the editorial advisory board; we know the authors were very appreciative of the valuable comments provided by the reviewers. We sincerely thank the reviewers for taking the time to read and comment on the submissions. This was an essential role and their contribution has improved the content and presentation of the chapters and thus the overall content of the book.

We would also like to thank the staff at IGI Global for their support during the entire process from original proposal to final publication.

Julie Prescott
University of Bolton, UK

Julie Elizabeth McGurren
Codemasters, UK

Section 1

Education, Computers, and Gaming

Profile 1: Carrie Warwick

Carrie Warwick has been working in the UK games industry since completing her degree in Games Art at the University of Bolton in the summer of 2013. She is currently a 3D artist at Rivet Studios, an innovative new games studio based in Manchester aiming to launch their first title.

From a very early age I found myself being introduced to computers, our very first being an Amiga 1200, and spending hours creating 'masterpieces' on Deluxe Paint. At the time they were simple squiggles and patterns, but this would have been my first experience creating digital art! The first video game console that we owned was the Amiga CD32, and I used to love playing games such as Simon the Sorcerer and Brian the Lion. A few years later when my dad got our first Windows PC, I remember spending every night after school playing our way through the levels of Tomb Raider together.

Throughout my GCSEs and A-Levels I always leaned towards more academic subjects as opposed to art subjects, and actually took psychology, biology and chemistry in college. All of my art knowledge was built up during my spare time and at this point in my life I never envisaged myself going into an art-based career. However, as art was where my interests lay, I did apply to study animation and illustration at the University of Bolton after finishing college, but as I had no portfolio to show for myself I backed out of the application process and worked full time for two years before I decided I wanted to get back into education and get a degree.

During my time out of education, I had plenty of time to consider where I wanted to go in terms of my career. I rekindled my love of video games, spending the evenings playing beautiful and rich games such as Assassin's Creed and Uncharted. I was blown away by their immersive and stunning environments, and I really wanted the opportunity to create something as wonderful as those games. I was also attracted to this career path by the prospect of a higher than average salary, and a clear career progression which can often be lacking in other job areas. I began to research courses that would help me to achieve my goal, and in September 2009 I started on the BA Games Art course at the University of Bolton. I chose the course as it offered a mix of both 2D and 3D art which was incredibly appealing to me.

On my course there were five other females, two of whom left the course to pursue other areas. I got along well with them and worked closely with one in many of our team projects. However, I always felt it easier to talk with the males on the course and actually found I tended to have more in common with them. I believe this probably comes from growing up being close to my dad and playing video games. When I was at school it was still seen as 'uncool' for girls to be playing games, therefore most of my talking about video games was with the guys.

Over the three years at University, I thoroughly enjoyed the course. I felt that the balance of 2D and 3D art which was taught allowed me to gain a fundamental understanding of art which in turn really helped to improve both my digital 2D and 3D work. In particular I took to the 3D side of the course, specifically environment modelling. It was during my second year that I decided that this was the area that I wanted to specialise in, and I focused my final year project on creating a game-ready 3D environment. I also found that I really enjoyed the technical aspects of games art more than the creative side, which I believe comes from my educational background of studying academic subjects which required me to be more methodical than creative.

During my final months at University I began approaching a number of studios, both local and national, and sent out e-mails with my CV and portfolio enquiring as to whether any job opportunities were available. I also applied to many of the larger studios which were advertising game artist positions. Rivet Studios came back to me and invited me in for a chat. Nervously, I went with examples of my work, and after a friendly and informal chat they gave me an art test which I worked on alongside my final university projects. When I'd finished this, they invited me back in to talk to me about how I'd gotten on, and I was overjoyed when later that same day they called me back to offer me a position! I was to start the day after my dissertation VIVA! As an excited young games artist fully aware of how difficult it is to break into this industry, I couldn't have been more grateful for how things had worked out.

I graduated a few months after I'd started my job with a 1st class honours degree, and two months into my three month probation period, I was offered a full time position at the studio.

I thoroughly enjoy working at Rivet Studios, which is a new studio located right in the heart of Manchester overlooking the town hall. The central location means there's always a buzz going into work. The atmosphere within the studio is very relaxed and everyone works and gets along well together as a team, both inside and outside of work. My role within the studio is as a 3D artist, but I also cover a lot of other roles as and when required such as 2D concept and 2D art, along with working inside Unity to create special effects.

As Rivet is a fairly small studio, I really feel that I'm being given a great opportunity to sample all roles within a games pipeline and learn new skills I might not even have considered before. One of the skills I have learnt since starting at the studio is how to effectively rig character models. This fits perfectly with how I like to work, and I've since been given the job of re-rigging all of the game's older, more complicated rigs to something simpler that our animator can work with.

When I first started at Rivet there were only seven full time members of staff, but in the time I've been there we've now grown to a team of eleven people in order to meet the crucial deadlines for our first release. Our team consists of three women and eight men, and I find that within my studio we are actively encouraged to become involved with all aspects of the game production pipeline. Everyone's opinions are respected and as such the relationship between all the staff members is incredibly friendly.

I don't feel that being a woman in the games industry is a barrier to advancing my career; in fact I believe that it may well be an advantage as the industry becomes more accepting of females who are aiming to start a career in games. The studio I work for actively encourages and seeks out female employees, and aims to someday have a 50/50 split between men and women. Rivet believes that in order to make fun games that will appeal to all audiences, it's important to reflect that demographic in the work place.

I believe the fact that I have no idea where the past few months have gone is testament to how much I'm enjoying working in the games industry. It's such a massively different experience to my past jobs in retail and customer service, and it's wonderful to see something that you've put so much time and hard work into be published and enjoyed by other people. As is always the case with any job, there are some days where it's stressful and I think to myself 'am I really cut out for this?', but then the payoff when you create something that people love is well worth the stress.

I'm currently learning the hard way that working in games can be incredibly demanding, both physically and mentally, but I believe that this is a small sacrifice to pay when working in a job role that you love. At Rivet, I've experienced my first 'crunch' period, which involved long, tiring hours staring at a Mac screen and hardly any time at home to relax before I was back in the studio again. It was very demanding and at times had a negative effect on my personal relationships, but I know that when I see our game released it'll have been worth the hours put in.

I have to admit that since starting full time work and getting my career rolling, I haven't had as much time for playing games as I'd have liked to, and currently a lot of my gaming time involves maintaining my crops and looking after my goats on Farmville2 for a few minutes in the morning before I start work! However, when it comes to AAA titles my favourite genre is definitely action and adventure, and I'm hoping very soon once I get some free time to play Assassin's Creed 3 and Last of Us. I've got quite a bit of catching up to do!

My future expectations of being part of the games industry are that it will continue to provide me with an exciting and innovative way to express my creativity. I am excited about the future and meeting like-minded people who will help to me to grow and improve as an artist. I would like to hope that someday I will be in a position to say that I've worked a particular title, and that I've been part of the team responsible for bringing a new experience to video game lovers and that I can help to inspire other females to get involved in this fantastic industry.

The long term goals of my career are to work for a large game studio, contributing to a highly successful game series. I'd love to experience the thrills of working in a AAA studio, especially overseas, and to be part of a big team all working towards a major project. Within the next couple of years I want to make a name for myself as a successful games artist, and hope that my work will be recognised. I don't feel disadvantaged knowing that for the time being I'll be working in what is still a male-dominated industry. I actually see this as a positive thing, as males tend to be more competitive and this will only lead me to challenge myself and strive to become better within my role and move up in this industry.

Profile 2: Elinor Townsend

Elinor Townsend graduated in 2013 and is currently working in her first full time position in the games industry as a programmer at games company Ninja Theory Ltd.

I've been playing games all my life. I started out playing educational games on a BBC microcomputer that my dad brought home from work. Hours were spent typing in the answers to simple maths questions in order to blast away brick walls, and remembering sequences of numbers to deliver mail in an old Postman Pat game. The witch from Granny's Garden terrified me every time I failed to solve puzzles correctly. Much of my childhood was spent playing games such as Prince of Persia, James Pond and two-player Lemmings with the boy who lived next door. My dad was always bringing home random games and consoles from car boot sales, and I was fortunate to grow up with a computer in the house.

It wasn't until I was thirteen that this game playing turned from just one of many childhood distractions into a serious hobby. I was hooked once I discovered Tomb Raider, again whilst playing at a friend's house. We used to take turns playing, swapping each time we died and excitedly squealing and throwing the controller to each other when a wolf or a Velociraptor jumped out at us and the "scary music" kicked in. Tomb Raider was what I'd always wanted from a game. It was the first time I really got lost in the game world, imagining that I was a gun-toting adventurer exploring ancient ruins. I got a PlayStation of my own for my birthday that year and spent the rest of my teens collecting demo discs from magazines, and using all the money I earned from my paper round on new games.

Although I enjoyed playing games, it never really occurred to me to consider a career in the games industry. I liked art and enjoyed playing around on the computer with Paintshop Pro, but I didn't have the sort of talent needed to be an artist. None of the subjects I was taught at school had any clear connection to game technology either. The computing class I took only covered word processing and PowerPoint presentations. I dabbled in web development in my free time, learning simple html, and I thought briefly about programming, but it wasn't taught at my school and I remember being told it was a boring subject.

I did well at school and had my mind set on going to university, but I didn't have a clear idea of what I really wanted to do in the future. The only thing I was really sure about was that I wanted to move away from home and see more of the world. Having spent so much time playing games and reading gaming magazines I had developed an interest in Japan, and so with that in mind I chose to study Japanese Studies and Business Studies at the University of Sheffield.

The course was a four year dual honours degree that included a year studying abroad at a university in Japan. The business side of the degree was a compromise I made with my parents, who were adamant I needed more employable skills than learning a new language alone would provide. My father was always bemoaning the fact that I ignored his advice to become a lawyer or an accountant as "that's where the money is". I took intensive Japanese language classes: spoken, grammar, and writing. I also took core business studies classes, but unfortunately there was no room in my timetable for the other Japanese classes offered such as history and literature. In my third year I was given a place at Rikkyo University in Tokyo and finally got my wish to live abroad.

The course at Sheffield was hard work, and I found that my heart was never really in it. Studying the language was a means to an end rather than something I was passionate about. I had a fantastic time in Japan and I feel like my experiences at university have helped develop my confidence and independence, but my disinterest in what I studied meant that when I graduated in 2005 I was still lacking any real career plan. While I enjoyed my time in Japan, I knew I didn't want to stay there and teach English, and translation work typically requires a Masters degree. In need of an income, I moved to Manchester with my boyfriend and took a job in a department store, where I worked for six months before accepting a job as a travel agent.

After a year and a half working in Manchester we made the decision to move up to Scotland and stay with my family while we got our careers sorted out. My boyfriend, who was interested in conservation work, spent a year volunteering with the Scottish Wildlife Trust and I continued working in the travel industry, this time for a business travel company, arranging travel for business clients. We got married, and once his volunteer work was completed my husband was accepted into the police force. With my husband starting out in a new career I had time to really reflect on where I was going in life. I was disappointed with myself, as I did not feel that I was reaching my full potential. My job was not challenging, and I felt bored and unmotivated. I am also very independent and admittedly quite competitive, and the idea that my husband would have all the earning power in our relationship made me dissatisfied.

I had continued playing games all this time, and had made a few friends through online gaming who worked in the games industry. It always sounded like an exciting career and one in which I thought I would feel truly productive. I was also aware of the good reputation of the gaming courses offered at Abertay University nearby. It was one of the first universities in the world to offer courses specifically tailored for the games industry, and many of the courses are Skillset accredited. I knew I didn't have the sort of skills needed to be an artist, but I had always been good at maths and physics, having achieved good grades in both when at school. I researched the programming courses offered at Abertay, specifically Computer Games Technology, and discovered that no prior programming experience was necessary, so I put in an application to enrol the following year.

Once I knew what I was going to be doing I really threw myself into it. I knew how much hard work university was already, and how important it was to have a clear idea of where I wanted to go after graduating. That autumn I attended an open day at the university, where I was shown around by a female student on the same course I would be taking, providing me with the opportunity to ask about the course and the university in general. I had seen a number of stories and news articles about how under-represented women were in the games industry, particularly in technical disciplines such as programming, so it was refreshing that the first person I met at Abertay University was also female and doing the same course as me.

In preparation for the degree, I did a beginners' C++ tutorial online and then asked a friend who was working as a games programmer for advice. He helped by giving me suggestions of small coding tasks I could work on. These were simple things like writing a programme to compute Fibonacci numbers, but they really helped me get a better feel for how to write code and go about solving programming problems. This gave me a big advantage when I started at Abertay, as I already had an understanding of the basic programming principles that were taught during the first year. This allowed me to focus on the Maths side of things. It was the first time in close to ten years that I had studied Maths, so I was understandably a little rusty.

Classes were large during the first year, as the majority of our modules were shared with other courses. There were somewhere in the region of thirty students on the Computer Games Technology course with me; however only four were female students.

As well as working hard at my studies, I also had in mind the fact that one of the hardest things about finding a job is having enough experience. Therefore, I applied and was accepted as an intern doing games testing with Denki, a local game developer. Denki had approximately twenty employees at the time, and I was working with their full time games tester helping to test Quarrel, a multi-player word game for Xbox Live. There were only two other women working there, both in administration, so my working environment was extremely male dominated, but I never felt that it affected my work. I worked at Denki a couple of days a week for a year and a half while I was studying, and it was my first proper experience of what game development was really like. I attended company meetings and learnt about what everyone was working on, as well as learning about bug tracking and reporting.

Denki was my first job in the games industry, and also my first experience of how tough the industry can be. The company failed to secure a publisher for the game we were working on, and in April 2010 they had to let nearly all of their staff go. It was really difficult to see so many colleagues losing their jobs when they had worked so hard to make a game we all believed deserved to succeed. I got to witness first-hand how touch and go developing games can be. Another reminder of this came four months later with the closure of Realtime Worlds, another well known games company local to Dundee.

In the summer following my second year at Abertay I took a programming internship with VEE-MEE in Edinburgh. VEEMEE are a games developer specialising in Playstation®Home development. I worked on a small team of six within the studio developing a multi-player, cover-based shooter for Playstation®Home called No Man's Land. VEEMEE had only one female member of staff, an artist who worked on a different team, and I remember being told by one coder there that he had in fact never met a female games programmer before.

This was my first time actually working as a programmer and it was extremely challenging. We were working in Lua, a programming language I had no experience of, so I had to learn that very quickly. I was paired with a senior programmer who worked closely with me, performing regular code reviews of my work and giving me help and advice as I went along. My programming abilities increased greatly with this help, and I really improved my coding style and my debugging skills. In addition, I gained valuable experience of working as part of a team.

I returned to university at the end of the summer, after a little over three months of working full time as a programmer, eager to try my new skills out in my coursework. Third year meant it was time to work on the group project, a year long project in which you worked with students from other disciplines such as art, design and production. My team had nine members, with one other female, again an artist. Our project was well received and I went on to form a team with a couple of people from that project to compete in a Scottish games development competition, Dare to be Digital, the next summer.

We didn't win any awards in the competition, but it was a great experience; working to a very tight schedule to create a game, which was then demonstrated to the public at the three day event, Dare Protoplay. This gave us the opportunity to meet with the public and let them play our game. I found that a lot of people were interested in the fact that as a woman I had chosen to become a programmer, and I felt like I was really representing my gender, promoting to parents the idea that the gaming industry is indeed a valid career path for their children, regardless of their sex. Often I've been asked what it is like to be a "female" programmer, and I never really know how to respond. I've never felt my gender has much to do with my work at all.

In my fourth and final year at Abertay I decided that I should work on my leadership skills, so I entered the IBM Business Challenge, a competition where teams of five make financial decisions about a fictional company each week, and compete against other teams to make the most profit each week. I took on the role of team leader in a team with four males from other courses at the university. We successfully made it to the national semi-finals, where we narrowly missed out on victory, coming in at second place.

My final year at university also meant that it was time to start looking for a job to move into once I graduated, and when I saw a notice in December that Ninja Theory, one of my most loved games developers, were looking for a junior programmer, I jumped at the chance to apply. I travelled down to Cambridge for my interview that January and was thrilled when I was offered the job two weeks later, commencing once I'd finished university.

I graduated from Abertay University with a first class degree in July 2013 and immediately began working at Ninja Theory as a graphics and engine programmer. I have now been with the company for almost seven months, and have loved every minute of it. Ninja Theory is a much larger studio than anywhere I've worked before, and although the majority of staff are still male the gender gap is much smaller, with women working in all disciplines at the company. I am currently the only female on my team, but I'm not treated any differently from anyone else.

I have been very fortunate in the opportunities presented to me when starting out on my career in the games industry and I don't feel like my gender has hindered me in any way. I have never felt uncomfortable in the male dominated environments that I've worked in, and have never experienced discrimination based on gender. Whilst I do not advocate positive discrimination, being female has potentially worked to my advantage, as a CV from a female programmer can stand out as a rarity. I do feel my choice of such a stereotypically male career is down to the sort of person I am, having once been described by a school teacher as very idiosyncratic! Indeed I was lucky that my parents always encouraged me to do whatever interested me, even if it wasn't a choice they particularly understood.

I'm still at the start of my career, but it's a career that is rewarding, both financially and emotionally. I work alongside like-minded people in a stimulating environment, and my work is something I truly feel passionate about. I love working as a games programmer, and firmly believe that choosing a career in the games industry was the best decision that I could have made. I hope that I will be a good role model for others looking for a rewarding and challenging career in the games industry.

Profile 3: Anna Ljungberg

Anna Ljungberg is originally from Sweden and has been working in the UK games industry for 18 months after graduating from Staffordshire University with a first in 'Game Artificial Intelligence'. She is currently based at Codemasters as a gameplay programmer, making racing games for a living and already has one released title under her belt.

As a young girl I grew up with my two older sisters. There was an age gap of 7 and 9 years respectively, meaning I was always the baby and had 3 mothers! Even though being a female dominated family, my sisters and I always thought spending time with our father doing "manly stuff" was the greatest thing ever! I always loved helping out washing cars, chopping wood and generally being in the garage playing with my own set of tools.

I grew up with a Nintendo NES and my sisters and I used to spend hours in front of a tiny TV trying to get as far as we possibly could, before it was time for dinner. I even remember my dad asking us "How did you know you had to jump on that block to get up into that cloud world? (Super Mario Bros 3)" and we replied, "You just know, dad". Playing games always came very naturally to me and to my middle sister, and we loved trying to find new shortcuts or hidden treasures.

Being a little girl, I was never told certain things were boy or girl toys, and I always found different things interesting, ranging from a whole mountain of cuddly toys to a mini Porsche radio controlled car. My parents never limited me, or tried to steer me towards any specific activities when I was younger, when I was 7 years old I started playing handball, and later I learned the double bass.

As I got older the NES and computer games became less important as I was busy with school, handball and the double bass. I didn't have another games console until the original Xbox, and by that time I was around 14 years old.

Computers have always been part of my life as my dad had his own company, writing software for the old Sharp computers. We were quite lucky in having a personal computer in the 80s and 90s. I remember putting old cassettes into the computer and playing all sorts of games, particularly Muc Mac. As my dad had an interest in technology, we were always exposed to brand new gadgets and were always shown how to use them properly, but were left to ourselves to figure out how to do things. Therefore, I have always found new technology exciting and not been afraid of experimenting with it.

At school I always had an interest in the science subjects, with Maths, Chemistry and Physics being my strongest. This led me to choose a science focused degree at the Swedish equivalent to college level (these are of 3 years duration in Sweden from the age of 16). At this age I found developing websites very interesting and I did a module in web development at college. I also remember wanting to do a module in programming, however, as I was the only student at my College applying for it, didn't run.

As I continuously got good grades in maths and the sciences, I was encouraged, by my teachers, during my final term at College to study "fine" university courses such as Law, Medicine or Engineering. However, nothing seemed to appeal to me, so I decided to take a year out and find out what I actually wanted to do with my life. During this year, I worked at a dairy in Sweden, and later decided to move over to England to be with my boyfriend of that time, and spent the rest of my gap year working at Barclays Bank as an office clerk.

While in England, I decided I would like to stay and complete a degree there instead of going back to Sweden. I went to an open day at Staffordshire University thinking I would do CGI and Animatronics or

Robotics. However, while talking to someone about the Robotics course and realising I found programming the most interesting, they kindly suggested I should go and check out the Games Programming or Software Engineering courses. So off I went to go to the Games Programming talk, where I was met by a lecturer (who later taught me), who immediately believed my boyfriend was the one interested in the course, and started talking to him. Once he realised it was me applying he said "This is a course with a lot of advanced maths and stuff, maybe you should check out Games Design downstairs". Quite demoralised and shot down, I left and decided to go to the games design talk, which did absolutely nothing for me. I remember thinking "I don't want to re-skin a bin lid to look like a pizza; I want to make it behave like a pizza". So, partly because I wanted to prove that lecturer wrong, and partly because the advanced maths that he had mentioned excited me, I decided to apply for the Games Programming course at Staffordshire University.

During my time at University I was the only girl on my course, alongside about 20 boys, this proved a bit difficult in the beginning. As people were making friends I was usually left out, however later on in the year, the dynamic seemed to have settled and I was not that scared after all. I believe as a female amongst a group of boys you feel like you have to prove that you are one of them and have similar interests and knowledge before you are accepted amongst the "brethren". Especially during my first year at University I felt like I had to prove myself, as both teachers and classmates weren't expecting me to be good at computers and programming. However, once the first grades were out and I was at the top of my class, the tone changed quite quickly, even from the teacher who once told me to go and do games design.

There were not many other girls at Staffordshire University especially within the computing areas, and I therefore found it quite hard to make friends, initially, outside of university study. However, as the years progressed my class shrunk significantly and we all found our places within the group; we started socialising and going on nights out together.

As part of my degree I went abroad to Germany to complete an industrial placement year with a small software company. This was my first experience of programming outside of university, as well as of working with large scale commercial software solutions. It was absolutely terrifying to begin with, however the people working at Intergral GmbH were absolutely fantastic, and guided me through both technical and professional challenges. I was the first female programmer that they had hired, and they weren't really sure what to expect (mostly because the swearing and language used generally by angry programmers), however they quite quickly realised I was just like them and I was never treated any differently to anyone else.

As I started my final year at University the daunting feeling of having to apply for jobs quickly approached, with the games industry being as it is at the moment, there was a slight panic spreading about getting a job as a games programmer. However I can't say I had much difficulty finding opportunities, I would like to say it had nothing to do with me being female but I do believe being a "rare breed" meant both recruiters and companies paid attention to my application and actually read my CV.

I went for a few interviews, and finally got a job as a gameplay programmer at Codemasters before even graduating with a first class honours degree in Game Artificial Intelligence from Staffordshire University in 2012.

As I joined Codemasters I was unsure what to expect as I had never been part of the games industry before, or held a proper job as a coder. I was also worried about the fact I don't play many "hard-core" games. I have never classed myself as a gamer, but usually play quite casual games, and was unsure if I would fit into the culture. I have also never seen myself as a *female* programmer, but just as a programmer, and as Codemasters is a larger company than I have ever worked at before I was worried that I was going to be "the girl" and not fit in with the groups.

Once I joined the gameplay programmers at Codemasters I believe the group balance and especially the language used was changed, however this is the same when anyone new starts. I found, for example, that if someone swore they looked at me in a sort of apologetic way, but once everyone released it did not bother me and that I was pretty much the same as everyone else, things were back to normal.

After only a few weeks I was given the responsibility of the extensive camera system that underpins all of the cinematic and driving cameras in our racing games, this opportunity was fantastic and I felt very grateful that as a graduate programmer I was given such responsibility. I also found that having ownership meant I cared more and wanted to do a good job on my own systems.

I am now one of the only people who knows the current camera system and I have become the go-to person for most camera related questions and issues. I believe feeling that I am personally needed in order to create great games is one of the things that make me want to stay in the industry instead of seeking a more traditional software engineering career.

When I joined Codemasters there was one other female programmer working on the same project, although we never felt like we had to hang out just because we happened to be of the same gender, it was nice having someone else to joke around and talk woman related stuff to. She unfortunately left and I am now the only female programmer left, something that is neither bothering nor pleasing me.

I can't say that working in the game industry has always been a goal of mine. Being a programmer I do find the work very interesting as it involves a lot of different aspects and is very varying, but I believe the most thrilling feeling is knowing what I produce will be played by people all over the world. These people will talk about the game that I worked on, maybe even my features meaning, if I do a bad job it might reflect on the review of the game or the community will pick up on it.

My main interest lies in the field of Artificial Intelligence and as I gain more experience, this is an area of programming that I would like to move towards and gain more knowledge in, be it in the games industry or not. However, being a recent graduate means that I learn new things every day and gain a lot of knowledge that University could never have taught me, something that I really enjoy.

Being a girl at a company focused on creating racing games is quite an experience, there are very few girls in the whole company, making the queues to the toilets very short, but the atmosphere very male dominated. During my whole life I have always had more male friends than female, mostly due to my interests being geared towards technology. Even at school I used to be out playing in the mud and climbing trees with mostly boys. Therefore I find the situation quite natural and I believe the people around me do too, as I have never felt like my gender has changed peoples opinion about me or that it has in any way affected my job.

The hardest part I found being a female in a male dominated workplace is socialising and making friends. I live with my boyfriend, quite a long way from work, meaning I also don't naturally meet people from work in town or on nights out. At the start of my time at Codemasters this was the hardest aspect but as time has progressed and I have got to know more people by working with them I've found this is no longer a problem.

I am a member of the Women in Games Jobs network, and have attended the yearly Women in Games conference twice, now. I don't believe that women in this industry are any more special or need more attention than women in any other industry, or males for that matter, but I do think it is important to encourage diversity. The amount of women in the industry should be the amount of women wanting to get in to the industry, which is quite significantly lower than the amount of men wanting to have a career in games. I am not part of the network because I feel the need to identify myself with other people in the same situation, but instead to encourage and be a role model to younger girls finding an interest in technology and especially games.

I never had a role model or someone I looked up to and wanted to become career wise, but I do believe the fact that my parents always encouraged me to do what I found interesting and did not push me into any field of study or activity, made the career choice a lot easier as I only had to decide what I wanted to do. Therefore, I do think it is important to give the same encouragement to young girls out there, who may not have the same courage and backing from their friends and family, and may require that extra push or piece of friendly advice to jump in there and follow their dreams.

Profile 4: Jo Daly

Jo Daly has been working in the games industry since 1996 and has many years experience in developing games as a texture artist, 3D generalist, character artist, concept artist, lead and manager. She is currently a lecturer on the BA Games Art course at the University of Bolton and is also developing an as yet unannounced iPad product with her partner (he is a games programmer – she chose wisely!).

While at school in East Kilbride my ambition was to work in a creative field but I had no specific end goal or real plan. I didn't know anyone who had a 'creative' job. Having left school I briefly had a summer job in an electronics factory. This was a very valuable experience as it gave me a sound and much needed dose of reality. It confirmed for me that I didn't want to work in an electronics factory or anything like it if I could possibly avoid it. The previously scary prospect of leaving the parental home to go to an art school in a new city I'd never been to suddenly became a more appealing prospect than the alternative employment prospects available to me at home.

At Grays School of Art, Robert Gordon University in Aberdeen, I spent the first year partaking in all available subjects, including sculpting, painting, print making, jewellery design and textile design. Although I very much enjoyed the Fine Art subjects they felt more of a creative indulgence to me at the time than a serious future career option so I opted to specialise, for the remainder of my degree, in textile design, something that I hoped might result in gainful employment at the end of the course. The textile design department there was predominantly female with regards to its students.

It was only during my years at University, starting around 1992 that I began to play computer games regularly. Having gotten my hands on a SNES I became completely enthralled by Super Mario Kart, Super Mario World, Super Probotector and Super Smash TV amongst others. We didn't have a computer in my family when I was at school, that wasn't unusual, I knew very few people that did have one. I also had no educational experience of computers whatsoever and despite the many, many hours of SNES game play at that time the notion of being involved in the creation of a computer game was unthinkable and didn't even occur to me as a potential career path.

Near the end of my degree I hand wrote my degree dissertation and paid someone to type it for me, on a typewriter, yes I am that old. It was quickly becoming obvious to me that I really needed to get with the programme and at least learn to use a computer at least to the extent of being able to write and print a job application, CV and covering letter.

During my Masters year the University expanded the use of computers beyond the Graphic Design department. I enrolled on a very basic evening class and had my first experience of using a Mac. On these art school Macs the University had installed Infini-D (Specular International). I experimented with the 3D aspect of the software in a very minor way but was focussed on the completion of my Masters and also on the freelance textile surface pattern design work I had secured through agents in London thanks to contacts provided by one of my lecturers at Grays.

Working with the agents in London was a great experience but I knew immediately that although London was exciting it would never feel like home to me. My lack of maturity, confidence, business knowledge and life experience meant that outside of London I had no idea where to take my textile design work beyond the freelance scenario. I knew I didn't want to live in London...so what next?

The freelance nature of my textile design work meant I had an irregular cash-flow and no pension to speak of, however it allowed me the freedom to work the hours that suited my somewhat itinerant lifestyle at the time. It was during one of my sojourns to visit a friend in Liverpool that the world of games development opened up before me. My friend was a games artist at Psygnosis. I visited the studio with him and I saw a potential new creative job, in an exciting, fun and cutting edge industry where artists could possibly have a secure job with a salary, pension and even the much-fabled end-of-game bonuses. I wanted to be part of all of that. I met some of the women on my friend's team and was unaware, still, that as women in games they were relatively rare.

To make the shift from textile design to computer games artist I needed to create a more relevant portfolio. A few small issues lay in my path. I had very few computer skills; I didn't own a computer and didn't have the funds to buy one. I needed to gain access to the relevant software and eventually I managed to find an interior design evening class at a college in Glasgow that used 3D Studio. There were no computer games courses at the time so I completed the interior design course but secretly also designed and built 3D models of space ships, robots and creatures alongside the proper coursework. There were no male students on this course.

I touted my newly created folio and after an interview, I was offered a junior position as a texture artist at a software development company called HammerHead Ltd in Southport. That makes the transition sound easy, it wasn't. It took time, determination, a lot of hard work, great support from my family and friends and a dose of good luck to secure my first games job.

When I joined HammerHead in 1996, it was a small company of around 10 people and I was the only woman in a development role. I enjoyed the camaraderie of the team and I was never made to feel left out or overlooked by the male group. It was at HammerHead that I was given the opportunity to learn how to create 16 colour textures using DPaint (Deluxe Paint) on an elderly Amiga and there, over time, with the help and support of my fellow artists t began to develop my modelling skills further, using Softimage. There was banter amongst the dev team at Hammerhead, but nothing untoward and during my time there, a few more women were added to the dev team. Although the number of women in the team remained comparatively small, I was never aware of any discrimination in employing women. Few women applied to work in games companies at that time, ability and potential were the determining factors in gaining employment.

After HammerHead I moved onto Jester Interactive in Liverpool and Mold (N Wales), Spiral House in Warrington and eventually to EANW (Electronic Arts North West) in Stockton Heath in 2002. In each of these studios the workforce was predominantly male and the working environment comfortable and informal. The team banter at times could be 'laddish' but having grown in confidence over the years I felt more than capable of dealing with it and felt very much one of the team. Most of the guys I have worked with in games development have been fun, clever, very hard working, talented and kind.

When applying for roles in the games industry it may even be suggested that being female might be an advantage. In an endless sea of male applicants the occasional female is certainly noticeable and possibly even memorable. Some men that I have worked with in games have suggested they prefer having a mixed gender team to create a less testosterone filled working environment and add a little social balance and decorum. I have certainly noticed a little flurry of excitement amongst some of the male team members when it becomes known that a new woman is being interviewed or is starting work on a team.

In my time at EA I was also seconded to the EA Chertsey studio. The Chertsey studio was much more corporate in atmosphere than any of the other studios I had previously worked in and had a sizeable onsite HR and Marketing departments. A good number of the employees in these departments were female and I felt there was a tangible difference in the studio vibe as a whole. I didn't feel it was better or worse, just noticeably different and more 'professional' in its approach.

In the small independent companies in my early career, there was no real management structure, no older, wiser heads in charge. We were mostly young and inexperienced and we were all learning and growing on the job. By the time I joined EA the industry was getting a little older and my contemporaries had gained experience and maturity. We had made many mistakes and learned from them and aimed to develop games more efficiently. Combined with this, games had also become an attractive career for management professionals from other industries and they brought systems and attitudes with them that also changed the approach to games development into a more organised one.

As the consoles and products changed, the team sizes changed and the art roles changed too. I had gone from being a texture artist to a 3D generalist and then became a character specialist. When the EA NW studio closed down in 2006 I was offered a role at Bizarre Creations in Liverpool as a character artist. Bizarre was a well-respected company with a great reputation as an employer. They had a very low staff turnover and released great games. It was also very close to my new home in Liverpool and I jumped at the opportunity.

Again, at Bizarre, the workforce was predominantly male but the women there were far from invisible. Of the few women in the dev teams a high proportion had been promoted into lead or management roles and a couple of the company directors were female. After a year or so I was offered the role of Character Team Manager. I was a little lost at first in my new role, I wasn't sure of the role's boundaries and responsibilities. I was conscious that I had gained this role having not been at the company for very long and was unsure if the team were happy about my promotion. I doubt I would have felt differently about this had I been male.

In my management role I was responsible for the day to day scheduling of the character modellers, riggers and animators across multiple concurrent projects (later I would look after the concept artists too) I dealt with pay reviews, personal development of staff and I also liaised with external companies when the product required content we didn't have the bandwidth for within BC itself. I also had to deal with disciplinary issues when they arose.

Would the role have differed had I been male? Would the team have felt as comfortable confiding their work and personal issues to me as some of them clearly seemed to? Did they find having a female manager better or worse than a male or did it even matter? I'd have to ask the team to find out for sure. I'd like to hope it wasn't an issue for them.

Although I have always been keen to ensure I present a positive view of the games industry from a female perspective I also need to mention that it wasn't perfect. I did face some outright sexism from a select few in my various roles. It would be very difficult for me to talk about these situations here without incriminating and accusing individuals. I'm not prepared to do that, especially in a forum in which they have no opportunity to respond. When these occasions arose I was rattled and even angry in some cases but I feel I generally addressed the various situations by firmly drawing a line in the sand explaining what I was willing to deal with as 'banter' and what, for me, crossed the line and was completely unacceptable. In most cases this was acknowledged and observed. My own experience of games development as a woman is that yes, there is some sexism but no more, I imagine, than I might expect had I worked in any other industry. Ask any woman in any job, sadly there's always a tale. In saying that, I'm not suggesting that we ignore this sexism, as a society we should be ridding ourselves of these attitudes but let's not make the assumption that it's far worse in games dev, I don't believe it is.

Having experienced a number of studio closures and redundancies over the years I was very sad to see Bizarre Creations close in 2011. Rather than jump immediately into another games development role I had made the decision to see what else was out there for someone of my skill set. There are fewer games art management roles available than there are games artist roles and with the games industry in flux I had no desire to chase employment abroad to Canada or even relocate in the UK as many of my workmates had.

I was also keen to see what job I could do that might improve my work/life balance. Games development does tend to involve very long working hours during crunch and few holidays and after many years of that lifestyle I was keen to see where else I might use my skills.

During my time at Bizarre I had some involvement in visiting various Universities as a games industry representative. I had also been invited to do some guest lecture spots and faced my long-standing public-speaking fear head on (resulting in hives and white knuckle, wobbly voiced delivery).

During some downtime after Bizarre closed I was invited to attend a validation event as an industry expert for the Games Art course at the University of Bolton and despite the public-speaking issue I decided to accept their offer of part-time lecturing work in the new 2011 academic year. I figured it would give me the chance to see if I liked the job whilst also giving me time to complete a part-time PGCE (Post Graduate Certificate of Education) at UCLAN.

2 years on and I am a full time lecturer at UoB where I lecture on ZBrush, Concept Art, final year dissertation, major project supervision and a computer games business module for final year games art, design and programming students.

The courses we deliver have a slightly higher proportion of females to males than I have experienced in the industry itself. Only time will tell how many of those students go on to gain roles in industry. The role is rewarding and the culture of academia is very different to the games industry. There is far more bureaucracy in academia. In games development, decisions are made and action taken, the new bureaucracy in academia has taken time to get used to. The work/life balance is significantly better in academia, the pay is worse but the pension is better. The holidays are far, far better. Academia seems less volatile and more secure than the games industry. As I have learned (twice) from experience with two games devs sharing a mortgage it is wise not to have your wages coming from the same company when redundancy and studio closure strikes. Staying current is the main issue for me now, I have to keep abreast of industry practices and software otherwise I will become obsolete as a developer and as a lecturer. This is a challenge but along with the students themselves it is what keeps the job interesting.

We visit schools and colleges to encourage new students to our courses. In some cases these are all girl schools. My experience so far has been that by the time they are leaving school, if students aren't already bought in to the idea of a career in games, it's probably already too late. We need to stimulate interest far earlier in their school subject choices. There is a current trend to encourage more girls to participate in STEM subjects. Hopefully this will result in us seeing more females on our games courses and in the industry itself. The recent huge rise of female gamers playing casual games may also have an impact. A large number of these gamers are mothers. If they can be encouraged to recognise themselves as gamers then there may be a chance that this will result in there being less of a 'geeky boy' image attached to the perception of a 'gamer'. This may in turn encourage their daughters to see playing computer games as an acceptable pastime for girls and eventually bring more females into the industry itself.

There are more and more females now in powerful positions within the industry, I'm hopeful that these women will be seen as role models and their presence will attract more females.

During my time in games and lecturing I have continued to play games to some extent. These days I tend to play more casual iPad games. I don't have the time or inclination to devote hours to lengthy console titles. I'm more likely to be found pouring over 'the art of…' books exploring glossy images of the concept art and character models than actually spending hours playing the game itself.

Now I'm about to embark on a PhD. This has been a long held ambition and will no doubt present many challenges for me. I'm looking forward to it.

Chapter 1
From the "Damsel in Distress" to Girls' Games and Beyond:
Gender and Children's Gaming

Alyson E. King
University of Ontario, Canada

Aziz Douai
University of Ontario, Canada

ABSTRACT

In this chapter, the authors critically assess the gendered nature of the products developed by the computer gaming industry. The chapter takes a historiographical approach to examining the nature of children's video and computer games as a type of toy that immerses children into current gender stereotypes even as they hold the potential for social change. New ways of bridging the gap between stereotypes and change is explored through a virtual world for children. In addition to an introductory section, the chapter is organized in three main sections: First, the authors place existing computer and video games into a broad and historical context. Second, the chapter takes into consideration feminist critiques of video games for adults. Third, the authors analyze the case of WebkinzWorld, a toy-based social-networking portal offering less gendered video game environments for kids. The authors argue that this mixed method analysis is important not only for computer game designers and marketers who aim to appeal to broad demographics, but also for educators, parents, and caregivers who need to understand the underlying or hidden messages of games for children.

INTRODUCTION: CHILDREN'S GAMES IN CONTEXT

Since the early 1980s with the advent of home computers, video and computer games, and information and communication technologies in general, researchers have sounded the alarm about the gender divide – not enough women employed in the field, technologies designed for men, few women studying in technology-related fields (in spite of increasing numbers of women enrolled in universities generally), hypersexualized and stereotyped female characters in video games, and so on. This lack of appropriate and fair representation of women in technological fields generally has been well-documented (Cassell & Jenkins, 1998; Dietz, 1998; Harvey 2011). In this chapter, we ask the question: how has the nature

DOI: 10.4018/978-1-4666-6142-4.ch001

of children's video games evolved in terms of gender? We take the approach that the products (i.e., computer and video games) developed by the game development industry are cultural texts. By taking a historiographical approach to examining the nature of children's video and computer games as a type of toy that immerses children into current gender stereotypes, we consider their potential for social change.

Feminist research in critical media literacy has illustrated how popular culture has worked to reproduce patriarchal power structures and gendered identities. Indeed, this research has highlighted the ways in which history and culture are linked together as part of the same process. Popular culture does more than simply reflect history; cultural texts make history because they are part of social processes and practices. In a similar way, readers of texts (i.e., audiences, gamers, viewers, etc.) interpret and produce meaning from those texts which then become components of history and society. This process is further complicated, as Alvermann et al. (2000) argue, because different people will interpret the same texts in different ways, even when those people apparently share similar cultures or belief systems. However, this complication also provides insight into how children can reinterpret and reinscribe alternative meanings into gendered toys. Similarly, gamers of all ages and genders regularly try to subvert the standard images portrayed by, for example, avatars that are gendered without real reasons for them to be gendered (Hatmaker, 2010; Beavis, 2005; Bryce & Rutter, 2003). Furthermore, as Bryce and Rutter (2003) demonstrate, there is often an oversimplification of arguments regarding the gendering of computer games because the full range of such games are not considered. Nonetheless, even though subversion occurs in game play, there is still concern regarding the effects that the immersive nature of video games has on children before they learn to manipulate such games and to understand the implications of stereotyped characters, images, and storylines.

Computer and video games constitute a form of play through which socialization takes place similar to traditional toys. Children begin to identify toys as being for girls or boys during their pre-school years, and gender roles become entrenched during their teens (Martin, Eisenbud, & Rose, 1995). Toys are ascribed gender roles that fit traditional social norms first by adults who are in charge of marketing toys and second by adults who are caregivers. Even if parents attempt to provide non-gendered play opportunities, once the child leaves home for daycare or school, she or he will quickly learn gendered social norms. Those social norms that designate items such as cars, trains, planes and construction sets as "boys' toys," teach boys to be in control of their environment because they can move and construct buildings and roads. Similarly, "girls' toys," such as dolls and kitchenware, teach girls that they are expected to care and nurture others through caring for babies, preparing food and cleaning. As Babcock and Laschever (2009) conclude, such "toycoding ... teach[es] girls to subordinate their needs to the needs of others and to teach boys to take charge of their environments" (p.71). Even though young children happily play with any toys available regardless of gender designations, it often does not take long before someone decides that any play that apparently crosses gender norms is inappropriate and the child is either subject to teasing or loses access to that toy.

Researchers have long argued that important human activities occur within play environments (e.g. Huizinga, 1950). Video games and play encourage children to take chances in permissive, enjoyable and pleasurable settings. As Kinzie and Joseph (2008) put it, "[a] game is an immersive, voluntary and enjoyable activity in which a challenging goal is pursued according to agreed-upon rules. The game provides a safe environment for taking chances and the opportunity to develop the knowledge and refine the skills required to succeed" (p. 644). Similarly, Prensky (2002) argues that "*whenever* one plays a game, and *whatever* game one plays, learning happens constantly, whether the players want it to, and are aware of it, or not. And the players are learning 'about life'" (p.1). As understanding has increased about how games help to develop and nurture high cognitive and motor skills, researchers have focused on how the incorporation of more educational games in the curriculum can help to bridge the digital gap between girls and boys at an early age in a safe environment. At the same time, however, non-educational, popular computer and video games developed for children have received less attention (Marsh, 2010). The focus has been primarily on games designed for adults.

We begin our analysis by examining the broad historical context of feminist critiques of video games for adults. This section reviews how "entrepreneurial feminism" and the "games for girls" movement both critiqued and offered an alternative to the male-dominated computer games through "pink" and "purple" games. Next, after assessing current data from the gaming industry, we argue that the "gender divide" has not been bridged despite an increase in female gamers. Finally, we analyze the case of Webkinz™ World, a toy-based social-networking portal offering a less overtly gendered video game environment for kids. We provide insights from a small group of children who play on Webkinz™ World to understand the viability of such models in transcending gender stereotypes and the stratified gender roles dominating the gaming industry.

VIOLENCE AND HYPERSEXUALITY IN GAMING: AN HISTORICAL CONTEXT

The early history of the mainstream computer/video gaming industry reveals not only an obsession with violence and gore, but a prevalent stereotypical treatment and marginalization of women in the gaming industry. In the early 1990s, Provenzo (1991) found that 92 per cent

of arcade games did not feature any female roles while only 6 per cent had females play the victim or the "damsel in distress" roles (cited in Cassell & Jenkins, 1998). In a content analysis of a sample of 33 popular Nintendo and Sega Genesis video games, Dietz (1998) discovered that violent themes and traditional gender roles dominated the portrayal of women. In addition to the "damsel in distress" role, women were overtly sexualized and objectified. Among the examples Dietz offers of how women are depicted as "visions of beauty with large breasts and thin hips" is the case of the football games Tecmo Super Bowl (1993) and Madden 95 (1994) as well as the pro-wrestling game, King of the Ring (1991):

The cheerleaders in Tecmo Super Bowl and the women in the parade after the championship game in Madden 95 as well as the female audience members in the wrestling game are shown wearing skimpy clothing. While there is a female paper carrier in Paper Boy 2 (1992), it is important to note that the video game also presents women in less than an egalitarian light. Not only is the title of the game itself exclusionary of women, but there is also a young woman in the game wearing a bikini, sun tanning in her yard. Incidentally, the paper carrier will score points if he/she is able to hit this young woman with a paper (Dietz, 1998, p. 435).

Laced with violence, computer game plots, largely revolving around action, adventure, simulation and role-playing, appear to have facilitated the negative treatment of women as well (Jenkins & Cassell, 2008).

While the gender gap in computer game use has long been documented, researchers have yet to fully grasp the implications of this digital divide on gender roles. Some very early studies have found significant differences in how much men and women use computers and videogames, linking these difference to the effects this has on differences in "spatial ability" (Terlecki &

Newcombe, 2005). According to Terlecki and Newcombe, spatial ability refers to the "skill in representing and transforming symbolic or nonlinguistic information through space" (p. 433). Their study warned that "if boys and men continue to choose to be involved in computer experiences that foster spatial ability, and girls and women do not, the gap in spatial performance may continue to grow" (p. 438). This type of research, however, has been critiqued as simply reaffirming "familiar gender assumptions and truisms" (Jenson & de Castell 2010, p. 52).

As recent research demonstrates, analyses of the gendered nature of video games are increasingly nuanced. As Carr (2006) points out, neither male nor female audiences are homogenous groups, yet female gamers are often treated as if they are (cited in Bouça, 2012). Games for girls tend to be viewed as a specialty market while the focus audience of most new games is assumed to be male. The idea of games for girls as being a specialty market must be questioned. Well-designed games will appeal to both girls and boys. For example, when games such as Angry Birds are examined, the ways in which girls and boys play, as well as the devices used, are remarkably similar (Bouça, 2012). However, in games such as Angry Birds, which might be categorized as arcade-style play, there is little opportunity for players to customize avatars or the game world, nor are there gendered characters or scenarios in the design. What is interesting with Angry Birds is that its popularity cuts across genders and ages. Although arcade-style games clearly have a continuing role with their attraction to players of all ages and genders, this may not the case with other types of games.

During the mid-1990s, a number of adult video games with positive female characters were launched, such as the fourth version of King's Quest (1994), Odyssey, and Hawaii High: The Mystery of the Tiki, the first video game to exclusively target girl gamers. The girls' game movement was undergirded by the proportional rise of women in computer companies as game developers, programmers, CEOs or entrepreneurs. This entrepreneurial feminism was embodied in a new wave of women-owned computer game companies such as HerInteractive, Girl Games, Girltech, and Purple Moon (Cassell & Jenkins, 1998). Such women business owners and leaders in the economic sector were at the forefront of transforming the business side of gender relations in the gaming industry:

Setting up a small business ... can represent an explicit rejection of the exploitative nature of the capitalist work process and labor market. In this sense, then, business proprietorship may be seen as a radical--albeit short-term and individualistic--response to subordination.... Thus, women who both own and manage business enterprises--especially those in male-dominated sectors--serve to undermine conventional and stereotypical notions about 'woman's place' (Goffee & Scase, 1985 p. 37; cited in Cassell & Jenkins, 1998).

As the number of female gamers increased, the female market attracted the attention of major industry players like Mattel and IBM. The sales of Mattel's Barbie Fashion Designer proved that the market for girls' computer games was too lucrative to ignore.

The relationship between the toy and gaming industries' gender divides, and their stereotypical treatment of girls are more explicit in the strategies that the girl game movement employed. In their overview of this relationship, Kafai et al. (2008) explain that the "so-called pink games for girls," displaying traditional feminine values and "gender-typed toy preferences," constituted a prominent aspect of the games for girl movement (p. xiv). The successful franchise games of My Little Pony and Powerpuff Girls are examples of the "pinking" of the gaming industry as well as the market opportunities available for this type of game. Another faction of the girls' game movement incorporated "girls' real-life interests in sharing secrets and building friendships" in video games (Kafai et al., 2008, p. xiv). Known as the "purple" games, these new designs have primarily targeted girls but de-emphasized the "ultra-feminine" values of the "pink" games. Some of its successful examples include the Nancy Drew games, Animal Crossing and Diner Dash. In addition to user-driven games, both the "pink" and "purple" games have expanded the female gaming community.

Video games that are intentionally designed to attract girls and women are often based on "culturally learned behaviour" (Chess, 2011) and simply serve to reinforce those behaviours. The same could, of course, be said about games that appear to be male-oriented; although not necessarily designed with the specific intention of attracting males, designers have been conditioned to assume a young male audience that has particular interests. Games designed with that audience in mind often play into stereotypes of a hypermasculine male audience. Indeed, some research clearly suggests that presumed preferences are not always accurate. For example, Denner et al.'s (2005) research that had young girls design their own video games illustrated "that game production can be a site of resisting and transforming traditional gender stereotypes" (p. 7; see also Harvey, 2011).

Dill and Thill (2007) suggest that because young people underestimate the impact of media portraying gender stereotypes, they are more likely to assume that because it is just a game or "harmless entertainment" it will not have a significant impact on their worldview. Yet, the evidence suggests that "[g]ender portrayals of video game characters reinforce a sexist, patriarchal view that men are aggressive and powerful and that women are not healthy, whole persons, but sex objects, eye candy and generally second-class citizens" (Dill & Thill, 2007, p. 854). Even with the shift towards female characters that are more aggressive, they are still "objectified, sexualized and trivialized" (Dill & Thill, 2007, p. 861). This point is important to consider for children's games because, as

Dietz (1998) has demonstrated, "feminine symbols become part of the female child's identity as do masculine symbols become part of the male's identity" (p. 427). It is not just that children learn gendered roles through play (Dietz, 1998, p. 426), but that computer and video games have an even more immersive quality than most other games.

With many games designed to engage children for up to 100 hours of interactive game play (Beasley & Standley, 2002), players may be immersed in the game world in ways that may have much greater impact on their socialization than other media such as film and television. Since children form their world views based on their accumulated experience (Beasley & Standley, 2002), video games have a significant influence on what children begin to view as normal. If a child consistently plays games that portray girls and women in hypersexualized clothing, poses, and activities, then this image of women will become part of the child's world view. Like Dietz (1998), Beasley and Standley found that in the Nintendo 64 and PlayStation games they studied, a dominant theme of the unimportance of women emerged, as did the well-documented hypersexualized, big busted female characters. Research on the effect of exposure to idealized women's bodies on girls has long demonstrated that there is a negative impact on girls and women's self-esteem and self-efficacy (Behm-Morawitz & Mastro, 2009); however, more recent research on the impact of video games on girls and women suggest that the ability to manipulate avatars and to actually play the character may have a mediating effect on that negative impact (Behm-Morawitz & Mastro, 2009). In other words, for some players, the immersion into the game may increase the likelihood that girls and women will identify with the character; for other players, the ability to transform avatars and to control the play may allow girls and women to undermine the stereotypes. Behm-Morawitz and Mastro (2009) found that women playing a sexualized character did not experience lower self-esteem, but did experience lower self-efficacy. In other words, the women in their study continued to feel good about themselves even though they felt less confident about their ability to accomplish tasks.

A PERSISTING "GENDER DIVIDE": CURRENT TRENDS IN THE GAMES DEVELOPMENT INDUSTRY

The fact that well-made games that appeal to both girls and boys are still hard to find is surprising, as is the persistence of the perception that girls and women do not play video games. In 1998, columnist Rebecca Eisenberg wrote about misguided efforts to create games that appeal to girls by using colour-coded packaging and stereotyped behaviours deemed appropriate for girls. By mirroring the toy industry's strategies, however, the computer game industry has not adequately bridged the gender's digital divide. Jenkins and Cassell (2008) observe that the girls' game movement failed to shake the perception that games and computers are "boys' toys" (p. 13). Except for "fringe" games, such as educational and serious games, computer games remain largely designed by men and for men (Harvey 2011). Eisenberg (1998) notes, however, that the vast numbers of girls and women who were playing video games, as well as the success of non-gendered games such as Sega's Sonic The Hedgehog and Broderbund's Where in the World is Carmen Sandiego suggests that games that include balanced characters and storylines will appeal to both girls and boys.

Almost two decades after the birth of the games-for-girls movement, the gender divide in the gaming industry does not appear to have been bridged. In its 2012 profile of Canadian gamers, the Entertainment Software Association of Canada (ESAC), the self-described "voice of the video game industry," revealed that "90% of Canadian kids and teens are gamers." In addition to a palpable increase in the number of gaming devices in Canadian households, the ESAC reports

a significant shift from computers to mobile and handheld gaming devices, such as consoles and cellphones. The differences in the type of device used by girls and boys are not huge: 44% of girls aged six to twelve are more likely to play video games on computers, while 35% boys of the same age use game consoles. Within the same age group, slightly more girls (30%) use cellphone or mobile devices, compared to 24% of boys. Similarly, there are some differences in the types of games played. The ESAC data indicate that a majority of boys (54%) prefer action-packed adventure video games, 32% of boys prefer "racing and fight" games, and 32% of boys play "shooter" games. In contrast, girls prefer "kid role-playing games" with 28% of girls playing "arcade games," and 26% playing some educational games and puzzles that challenge mental abilities. At the early age of six to twelve years, the "gender divide" in the nature of video game playing implies that boys are more likely than girls to prefer action-packed and competitive games that involve violence; girls are more likely than boys to be attracted to educational and problem solving games and puzzles. It is unsurprising to see that this gender divide persists among teen and adult gamers, but caution is needed here. Children's game choice will also be filtered by their parents who approve or veto purchases.

The impact of adult influences on children's choices is unclear, but the changing demographics of adult gamers may indicate future changes in children's gaming choices. The gap between the number of men and women who play video games seems to be narrowing. In 2011, 38% of Canadian women and 62% of men played video and computer games; in 2012, 46% of women and 54% of men reported playing computer and video games (ESAC, 2011; ESAC, 2012). Among children aged six to twelve in 2012, although boys were more likely to play every day (41% vs. 17% of girls), more girls reported playing video games a few days per week (58% of girls and 48% of boys) (ESAC, 2012). Even though there continues to be some gender differences in types of games and device used for playing, those differences are no longer as large. It is important to question the statistics and not take them at face value (Harvey, 2011). For example, are girls more likely to model their game play on their mothers' habits or do their game choices reflect an innate preference for certain types of games? What other family dynamics may be taking place that encourage girls and women to play primarily on computers or hand-held devices rather than game consoles? Why do girls and women choose to play arcade-style games that can be completed quickly and do not require extensive time commitments that extend over days, weeks or months?

The gender bias in the game development industry's workforce may contribute to the gendered nature of game products. Current statistics about the representation of women in the Canadian gaming industry's workforce are difficult to obtain, but some researchers estimate that women constitute between 10% and 15% (Dyer-Witherford & Sharman, 2005). In their survey of the Canadian digital game industry, Dyer-Witherford and Sharman conclude that "[g]aming's continuing male bias is not only a limit to market expansion and an obstacle to girls and women learning digital skills, it is also a potential source of workplace turbulence inside games companies" (2005, p. 203). In justifying the lack of women in the gaming industry, male game designers often perceive women as incapable of appreciating the "feedback loop" between those who produce the games and those who play (Dyer-Witherford & Sharman, 2005, p. 203). Faced with this persistent gender divide in the gaming industry, an important question remains: What are the implications of this gendered digital divide?

According to the American group National Center for Women & Information Technology (NCWIT), "[t]he percentage of computing occupations held by women has been declining since 1991, when it reached a high of 36 percent" (p. 14). Even when women are successful in attaining a job in the computing or high tech fields, they are almost twice as likely as men to leave their jobs (NCWIT, 2009, p. 16). The reasons identified by NCWIT for these disparities include: unconscious bias, stereotype threats ("the fear or anxiety that our actions will confirm negative stereotypes about our 'group' or about ourselves as members of a group" (p. 25), gender- or color-blindness, the glass cliff, isolation, supervisory relationships ("Employees leave managers, not companies"), bias in promotion/performance review processes, competing responsibilities (i.e., being required to put in more time face-to-face and/or online which restricts ability to juggle family life with work life), and dual tech career households (i.e., "nearly 70 percent of partnered mid-level technical women (vs. 33 percent of men) have partners who also work in technology") (NCWIT, 2009, p. 16; see also Harvey, 2011).

The fact of fewer women working in the industry may also be explained by the low number of women studying in related fields. According to Statistics Canada, "[i]n the STEM fields of 'science and technology,' younger women held the majority (58.6%) of university degrees compared with the share of 34.9% held by older women. Younger women also had a larger share (23.1%) of university degrees in 'engineering and engineering technology' compared with women's share in the older age group (8.5%). In 'mathematics and computer sciences,' the shares held by women were similar in the younger and older age groups at 30.4% and 29.3% respectively" (2013a, p. 2). However, the field of "mathematics, computer and information sciences" was one of only five fields in which males outnumbered females in postsecondary enrolment in 2011. In all other fields, women students outnumbered men (Statistics Canada 2013b). According to the 2012 British Academy of Film and Television Arts (BAFTA) careers survey, "[w]hile 38% of 16-24 year old males have, at some time, wanted to enter the games industry, just 9% of females have ever considered it. Similarly, just 4% of female respondents are currently doing a course, work experience or job related to games, compared to 18% of males" (p. 5). Even when women consider the field as a career possibility, the BAFTA survey found that "[c]ompared to 14% of males, 21% of females who had previously considered a career in film, television or games were discouraged by parents, family or friends. Over a quarter of females (28%) felt that they would not fit in to the industry, compared to just one in five males (20%)" (p. 15). Consider that these statistics are from a point in time some 20 or 25 years after the issue was first identified as a potential problem, the question remains: why are women so under-represented in the game design industry?

Given that relatively few women are studying in the field, it stands to reason that few women are employed in the field of game development. However, efforts are being made to recruit more balanced representations into the game development industry, such as Interactive Selection who specifically recruit more women into the field (see Interactive Selection, 2013). Another non-profit group, the Women in Games Jobs, began in 2009 and "works to recruit, retain and support the progression of women in the games industry by positively and actively promoting female role models and giving encouragement and information to those women seeking to work in games" (Women in Games, 2013). The lack of women in the industry is further complicated because few women seem to even consider game design as a viable career option (Terlecki & Newcombe, 2005; Dyer-Witherford & Sharman, 2005).

Men are the majority in the game development workforce (see the UK's Skillset 2011 report). Although the issue of gendered products is recognized by the industry and the efforts to create games targeted at girls are laudable, there is a tendency to essentialize what girls want. Not all girls are attracted to the Barbie-style fashion world, just as not all boys love the violent video games. The video games that make the news on a regular basis tend to be those on the extreme end of violence spectrum, which are not targeted at young children of any sex. If one looks at the games that are specifically designed for children, the gendered nature of the characters is not always as overt as in those designed for adult males. While games such as Super Mario Bros and the Barbie virtual world have been critiqued for their gender stereotyping of characters and activities, other games and game sites, such as Webkinz World, Poptropica, Portal 2, or Minecraft, have received less attention. Therefore, computer games that offer less gendered exemplars need to be both researched and considered as a guide in the game development industry.

Our focus here has been on mainstream games backed by large corporate toy companies. There is, however, considerable research on non-mainstream games and digital play environments that suggest that collaborative and participatory online relationships have important potential to change the nature of gaming (Pearce et al., 2007). For children's games and virtual worlds, however, such openness and lack of constraints raises fears of setting children up in vulnerable situations. Sites such as Webkinz World take care to reassure parents that their children can play in their virtual world in safe ways. As a result, much of the openness and flexibility inherent in adult spaces such as The Well (created in 1985) or Second Life (created ca. 2001) is lost in sites for children. Nonetheless, virtual worlds such as Webkinz World provide opportunities for children to express a degree of creativity and to merge their real world experiences and identity with their virtual play.

THE CASE OF WEBKINZ™ WORLD

Aimed at girls and boys aged five to twelve, Webkinz World is an online virtual world created by the Canadian toy company Ganz that is linked to a physical plush toy purchased in real-world stores. Each toy comes with a code that allows the owner of the toy access to the online world. Most of the plush toys are animals, while others released in later years are fantasy characters (i.e., dragons, Zingoz, Zumbuddies). The physical toys are represented by a look-alike avatar in the virtual world. In many ways, the gendered norms of Webkinz World are much less overt than in other games; however, the focus on shopping, house design, décor, and fashion tends to reinforce the consumer culture that has been historically gendered as feminine (Carrington & Hodgetts, 2010). The potential for non-gendered play is seen in the fact that the children can control the gender of the characters, the clothes they wear, and the décor of their virtual homes. When a child accesses the virtual world, he or she enters the secret code attached to the toy; in this way, the child 'adopts' her or his pet, names it and assigns it a gender. The date of adoption becomes the pet's birthday, which is celebrated each year with a piece of cake and a gift. Children can play in fourteen languages, including English, French and Spanish – a fact that underlines the importance of understanding the impact of this game site. Webkinz World was envisioned by Ganz president Howard Ganz, with the development team led by creative director Karl Borst, and launched in 2005. It has since won several industry awards and continues to be ranked among the top ten websites visited by American tweens, in spite of some decline in popularity (Traylor, 2012; Traylor, 2013)

To supplement our exploration of the nature of Webkinz World through adult eyes, we also invited four children to share their points of view with us. The focus group was composed of a convenience sample of two girls (both aged 11) and two boys (aged 8 and 9). The small sample included one of the authors' two children, as well as two friends from school and daycare. The children live with their respective middle-class families in a small town in Ontario, Canada. All four have strong computer literacy skills and enjoy a variety of computer and video games, but their screen time is limited to one to two hours per day by their parents.

While the children provide a small homogeneous sample, their responses and experiences provide insight into how children can make choices as they navigate the virtual world and how they connect their real-world toys with the virtual avatars.

The design of the virtual world allows for individual preferences to be at the forefront of the game play; children choose which games to play, products to purchase with virtual Webkinz World cash (Kinzcash), rooms to design, and so on. Indeed, Karl Borst describes virtual worlds as needing to be "a sandbox of interactive systems that allow players to choose the experience that they wish to make, while remaining a cohesive world" (Traylor, 2012, p. 8). At the same time, the product is structured such that children are encouraged to visit daily and to purchase a new plush toy at least annually: the more one plays and spends, the more Kinzcash and gifts one earns. While all the children in this focus group enjoyed playing in Webkinz World, with the limited screen time they were allowed, they tended to only visit on a daily basis when the toys were new. However, all the children had multiple stuffed toys acquired as gifts or purchased with spending money over a period of several years indicating ongoing interest in acquiring the real-world and virtual toys used in Webkinz World. Similar to other game sites' efforts to create "stickiness" (Marsh 2010, p. 34), daily visits are encouraged by several of the games, as well as by the idea that one must visit regularly in order to care for one's pets (such as, by feeding, grooming, playing, and putting to bed). Further incentive for daily visits is found in the fact that by playing games and becoming good at them, one can earn KinzCash that can be used to buy furniture and appliances, food and beverages, toys and games, and clothes that can be placed in the virtual home. Each new pet comes with a room, plus a few gifts. Additional rooms can also be purchased. These rooms can be indoor or outdoor, as well as underwater rooms for water creatures or rooms in trees for flying animals. Indoor rooms can be named and furnished to represent bedrooms, kitchens, dining rooms, play rooms, school rooms and so on. Similarly, outdoor rooms can be transformed into beaches, flower or vegetable gardens, or playgrounds. Children can purchase seeds to grow vegetables, which can then be fed to their pet(s). Furniture may be generic or thematic; for example, at the height of the Harry Potter craze, children could purchase castle-themed furniture and decorations that evoked the feel of Hogwarts. In some ways, the virtual house takes on the feel of building a dollhouse or Lego structure. The child can design the house layout within certain parameters and then proceed to decorate and design room layouts. While the virtual home may not have the versatility of building with Lego bricks, it is less frustrating to design and decorate than a physical dollhouse.

The digital online space provides a variety of games that allow participants to earn Kinzcash; some of the games, if they were the primary game, may be seen as gendered, such as cooking using recipes in a cookbook, kitchen equipment (that the child has chosen to purchase) and the pet's food. The food created by the child can then be fed to the virtual pet, who will react with a comment such as "I don't think I like that" or "That was yummy! You take such good care of me." Similarly, a fashion show competition can be played with other players who are online. Chat rooms are also available, but limited interactions are allowed. While all of these games could be viewed as gendered, reflecting a site architecture that embeds values and social norms through the coding used by designers (Harvey, 2011), the games are open to all players and both girls and boys engage in them. Nonetheless, some gender preferences are apparent.

The small sample of children included here revealed that while some gender stereotyped choices were made, the wide range of activities held the potential to challenge those stereotypes. The real-world stuffed toys are generally gender neutral. Male and female children could have the same stuffed toy and designate them as different

genders with different names. For example, in our small sample, both girls chose to name their pets by splitting them equally with girl names and boy names, while both boys only used male names.[1]

Online, there are a number of games that the children in the focus group enjoy playing, including ones that involve different types of learning. Anna[2] enjoys playing games like Home Before Dark which involves connecting pieces of a path from the park to the pets' homes. The more pets that make it home before dark, the more points the player gets. It is a challenging game that develops some spatial recognition skills and requires the player to visualize what will happen a few steps ahead. For Anna, the games that are drill-oriented and aimed at developing content knowledge hold little interest. Quizzy's Corner, for example, is a game where the child answers questions on different subject areas, organized by age categories. Quizzy's Corner also holds little interest for Anna's younger brother, Bill (age 8), who is still developing his reading skills. Anna enjoys playing with the interactive books that can be read by the player who can turn the pages as she reads and with the cookbooks, which allow her to experiment with the recipes. For Bill, the games most enjoyed are those that require little textual reading and that require a degree of speed and skill. His favourite arcade game is Zingoz, but he also enjoys the Battleship game which is a game of logic that is purchased and placed in a pet's room. Bill tends to experiment with games until he figures it out, rather than reading directions. He is very good at problem solving and reading the icons and symbols to figure out how games work. What is particularly interesting is that girls and boys can choose how and what to play; there is nothing overt that cues the child to select gendered games (i.e., there is not a 'girls zone' or 'boys zone' as might be seen, for example, in large toy stores).

The children also enjoy playing the games that can only be visited once a day. These games are modelled after games of chance. For example, the

Wheel of Wow brings to mind a roulette wheel and the Wishing Well resembles a slot machine. Although no gambling or wagering is involved – the children lose nothing by playing – some researchers fear that such games are being normalized and are teaching children at a very young age to enjoy games of chance. These games, while not gendered, are socializing children to accept that gambling is a fun and safe activity. The Webkinz FAQ site, however, includes a comment that because "[g]ambling requires that a player put in a wager to play, and hence have the chance to lose that wager" none of their games fit that definition (2013). Gendered play, in the case of Webkinz World, is more likely to take place because of previously internalized gender roles then due to gendered design elements. The limitations embedded in some aspects of the game play, such as the lack of action and fast-paced competition, may cause some children to become bored with this virtual world and to move on to other video and computer games. Additionally, children may eventually grow out of this style of game play (although there is some anecdotal evidence that many adults enjoy playing in Webkinz World) as the target audience is children aged five to twelve.

Offline, the children extend the Webkinz play by regularly acting out fairly elaborate story lines. At daycare, for example, Anna, Lisa and their friends planned a wedding between Anna's black-and-white cat, Pippin, and her friend's black-and-white cat, Emory. On the day of the wedding, all the girls and boys in their room at the daycare brought in one or two Webkinz pets to be in the audience or to be part of the wedding party. After the wedding, the older girls wrote stories about the event and drew pictures of the participants to put in a Webkinz fan magazine they created. In addition to the wedding story, they created advertisements, beauty tips, and posters of 'famous' Webkinz, in the style of a gossip magazine. Marsh (2010) notes that it is difficult to separate play in the 'real' world from that in the 'virtual' world, arguing that it is useful to see children's play as a continuum that flows between worlds. Arguably, offline play allows for more creativity than anything on the website. For instance, on the website, children can 'write' their own stories, but only using prewritten phrases and words. Similarly, messages sent by Kinzpost and in the Chat room are limited to canned, generic phrases. The children find it frustrating to be so limited in how they can interact on the site. Yet, for parents and teachers, the use of predetermined expressions is seen as providing a level of protection for the children; fears about online safety are alleviated.

Although both girls and boys play Webkinz World, the connection with a plush toy is likely to attract girls longer than it will boys given that it is usually more socially acceptable for girls to continue to collect such toys well into their teens. As Carrington & Hodgetts (2010) point out, with girls particularly targeted by such consumer-oriented game sites, they "are being taught that particular types of effort are required to earn currency; that the purpose of currency is to purchase identities and other consumer items, and that they are rewarded with friendship, success and happiness for these displays of gender, identity and consumption" (p. 680). Although Webkinz World is not overtly gendered, such sites do not encourage girls to move beyond the stereotypical roles that have disempowered girls and women for generations and, at the same time, may be drawing young boys into the consumer culture. As de Castells et al. (2007) have pointed out, when a girl is focussed on a particular activity, that activity is "where her intelligence is at work" (p. 597). This point highlights the need to look critically at play as a place of learning. No longer should such video games be dismissed as "just play." Designers of games must look beyond simply adding content to being more critical about how design and content work together to create an immersive environment that does not simply recreate the world as it is, with its ongoing patriarchal power structures and lack of equity. Even though Webkinz World is not as explicitly gendered as sites such as BarbieGirls, it still plays a role in the enculturation of children into stereotyped roles (Carrington & Hodgetts, 2010; Harvey, 2011). In addition, and perhaps more subtly, the site draws children into a consumer culture (Black & Reich, 2013; Briton, 2010) that encourages spending and gambling. Not only must one purchase the real plush toy, but then a player must play games and undertake various activities to earn money to purchase virtual consumer goods.

Some virtual world-type games seemed to hold promise for experimentation in alternative gender identities, but such games have since been demonstrated to tend to reproduce sexualized gender stereotypes and traditional power structures (Hayes, 2007). Webkinz World is different from adult games where the avatar represents the individual player; rather, the Webkinz avatars represent the plush toys purchased in the real world. In effect, therefore, the child is playing with an online version of the toy not enacting an alternative self-identity in the way that adults have engaged in identity experimentation in some multi-player games.

CONCLUSION

The case study of Webkinz offers an important lesson about gaming and gender: it is possible for games to nurture children's ability to transcend the stereotypical gender roles and foster a greater engagement with technology among girls; however, the consumer-orientation of Webkinz World also reinforces the feminine stereotype of girls loving to shop and encouraging an overall consumer behaviour among all players. Nonetheless, the case of Webkinz World illustrates the blending of virtual and real-world play and its potential to help children in their learning by developing, for example, multiliteracies skills. In their study of how children navigate the world of Webkinz, Wohlwend et al. (2011) similarly conclude that: "Web/toys merge play and discourses with technologies and literacies that coordinate meanings

with others across time and space. These converged texts shape children's identities and teach them how to read and respond in particular ways in digital worlds" (p. 161). Moreover, the nature of play is itself transformed: as our case study of Webkinz also highlights, connecting the "offline" and "online" environments extends the nature of play as gamers work on elaborate story lines.

Where does this leave the "gender divide" debate in the field of computer and video games for children? As this chapter has demonstrated, there has been palpable improvement and progress in the representation of women in computer games due to the hard work of a generation of women who "infiltrated" and challenged the industry's stereotypical treatment of females. The exponential growth in the number of female gamers has also aided in the campaign for "fair" and "positive" representation. Yet, the industry's own statistics reveal that the path to full equality between the number of men and women employed in the game development industry is still long. Taking stock of these shifts, we have argued that the mixed methods analysis is important not only for computer game designers and marketers who aim to appeal to broad demographics, but also for educators, parents, and caregivers who need to understand the underlying or hidden messages of games for children.

REFERENCES

Alvermann, D. E., & Hagood, M. C. (2000). Critical media literacy: Research, theory, and practice in new times. *The Journal of Educational Research, 93*(3), 193–205. doi:10.1080/00220670009598707

Ashcraft, C., & Blithe, S. (2010). *Women in IT: The facts*. National Center for Women & Information Technology.

Babcock, L., & Laschever, S. (2009). *Women don't ask: Negotiation and the gender divide*. Princeton, NJ: Princeton University Press.

Bandura, A. (1994). Self-efficacy. In V. S. Ramachaudran (Ed.), *Encyclopedia of human behavior* (Vol. 4, pp. 71-81). New York: Academic Press. (Reprinted in H. Friedman [Ed.], *Encyclopedia of mental health.* San Diego: Academic Press, 1998). Retrieved from http://www.uky.edu/~eushe2/Bandura/BanEncy.html

Beasley, B., & Standley, T. C. (2002). Shirts vs. skins: Clothing as an indicator of gender role stereotyping in video games. *Mass Communication & Society*, *5*(3), 279–293. doi:10.1207/S15327825MCS0503_3

Beavis, C. (2005). Pretty good for a girl: Gender, identity and computer games. In *Proceedings of DiGRA 2005 Conference: Changing Views – Worlds in Play*.

Behm-Morawitz, E., & Mastro, D. (2009). The effects of the sexualization of female video game characters on gender stereotyping and female self-concept. *Sex Roles*, *61*, 808–823. doi:10.1007/s11199-009-9683-8

Black, R. W., & Reich, S. M. (2013). A sociocultural approach to exploring virtual worlds. In G. Merchant, J. Gillen, J. Marsh, & J. Davies (Eds.), *Virtual literacies: Interactive spaces for children and young people.* New York: Routledge.

Bouça, M. (2012). Angry birds, uncommitted players. In *Proceedings of DiGRA Nordic 2012 Conference: Local and Global – Games in Culture and Society*.

British Academy of Film and Television Arts. (2012). *The BAFTA career pathways survey: Career pathways in film, television and games: A report published by the British Academy of Film and Television Arts.* Retrieved from http://static.bafta.org/files/career-survey-booklet-v8-online-1569.pdf

Briton, D. (2010). The virtual expanses of Canadian popular culture. In B. Beaty, D. Briton, G. Filax, & R. Sullivan (Eds.), *How Canadians communicate III: Contexts of Canadian popular culture* (pp. 319–352). Edmonton, Canada: Athabasca University Press.

Bryce, J., & Rutter, J. (2003). Gender dynamics and the social and spatial organization of computer gaming. *Leisure Studies*, *22*, 1–15. doi:10.1080/02614360306571

Carrington, V., & Hodgetts, K. (2010). Literacy-lite in *BarbieGirls™*. *British Journal of Sociology of Education*, *31*(6), 671–682. doi:10.1080/01425692.2010.515109

Cassell, J., & Jenkins, H. (1998). Chess for girls? Feminism and computer games. In J. Cassell, & H. Jenkins (Eds.), *From Barbie to Mortal Kombat: Gender and computer games* (pp. 2–45). Cambridge, MA: MIT Press.

Chess, S. (2011). A 36-24-36 cerebrum: Productivity, gender, and video game advertising. *Critical Studies in Media Communication*, *28*(3), 230–252. doi:10.1080/15295036.2010.515234

Computer and video games. (n. d.). *Science Daily*. Retrieved from http://www.sciencedaily.com/articles/c/computer_and_video_games.htm

de Castell, S., Jenson, J., & Taylor, N. (2007). Digital games for education: When meanings play. In *Situated Play, Proceedings of DiGRA 2007 Conference*.

Denner, J., Bean, S., & Werner, L. (2005). Girls creating games: Challenging existing assumptions about game content. In *Proceedings of DiGRA 2005 Conference: Changing Views – Worlds in Play*.

Dietz, T. L. (1998). An examination of violence and gender role portrayals in video games: Implications for gender socialization and aggressive behavior. *Sex Roles*, *38*(5/6), 425–442. doi:10.1023/A:1018709905920

Dill, K. E., & Thill, K. P. (2007). Video game characters and the socialization of gender roles: Young people's perceptions mirror sexist media depictions. *Sex Roles*, *57*(11/12), 851–864. doi:10.1007/s11199-007-9278-1

Dyer-Witheford, N., & Sharman, Z. (2005). The political economy of Canada's video and computer game industry. *Canadian Journal of Communication*, *30*(2), 187–210.

Eckert, P., & McConnell-Ginet, S. (2003). *Language and gender*. New York: Cambridge University Press. doi:10.1017/CBO9780511791147

Eisenberg, R. (1998). Girl games: Adventures in lip gloss. *Gamasutra*. Retrieved from www.gamasutra.com/view/feature/3252/girl_games_adventures_in_lip_gloss.php

Harvey, A. (2011). Architectures of participation in digital play: Social norms, gender, and youth gameplay. *Information Communication and Society*, *14*(3), 303–319. doi:10.1080/1369118X.2010.542821

Hatmaker, T. (2010). *The (gender) trouble with video game avatars*. Retrieved from http://www.autostraddle.com/the-gender-trouble-with-avatars-56108/

Huizinga, J. (1955). *Homo Ludens: A study of the play element in culture*. Boston: Beacon Press.

Interactive Selection. (2013). *Interactive promotes women in games development*. Retrieved from http://www.interactiveselection.com/women.asp

Jenkins, H., & Cassell, J. (2008). From quake grrls to desperate housewives: A decade of gender and computer games. In Y. Kafai, C. Heeter, J. Denner, & J. Sun (Eds.), *Beyond Barbie and Mortal Kombat: New perspectives on gender and computer games* (pp. 5–20). Cambridge, MA: MIT Press.

Kafai, Y. B., Heeter, C., Denner, J., & Sun, J. Y. (2008). *Preface: Pink, purple, casual, or mainstream games: Moving beyond the gender divide. Beyond Barbie and Mortal Combat: New perspectives on gender and gaming*. London: The MIT Press.

Kinzie, M. B., & Joseph, D. R. (2008). Gender differences in game activity preferences of middle school children: implications for educational game design. *Educational Technology Research and Development*, *56*(5-6), 643–663. doi:10.1007/s11423-007-9076-z

Marsh, J. (2010). Young children's play in online virtual worlds. *Journal of Early Childhood Research*, *8*(1), 23–39. doi:10.1177/1476718X09345406

Martin, C., Eisenbud, L., & Rose, H. (1995). Children's gender-based reasoning about toys. *Child Development*, *66*, 1453–1471. doi:10.2307/1131657 PMID:7555224

Pearce, C., Fullerton, T., Fron, J., & Ford Morie, J. (2007). Sustainable play: Toward a new games movement for the digital age. *Games and Culture*, *2*, 261–278. doi:10.1177/1555412007304420

Prensky, M. (2002). *What kids learn that's positive from playing video games*. Retrieved from http://www.paaco.org/ArticlesBooksCourses/What_Kids_Learn_That_s_POSITIVE_from_Playing_Video_Games.html

Skillset. (2011). Computer games sector: Labour market intelligence digest. *The Sector Skills Council for Creative Media*. Retrieved from http://www.creativeskillset.org/uploads/pdf/asset_16891.pdf?4

Smith, P. K. (2013). *The encyclopedia on early childhood development*. Retrieved from http://www.child-encyclopedia.com/pages/PDF/play.pdf

Statistics Canada. (2013a). 2011 national household survey: Education in Canada: Attainment, field of and location of study. *The Daily*. Released June 26, 2013. Retrieved from http://www.statcan.gc.ca/daily-quotidien/130626/dq130626a-eng.pdf

Statistics Canada. (2013b). Public postsecondary enrolments and graduates, 2010/2011. *The Daily*. Released January 23, 2013. Retrieved from http://www.statcan.gc.ca/daily-quotidien/130123/dq130123a-eng.pdf

Terlecki, M. S., & Newcombe, N. S. (2005). How important is the digital divide? The relation of computer and videogame usage to gender differences in mental rotation ability. *Sex Roles*, *53*(5-6), 433–441. doi:10.1007/s11199-005-6765-0

Traylor, S. (2012, November). Inside the World of Webkinz: An interview with creative director Karl Borst. *Children's. Technology Review*, 6–8.

Traylor, S. (2013). *Tween virtual worlds by the numbers*. 360Blog. Retrieved December 9, 2013, from http://www.360kid.com/blog/2013/08/

United Nations. (1989). *Convention on the rights of the child*. Retrieved from https://treaties.un.org/doc/Publication/UNTS/Volume%201577/v1577.pdf

Webkinz. (2013). *Frequently asked questions: For parents*. Retrieved December 9, 2013, from http://www.webkinz.com/faq/j.html#6

Wohlwend, K. E., Vander Zanden, S., Husbye, N. E., & Kuby, C. R. (2011). Navigating discourses in place in the World of Webkinz. *Journal of Early Childhood Literacy*, *11*(2), 141–163. doi:10.1177/1468798411401862

Women in Games Jobs Network. (2013). *About women in games jobs*. Retrieved from http://www.womeningamesjobs.com/?page_id=2

ADDITIONAL READING

Alvermann, D. E., & Hagood, M. C. (2000, Jan/Feb). Critical media literacy: Research, theory, and practice in "new times.". *The Journal of Educational Research*, *93*(3), 193–205. doi:10.1080/00220670009598707

Babcock, L., & Laschever, S. (2009). *Women don't ask: Negotiation and the gender divide*. New Jersey: Princeton University Press.

Bandura, A. (1994). Self-efficacy. In V. S. Ramachaudran (Ed.), *Encyclopedia of human behavior* (Vol. 4, pp. 71-81). New York: Academic Press. (Reprinted in H. Friedman [Ed.], *Encyclopedia of mental health*. San Diego: Academic Press, 1998). Retrieved from http://www.uky.edu/~eushe2/Bandura/BanEncy.html

Beasley, B., & Standley, T. C. (2002). Shirts vs. skins: Clothing as an indicator of gender role stereotyping in video games. *Mass Communication & Society*, *5*(3), 279–293. doi:10.1207/S15327825MCS0503_3

Beavis, C. (2005). Pretty good for a girl: Gender, identity and computer games. Proceedings of DiGRA 2005 Conference: Changing Views – Worlds in Play.

Behm-Morawitz, E., & Mastro, D. (2009). *The effects of the sexualization of female video game characters on gender stereotyping and female self-concept. Sex Roles*. Online.

Black, R. W., & Reich, S. M. (2013). A sociocultural approach to exploring virtual worlds. In G. Merchant, J. Gillen, J. Marsh, & J. Davies (Eds.), *Virtual literacies: Interactive spaces for children and young people*. New York: Routledge.

Bouça, M. (2012). Angry birds, uncommitted players. Proceedings of DiGRA Nordic 2012 Conference: Local and Global – Games in Culture and Society.

Bryce, J., & Rutter, J. (2003). Gender dynamics and the social and spatial organization of computer gaming. *Leisure Studies*, *22*, 1–15. doi:10.1080/02614360306571

Carrington, V., & Hodgetts, K. (2010). Literacy-lite in *BarbieGirls™*. *British Journal of Sociology of Education*, *31*(6), 671–682. doi:10.1080/0142 5692.2010.515109

Cassell, J., & Jenkins, H. (Eds.). (1998). *From Barbie to Mortal Kombat: Gender and computer games* (pp. 2–45). Cambridge, MA: MIT Press.

Chess, S. (2011). A 36-24-36 Cerebrum: Productivity, gender, and video game advertising. *Critical Studies in Media Communication*, *28*(3), 230–252. doi:10.1080/15295036.2010.515234

de Castell, S., Jenson, J., & Taylor, N. (2007). Digital games for education: When meanings play. Situated Play, Proceedings of DiGRA 2007 Conference.

Dietz, T. L. (1998). An examination of violence and gender role portrayals in video games: Implications for gender socialization and aggressive behavior. *Sex Roles*, *38*(5/6), 425–442. doi:10.1023/A:1018709905920

Dill, K. E., & Thill, K. P. (2007). Video game characters and the socialization of gender roles: Young people's perceptions mirror sexist media depictions. *Sex Roles*, *57*(11/12), 851–864. doi:10.1007/s11199-007-9278-1

Dyer-Witheford, N., & Sharman, Z. (2005). The political economy of Canada's video and computer game industry. *Canadian Journal of Communication*, *30*(2), 187–210.

Harvey, A. (2011). Architectures of participation in digital play: Social norms, gender, and youth gameplay. *Information Communication and Society*, *14*(3), 303–319. doi:10.1080/1369 118X.2010.542821

Huizinga, J. (1955). *Homo Ludens: A study of the play element in culture*. Boston: Beacon Press.

Marsh, J. (2010). Young children's play in online virtual worlds. *Journal of Early Childhood Research*, *8*(1), 23–39. doi:10.1177/1476718X09345406

Martin, C., Eisenbud, L., & Rose, H. (1995). Children's gender-based reasoning about toys. *Child Development*, *66*(5), 1453–1471. doi:10.2307/1131657 PMID:7555224

Pearce, C., Fullerton, T., Fron, J., & Ford Morie, J. (2007). Sustainable play: Toward a new games movement for the digital age. *Games and Culture*, *2*(3), 261–278. doi:10.1177/1555412007304420

Terlecki, M. S., & Newcombe, N. S. (2005). How important is the digital divide? The relation of computer and videogame usage to gender differences in mental rotation ability. *Sex Roles*, *53*(5-6), 433–441. doi:10.1007/s11199-005-6765-0

KEY TERMS AND DEFINITIONS

Children: According to the United Nations' Convention on the Rights of the Child adopted in 1989, "a child means every human being below the age of 18 years unless, under the law applicable to the child, majority is attained earlier."

Computer Games: *Science Daily* defines computer games as "a computer-controlled game where players interact with objects displayed on a screen for the sake of entertainment. It also includes games which display only text or which use other methods, such as sound or vibration, as their primary feedback device, or a controller (console games), or a combination of any of the above" (Computer and video games, n. d.).

Feminism: As a social and political movement, feminism advocates equal rights between men and women rights in all spheres of life. While there are different strands of feminism, they all share a critique of patriarchy and male dominance in private and public life.

Gender: Gender refers to the socio-cultural categorization of people into male and female with each having a different set of gender roles and social expectations. According to Eckert and McConnell-Ginet (2003), "[g]ender is embedded so thoroughly in our institutions, our actions, our beliefs, and our desires, that it appears to us to be completely natural..... Gender is not something we are born with, and not something we have," but something we daily *do* and *perform*.

Play: According to *The Encyclopedia on Early Childhood Development* (Smith, 2013) play is "a spontaneous, voluntary, pleasurable and flexible activity involving a combination of body, object, symbol use and relationships. In contrast to games, play behaviour is more disorganized, and is typically done for its own sake (i.e., the process is more important than any goals or end points)."

Stereotypes: A stereotype refers to simplistic assumptions and generalizations about a person or a thing. Gender stereotypes refer to these socially-constructed beliefs about the attributes and roles of men and women. For instance, while men are stereotypically expected to be strong and the provide for their families, female stereotypes traditionally include the generalization that all women have to be loving, nurturing, sexy, marriage-seeking, and have children.

ENDNOTES

[1]   Some parts of this research were presented at the Canadian Society for Studies in Education Annual Meeting, 2009.

[2]   All names are pseudonyms.

Chapter 2
Women and Men in Computer Science:
The Role of Gaming in their Educational Goals

Jill Denner
Education, Training, Research, USA

Eloy Ortiz
Education, Training, Research, USA

Linda Werner
University of California, Santa Cruz, USA

ABSTRACT

Playing digital games is described as a pathway to computer science (CS) classes and majors, but not all gamers want to study CS. The goal of this chapter is to explore which gaming motivations and practices are most strongly related to an interest in studying computer science, and whether the connection between gaming and computer science is similar for men and women. The data are from 545 male and female gamers taking an introductory computer science class at one of 15 community colleges in the US. Survey responses were analyzed to provide a picture of what, how often, and why they play, and interviews from 39 of the most avid gamers were analyzed for why and how they play. The results show that, on average, men play more frequently than women, and there are gender differences in the type of games they like to play and why they play them. However, playing more frequently was not associated with greater interest in studying CS for either gender. Interest in CS was highest among men who were motivated to play in order to increase skills, be with friends, connect with the game features, and by the art or graphics. However, CS interest was highest among women who consider themselves to be more serious gamers, play racing and puzzle games, play on a game console, and are motivated by fun, relaxation and social interaction. The results can inform efforts to increase the number of women that pursue computer science. The chapter concludes with recommendations for future research on how game play and interest in CS are related.

DOI: 10.4018/978-1-4666-6142-4.ch002

BACKGROUND

Women's enrollment in computer and information sciences (CIS) majors and completion of CIS undergraduate and graduate degrees has declined in the US over the last 20 years (National Science Foundation, 2013). Prior research has suggested that enrollment and retention in college-level computer science is related to students' experience and interest in digital gaming. In particular, women's underrepresentation is widely believed to be due, in part, to a lack of computer game play (Carter, 2006; Lynn, Raphael, Olefsky, & Bachen, 2003). Until recently, males reported more frequent game play and were more likely to cite that as a source of motivation and preparation to pursue a computer science (CS) major (Margolis & Fisher, 2002; Natale, 2002; Tillberg & Cohoon, 2005). A recent quantitative study of community or 2-year college students found that intention to pursue computer science studies was predicted by computer gaming, for both women and men (Denner, Werner, O'Connor, & Glassman, 2014). However, other studies have challenged the connection between gaming and CS.

In order to understand how playing computer games is related to educational goals, it is important to understand students' motivation to play certain types of games--whether it is for entertainment, to learn something, or to reduce stress (Sherry et al., 2006). More recent and in depth studies of gaming are needed to understand how and why students play, as well as whether there are gender differences in the role that computer game play has in students' interest in a computer-related major. The next section includes a review of relevant research on what male and female gamers play, why they play, and the implications of this research for understanding the connection between gaming and interest in studying computer science.

Different Types of Game Play

Talking about gaming in general is like talking about sports—there is great variation in the kinds of games that are available, and a range of play experiences is available both within and across game genres. In this chapter we are talking about all kinds of digital games, including what the Entertainment Software Association refers to as video games (those using game consoles) and computer games (those playable on personal computers including mobile multi-purpose devices). In 2012, the best selling video game genres were: action (22%), shooters (21%), sports (15%) and adventure (8%), and the best selling computer game genres were role playing (28%), casual (27%), and strategy (25%) games (Entertainment Software Association, 2013). Action games include a range of play experiences, from fighting games (Mortal Kombat) to platform games (Super Mario Brothers), but usually involve completing discrete levels, having limited lives, and scoring points. Shooter, otherwise known as First Person Shooter (FPS) games (the player's view is through the eyes of their character) such as Call of Duty include discrete local campaigns or storylines for the player to complete, and online cooperative and battle modes. Sports games such as the Madden NFL series are often played on a game console, and there are options to play online with or against other people. Adventure games such as Tomb Raider and Assassin's Creed include exploration, solving environmental puzzles and collecting objects. Role playing games include the Final Fantasy series and World of Warcraft games which include developing characters actions and abilities through experience and training while completing a long range storyline. Casual games are usually played on a personal computer or mobile device and require little time to learn and complete; they are often puzzle games, which involve problem solving skills (e.g., pattern recognition, word completion), like Bejewelled. Strategy games, such as the Sims and Civilization, feature the player using tactics and strategic and economic planning to complete the goals of the game.

There is some evidence of gender differences in gaming practices. For example, one study finds that girls and women are more likely to play simulations, puzzle games, and racing games, and less likely to play first person shooters or sports games (Cragg, Taylor, and Toombs, 2007) but this was based on a small sample, particularly few females. A large study found that adult women play puzzle games more often than men, but men like shooter, sports, racing, strategy, adventure, and role playing games more (Lucas & Sherry, 2004). Similarly, studies of middle school children find that girls prefer games that involve exploration and creativity, while boys prefer games that include strategy, action, and competition (Kinzie & Joseph, 2008; Olson, 2010). A study of college students found that females are more likely than males to say they prefer to play games in small chunks of time (Winn & Heeter, 2009). However, most of these findings are based on data collected more than a decade ago, and do not reflect the pervasiveness of gaming, particularly the short (casual) games that have been developed for play on mobile devices.

Despite some overall differences in game play between men and women, there is also a great deal of overlap, and research suggests that other factors besides biological sex are playing a role. These studies suggest that it may be more productive to look at variation within gender. As Hayes (2005) describes, there is not one female style of playing…women bring different experiences and motivations to their game play, which affects how they play. This variation is due to a number of factors, including age and the social context (Yee, 2008). Thus, descriptions of gaming practices and preferences need to be situated in the context of where and with whom it occurs, rather than assuming there are biological gender differences

and talking about less competent and more competent gaming performances (Thornham, 2008). In addition, examinations of gender differences in game preferences must take into account prior experience (Denner et al., 2014). Jenson and de Castell (2010) provide a clear argument for why it is important to know how game technologies are used, including when and with whom people play, whether gaming is disruptive or conducive to everyday lives, as well as the range of play within gender. In the next section, we describe research that suggests players' motivations may be more important that simple demographic categories.

Motivation for Playing

Several theoretical perspectives have been used to explain why there are gender differences in gaming behavior. Lucas and Sherry (2004) describe a model in which video game play is a way of seeking gratification for needs, including dominance or social interaction. Others have documented how a game's characters, especially oversexualized female characters in action and strategy games, have a strong influence on why these genres are more appealing to men (Hartmann & Klimmt, 2006; Ogletree & Drake, 2007). And still others explain gaming behavior by looking at gender norms and expectations for sex-typed play, and the way that gaming spaces are still viewed as male dominated (Fullerton et al., 2008; Taylor, Jenson, & de Castell, 2009; Walkerdine, 2007). In this section, we summarize research on the various motivations that female and male gamers have for playing.

Sherry et al (2006) identified an empirically valid set of traits for video game uses and gratifications with data from 18-22 year old undergraduates in the US: *arousal* (stimulate emotions as a result of fast action and high quality graphics), *challenge, competition* (to show others how good they are), *diversion* (relax, escape, boredom), *fantasy* (do things they cannot in real life), and *social interaction*. They studied these reasons with middle, high school and college students, and found that challenge was the number one reason for playing. The biggest difference between men and women was that men ranked all gratifications higher than women; while the order was similar, males ranked social interaction higher. Using a British sample with a range of ages, Cragg et al (2007) found similar motivations to what Sherry et al found: Challenge, escape, competition, graphics. In a study of college students that were primarily female, Hoffman and Nadelson (2010) found that the three main reasons that people play games are to escape and have fun, to make social connections, and to have a sense of achievement, but they found that females were more likely to be motivated by socializing, rather than by the game play itself. Olson (2010) found similar results in middle school: the greatest motivation for both boys and girls was to have fun, followed by competition and challenge for boys, and avoiding boredom for girls. In none of these studies was storyline found to be one of the reasons that players were attracted to certain games.

Motivations for play vary depending on the type of game or platform being used. Yee (2008) identified three primary reasons for playing massively multiplayer online games: achievement, social connections, and immersion. He found that males were more likely to talk about achievement, and females were more likely to talk about the relationship aspect of social connection and the customization aspect of immersion. Williams, Consalvo, Caplan, & Yee (2009) also found that women were more likely to play online games for social interaction than men, while men were more likely to play for achievement. However, Yee (2008) suggests that these gender differences are better explained by age (the males were younger than the females) and there were no gender differences in motivation to socialize, collaborate, explore, follow a storyline or escape/relax. In summary, these studies find more overlap than difference in the motivations of females and males for gaming behavior. Where there is difference, it

follows closely with wider societal norms about male achievement and female social connectedness (Hare-Mustin & Marecek, 1988).

The Connection between Gaming and Computer Science

Gaming and gamification are now widely regarded as a promising educational strategy (Gee, 2007; Khine, 2011). In an effort to understand why fewer women than men are pursuing computer science in many developed countries, some studies have looked at influence of gaming. One study found that the amount of time playing games has only a small relationship with interest in computing (DiSalvo, Crowley, & Norwood, 2008). Another concluded that gaming experience does not predict performance in CS classes (Beyer & Haller, 2006). Still other studies suggest the relationship varies by gender. For example, frequency of game play was associated with choice of a computing major for men, but not for women (Ogan, et al., 2006) and interest in computer games was the strongest influence on male (but not female) pursuit of CS (Carter, 2006).

More in-depth studies of gaming practices suggest that it may be the type of play, rather than the amount, that is important. Women and men are playing games in equal numbers (Entertainment Software Association, 2013) but in different ways (Kafai, Heeter, Denner, & Sun, 2008; Lenhart et al., 2008). Certain types of digital games, such as those that take a long time to learn and master, may be more likely to promote the kinds of thinking and problem solving skills (Denner & Bean, 2006; Granic, Lobel, & Engels, 2013) that prepare students to succeed in CS classes. With the vast array of game types and gaming devices, there is a range of opportunities to engage in tinkering and the cycles of problem solving and failure that are a part of learning to program (Denner & Werner, 2007; Margolis & Fisher, 2002). For example, casual games are easy to learn, have less complex game play and a shorter duration (Juul, 2012), and may be more likely to have emotional than cognitive benefits of games with a steeper learning curve, like first-person shooter games (Granic et al., 2013). On the other hand, first-person shooter games may increase spatial cognition skills, which are important in many mathematics and engineering fields (Feng, Spence, & Pratt, 2007; Wai et al., 2010). Because not all people who play games are interested in studying computer science, it is important to understand what aspects of gaming, if any, play a role in their educational goals.

Summary

Studies suggest that while gaming leads to an interest in computer science by some, not all gamers want to study CS. Little is known about whether there are certain types of games or game play that are more closely associated with an interest in CS, and whether this association is different for women and men. Prior research on the role of computer gaming in CS pathways has been limited by reporting only frequencies rather than looking at what types of games they play, why they play, and who they play with. Therefore, it remains unclear whether certain kinds of gaming practices are better preparation or more likely to lead students to pursue CS. In addition, previous studies are not recent enough to include mobile gaming. Research on gaming has also been limited by a focus on male students, who are considered the most avid gamers.

The goal of this study is to better understand the conditions under which playing digital games is related to a long-term interest in studying CS. To this end, we studied gamers taking a college-level introductory computer programming class and analyzed why they are playing, how they are playing, and if gaming was connected to CS interest. Our research question was: *What kinds of game play and motivation are related to greater interest in computer science, and how does this vary by gender?*

METHODS

Participants

Data were collected from 741 community college students (26% female). For the analyses in this chapter, we included survey data from the 545 students who play games at least once/week, and interview data from 39 avid gamers. This meant dropping 90 women (48% of the original sample) and 101 men (18% of the original sample) who said they play no computer games in a typical week. Most of the 545 students (82%) were male; 5% were African American, 33% Asian/Pacific Islander, 22% Latino/a, and 46% white. The students ranged in age from 15-61 (average=23.22). The majority (74%) attend college full time, 22% attend part time, and 13% already have a college degree. Half of the interviewees were female (51%) and their race/ethnicity by intention are in Table 1.

Procedures

In the Fall of 2010, students attending the first or second day of 26 introductory computer programming classes at 15 community colleges across California were invited to participate in a longi-

Table 1. Numbers interviewed based on high or low intention to transfer

	Female	Male	Total
High Intention	8	9	17
White	4	3	7
Asian	3	5	8
Latino	0	1	1
Other	1	0	1
Low Intention	12	10	22
White	8	7	15
Asian	2	1	3
Latino	1	1	2
Other	1	1	2
Total	20	19	39

tudinal study. What these classes had in common was that they had no programming prerequisite, they had a computer language-specific focus (e.g., C++ or Java), and the instructor agreed to allow in-person recruitment. Of the 1,723 students that were invited, 741 (43%) students completed the baseline (T1) online survey, and 191 (26%) were female. There were high participation rates (72% or more) at four of the 15 community colleges because the instructors allowed students to complete surveys during their lab classes. Students received a $25 gift card upon completion of each survey.

A subgroup of students were invited to participate in a telephone interview. We selected the most avid gamers, with a balance of women and men; half of whom had high intention to pursue further CS education, and half that did not. We originally invited 62 women and men from 11 colleges to participate in an interview; all played 4+ days per week. Of the 33 women, 2 declined, 11 did not respond, and 20 were interviewed. Of the 29 men, none declined, 10 did not respond, and 19 were interviewed. High intention to transfer and major in CS was determined by a response of "probably" or "definitely" to the question "Do you plan to pursue a computer-related major at a 4-year college or university?" All other responses were coded as low intention.

Measures

Frequency of Game Play: Students responded to two questions about how often they play video games, and then rated how often they play in specific ways or on certain devices. The first question was "In a typical week, how often do you play video games?" Responses ranged from 1=never to 5=every day. The second question was "Thinking about yesterday, about how many hours would you say you spent playing video games?" Responses ranged from: 1=none, 2=less than one hour, 3=1-2 hours, 4=3 or more hours.

Game Type: Following the prompt "Which of the following types of video games do you enjoy playing?" students were asked to choose all that apply from a list of 11 types (e.g., sports games, racing games, online role-playing games, puzzle games, and educational games). In addition, students were asked "In a typical week, how many hours do you spend playing the following types of games or game devices?" Options include: game console (e.g., Nintendo, Playstation, Dreamcast, Xbox, Wii, etc), casual games via electronic devices (e.g., solitaire, bejeweled), and massively multiplayer online games. Responses ranged from 1=none to 4=21 hours or more.

Motivation for Game Play: Participants were asked to report the importance of different game features in response to this sentence: "For each item below, indicate how important that feature is to you" (e.g., playing games with friends or other people, the challenge of the game, the art of the game). Responses for each item ranged from 1= not at all important to 5 = very important.

Intention to Pursue Computer Science: This was measured with one item: "Do you plan to pursue a computer-related major at a 4-year college or university?" Responses ranged from 1= definitely not to 5= definitely.

Interview Questions: A series of open-ended questions were used to gather information about what and why they play, how they think about gaming (their identity), and the extent to which they see a connection between gaming and studying computer science. Questions included "How would you describe the type of video games you like to play the most?" "What is it about these games that you like the most?" "How would you describe your motivations for playing?" "How would you describe other peoples' reactions to your playing video games as an adult?" "Do you think that playing computer games had anything to do with your decision to take a computer programming class?" The interviews were done on the telephone and audio-tape recorded.

Data Analysis

Survey Data: Initial analyses were conducted separately for female and male students. Simple frequencies were run to describe how often and what students play, as well as their motivations for playing. T-tests (for continuous variable) and crosstabs analysis (for categorical variables) were used to compare students with "high" (probably or definitely) and "low" intention to pursue CS on the gaming practices and motivations variables. Additional analyses of the association between CS intention and gaming were run, in order to control for the frequency of game play. Analyses of Covariance were used to identify significant differences in intention to pursue CS between those who do and do not play a certain type of game (e.g., strategy). For continuous variables, regression analyses were run to identify correlations between game preferences (e.g., game console, mobile) and motivations (e.g., importance of challenge) with intentions to study CS, controlling for frequency of game play.

A cluster analysis was performed on key variables to identify different types of gamers. The variables were selected based on two criteria: 1) their expected importance for distinguishing gaming groups (from the literature review) and 2) the independence of the variables (i.e., correlated less than r=.20) so that they do not represent the same concept (Sambandam, 2003). Students were clustered on eight variables. Three variables measured frequency of game play (casual games, online role playing games, and console games) and four measured motivation for game play (solving puzzles, playing with friends, being physically active and escaping into another world. Because the response scale was not consistent across variables, and because cluster analysis assumes that the distribution is normal, the variables were transformed before they were included in the analysis.

To identify the appropriate number of cluster groups to adequately describe patterns of gaming practices and motivation we followed a series of steps to test the stability and replicability of the cluster solution. The data were analyzed with Ward's agglomerative method and a squared Euclidean distance measure. A scatterplot was used to identify the amount of variance explained and the increase in error due to each cluster addition, and to identify a range of possible cluster solutions. Finally, theoretical and statistical considerations guided the selection of an optimal cluster solution, using criteria suggested by Bergman et al (2003).

To examine the association of patterns with outcomes, clusters were compared on demographics, educational goals, as well as additional types of game play and motivations for play, to explore which types of game play are related to interest in pursuing computer science. The analyses were done using ANOVAs with a Tukey post hoc test to see which variables significantly differentiate the clusters.

Interview Data: The interviews were transcribed, and coded for key themes. The analysis followed a multi-step process, as suggested by Auerbach & Silverstein (2003): (a) state your research concerns and conceptual framework, (b) select the relevant text for further analysis, (c) record repeating ideas by grouping together related passages, (d) organize themes by grouping repeating ideas into categories, and (e) develop theoretical constructs by grouping themes. Percentages were used to describe the proportion of the sample represented by each category. Quotes are presented to illustrate normative responses for a particular theme.

RESULTS

Gaming Practices and Preferences

As a reminder, students were included in this analysis if they played games at least once a week in a typical week. The frequency of game play varied within gender, as shown in Tables 2 and 3. In a typical week, men play more on more days than women; on average men play 2-3 days and women play just over one day (p<.0001). Although half the women play only one day a week, the other half are more frequent gamers. Men also reported playing more hours yesterday than women (p<.0001).

As shown in Table 4, there were several gender differences in game genre preferences. The most popular genre was first person shooters (FPS), mainly because these were so popular with men. The types of games that women enjoy playing the most were puzzle, adventure, party, or racing games, but about one third of the women also report playing shooter, strategy, and online role playing games. The most common games that men enjoyed playing were first person shooters (FPS), adventure, strategy and role playing games, but one third also play puzzle games. Students responded to a list of 12 game types. On average, men said they enjoyed playing 5.20 types, and women enjoyed playing 4.72 types; the difference in the range of game types they enjoy playing was not significant.

As shown in Table 5, both men and women report playing games on the Internet more than anywhere else (range is: 1=none to 4=21 hours or more). There were some gender differences in where else and what they play. On average, men reported they play significantly more hours each week on the Internet, the computer, a game console, and on Massively Multiplayer Online (MMO) games. Women spend more time playing casual games than men. Both women and men spent the least amount of time playing serious games (e.g., educational games).

The interviews provided insight into the social factors that influence students' gaming practices and preferences. For example, there was a real range in how both men and women talked about others' perceptions of their gaming. Perhaps because they play more, men were more likely to talk about the negative perceptions that others have of their gaming--in our interviews with the most avid gamers, more men (37%) than women

Table 2. Frequency of game play on a typical week

	Women	Men	All
One day	49%	26%	30%
2-3 days	31%	34%	34%
4-6 days	10%	20%	18%
Everyday	10%	20%	18%

Table 3. Hours played yesterday

	Women	Men	All
None	42%	29%	31%
Less than 1 hour	32%	20%	22%
1-2 hours	17%	30%	28%
3 or more hours	8%	21%	19%

Table 4. Game genres that students enjoy playing

	Women	Men	All
Puzzle	79%	33%	41%
Adventure	55%	72%	68%
Party	52%	28%	32%
Racing	51%	48%	48%
FPS	33%	82%	73%
Strategy	31%	62%	56%
Role playing	31%	50%	44%

Table 5. Number of hours/week students play certain games or devices

	Women	Men	All
Internet**	1.95	2.24	2.18
Computer*	1.66	1.84	1.81
Mobile device	1.70	1.71	1.71
Game console**	1.66	1.90	1.85
MMOs**	1.47	1.81	1.75
Casual games***	1.65	1.33	1.39
Serious games	1.22	1.11	1.13

*$p < .05$, **$p < .01$, ***$p < .001$

(25%) talked about the negative perceptions that other people have of their gaming. For example, a male gamer said: "People think that if you're playing MMO, you can have no life." When women talked about others' perceptions of their gaming, many described it as a norm among their friends: "Most of my friends, they all play video games. So when we play together we usually go to each other's houses and play and play online." However, several of the women said that they kept their gaming behavior a secret. "…most of the time no one understands, so I ….I don't really play outside of the house. I keep my school and my outside life separate from my video game life." A few describe how others were surprised that they were female and knew how to play certain types of games. For example, one woman said "I think a lot of people get really surprised when they find out that I play a lot of games…..I guess to them I don't really seem like the type that would play a lot of games when they see me….I guess part of it is because I'm a girl." These quotes show the importance of studying not only the frequency and type, but also the social context of gaming behavior.

Gaming Motivations

As shown in Table 6, there were differences both across and within gender in students' motivations to play. Solving puzzles was the most important game feature for women, and was rated significantly higher by women than by men. Other important game features for women were the challenge, leveling up (increasing skills and getting to the next level of the game), and the art/graphics. The interviews suggested that for women who played mostly casual games, their motivation was primarily to relax by playing quick puzzle games and reach new levels. As one woman said "I guess it's like the problem solving is really satisfying, or you know, meeting challenges and satisfying it." But for women who also played Role Playing games, MMOs, and shooter games, the motivation had more to do with competing and being challenged, as well as interacting with other people. Although women did not rank "playing with friends" as an important feature, it was common

Table 6. Most important game features

	Women	Men
Solving puzzles***	4.17	3.72
Challenge***	4.06	4.35
Leveling up	4.03	4.17
Art/graphics**	4.00	4.36
Exploring	3.97	4.13
Following storylines*	3.70	4.01
Action***	3.53	4.34
Playing with friends***	3.52	4.13
Competing***	3.48	4.01

$*p < .05, **p < .01, ***p < .001$

in the interviews for them to describe playing with girl and boyfriends in their interviews: "I actually play with my boyfriend most of the time because we live in the same room and his computer is directly on the opposite wall of mine." However, most said their motivation was to "…challenge myself. I don't really play much with others. My friends don't really like video games."

For men, the most important game features were the art/graphics, the challenge, and action. This sentiment was shared by many in the interviews: "Easy games are boring…personally I like it to be a bit more challenging than normal." The men also frequently talked about the importance of game quality—many stated that they would not play a game without a good storyline, developed characters, and a high production value. As one man with high intention stated "I think first person shooting games are just exciting. When I play it I feel like I'm in it, like I'm the one holding the gun and into the motion. And for RPG, usually RPG has great graphics and I enjoy it and usually has story lines as well. So I enjoy like reading and enjoying the story." Another stated "I have picked up games where it had horrible storylines and it didn't grab my attention and I wouldn't play it past day one." They also described many other motivations, including relaxing, interacting with other people, competing, and solving difficult problems. These motivations are consistent with their responses in the surveys, which showed that many men play more MMOs and rank the feature of 'playing with friends' to be important.

These findings partially explain why both men and women play so many different types of games; they choose a game based on their current motivation for playing. As a female student explained "It really depends on the type of game. I guess like for something like World of Warcraft, it was I liked talking to my friends a lot. And then I liked exploring and just like being able to get better gear playing. And then like ....a single player game, which I don't do really that often....then that will be more for the story." Similarly, most of the interviewees described a range of motivations for game play, which shows the limitations of categorical questions about motivation.

How Gaming Practices and Motivations Relate to Intention to Pursue CS

Intention to pursue CS was not related to overall frequency of game play in a typical week, or the number of hours played the day before, for either men or women. This suggests that students who played more than one hour a week were not any more likely to express interest in studying CS. However, CS intention was related to what and why students played, and the preferred game types and features that were associated with greater intention differed for men and women.

Based on their survey responses, *women* who have high intention (they said they 'probably' or 'definitely' intend to pursue a CS major) are more likely to engage in certain types of gaming practices. For example, they were more likely to play racing (X^2 (1,82)=5.02, p<.05) and puzzle games (X^2 (1,82)=4.22, p<.05), and they reported playing on a game console more often (t(77)=.63, p<.05) than women with low intention. The interview data were used to elaborate on these findings. Women with high intention were more likely to talk about

themselves as a serious or moderate gamer, while women with low intention were equally as likely to describe being a casual gamer. In addition, in their interviews, women with high intention were more likely to say that making a game was the reason they took the Introductory programming class, were more likely to say they try and problem solve when stuck in a game, to state they prefer a medium (not easy) level of game difficulty, and to be motivated to play to have fun and to interact with friends. They were also more likely to talk with pride about being one of few females that played certain types of (male-dominated) games.

Although many of these women also played casual games, it was the addition of other game genres, particularly online competitive games, and console-based role playing games, as well as their reasons for playing puzzle or casual games, that made their gaming different. They were more likely to play real time strategy games, play a range of game genres including MMORPG and shooter games, and to use an online game site to download games, such as Steam. Although it was most common among men with high intention to study CS, one woman with high intention connected her interest in puzzles to her pursuit of computer programming: "I was a cultural anthropology major and it felt like I was just talking about problems and studying problems and not really solving any problems. And so to me like programming was like doing a bunch of little puzzles. And so it was really satisfying to have a bunch of little problems that were solvable."

Women who have low intention to pursue CS rated the importance of immersion, in-game accomplishments, competition with others, relieving boredom, and personal accomplishments higher than women with high intention. In their interviews, they were more likely to play short (casual) games, as well as Simulations. They preferred games that are easy to learn, quick to go in and out of, and although they are motivated by getting to the next level, they game in order to relax or keep their brain active, and do not want it to be so hard that they get frustrated. These women were also more likely to talk about a boyfriend or husband that played a lot of games, and how their gaming is likely the result of the male partner buying a console or spending a lot of time playing. They like the social aspect of gaming, but due to the types of games they tend to play, it is often alone (except for games like Words with Friends). Women with low intention were also more likely to say that they took the programming class to fulfill a requirement for their major (e.g., Accounting) rather than because they were interested in studying CS.

Although certain gaming practices and preferences were more common among women who intended to pursue CS, gaming alone did not explain intention. Some of the women with high intention reported gaming practices that looked more like those with low intention. For example, these women played more casual games, as well as board and card games that were turned into digital games (e.g., Yugioh). Their reasons for pursuing CS were due to an interest in math and programming, rather than to an interest in gaming.

The data also suggest that certain gaming practices and preferences are common among men who are interested in studying CS. Men with high intention ranked the following game features as more important than men with low intention to pursue CS: the challenge ($t(1,441)=2.91, p<.01$), leveling up ($t(1,440)=2.77, p<.01$), playing with friends ($t(1,441)=2.43, p<.05$), connecting with characters ($t(1,441)=2.32, p<.05$), taking on a new role ($t(1,441)=2.09, p<.05$), personalizing characters ($t(1,440)=2.08, p<.05$), and the art/graphics ($t(1,441)=2.16, p<.05$). In their interviews, men with high intention were more likely to say they play MMORPG and shooter games, and that they are motivated to play by fun and the storyline, as well as in-game accomplishments. As one man with high intention explained his motivation for playing "…it's getting engaged in a really cohesive environment that carries itself throughout…you kind of get lost in the story, in the characters, with at the same point as with the interaction between whatever the combat system is in trying to figure out how that works and how to do the best in that game." Perhaps because they play MMOs, they were also more likely to talk about being part of a gaming community, and being "addicted" to gaming and that others have negative perceptions of their game play.

Interviews with men who do not intend to pursue CS show the ways in which their gaming practices and motivations differ from men with high intention. They were more likely to say they play puzzle and real time strategy games, to be motivated by escaping and relaxing, and to recognize that some people hold negative perceptions of gaming. Based on their survey responses, *men who have low intention to pursue CS are more likely to play serious games than men with high intention* ($t(1,444)=1.79, p=.07$). The interviews also showed that gaming was not always the most important factor in students' educational plans. For example, they were not pursuing CS for reasons that included needing to graduate quickly, limited finances, viewing themselves as not "good" at memorizing, or viewing CS as too detailed and complex, and requiring too much time.

Additional statistical analyses were used to determine whether the above findings, based on interviews and mean-difference analyses of surveys, would be replicated. Cluster analysis of gaming practices and preferences was used to differentiate students with low and high intention to pursue CS. The analysis resulted in five clusters; four were all-male due to the larger sample size. There were significant differences in intention to pursue CS between three of the clusters: one all-male cluster had significantly higher intention than one of the three other all-male clusters, and higher intention than the all-female cluster. There was a clear pattern of gaming behavior among the high intention males; they were younger, played games more hours each week, were more likely to play MMOs, and less likely to play on a gaming console. The males with high intention were also more motivated by competing, playing with friends, and leveling up than the female cluster or the one male cluster whose members had significantly lower intention to pursue CS. Compared to the high intention males, the females played more casual games, puzzle games and party games, and were more motivated by solving puzzles, escaping, and following storylines.

In addition to looking for patterns in the data, the most avid gamers were asked directly about whether their interest in studying CS was related to their gaming. For some, the connection was clear. One female with high intention said "I wanna make people happy by making games. And it seems like a really big industry to get into." And a man with high intention that playing games had something to do with his decision to take a programming class: "I certainly think it has a positive effect on that because it's interacting with computers be it Nintendo or x-box or an actual PC running, whatever, operating sytem. That it provides a way for you to interact with it...so it might make you think 'Well, you know what, I want to learn more about this or I want to figure out how these things work better.'" Another high intention male stated "I was thinking like if I can complete a major maybe I can end up in a video game making company so that I can really get involved in making an awesome video game and stuff." Others were less certain that gaming influenced their enrollment in the class. As one low intention woman said "I think it ties in a little bit, but it wasn't the main reason I wanted to do it. I kind of just out of curiosity wanted to see if it was something that I would enjoy doing. And it kind of came across that though because I had been gaming and somebody had kind of mentioned it."

DISCUSSION

The results show that among gamers who are taking an introductory computer programming class, there is great variation in how and why they game, and certain practices and motivations are associated with greater interest in pursuing CS. The results also show that although certain types of gaming are associated with intention to study CS, there is great variation both within and across gender. The following section explores these findings in the context of other research.

Gender Differences and Similarities in College Students' Game Play and Motivation

The findings confirm prior research that shows differences in what women and men report about the frequency and type of games they enjoy playing, but we interpret these findings in light of research that suggests gender "difference" can be more about performance than about an inherent truth. For example, responses to questions about gaming behavior are influenced by societal norms and expectations (Pelletier, 2008; Walkerdine, 2007) and apparent differences may be a result of different associations with the terminology. For example, men and women both like competition, but it may mean something different to them in the context of gendered games (Jenson & de Castell, 2008; Laurel, 2008). In fact, while we found that men in community college CS classes play computer games more often than women in the same classes, there is great variation within gender. A large percentage of the women are also playing games frequently, and the amount of play time alone is not indicative of the extent to which they embrace a gaming identity. However, women were also more likely to say that they played alone, or hid their game play from their friends, which shows their awareness that it is less socially acceptable in many communities for females to be gamers.

In this sample of college students, the most popular types of games were similar to those identified in earlier research (Cragg et al., 2007; Lucas & Sherry, 2004). The games that women say they enjoy the most are puzzle games, while men say they enjoy first person shooter games the most. Therefore, one reason for why more men than women intend to pursue CS may have to do with the fact that their gaming preferences prepare them with a way of thinking that is more conducive to CS (Kell et al., 2013), while the puzzle games that women prefer are more likely to improve mood (Granic, 2013). An important difference between these two game genres is that puzzle games are more likely to be colorful, and have no opportunities for conflicts or dominance over other players, while first person shooter games are more likely to have a storyline (usually one that focuses on combat or science fiction), and to be violent. Another key difference between puzzle and shooter games is that the latter usually takes place in 3-dimensional space, and requires the player to put themselves into another person or object's viewpoint; this requires spatial skills that research shows lead to the kind of creativity and technical innovation that are essential for productive careers in science, technology, engineering and mathematics (Kell et al., 2013; Wai et al., 2010). However, because most students play more than one game genre, there was also a great deal of overlap in what men and women enjoy playing, and the data in this study cannot be used to conclude that game play leads to CS; only that a certain type of play is more common among those interested in CS.

The findings are mostly consistent with prior research on gaming motivation that show variation within and across gender. Like others have found (Van Looy, Courtois, & Vermeulen, 2010; Olson, 2010; Sherry et al., 2006) men ranked all motivations higher than women, suggesting that we need to include additional response options on the survey in order to better understand the gaming motivations of women. Like others (Thornham, 2008) have found, the women talked about their choice of gaming genre as a function of individual preference rather than being motivated by the features of what makes up a good game, while men were more likely to describe their game choices in terms of social/cultural or financial terms. But

both men and women talked about liking to be challenged, but in a different way. Solving puzzles was the most important game feature selected by women, so it is not surprising that they like to play puzzle games the most, a finding that is similar to a study by Lucas and Sherry (2004)—the women in that study ranked "getting to the next level" as their greatest motivation. Like others have found (Olson, 2010; Sherry et al., 2006), men in this study were most motivated by the game challenge, the action, and the graphics, such as those commonly found in shooter games. However, men frequently talked about the importance of storyline, in contrast to what Cragg et al and Sherry et al found. This finding may be a result of the frequent interest in the story-driven MMOs among our male participants.

There were some notable gender differences in how they thought their gaming was viewed by other people. Men were more likely to talk about concerns related to how much time their gaming is taking up, a finding that is similar to other studies (Cragg et al., 2007). In contrast, none of the women who were interviewed talked about being judged in a negative way for gaming. This may be partly because women tended to play less frequently and to hide their gaming, but it may also be because, like other studies have found, many women who play the longer duration games like MMOs are often playing with other people in the room (Yee, 2008). In our study, these other people were usually boyfriends who encouraged and supported the game play.

Gaming and Computer Science

The findings challenge assumptions that more game play leads to greater interest in CS. In research with the same sample that also included non-gamers, we found that gaming frequency was predictive of interest in pursuing CS (Denner et al., 2014). However, the current study, which includes only people who play games at least once a week, suggests that the amount of gaming is not important. Those who played games every day were not any more likely to intend to pursue CS than those who played once a week. For both men and women, what was more important than frequency in explaining the connection between gaming and CS interest, was the extent to which the person identified as a gamer. The findings are similar to those by Royse et al. (2007) who described three levels of game consumption by women: power gamers (place high importance on gaming; familiar with different genres; like challenges; take pleasure in making a stereotypical female character strong), moderate gamers (gaming is not a part of their identity; like to control environment not characters, use to escape and cope with daily life; reject violence), and non-gamers. In our study it was the power gamers that were most likely to intend to study computer science. These findings suggest that while there is some connection between playing games and an interest in CS, more frequent game play will not necessarily lead to even greater interest.

The results suggest there are different patterns of game play, depending on whether a student intended or did not intend to study CS. Women who played a wide range of games, who enjoyed the challenge and competition, and who were motivated to play by fun, relaxation, and social interaction were more likely to say they wanted to study CS. Women who wanted to study CS were also more likely to be interested in the structure and mechanics of the game than with just playing the game the developer created, and less likely to be solely interested in casual games. Men who play MMOs, were younger on average than their classmates, and who played the greatest range of games were more likely to say they intend to study CS. Men with the highest intention were motivated to play by competition, challenge, and social interaction, as well as the features of the game (e.g., the art and ability to personalize or connect with the characters). Men with high intention were less likely to say they played serious games or on a game console. It is not clear from

our data whether age is the most important factor—younger students were more likely to want to continue their studies, while older students were more likely to be taking the programming class to enhance their career but not to change it. An interest in making games appeared to lead some people in the direction of CS, but a more common explanation for both men and women was an interest in solving puzzles that seemed to drive both an interest in playing games AND an interest in CS.

Limitation of this study are that we looked at variation in the type of games they played and what equipment they played on, but did not collect detailed information on HOW and with whom they played certain types of games. Play style is important to measure because the player can rely on the help features and stay within the game as it was developed, or he/she can take advantage of opportunities to change the gaming features or modify how the game is played or their identity within it. Juul (2012) talks about the importance of looking at both *what* games are played and *why* they play, but also looking at the interaction between the game and the player—how they play. Similarly, our analysis lacks detail about the social context of game play--who the participants play with. Although the interviews provided some information, this information was not gathered systematically and was only collected from a sub group of the most avid gamers.

The results of this study challenge the widely held belief that there is a simple association between video game play and an interest in computer science. We found that frequency of game play alone cannot be used to explain gender differences in the pursuit of a computer science degree. In fact, gaming practices alone do not determine an interest in computer science; there are certain gaming motivations and genre preferences that are associated with that interest. Thus, the simple inclusion of game programming into the curriculum will not necessarily increase diversity in CS. The results also challenge the common reliance on a gender "difference" frame to understand gaming behaviors. The results show that women are playing games, and that there is greater variation in what they play within than across gender. Efforts to increase the number of women that pursue computer science should target the group of women who are power gamers—those who like a challenge and embrace a gamer identity. Future research on the connection between gaming and computer science should explore a wider range of motivations for play, as well as the growing number of games that defy categorization (e.g., indie games), in order to better understand the consistent finding that men have higher motivation scores. In addition, future research should look more deeply into game genre preferences—not just what, but how they play--in order to more fully understand how game play and interest in CS are related.

REFERENCES

Auerbach, C. F., & Silverstein, L. B. (2003). *Qualitative data: An introduction to coding and analysis*. New York: NYU Press.

Bergman, L. R., Magnusson, D., & El-Khouri, B. M. (2003). *Studying individual development in an interindividual context: A person-oriented approach*. Mahwah, NJ: Erlbaum.

Beyer, S., & Haller, S. (2006). Gender differences and intragender differences in Computer Science students: Are female CS majors more similar to male CS majors or female nonmajors? *Journal of Women and Minorities in Science and Engineering*, 12(4), 337–365. doi:10.1615/JWomenMinorScienEng.v12.i4.50

Carter, L. (2006). Why students with an apparent aptitude for computer science don't choose to major in computer science. *ACM SIGCSE Bulletin*, 38(1), 27–31. doi:10.1145/1124706.1121352

Cragg, A., Taylor, C., & Toombs, B. (2007). *Video games: Research to improve understanding of what players enjoy about video games, and to explain their preferences for particular games*. London: British Board of Film Classification.

Denner, J., & Bean, S. (2006). Girls, games, and intrepid exploration on the computer. In E. M. Trauth (Ed.), *Encyclopedia of gender and information technology* (pp. 727–732). Hershey, PA: Idea Group Reference. doi:10.4018/978-1-59140-815-4.ch113

Denner, J., Ortiz, E., Campe, S., & Werner, L. (2014). Beyond stereotypes of gender and gaming: Video games made by middle school students. In H. Agius, & M. Angelides (Eds.), *Handbook of digital games*. New York: Institute of Electrical and Electronic Engineers. doi:10.1002/9781118796443.ch25

Denner, J., & Werner, L. (2007). Computer programming in middle school: How pairs respond to challenges. *Journal of Educational Computing Research*, 37(2), 131–150. doi:10.2190/12T6-41L2-6765-G3T2

Denner, J., Werner, L., O'Connor, L., & Glassman, J. (2014). Community college men and women: A test of three widely held beliefs about who pursues computer science. *Community College Review*.

DiSalvo, A., Crowley, K., & Norwood, R. (2008). Learning in context: Digital games and young black men. *Games and Culture*, 3(2), 131. doi:10.1177/1555412008314130

Entertainment Software Association. (2013). *2013 sales, demographics, and usage data*. Retrieved from http://www.theesa.com/facts/pdfs/ESA_EF_2013.pdf

Feng, J., Spence, I., & Pratt, J. (2007). Playing an action video game reduces gender differences in spatial cognition. *Psychological Science*, 18(10), 850–855. doi:10.1111/j.1467-9280.2007.01990.x PMID:17894600

Fullerton, T., Fron, J., Pearce, C., & Morie, J. (2008). Getting girls into the game: Toward a virtuous cycle. In Y. Kafai, C. Heeter, J. Denner, & J. Sun (Eds.), *Beyond Barbie and Mortal Kombat: New perspectives on gender and gaming* (pp. 161–176). Cambridge, MA: MIT Press.

Gee, J. P. (2007). *Good video games and good learning*. New York: Peter Lang.

Granic, I., Lobel, A., & Engels, C. M. E. (2013). The benefits of playing video games. *The American Psychologist*. doi: doi:10.1037/a0034857 PMID:24295515

Hare-Mustin, R. T., & Marecek, J. (1988). The meaning of difference: Gender theory, postmodernism, and psychology. *The American Psychologist*, *43*(6), 455–464. doi:10.1037/0003-066X.43.6.455

Hartmann, T., & Klimmt, C. (2006). Gender and computer games: Exploring females' dislikes. *Journal of Computer-Mediated Communication*, *11*(4), 910–931. doi:10.1111/j.1083-6101.2006.00301.x

Hayes, E. (2005). Women, videogaming, and learning: Beyond stereotypes. *TechTrends*, *49*(5), 23–28. doi:10.1007/BF02763686

Hoffman, B., & Nadelson, L. (2010). Motivational engagement and video gaming: A mixed methods study. *Educational Technology Research and Development*, *58*(3), 245–270. doi:10.1007/s11423-009-9134-9

Jenson, J., & de Castell, S. (2008). Theorizing gender and digital gameplay: Oversights, accidents, and surprises. *Eludamos: Journal for Computer Game Culture*, *2*(1), 15–25.

Juul, J. (2012). *A casual revolution: Reinventing video games and their players*. Cambridge, MA: MIT Press.

Kafai, Y., Heeter, C., Denner, J., & Sun, J. (Eds.). (2008). *Beyond Barbie and Mortal Kombat: New perspectives on gender and gaming*. Cambridge, MA: MIT Press.

Kell, H. J., Lubinski, D., Benbow, C. P., & Steiger, J. H. (2013). Creativity and technical innovation. *Psychological Science*, *24*(9), 1831–1836. doi:10.1177/0956797613478615 PMID:23846718

Khine, M. S. (2011). *Learning to play: Exploring the future of education with video games*. New York: Peter Lang.

Kinzie, M. B., & Joseph, D. R. D. (2008). Gender differences in game activity preferences of middle school children: Implications for educational game design. *Educational Technology Research and Development*, *56*, 643–663. doi:10.1007/s11423-007-9076-z

Laurel, B. (2008). Notes from the utopian entrepreneur. In Y. Kafai, C. Heeter, J. Denner, & J. Sun (Eds.), *Beyond Barbie and Mortal Kombat: New perspectives on gender and gaming* (pp. 21–32). Cambridge, MA: MIT Press.

Lenhart, A., Jones, S., & Macgill, A. (2008). Adults and video games. *Pew Internet and Family Life Project*. Retrieved on December 9, 2011 from http://www.pewinternet.org/Reports/2008/Adults-and-Video-Games.aspx

Lucas, K., & Sherry, J. L. (2004). Sex differences in video game play: A communication-based explanation. *Communication Research*, *31*(5), 499–525. doi:10.1177/0093650204267930

Lynn, K. M., Raphael, C., Olefsky, K., & Bachen, C. M. (2003). Bridging the gender gap in computing: an integrative approach to content design for girls. *Journal of Educational Computing Research*, *28*(2), 143–162. doi:10.2190/79HP-RVE7-3A9N-FV8C

Margolis, J., & Fisher, A. (2002). *Unlocking the clubhouse: Women in computing*. Cambridge, MA: The MIT Press.

Natale, M. J. (2002). The effect of a male-oriented computer gaming culture on careers in the computer industry. *Computers & Society, 32*(2), 24–31. doi:10.1145/566522.566526

National Science Foundation. (2013). *Women, minorities, and persons with disabilities in science and engineering: 2013*. Retrieved December 3, 2013 from http://www.nsf.gov/statistics/wmpd/2013/pdf/nsf13304_full.pdf

Ogan, C., Robinson, J. C., Ahuja, M., & Herring, S. C. (2006). Gender differences among students in computer science and applied information technology. In J. M. Cohoon, & W. Aspray (Eds.), *Women and information technology: Research on underrepresentation* (pp. 279–300). Cambridge, MA: The MIT Press. doi:10.7551/mitpress/9780262033459.003.0009

Ogletree, S. M., & Drake, R. (2007). College students' video game participation and perceptions: Gender differences and implication. *Sex Roles, 56*, 537–542. doi:10.1007/s11199-007-9193-5

Olson, C. K. (2010). Children's motivations for video game play in the context of normal development. *Review of General Psychology, 12*(2), 180–187. doi:10.1037/a0018984

Pelletier, C. (2008). Gaming in context: How young people construct their gendered identities in playing and making games. In Y. Kafai, C. Heeter, J. Denner, & J. Sun (Eds.), *Beyond Barbie and Mortal Kombat: New perspectives on gender and gaming* (pp. 145–159). Cambridge, MA: MIT Press.

Royse, P., Lee, J., Undrahbuyan, B., Hopson, M., & Consalvo, M. (2007). Women and games: Technologies of the gendered self. *New Media & Society, 9*(4), 555–576. doi:10.1177/1461444807080322

Sambandam, R. (2003). Cluster analysis gets complicated. *Marketing Research, 15*(1), 16–21.

Sherry, J. L., Lucas, K., Greenberg, B. S., & Lachlan, K. (2006). Video game uses and gratifications as predictors of use and game preference. In P. Vorderer, & J. Bryant (Eds.), *Playing video games: Motives, responses, and consequences* (pp. 213–224). Mahwah, NJ: Erlbaum.

Taylor, N., Jenson, J., & de Castell, S. (2009). Cheerleaders/booth babes/Halo hoes: Pro-graming, gender and jobs for the boys. *Digital Creativity, 20*(4), 239–252. doi:10.1080/14626260903290323

Thornham, H. (2008). It's a boy thing. *Feminist Media Studies, 8*, 127–142. doi:10.1080/14680770801980505

Tillberg, H. K., & Cohoon, J. M. (2005). Attracting women to the CS major. *Frontiers: A Journal of Women Studies, 26*(1), 126-140.

Van Looy, J., Courtois, C., & Vermeulen, L. (2010). *Why girls play video games: A gender-comparative study into the motivations for and attitudes towards playing video games*. Paper presented at the Future Reality of Gaming (FROG) conference, Vienna.

Wai, J., Lubinski, D., Benbow, C. P., & Steiger, J. H. (2010). Accomplishment in science, technology, engineering, and mathematics (STEM) and its relation to STEM educational dose: A 25-year longitudinal study. *Journal of Educational Psychology, 102*, 860–871. doi:10.1037/a0019454

Walkerdine, V. (2007). *Children, gender, video games: Toward a relational approach to multimedia*. New York: Palgrave Macmillan. doi:10.1057/9780230235373

Williams, D., Consalvo, M., Caplan, S., & Yee, N. (2009). Looking for gender: Gender roles and behaviors among online gamers. *The Journal of Communication, 59*(4), 700–725. doi:10.1111/j.1460-2466.2009.01453.x

Winn, J., & Heeter, C. (2009). Gaming, gender, and time: Who makes time to play? *Sex Roles*, *61*, 1–13. doi:10.1007/s11199-009-9595-7

Yee, N. (2008). Maps of digital desires: Exploring the topography of gender and play in online games. In Y. Kafai, C. Heeter, J. Denner, & J. Sun (Eds.), *Beyond Barbie and Mortal Kombat: New perspectives on gender and gaming* (pp. 82–96). Cambridge, MA: MIT Press.

ADDITIONAL READING

Cohoon, J. M., & Aspray, W. (Eds.) (2006). Women and information technology: Research on underrepresentation (pp. 279-300). Cambridge, MA: The MIT Press.

Feng, J., Spence, I., & Pratt, J. (2007). Playing an action video game reduces gender differences in spatial cognition. *Psychological Science*, *18*(10), 850–855. doi:10.1111/j.1467-9280.2007.01990.x PMID:17894600

Granic, I., Lobel, A., & Engels, C. M. E. (2013). The benefits of playing video games. *The American Psychologist*. doi: doi:10.1037/a0034857 PMID:24295515

Jenson, J., & de Castell, S. (2008). Theorizing gender and digital gameplay: Oversights, accidents, and surprises. *Eludamos: Journal for Computer Game Culture*, *2*(1), 15–25.

Juul, J. (2012). *A casual revolution: Reinventing video games and their players*. MIT Press.

Kafai, Y., Heeter, C., Denner, J., & Sun, J. (Eds.). (2008). *Beyond Barbie and mortal kombat: New perspectives on gender and gaming*. Cambridge, MA: MIT Press.

Margolis, J., & Fisher, A. (2002). *Unlocking the clubhouse: Women in computing*. Cambridge, MA: The MIT Press.

Ogletree, S. M., & Drake, R. (2007). College students' video game participation and perceptions: Gender differences and implication. *Sex Roles*, *56*(7-8), 537–542. doi:10.1007/s11199-007-9193-5

Trauth, E. M. (Ed.). (2006). *Encyclopedia of Gender and Information Technology* (pp. 727–732). Hershey, PA: Idea Group Reference. doi:10.4018/978-1-59140-815-4

Vorderer, P., & Bryant, J. (Eds.), *Playing video games: Motives, responses, and consequences* (pp. 213–224). Mahwah, NJ: Erlbaum.

KEY TERMS AND DEFINITIONS

Community College: Two-year public colleges.

Computer Science: The study of the principles and uses of computers and computation.

Educational Goals: Plans to pursue certain fields of study.

Gaming: Playing computer games.

Gender: The state of being male or female, typically used with reference to social or cultural factors, rather than biological ones.

Motivation: The reasons given for interest or behavior.

Chapter 3
The Only Girl in the Class!
Female Students' Experiences of Gaming Courses and Views of the Industry

Lauren Elliott
University of Bolton, UK

Julie Prescott
University of Bolton, UK

ABSTRACT

Four female students studying a games course at one UK University took part in a qualitative study of face-to-face semi-structured interviews. Although a small sample, the study provided an interesting insight into the experiences of the females on the course as well as their views of entering (or at least potentially entering) the male dominated computer games industry. The findings related by the chapter reveal that females choose to study games because they enjoyed playing games. Despite all participants experiencing the course positively, there was some apprehension about going into the industry. Interestingly, the study suggests the male dominated working environment may be off-putting to women, even to women studying and interested in going into that area of work. The main themes that emerged in regard to the negativity associated with the industry were the long hours culture and potential sexism within the industry.

INTRODUCTION

There have been a number of studies looking at the female presence in the gaming industry, or lack of, much of which explains that the male dominated environment and work conditions puts many women off going into industry. This is mainly due to the long hours culture associated with the industry and the lack of flexible working practices available. The fact that females are greatly outnumbered in this sector should be taken seriously, as well as the lack of females studying games courses at university level which has been hugely overlooked. There are now a number of game courses available which prepare people for a career in games, giving these students the option of entering the industry through the pathway of higher education. However, despite an educational route into the games industry, there is a distinct lack of females on these courses. For instance,

DOI: 10.4018/978-1-4666-6142-4.ch003

according to 2012/13 UCAS (University and College Admissions Service) data, of all students who applied to university via UCAS, one gaming course offered nationwide had 241 males accepted to study compared to only 25 females. These statistics are similar of all gaming courses offered in the United Kingdom (UCAS, 2013). This is clearly an issue as the gender difference in higher education will have a knock on effect into the industry, increasing the male dominance within the gaming sector.

It is important, then, to ask what the experiences of the females currently on these courses are and if there is anything that could be done to improve the recruitment of female students into gaming courses and their retention when they are there. This chapter aims to explore these issues through a qualitative study of female students currently studying a games course at university in order to investigate the experiences of female gaming students.

BACKGROUND

Male-Dominated Workforce

The games industry is a male dominated environment, the few females that are employed in this workplace are typically working in non-developmental roles such as administration rather than a role which needs technical ability and a higher level of skill such as developmental roles e.g. programming, design or production (MCV, 2008; Gourdin, 2005; Dyer-Witheford & Sharman, 2005; Haines, 2004). Gender occupational segregation suggests that due to gendered stereotypes there are male and female jobs/roles and as such males and females traditionally prefer to work in what are considered gender congruent roles. Prescott and Bogg (2012) (amongst others) suggest that gender occupational segregation exists across the information and communication technology (ICT) sector and across the wider STEM (Science,

Technology, Engineering and Technology) sector. They also state that this issue is not geographically exclusive; these sectors were found to have gender occupational segregation across the UK, Europe and USA. This gendered occupational segregation has also been found to exist within the computer games industry with women concentrated in non-developmental roles as opposed to developmental roles (Prescott & Bogg, 2011).

Nature of the Industry

It is argued that females are not entering the computer games industry because the nature of the industry is particularly restrictive to females. The long-hours culture appears to be a key element of the games industry (Prescott & Bogg, 2010) and also seems to be the main deterrent too. Consalvo (2008) argued that the long hour's culture and crunch time within the industry are the biggest challenges to women in the games industry, especially women with children. However, this is also prominent in other industries for example the ICT sector, which we have already mentioned, is segregated, and renowned for its long hour's culture (Valenduc et al., 2004). The long hours culture leads to another key issue that of work-family conflict which research suggests affects women more than men (Innstrand et al., 2009). It has been noted that among the lack of females in the industry, there is a greater lack of women with children. This is also true of the wider ICT and STEM sector (Deuze et al., 2004; Haines, 2004; Krotoski, 2004; Gourdin, 2005; Consalvo, 2008; Prescott &Bogg, 2010). It could be speculated that the occupational structure of the industry including the long hours, potential need to relocate and the lack of flexible working practices is a key reason for the lack of women with children or women delaying having children, and as such should be targeted as a need of change in order for the industry to maintain and appeal to a more diverse workforce (Consalvo, 2008; Prescott &Bogg, 2010).

Stereotype Threat and Solo Status

One reason put forward as to why women may prefer working in gender congruent (traditional) occupations is the concept of stereotype threat. Stereotype threat occurs when an individual's actions confirm a stereotype about a particular group (Steele & Aronson, 1995). Stereotype threat may be elicited by any cue, overt or covert that increases the salience of a negative group stereotype. Both social identity theory (Taifel & Turner, 1986) and self-categorization theory (Turner et al., 1987) put forward that individuals have two sources of identity; personal identities that are unique to the individual and various social identities due to membership of social groups. According to social identity theory, people are motivated to maintain both positive personal and positive social identities. Negative group stereotypes are therefore viewed as a threat to one's social identity.

Performance expectation plays an important role in research on stereotype threat. Negative stereotypes can harm performance due to an increase in anxiety. Keller (2002) suggests that stereotype threat can be reduced or eliminated when negative stereotype expectations are irrelevant to the testing situation. However, research has found that by making a group's achievements salient can lessen the negative aspect of the threat. This, in turn, increases performance, perhaps due to an increase in confidence and a reduction in anxiety. For example, McIntyre, Paulson & Lord (2003) conducted two studies with American college students. They found in study one that women performed better on a maths test when they were first told that women were better than men in psychology experiments. In study two, they found that women also performed better on a math's test when they first read about four women who had succeeded in four male dominated occupational fields. Steele, James & Barnett (2002) found female undergraduates in male dominated academic areas had higher levels of stereotype threat than women in female dominated areas and

men in either area, suggesting gender was salient for the women in the male dominated areas. Making gender salient has also been found to impact on women's preference of art over maths (Steele & Ambady, 2006) and women also did better on a visual-spatial task when they were told there was no gender difference on the task (Campbell & Collaer, 2009).

According to Campbell & Collaer: *'performance can be improved, not only through education and training for the skills being tested, but also by simply changing the context in which we present these tasks' (p443)*. In the main, the research on stereotype threat tends to support this view. Even women who are highly motivated in a subject area can be affected by stereotype threat (Good, Aronson & Harder, 2008). However, Dar-Nimrod & Heine (2006) found that stereotype threat on women's mathematic performance is reduced, when women are represented with accounts of the origins of stereotypes. Recent research suggests that role models can undo stereotype threat when group members think the role model deserves the achievement, but not when group members think the achievement is undeserved (Taylor et al., 20011). Taylor et al. (2011) called this the 'Hillary Clinton effect', suggesting attribution has a moderating effect on stereotype threat. This study also supports the 'Obama effect' reported by Marx et al. (2009) and highlights the non-specific nature of role model success for undoing stereotype threat.

Most women will no doubt recognize their membership to the social category 'women'. However, women will vary in the extent to which they consider this social category membership as important to their self-identity. Schmader (2002) hypothesized that individuals would be more susceptible to negative stereotype threat depending on how highly they identified with the group to which the negative stereotype refers. In a study of male and female college students, Schmader found that individual differences in gender identification moderated the effects of gender identity relevance on women's, but not men's, maths performance. Women with high levels of gender identification performed worse than men, but women with low levels of gender identification performed equally to men. When faced with threats to their social identity, individuals who are highly identified will engage in behaviours to protect that identity. This suggests that women who feel they must act as representatives of their gender are motivated to perform better on tasks than women who are not as closely identified with their gender. More recently, Oswald (2008) found that strongly gender identified college women liked feminine occupations significantly more than less strongly identified women. According to Oswald (2008) because stereotype activation is a significant contributing factor as to why women pursue gender traditional occupations rather than non-traditional. The harmful impact of gender stereotypes therefore, should be reduced through an increase in women's participation in non-traditional occupations (Oswald & Lindstedt, 2006).

Due to the lack of women within the computer games industry and on the educational courses related to a career within games, the psychological construct of solo status is also worth considering. Solo status is important to consider since being the only woman in a group heightens gender stereotypes and can result in stereotypical task performance. When an individual is the only one of his or her social category in a group then they have solo status (for example being the only member of your race or gender in a group). Solo status has been related to both improved (Craig & Rand, 1998; Fuegen &Biernat, 2002) and decreased performance (Sekaquaptewa &Thompson, 2002, 2003). The inconsistencies in the research could perhaps suggest there are moderating factors to the effect of solo status, as with stereotype threat. For example, variables including gender, group stereotypes, and group status, have been shown to moderate the effect of solo status on individual performance (Crocker & McGraw, 1984; Sekaquaptewa & Thompson, 2002; Yoder, 1994). More

recently, White (2008) found cognitive appraisals had a moderating effect on solo status. Results from two separate experiments suggest that for individuals who feel challenged, but not threatened by their work, cognitive appraisal can help moderate the effect of solo status (White, 2008).

Academic Issues

It is clear to see that women face numerous hurdles when entering the industry and it is seen to be no different for those entering academic courses into computer games. Hayes (2005) has described how the expected stereotypical behaviours that women face are off-putting to them and this is acting as a deterrent for choosing to study computer games courses. When looking at computing courses, Hess & Miura (1985) posit that females are becoming discouraged even before they've chosen a subject because of the dominated male environment they can expect to be working in after the educational course. However, other researchers suggest that it is the skills that women possess that puts them off applying for computing courses, and that women feel inferior when it comes to computer literacy more than men (Sackrowitz & Parelius, 1996). There is also the suggestion that women prefer to work with humans not machines and thus they are not interested in computers (Hess & Miura, 1985) which could be preventing them from entering this particular industry. There is also a lack of females teaching computing and technology related courses, which results in a lack of female educational role models (Frenkle, 1990). Frenkle (1990) highlighted how in computing courses, although there appears to be more women entering the IT sector and computing jobs, the entry into academic jobs and onto educational courses is declining or has a very little uptake for females. This is a problem because, as with the industry, academia needs a variety of people working within it and a diverse workforce can provide a better education for the students, both male and female. The industry also needs employees who are skilled and have knowledge and experience of the processes involved in computer games development and the graduates who have these skills need to be more diverse in order to bring new ideas and points of view to each element of the gaming industry. Table 1 shows UK data on the gender composition of computer science by education and career stage at UK higher education institutions, 2006/07. It is clear from this data that the proportion of females studying computer science degrees at undergraduate level is significantly lower than their male counterparts. This underrepresentation is dramatically affecting the numbers of females in academic positions.

At present in the UK, the press is particularly interested in the lack of digital literacy among the population and computer sciences being taught in the UK education system. The UK has been recently criticized for not providing children with the skills and motivation to pursue science, engineering or technology to degree level or pursue careers in these areas (Murray, 2012). This is viewed as necessary. For instance, Livingstone & Hope (2011), advocate an increase in ICT in schools in order to give the UK a competitive edge in ICT industries, such as computer games. The

Table 1. Gender composition of computer science by education and career stage at UK higher education institutions, 2006/07

Career Stage	Female Proportion (%)	Male Proportion (%)
GCSE Awards (England)	47.8	52.2
A-level Awards (England)	36.3	63.7
UK Full-time Undergraduates	15.3	84.7
UK Full-time Postgraduates	18.8	81.2
UK University Researchers	20.0	80.0
UK University Lecturers	24.8	75.2
UK University Senior lecturers and researchers	19.2	80.8
UK University Professor	14.1	85.9

(UKRC, 2008)

lack of girls choosing ICT in secondary school is related to gender differences in access to, use and experience of computers. Indeed, within the home, it has been reported that boys tend to have greater access and use IT more (BECTA, 2008). In the UK, the Guardian newspaper in 2012 started a 'digital literacy campaign' (commenced, January 2012) to improve IT and computer science teaching in schools and universities. Indeed many UK supermarkets have voucher schemes in place to help buy computing equipment for schools (Smithers, 2011). With regard to educating children for SET careers, it is apparent that not all of the UK is at the same level. Scotland, has been highlighted as leading the way for teaching computer science, with primary schools (children aged 4-11), teaching children basic computer science (Shepherd, 2012).

Women and girls are increasingly engaging in technology, especially the Internet and Web 2.0 tools such as social networks, blogs and wikis. It is apparent that girls need to be encouraged to become drivers of technology, through knowledge of how computers work, as well as computer use. It is especially pertinent that children are taught the value of computer science and technology in today's society. However, the issue of educating children, is not confined to the UK, it is striking how the situation is similar globally. For example, research has looked at why girls are not interested in IT in an American context (e.g. Barker & Asprey, 2006); an Australian context (e.g. Miliszewska & Moore, 2009) and Gras-Valazquez et al (2008) looked at why girls were not attracted to IT in five European countries.

The situation within schools is not confined to computer science and technology. It extends to attracting girls to pursue science and engineering subjects, to develop their interest at an early age. Globally according to the Program for International Student Assessment (PISA, 2006), both genders at age fifteen place an equal value on science, however at university level the discrepancy between the genders opting for science and technology subjects is more noticeable. The percentage of female graduates in science and technology varies across Europe and Internationally. The average percentage of female graduates in science and technology in Europe was 33% in 2005 (UNESCO, 2005), behind South Africa (37%) and Brazil (37%). With regard to computer science and technology there is a general need to break the 'toys for boy's' view of computers and technology. Throughout the STEM sector, there is a need to move away from gendered stereotypes concerning abilities and appropriate career choices based on gender. Through more gender inclusive socialization within schools and within the home children will accept that they can pursue a wide range of careers and help in the eradication of gendered occupational segregation.

Computer Confidence

Touching on the idea of skills being a reason why females are not entering computing and gaming courses, some studies have implicated a lack of confidence with computers being an issue. Early research by Chen (1986) studied a sample of students from five high schools and found that although males and females were perceived to have similar levels of interest in computing, males held stronger, more confident attitudes towards with computers than females did. Sackrowitz & Parelius (1996) found female students still entered introductory computer science classes with weaker skills and less involvement with computers than their male peers. Nearly two decades later, Beyer et al. (2003) found that surprisingly, males who were non-computer majors had higher confidence levels with computers than female computer majors. Gibbs (2013) posits that there has been a general increase in computer self-efficacy and computer confidence with no differences between the genders. This shows a narrowing of the gender gap in computing, which they argue, could be due to better education at earlier levels. For instance, ICT is now taught in primary schools to enable children to gain a full grasp of computers and

the modern way they are used within society, the UK Government has also decided to change the name of these classes from ICT to Computing in order to "improve the status of the subject...[and] more accurately reflect the breadth of content" (Department for Education, 2013).

The evidence suggests how computer confidence and lack of skills can act as a deterrent to female students and this could be implied as a factor as to why there is a lack of female presence in gaming courses and female gaming academics.

Recruitment onto Games Courses

The literature presented has attempted to uncover issues for the lack of females on computer games courses and subsequently potential reasons why there is an underrepresentation of females in the computer games industry. One important reason for women not enrolling on gaming courses may actually lie within the recruitment process. An issue highlighted in regard to the underrepresentation of females on computing courses in the USA (Scragg & Smith, 1998). Roberts, Kassianidou & Irani (2002) agree with the suggestion that there is a problem in the recruitment processes. They put forward a number of 'effective steps' that faculties can employ to increase the recruitment of women in computer science. They suggest universities should use the following four techniques to improve recruitment and retention of female students in the computer sciences;

- Increasing the number of women enrolled in computer science, as opposed to the percentage.
- Redesigning the introductory sequence to make it accessible to a much wider audience.
- Provide role models for undergraduate women at every level of the educational process, including those who are only one or two years more advanced in age and experience.

- Establish several bridge programs that target students, both women and minorities, who are at greater risk of leaving technical fields.

It should be considered, then, that because of the massive gap in ratio of male to female students, seen in previous statistics, perhaps the advertising techniques used by institutions are aimed at more of a male demographic and this then bypasses the female interest. It is clear from the literature presented that there is a lack of females studying computer related and gaming courses, not just in the UK but worldwide . There have as yet (at least to our knowledge) been no studies looking at the view and opinions of females on gaming courses and what their experiences of the course and expectations of the industry are. Therefore this chapter provides a unique insight into the area.

METHODOLOGY

Participants

The study entailed face to face semi-structured interview with four female participants out of the possible twenty (a response rate of 20%) who were enrolled on one of three gaming courses at a university in the North West of England. The three courses offered were Games Design, Games Art and Games Programming, three participants were studying Game Design and one Games Art. All the females volunteered and signed an informed consent form prior to the interview being conducted. The age range of the female students involved was from 20 to 29 years old. One participant was in her first year of study and the other three were completing their final year. Three participants described themselves white-British in ethnicity and one mixed race. Only one of the participants mentioned she had children.

The Questions

The interview questions were split into three categories; Why Games?, Experiences on the Course and Further Career. For the first section (why games?) the questions asked were;

- Why did you choose to study games?
- How did you apply for the course (e.g. via UCAS or direct applicant to the university)?
- Was your course advertised to you, if so, how well was it advertised?
- Do you play computer games for leisure? If yes,
  ○ Do you think this has influenced your decision to study computer games?
  ○ What type of games do you tend to play?
- What qualifications did you need to get onto the course?
- What do you want to do when you finish the course?

The second section (experiences on the course) asked;

- How many females are on your course?
- What do you feel is the general reaction of the male course members having females on the course?
- In your opinion do you feel you have been treated differently because you as a female are a minority on the course? If yes, please explain.
- Have you encountered anything you might describe as sexist behaviour? If yes, please explain.
- Have you ever felt intimidated being a female on the course? If yes, please explain
- Do you feel you are at a disadvantage being a female on the course? If yes, please explain
- Can you think of any positive benefits for being a female on the course?

And the last section (further career) asked;

- What are your career goals/aspirations?
- Why do you want to work in games?
  - If you don't want to work in games, why not?
  - Which sector/industry do you want to go into?
- If you do want to work within the games industry in what area?
- Since the computer games industry is male dominated –do you think you will experience prejudice for being a women within the games industry? If yes, please explain
- Do you think it is beneficial for the industry to have a more diverse workforce?
- In what ways do you think more women working within the computer games industry could benefit the industry and the games that are made?
- How do you feel about working in a male dominated environment?
- What are your expectations about being a part of the games industry, what do you hope to achieve?

Since the interviews were semi-structured, additional questions were included in the interviews that were not part of the schedule; these have been noted in bold. All the interviews were digitally recorded and transcribed verbatim. Thematic analysis was conducted, identifying common themes from the data (Braun & Clarke, 2006).

FINDINGS

Choosing to Study Games

Most of the participants chose to pursue their course because they already had an interest in games/ gaming. Some mentioned that it was a permanent feature in their life since they were younger so it was logical to them to enrol on the course.

Because I love games just because I wanted to do it really, I've always played games to be honest since I can remember. At first just kind of anything because when I was younger I was just limited to whatever my dad bought so it was just kind of Nintendo games like supermario, things like that. Then as I got a bit older and I had jobs and things I started playing a lot of role playing games. (Interview 1)

Since I was little I wanted to [make] games I was like the best way is probably going through a course. (Interview 3)

Well, since I was younger I've had a family who were really into their games, 3d modelling and what not, so I've kind of been brought up in that sort of environment. Whereas if I wasn't I probably wouldn't [have chosen games] – I'm not sure. (Interview 2)

All but one of the participants felt that the course hadn't been advertised to them and that they had actively search for the course. The participants described different life events that had lead them to look for the course and some of the participants felt that more could be done to encourage females onto these courses.

I think maybe advertising on even like girl gamer forums like advertising on there or having female students at perhaps open days or going in to colleges because I would presume that it's the male tutors or male student that are going I've never been asked to go and I think that having a male and female student talking about it would maybe help the girls think well I can do that as well. (Interview 1)

It would be great if they could advertise it more because there's a lot of students out there who would kill to do something like this but they don't know where to start. (Interview2)

All four participants played computer games for leisure and said that this had strongly influenced their decision to study games at university, sparking an increased interest in the subject. One participant felt that being in the computer games industry where she would be making games as well as playing games for leisure wasn't going to be an issue in terms of downtime.

(Do you think that being in the games industry and playing games for leisure will be an issue then?) it doesn't bother me, like if I've got a project on that's near a deadline I don't sleep very much, just lay in bed thinking of ideas for the project but because It's something I'm interested in it doesn't matter. (Interview 1)

When asked what they wanted to do after they had finished the course, the responses were varied but there was an underlying uncertainty of whether to enter the industry from some of the participants.

I'd really like to go into tutoring, do a PhD and maybe study different aspects of games as well. (Is there anything that entices you to going into tutoring rather than the industry itself?) Its two things really, the first thing is that the industry isn't very family friendly and I have a family. The second thing is I think that it kind of plays to my strengths of organising and relaying information to other people- I really enjoy that. (Interview 1)

I did want to; well it's kind of hard to say. We did have guest lecturers in and they were talking about how it works now, like it works more like they recruit you when you're needed unless you're permanent staff. Its whether or not I go with that path or go as more of an indie developer. (So does the job stability concern you of potential jobs?) It does but getting in seems quite hard, you've got to have quite a lot of contacts was what we were told and you've really got to push yourself to get publicised and you've really got to be good at it

and stuff. I think that if you just decided if you wanted to be an indie developer it's not too hard but it's until you get that first sale you're kind of funding yourself off nothing. (Interview 3)

Experience of Being Females on Male Dominated Courses

The female students were in the minority on their courses and in some cases they didn't know of any other females until they had been on the course for a little while.

For the first month I didn't even know there was another girl on specifically games design and when I met her I was like 'oh my god you're a girl!' (Interview 3)

There was none to start with on mine but now the HND has joined us there's one other girl. (Interview 1)

Participants didn't view being the only female (or one of few females) on the course a problem, on the converse it was viewed somewhat as an advantage in terms of standing out,

I mainly hang around with the guys anyway so it doesn't bother me if there isn't that many girls.' (Interview 3)

No, no not at all, in fact I think it gives me more of an advantage to be honest. (how so?) well because teenage, I don't want to say they all look alike but teenage lads can look quite similar so I can see from a tutors point of view that it's very hard to learn all their names and interests, and strengths and weaknesses are, but for me being the only girl I stick in their heads. (Interview 1)

The general reaction of the male course members to having females on the course was described fairly positively.

Different really, I can honestly say that I've not had a single negative experience from one of my fellow course members. Not one, not based on my gender anyway. But I did find at first, especially young lads, certain ones are not comfortable talking to the opposite sex and it tended to be the older ones who were more comfortable in themselves that would come and talk to me and it has taken the younger ones basically until this year to speak with me. (Interview 1)

They're very shy guys so there was one particular guy who was sat near me who was trying so hard to talk to me ...so I don't know if they felt the need to try and include me. (Interview 2)

I think at first it was more "oo a girl wants to study this" but I think now it's like they know you know what they know so it's like we've all got the same understanding were all the same and we're all here to learn so. (Interview 3)

However, one participant commented that some of her peers had made advances towards her but she had shaken it off as an everyday thing.

I mean they have tried it on but I think with any female they'll do that regardless, but they know not to. (Interview 2)

All the girls said that they didn't feel intimated or at a disadvantage being a female on the course and that they hadn't encountered any sexist behaviour either. However, two of the participants expressed views of sexist behaviour happening within the industry, despite experiencing this first hand.

No I mean I'm not really uppity on that kind of stuff like when the guys are going on about boobs and stuff it's kind of like boobs yep boobs are there. (Interview 3)

You hear a lot about it [sexism], I can honestly say that I've never experienced it personally but yeah you do hear about it in industry and it is worrying to think. I do have the worry that this is an industry that is very dependent on people doing long hours and people doing overtime and I do have a general sense that are they going to [be sexist/discriminate], not just because I'm female but because I've got a child as well; is it going to be 'well she's actually going to be quite good but do we want to take her on, because she's not going to put the hours in? (Interview 1)

When asked about being treated differently because of their gender, either for positive or negative reasons, by peers or lecturers the female students felt that they had been treated differently but in more positive than negative ways

Yeah, I think in a sense they do look after me [her peers], they look out for me, they make sure I'm okay, but at the same way I think, it's weird because I'm a lot older than them' (Interview 2)

'I have had tutors come to me and say that it's beneficial to have me on the course because they [the younger male students] need to learn to work with people but it's not been anything like singling me out. (Do you think it's because they've had so many males over the years?) yeah, like one of the tutors has said to me that he's disappointed because the intake he's got at the moment is lacking in female students and the males tend to have a specific type of game that they're into he said that you don't get that variety [with only male students]. (Interview 1)

Positive benefits of having females on the course were viewed by the female participants as bringing different skills and qualities such as leadership and an eye for detail.

I think that females tend to want to be, not bossy, but want [to be in] leadership [rolls] more naturally than especially young lads do. And I think if it was a course full of females that would cause problems because everybody would want to be the leader and everybody would want to, kind of, have it done their way but really because I'm naturally swayed towards that and they [the lads] don't it works nicely because there's a person who organises it and the rest of the people follow. (Interview 1)

Definitely…I think when people are asking for help and doing module work… it's easier for a women to pick out finer details as a man wouldn't he's just like get the job done yeah slap bang, whereas I'm like hold on what about this and what about that and we kind of help each other with both our work because I'll see things they don't see and they see thing that I don't. (Interview 2)

There was a sense that being a woman should not matter as it is your knowledge and skills that are important. Indeed one participant felt that being a female student or indeed a female working in the industry was not an issue since it is the work that matters more to herself, her peers and her lecturers.

[speaking about a female lecturer] I think she's probably in the same boat of the industry being guy heavy anyway so you either get on or you don't so it's just it doesn't really matter what gender you are at the end of the day. (Interview 3)

I just want to be on the same level as everyone else. I've got the same knowledge as everyone else like obviously people know different things and they apply it in different ways. (Interview 4)

I personally haven't been treated any differently and I wouldn't want to be either because its then like 'oh you're a girl' (Interview 2)

Career Aspirations and Goals

When asked about career goals three of the girls expressed an interest in going into the industry but as mentioned earlier they highlighted concerns.

I would like to work for a games company as a character or concept artist why? Because I've spent the time and effort learning the skills I need to work in games. I would like to be part of a project and see something published which I helped to create. (Interview 4)

If you've got the strong passion for what you're doing then you can do it and it is a hard industry to get into you've got to really stand out but I think if you succeed in that you can get far in it… my aim is to get to Canada if I can. (Interview 2)

Well they're kind of changing at the moment. It was originally to go into industry but I'm not sure whether or not to follow that path. (Is there any particular reason why not?) it's more the fact that I'm not sure if its stable at the moment, I mean XXX [a lecturer] did mention that sometimes girls do have the advantage because obviously they're so far and few between so it's more or less. I wouldn't have minded setting up an indie company and creating a game or something and hoping that we get somewhere and if not then go into industry or something. (Interview3)

The participant who mentioned she had children discussed concerns with working in an industry notorious for long hours, suggesting the industry was not family friendly. In particular, even before entering the industry she felt that the industry wasn't for her at least at this stage in her life and was interested in becoming a games tutor/ lecturer. Another woman also expressed views on the family issues within the industry but from an employer's point of view.

If I was a man and was to employ a women for my games company, the first thing I'd think about is like forget the skills, forget the talents, forget the differences a woman has, because projects could be a year- two years, so if it was like a two year/ three year project you've got your strict deadlines. If they were to possibly get pregnant or anything like that, you know they get hormonal they could totally flunk out on their work, they could cause stress in the workplace and they could have their maternity leave and that's it. The stuff she's been assigned to is gone, so who else are they going to rely on they've got another year, strict deadlines by the end of a few months. So I think in that way I'm not sure if men will be a bit like shall we see what she's on, is she married – they need to find out about your personal life first. Which is unfair but it happens if you're a woman- what can you do? You can't, you either choose your career or family life, it's more difficult for women than men. (Interview 2)

The main benefit of more females working in the industry where pointed out by participants which centred around de-sexualising female characters within the games themselves.

It might help to even out the over sexualised characters and any sexism within the game design. (Interview 4)

Yeah I would say so because I really hate it when I see all these games like Just Dance and it's always aimed at women and it's like it is fun but it's, like so bad! I've got this annoying thing now where I've done the course and you pick up on things in the game and it's like I don't know why they've made this decision its totally wrong- was it the shortcut or something? Games like that really grind me and it's like (almost like a man's view of what a women would want really?) yeah it is it's like they need more women to just go well maybe they don't, maybe they don't want outfits like in RPG's when the outfits are just breastplates

and they have the same defence- that always confuses me as well how come they have really cool armour and I've got just a bra that protects me? (Interview 3)

With regard to their future career aspirations, some of the women touched upon the previous issues of the hardship of entering the games industry and others described aspirations and goals they wanted to achieve.

It's mainly see what I can do at the moment like that's the short term goal but obviously I would like to have a game out at some point. Yeah, even just have my name in the credits and just go oh look that's me. Even XXXX (a lecturer) has his company and he's set it up so we can have six weeks experience so that was kind of nice of him and hopefully we can have our names in his credits. (Interview 3)

Well I don't want to be too narrow, I think with this sort of industry you can't be too narrow you have to be open and for you to be the person who decides to do that- it's a very slim chance. You have to be in industry for a very long time before you decide to tweak ideas that's the problem so in industry it would take you a very long time. I've not got any particular thing but I mean I'm open to anything as long as I'm enjoying it I just want to be part of a team, all having a laugh and working together getting things done putting ideas out onto a screen and everyone's loving it. (Interview 2)

Really I would like to get rid of the whole 'we work this way so if you've got a family you've not got a place here' I think it's wrong and a bit backwards to be honest. It really would be nice if we could get to a point of people working normal hours and people could have lives and have families rather than thinking I don't know if I can go into industry because I'm not going to see my daughter or whatever, but that's a big change for one person to make but that the ideal scenario. (Interview 1)

RECOMMENDATIONS

It is apparent that all the female students interviewed want to work in the area of games and have a real interest and passion for games, however they were concerned about entering the industry due, in the main, to the long hours culture associated with the industry and the view that the industry is not a family friendly work environment. More research is needed on female game students' experiences of their courses and also on their views and expectations of working in the industry. This may help the industry eradicate some of its working practices which may indeed be limiting the diversity of its workforce. As Prescott & Bogg (2010) have noted elsewhere, it is paramount that the industry highlights the many benefits it can offer women as an interesting and enjoyable career.

FUTURE RESEARCH DIRECTIONS

Gaining the views of women at differing stages in their career is important. There is a paucity, perhaps no research that has gained the views, and experiences of female students undertaking game courses at university level. This chapter therefore provides a unique viewpoint being a minority from female students on games course and their views about potentially working in the male dominated games industry. More research is needed in this area. The current study is limited due to its small sample size. Future research may consider gaining the views of women studying games at a number of universities rather than just one in order to increase the sample size and the generalizability of the findings. Although previous research has considered the views of children potentially working in computer science and other technology disciplines; future research may want to consider the views of children who play games and how they view a career in the games industry. All the students in this study had entered games

due to having an interest in games therefore understanding the views of children who play games may prove insightful.

CONCLUSION

Although limited due to the small sample size, this study offers a unique insight into the experiences and views of female game students. What is particularly interesting from the interviews is the apprehension the females have about entering the industry. This is despite not experiencing any negativity for being a female, yet being very much in the minority currently on their university course. Interestingly it is the issue of work life balance which raises concerns. There is also the issue of potential sexism within the industry, but again, this on the whole is centred around having a family rather than being female. This is an important issue as many females may be put off studying games related disciplines due to the issues involved with the industry for female employees and the pressure to choose between either a family or a career in games.

It is apparent from the low number of female students on games courses at this and other UK universities, that more needs to be done to attract and encourage girls onto gaming courses at university level. However despite the participants in this study being either the sole female on the course or being very much in the minority, there were no negative only positive experiences mentioned by the female students of being on the games courses. The participants felt welcomed and accepted on the course, bringing to the course different skills and qualities. There was, however, some negativity expressed in regard to working in the industry as mentioned previously. The female students were keen to see more females enter the industry in order to tackle the issue of sexualised representation of females within games, and better games to females generally.

REFERENCES

Bartol, K. M., & Aspray, W. (2006). The transition of women from the academic world to the IT workplace: A review of the relevant research. In J. M. Cohoon, & W. Aspray (Eds.), *Women and information technology: Research on underrepresentation* (pp. 377–419). Cambridge, MA: MIT Press. doi:10.7551/mitpress/9780262033459.003.0013

BECTA. (2008). *How do boys and girls differ in their use of ICT?* (Research report). *BECTA, Coventry.* Retrieved from http://www.vital.ac.uk/community/file.php/872/gender_ict_briefing.pdf

Beyer, S., Rynes, K., Perrault, J., Hay, K., & Haller, S. (2003). Gender differences in computer science students. *ACM SIGCSE Bulletin, 35*(1), 49–53. doi:10.1145/792548.611930

Braun, V., & Clarke, V. (2006). Using thematic analysis in psychology. *Qualitative Research in Psychology, 3*(2), 77–101. doi:10.1191/1478088706qp063oa

Campbell, S. M., & Collaer, M. L. (2009). Stereotype threat and gender differences in performance on a novel visuospatial task. *Psychology of Women Quarterly, 33*(4), 437–444. doi:10.1111/j.1471-6402.2009.01521.x

Chen, M. (1986). Gender and computers: The beneficial effects of experience on attitudes. *Journal of Educational Computing Research, 2,* 265–282. doi:10.2190/WDRY-9K0F-VCP6-JCCD

Consalvo, M. (2008). Crunched by passion: Women game developers & workplace challenges. In H. Kafai, Denner & Sun (Ed.), Beyond Barbie & Mortal Kombat: New perspectives on gender & gaming (pp. 177-192). Cambridge, MA: The MIT Press.

Craig, K. M., & Rand, K. A. (1998). The perceptually privileged group member: Consequences of solo status for African Americans and Whites in task groups. *Small Group Research, 29,* 339–358. doi:10.1177/1046496498293003

Crocker, J., & McGraw, K. M. (1984). What's good for the goose is not good for the gander: Solo status as an obstacle to occupational achievement for males and females. *The American Behavioral Scientist, 27*(3), 357–369. doi:10.1177/000276484027003007

Dar-Nimrod, I., & Heine, S. J. (2006). Exposure to scientific theories affects women's math performance. *Science, 314,* 435. doi:10.1126/science.1131100 PMID:17053140

Department for Education. (2013). *Consultation on the order for replacing the subject of ICT with computing government response (Report).* Crown.

Deuze, M., Martin, C. B., & Alen, C. (2007). The professional identity of gameworkers. *Convergence: The International Journal of Research into New Media Technologies, 13*(4), 335–353. doi:10.1177/1354856507081947

Dyer-Whitheford, N., & Sharman, Z. (2005). The political economy of Canada's video & computer game industry. *Canadian Journal of Communication, 20,* 187–210.

Frenkel, K. A. (1990). Women and computing. *Communications of the ACM, 33*(11), 34–46. doi:10.1145/92755.92756

Fuegen, K., & Biernat, M. (2002). Re-examining the effects of solo status for women and men. *Personality and Social Psychology Bulletin, 28*(7), 913–925. doi:10.1177/014616720202800705

Gibbs, S. (2013). Computer self-efficacy-Is there a gender gap in tertiary level introductory computing classes? *Journal of Applied Computing and Information Technology, 17*(1).

Good, C., Aronson, J., & Harder, J. A. (2008). Problems in the pipeline: Stereotype threat and women's achievement in high-level math courses. *Journal of Applied Developmental Psychology, 29*(1), 17–28. doi:10.1016/j.appdev.2007.10.004

Gourdin, A. (2005). Game developers demographics: An exploration of workforce diversity. *International Game Developers Association.* Retrieved from http://archives.igda.org/diversity/IGDA_DeveloperDemographics_Oct05.pdf

Gras-Velazquez, A., Joyce, A., & Derby, M. (2008). Women and ICT: Why are girls still not attracted to ICT studies? *European Schoolnet, Brussels.* Retrieved from http://blog.eun.org/insightblog/upload/women_and_ICT_FINAL.pdf

Haines, L. (2004). Why are there so few women in games? [Report]. *Media Training North West.* Retrieved from http://archives.igda.org/women/MTNW_Women-in-Games_Sep04.pdf

Hayes, E. (2005). Women, video gaming and learning: Beyond stereotypes. *TechTrends, 49*(5), 23–28. doi:10.1007/BF02763686

Hess, R. D., & Miura, I. T. (1985). Gender differences in enrolment in computer camps and classes. *Sex Roles, 13*(3-4), 193–203. doi:10.1007/BF00287910

Innstrand, S. T., Langballe, E. M., Falkum, E., Espnes, G. A., & Aasland, O. G. (2009). Gender-specific perceptions of four dimensions of the work/family interaction. *Journal of Career Assessment, 17*(4), 402–416. doi:10.1177/1069072709334238

Keller, J. (2002). Blatant stereotype threat and women's math performance: Self-handicapping as a strategic means to cope with obtrusive negative performance expectations. *Sex Roles, 47*(3/4), 193–198. doi:10.1023/A:1021003307511

Krotoski, A. 2004. *White paper: Chicks and joysticks.* London: Entertainment & Leisure Software Publishers Association (ELSPA).

Livingstone, I., & Hope, A. (2011). *Next gen: Transforming the UK into the world's leading talent hub for the video games and visual effects industries.* London: NESTA.

Marx, D. M., Ko, S. J., & Friedman, R. A. (2009). The 'Obama effect': How salient role model reduces race-based performance differences. *Journal of Experimental Social Psychology, 45,* 953–956. doi:10.1016/j.jesp.2009.03.012

McIntyre, R. B., Paulon, R. M., & Lord, C. G. (2003). Alleviating women's mathematics stereotype threat through salience of group achievements. *Journal of Experimental Social Psychology, 39,* 83–90. doi:10.1016/S0022-1031(02)00513-9

MCV. (2014). *Recruitment special: Industry salary survey.* Retrieved from http://www.mcvuk.com/news/read/recruitment-special-industry-salary-survey

Milliszewska, I., & Moore, A. (2010). Encouraging girls to consider a career in ICT: A review of strategies. *Journal of Information Technology Education, 9,* 143–166.

Murray, J. (2012). Pupils need to understand computers, not just how to use them. *The Guardian.* Retrieved January 12, 2012, from http://www.guardian.co.uk/education/2012/jan/09/computer-studies-in-schools

Oswald, D. L. (2008). Gender stereotypes and women's reports of liking and ability in traditionally masculine and feminine occupations. *Psychology of Women Quarterly, 32*(2), 196–203. doi:10.1111/j.1471-6402.2008.00424.x

Oswald, D. L., & Lindstedt, K. (2006). The content and function of gender self-stereotypes: An exploratory investigation. *Sex Roles, 54,* 447–458. doi:10.1007/s11199-006-9026-y

PISA. (2006). *Science competencies for tomorrow's world. The programme for international student assessment.* OECD. Retrieved from http://www.oecd.org/dataoecd/15/13/39725224.pdf

Prescott, J., & Bogg, J. (2010). The computer games industry: Women's experiences of work role in a male dominated environment. In A. Cater-Steel, & E. Cater (Eds.), *Women in engineering, science & technology: Education & career challenges* (pp. 138–158). Hershey, PA: IGI Global. doi:10.4018/978-1-61520-657-5.ch007

Prescott, J., & Bogg, J. (2011). Segregation in a male dominated industry: Women working in the computer games industry. *International Journal of Gender. Science and Technology, 3*(1), 205–227.

Prescott, J., & Bogg, J. (2012). *Gendered occupational differences in science, engineering, & technology careers.* Hershey, PA: IGI Global. doi:10.4018/978-1-4666-2107-7

Roberts, E. S., Kassianidou, M., & Irani, L. (2002). Encouraging women in computer science. *ACM SIGCSE Bulletin, 34*(2), 84–88. doi:10.1145/543812.543837

Sackrowitz, M., & Parelius, A. (1996). An unlevel playing field: Women in the introductory computer science courses. *SIGCSE '96 Proceedings of the Twenty-Seventh SIGCSE Technical Symposium on Computer Science Education, 28*(1), 37-41.

Schmader, T. (2002). Gender identification moderates stereotype threat effects on women's math performance. *Journal of Experimental Social Psychology, 38*, 194–201. doi:10.1006/jesp.2001.1500

Scragg, G., & Smith, J. (1998). A study of barriers to women in undergraduate computer science. *ACM SIGSCE Bulletin, 30*(1), 82–86.

Sekaquaptewa, D., & Thompson, M. (2002). The differential effects of solo status on members of high- and low-status groups. *Personality and Social Psychology Bulletin, 28*(5), 694–707. doi:10.1177/0146167202288013

Sekaquaptewa, D., & Thompson, M. (2003). Solo status, stereotype threat, and performance expectancies: Their effects on women's performance. *Journal of Experimental Social Psychology, 39*, 68–74. doi:10.1016/S0022-1031(02)00508-5

Sheperd, J. (2012). ICT lessons in schools are 'highly unsatisfactory', says Royal Society. *The Guardian.* Retrieved January 12, 2012, from http://www.guardian.co.uk/education/2012/jan/13/ict-lessons-uk-schools-unsatisfactory

Smithers, R. (2011). *Should we collect vouchers to fund equipment for schools?* The Guardian Mortarboard Blog. Retrieved 19 March, 2014 from http://www.theguardian.com/education/mortarboard/2011/feb/16/should-we-collect-school-vouchers

Steele, C. M., & Aronson, J. (1995). Stereotype threat and the intellectual test of African Americans performance. *Journal of Personality and Social Psychology, 69*(5), 797–811. doi:10.1037/0022-3514.69.5.797 PMID:7473032

Steele, J., James, J. B., & Barnett, R. C. (2002). Learning in a man's world: Examining the perceptions of undergraduate women in male-dominated academic areas. *Psychology of Women Quarterly, 26*, 46–50. doi:10.1111/1471-6402.00042

Steele, J. R., & Ambady, N. (2006). Math is hard! The effect of gender priming on women's attitudes. *Journal of Experimental Social Psychology, 42*, 428–436. doi:10.1016/j.jesp.2005.06.003

Tajfel, H., & Turner, J. C. (1986). The social identity theory of intergroup behaviour. In S. Worchel, & W. G. Austin (Eds.), *Psychology of intergroup relations* (2nd ed., pp. 7–24). Chicago: Nelson-Hall.

Taylor, C. A., Lord, C. G., McIntyre, R. B., & Paulson, R. M. (2011). The Hillary Clinton effect: When the same role model inspires or fails to inspire improved performance under stereotype threat. *Group Processes & Intergroup Relations*, *14*(4), 447–459. doi:10.1177/1368430210382680

Turner, J. C., Hogg, M. A., Oakes, P. J., Reicher, P. J., & Wetherall, M. S. (1987). *Rediscovering the social group: A self-categorization*. Oxford, UK: Blackwell.

UCAS Communications and Public Affairs. (2013). *2013 cycle applicant figures – June deadline* [Report]. UCAS Communications and Public Affairs.

UKRC. (2008). *Women's underrepresentation in SET in the UK: Key facts*. UK Resource Centre for Women in Science, Engineering and Technology. Retrieved January 2, 2008, from http://www.theukrc.org/resources/key-facts-and-figures/underrepresentation

UNESCO. (2005). *Towards knowledge societies: UNESCO world report*. United Nations Educational, Scientific and Cultural Organization. Retrieved February 1, 2012, from. http://unesdoc.unesco.org/images/0014/001418/141843e.pdf

Valenduc, G., Vendramin, P., Guffens, C., Ponzellini, A., Lebano, A., & D'ouville, L. et al. (2004). *Widening women's work in information and communication technology*. Namur, Belgium: European Commission.

White, J. B. (2008). Fail or flourish? Cognitive appraisal moderates the effect of solo status on performance. *Personality and Social Psychology Bulletin*, *34*(9), 1171–1184. doi:10.1177/0146167208318404 PMID:18678859

Yoder, J. D. (1994). Looking beyond numbers: The effects of gender status, job prestige, and occupational gender-typing on tokenism processes. *Social Psychology Quarterly*, *57*(2), 150–159. doi:10.2307/2786708

ADDITIONAL READING

Acker, J. (1990). Hierarchies, jobs, bodies: a theory of gendered organizations. *Gender & Society*, *4*(2), 139–158. doi:10.1177/089124390004002002

Adam, A., Richardson, H., Griffiths, M., Keogh, C., Moore, K., & Tattersall, A. (2006). Being and 'it' in IT: gendered identities in the IT workplace. *European Journal of Information Systems*, *15*(4), 368–378. doi:10.1057/palgrave.ejis.3000631

Adya, M., & Kaiser, K. M. (2005). Early determinants of women in the IT workforce: a model of girls' career choices. *Information Technology & People*, *18*(3), 230–259. doi:10.1108/09593840510615860

Ahuja, M. K. (2002). Women in the information technology profession: A literature review, synthesis and research agenda. *European Journal of Information Systems*, *11*, 20–34. doi:10.1057/palgrave.ejis.3000417

Anderson, N., Lankshear, C., Timms, C., & Courtney, L. (2008). 'Because it's boring, irrelevant and I don't like computers': why high school girls avoid professionally-oriented ICT subjects. *Computers & Education*, *50*(4), 1304–1318. doi:10.1016/j.compedu.2006.12.003

Bagihole, B., Powell, A., Barnard, S., & Dainty, A. (2008). *Researching cultures in science, engineering and technology: an analysis of current and past literature. UK resource center for women in science, engineering and technology*. UKRC Research Report Series.

Benyo, J., White, J., Ross, J., Wiehe, B., & Sigur, M. (2009). *A New Image for Computing. ACM Bulletin*. WGBH Educational Foundation and the Association for Computing Machinery.

Berg, A. J., & Lie, M. (Eds.). (1994). *Technological flexibility: bringing gender into technology (or was it the other way round)? Bringing technology home - gender and technology in a changing Europe*. Buckingham: OUP.

Blickenstaff, J. C. (2005). Women and science careers: leaky pipeline or gender filter? *Gender and Education, 17*(4), 369–386. doi:10.1080/09540250500145072

Camussi, E., & Leccardi, C. (2005). Stereotypes of working women: the power of expectations. *Social Sciences Information. Informa-tion Sur les Sciences Sociales, 44*(1), 113–140. doi:10.1177/0539018405050463

Ceci, S. J., & Williams, W. M. (2011). Understand-ing current causes of women's underrepresentation in science. *Proceedings of the National Academy of Sciences of the United States of America, 108*(8), 3157–3162. doi:10.1073/pnas.1014871108 PMID:21300892

Ceci, S. J., Williams, W. M., & Barnett, S. M. (2009). Women's underrepresentation in sci-ence: socio-cultural and biological consider-ations. *Psychological Bulletin, 135*(2), 218–261. doi:10.1037/a0014412 PMID:19254079

Denner, J. (2011). What predicts idle school girls' interest in computing? *International Journal of Gender. Science and Technology, 3*(1), 53–69.

Eccles, J. (1994). Understanding women's educational and occupational choices. *Psy-chology of Women Quarterly, 18*(4), 585–609. doi:10.1111/j.1471-6402.1994.tb01049.x

Faulkner, W. (2001). The technology question in feminism: a view from feminist technology stud-ies. *Women's Studies International Forum, 24*(1), 79–95. doi:10.1016/S0277-5395(00)00166-7

Faulkner, W. (2007). 'Nuts and bolts and people': Gender-troubled engineering identi-ties. *Social Studies of Science, 37*(3), 331–356. doi:10.1177/0306312706072175

Faulkner, W., & Lie, M. (2007). Gender in the in-formation society: Strategies of inclusion. *Gender, Technology and Development, 11*(2), 157–177. doi:10.1177/097185240701100202

Galpin, V. (2002). Women in computing around the world. *ACM SIGCSE Bulletin, 34*(2), 94–100. doi:10.1145/543812.543839

Griffiths, M., Moore, K., & Richardson, H. (2007). Celebrating heterogeneity?: a survey of female ICT professionals in England. *Information Communication and Society, 10*(3), 338–357. doi:10.1080/13691180701409945

Harries, R., & Wilkinson, M. A. (2004). Situating gender: students' perceptions of information work. *Information Technology & People, 17*(1), 71–86. doi:10.1108/09593840410522189

Hirshfield, L. E. (2010). She Won't Make Me Feel Dumb: Identity Threat in a Male-Dominated Discipline. *International Journal of Gender. Sci-ence and Technology, 2*(1), 6–24.

Jorgenson, J. (2002). Engineering selves: Ne-gotiating gender and identity in technical work. *Management Communication Quarterly, 15*(3), 350–380. doi:10.1177/0893318902153002

Kanter, R. (1977). *Men and women of the corpo-ration*. New York: Basic Books.

Kelan, E. K. (2007). Tools and toys: communi-cating gendered positions towards technology. *Information Communication and Society, 10*(3), 358–383. doi:10.1080/13691180701409960

Kirkup, G., Zalevski, A., Maruyama, T., & Batool, I. (2010). *Women and Men in Science, Engineering and Technology: The UK Statistics Guide 2010*. Bradford: Uk Resources Centre for Women In Science and Technology.

Michie, S., & Nelson, D. L. (2006). Barriers women face in information technology ca-reers: Self-efficacy, passion and gender biases. *Women in Management Review, 21*(1), 10–27. doi:10.1108/09649420610643385

Natale, M. J. (2002). The effect of a male-orientated computer gaming culture on careers in the computer industry. *Computers & Society*, 24–31. doi:10.1145/566522.566526

Plant, S. (1998). *Zeros and ones: digital women and the new techno culture*. London: Fourth Estate.

Powell, A., Bagihole, B., & Dainty, A. (2009). How women engineers do and undo gender: consequences for gender equality. *Gender, Work and Organization*, *16*(4), 411–428. doi:10.1111/j.1468-0432.2008.00406.x

Powell, A., & Bagihole, B. M. (2006). The problem of women's assimilation into UK engineering cultures: can critical mass work? *Equal Opportunities International*, *2*(8), 688–699. doi:10.1108/02610150610719146

Rose, M. (2007). Why so fed up and footloose in IT? Spelling out the associations between occupation and overall job satisfaction shown by WERS 2004. *Industrial Relations Journal*, *38*(4), 356–384. doi:10.1111/j.1468-2338.2007.00453.x

Singh, K., & Allen, K. R. (2007). Women in computer-related majors: A critical synthesis of research and theory from 1994 to 2005. *Review of Educational Research*, *77*(4), 500–533. doi:10.3102/0034654307309919

Tattersall, A., Keogh, C., & Richardson, H. (2007). *The gender pay gap in the ICT industry University of Salford*. UK: Greater Manchester.

Thewlis, M., Miller, L., & Neathey, F. (2004). *Advancing women in the workplace: statistical analysis. WorkingPaper Series No. 12. EOC.* Manchester: Equal Opportunities Commission.

Trauth, E. M. (2002). Odd girl out: an individual differences perspective on women in the IT profession. *Information Technology & People*, *15*(2), 98–118. doi:10.1108/09593840210430552

Trauth, E. M., Quesenberry, J. L., & Huang, H. (2008). A multicultural analysis of factors influencing career choice for women in the Information Technology workforce. *Journal of Global Information Management*, *16*(4), 1–23. doi:10.4018/jgim.2008100101

Trauth, E. M., Quesenberry, J. L., & Morgan, A. J. (2004). Understanding the under representation of women in IT: Toward a theory of individual differences. In M. Tanniru & S. Weisband (Eds.), *Pro- ceedings of the 2004 ACM SIGMIS Conference on Computer Personal Research* (pp. 114-119). New York: ACM Press.

Turkle, S. (1988). *Computational reticence: why women fear the intimate machine. Technology and women's voices - keeping in touch. C. Kramarae* (pp. 41–61). London: Routledge and Kegan Paul.

Wajcman, J. (1991). *Feminism confronts technology*. Cambridge: Polity Press.

Wajcman, J. (1998). *Managing like a man*. Oxford: Blackwell.

Wajcman, J. (2000). Reflections on gender and technology studies: In what state is the art? *Social Studies of Science*, *30*(3), 447–464. doi:10.1177/030631200030003005

Wajcman, J. (2004). *TechnoFeminism*. Cambridge: Polity.

Wajcman, J. (2007). From women and technology to gendered techno science. *Information Communication and Society*, *10*(3), 287–298. doi:10.1080/13691180701409770

Wajcman, J. (2009). Feminist theories of technology. *Cambridge Journal of Economics*. doi: doi:10.1093/cje/ben057

KEY TERMS AND DEFINITIONS

Education: Education into STEM and computer games viewed as an important route into the industry through gaining an interest and skills in the area.

Gendered Occupational Segregation: Refers to the representation that some jobs are viewed as male and traditionally undertaken by men and other jobs are viewed as female jobs and therefore traditionally done by women.

Industry: Referring to the computer games industry, a term to refer to the industry that makes computer games.

Long Hours: Culture of long hours that may be used to demonstrate career commitment.

Male Dominated: Refers to male dominated occupations and industries that are viewed as being traditionally male. Where the majority of the workforce within that occupation or industry is male.

Recruitment: Recruitment into the industry is an important issue when considering the underrepresentation of women. More attention needs to be paid to how to best utilise recruitment strategies in order to appeal to a wider, more diverse audience.

Section 2

The Experience of Women Working in the Computer Games Industry:
An International Perspective

Profile 5: Fiona Cherbak

Fiona Cherbak has two decades of experience in entertainment business development, marketing, staffing and strategic planning for interactive games, feature films, television, theme park shows, music production and theatre arts. As president of marketing and media firm ThemePark Studios, she spearheads fund-raising, marketing and publicity campaigns for a cross-section of interactive, film and tech companies and organizations. Presently she is co-producer and promoter of the Boston Festival of Indie Games.

My early path into the games industry was both predictable and circuitous. From an early age, I knew I was bound for a career in arts and entertainment, primarily because I had been highly exposed to these industry sectors as a young person growing up in and around performing, visual and technical arts in Southern California. In addition, my mother had an established career as a commercial illustrator in book publishing and major consumer brand packaging, as well as a concept artist for the TV and film studios. This meant I already had a fair idea of the challenges and benefits of working in these sectors: being project-based, learning how to identify new business, managing client relationships, hitting deadlines, needing to set up a functional workspace, laboring long hours, and dealing with vagaries of the fickle entertainment business, in all its glory.

Early in my career, after realizing I was not quite technically-minded enough to succeed as a fledgling animator, I ventured into project management and marketing areas of the entertainment business, essentially roles where I supported and enabled the creative staff who were working in production. This pattern began at Universal Studios, where I worked as a project coordinator in the Planning & Development division, basically the department that designed and built theme parks. My primary job was to provide resources to the artistic staff and the show producers. Not long after, I found myself in similar project coordinator role at the Walt Disney Studios in Burbank, when I was added to the internal marketing team billed as Corporate Synergy & Special Projects, a carefully designed task force that worked directly with executive management at the corporate headquarters to develop cross-marketing initiatives across thirty-five business divisions worldwide.

It was at this juncture that my professional life changed forever. While working on marketing events and programs for the Disney corporate group, I happened to learn more about the Disney animated film division. Already trained in animation and accustomed to supporting the needs of creative teams, I jumped at the chance to transfer into the Human Resources department at Walt Disney Feature Animation. It was here that I cut my teeth on the recruiting side of the business, which was highly competive at that time. Major film studios around the world were battling each other to find and retain the best animators. We were working extremely hard to attract top-tier animation talent to work on seven feature films all in various phases of development, pre-production and production, including *The Lion King, Pocahontas, Hunchback of Notre Dame, Mulan* and other important Disney animated features. This entailed reaching out to a global market of potential job candidates, and learning how to market and advertise to, and solicit animation professionals through various channels. I became completely hooked on recruiting artists, writers and "CG" (computer graphics) programmers. It was a completely rewarding experience and I felt I had found my niche.

A few years later, I had the opportunity to relocate from the west coast of California to Austin, Texas, mainly a move to facilitate an improved life for my young family. As a young woman working in Hollywood at major studios, I found my time too overloaded with work and not enough support, either professionally or personally, to sustain a healthy balance. My son was a year old, and the prospect of raising him in Los Angeles seemed increasingly difficult. Moving to clean, safe, progressive Austin provided a breath of fresh air and a promising new horizon. The only trouble was that I'd left behind a huge entertainment business centered in California that was simply not available in central Texas. I suddenly felt like I had made a big mistake. That was, until I learned about local game company Origin Systems. Founded by games industry legend Richard Garriott in the early 80's, the studio was famous for game titles such as its Ultima franchise. Their base was in Austin, where they had built up a world-class team of nearly 200 game developers.

To make ends meet, I had started a small consulting business, using all my hard-earned skills from Hollywood to provide contract marketing, publicity, booking and event services to a wide range of clients in Austin, including filmmakers, musicians, book authors and tech start-ups. Whilst writing a news column on the local film scene for a weekly newspaper, my editor asked me to write an article on the "new" SXSW Interactive portion of the world-renowned SXSW music conference in Austin. I reached out to the head of marketing at Origin Systems, who assisted me in setting up an interview with a senior game producer at the studio I was also given the opportunity to showcase artwork from their latest games in the newspaper, alongside the final article.

This chance encounter with one of the Origin Systems management team was an incredibly lucky break. In addition to helping me get in the door with Origin Systems, where I went on to provided contract marketing and publicity services on multiple game products for several years, this producer also introduced me to a local game recruiting agency that was doing remarkably well, had an excellent reputation and seemed to need some experienced help. I signed up right away, excited to apply my previous recruiting skills to this "new" games industry.

Representing the agency, I attended my first Game Developers Conference within a few months of starting work. Truly my big coming out, this was an eye-opening experience, one that taught me that the games industry was just as sprawling, diverse, complicated, exhilarating and challenging as other major entertainment sectors such as film, TV and music. Attending GDC made me realize that there was a long-term potential for my career in the games space, and that with careful planning and a commitment to carefully building my profile, I could likely do quite well. What proceeded was a multi-year experience of filling hundreds and perhaps thousands of crucial production positions for a wide variety of game studios and publishers, a worthy trade that I continue to fulfill to this day.

That was a decade ago. The road since then has been wide and curvy at the same time, affording me the ability to make a healthy income, at times considerable, all the while increasing my reach within the games industry and making a credible name for myself. As I had learned from the Hollywood business, earnest self-promotion and building a community profile were absolutely critical steps in the process of being recognized, respected and sought out for business services in the industry. I've discovered several methods for maintaining this self-marketing effort, in addition to building a reputation for doing good work in the recruiting business. With a stolid commitment to professional integrity, I strive to balance between daily work and promoting my profile within the industry.

Crafting an annual plan, I was vigilant in submitting speaking proposals to various professional events, making myself available to speak to games and mainstream media outlets about hiring issues in the industry, and to participate in important programs and organizations that could benefit from my support. These efforts included being part of the early founding group behind Women in Games International, producing numerous 'women in games' seminars and conferences around the U.S., serving on the advisory boards for SXSW Screenburn and SIGGRAPH, speaking to students and young people at various colleges and industry events, serving as the chair for IGDA's Women in Games Special Interest Group, writing articles on the industry's hiring practices and diversity issues and attending a minimum number of industry conventions each year, to stay connected to the game professionals, clients and groups that I supported.

To be clear, this is incredibly hard work. The actual process of recruiting and placing experienced talent at all levels at numerous studios is an enormous task, highly time-consuming and sometimes quite complicated. Hiring managers at game studios are sometimes not clear on their objectives, or not highly trained in basic human resources, thus making the process of identifying and interviewing qualified staff quite challenging for them, and for their recruiting team. Job candidates, especially those in demand, can be unrealistic or unclear in their expectations for a new employer, or simply have extensive considerations that need to be managed before they will accept a job offer.

In my constant quest to continually learn and develop additional skills to pull from, I took on recruiting roles within game studios, both full-time and contract, so I could more fully experience game production from the inside out. This proved to be a worthy choice, as I was finally able to see and hear first-hand what was happening in production on a daily basis. This insider insight became my invaluable tool for becoming even more in tune with the specific needs of game production, and pushed me to gain knowledge that improved my ability to help teams make the right hiring choices. This included learning the details of Agile production methodology, attending production meetings, asking for and receiving mentorship from senior staff, managing projects, participating in human resources and operations tasks, and being willing to do what was needed when called upon by studio management.

Along the 'way, I've often been asked what it is like to work in an industry that is predominantly filled with male counterparts. It's an interesting question for me, since I have worked in traditionally male-dominated work environments since my early career days. It simply has been the norm for me. In general, I've learned a great deal through the years on how to communicate with both men and women in professional environments, and recognize the differences that are sometimes too subtle to describe clearly. While those differences obviously exist, my thought has always been to strive for general equity, as well as for progress for any group of individuals that may be overlooked or receiving less than favorable treatment in the workplace due to their minority position. Common rule of thumb has been that in any scenario where one group is extensively outnumbered by another, there are inherent, inescapable issues.

Truth be told, most of my mentors and supporters throughout my career have been men, but there have also been women who acted as important role models and teachers for me. My goal has been to treat each with respect and gratitude, and to take away from those relationships what I could that would enable other women to do well and even better than me in the games industry. There is no visible enemy when it comes to gender equality, but more of a relaxed malaise that comes from complacency, ignorance or doubt. My quest has been to spread a continual message that there is a pervasive need to stay alert of the issues, and remain diligent about addressing and even solving these issues when they arise. The key to success in this area is communicating in such a way that your intended audience listens and responds positively.

In summation, I can wholeheartedly say that the games industry in an extremely worthwhile endeavor for women to undertake, especially if they are dedicated professionals with a clear understanding of the competive marketplace, the blue chip level of knowledge required to excel, and a preparedness to learn, experience and gain from their peers and managers. The games industry, like other entertainment sectors, is a "people" business, meaning it is very much about the relationships that are developed and maintained. It's also an environment of both vibrant camaraderie and encouraged self-learning when it comes to the actual craft of making games. Ask, and you will learn. Game developers are interested in sharing their knowledge, and most prefer to see their colleagues reaching for a higher level of achievement. Given the team nature of game production, the entire group benefits as a whole, the more capable, enthusiastic and committed their peers are about the production process.

Profile 6: Sheri Graner Ray

Sheri Graner Ray is an award-winning game designer/developer. She is also the author of Gender Inclusive Game Design: Expanding the Market and is a sought after speaker on gender and games. In the game industry since 1989, she has served in many capacities from writer/designer to Director of Product Development. She has more than 30 titles to her name and is currently the CEO and founder of Zombie Cat Studios, based in Austin Texas

On a fall evening in 1989, after my weekly Dungeons and Dragons game had ended for the night, the players were packing up their dice and books when the guy who was the newest addition to the group approached me.

"You know, my company has an opening for a writer," he said, "and with all the writing you've been doing for this weekly game, I think you'd be a natural. Want me to take your resume in?"

A week later I had my interview at Origin Systems, with Warren Specter. I had my offer later that day. So I gave my notice at my job with the American Diabetes Association and two weeks later I started as a "writer" on the Ultima games at Origin Systems.

At the time, I thought it was a lark and that I'd just ride the ride as long as it lasted. I mean, really. Make a career out of something I'd been doing for my gaming group for free? Surely this would never last!

Well, 25 years later I'm still here and I still wonder how I got so lucky to have a career doing something I dearly love!

When I started at Origin Systems, the Ultima team was in crunch on Ultima VII. I was asked to help out by researching the correct usage of "thee" and "thou" and then editing the conversations in the game to reflect this. That wasn't as easy as it sounds because "in those days" there wasn't an internet to consult. I ended up spending some afternoons in the UT library, looking for the grammatical rules.

It was during my time at Origin that I began to get interested in understanding the female game market. It started when I realized that, judging by the registration cards that had been returned to us, The Ultima series seemed to have more female players than the others. This intrigued me and I began my research into why. Truthfully, it was kind of selfish. I loved the games and didn't understand why more females didn't play them. I wanted to share them with my friends, so I figured we just had to find out what was stopping them from playing.

In 1993, I had an opportunity to go to work for American Laser Games in Albuquerque, New Mexico. "ALG" had a new division starting up called "Her Interactive." It was being headed by Patricia Flowers; the wife of the president of ALG. Patricia had five children, three of them girls. As she watched her children play, she saw that there was no computer entertainment aimed at the girls market. This, she believed was a tremendously great business opportunity and so she set about opening Her Interactive. I was brought on as a designer and producer for Her Interactive's first title, "McKinsey and Co". McKenzie & Co. was the first game for girls produced here in the US, releasing one full year ahead of Barbie Fashion Designer.

After I had been with Her Interactive for a year, I was promoted to Director of Product Development. We did a game based on the now extremely popular Vampire Diaries license and also released the first in the long running series of Nancy Drew games. The initial design I did on the Nancy Drew title served as a model for the game series and is still being used today.

During my time at ALG and Her Interactive I founded the IGDA's "Women in Games Committee", which went on to become the Women in Games Special Interest Group (SIG) and I served as the list administrator for more than ten years.

However, American Laser Games was primarily in the business of producing stand-up arcade games and the late nineties weren't good for that market. They had to declare bankruptcy and in 1998 my husband and I returned to Austin Texas with the idea of starting our own development house.

Unfortunately for us, that was also the time when Purple Moon and Girl Games, the other two major "games for girls" companies were both shut down. Even Mattel sold off their interactive department and the game industry turned its collective back on the idea of games for girls. This left me looking for work. I also took that time to gather up what I had learned while at Her Interactive and put it into a book called "Gender Inclusive Game Design – Expanding the Market."

I also used that time to work with the Austin Game Conference to put together and chair the first Women in Games Conference held in the US. We put it on in Austin Texas and had over 165 women in attendance. That conference was the springboard for a new organization, Women in Games International which I founded. I was lucky to have Ellen Guon Beeman, Mia Consolvo, Laura Fryer and Kathy Astromoff serve as my advisory board for this organization.

When my book came out, it received very good reviews and in 2005 was nominated for a Game Developers' Choice Book of the Year award. Additionally I was honored with the Game Developers Choice award for my work in community. I don't think I've ever been as nervous as when I was told I'd have to get up in front of several thousand people and give an acceptance speech!

After a year of unsuccessfully trying to start my own company, I ran into Gordon Walton at a talk I was giving at the University of Texas. He told me he was starting a new group at Sony Online Entertainment to put together an original IP MMO. He offered me the chance to be his Content Lead on the project and I jumped at it! During the next 18 months we worked hard building a full MMO from the ground up. We had the Star Wars Galaxies code base to build on and that made it somewhat easier, but as any of you who work with code know, it also made it harder. The game was coming along well when we received notice that Star Wars Galaxies needed additional manpower to get its next release out the door. So our project was side-lined and we were all moved onto the Star War Galaxies project. I started there by working on a revamp of the tutorial and was then promoted up to content lead for the entire project.

After three years with SOE, I was offered the opportunity to work with Cartoon Network on initial creative concept work for their MMO, FusionFall. I spent a year working with that project. It was so much fun to tell people that watching cartoons was part of my work! When that contract ended, a stream of additional contracts started including CCP/Whitewolf, TellTale Games, Fresh Games, KingsIsle, Kraft Foods, the US Military and many others. I worked with MMOs, puzzle games and finally with serious games. My title GeoCommander, done with the US Navy, placed first in its category at the 2008 Serious Games Summit.

Then in 2008, I ran into Jesse Schell at GDCOnline in Austin. He and I started talking about a game he was working on. After the conversation ran on for a while, we decided to continue the discussion over dinner. Dinner lasted almost three full hours with us redesigning the game concept he'd been working on. It was a fabulous meeting and I had a lot of fun bouncing design ideas with him so I was thrilled when he called the next day and offered me a position as a designer with his company. I told him that I was honored but that I couldn't see my way clear to move to Pittsburgh. He thought about it a moment and then offered to have me work from Austin and, in time, perhaps set up an Austin satellite studio.

After a year of working with Schell Games, Jesse offered me the opportunity to serve as his Design Director. This was an amazing opportunity as I had the chance to work on everything from small social games to educational games to location based attractions in major theme parks. I also got the chance to mentor some of the finest young design talent around.

After five years of working with Schell Games, Jesse and I decided that the long distance working was not as effective as an onsite manager for the design team. We decided that I would remain as a consultant for Schell games while beginning to pursue my own projects.

Currently I still work with Jesse and Schell Games and I am also in the process of exploring the indie games market. My little start up studio is called Zombie Cat Studios and has eight people besides myself working there. We are doing contract work on educational and social games and at the same time exploring some original IP for the tablet market. Stay tuned!

Profile 7: Lindsey "Lindz" Williamson Christy

Lindsey Williamson Christy has been working in the Vancouver publishing, games and film industries since 1997. She has over 16 years of project management experience working on several blockbuster films and AAA game titles. She is currently an instructor at the Vancouver Film School in the Entertainment Business Management program.

I never really planned on getting into video games or visual effects, it just sort of happened and I'm very thankful that it did. Now that I'm taking a break from my career to be a Mom and I'm watching the industry crumble apart, redefine and rebuild itself , I'm not sure if I'll return to the game industry. I've spent 11 years working on console games and most recently in the last 2 years made the jump into 3D conversion and visual effects for the film industry. It's been an amazing roller coaster ride of a career that I've loved and loathed but never regretted.

I started at the University of British Columbia in 1991 and at the very green age of 17, I was completely clueless as to what I wanted to do with my life, but everyone told me that the next 4 years would help me define my career. Unfortunately, 4 years later, having graduated with a BA in Russian History very few doors to a future career were opening for me. Determined to do something, I started thinking about what I loved to do, what got me excited, and thanks to some photography and graphic arts classes in high school I decided that magazines were where my passion lay. I applied to The Simon Fraser University to begin my masters in Publishing, it was a brand new programme and I was positive that this would set me on the right path. However, my application was denied due to my lack of experience. Frustrated that I couldn't get a job or further my education due to lack of experience, I decided I needed to find a way to create my own experience.

I decided an internship would be the best way to break in, who doesn't love free employees? Bear in mind this was 1995 and the internet was barely a blip, so I had to do all my research and canvassing the old fashioned way, I didn't even have an email address or a cell phone. I spent hours at the library researching which magazines & newspaper took interns, mailed off applications and cover letters and waited patiently at home by the phone for someone to call me. After what seemed like endless rejection letters the phone finally rang, it was a local publisher that printed a series of travel magazines who said they would be thrilled to have me for a 3 month internship starting the following week. This brief encounter was to set the wheels in motion for my future career in games. The Production Manager, Kirsten Forbes, was a smart, tough, worldly woman who liked to take a chance on young talent, especially those willing to work their butts off for free. I learned everything I could about magazine publishing in those 3 short months and left work one day, for a job interview at another local weekly newspaper called Business in Vancouver. My interview at BIV was short and sweet; basically I was asked could I use Photoshop and if was I free that weekend. I answered yes and they tossed me a set of keys.

I quickly realized that I was an adequate graphic artist but I wasn't going to win awards, so I started volunteering for the Western Magazine Association in an effort to network and hopefully work my way out of the advertising department. One night at the Western Magazine Awards Gala which I got to attend as a volunteer I bumped into Kirsten, she dragged me over to her table and next thing I knew I was drinking with the publisher and editors of the 2 biggest magazines in town - Vancouver Magazine & Western Living Magazine. The night became a blur but a few weeks later I heard that Van Mag needed an Assistant Production Manager. Through Kirsten's recommendation I got an interview with the very stern German production manager. I was nervous and wasn't sure if the interview was going well but as luck would have it, the publisher just happened to walk by and saw us sitting in the boardroom. He stuck his head in, said hello and that he was happy to see me at the office. I couldn't believe that he remembered me and I'm positive that is the only reason I got hired at Telemedia/Transcontinental Publishers. I'd worked there for almost a year as an Assistant Production Manager when the Production Manager was stricken with breast cancer and had to take a leave of absence. During this time I worked my butt off covering her job, and my own, as the company was paying her during her leave and didn't want to take on the additional burden of hiring a replacement. In the end it worked in my favour, my boss decided after battling cancer for 9 months that she was going to retire and I was awarded the position of Production Manager for Vancouver Magazine & Western Living Magazine.

I loved making magazines; I loved everything about it except the pay cheque. Magazines in Canada don't make money; it's a huge country with a small population that borders the biggest producer of pop culture in the world! If a magazine can't make money they have to keep costs low and therefore salaries are low. So after 3 years when the phone rang and it was Kirsten asking "Hey, do you want to do basically the same job and get paid twice as much?" how could I possibly say no?!

So that was 2000, Y2K, the year that it was all supposed to end, for me it was the beginning. I started at Radical Entertainment on Dec 11, 2000, it was my 27th birthday. Radical had been around since 1995 and had had some ups and downs but when I joined they were on the upswing again. They had 3 projects on the go and I was joining the super secret sequestered team called 'Hairclub'. The name was a goofy reference to Fight Club but it's a name that stuck to our team for 10 years. I had joined a team of 40 guys working on a fighting game for a movie that was coming out in 16 months. The game was proving to be a challenge since the movie was tied to Steven Spielberg and everyone was paranoid about leaks. It was also going to be one of the first titles that Radical released as an Xbox exclusive launch title. The pressure was on and I had no idea what I was doing. Running a team of 40 software developers was only vaguely like making a magazine in that I had to get a group of people to agree on making a product, in budget and by a certain date, but that is where the similarities ended.

Making games is crazy and hard and crazy hard. When making a magazine there was a formula and a cycle to follow, I had a formula to figure out how many pages we could afford based on how many ads were sold and there was a budget for editorial to fill in the gaps between ads. The timeline was set, we publish 10 times per year, each month had a theme and it was pretty straight forward from there. With Games you have a lot of vagueness and ambiguity because a lot of the time you have to wait months and months before you actually have something you can look at and then ask the vital question, "Is it fun?" All the while you are burning through your budget and the deadline is looming and you not really sure if it's all going to come together or not and who knows if it will sell?

My first title, the Xbox launch title, in the end was cancelled, the movie that it was tied to came out as we had just hit Alpha. As a treat we took the team to see the film and I remember the moment we all walked out of the theatre and stood in shock and disbelief. None of what we were told would be in the film was actually in the film, it had all been cut. We were making a fighting game for a feel good movie about a robot boy & his bear. The producer quickly got on the phone to the publisher and we all headed to the bar to get very drunk. A week later we found out the game was cancelled. That blow initially hurt, its always devastating to a team to see something that has been consuming their lives for months if not years, just get tossed away, usually based on a sales & marketing forecast. Often it's cheaper to write off the development cost than to spend the marketing money to try to generate the sales. It's been my experience at Radical that about 25% of games are cancelled well into production for that reason. In the end though 'Hairclub' persevered and the engine we built for that ill fated fighting game went on to be used in The Hulk, The Incredible Hulk Ultimate Destruction, Prototype and Prototype2 and a couple other games that also never saw the light of day.

In 2004 I met my husband at Radical and we went on to get married in 2007 and then in 2010 I got pregnant. At this point I was working on P2 as the Senior Development Director managing a team that would eventually grow to be over 150 people. Radical had been through 2 mergers in the past 2 years and the last one with Activision hadn't been going well. Activision, after the merger with Vivendi/Universal, had forced Radical to downsize from 4 teams to 2 and then 18 months later we were forced once again to downsize to 1 team. 'Hairclub' was the remaining team. I watched as my boss the Executive Producer, the studio president, Kirsten who was an EP on another team and countless friends and co workers were laid off. I was pregnant at the time and I had to hand out the severance letters and help people pack up their desks after having worked with them for a decade. It was a horrible experience and at the time all I could focus on was just getting on my maternity leave. I knew that my time a Radical was also over - I was just going to disappear into the Mommy fog.

Re entering the workforce after having a child is a challenge, you are sleep deprived, exhaustion is the norm and your attention is divided, you don't get to just worry about your needs, there's this little insistent being that is depending on you for everything. Before having a kid all I had to worry about in the morning was getting a shower and walking the dog, and I had worked in games for the last 10 years so no meeting ever started before 10am. Well I was in for a shock when I jumped into the film industry. The film industry is 24/7, it doesn't stop and it expects you to give 120% all the time. I was used to crunching on games and working 6 days a week 10 & 12 hour days but that was always for a few short months and then it would normalize. The film industry does not work that way, its 12 to 16 hour days, 7 days a week and you need to be reading emails constantly even when you are not in the office. I learned all of this the hard way and also while I was trying to work only 4 days a week in the office so I could be a good mom and spend time with my child. Not to mention that I was still breast feeding and my child seemed to hate sleeping. On top of that Gener8 was a start up and it was having growing pains that needed more of my time than I could give. Needless to say after 2 years of sucking at being a mom, ignoring my husband, barely getting by at the office and suffering through a pretty severe bout of depression I called it quits. It was the best decision for the company and my family. I don't regret it but I do sometimes miss being the career driven woman I used to be. My husband always refers to me as the bread winner as my salary has always been higher than his but I've come to realize that at this time my best contribution to my family is not my pay cheque. I miss having the income but at the same time nothing can replace watching my son grow and learn. I love holding his little hand as we walk to preschool together.

I never really faced sexism in the games industry, possibly because I never allowed myself to be a victim. My team was always 95% male, I was always in a position of authority and I always felt respected. I've always been a tomboy, I swear like a trucker and used to be able to keep up with the boys, and so fitting in with the guys was never an issue for me. The stereo types of Booth babes and hyper sexual-ized images of women never really played into my career at Radical, we just didn't make those types of games. I can say now however that ageism is an issue for me and feels to be a limiting factor. I'll be turning 40 this year and I can feel that the young start up companies are weary of hiring a 40 year old mom because they wonder if I'm to be able to work the 60 hour work weeks like I did 10 years ago. As a veteran in the industry, my position translates to a high salary and with today's current economy and fast paced consumer market it's become more difficult for me to compete with all the young and eager new graduates. Production budgets are tight, team sizes are small and everyone is looking to make the next Angry Birds. Currently, I'm taking from time off from the industry and teaching at Vancouver Film School part time which is affording me the opportunity to spend more time with my family and allowing me to plan out the next stage of my career, while the industry reboots itself.

Profile 8: Julie McGurren

Julie McGurren has been working in the UK games industry since 1999 and has more than 14 years experience in developing AAA racing titles as an artist, lead and manager. She is currently a producer at the games company Codemasters.

I grew up playing games from 'Orc Attack' on the Atari 600 in the early 80s, where loading games from the cassette deck took an age, to the handheld Donkey Kong on Nintendo Game and Watch following through to the Sega Mega Drive console at the turn of the '90s. Many hours were spent chasing rings in Sonic the Hedgehog or casting spells in Mickey Mouse World of Illusion. I spent so much time playing Sonic the Hedgehog trying to beat Dr Robotnik I used to catch rings in my sleep! Games were never a vocation I considered growing up, and I imagine that ultimately this was because I had no idea of how you would go about getting work in the industry.

My educational path took me in an artistic direction upon leaving school, and after completing a 2 year BTEC course that explored numerous art disciplines (sculpture, photography, graphic design, 3D Design etc) my university degree from 1993 at the University of Teesside was 'Interior Design'. During my first year, alongside traditional drafting and illustration methods, I was introduced to 3D modelling in C.G.A.L (Computer Graphics and Animation Language). C.G.A.L was a computer language especially designed to help the user produce still and animated images within a Computer. It was a command line driven editor and required more expertise in understanding how to use the language rather than delivering any creative output.

The following year, the university purchased copies of Softimage (Forerunner to XSI), a 3D modelling package that was tools based and the creation of objects and environments became a much more creative process. The goal being to use the software to help visualise the designs conceived on my interior design course. I saw these packages as more of a tool similar to that of a pencil or paintbrush; it was another way to bring your ideas to life.

I left university in 1995 with a 2.1 in Interior Design but never found work in my discipline; I worked in a supermarket and shoe shop as a sale assistant for 2 years. A number of fellow graduates from my university degree had continued their studies in 3D on a Masters course in Computer Graphics at Teesside University, and almost immediately had found work in games companies across the UK, paying good salaries. Taking a lead from my colleagues, I started to see that a job within the games industry could be a solid career path for someone from a creative discipline.

I gained a place on the Masters course (MSC Computer Aided Graphical and Technological Applications) back at Teesside University in 1997 and this allowed me to complete a year of focussed study creating computer graphics and understanding its principles. I was funded to complete the course by the ESF (European Social Fund) and at this time only a few universities in the UK (most notably The University of Teesside and The University of Bournemouth) were offering a course that allowed students to study computer graphics. The funding allowed me to complete the course with minimal debt and take an opportunity to study within a new and exciting discipline.

The course was difficult and challenging as the focus was not just the creation of 3D assets but also the study of graphical mathematics and the coding language C, both of which demanded a high level of study to aid my progression through the course. I would argue that the graphical maths element was the most challenging study I have ever undertaken.

The students on the course were predominantly male but there were a small proportion of female students from a variety of creative and scientific backgrounds. Whilst I was aware we were in a minority on the course, growing up as a teenager I had always had a large proportion of male friends, and during my degree the ratio of male to female students was always higher. I had always felt comfortable with this demographic and never felt challenged because of it.

A few months after completion of the MSc I attended a number of interviews across the country at games companies and I recall I was even interviewed at this early stage by a female art director. I remember peppering my CV with comments and information that made me sound 'cool' and 'quirky', with the hope that this would spark an interest and make me appear that I could be one of the guys on the team. At university I rode to lectures daily on an old BMX and I included this in the interests section!

It was an interview at the Liverpool based Bizarre Creations in Feb 1999 that led me to my first job. I was aware of the company and their products as I had been playing their F1 games on the Sony PlayStation. I had a small portfolio of 3D work alongside my traditional artwork and knowledge of the built environment gained during my undergrad degree. At this point, a job within games as an artist was attainable, even with minimal 3D experience. Games courses were few and far between and most artists came into the industry via a variety of backgrounds some with no 2D or 3D skills just a strong traditional art portfolio that illustrated a creative ability. I do believe when my CV landed on the desk at Bizarre it probably attracted attention as I was female and very much a rarity in the late 90s, I like to think the BMX comment probably helped too! I was thrilled to be given the opportunity to join a successful team and my games career began as a 3D artist making content for Metropolis Street Racer (MSR) on the Sega Dreamcast.

The company consisted of 22 people working on 2 projects, with 2 female staff in administration/human resource/management roles. I was the first female to work directly within the teams creating game content and whilst my Masters course had given me a solid grounding in 3D the learning curve was steep. I did find that there was a competitive nature amongst the art group and a reluctance to share knowledge, and I wonder if I was more sensitive to this being the only female within the team. The company however was relaxed and very informal, the jokes were often lewd and the banter very blue but I found the environment easy to work in and never felt uncomfortable about how the male staff around me behaved, or treated me. Whilst the young male staff around me socialised outside of work I never found myself involved in these groups or was rarely invited to join unless it was an official /corporate event organised by work.

The small team were very committed to the project and long hours were the norm. Unfortunately, the development of the MSR project was pushed way beyond its slotted release date and finally came out in October 2001 - almost a year and a half late. By this time the Dreamcast was failing and sales for the game were low. The MSR game however morphed into Project Gotham Racing that began a 6 year relationship between Bizarre and Microsoft creating the PGR series for the Xbox and 360 consoles.

As the scale of the projects grew so did the team sizes and the 3D art role morphed into a more senior position with management and people responsibilities including the hiring of new staff. As the art team grew I was charged with looking after 4 artists alongside managing my own day to day work.

As a female, I would say I was naturally the most organised of the art group and I gravitated towards keeping the team running as opposed to completing my own work. I believe this led me to become the art manager after 3 projects, a role that I started upon development of PGR3. This position coincided, I believe, with the natural growth of the company and the scale of the games we were creating. Whereas the structure had remained relatively flat for 3/4 years, the growth in numbers brought about the need to manage the team and an increasing workload.

Taking on the additional responsibility was a challenge, primarily because I was now responsible for a predominantly male team (there was one other female artist at this point), including a number of team members I had worked with from the outset of my career. Having been involved in the early days of Bizarre I never felt awkward or shy surrounded by the large male workforce but I now felt I had something to prove. The role of 'Art Manager' was a new position within the company with no specific role to follow, it was left for me to determine what the position should entail and for the most part it felt like the position was being made up as I went along, making pitfalls and learning from my mistakes.

I remained at Bizarre Creations for nearly 12 years continuing as an Art Manager and it was only due to the company's closure in 2011 that I left. When I started at Bizarre the total ratio of males to females was 1 in 8. Interestingly, in 2011 when Bizarre Creations closed, the proportion of female to male staff was similar to when I first started, approximately 1 in 10.

When Bizarre closed I along with the other employees was made redundant and interestingly, I felt at this time, more at odds with being female. Having spent 12 years in one company suddenly I felt exposed and unsure if my experiences and skills would carry over to another company. With no tangible skills i.e. a portfolio to offer I found it hard to sell myself and lacked the self-belief and confidence to put myself out in the jobs market. I was very fortunate that I was offered a position with another UK based studio, Codemasters whose primary output was racing titles. Codemasters, like Bizarre, is world renowned for its racing products and is responsible for the DIRT, GRID and current F1 franchises.

Due to the nature of the Codemasters Company the size of the business was much larger than that of Bizarre and it was daunting to be put amongst the large team size in a relatively senior position. I found it difficult to settle into a team and company with a very different set of processes to that which I was used to. I only knew one way to do things, how it had been done at Bizarre and it felt like I was starting over and beginning my career from scratch. It took nearly a year for me to feel at home within the new environment. The position of Art Producer was new to the company and I found myself having to dictate a little as to what the role was about and what my responsibilities were. I am now nearly 3 years into this role. I feel no different at this company than at Bizarre, my challenges aren't because I work at Codemasters they are just the natural course of game development and as always a lack of time to develop the product!

Codemasters has a number of females within the development teams but numbers are minimal and sadly these have dwindled in recent months. Due to some of the more traditional disciplines we have on site e.g. human resources, marketing, finance, admin, there are a reasonable proportion of women who work within the Codemasters business and we are not such a rarity within the office.

During my time at Bizarre I was heavily involved in the recruitment of artists and C.Vs were few and far between from female applicants. In my experience, introducing females into the workplace often changes the dynamic of a group; it introduces new ways of thinking and throws different opinions into the mix. It's interesting to watch the males react to a new female team member and for a few weeks the banter will die and the team quieten as they get used to the female stranger within the group! Of those women that had been employed at Bizarre, I would say generally they gravitated to the top of the pile and became leads and seniors more quickly than their male counterparts. I would also note that the same is also true within Codemasters with a number of the key art lead positions held by females during my time with the company.

I have never felt my progression has been impeded because I am female, and I believe some of my progression has been enhanced because of it, for example my move into art management. I enjoy the working environment and don't feel awkward as a female working within a predominantly male workplace. Being one of the only females within a team can feel quite special and interestingly I have found myself wary of new female employees, it can feel like you are being usurped when others join the group and I may have missed opportunities to bond with other female staff because of this.

I have a partner and our respective careers have often forced us to do long hours. As such, the commitment that I need to give at certain times during the development cycle has always been a part of working in the industry and this has never caused an issue in my personal life. This development cycle, whilst tough and often tiring can also be a time of camaraderie for a team, I don't find being at work for long hours difficult, it's just the time it takes away from getting other things done. I set myself limits on what I work during these busy periods and will always go home to eat as opposed to adopting the fast food takeaway approach. This allows me a level of control over the work during the busy times and gives me some clarity and focus.

I have been fortunate to progress in my career and be rewarded financially with bonuses that can be one of the great perks of working within games. This has given me financial freedom to pick and choose quite freely on holidays, clothes, impulse buys and also helped when I needed a deposit to buy a house. I feel lucky to have been involved in such an exciting industry and fortunate to work on games that have been critically acclaimed, sold in excess of 1 million units and have been popular with the gaming community. The thrill of walking into a store and seeing your game on the shelf or seeing your game advertised on the TV is an incredibly proud moment.

I don't believe you need to be a gamer to work in games you just need to be passionate about what you do, for me I was passionate about my art and this led me to a career in games. I don't play games like I used to and as my role has changed so has my passion. Whilst my output is less tangible in a production role I am driven by the thrill of working within a team to deliver games played my people across the globe and ultimately that's what gets me out of bed.

Profile 9: Althea Deane

Althea Deane has been working in the games industry since 2000 as a character animator. She has worked at a number of companies in this time, and has credits on many published titles. She is 46, unmarried, and currently working as a self-employed freelance animator, based in Liverpool.

I didn't play many computer games as a child, as they were in their infancy. The odd go on a Space Invaders or Asteroids machine in an arcade was as far as my interest extended. From a fairly early age I was primarily interested in art, and hoped to become an illustrator one day. As I grew up, home-computing became more common, but I was fairly Luddite in my attitude and didn't find it at all interesting when there were paints and paper calling me as an alternative. (My elder brother, incidentally, grew up to write software, so it's possible that I was just being contrary!)

I studied for a BA Honours degree in Illustration in Manchester, and drifted into animation, primarily down to the extraordinary luck of there being an internationally famous animation studio about ten minutes' walk from my home in Chorlton-cum-Hardy, Manchester. Cosgrove Hall Films was responsible for some of the television cartoons of my childhood, such as Dangermouse and Duckula. I began as a Cel-painter in 1990 and gradually worked my way up to an animator of the 2D, pencil and paper variety. Although Cosgrove Hall had moved to the use of computers for the colouring and rendering of animation in the mid-nineties, it wasn't until around 1998 that they began to dabble with actually animating on them, and I was given the opportunity to learn to use Flash. This involved drawing on a Wacom tablet which was a struggle, as you looked at a screen while drawing rather than at your hand. I still find this hard! I also learnt the rudiments of 3D Studio Max, which was a huge learning curve, dealing as it did with not just the technological aspects, but working with a 3D model too. (Cosgrove Hall had long been famous for its puppet series' using 'real' jointed and constructed models such as the ones in The Wind in The Willows, but it was a different department to 2D, and I'd never been involved in any of the productions.)

Around this time, the writing seemed to be on the wall for animation in the UK, with a lot of work designed and written here, but made cheaply overseas. I had heard tales of the bonanza times in the games industry, where companies were allegedly crying out for experienced animators to add some class to their products, so I decided to see if I might do better if I moved into games. I still wasn't playing many games, but what I had seen of Tomb Raider had amazed me with its depth and relative sophistication of movement, even if I did keep getting eaten by wolves at the same point every time!

I started at Warthog PLC in Cheadle, Manchester in late 2000 working on a Looney Tunes game, which was right up my street. I was shocked to find that, as well as working in a building which was sheathed in plastic sheeting on the inside and undergoing redevelopment as we worked, I was one of only three women in the entire workforce of ninety-eight. Although I wasn't daunted by this, it was a big change from working in television animation, where the ratio was more like 50/50 men to women. However, the atmosphere was friendly and I soon adapted. Plus the Ladies' loo was always free!

I worked on a number of projects at Warthog, mostly using Maya, which I found I preferred to Max. These included 'toon' style games, such as the Looney Tunes and Animaniacs, plus a couple of Harry Potter games. I did some lip-syncing on the latter which I found interesting and enjoyable, even if the kid playing Harry did have adenoids. I also worked on cut-scenes and in-game animations. Adapting to in-game animations was a leap, as I'd never before had to produce animations that looked right, not just from the front, but from every conceivable angle! It was a couple of weeks before I got into the habit of checking the back views of what I'd produced, as I finally got my head around the concept of working in three dimensions.

I was at Warthog for about three and a half years, until I was made redundant in the third round of a series of redundancies that marked the decline of the company. I'd enjoyed my time there and learnt a lot, as well as having met a lot of people who I would encounter again in other companies and other locations. I'd also learned about the differences between television animation production, and games production. The culture was rather different; a lot more male, sometimes bordering on the 'laddy'. Although I didn't experience any negative sexist behaviour personally, I did find the odd girly calendar or unpleasantly explicit screensaver a bit off-putting. However, the industry has matured since then, in my opinion. Or the people in it have, at any rate. I have also noted at a number of companies a lot of casual 'humorous' homophobia, which simply didn't happen in television production, and is totally unacceptable in this day and age. Another difference was the habitual long hour's culture, and the concept of 'crunch' time. I was mildly horrified to discover that it was accepted that there were times when people were expected to work late every night and all weekend for no extra pay, just the vague lure of a bonus at some distant future point that didn't always materialise. I have always thought that if a project is properly planned and scheduled, weeks and weeks of unpaid overtime is not needed, and is merely exploitative. Of course, there will be times when some staff need to work extra time to finish something, but in my opinion that should be the exception, not the rule, and rewarded if not financially then with time off in lieu.

After Warthog, I did a brief stint at Eurocom in Derby, but soon moved back up north to work at Sony in Liverpool. I thoroughly enjoyed most of my time at Sony. The company had a mature yet relaxed atmosphere, and my co-workers were a good bunch. I was slightly less outnumbered at Sony, with a couple of women on the art side, one female coder and an entire phalanx of women in the administrative roles. While I was at Sony I learned to use MotionBuilder, which takes motion-capture data and applies it to games models - a technique becoming increasingly popular as the technological capabilities of games consoles moves on and demands greater realism year on year. I also had the opportunity to work in Holland for some months, helping out on Killzone 2 at the Sony-owned Guerrilla Games in Amsterdam. Luckily I live near Liverpool airport, so the weekly commute via EasyJet wasn't too much of a strain, and I have retained to this day the ability to fall asleep on a plane before the safety demonstration has even reached the bit about the life-jacket and whistle. Oddly, for such a cosmopolitan city as Amsterdam, I found the atmosphere at Guerrilla at the time not particularly friendly, but that was offset by the fabulous setting on the Herengracht in the old centre of the city, and the companionship of the other 'foreigners' flown in by Sony to help out. The delicious free lunches helped, too. However, I was glad to come back after seven months as the travelling did get pretty tiring, and Amsterdam in December is cold with a dankness that penetrates to the bone. Also, the unisex toilets at work freaked me out!

I remained at Sony until March 2010, when I was again made redundant. Being made redundant is just part of being in the games industry, it transpires. It's happened to me three times in total, but I have friends who are almost in double figures. The boom and bust nature of the industry can be wearing, and I personally feel that it may be one of the reasons that women, (and men, come to that), don't always stay in games. I know a number of people who have left to work in Academia, or do other things entirely. Of course, there is generally work to be found elsewhere in the country, but for people with mortgages and especially those with kids, upping sticks and moving every few years is not very appealing. For myself, having being made redundant and saddled with a mortgage of my own on a property worth less than I'd paid for, due to the housing bubble bursting, I found that permanent employee contracts were hard to come by. However, I have been working solidly since May 2010 as a freelance character animator on short-term contracts for projects such as 007 Bloodstone and Motorstorm Apocalypse. I'm currently working on a cute pets game which should be out next year, after which I'll probably again be looking around. Ironically, the television animation industry which I abandoned to work in the booming games industry seems to be doing pretty well in the north-west, and I'm considering making a move back into that side of things. Less guns, more gags!

On a more personal level, I've mostly enjoyed my career in games, and have found it rewarding. The gender imbalance seems to be no better now than previously, but that shouldn't put off any women who want to get into the industry - it's still quite a young industry, but has been maturing and becoming more family-friendly over the last ten years, although I do feel that the recession may have set back progress somewhat. However, as a single, child-free woman, I haven't had to face the issues that many women have. A more flexible attitude to part-timers or working from home would benefit women, but those are things that appear yet to be embraced in the games industry. As for my own future plans, those remain fluid, but then they have to - it's the nature of the business.

Profile 10: Dianne Botham

Dianne Botham has been working in the games industry as an Environment Artist since 2002 and has created art work for seven AAA tiles for two different game developers in the UK. She was employed by Bizarre Creations for almost nine years as an Environment and Principal Artist until the company's closure in 2011, and currently works as an Environment Artist at Ninja Theory.

From about the age of seven, I started to play electronic games, the first being "Simon" developed by Milton Bradley. After this, I progressed onto "Space Invaders 1000", "Pac man 2" and "Tomytronic 3D" handheld games. I can even remember prior to this, playing a lot on my older brothers' Grandstand TV console.

As a young teenager, I persuaded my parents to buy me a 48k Sinclair Spectrum for which I collected about thirty games, "Manic Miner" and "Trashman" being my favourites. As I headed into my mid-teens, I gave up on games and concentrated more on my education and socialising with friends.

It was around my early 20's when I started to play games again, I bought a Sega Megadrive after playing one at a friend's house and I became addicted. I never had any intention of working within the games industry at this point. I thought games were just created exclusively by programmers which was largely true at the time. It was only when games started to be developed with 3D graphics that I became interested in them for their art work. I remember playing Doom at a friend's house and being impressed by how far the graphics had improved since the Megadrive.

My favourite subjects at school were Maths, Art and Craft Design technology. These skills led me to study for a HND in Product Design at University. I then went on to complete a Bachelor of Arts in Design Studies with Visual Studies. After struggling to find a job in this discipline, I studied for a teaching certificate in Adult and Further Education which was of one year's duration. After only two years of teaching, I decided to change my career path as I wanted a job that would allow me to be more creative.

I wanted to learn 3D animation, that was my goal, but I couldn't even use Photoshop at this point, so I studied for a University Certificate in Multimedia Technology at Liverpool John Moore's University. I thoroughly enjoyed this course; it was nine months long and involved learning various computer art packages including Photoshop, Illustrator, Adobe Premier, Director, Flash and Infini D (a 3D art package). I developed some basic programming skills on this course, namely HTML, CSS, Java Script, Dreamweaver, Flash Action Scripting and Director Scripting Lingo. I even made a few games using Director and Flash. On the back of these new skills, I acquired a job as a Multimedia Designer, which mainly involved web design, but my passion was still with 3D art. I taught myself how to use 3DS Max, then decided to try and start a career in film or games, but felt that my skills were not adequate enough to get my foot in the door of either industry. My knowledge of 3DSMax was still quite basic at the time, so I applied to do a Master's Degree in Digital Games at Liverpool University. This course consisted of various modules including; Games Design, 3D Modelling and Texturing, Character Design and Animation, History and Critique of Games, Game Production, CGI for Film and Sound Design. It was partly practical, creating art assets and environments, and partly theoretical, writing essays and a dissertation. Obviously, I found the practical side much more enjoyable.

Near the beginning of this course my aim was to become a Character Artist/Animator, but by the end of the course, I was more focussed on becoming an Environment Artist as I enjoyed that speciality a lot more.

The course was twelve months long and very demanding and intense. I put the rest of my life on hold whilst studying for my Master's degree. I worked from when I woke in the morning until I went to bed, seven days a week. The only time I allowed myself off from studying was one evening a week. It was a very tough year.

Shortly after completing my Master's degree, I was fortunate enough to be offered three jobs within the games industry, one of which was at Bizarre Creations which I accepted. They had their own in-house editor for modelling at Bizarre at this time which was similar to Soft Image. I managed to learn how to use this in about two weeks. A couple of years later, we switched to Maya and I have been using this package for modelling ever since. Due to the demands of the job, I have learned how to use various other modelling and sculpting packages in the past ten years. It is important to keep up to date with the latest technology in this industry.

In 2002, when I began my new career, it was quite rare for women to be employed within the games industry unless they were in the Human Resources Department. For my first couple of years at Bizarre, I was one of only two women working on the development team. This didn't bother me because I already had experience of being in the minority; whilst studying for my HND in Product Design I was one of only three women in a class of thirty students. Throughout my time at university, I had equal amounts of both male and female friends. On my master's degree the women actually outnumbered the men, but this was a rarity.

The number of women working at Ninja Theory is greater compared to that at Bizarre Creations and a lot of other game studios, not just in the art department, but in the programming, production and design departments too. I believe that one reason for this could be due to the style of games that are made at Ninja Theory which are very creative and usually fantasy/story driven.

Whilst studying for my master's degree, I completed an assignment based on women in the games industry. I came across many theories as to the type of video games women prefer to play and why, many of which I thought to be totally untrue and outdated. One theory which I do believe that could be true on this subject is that in general, women prefer to play games which are story and character driven. These two features are quite prominent in recent Ninja Theory games. (This theory is not taking into account mobile gaming). If these types of games are more attractive to play, then they are also more attractive to make, encouraging more women to apply to the company.

I very rarely play games these days and have not played them much in the past five years, but some of my favourite games include the Splinter Cell Series, Enslaved, Silent Hill, Mass Effect and Tomb Raider. Most of my spare time is taken up by exercising and socialising. I don't believe that you need to be an avid gamer in order to develop good art work for games, but it is important to stay abreast of what is going on within the industry.

In my experience, I think that attitudes towards women working in the games industry haven't altered over the past twelve years, but then I have never experienced any negativity towards women working in the industry. Nothing has ever stood out as being unusual about the situation to me. I have only experienced working within two games companies though and this may not be the case elsewhere.

I have never felt undervalued as an artist because of being female; I have always got on well with my team members and have never felt segregated from the rest of my colleagues because of being female. The game companies I have worked at have both been very professional.

Working in the games industry can be very demanding on your time, with lots of overtime and deadlines to meet. We were expected to work very long hours at Bizarre Creations during crunch time, which sometimes lasted for around six months at a time and this is the case in most game studios. Working an extra 20 hours a week is not much fun. Fortunately, at Ninja theory, this is not the case. We still have crunch times, but not nearly as severe as that of my days with Bizarre.

A lot of my female friends in the industry have been very successful and gender was not an obstacle for them. Many of my female colleagues and friends working in other game studios moved into the managerial side of game production. I personally, have no desire to become a manager as I want to create art.

I am very critical of my own work and I am always striving to improve my skills and learn new and faster techniques. I do welcome promotion but only if I am still allowed to be creative on a daily basis. My career goals have not altered much during my time in the games industry. My main goal is to be creative and be the best artist that I can be.

Profile 11: Joy Dey

Joy Dey has been working in the games industry for just over 5 years. Following completion of a degree in Game Development she has held roles at a number of different companies working within QA as a Localisation Technician and a Senior QA Tester. At the end of 2013 Joy realised a career dream and was offered a role as a designer at Headstrong Games. Originally from Sweden she is now based in the UK.

My mother is from Bangladesh, but I was born and raised in Sweden and as such I have always had a mix of cultures in my life. My mother is very religious (she is a Hindu) but Sweden is a Christian country so I have always experienced a religious mix, in school I learned about Christianity and at home I learned about Hinduism. I wouldn't say that I'm religious, but if someone asked me then I would say that I'm Hindu even though I don't celebrate any Hindu events or follow any of the "rules".

I've always loved games and in High School (at 16 years old) I chose a study route that would make it possible for me to get in a Game related study in University. I knew that I wanted to work with something that I enjoyed which is why I chose Games.

I studied in Sweden. I started off 3 years in Västerås where I studied Games Programming and in my 3rd year I realised that it wasn't what I wanted to do so I studied Games Design for a year and got a Bachelor Degree in Games Design.

After graduating from University it was really difficult to get that first gaming job. I sent my CV to a lot of companies in Sweden but I didn't even get a response from most of them. Looking back on it now I realize that I did not have the right approach, I believe I was not specific about the kind of role I wanted to apply for. I applied for a Localization Tester job for EA in Madrid and I really tried to sell myself for once. This went a lot better than my previous applications, I got a phone interview and then I got the job! This was my first step into the industry.

When working in a different country I feel it's important to learn the language. Luckily when I moved to Spain I already knew some Spanish from what I had learnt in school, but also from a language course I did in Spain back in 2004. The culture in Spain is so different from the culture in Sweden - the food, the people even the weather and it made a huge difference! I lived with a Spanish girl in Madrid and I learnt a lot about the culture from her. Apart from my roommate I didn't really have many Spanish friends and I ended up hanging out with people from work who were all from different countries in Europe.

After 2 years in Spain I got a job as a Localisation QA Technician at Disney Interactive Studios in London so I moved to the UK. Sadly, after just a few months they decided to close down our department and I had to look for another job. That is when I got a job at Headstrong Games as a Senior QA Technician. I worked on and off at Headstrong for 2 years, and worked for a short period at Microsoft Studios. On my third contract at Headstrong Games I was offered a designer role which is where I'm currently working.

Headstrong Games is an independent studio based in Borough, South East London and is part of Kuju Entertainment Ltd. It currently has over 40 employees and is working on two unannounced console titles. There are not too many women employed at Headstrong, there are 6 women; 4 artists, 1 designer and 1 QA technician. There are however additional female staff who work in HR, finance and administration in our parent company which exists within the same building.

When I joined the design team at Headstrong I spent the first couple of weeks learning about the project from a design point of view. My responsibilities so far have mainly been to script certain areas of the game. As the project moves along I have been given more responsibilities and am taking ownership of certain features.

My goal was always to work in Design but I'd read and was told that the way in was through QA. I did not really work on my own projects and I don't have a Portfolio which I'm sure would've helped me back in the days for an entry level role as a Designer. However starting as a QA gave me experience of working in the industry and learning a lot about it without having the added pressure that designers have. I could focus on judging the quality of the game instead of having to come up with ways to improve it. I was very comfortable as a QA but I was very happy when I got the opportunity to join the design team.

I have now worked in the gaming industry for 5 years in 5 different companies and I have really enjoyed it and it has definitely met my expectations. I expected it to be fun and that it would be something that I looked forward to when I woke up in the morning. I do enjoy taking holidays but I don't dread going back to work again. The people in this industry seem so much more relaxed than the other industries that I have experienced. Although some places have been more fun to work at than others!

I have never thought about my gender being any kind of issue in this industry. I grew up with two brothers and my mum was a single mother so I spent a lot of time with my brothers. I used to go everywhere with them so I ended up doing a lot of boy stuff as a kid. We played football, video games and climbed anything that could be climbed. I have always found it easier to become friends with boys than with girls, mainly because of my interests. I was never into fashion, makeup and other, what were considered girl interests, and because of this I usually ended up being the only girl in some classes in school that we were allowed to choose ourselves. The same was also true during my University studies. I have always felt like I was equal to the boys and there was no special treatment (either positive or negative) towards me because I am a girl.

I have not been active in any women in games related issues since I don't personally think there is an issue. I think it's just natural that more men have the desire and interest to work in the gaming industry than women. There will always be professions and industries that are more appealing to one gender.

In recent years I have attended the Women in Games conference but to be honest I was quite disappointed. It was probably because it was nothing like I expected it to be. Looking at the conference from the outside it was impossible to tell that it was a conference about gaming. Looking at the conference from the inside didn't make it any more obvious! I expected there to be gaming posters or cardboard figures, and companies handing out gaming goodies. The only goody bag, we did get contained brochures about how to get involved with recruiting more women into the industry. I thought there would be demos or even some information about projects the different companies are working on, but there was none. The topics that were raised weren't about gaming. For me the conference could've been about women in any male dominant industry.

I did however enjoy the round table section of the Women in Games conference because we finally talked about games! In my opinion the topic of this conference shouldn't be "there are not enough women in this industry", it should be about "we are women in this industry who have done well and I will teach you how to achieve it". This would also be a great opportunity for women who feel like they are being treated differently, because of their gender, to learn how to overcome it from women who have either gone through the same or have found a way to not be affected by it. This conference should teach women skills that could help them to get further in this industry and an opportunity to show off their work. The conference is also for students that want to get into the industry and it would be an opportunity for companies to advertise themselves and not just for the students to show off their work. The few students I did see were artists or 3D modellers; it would be great to see students doing game design or programming.

I play a lot of games on a lot of different platforms. I own a PS3, Xbox 360, Wii U, 3DS and some older consoles that I don't use anymore. I have also just received my PS4! I am currently playing Kingdom Hearts Final Mix on the PS3, A kingdom for Keflings on the Xbox 360, Zelda the Windwaker and Super Mario Bros U on the Wii U, Luigis Mansion and Pokémon X on the 3DS, and Contrast on the PS4. I am also playing Candy Crush on my android phone. My favourite genre is JRPG, and my favourite games series is Kingdom Hearts.

I am now 29 years old and live in Woking, whilst working in London. I have a partner who also works in the games industry and we have a 1 year old son. This is one of the reasons I had to leave Headstrong once, and I stayed at home with my son for 5 months before I went back to work. My son now stays with a child-minder whilst I am at work. Working while having children makes a bit of a difference. I can't always do overtime because I need to get back home to my son, and weekend work (which is quite rare anyway) is not an option. I also have to save my holidays in case he gets ill. One thing I have noticed, since having my son is that children make you even more creative. Children need entertainment or distractions and I have had to be quite creative with the things I have had around me to entertain him. I have found this has actually made me even more creative at work where I tackle problems in ways that I wouldn't have done before. I also feel that I have more patience now, both when it comes to dealing with issues and people.

I still have a lot to learn in design but I'm enjoying every moment of it. At first I had to get used to the different mindset that I'm not looking for bugs anymore, I am actually supposed to avoid creating them. My dream was to become a designer so I am living the dream right now. I would like to stay on this path so I guess my next goal would be to become a lead designer one day!

Profile 12: Hannah Payne

Hannah Payne has been working in the games industry since 2010. With experience in both art and design roles primarily in mobile games, she now works as a junior artist at mobile game developer, Kwalee.

I have loved games and drawing from a young age, ever since my parents bought an Amiga 1200 when I was about 4 years old. Being so young I wasn't particularly good at most of the games we had, so the first ones I played were things like Fun School and Noddy's Big Adventure. I also remember playing Wizkid, James Pond and Lemmings, and filling disk after disk with Deluxe Paint portraits of our cats. I also have fond memories of the Dizzy and Monkey Island games, Shadow of the Beast and Alien Breed, but I was a bit young to play these and so mainly took the role of spectator (the Shadow of the Beast II intro still gives me nightmares!).

A few years later, we got our first family PC, and I started playing games like Tomb Raider and the Final Fantasy series. Lara Croft became a kind of a role model for me at the time, and the Final Fantasy games inspired me artistically with their imaginative creature and character designs. I got into playing The Sims in a big way when I was about 13, and after downloading enormous amounts of custom content I decided to try making my own custom characters. My parents very kindly bought me my first piece of 3D modelling software (MilkShape 3D) and with the aid of various tutorials I was able to learn the process of editing the existing game meshes, drawing new textures, exporting them correctly and then getting them to show in-game. This was partly what got me interested in how games are made, but at that stage it didn't occur to me that you could do it professionally.

As I progressed through school and then sixth form, I prioritised Art and IT as subjects. The fine art course at my school focused on teaching traditional skills like painting and ceramics, but in my personal work I ventured more into digital art and got my first graphics tablet on my 16th birthday. When I reached the end of sixth form and started looking at universities, I thought more seriously about getting into games as a career. I was surprised to find that there were courses perfectly tailored to this and I applied to a few, but after attending various open days the one that really stood out was the Computer Games Design course at the University of Wales, Newport.

One of the entry requirements was the completion of a foundation art year, which I took at a local college. This gave me the chance to explore many different ways of working and try a variety of media that I hadn't tried at school (such as printmaking, etching and photography) but although the course was enjoyable, it wasn't particularly focused on what I wanted to do. I completed the course in 2007 then went on to university.

The course leaders at Newport were passionate about the subject, and were keen to give us a solid grounding in general design principles as well as the industry-standard practical knowledge we'd need later on. Including myself, there were 4 female students on the course, though this later went down to 3 as class numbers in general dwindled over the years. The class as a whole was made up of people from many different backgrounds, so the fact that we were in a minority as females never really stood out. I was never aware of any competitiveness or rivalries, and although we moved in different circles of friends we all got along well.

The projects on the course were varied, starting with simple illustration and animation tasks before moving on to larger projects that involved making playable games. This meant working in a team, recruiting programmers and getting some experience with full art production pipelines. It was as close to working in a studio as you could get at that stage, and this was also where I met my partner. We collaborated on a number of projects, including the major practical project in our final year. The brief was to create a playable game from scratch using any engine, and we were given complete artistic freedom. We chose the Unreal Development Kit and recruited a programmer from the 'modding' community, and came up with ColourRunners; a free-roaming, first-person exploration game where players create a path of ink that allows them to run around the environment (including up walls) and uncover hidden messages.

I graduated with a first in 2010, and my parents were kind enough to let me and my partner both move in with them (along with our five pet rats) while we looked for jobs and worked on our portfolios. We continued to work on ColourRunners in our spare time, partly to create a more polished portfolio piece and partly to prepare it for exhibition at the GameCity festival in Nottingham. This was a fantastic experience, if rather nerve-wracking. We got to show our game in the main square alongside some of our fellow students' work, and gain some insightful feedback from both the public and some visiting games industry veterans.

University had been invaluable in building up a body of work for my portfolio, and the lecturers had provided plenty of in-depth advice on the best way to write up a CV and present artwork. Even so, looking back I was quite naïve to think that I was ready for some of the roles I was applying for, as no amount of university group work will really prepare you for a working studio environment. After six months however, I had an interview at Silverball Studios and was lucky enough to get my first industry job.

The studio was small (consisting of around 12 people) and remote, situated in a converted barn in a tiny village, right next to a working farm (it wasn't unusual to find chickens and sheep wandering amongst the cars outside). The company focused on making family-friendly console games and apps for various publishers, so I was able to gain a little experience with all of the major platforms. It was an all-male development team and everyone was far more experienced than I was which was rather daunting for a graduate, despite everyone being perfectly friendly. The team was roughly split in half between program-mers and artists, but initially I worked as a designer. Being new to the industry and the only designer (it was a completely new role at the company) I did feel a bit isolated from the rest of the team at times. My job mainly involved writing up design and pitch documents and making PowerPoint presentations. It wasn't what I wanted to be doing ideally, but it still gave me a chance to flex my creative muscles and get a feel for working in a studio environment. Later on, an art position opened up, and, with the help of some very supportive colleagues, I began the transition into a role which was far more varied and more in line with what I wanted to do. There were still occasions when I'd be needed to write documents and make presentations, but in general I became a lot more involved in development. I created concept art, modeled and animated 3D assets, and designed and implemented UI. During my time there, I mainly worked on Mensa Academy and Frogger Pinball, as well as some of the promotional work for the remas-tered Pro Pinball project. I spent a happy two years there before the company closed at the end of 2012.

After the closure of the company, I spent a couple of months taking on various freelance art jobs while I looked for something permanent. My experiences at work (and university) so far had shown that a perk of working in smaller teams is being more involved in the project at all stages of development. I knew a small team was where I wanted to stay and the mobile development sector was a perfect fit.

Eventually I saw a vacancy for a 2D/3D artist at Kwalee, a relatively new mobile developer, and was thrilled when I got the job. As soon as I saw the studio my first impression was of a friendly, creative atmosphere and the fantastic tech resources the team are given to work with. Everyone on the team is approachable, easy to talk to, and passionate about their projects. It's another small company (made up of around 20 people) and most are programmers and designers, but I work within a team of 4 artists.

Again, most of the permanent staff members are male, apart from one other female on the art team. There is a sense of camaraderie among the artists, with feedback and support always on hand, and everyone is passionate about art in their personal lives so it never feels like just a job. Our team leader is keen to get us focusing and improving on our weaknesses, as well as going on training days and attending life drawing sessions to cultivate our skills.

My responsibilities at the company are again quite varied, and I find I'm never doing the same task for more than a few days at a time. My work ranges from 2D illustration and concept art to 3D modelling and animation, and I'm generally given a lot of creative freedom. In addition to this, I often need to liaise with the rest of the team (not just the artists) both for feedback and to fix any issues.

On the whole, working in the games industry has met my all of my expectations. In particular, I knew that I'd be in the minority gender-wise as this has largely been the case in my life up until now. I've never seen this as a negative, however, as I've never personally experienced any different treatment to my male colleagues and not been on the receiving end of any negative comments. I know my positive experience is far from unique, but at the same time I know that everyone isn't so fortunate and we are generally under-represented in the industry. I'm also on the Women in Game Development mailing list, which allows me to stay aware of the issues facing women in the development community.

As for my other expectations, it is (as I'd hoped) a friendly and relatively informal environment, and despite all of the warnings about intense crunch periods and stories of people sleeping under their desks, I've personally not encountered anything of the sort. It can sometimes be demanding (particularly if you have a bout of art block to contend with) and there can be late nights if a deadline is looming, but ultimately you're getting to create art for people to enjoy, and having that work released into the world is exciting and incredibly rewarding.

I now live in Leamington Spa with my partner (who also works in the industry) and a rather lazy three-legged cat. My work hasn't changed how I feel about games as a hobby, and I still play them often. I feel incredibly lucky to be doing what I'm doing and my experience of the industry so far has been a very positive one. I'm hoping this will be the case for many years to come.

Chapter 4
A Look inside the Current Climate of the Video Game Industry

Vachon M.C. Pugh
Electronic Arts, USA

ABSTRACT

The issue of the lack of women in the video game industry has been a hot topic for quite some time. For the past twelve years, Game Developer Magazine has published their annual Game Developer Salary Survey, which not only lists the average salaries for each department; but also breaks down each department by gender. By examining the salary surveys for the past four years (2009-2012), an initial assessment can be made on the amount of women working in the game industry, and in what disciplines. The purpose of this chapter is to assess the current climate of the video game industry, and briefly discuss possible causes of the lack of women in this particular field.

INTRODUCTION

While women account for 45% of today's gamers (Entertainment Software Association, 2013), there is still an underrepresentation of women in the game industry. This anomaly does not restrict itself to just one area of the industry, but affects the industry as a whole. While the exact reason for this is still yet to be discovered, even a quick glance at any of the annual Game Developer Salary Surveys make it readily apparent that the video game industry is a male dominated field. Not only is this the issue in the United States, but the industry climate in the UK and Britain are

strikingly similar (Sector Skills Council, 2012). However, before attempting to solve the issue of the lack of women in the game industry, we must first take a closer look at the industry itself. For the past twelve years, Game Developer Magazine has published its annual game developer salary survey. However, while there are twelve years of data that have been collected, only the 2009 through 2012 surveys will be discussed, so that recent data can be used. With a ±3.06% margin of error for the 2009 survey (Sheffield & Fleming, 2010), a ±2.7% margin of error for the 2010 survey (Sheffield & Newman, 2011), a ±2.4% margin of error for the 2011 survey (Miller,

DOI: 10.4018/978-1-4666-6142-4.ch004

2012) and a ±2.6% margin of error for the 2012 survey (Miller, 2013), all of which are at a 95% confidence level, the surveys acknowledge that the results may be slightly skewed due to the fact that respondents self-report their own salaries. However, the information presented still paints a fairly accurate representation of the current state of the industry. Using this information we will focus on the gender breakdowns in each area to get a better idea of the presence of women in the industry today.

BACKGROUND

The topic of women in the game industry has been a hot topic for some time now. There have been several articles that have discussed this issue, and the opinion the game industry has on the lack of women in the industry. For example, in an interview by Tyler Dukes (2010), IBM Gaming and Interactive Manager Phaendra Boinodiris shared her opinion on the topic. When asked why she thought the industry didn't market appropriately to women, she suggests it is due to the fact that so few women working in these companies, and that if there were more women employees, there would be a bigger shift in the marketing of video games towards a wider audience (Dukes, 2010). This supports the idea that one of the benefits of bringing more women into the industry could provide increased marketability for games. She also goes on to suggest that one reason women are so reluctant to pursue careers in the game industry is the stigma the industry has for being a boy's club (Dukes, 2010), and that making the industry more inclusive could result in new types of games being developed that have never been seen before (Dukes, 2010).

In another article, Mary K. Pratt (2007) talks about how the computer game industry is looking to women for fresh insights. In it, Sheri Graner Ray, game designer and developer at Sirenia Consulting, states "If we want to have [game]

titles that reach a diverse audience, our workforce has to reflect that diversity", (Pratt, 2007, p.1). Again, this suggests that bringing more women into the industry could enable games to appeal to a wider audience. Even the creators of the massive multiplayer online role-playing game (MMORPG) Eve Online planned to hire on more people in order to bring more women into the workplace, since women only made up 16% of their staff (Pratt, 2007). Peter Gollan, CCP Games director of marketing for North America, agrees that bringing more women into the industry will be beneficial, stating "If you want to bring in content that's more engaging to women, you have to bring in more women" (Pratt, 2007, p.2).

Lastly, Sophia Tong (2008) sat down with several panelists from the Penny Arcade Expo 2008, and talked about some of the challenges facing women in the game industry. The panelists suggested that women who are already in the workplace "need to be respectful of each other and not feel threatened when another female joins the group" (Tong, 2008, p. 1). Linsey Murdock, a game designer at ArenaNet, also feels that "young girls should be encouraged to pursue math and science for potential careers in the game industry [….] We need to show them that it's alright and it's acceptable…it's not geeky or weird" (Tong, 2008, p.2). This suggests that one possible way to increase the number of women in the game industry is to interest them at a younger age, and teach them that it is alright to want to pursue careers in STEM related fields. Even Phaendra Boinodiris believes that this is important as well, and has spoken at elementary and middle schools about this, enforcing the idea that "[If] you encourage young women, young girls to play these games, to design their own games, [...] hopefully they'll be able to see why having a field in computer science or math or physics would be interesting" (Dukes, 2010, p.4).

These opinions are only a few of the many voices in the game industry that have spoken out about the issue of the lack of women in the game industry. Even though they represent only a tiny fraction of the industry, the message they are trying to get across is the same—that the industry is in need of more women employees and that having more women will be highly beneficial.

GENDER BREAKDOWN BY DEPARTMENT

Programmers

The female presence in the programming department is the lowest of all the disciplines. The number of women has declined over the past four years from 5% in 2009 to 4% in 2013 (Sheffield & Fleming, 2010; Miller, 2013) This is interesting because according to Nirmala Kannankutty from the National Science Foundation, women make up 45% of all scientists and engineers in the United States (2006). According to the Game Developer surveys, programmers of both genders with less than three years of experience made up 27% of the industry last year, up from 20% in 2011; while those with more than six years of experience is down from 42% to 37% in 2012 (Miller, 2012; Miller, 2013). However, this still does not answer the question of why there are so few female engineers in the video game industry when there are many qualified individuals available. Possible causes for this will be discussed later in this chapter.

Artists and Animators

The art and animation department saw an increase in female employees in 2012. Much higher than the programming department, women accounted for 16% percent of artists and animators in the game industry in 2012, up 13% from 2011(Miller, 2013; Miller 2012). On a positive note, the number of women in the art department has doubled from 8%in 2009 (Sheffield & Fleming, 2010). The survey also reports that 80% of artists and

animators reported being in the industry three years or more (Miller, 2013), which could mean that in addition to women continuing to stay in the industry in this field, there are more joining the field as well.

Game Designers

The female presence in the design department saw a slight drop from 8% in 2009 to 7% in 2010 (Sheffield & Fleming, 2010; Sheffield & Newman, 2011). However, for the past two years, it has held constant at 11% (Miller, 2013; Miller, 2012). Unfortunately, there is not enough information available to make any inferences as to why the number has not increased over the past year. Instead, the takeaway is that the number has still slightly increased over the past four years.

Producers

The next field up for discussion is production. Out of all the creative disciplines in the game industry, production has historically held the highest percentage of women. Women accounted for 18% of the field in 2009, and saw a slight decline over the next two years at 17% and 16% in 2010 and 2011, respectively (Sheffield & Fleming, 2010; Sheffield & Newman, 2011,Miller, 2012). However, 2012 broke the decline, showing an increase in women to 23% (Miller, 2013). Miller suggests that this increase could be due to the importance of design in mobile and free-to-play games (2013).

Audio Professionals

Grouped together in the audio professionals' area are directors, composers, and designers who develop audio for video games. Not only does this field require creative skills, it requires technical skills as well to use the software and various tools needed for creating the various sounds heard by the player in a video game. While women made up about 12% of the department in 2009, their presence dropped by half to only 6% in 2010 (Sheffield & Fleming, 2010; Sheffield & Newman, 2011). The number jumped slightly in 2011 to 7% (Miller, 2012) but saw another sharp decline to only 4% in 2012 (Miller, 2013). Miller suggests that this could be due to the limited amount of audio positions available (2013), however there is not enough information available to support this theory.

QA Testers

Next is the Quality Assurance (QA) Testing department. Since this is the easiest area of the industry to get into, it is most commonly used as a stepping stone to get into other areas of the industry (Sheffield & Fleming, 2010). Female presence in this field dropped from 11% to 5% between 2009 and 2010 (Sheffield & Fleming, 2010; Sheffield & Newman, 2011) and had a brief jump to 13% in 2011 before falling back to 7% in 2012 (Miller, 2012; Miller, 2013). One important note for this area is that most QA testers are on contract, with leads being the most likely to be salaried, which could explain the sudden increases (Sheffield & Newman, 2011). Another explanation for the drop of female presence in this area could be attributed to the fact that they have moved on to other positions, since again the QA area is most often used as a means to get a foot in the door in the industry.

Business and Legal

While the last department is not part of the core creative disciplines in the game industry, the roles within are still an integral part of the industry. The business and legal department combines all related positions such as marketing, chief executives, legal, human resources, licensing, IT, and various other positions. The business and legal department also saw a drop in the number of women, down from 25% in 2009 to 14% in 2010 (Sheffield & Fleming, 2010; Sheffield & Newman, 2011), but has held steady at 18% for the past two years (Miller, 2012; Miller, 2013). Since this area is extremely business focused and does not usually require the extreme time commitments and long work hours that are customary of the creative disciplines in the industry, it is no surprise that it has the second highest percentage of women out of all the departments; surpassed only by the production department's 23% (Miller, 2013). However, this number still pales in comparison to the actual number of women in business and legal professions in the country. According to the U.S. Department of Labor and the U.S. Bureau of Labor Statistics recent assessment, women make up 42.7% of business professionals in the labor force and 49.7% of legal professionals (2010). Once again, this supports the idea that there are qualified individuals available; however why they choose other fields than the video game industry is still an area that deserves further exploration.

What These Numbers Mean

These numbers clearly demonstrate how sparsely women are scattered throughout the industry. It is important to keep in mind that this is not a definitive list on the full capacity of women in the industry; there are other roles that women occupy as well such as through outsourced tasks and other contract work, but while acknowledged will not be explored in detail within this chapter, instead the focus will be kept on the core areas of the game industry.

The lack of women in the industry is apparent from data gathered in the Game Developer Salary Surveys. While it shows how few women there are, it doesn't show what could possibly be causing this anomaly. Therefore, there must be other factors affecting why women choose careers in other industries instead of the game industry. The next step in hopefully remedying this problem is to investigate the root causes behind the low female presence. Once the cause has been identified, then the appropriate steps can be taken to resolve the issue.

POSSIBLE CAUSES

There have been several speculated causes for the lack of women in the video game industry. Lack of interest, anticipated work/family conflict, and the overall social stigma of the industry environment have all been named as possible reasons, and each will be discussed in detail. There has been a limited amount of actual scientific research that has been done into each of these supposed reasons, so much is speculation. However, this also demonstrates the need for further research into these areas. One key point that must be stressed is that until the root cause(s) of the lack of women in the video game industry is found, the issue will never be truly fully resolved.

Lack of Interest

Some people believe that the reason that there aren't many women in the video game industry because they just aren't interested in it. However, the fact still remains that women make up around 45% of today's gamers (Entertainment Software Association, 2013), and women age 18 or older account for 31% of the game-playing population while boys age 17 or younger only account for 19%(Entertainment Software Association, 2013). Therefore, at first glance it seems that there is not much fact to this statement. It is clear that women are interested in video games; however whether or not they are actually interested in joining the industry is a different question. Recent information also suggests that female interest could be picking up; for example, Southern Methodist University's January 2010 cohort was 20% female (IGN Entertainment Games, 2010). While this is definitely a step in the right direction, only time will tell whether this is the beginning of an actual trend or if it is just another random occurrence.

Brenda K. Hawks and Joan Z. Spade did a study to examine several hypotheses in regards to differences in career interests amongst men and women, and whether or not the anticipated role

conflicts of men and women affected their career choices as well (1998). They surveyed both male and female students in their first year introductory engineering course, and asked questions on things such as their interests, how they felt about their abilities, the course curriculum, and family and work conflicts, and if they thought these factors would affect their ability to become successful engineers (Hawks & Spade, 1998). What Hawks and Spade discovered is that the women pursuing the engineering path were quite interested in the field, but were more concerned with work and family roles conflicting with their ability to succeed in the field (1998). They also discovered that women were more likely than men to consider lack of confidence in their abilities as more of a barrier to their success (Hawks & Spade, 1998), again suggesting that lack of interest is not a significant enough explanation for the lack of women in the industry, but that there are other underlying issues as well, such as lack of confidence in their skills and abilities, and anticipated work/family conflict, both which will be discussed further in this paper.

While Hawks and Spade (1998) suggest that lack of interest is not a major issue in the lack of women in STEM related careers such as engineering, there is other literature that suggests that women are just not interested in STEM. In a research paper by Jacob Clark Blickenstaff (2005), he examined various literatures that attempted to explain the lack of women in STEM careers. Two studies he examined suggest that girls are less interested in STEM careers. The first was a meta-analysis by Molly Weinburgh (1995), in which she discovered that girls do have a more negative attitude towards science than boys, despite the small effect size (as cited in Blickenstaff, 2005). This could suggest a lack of interest in STEM; however Weinburgh also noted that girls seemed to favor biology over other sciences (as cited in Blickenstaff, 2005). The second article that Blickenstaff cited was a 1995 study conducted by Dale Baker and Rosemary Leary on primary and secondary school girls and their attitudes towards science. Baker and Leary found that girls were more interested in life sciences such as biology and zoology, rather than physical sciences (as cited in Blickenstaff, 2005), and that this could be due to the female desire to care for people and animals (as cited in Blickenstaff, 2005). Again, like Weinburgh's study (1995), this suggests that there is a lack of interest in girls towards science and STEM, however it also acknowledges the female preference towards biological and life sciences.

The usefulness of both sides of the lack of interest argument is that it helps provide more options for the solution to the lack of women in not only the video game industry, but other STEM fields as well. For example, if lack of interest is in fact a major contributing factor to this problem, then actions can be taken to increase women's interests in this area. However if it is not a major issue, it also provides a different direction to look into when attempting to come up with a solution to this problem. For the purpose of this chapter, all possible avenues must be considered when suggesting various methods to improve the gender differences in the video game industry; therefore the possible explanation of lack of interest is worth examining.

Anticipated Work/Family Conflict and the Social Stigmas of the Video Game Industry

These two issues are by far the most commonly brought up theories in the attempt to explain the lack of women in the game industry. It is common knowledge that our society deems it mainly the woman's responsibility to care for the family, and handle family responsibilities at home; therefore many women choose career paths that allow them to balance both areas effectively. The video game industry is notorious for its long hours during crunch time and the largely male dominated environment, which are not among the most appealing work conditions for the average woman. Scandals such as the Rockstar Wives (Rockstar

Spouse, 2010) and EA Wives (EA Spouse, 2004) issues are prime examples of the negative image the industry has acquired over the years. Joe Sapp of the International Game Developers Association (IGDA) has voiced their concerns on the issue, stating that "In any studio, the IGDA finds the practice of undisclosed and constant overtime to be deceptive, exploitative, and ultimately harmful not only to developers but to their final product and the industry as a whole. While our research shows that many studios have found ways to preserve quality of life for their employees, unhealthy practices are still far too common in our industry" (Sapp, 2010). The fact that the industry is renowned for crunch time and long hours is a definite deterrent for women who have families of their own and must split their time between family and work. A recent study was conducted by Julie Prescott of the University of Liverpool which consisted of a survey of 450 women currently working in the game industry in the UK, U.S, Europe, Canada, Australia, and several other countries. The survey showed that 43% felt that the long hours and crunch time at work negatively impacted their well-being, 80% felt that long hours and crunch time were typical of the industry, and 60% felt that the industry could stand to improve their work-life balance policies (Crossley, 2010). Prescott also feels that "Flexible working practices would not only improve the image of the industry as a family-friendly working environment, but could also assist in retaining more women, especially those with or considering having children" (Crossley, 2010, p.2). As stated earlier, the video game industry climate in the U.S., UK, and Europe are quite similar—all are largely male dominated and have a less than stellar reputation when it comes to how the industry is viewed. Therefore industries in a variety of areas could benefit from the methods proposed in this chapter.

The issues of work-family conflict and work-life balance have been reviewed in several different studies, all with similar results. For example, a 2006 study by Rachel Gali Cinamon showed that young women aged 18-28 anticipate work interfering with family more than family interfering with work, and also demonstrated less confidence in themselves being able to effectively balance the two (Cinamon, 2006). This again supports the notion that women are more likely to consider career paths that will allow them to effectively balance both job and family responsibilities, and are less likely to pursue career paths with high anticipated levels of work-family conflict. This also suggests that the game industry could benefit from having more family friendly practices, or FFP's, in place in order to attract more women to the industry. This is not to say that this is the only way of solving the issue of the lack of women in the industry, and instead will apply more to women who already have career paths that could be applied to the game industry instead of young girls who have yet to decide on their career path. However, it is important to take into consideration both age groups so that all can benefit from these ideas. Another study by Anne Bourhis and Redouane Mekkaoui surveyed 110 part time college students (66 women, 44 men), and presented them with five different career choices from four different companies (2010). Each option had a different set of FFP's, with the fifth option being no FFP's at all. Results showed that organizations with FFP's such as flexible scheduling, on-site child care, generous personal leaves, and teleworking, were found more attractive by not only women but men as well, with flexible scheduling and personal leaves ranking the highest (Bourhis & Mekkaoui, 2010). Taking into consideration that the video game industry is not an industry with many FFP's, it is understandable why many women may shy away from this career path, especially those with children or those planning to have children. Again, the biggest deterrent amongst adult women joining the video game industry seem to be the long hours that are typical of the industry, on top of the anticipated work-family conflict that many women believe they will encounter if working in the industry.

CONCLUSION

This chapter has covered many different aspects of the issue of the lack of women in the video game industry. It has examined the gender breakdown of each department, explored the relationship between STEM and the video game industry, and looked at possible causes of this problem. The main takeaway message from this review is that the root cause of the problem of the lack of women in the game industry is still yet to be discovered, despite some speculations that have been tested in a limited capacity.

FUTURE QUESTIONS/RESEARCH

There are several things that could stand to be further researched in this issue. The first and most important thing is that the root cause of the problem needs to be discovered. This is not to say that there is only one reason behind the lack of women in the game industry, and this article provides suggestions that should be further looked into such as lack of interest, work-family conflict, and the social stigmas of the industry. It is important to note that these are only speculations, and there is no concrete scientific evidence to support these claims; however based on the anecdotal evidence provided, they provide a valid starting point.

One possible way to gather data would be to survey a number of females on their feelings about pursuing careers in the video game industry. Possible subjects could be selected from females who are already current gamers, in addition to females who are not gamers but are interested in industry related fields. By selecting participants who are both gamers and non-gamers, possible correlations between interest and industry retention could be identified. The result s of this survey could also help confirm whether or not lack of interest plays a definitive part in whether or not a woman chooses to pursue a career in the industry.

In addition to surveying women who are not already in the industry, it might also be beneficial to survey women who are in the industry to assess their reasons for pursuing careers in the field. Although women are present in the industry in limited numbers, by learning what motivated them to join the field despite the negative social stigmas that surround it the information gained could be used to change the gender balance in a positive manner, and empower more women to follow suit as well.

REFERENCES

Blickenstaff, J. (2005). Women and science careers: Leaky pipeline or gender filter? *Gender and Education, 17*(4), 369–386. doi:10.1080/09540250500145072

Bourhis, A., & Mekkaoui, R. (2010). Beyond work-family balance: Are family-friendly organizations more attractive? *Relations Industrielles. Industrial Relations, 65*(1), 98–117. doi:10.7202/039529ar

Cinamon, R. (2006). Anticipated work-family conflict: Effects of gender, self-efficacy, and family background. *The Career Development Quarterly, 54*(3), 202–215. doi:10.1002/j.2161-0045.2006.tb00152.x

Crossley, R. (2010). *Female count of UK dev workforce 'falls to 4%'*. Retrieved January 27, 2010 from http://www.develop-online.net/news/35806/Female-count-of-UK-dev-workforce-falls-to-4

Dukes, T. (2010). *Female role in gaming industry grows*. Retrieved September 23, 2010 from http://scienceinthetriangle.org/2010/09/female-role-in-gaming-industry-grows/

Entertainment Games, I. G. N. (2010). *SMU graduate program shows women's interest in video game development careers on the rise* [Press Release]. Retrieved January 27, 2011 from http://games.ign.com/articles/106/1068196p1.html

Entertainment Software Association (ESA). (2013). *Essential facts about the computer and video game industry: 2013 sales, demographic and usage data*. Retrieved August 28, 2013 from http://www.theesa.com/facts/pdfs/ESA_EF_2013.pdf

Hawks, B., & Spade, J. Z. (1998). *Women and men engineering students: Anticipation of family and work roles. Journal of Engineering Education, 87*(3), 249-256. Retrieved May 24, 2011 from http://www.jee.org/1998/july/570.pdf

Kannankutty, N. (2008). *Unemployment rate of U.S. scientists and engineers drops to record low 2.5% in 2006*. Retrieved January 9, 2011 from http://www.nsf.gov/statistics/infbrief/nsf08305/

Miller, P. (2012). *Eleventh annual game developer salary survey*. Retrieved August 13, 2013 from http://twvideo01.ubm-us.net/o1/vault/GD_Mag_Archives/GDM_April_2012.pdf

Miller, P. (2013). *Twelfth annual game developer salary survey*. Retrieved August 13, 2013 from http://twvideo01.ubm-us.net/o1/vault/GD_Mag_Archives/GDM_April_2013.pdf

Pratt, M. (2007). *Computer game industry looks to women for fresh insights*. Retrieved September 23, 2010 from http://www.computerworld.com/s/article/293317/Computer_game_industry_looks_to_women_for_fresh_insights

Rockstar Spouse. (2010). *Wives of Rockstar San Diego employees have collected themselves*. Retrieved January 27, 2011 from http://www.gamasutra.com/blogs/RockstarSpouse/20100107/4032/Wives_of_Rockstar_San_Diego_employees_have_collected_themselves.php

Sapp, J. (2010). *IGDA: Regarding overtime concerns at Rockstar San Diego*. Retrieved January 27, 2011 from http://www.igda.org/igda-regarding-overtime-concerns-rockstar-san-diego

Sector Skills Council for Creative Media. (2012). *2012 creative skillset employment census of the creative media industries* [Data File]. Retrieved August 14, 2013 from http://courses.creativeskillset.org/assets/0000/2819/Census_report_6.pdf

Sheffield, B., & Fleming, J. (2010). Ninth annual game developer salary survey. *Game Developer Magazine, 17*(4), 7–13.

Sheffield, B., & Newman, R. (2011). Tenth annual game developer salary survey. *Game Developer Magazine, 18*(4), 7–13.

Spouse, E. A. (2004). *EA: The human story.* Retrieved January 27, 2011 from http://ea-spouse.livejournal.com/274.html

Tong, S. (2008). *Women in the game industry.* Retrieved September 23, 2010 from http://www.gamespot.com/news/6197045.html?tag=result,title,0

ADDITIONAL READING

BeedeD.N.JulianT.A.LangdonD.McKittrickG.KhanB.DomsM.E. (2011)

Broyles, P. (2009). The gender pay gap of STEM professions in the United States. *The International Journal of Sociology and Social Policy, 29*(5/6), 214–226. doi:10.1108/01443330910965750

Burke, R. J. (2007). *1. Women and minorities in STEM: a primer. Women and Minorities in Science, Technology, Engineering, and Mathematics: Upping the Numbers, 1.* London: Edgar Elgar Publishing. doi:10.4337/9781847206879

Dunlop, J. C. (2007). The US video game industry: Analyzing representation of gender and race. [IJTHI]. *International Journal of Technology and Human Interaction, 3*(2), 96–109. doi:10.4018/jthi.2007040106

Espinosa, L. L. (2011). Pipelines and pathways: Women of color in undergraduate STEM majors and the college experiences that contribute to persistence. *Harvard Educational Review, 81*(2), 209–241.

Fassinger, R. E., & Asay, P. A. (2006). Career counseling for women in science, technology, engineering, and mathematics (STEM) fields. In W. B. Walsh, & M. J. Heppner (Eds.), *Handbook of career counseling for women* (2nd ed., pp. 427–452). Mahwah, NJ: Lawrence Erlbaum.

Flanagan, M. (2005). *Troubling 'games for girls': notes from the edge of game design.* Unpublished proceedings of Digital Games Research Association.

Fullerton, T., Fron, J., Pearce, C., & Morie, J. (2008). Getting girls into the game: Towards a 'virtuous cycle'. Beyond Barbie and Mortal Kombat: New perspectives on gender and computer games, 161-176.

Glass, C., & Minnotte, K. L. (2010). Recruiting and hiring women in STEM fields. *Journal of Diversity in Higher Education, 3*(4), 218. doi:10.1037/a0020581

Griffith, A. L. (2010). Persistence of women and minorities in STEM field majors: Is it the school that matters? *Economics of Education Review, 29*(6), 911–922. doi:10.1016/j.econedurev.2010.06.010

Johnson, D. R. (2011). Women of color in science, technology, engineering, and mathematics (STEM). *New Directions for Institutional Research,* (152): 75–85. doi:10.1002/ir.410

Mavriplis, C., Heller, R., Beil, C., Dam, K., Yassinskaya, N., Shaw, M., & Sorensen, C. (2010). Mind the Gap: Women in STEM Career Breaks. *Journal of technology management & innovation, 5*(1), 140-151.

McNeely, C. L., & Vlaicu, S. (2010). Exploring institutional hiring trends of women in the US STEM professoriate. *Review of Policy Research*, 27(6), 781–793. doi:10.1111/j.1541-1338.2010.00471.x

Milgram, D. (2011). How to Recruit Women and Girls to the Science, Technology, Engineering, and Math (STEM) Classroom. *Technology and Engineering Teacher*, 71(3), 4–11.

Perna, L. W., Gasman, M., Gary, S., Lundy-Wagner, V., & Drezner, N. D. (2010). Identifying strategies for increasing degree attainment in STEM: Lessons from minority-serving institutions. *New Directions for Institutional Research*, (148): 41–51. doi:10.1002/ir.360

Sassler, S., Glass, J., Levitte, Y., & Michelmore, K. (2011). *The Missing Women in STEM? Accounting for Gender Differences in Entrance into STEM Occupations*. Population Association of America Presentation.

Stout, J. G., Dasgupta, N., Hunsinger, M., & McManus, M. A. (2011). STEMing the tide: using ingroup experts to inoculate women's self-concept in science, technology, engineering, and mathematics (STEM). *Journal of Personality and Social Psychology*, 100(2), 255. doi:10.1037/a0021385 PMID:21142376

Szelényi, K., & Inkelas, K. K. (2011). The Role of Living–Learning Programs in Women's Plans to Attend Graduate School in STEM Fields. *Research in Higher Education*, 52(4), 349–369. doi:10.1007/s11162-010-9197-9

Thompson, C., Beauvais, L., & Lyness, K. (1999). When work-family benefits are not enough: The influence of work-family culture on benefit utilization, organizational attachment, and work-family conflict. *Journal of Vocational Behavior*, 54(3), 392–415. doi:10.1006/jvbe.1998.1681

Women in STEM: A gender gap to innovation. *Economics and Statistics Administration Issue Brief 4(11)*.

Xu, Y. J. (2008). Gender disparity in STEM disciplines: A study of faculty attrition and turnover intentions. *Research in Higher Education*, 49(7), 607–624. doi:10.1007/s11162-008-9097-4

KEY TERMS AND DEFINITIONS

Crunch Time: A critical time period (typically towards the end of the development cycle) where it is necessary to work longer hours than usual.

Family Friendly Practices (FFP): Various programs put in place by the employer in an attempt to help employees balance work and family roles—such as mental health programs, maternity/paternity leave, and childcare options.

Game Industry: An entertainment industry that focuses on the software development of video games.

Gender: The state of being male or female (typically used with reference to social and cultural differences rather than biological ones).

STEM: An acronym referring to careers in the fields of science, technology, engineering or math.

Work/Family Conflict: A form of interrole conflict in which the role pressures from the work and family domains are mutually incompatible in some respect.

Chapter 5
The Experiences of Women Working in the Computer Games Industry:
An In-Depth Qualitative Study

Julie Prescott
University of Bolton, UK

Jan Bogg
University of Liverpool, UK

ABSTRACT

This chapter provides a unique understanding of women working in the computer games industry. In depth interviews were undertaken with seven female game workers based in the UK. The women were interviewed as part of a larger study focusing on women in this male dominated industry. The issues detailed in this chapter focus on the industry as a viable career for women, the experience of being a woman working in games and the working environment; including work life balance issues, experiences of discrimination and experiences of sexism. The research discussed is related to attracting and retaining women in games development. The issues are of relevance to employers, professional bodies, policy makers and researchers of the games industry and the wider ICT and SET industries. Recommendations from the findings and future research directions are provided.

INTRODUCTION

I think generally because games are played in the most part by men it is probably perceive that they are mainly made by men which I suppose to a certain degree they are (Interview 7).

The games industry has a pervasive impact upon popular culture, which is influenced by, and influences other media and popular culture including TV, books and films. The industry is an important and growing industry with connections with other cultural sectors such as music and film as

DOI: 10.4018/978-1-4666-6142-4.ch005

we have previously highlighted in chapter two. The games industry has accelerated from small firms and individuals programming in their bedrooms to an industry dominated by multinational hardware producers such as Sony and Microsoft (Johns, 2006).

It is well recognised that the computer games industry like other technology based careers, is a male dominated industry. This is a global issue (USA-Gourdin, 2005; UK-Skillset, 2009; Canada-Dyer-Witheford & Sharman, 2005; Australia-Genieve, 2012). With the increasing rise in the popularity of computer games as a leisure pursuit to both male and female audiences, it is a concern of many that this gender disparity exists in such a culturally influential industry. It is important for women to have a voice in all areas of the economy and the cultural landscape. The games industry is a particularly important industry as highlighted by Prescott & Bogg (2013).

There have been a number of reasons put forward for the under representation of women in the computer games industry. Including the long hour's culture, the lack of flexible working practices, the image of the industry and computer games generally being targeted for males, the lack of games that appeal to females, as well as the sexual representation of females within the games themselves. Many of these issues arouse in the current study and so it is deemed important to briefly discuss some of these issues to give readers a brief background.

BACKGROUND

Gendered Occupational Segregation

Not only are women under represented within the industry but previous research has found that women that do tend to work in the industry tend to be concentrated into certain roles. These roles tend to be in non-developmental roles such as hu-man resources and administration rather than core developmental roles needing technical ability and roles which influence the game making process such as programming, design and production (MCV, 2008; Gourdain, 2005; Dyer-Witheford & Sharman, 2005; Haines, 2004). Gendered occupational segregation refers to the representation that some jobs are viewed as male and traditionally undertaken by men and other jobs are viewed as female jobs and therefore traditionally done by women. Gender occupational segregation has been found to persist in the information and communication technology (ICT) and the wider science, technology, engineering and mathematics (STEM) sectors including in the UK, USA and across Europe (Prescott & Bogg, 2012).

Computer games may be a good way to encourage and attract girls to the industry since gaming can enable the development of IT skills as well as help develop an interest in computers. Fullerton et al (2008) argue that more women would be interested in games if more games existed that girls and women liked to play and if work environments could be found that were more supportive of their values and work styles. The authors refer to this as the 'virtuous cycle' "*making games that appeal to women and girls attracts more women to work on games, resulting in the creation of more games that appeal to women and girls*" (Fullerton et al, 2008, p.141).

The Male Dominated Working Environment

Practices inherent to male dominated industries and occupations including the computer games industry include the long hour's culture, the potential need to relocate and the lack of flexible working practices (Prescott & Bogg, 2010). One strategy for increasing the diversity of games is to increase the diversity of those involved in all aspects of game design and production. The organisational structure has been highlighted as in need of change for computer game companies to appeal to and maintain a more diverse workforce (Consalvo, 2008).

Combining work with other roles especially motherhood, has been viewed as a major disadvantage to women in the workplace. Family demands may interfere with women's careers, leading them to perhaps refuse overtime, rearrange their working day, or refuse extra work, all of which can be viewed as being less committed to the job. Women have been found to have more work-family conflict than men (Innstrand et al. 2009). Women's extra domestic responsibilities can create work overload, effecting women's experience of work and possibly reducing their career promotional opportunities. These issues are especially prominent for women with or considering having children. It has been acknowledged that there is a lack of women with children working in the games industry as there is in the wider ICT and SET sectors (Deuze et al. 2004; Haines 2004; Krotoski 2004; Gourdin 2005; Consalvo 2008; Prescott & Bogg 2010). However, it is unclear from the limited research into women working in the computer games industry whether women who enter the industry do not want children or they do not have children due to their careers.

Associated with the lack of flexible working practices within the industry is the issue of long hours. A long hours culture appears to be especially prominent in male dominated occupations and industries, such as the ICT sector (Valenduc et al. 2004) and computer games industry (Consalvo 2008; Prescott & Bogg 2010). According to research by Consalvo (2008) the long hours culture and crunch time are the biggest challenges to women in the games industry.

Games For The Girls

Women in particular are increasingly making up the gamer population. Women have been found to like the more family friendly Nintendo consoles, with recent figures reporting that women represent 51% of Wii users and 53% of DS users (ESA, 2011b). There are a number of gender dif-

ferences that exist within games culture (Prescott & Bogg, 2013). Games are generally still viewed as a male pursuit and females are less immersed in the culture of games.

A gender difference in computer game involvement has been observed in many countries including America, the UK and throughout Europe. For example, studies have found gender differences in interests in computer games, confidence in computer games and the amount of time spent playing computer games (Bonanno & Kommers, 2008; Angelo, 2004; Krotoski, 2004; Natale, 2002; Schott & Horrell, 2000). Women have also been found to be more likely to play with a partner (Yee, 2006) and more likely to have been introduced to gaming by their male partner (Ogletree & Drake, 2007). Suggesting a gender divide in that gaming is viewed as a male pursuit with males often introducing females to the leisure activity. The image of computers and computer games have also been found to be gender specific, with research finding that children of both genders perceive computer users as male (Mercier, Barron & O'Connor, 2006). Men are also considered more computer literate and computer confident than women, due to playing computer games (Natale, 2002).

However, it is recognised that female game teams produce games that appeal to female gamers (Consalvo, 2008; Fullerton et. al., 2008). Game design teams that have more women in key design and production roles have produced products female gamers tend to enjoy (i.e. The Sims game produces by Maxis). It has been suggested that the unconscious decisions made by the male and female team at Maxis produce a different game than that made by an all or predominately male design team (Jenkins, 2001). The industry it seems creates a feedback loop, which affects games content.

Denner & Campe (2008) developed the Girls Creating Games (GCG) programme in order to help increase interest, confidence and skills in IT for 126 girls aged 11-14 in America. The girls had to work in pairs to create a computer game with an interactive story structure, which limited the games they could make. The authors found that girls made games with three main themes; competition and conflict, real-world applications and challenges to gender stereotypes. The girls tended to like to solve real world problems in real world settings. Their games also tended to have bright vivid colours and they won through achievement rather than competition. Most of the games allowed the player to choose the gender of the character and they found girls seek to explore different identities and experiment with different notions of femininity. This potential need to explore identity is explored in more detail in the next chapter.

Similar findings have also been found by Heeter et al. (2009) in a study of 5th and 8th graders in America. Heeter et. al., found that the designer's gender did influence the design outcome of games. Through mixed methods research, the results suggest that girls expected that they would find the girl-designed games significantly more fun than the boy-designed games and vice versa for the boys in the study. A significant finding from the study is that girls tended to design games with both girls and boys in mind, whereas boys designed for just boys. Their findings support the first half of the 'virtuous cycle' as proposed by Fullerton et al. (2008), in that, games designed by women are more likely to attract women than games designed by men. Fullerton et al. (2008) argue that more women would be interested in games if more games existed that girls and women liked to play and if work environments could be found that were more supportive of their values and work styles. The authors refer to this as the 'virtuous cycle'; making games that appeal to women and girls attracts more women to work on games, resulting in the creation of more games that appeal to women and girls (p.141).

The study therefore attempts to understand the unique perspective of women working in the computer games industry. In depth qualitative interviews were undertaken with seven female game workers based in the UK.

METHODOLOGY

Participants

The study consisted of in depth face to face semi-structured Interviews with seven females working in the production of computer games. All of the women volunteered to participate. All the women completed a biographical details sheet which gained personal and professional biographical details. All signed a consent form prior to the Interview. The age ranges of the women interviewed ranged 30 to 41. With regard to their ethnic origin, one of the participants was Chinese; the remaining six were White British. At the time of the Interviews, two of the participants were single, two were married and three lived with their partners. All described themselves as heterosexual, only one had children and she had one child. None of the women described themselves as being a lone parent, carer for another dependent or had any health problems. Three months was the least amount of time in their current post and 5 ½ years the longest. Four of the women had not been promoted in the past 5 years, two had been promoted once and one participant had been promoted twice in the past 5 years. Two of the women were art managers, one was an art lead, one was a character artist and rigger, one was an environment artist, one a programmer and one was a sound designer. One of the women had been in the games industry for 13 years, one 12 years, one 9 years, one five and half years, one three and half years, one for a year and one 6 months. All of the women had a degree, five had master's degrees and one (the programmer) had a PhD.

Female Game Playing Characteristics

All but one of the women played computer games for leisure, although three of them said they didn't play so much now because they worked in the industry and wanted to do 'other stuff' for leisure and one woman only played handhelds when she was bored i.e. at the airport. All of the six women, who played, played very different types of games and none of them played driving games which they are involved in the development of. One played puzzles and adventure, one skating and extreme sports, one super Mario, one action and adventure, one shooter's and platform games and one handhelds but she did not specify the game genre she preferred.

The Interviews

Areas

The interview areas were based on understanding the participants 'world':

- Perceptions of the industry.
- Perceptions of career.

Questions

Questions focused on how the women thought the games industry is perceived as a potential career to other women? What the women enjoy about working in the industry? What they dislike? Do they think it is different for women than men working in the industry? What they think women bring to the industry? If they thought the industry would benefit with more women in it?

Analysis

All the interviews were digitally recorded and transcribed verbatim. Analysis was conducted using NVivo version 6. Interview duration was approximately one and a half hours. Interpretive phenonomological analysis (IPA) was used to understand the women's perspective (Eatough & Smith, 2007).

In brief, IPA involves interpretation and shares cognitive psychology and the social cognition approaches in social psychology. It involves detailed

examination of the participant's world, it attempts to explore personal experience and the individual's personal perception of their world, as opposed to any attempt by the researcher to be objective about the event. Equally, IPA also recognises the active role of the researcher in the process. To accomplish this two-stage interpretation process, or double hermeneutic, is involved. The participants are trying to make sense of their world; the researcher is attempting to make sense of the participants, trying to make sense of their world.

IPA studies are conducted on small sample sizes, detailed case-by-case analysis of individual transcripts is undertaken, the aim is to describe the perception and meaning to participants of events, rather than make more general claims. The participants will be a fairly homogeneous sample, identified by purposive sampling; therefore the research questions will be significant to the group and their 'word' (Eatough & Smith, 2007).

Findings

The findings have been sectioned into four key themes:

1. The games industry as a career for women.
2. The experience of being a women in the computer games industry.
3. Discrimination and sexism experienced by the women.
4. The working environment and family issues.

The Games Industry as a Career for Women

All of the women interviewed felt it was important for women to be involved in technology. Reasons given for why women should be involved in technology focussed on the importance technology has in society;

Women don't want to be left behind, technology is important in society today and women should and need to be a part of that (Interview 5).

Technology is powerful (Interview 6).

Technology is going to happen so women might as well be involved they don't want to be left behind everybody else (Interview 3).

There was also the recognition by the women that the field of technology in general was male dominated;

Because to date the field of technology is male dominated and women may find this off putting. (Interview 3).

Part of the reason that there are fewer women is (I believe) that women are not encouraged to pursue technical studies as often in school. That's changing, but up to this point, games have often been considered very technical fields that require a lot of math and science knowledge (Interview 4).

In particular the women felt the computer games industry was still very much perceived as a male domain and therefore an industry women would not necessarily view as a potential career;

Women do not view working in the game industry as a realistic career choice. It's very hard to break in, and even harder if don't already run in certain circles. Although there is a concerted effort by a few companies to hire outsiders in most cases they are still looking for a specific type, namely gamers. As marketing does not target women as much, there are fewer female gamers, and so there are fewer "qualified" female candidates. I think this is changing with the success of the Wii, and some developers are scrambling to figure out the female demographic. Watch the hilarity ensue! (Interview 3).

I don't think a lot of women see it as a potential career, it may be a bit different now but certainly when I was at school technology was very much something that boys did (Interview 5).

This lack of appeal to women was also in part down to the games companies making games that appeal to a more male audience;

I think we've been in a viscous cycle for a long time now where the majority of game developers are male, so they make games that appeal to them-selves. Companies see the success of these games and push to make more like it. They're not willing to risk losing millions on new, female friendly products. Women don't pick up the testosterone laced games and never develop an interest in the field. In fact, most game stores set up their interiors specifically to attract men (music, advertisements, colour schemes). It's hard to pin-point how such a male dominated market came to be, especially considering the huge success of female friendly games such as the "King's Quest" series back in the 1980s (Interview 5).

I think it's true that a lot of games are still de-signed with a sexist male audience in mind, very sexualised/stereotyped female characters.. but it must also be noted that most women in society accept these sexualised and unrealistic portrayals of women in the media too (Interview 7).

As so few girls play games in the first place few are likely to see it as a career path. Most of my female friends are largely unaware that such a career even exists. If they are aware of it they will find a place with excessive working hours, in many cases poorly paid compared to equivalent jobs elsewhere, and where they are continually told by the media and their colleagues that it is extremely strange that they should be there at all (Interview 3).

The fact that games were viewed as being for a male audience impacted the potential to attract more women into the industry;

The number of games made for a male audience is significantly higher than those made for female audiences - while a lot of women do have tastes that gear towards male-dominated games, for a significant portion of women that's a total turn-off. So because they think that video games are all about either sexy chicks in leather or violent bloodbaths, they avoid the whole industry. However, that is fast changing - the number of women going into the industry gets exponentially bigger as more types of games are made (Interview 1).

Well at the moment the majority of the games we sell are still for boys possibly the introduction of more females in the industry would encourage more girls to play them as well as it may have an influence on the content of the game in the long term (Interview 3).

There is a preconceived notion that it is men that play games and it is men who make games (Interview 7).

Yes, it is different being a female. Usually you are creating games targeted at a male demographic. This may seem to be a practical and typical aspect of any business from a marketing point of view, but from a social standpoint it creates all sorts of inequities and recursive problems (Interview 2).

I guess because it started off as quite an exclusive science/math/computers sort of industry.. games got created by small groups of guys and were considered kind of a 'boy' thing back in the 80s and all through the 90s, games were mostly being designed with a male target audience in mind and so mostly men were inspired to want to work in the videogame industry. I mean we still live in a bit of an action man vs. barbie society where science

and sport is considered more of a 'guy' thing and humanities and textiles are considered a 'girl' thing. But the gap is still closing (Interview 3).

However it was also recognised by some of the women that the computer games industry was becoming more and more open to women as a career;

The gaming industry *was* mostly considered a "boys club" where women weren't wanted or included. This has changed drastically in the last few years. Young women who are gamers are more accepted as viable players now and, as such, grow into women who become viable developers (Interview 2).

I think more and more women are getting into games now, I think it is developing (Interview 1).

One woman felt that the industry was appealing to more women due to the increased visibility of games in society generally;

Because there are more game consoles at home it might seem a more appealing career to women but the female applicants we get here is tiny compared to men (Interview 5).

College courses were also viewed as helping to increase the number of women interested in pursuing the industry as a viable career;

Less women were pursuing careers in, say, programming. And there was a lack of knowledge about how to go about entering gaming as an industry. Now, more attention is brought to the industry as a whole, even through schools. At a convention, I had a girl come up to me at an autograph signing and actually say, "I had no idea there was a job like yours, and now that I know, I want it!(Interview 4).

Due to the games course and there is more of a presence of games on television as well, it's more obvious in the shops now so I think women now do see it as a career option (Interview 3).

Now that there are a lot of courses out there I think that will make it more accessible to women. (Interview 6).

Indeed, a number of the women interviewed got into the games industry themselves through courses;

Through my master's degree I became aware of how much technology had moved on and when I applied for my masters I wanted to go into special effects but as I progressed through my masters I became more interested in the game side of it and so applied in it when I left (Interview 5).

I got into the industry through my animation course. Since I have been little I have always enjoyed drawing characters and I loved cartoons and Disney. I just had a really good imagination and when I found I could study animation I did that. (Interview 1).

The Experience of Being a Woman in the Computer Games Industry

All of the women thought that it was different for women than men working in the industry;

I think being a female in the games industry gets you a lot of attention, as you are in the minority these days.. But it's all to your advantage, you have a better chance of getting a job and more guys offering to buy you a drink. I don't think your skill expectations are any different, though you might be more likely to be asked to represent the company at the events to show off their diversity (Interview 1).

You are always very obvious as a woman working in the games industry. At the very least people show obvious surprise that you are there. People are often unsure how to react to you. You are an obvious talking point especially when first joining a games company - it takes a long time to blend in. When you do achieve 'part of the furniture' status the opposite seems to happen and people tend to forget that you're female at all, which equally takes some getting used to (I've lost count of the times I'm referred to as 'gentlemen') (Interview 4).

It is different for women in the industry I would say. There's a LOT fewer of us to begin with (Interview 3).

Being a female and 'different' was not necessarily always viewed as a disadvantage, with advantages of being a woman in a male dominated work environment including getting noticed and treated with more respect;

It does get you noticed, but you are also more likely to face prejudice because of it. And you are expected to answer for over 50% of the world's population, which is just silly. (Interview 6).

In my opinion, I'm actually treated with more respect, because I'm one of the "few" women in gaming. I'm also a boss in some fashion, overseeing the production of the game (Interview 7).

One woman felt that being a woman was beneficial because women climb the ladder quicker because they are the minority in the workforce;

There's obviously some difference but I think women get up the ladder more because they try harder and want to prove themselves more than men (Interview 4).

The women interviewed felt women bring numerous qualities to the industry which tended to centre on a different perspective, different view point and a different way of looking at things;

I think women bring a huge amount to the industry, a completely different perspective to men, different concerns and appreciations and a different way of looking at things (Interview 5).

More women make it a more professional environment and they also bring another point of view. Like looking at a game and thinking 'well I wouldn't want to play something like that (Interview 6).

All the women felt the industry would benefit from more women in the industry as more women in the industry would also help change the image of the industry as a male domain and games as for boys general;

The benefits of more women in the industry would be in changing the image people have of the games industry (Interview 4).

I think because the female market is so big it they want to earn more profit they should explore the female market and so they should hire more females to do the story design and that kind of thing (Interview 2).

When I'm out meeting people in the real world, I often get the comment, "but you don't look like a game developer." I think the general public has a very unattractive, out of shape, and uber-geeky image of women in the game industry (Interview 1).

The women felt the industry could help attract more female developers by making less gender specific games, and more games that appeal to females.

Well making them less gender specific like at the moment we are talking about making a racing game and we were talking in broad terms of what the reward would be when you win the race and part of the reward would be you get to have these hot chicks in hot pants and that is very gender specific. And historically before tomb raider came out people were saying you can't have a woman protagonist, blokes aren't going to want to play that it's a complete none started and obviously it turned into a world wide phenomena. And until well its not to appeal to a specific gender its more open then you aren't going to appeal to women as much as men. At the moment people are oh let's make Barbie or the box pink, ok that's going to appeal to a very small section of little 8 year old girls and until the games industry grows up and realises women aren't a distinct group of people and they are just people they aren't going to get a handle on it (Interview 5).

Lara Croft she is an example of how the guys in the industry see women and all their characters tend to look like her and it's not until I come onto the characters team were I sort of made the women a little bit less stereotypical, they actually look like a normal looking women with maybe a little bit of hips and a little midriff but they are looking more like a woman now than Lara croft whose proportions were all wrong and I think that's where you see men being quite sexist and stuff. There is quite a lot of immaturity in them as well the way; they seem to be more immature in the games industry a lot of the guys (Interview 1).

One of the main reasons given for the disparity between the numbers of men and women in the industry was due to the perception that men like and play games therefore men want to make games;

In my understanding a lot of men like games so they like to make games (Interview 2).

What the women enjoyed most about their jobs was mostly the creative element with many also citing the industry is fun;

It's fun, its creative and I couldn't bear to do something like banking or accounting (Interview 5).

It's quite a creative industry, it's quite a fun industry, it's a fun job and it's a challenging job (Interview 6).

It was also viewed by one woman as interesting because the technology associated with games was always changing;

It changes all the time you are constantly keeping up, even if you are in the same role because the consoles change. (Interview 3).

The following quotes suggest that it takes a certain type of woman to be able to work in the male dominated games industry;

It can be very beneficial for a woman to work in a male-dominated company, but that really does depend on her support system and her own personality. I've always worked in male-dominated companies so I'm comfortable in this world and feel it is helping me grow into a stronger individual who won't back down to pressure. For other women, however, it can lead to them feeling suppressed or overlooked in the workplace (Interview 4).

Because most games are made by boys for boys I suppose a lot of girls would see it as, well when I tell people what I do they are shocked and so girls would maybe think it would be quite hard being a girl in a male environment, so I suppose it takes a certain type of person to do it really (Interview 4).

Understand that, for now, you may be the only woman in the office. You need to be okay with that. You need to have a sense of authority, but you needn't overdo it (Interview 6).

Interestingly, when asked about the type of woman that might be attracted to working in the industry all of the women interviewed mentioned the term 'tomboy' to describe themselves and/or other women in the industry, suggesting it takes a certain type of woman to work in the industry;

I think I am quite tomboy anyway so it might affect a really girlie girl who can't sort of stand up and give banter back. I also have a lot of hobbies that are male dominated too so I am use to male company. I think I prefer working with males than females anyway as females can be bitchy, so it is nicer not having too many women (Interview 1).

All the girls I have met in the industry are quite similar, I have not met any girly girls that act girly (Interview 2).

Girls in the industry are more tomboyish, well none of my friends that work in games are very girly (Interview 4).

Gamer girls' and 'Female Otaku' are kind of a stereotype, more socially acknowledged in Asia. You will often find 'tomboyish' females such as myself, as well as women who are interested in aspects of games that tend to appeal to females, such as RPGs with 'bishonen' and medieval fantasy games. And occasionally you will also find women who are in the industry with little interest in videogames, but want to get a well paid '21st century industry' job in a rising industry because they think it will make them appear successful (Interview 5).

Other attributes the women felt women needed to work in the industry was a 'thick skin', as well as resilience and not to be easily offended;

The games industry as a whole can be a bit of a boy's club, but I wouldn't necessarily describe any of the men I've worked with as particularly sexist. The women here usually do possess thicker skins, as you say, but that's not really the result of male oppression so much as it is the nature of gaming in my opinion - when you game, especially online, there's a fair amount of trash talk you have to be able to indulge in, a good-natured rivalry and the expectation that you will give as good as you get (Interview 1).

When I first started I was told that women need resilience and to be 25% better than men just to prove themselves equal (Interview 5).

I would say somebody who wanted a 9 to 5 job wouldn't want it and a little bit of tomboyish to a certain extent because I don't think it's the kind of industry if you're going to be offended by a bit of bad language or a rude reference (Interview 6).

When discussing the skills women needed to work in the industry there was a suggestion by some women that a 'boys club' exists within the industry;

The same skills as everyone else, plus exceptional social skills and a lot of patience. This is unfair, but to break into a lead or director roll you have to know the right people, and this is harder when most of your co-workers are male and you don't socialize with them normally. This problem extends beyond the scope of the video game industry, and into broader gender roles (Interview 2).

Gendered role segregation was recognised by the participants, with the acknowledgement that women who worked within the industry tended to be in female dominated roles such as human resources, administration and marketing and women in a developmental role being concentrated in art.

Yes. I notice this more and more as I attempt to progress further. There is a fair amount of women in HR and non-developer roles, but they have a limited effect on the content that is created. Environmental Art, which is considered entry level work at many places, also has a relatively high percentage of women, at least in my experience. I've never met a female character artist. I know they exist because I've heard of a few, but they are very rare. Concept artists, Lead Artists, and Designers, all of which have direct input on the content of a game, are positions predominantly occupied by men. I'm not a programmer, but from what I've heard there are hardly any women in that field, although I do know a couple (Interview 4).

Usually if girls work in games at all they work in admin or hr. You get a small number of artists. In the two games companies I have worked for I have been the only female programmer (in my previous company out of 100 people I was the only female not working in admin - which was on a separate floor) (Interview 4).

Women in the games industry tend to gravitate towards departments like Production, Art, Finances, etc... areas that are often more support structures or areas that require less technical ability and a greater amount of human relations. I wouldn't say that's expected of them, but more accurately those are the areas that they feel more comfortable entering into (Interview 5).

We have far more women in the marketing department than we do in game development. As far as development goes, about half of the managers and game designers are female. Women are somewhat rare among artists (especially 3D artists) and extremely rare among the programmers (Interview 7).

Developmental roles such as testing and programming where viewed as having very few women and being extremely male dominated;

There are hardly any female testers that really is male dominated, that is boys territory and they are all really young (Interview 3).

I think it is a hard industry to get into. I mean in terms of maybe artists or audio that seems to be better but programming I think is really difficult (Interview 2).

The whole time I have been in the industry I think I have meet five female programmers, the majority of women are artists or admin or personnel. I don't know any female designers at all. They are very, very rare (Interview 3).

Discrimination and Sexism Experienced by the Women

Disturbingly a number of the women interviewed recounted specific instances of overt discrimination and sexism whilst working in the games industry.

I was not picked to go on a research trip because the lead wanted to be with his mates and they didn't want a girl there as they would be wanting to go to strip clubs and stuff. (Interview 4).

I think there are aspects of being a female were they will argue less aggressively with you because they think you will burst into tears or something or on the other hand there are ones that will do

because they want to make you cry. On a stupid point in some companies they actually have a list of people they have made to cry and you get double points if it is a girl (Interview 3).

Going back to my very first position in the games industry, I had a very long and awkward Interview at the company I eventually ended up at and some months down the line I was talking to one of the guys who had Interviewed me just joking about this horrendous Interview and he said oh well we weren't sure about employing a girl, because we have had a girl before and it hadn't worked out which is absolutely horrendous talk about being tarred with the same brush. And that's the only time I really felt oh my god (Interview 5).

The Working Environment and Family Issues

An issue frequently cited as major reason for the minority status of women working in the developmental side of the computer games industry relates to work life balance issues. Many of the women in the current study reflected on the difficulties they could image for women with children working in the industry;

I think it would be hard to have kids and be in this industry. I don't know whether it is the natural personality of the type of person that is attracted to the industry I don't know but that is something I am aware of (Interview 5).

If you had children it would be a very difficult industry to work in (Interview 6).

Related to the difficulties of being a mother in the industry was the long hours associated with the industry and this was acknowledged as being an expected condition of working in the industry which all the women interviewed acknowledged;

Well, the first rule of the gaming industry is that everyone who gets into it LOVES gaming. Making games requires most folks to spend inordinate amounts of time at work, usually a minimum of 45 hours with a maximum during the worst crunch time of 60-70 hours. You only do that if you absolutely love playing games. So I would say that the majority of women in the industry are dedicated to playing games or thinking about games/puzzles all the time (Interview 3).

I suppose the toughest thing about working in the industry is the, it can always be quite pressured over a short period of time, usually the crunch period towards the end of the project (Interview 7).

The long hours are tough, it varies an awful lot between 50 hours and it could be up to 70 hours per week (Interview 5).

It's got long hours but that is to be expected (Interview 6).

One of the women suggested that without the long hours culture more women would be attracted to the industry as a career;

I think if they reduced the working hours a little bit so it will attract women (Interview 2).

RECOMMENDATIONS

It is apparent that the women interviewed enjoyed working in the computer games industry despite the major drawback of the long hours. The industry would benefit by highlighting the many benefits of working in the industry to potential female employees. This point has been previously highlighted elsewhere by the authors (Prescott & Bogg, 2010) but is a point worth reiterating.

FUTURE RESEARCH DIRECTIONS

Hearing the voices of women who work in the games industry is important to understand their experiences and views. It also enables insight into work practices that may need to change or be addressed by organisations within the industry in order to make the industry more appealing as a viable career to women. Future research may consider gaining the views of women who have left the industry in order to gain a fuller insight into why women leave the industry. Again this might benefit the industry in understanding what makes women leave in order for the industry to try and eradicate working practices that discriminate against women in the industry. It might also be valuable to understand the experiences of women who are senior members of women in games organisations such as WIGI (Women in Games International) as well as the executive women in games organisations in order to broader insight into the industry and perhaps a deeper understanding of the situation. This may also provide a deeper history of the industry and its workforce.

Motherhood may be an issue for women continuing to work in a developmental role within the games industry. Only one of the women interviewed currently was a mother. However, many of the other women felt that having children would be difficult especially given the long hours that they worked. The lack of part-time working and other flexible working practices has been previously highlighted as an issue for women working in the industry (Prescott & Bogg, 2010).

CONCLUSION

This study offers a unique insight into the experiences of women working in the computer games industry from the view point of seven women currently working in a variety of roles within the industry, what is apparent from the study is that there are a number of reoccurring issues relating to work life balance issues, in particular the long hours culture associated with the industry that many women considering a career within the industry may find off putting. What is perhaps surprising from the findings is the overt instances of discrimination and sexism some of the women interviewed had been subjected to whilst working in the industry.

Interestingly the women interviewed all viewed themselves and other females working in the industry as being 'tomboyish' and different from other women in that they were not very girly girly or feminine. The women felt it took a certain type of woman to be able to work in this male dominated industry as it was a tough male domain to work in and they needed to have 'thick skins' and in essence be more masculine.

It is clear that the women interviewed felt that gendered occupational segregation existed within the industry in that women tended to be concentrated into more traditionally female roles such as human resources, administration and marketing. It was also viewed that women in developmental roles tended to be concentrated in what also might be considered a more traditionally female role, that of artist.

It is also apparent that another major factor for the gender disparity within the games industry is the fact that computer games, despite an increasing female gamer population, are still viewed as a male leisure pursuit. As games are viewed as being largely a male leisure and entertainment pursuit, making games in turn is also viewed as being a male career. What is encouraging is that a number of the women interviewed had worked in the industry for over or near to a decade and these women did view the industry as changing and becoming a more appealing and viable career for females. This appeal was in the main due to computer games becoming a mainstream activity. On the other hand, the women also recognised the irony that the industry needed to develop more female friendly games, in order to attract and en-

courage future female developers, future women game developers, who in turn would develop more games that appeal to women and girls.

REFERENCES

Angelo, J. (2004). *New study reveals that women over 40 who play online games spend more time playing than male or teenage gamers.* Business Wire.

Bonanno, P., & Kommers, P. A. M. (2008). Exploring the influence of gender & gaming competence on attitudes towards using instructional games. *British Journal of Educational Technology, 39*(1), 97–109.

Consalvo, M. (2008). Crunched by passion: Women game developers & workplace challenges. In H. Kafai, Denner & Sun (Ed.), Beyond Barbie & Mortal Kombat: New perspectives on gender & gaming (pp. 177-192). Cambridge, MA: The MIT Press.

Denner, J., & Campe, S. (2008). What games made by girls can tell us. In Y. B. Kafai, C. Heeter, J. Denner, & J. Y. Sun (Eds.), *Beyond Barbie & Mortal Kombat: New perspectives on gender & gaming* (pp. 129–144). Cambridge, MA: The MIT Press.

Deuze, M., Martin, C. B., & Alen, C. (2007). The professional identity of gameworkers. *Convergence: The International Journal of Research into New Media Technologies, 13*(4), 335–353. doi:10.1177/1354856507081947

doi:

Dyer-Whitheford, N., & Sharman, Z. (2005). The political economy of Canada's video & computer game industry. *Canadian Journal of Communication, 20*, 187–210.

Eatough, V., & Smith, J. A. (2007). Interpretative phenomenological analysis. In C. Willig, & W. Stainton Rogers (Eds.), *Handbook of qualitative psychology* (pp. 179–194). London: Sage.

ESA. (2011). *Essential facts about games & violence*. Entertainment Software Association. Retrieved from http://www.theesa.com/facts/pdfs/ESA_EF_About_Games_&_Violence.pdf

Fullerton, T., Fron, J., Pearce, C., & Morie, J. (2008). Getting girls into the game: Towards a virtuous cycle. In H. Kafai, Denner & Sun (Ed.), Beyond Barbie & Mortal Kombat: New perspectives on gender & gaming (pp. 161-176). Cambridge, MA: The MIT Press.

Geneve, A. A. (2013). *Women's participation in the Australian digital content industry* (PhD thesis). Queensland University of Technology, Australia. Retrieved from http://eprints.qut.edu.au/60898/1/Anitza_Geneve_Thesis.pdf

Gourdin, A. (2005). *Game developers demographics: An exploration of workforce diversity*. International Game Developers Association. Retrieved from http://archives.igda.org/diversity/IGDA_DeveloperDemographics_Oct05.pdf

Haines, L. (2004). Why are there so few women in games? *Research for Media Training North West September*. Retrieved from http://archives.igda.org/women/MTNW_Women-in-Games_Sep04.pdf

Heeter, C., Egidio, R., Mishra, P., Winn, B., & Winn, J. (2009). Alien games: Do girls prefer games designed by girls? *Games and Culture*, *4*(1), 74–100. doi:10.1177/1555412008325481

Jenkins, H. (2001). *From Barbie to Mortal Kombat: Further reflections*. Retrieved from http://culturalpolicy.uchicago.edu/papers/2001-video-games/jenkins.html

Johns, J. (2006). Video games production networks: Value capture, power relations & embeddedness. *Journal of Economic Geography*, *6*(2), 151–180. doi:10.1093/jeg/lbi001

Krotoski, A. (2004). *Chicks & joysticks: An exploration of women & gaming* (Entertainment & Leisure Software Publishers Association White Paper).

MCV. (2008). *Salary survey*. Retrieved from http://www.mcvuk.com/news/29399/Industry-salary-survey

Mercier, E. M., Barron, B., & O'Connor, K. M. (2006). Images of self & others as computer users: The role of gender & experience. *Journal of Computer Assisted Learning*, *22*(5), 335–348. doi:10.1111/j.1365-2729.2006.00182.x

Natale, M. J. (2002). The effect of a male-orientated computer gaming culture on careers in the computer industry. *Computers & Society*, *20*, 24–31. doi:10.1145/566522.566526

Ogletree, S. M., & Drake, R. (2007). College students' video game participation & perceptions: gender differences & implications. *Sex Roles*, *56*(7-8), 537–542. doi:10.1007/s11199-007-9193-5

Prescott, J., & Bogg, J. (2010). The computer games industry: Women's experiences of work role in a male dominated environment. In A. Cater-Steel, & E. Cater (Eds.), *Women in engineering, science & technology: Education & career challenges* (p. 138). Hershey, PA: IGI Global. doi:10.4018/978-1-61520-657-5.ch007

Prescott, J., & Bogg, J. (2012). *Gendered occupational differences in science, engineering, & technology careers*. Hershey, PA: IGI Global. doi:10.4018/978-1-4666-2107-7

Prescott, J., & Bogg, J. (2013). *The gendered digital divide and the computer games industry*. Hershey, PA: IGI Global. doi:10.4018/978-1-4666-4534-9

Schott, G., & Horrell, K. (2000). Girl gamers & their relationship with the gaming culture. *Convergence: The International Journal of Research into New Media Technologies, 6*(4), 36–53. doi:10.1177/135485650000600404

Skillset. (2009). *2009 employment census: The results of the seventh census of the Creative Media Industries December 2010.* The Sector Skills Council for Creative Media.

Valenduc, G., et al. (2004). *Widening women's work in information and communication technology, European Commission.* Retrieved from http://www.ftu-namur.org/fichiers/D12-print.pdf

Yee, N. (2006). Motivations for play in online games. *Cyberpsychology & Behavior, 9*(6), 772–775. doi:10.1089/cpb.2006.9.772 PMID:17201605

ADDITIONAL READING

Women and Computer Games

Beasley, B., & Standley, T. C. (2002). Shirts vs.skins: clothing as an indicator of gender role stereotyping in video games. *Mass Communication & Society, 5*(3), 279–293. doi:10.1207/S15327825MCS0503_3

Brathwaite, B. (2010). *Women in games: from famine to Facebook.* Retrieved from http://www.huffingtonpost.com/brenda-brathwaite/women-in-games-from-famin_b_510928.html

Bryce, J., & Rutter, J. (2002). The gendering of computer gaming: experience & space. In S. Fleming, & I. Jones (Eds.), *Leisure cultures: investigations in sport, media & technology* (pp. 3–22). Leisure Studies Association.

Bryce, J., & Rutter, J. (2003). Gender dynamics & the social & spatial organization of computer gaming. *Leisure Studies, 22*, 1–15. doi:10.1080/02614360306571

Bryce, J., Rutter, J., & Sullivan, C. (2005). Gender & digital games. In J. Rutter, & J. Bryce (Eds.), *Understanding Digital Games.* London: Sage.

Clegg, S., & Trayhurn, D. (2000). Gender and computing: not the same old problem. *British Educational Research Journal, 26*(1), 75–89. doi:10.1080/014119200109525

Crawford, G., & Gosling, V. (2005). Toys for boys? women's marginalization and participation as digital gamers. *Sociological Research Online, 10*(1), 1–13. doi:10.5153/sro.1024

Cunningham, S. (2000). Re-inventing the introductory computer graphics course: providing tools for a wider audience. *Computers & Graphics, 24*(2), 293–296. doi:10.1016/S0097-8493(99)00164-8

Dietz, T. L. (1998). An examination of violence and gender role portrayals in video games: implications for gender socialization and aggressive behaviour. *Sex Roles, 38*(5/6), 425–442. doi:10.1023/A:1018709905920

Divinch, J. (2008). *The divinich tapes: females representation in games across genres, consoles.* Retrieved February 18, 2009, from www.gamasutra.com

Dovey, J., & Kennedy, H. W. (2006). *Game Culture: computer games as new media.* Berkshire: Open University Press.

Erfani, M., El-Nasr, M.S., Milam, D., Aghabeigi, B., Lameman, B.A., Riecke, B.E., Maygoli H., & Mah, S. (2010) The Effect of Age, Gender, and Previous Gaming Experience on Game Play Performance. *Human-Computer Interaction IFIP Advances in Information & Communication Technology, 332*/2010, 293-296, doi: 10.1007/978-3-642-15231-3_33

Jansz, J., Avis, C., & Vosmeer, M. (2010). Playing The Sims2: an exploration of gender differences in players' motivations & patterns of play. *New Media & Society, 12*(2), 235–251. doi:10.1177/1461444809342267

Jenkins, H. (2006) *Reality bites: eight myths about video games debunked.* Retrieved from http://www.pbs.org/kcts/videogamerevolution/impact/myths.html

Jenkins, H. (1999). Voices from the combat zone: Game grrlz talk back. In J. Cassell, & H. Jenkins (Eds.), *From Barbie to Mortal Kombat: Gender & computer games* (pp. 328–341). Cambridge, MA: MIT Press.

Jenson, J., & deCastell, S. (2010). Gender, simulation, & gaming: research review & redirections. *Simulation & Gaming, 41*(1), 51–71. doi:10.1177/1046878109353473

Jenson, J., & de Castell, S. (2010) Girls@play: An ethnographic study of gender and digital gameplay. Handbook of Research in the Social Foundations of Education. Steve Tozer, Bernardo P. Gallegos, Annette Henry, Mary Bushnell Greiner, & Paul Groves Price (Eds.), p. 504-514. doi: doi:10.1080/14680777.2010.521625

Kafai, Y. B., Heeter, C., Denner, J., & Sun, J. Y. (2008). *Beyond Barbie and mortal kombat: new perspectives on gender and gaming* (p. 152). London, Massachusetts: The MIT Press.

Work Life Balance Issues

Cunningham, M. (2007). Influences of women's employment on the gendered division of household labour over the life course: evidence from a 31-year panel study. *Journal of Family Issues, 28*(3), 422–444. doi:10.1177/0192513X06295198 PMID:18458763

De Ruijter, E., & Van der Lippe, T. (2007). Effects of job features on domestic outsourcing as a strategy for combining paid and domestic work. *Work and Occupations, 34*(2), 205–230. doi:10.1177/0730888406296510

Hamilton, E. A., Gordon, J. R., & Whelan-Barry, K. S. (2006). Understanding the work life conflict of never married women, without children. *Women in Management Review, 21*(5), 93–415. doi:10.1108/09649420610676208

Keene, J. R., & Reynolds, J. R. (2005). The job costs of family demands: Gender differences in negative family-to-work spillover. *Journal of Family Issues, 26*(3), 275–299. doi:10.1177/0192513X04270219

Liff, S., & Ward, K. (2001). Distorted views through the glass ceiling: The construction of women's understandings of promotion and senior management positions. *Gender, Work and Organization, 8*(1), 19–36. doi:10.1111/1468-0432.00120

Rapoport, R., Bailyn, L., Fletcher, J. K., & Pruitt, B. H. (2002). *Beyond work-family balance: Advancing gender equity and workplace performance.* San Francisco: Jossey Bass.

Shapiro, M., Ingols, C., & Blake-Beard, S. (2008). Confronting career double blinds: implications for women, organization, and career practitioners. *Journal of Career Development, 34*(3), 309–333. doi:10.1177/0894845307311250

Wallace, J. E., & Young, M. C. (2008). Parenthood and productivity: a study of demands, resources and family-friendly firms. *Journal of Vocational Behavior, 72,* 110–122. doi:10.1016/j.jvb.2007.11.002

Wharton, A. M., & Blair-Loy, M. (2006). Long work hours and family life: a cross-national study of employee' concerns. *Journal of Family Issues, 27,* 415–436. doi:10.1177/0192513X05282985

Wickham, J., Collins, G., Greco, L., & Browne, J. (2008). Individualization and equality: women's careers and organizational form. *Organization, 15*(2), 211–231. doi:10.1177/1350508407086581

KEY TERMS AND DEFINITIONS

Flexible Working: Practice that facilitates a work life balance.

Games Industry: Computer or video games industry.

Gendered Occupational Segregation: Refers to the representation that some jobs are viewed as male and traditionally undertaken by men and other jobs are viewed as female jobs and therefore traditionally done by women.

Long Hours: Culture of long hours that may be used to demonstrate career commitment.

Work Life Balance: The balance of work and other life or role commitments.

Chapter 6

Career Development among Japanese Female Game Developers:
Perspective from Life Stories of Creative Professionals

Masahito Fujihara
Senshu University, Japan

ABSTRACT

The purpose of this chapter is to clarify the process of female developers' career development and their characteristics based on the life stories of creative professionals employed in the Japanese gaming industry. This study followed a one-to-one semi-structured interview format and employed a qualitative methodology. The survey was conducted on 21 female game developers who have more than five years work experience in the Japanese gaming industry. One of the most important analytical results of the study is the behavioral characteristics of female game developers in their career development are that they support persons who have similar problems in the workplace, and they contribute to mentor game developers in the next generation. In conclusion, female game developers do not have clearly defined career goals; however, they have the ability to alter their work situation, and evaluate and manage it if needed. Therefore, it is important that female game developers have diverse role models. Further research directions are discussed.

INTRODUCTION

In the digital gaming industry, the relationship between the market share of game hardware and game software packages is affected by the interaction between demand and supply, have been pointed out "network externality" (Tanaka, 2000a).

DOI: 10.4018/978-1-4666-6142-4.ch006

Network externality is a phenomenon in which user benefit rises when consumers who use some goods increase. For example, if many people buy a particular game hardware, then game software companies adapt to develop games for that particular hardware. As a result, game software for the hardware of a wide selection is supplied, and a good cycle that the hardware is sold more than ever is generated. Therefore, the hardware and software businesses are separated in the Japanese gaming industry. As a result, the Japanese game software market grew rapidly until the early 1990s because various venture-capital companies were able to enter the digital gaming field (Shintaku, 2005). However, the game software that won a big market share began to show a tendency to limit the genres of video games produced by particular companies, and much of it was developed mainly by large companies starting around 1995 (Tanaka, 2000b). Because of this, Japanese game companies no longer achieved significant sales and did not release innovative products. Therefore, they developed two strategies: first was to make products that were similar to existing products, and second was to create novel products that complemented already existing products because a "moderate differentiation" would create added value (Yonekura & Ikuine, 2005).

These changes denote that the environment surrounding game development has transformed. That is, game companies can no longer survive only by developing and selling games; it is becoming increasingly important for them to make prompt decisions based on management strategies such as multi-platform development and online service adaptation. The need for creative human resources to resolve these issues is an important factor in the gaming business. However, according to Kobashi (1996), who is a pioneer researcher of the Japanese gaming industry, the Japanese game development process were named "self-sacrificial process model." She pointed out that Japanese game developers deal with a number of different tasks in a short period of time. The Japanese game software is designed for fun, which includes a consideration of level design, game balance, a balance of logic and ambiguity, and playability. It is completed by skillfully tuning it many times by game developers. Therefore, Japanese game development needs a lot of time to ensure high-quality.

An important aspect of game development is for a company to have diversity in the composition and creativity of the developers. Therefore, on the basis of previous studies, I will consider career development among Japanese female game developers in this paper.

In recent years, the number of female professionals and creators has been increasing steadily in the gaming industry. Research on the status of female game developers can thus clarify various aspects of their career development. Researchers have therefore begun to pay more attention to the career development of female developers in the gaming industry throughout the world.

The number of female developers in the gaming industry is extremely low. Out of the total number of developers, the proportion of female developers stands at 12.8% in Japan (Fujihara, 2010), 11.2% in the USA (Gourdin, 2005), and 4% in the UK (Prescott & Bogg, 2010; Skillset, 2009). The percentage has been similarly low in Canada, at 10%–15% (Dyer-Whitheford & Sharman, 2005), and less than 10% in Australia (Geneve, Nelson, & Christie, 2008). However, Prescott & Bogg (2010), the leading researchers on female workers in the gaming industry, pointed out that, "Games companies need to broaden out their recruiting scope and attract talent from other new industries and seduce more diverse groups into game teams, particularly women and ethnic minorities" (p. 143).

Game developing is clearly a high-risk, high-return business. Thus, despite game publishers' strategy of releasing only hit titles of series and remakes in similar genres, the Japanese consumer gaming market has recently been shrinking (CESA, 2013). In such circumstances, it is therefore vitally important for Japanese companies to employ diverse management that goes beyond customary gender requirements, especially so that they can provide a variety of gaming entertainment for young and old around the world. Namely, they should follow the approach mentioned by Prescott and Bogg (2010) and draw upon the talents of a variety of game developers. There is a clear need to focus on female developers in the Japanese gaming industry.

The purpose of this chapter is to clarify the process of female developers' career development and their characteristics based on the life stories of creative professionals employed in the Japanese gaming industry.

METHODOLOGY

The target of this study is female developers in the Japanese gaming industry. In this chapter, the term "developer" is defined as a creative professional who is responsible for planning, developing, and managing the games. More specifically, developers are the programmers, artists, game designers, directors, and producers in this business. According to Fujihara (2010), Japanese female game developers have an average of 5.1 years work experience in the industry. Therefore,

the target person of this study has more than five years of work experience in the gaming industry.

However, it is difficult to identify this target person because there is no register that lists the names of female game developers. Therefore, for this study, the next best option was to identify these individuals by considering the distribution of basic attributes such as age, occupation, and job title. First, they were identified through my website and SNS (social networking service), which yielded applications from two target persons. Second, female game developers introduced 9 target persons to me. Third, the heads of the public relations departments and the human resources departments at game companies introduced 10 target persons to me. The target persons were identified by combining the snowball sampling; samples were acquired through my website and personal networks, and then eliminating the arbitrariness of those surveyed. This study was then conducted with 21 female game developers.

Figure 1. Japanese market for household games
Figure 1 adapted by author from CESA games white paper.

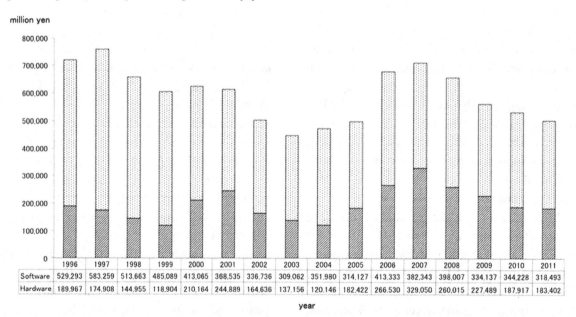

	1996	1997	1998	1999	2000	2001	2002	2003	2004	2005	2006	2007	2008	2009	2010	2011
Software	529,293	583,259	513,663	485,089	413,065	368,535	336,736	309,062	351,980	314,127	413,333	382,343	398,007	334,137	344,228	318,493
Hardware	189,967	174,908	144,955	118,904	210,164	244,889	164,636	137,156	120,146	182,422	266,530	329,050	260,015	227,489	187,917	183,402

This study followed a one-to-one semi-structured interview format and employed a qualitative methodology. Interviews were conducted over three months, with each interview lasting from 42 to 108 minutes (75 minutes on average for each interviewee). After obtaining the interviewee's consent, I recorded the interviews with an IC recorder and then transcribed them verbatim. The number of letters in the transcripts was approximately 400,000 in Japanese (21,000 on average per interviewee). This study was conducted between October and December 2010.

Overviews of the interviewees are as follows (Table 1). Average age of interviewees is 34.05 years (SD = 5.15). Level of education is 1 master's degree, 13 bachelor's degrees, 5 diplomas, and 2 high school degrees. Graduation year is 1998 (SD = 4.89). University major is 19 from liberal arts and 2 from science. Family structure is 8 single, 9 married without children, and 4 married with children. Occupations are 2 computer programmers, 11 artists, 2 planners, 2 directors, 3 producers, and 1 manager. Job titles are 15 staff (including 4 project managers), 2 chief clerks, 2 subsection managers, 1 section manager, and 1 executive. Size of studio is 14 medium-sized companies (300 employees or less) and 7 large-sized companies (300 employees or more).

The transcript data was analyzed based on the life story approach (Sakurai, 2005, pp. 155–183). First, I identified concepts and categories by comparing the interviewees' life stories. Then, I found a structure linking the stories and their meanings to clarify the variation in core concepts and categories. Second, I interpreted the meaning of the life stories, focusing on the words as signs that showed mutual action between interviewer and interviewee. Third, I considered the interviewees' interest in digital games, their reasons for entering the gaming industry, their outlook on making a career transition, and the characteristics of their career development, paying particular attention to the events and meanings that affected the course of their career.

RESULTS AND DISCUSSION

External Career Development Process

The female game developers had work experience of 5.2 years on average at their first company, and their total work experience until now is 11.7 years on average. After their first job, 14 of them moved to a second company (gaining work experience of 3.2 years on average); 9 moved to a third company (gaining work experience of 3.9 years on average); 7 moved to a fourth company (gaining work experience of 5.9 years on average); 3 moved to a fifth company (gaining work experience of 2.9 years on average); and 1 moved to a sixth company (gaining work experience of 5.8 years). Regarding their work experience in the gaming industry, as they built their career as game developers, 16 of them had work experience of 6.2 years on average at their first company. Following their first job, 10 of these 16 moved to a second company (gaining work experience of 4.1 years on average); 8 moved to a third company (gaining work experience of 4.2 years on average); 6 moved to a fourth company (gaining work experience of 6.8 years on average); 3 moved to a fifth company (gaining work experience of 2.9 years on average); and 1 moved to a sixth game company (gaining work experience of 5.8 years). Since graduation from university, technical college, and high school, until now, they accumulated an average of 11.1 years of work experience at game companies. It is noteworthy that the female game developers had more work experience at their first company, which suggests that they built their career while simultaneously exploring the field (Table 2).

Only 6 developers—planners, programmers, and two artists—had work experience at just one company. Five of them entered the gaming industry via other industries, and 10 of them changed workplaces within the gaming field. Based on the above facts, most of the female game developers appear to have established their careers at companies outside the gaming industry.

Table 1. Interviewee Overview

No.	Age	Level of education	Year of graduation	Discipline	Family structure	Occupation	Designation	Size of studio
A	42	University	1991	Literature	Husband	Producer	Section manager	L
B	29	University	2004	Literature	Husband & Grandmother	Director	Staff	M
C	24	High school +S	2004	General course	-	Programmer	Chief clerk	M
D	36	University +S	1997	Physics	Husband & Child (3 y/o)	Artist	Subsection chief	M
E	29	Technical college	2002	Fine Arts	-	Artist	Staff	M
F	34	Technical college	1999	Fine Arts	Younger brother	Artist	Staff	M
G	47	University	1985	Fine Arts	Husband & Child (18 y/o)	Manager	Executive	M
H	32	University	2001	Fine Arts	Husband	Artist	Staff	M
I	27	Technical college	2004	Fine Arts	-	Planner	Staff	L
J	38	Master	1997	Science & Engineering	Husband	Planner	Chief clerk	L
K	37	University	1996	Language	Husband	Producer	Staff	L
L	36	High school +S	1994	Fashion	Adopted child	Artist	Staff (M)	M
M	31	Technical college	2003	Tourism	Husband	Producer	Subsection chief	M
N	37	University	1995	Fine Arts	Husband	Artist	Staff	L
O	37	University	1999	Fine Arts	Husband	Artist	Staff	L
P	31	University	2002	Fine Arts	-	Artist	Staff (M)	L
Q	33	University	2000	Fine Arts	Husband & Child (1 y/o)	Artist	Staff (M)	M
R	29	Technical college	2003	Fine Arts	-	Programmer	Staff	M
S	34	University	1998	Fine Arts	Husband & Child (0 y/o)	Artist	Staff	M
T	33	University	1999	Psychology	-	Director	Staff (M)	M
U	39	University	1991	Fashion	Husband	Artist	Staff	M

"S" in level of education refers to a private educational institution that is not based on the School Education Act.

"M" in size of studio refers to project manager.

In terms of occupation, the female game developers took either of the following two types of career paths: (1) management positions such as producer and director, and (2) development positions such as planner, programmer, and artist. Those in management built a general management career, holding positions such as assistant producer, assistant director, and planner, after majoring in humanities fields such as literature, languages, psychology, fine arts, and tourism. They have an average of 13.7 years of work experience (12.5 years on average within the gaming industry). For those in development, after majoring in fine arts, physics, 3D computer graphics, or fashion studies,

Table 2. Career paths of Japanese female game developers

	Average age of graduating from school (y/o)	Work years at the first company (years)	Work years at the second company (years)	Work years at the third company (years)	Work years at the fourth company (years)	Work years at the fifth company (years)	Work years at the sixth company (years)	Total work years (years)
N	21	21	14	9	7	3	1	-
		16	10	8	6	3	1	
Mean	22.3	5.2	3.2	3.9	5.9	2.9	5.8	11.7
		6.2	4.1	4.2	6.8	2.9	5.8	11.1
S.D.	1.7	3.7	2.6	4.9	6.7	1.6	0.0	4.9
		3.5	2.6	5.1	6.8	1.6	0.0	4.2
Min	18.0	0.5	0.3	0.3	0.3	1.0	5.8	6.0
		0.5	1.0	0.3	0.3	1.0	5.8	5.7
Max	26.0	13.0	9.5	17.5	20.0	5.0	5.8	25.0
		13.0	9.5	17.5	20.0	5.0	5.8	23.0

Each row of table has been divided into two sections.
The upper section of each row denotes total of interviewees' work term of all work.
The lower section of each row denotes total of interviewees' work term of the gaming industry.

they established a specialized development career, holding positions such as planner, programmer, artist, and technical artist. They have an average of 10.9 years of work experience (12.3 years on average within the gaming industry).

One of the factors that define the career development of female game developers is work style. Their average number of work hours per week is 54 (63 during crunch time) in management jobs and 45 (59 during crunch time) in development jobs. In terms of the position, managerial positions are 50 hours (62 hours during crunch time) and staff positions are 47 hours (60 hours during crunch time). Regarding family structure, single females work 48 hours per week (62 hours during crunch time); married females with no children work 50 hours (62 hours during crunch time); and married females with children work 42 hours (54 hours during crunch time) (Table 3). Although most of the female game developers are currently working in a discretionary labor system, the work style of those who are married with children is flex-time or part-time; therefore, their hours are shorter than those of the other developers.

The female game developers play various roles in their lives, and accordingly, they have various sense of values such as being life-oriented, work-oriented, and having a work-life balance, which may experience psychological conflict. Therefore, it is considered that their outlook and behavior form their internal career development process.

Internal Career Development Process

Japanese female game developers became interested in the gaming industry when they were students in primary schools or in university, or early in their careers. Those who first began playing digital games in elementary school or junior high school developed an interest in gaming at that time, while those who became attracted to the industry as students in technical school or university had played digital games by sheer chance. Moreover, those who were in their early careers did not originally have an interest in digital games, but discovered that they could display and employ their skills in the industry and then moved

Table 3. Work styles of Japanese female game developers

Group	Division	N	Average age (y/o)	Fix-time (%)	Flex-time (%)	Discretionary labor system (%)	Average work hours (crunch time) (hours per week)	Average commuting time (minutes)
Type of job	Management job	6	37	16.7	16.7	66.6	54 (63)	44
	Development job	15	33	26.7	26.7	46.6	45 (59)	40
Position	Managerial position	6	36	33.3	16.7	50.0	50 (62)	33
	Staff	15	33	20.0	26.7	53.3	47 (60)	45
Family Structure	Single	8	30	25.0	12.5	62.5	48 (62)	36
	Married without child	9	36	0.0	44.4	55.6	50 (62)	47
	Married with child	4	38	75.0	0.0	25.0	42 (54)	40

into that field. It can thus be said that all of these female game developers encountered their careers largely by accident.

I did not have PlayStation when I was a child. But I played digital games because my elder brother played them. Then, I borrowed Final Fantasy XII with PlayStation from my elder brother's friend by chance. It was interesting to me. So, I bought PlayStation. I was playing Final Fantasy at my friend's house when I was an elementary student. I was hooked on it when I was 13 years old (I).

I started looking for a job when I was a university art student. PlayStation had just been released by Sony Computer Entertainment, and thereafter it sold over one million copies. In those days, even people who did not often play digital games had started playing them. Then, I played it a little bit and felt like the graphics were really beautiful. When I was looking for a job, glancing at a recruiting advertisement at our arts university, I noticed that a gaming company was recruiting us for the first time (O).

When I worked at the travel agency, I had been studying for a certification to be a travel agent, although, in those days, I had thought about finding another job in the travel industry. Then, on my way home from paying courtesy visits to my customers, I dropped into the TSUTAYA where there was a shop that rented CDs and DVDs. Unexpectedly, they sold package games there. So, I bought a package game. I just bought it by chance rather than really wanting it. It had been stacked up there right after being released. I bought it to play digital games because I had not played them for a long time. It was really accidental for me (M).

The reasons why female game developers enter the gaming industry are as follows: they feel that digital games have possibilities as a form of interactive media; they expect to take advantage of the opportunity to express their individuality in the gaming industry; and they have personal networks in this field. In particular, persons who become involved in the business through personal connections have longer experience working as developers at a game company, which suggests that they are aware of the value of building and maintaining personal networks.

I am a greedy person who wants to try various things such as sounds, images, and visual arts, and not work on one thing intensively. As a result, I decided to enter the gaming industry after graduating from an arts university because it seemed that digital games have a lot of elements (P).

I started to play digital games when I was a university student because I did not have enough money to buy them before. However, I have been hooked on digital games ever since I played them by chance. I like movies, novels, and books; therefore, I was caught up in digital games that can be played interactively. At that time, when I played RPG for teenage girls through the Super Nintendo Entertainment System, I noticed accidentally that there was a very interesting package game, and then I was hooked on it. It changed my life (K).

When I took an employment interview examination for artists, I felt that I wanted to work with the very attractive interviewer. He said to me that I could entertain people by drawing graphic arts. At that time, I thought that media as digital games might entertain people, and would expand as a form of play in society. It made me feel like it was a big dream, as big as infinity, and very attractive (Q).

I couldn't choose my career in the gaming industry when I was a university student, because the gaming industry was not yet formed in Japan. In those days, Dragon Quest was just released and was gaining in popularity. It was an era in which we didn't have any models for entering the gaming industry. In such a situation, I wanted to work with a wide variety of related media such as visual images and picture books; however, I got involved with the gaming industry. In other words, it was by chance that I got into the gaming industry because I worked in digital games related with education, and for no other reason. Thereafter, I was able to establish a personal network with various staff members and business connections as colleagues, to develop educational

games. They were programmers, artists who could draw dot images, and directors like me, or small visual image and development companies. In those days, my interest in digital games grew steadily through interacting with developers in the gaming industry. It was my trigger to get into the gaming industry (G).

The female game developers' career transitions are considered based on Schlossberg (2000) in terms of three aspects: anticipated transitions, unanticipated transitions, and non-events. Regarding anticipated transitions, the category of childbirth was extracted. The developers who have children intentionally create a new environment in which they can balance work and family life and obtain help from their families, because they have no role models at their workplace. Concerning unanticipated transitions, the following categories were extracted: work experience to encourage the developers' growth, a boss who acted as a mentor, and the opportunity to move up in their position. As far as making a change in their job to grow in their career, they take a new job to feel more enjoyment in their work, and to develop a more flexible attitude toward their situation. As far as having a boss who mentors them, these women construct strong relationships of mutual trust with their boss, which helps them advance in their career. In moving up in their position, they expand their focus from developing their skills to enhancing their organizational abilities. Regarding non-events, the categories of change in job title, career plateau, and childbirth were extracted. The transition of childbirth is included in both events and non-events as it has multiple meanings.

First, I was filled with anxiety about my work because it was affected by childbirth and childcare. So, somehow…I was worried about whether my studio will accept me, whether I will be able to balance my work and family life. The former worry was an unprecedented case at my studio. I have an attachment to my studio, because it is possible to do work that I like in a small-scale studio, there is a feeling that I can build my work by myself. But I can't compare work environments because I don't have experience working at other studios. In addition, maybe I was hesitant to change my workplace because it was very hard for me. (Omission) The latter worry had to do with my work-life balance. My mother helped me. She lived near my home, so she could come there within one hour. I gave up leaving my child at the government authorized nursery school because it was not near my home. So, I left my child at a private nursery school from 8:30 to 19:30 near the station near my studio. It's a convenient place, but it cost a lot. I don't have to worry about leaving my child there, but I worry whether my child will get into an elementary school, because I have to leave my child in after-school childcare. But there is no option of leaving children there because it closes earlier than nursery school. What should I do? Education and childcare during summer holiday in an elementary school when I work at the studio. I have so many things on my mind now (D).

When I heard about personnel transfers, I felt like it was a demotion. It seemed that I was a person who was sacrificed for restructuring when my company had to reduce operations. At the time, I felt betrayed. But it seemed that it was the company's management policy, and I could understand that the other section needed a female middle manager. Therefore, I thought that the intention was to cultivate barren land again. So, I gave up and accepted it partly. I was trying to work as cheerfully as possible, moving to another section without a word of complaint. (Omission) Although I had some feelings, I moved there smoothly. As a result, I thought that it was a very good personnel transfer. Because I could learn a lot of things that I would never know if I worked only in game development. I accepted moving there with a positive outlook, and I thought that I could take a lot of good things from it (J).

I experienced my transition when I reached the fifth year of my career. I was worrying about how to improve my skills even more now, because I could not take enough time to study for harder work. (Omission) I didn't have complaints against the company, although it was tough to work there. But this job was worth doing because I was entrusted with a lot of tasks. As a result, I decided to continue my job so that I could learn a lot more from that experience than if I left the company, because I gained precious experience throughout the five years, and also had a job to do now. In addition, I thought that I would be able to take enough time for studying and improving my work efficiency if I became a skilled worker. It seemed like I would be even busier working in a new environment if I moved to another company. So, I could overcome the hardships in my fifth-year career transition. But I feel pressured. I can't understand how to change personally, but people are changing when I compare myself with others of my generation (E).

I thought that I would get married with my husband and expect my child. But I was worried…because I could not be expecting a baby. (Omission) I had mingled feelings of anxiety, impatience, and expectation because I had to give birth to my child; the stork might bring my baby someday. I had sought a doctor's advice during my physical examination only once because it might be difficult at my age. I kept telling myself that I should not give up. My colleagues asked me, 'Is your baby coming soon?' (Omission) I was worried about my health. But my doctor told me, 'There is nothing wrong with you!' So, I had no choice but to believe it (Q).

This study found that Japanese female game developers display the following ten characteristics regarding their careers: (1) They continue to challenge the market by behaviorally adapting to their environment and role. (2) They enjoy work and have a positive frame of mind. (3) They desire to place more emphasis on the quality of work rather than the quantity. (4) They display their creativity in their organizations. (5) They reflect on their careers objectively. (6) They work at explaining themselves to others. (7) They manage various relationships with other people. (8) They have the desire to do anything they can for the future by acting through trial and error, while at the same time treasuring the present. (9) They do not conform to gender stereotypes. (10) They act as leading role models for other creative professionals.

I think it is important that I deal with work flexibly in the organization. Because I have been entrusted with a lot of various jobs at my studio, it seems that I have been expected by my bosses and colleagues to use my ability. So, I have come to use positive thinking, like believing that I can produce some better results, try to learn new technologies that I don't know. (Omission) First of all, we receive a salary every month if we work hard, so we have been stable in our daily life. So, I will be not able to work immediately if I don't try to devote myself to my studies every day. It will mean that I'm not a creator (O).

I want to do my best so that all of our colleagues can work happily together. A lot of my senior colleagues at the studio left me and moved to another studio. So, I will never make my junior colleagues feel like this. I will work as long as I have the strength. Because this work requires physical strength (C).

I have observed the career development of my senior colleagues in the gaming industry. Because they aren't of retirement age yet, I cannot have my own career perspective on how I can play a role in game development in the future. But I have developed my career by making my best effort since I came across this work. So, I'm always thinking about how I can show my career path and perspective in the future for my junior colleagues (A).

CONCLUSION

For most of these Japanese female game developers, their original experience of playing digital games was in the past, and they found opportunities to take advantage of their skills in the gaming industry, which led to their entry into the industry. Then, they built their early and middle careers, taking time to develop professionally. However, it is difficult to provide a typical career pattern for Japanese female developers as there appear to be various individual styles of career progression.

As for the personal characteristics that these female developers display regarding career development, they enjoy their work because they have a positive attitude that allows them to be flexible and accept various changes; they continue to develop their skills and evaluate their career objectively; and they form valuable personal relationships. In addition, they respect individuality and being themselves, rather than conforming to the stereotypical feminine image, and they seek to understand themselves in relation to their colleagues.

For these female developers, the life transition of having a child has multiple meanings, which include both hope and anxiety. They show a willingness to explore new possibilities and to confronting the present, past, or future. In particular, females who have given birth and are caring for their children intentionally create an environment that allows work–life balance, thus improving their quality of work. However, this can cause emotional conflicts in terms of their career development as professionals. Therefore, they may attempt to overcome this by taking care of themselves, receiving support from their family at home, and relying on a support system at their workplace.

These women aim to be leading role models at their workplace because there are few female developers in the Japanese gaming industry; this motivates them to play this part. Thus, the behavioral characteristics of female game developers in their career development are as follows: they support persons who have similar problems in the workplace, and they contribute to mentoring game developers in the next generation. In other words, it is possible to find "generativity" in the outlook and behavior of Japanese female game developers.

In conclusion, female game developers do not have clearly defined career goals; however, they have the ability to alter their work situation, and evaluate and manage it if needed. Therefore, it is important that female game developers have diverse role models.

FUTURE RESEARCH DIRECTIONS

The gaming industry is affected by technology advances, because of which the environment surrounding the Japanese gaming industry has rapidly changed. In recent years, the social gaming industry has been gaining power because of increasing use of smart phones and easy access to the Internet. In Japan, household games and social games are forming each industries while intermingling. The Japanese gaming industry is changing from complete packages to online services.

Accordingly, female Japanese game developers' work style and career development is expected to change. Some developers will create household games, while others will create social games. Thus, female game developers' area of work may improve.

Therefore, we should continue research about career development among female Japanese game developers.

REFERENCES

Computer Entertainment Supplier's Association (CESA). (2013). *2012 CESA games white paper.*

Dyer-Whitheford, N., & Sharman, Z. (2005). The political economy of Canada's video and computer game industry. *Canadian Journal of Communication, 20*, 187–210.

Fujihara, M. (2009). Career development of producer in the Japanese gaming industry. *Journal of career design studies, 5*, 5–21. (in Japanese).

Fujihara, M. (2010). Issues of career development and career awareness among Japanese game developers. *Research Report on the Application of Advanced Technology in Digital Content Creation*, 253–300. Digital Content Association Japan. (In Japanese).

Geneve, A., Nelson, K. J., & Christie, R. J. (2008). *Passion, women and the games industry: Influences on women's participation in the Australian Digital Content Industry.* Paper presented at Women in Games, Warwick, UK.

Gourdin, A. (2005). *Game developers demographics: An exploration of workforce diversity.* International Game Developers Association.

Kohashi, R. (1996). *Household gaming industry in Japan: Organizational structure and the process* (Doctoral thesis). Graduate School of Business Administration, Kobe University, Japan. (in Japanese).

Prescott, J., & Bogg, J. (2010). The computer games industry: Women's experiences of work role in a male dominated environment. In A. Cater-Steel, & E. Cater (Eds.), *Women in engineering, science and technology: Education and career challenges* (pp. 138–158). Hershey, PA: IGI Global. doi:10.4018/978-1-61520-657-5.ch007

Sakurai, A. (2005). To interpret the interview text. In A. Sakurai, A., & T. Kobayashi T. (Eds.), Life story interview: Introduction to qualitative research (pp. 129-183). Tokyo: Serica Shobo. (in Japanese).

Schlossberg, N. K. (2000). *Overwhelmed: Coping with life's ups and downs*. Lanham, MD: Lexington Books.

Shintaku, J. (2000). Development of the software market by venture-capital company. In *Economic analysis of the gaming industry: Strategy and structure of the content industry development* (pp. 97–115). Tokyo: Toyo Keizai Shinpo Sha. (in Japanese).

Skillset. (2009). *2009 employment census: The results of the seventh census of the creative media industries December 2009*. The Sector Skills Council for Creative Media.

Tanaka, T. (2000a). *A demonstration of network externalities between hardware and software. Economic analysis of the gaming industry: Strategy and structure of the content industry development* (pp. 41–94). Tokyo: Toyo Keizai Shinpo Sha. (in Japanese).

Tanaka, T. (2000b). *The background and concentration into big companies. Economic analysis of the gaming industry: Strategy and structure of the content industry development* (pp. 117–143). Tokyo: Toyo Keizai Shinpo Sha. (in Japanese).

Yonekura, S., & Ikuine, F. (2005). Japanese game software industry: Trap of series strategy. *Hitotsubashi Business Review, 53*(3), 52–69. (in Japanese).

ADDITIONAL READING

Akagi, M. (2005). *It started from Pong: Origin of arcade TV games*. Amusement Press. (in Japanese).

Computer Entertainment Supplier's Association. (CESA). http://www.cesa.or.jp/index.php/en

Computer Entertainment Supplier's Association (CESA). (1998). *'98 CESA Games white paper (Japanese Ed.)*.

Computer Entertainment Supplier's Association (CESA). (1999). *'99 CESA Games white paper (Japanese Ed.)*.

Computer Entertainment Supplier's Association (CESA). (2000). *2000 CESA Games white paper (Japanese Ed.)*.

Computer Entertainment Supplier's Association (CESA). (2001). *2001 CESA Games white paper (English Ed.)*.

Computer Entertainment Supplier's Association (CESA). (2002). 2002 *CESA Games white paper (English Ed.)*.

Computer Entertainment Supplier's Association (CESA). (2003). 2003 *CESA Games white paper (English Ed.)*.

Computer Entertainment Supplier's Association (CESA). (2004). 2004 *CESA Games white paper (Japanese and English Ed.)*.

Computer Entertainment Supplier's Association (CESA). (2005). 2005 *CESA Games white paper (Japanese and English Ed.)*.

Computer Entertainment Supplier's Association (CESA). (2006). 2006 *CESA Games white paper (Japanese and English Ed.)*.

Computer Entertainment Supplier's Association (CESA). (2007). *Project Report on the Human Resource Development in the Game Industry.*

Computer Entertainment Supplier's Association (CESA). (2007). 2007 *CESA Games white paper (Japanese and English Ed.)*.

Computer Entertainment Supplier's Association (CESA). (2008). *Project Report on the Human Resource Development of New Graduate Developers in the Game Industry.* (in Japanese).

Computer Entertainment Supplier's Association (CESA). (2008). 2008 *CESA Games white paper (Japanese and English Ed.)*.

Computer Entertainment Supplier's Association (CESA). (2009). 2009 *CESA Games white paper (Japanese and English Ed.)*.

Computer Entertainment Supplier's Association (CESA). (2010). 2010 *CESA Games white paper (Japanese and English Ed.)*.

Computer Entertainment Supplier's Association (CESA). (2011). 2011 *CESA Games white paper (Japanese and English Ed.)*.

Computer Entertainment Supplier's Association (CESA). (2012). 2012 *CESA Games white paper (Japanese and English Ed.)*.

Computer Entertainment Supplier's Association (CESA). (2013). 2013 *CESA Games white paper (Japanese and English Ed.)*.

Digital Games Research Association Japan. (DiGRA JAPAN). http://digrajapan.org/

Enterbrain global marketing office. (2005). *Famitsu game White Paper 2005*. Enterbrain. (in Japanese).

Enterbrain global marketing office. (2006). *Famitsu game White Paper 2006*. Enterbrain. (in Japanese).

Enterbrain global marketing office. (2007). *Famitsu game White Paper 2007*. Enterbrain. (in Japanese).

Enterbrain global marketing office. (2008). *Famitsu game White Paper 2008*. Enterbrain. (in Japanese).

Enterbrain global marketing office. (2009). *Famitsu game White Paper 2009*. Enterbrain. (in Japanese).

Enterbrain global marketing office. (2010). *Famitsu game White Paper 2010*. Enterbrain. (in Japanese).

Enterbrain global marketing office. (2011). *Famitsu game White Paper 2011*. Enterbrain. (in Japanese).

Enterbrain global marketing office. (2012). *Famitsu game White Paper 2012*. Enterbrain. (in Japanese).

Enterbrain global marketing office. (2013). *Famitsu game White Paper 2013*. Enterbrain. (in Japanese).

Fujihara, M. (2009a). Change of the Japanese game industry and the human resource management. *Research Report on the Application of Advanced Technology in Digital Content Creation*, 230–260. Digital Content Association Japan. (in Japanese).

Fujihara, M. (2009b). Producers' career development in the Japanese game industry. *Journal of Career Design Studies*, 5, 5–21. (in Japanese).

Fujihara, M. (2010a). Issues of career development and career awareness among Japanese game developers. *Research Report on the Application of Advanced Technology in Digital Content Creation*, 253–300. Digital Content Association Japan. (in Japanese).

Fujihara, M. (2013). Career development among Japanese female game developers: Perspectives from life stories of creative professionals. *Journal of Information Studies, Interfaculty Initiative in Information Studies. The University of Tokyo*, 85, 45–95. (in Japanese).

Game Amusement Society. (GAS). http://www.gameamusementsociety.org/

Ikuine, F. (2012). *Dilemma of development productivity: Innovation pattern of digital age*. Yuhikaku Publishing. (in Japanese).

International Game Developers Association Japan. (IGDA Japan). http://www.igda.jp/

Ishijima, T. (2009). How to walk in the game industry. *Diamond*. (in Japanese).

Japan Amusement Machinery Manufacturers Association. (JAMMA). http://www.jamma.or.jp/english/

Japan Association of Simulation And Gaming. (JASAG). http://jasag.org/en/

Japan Online Game Association. (JOGA). (2013). *JOGA online game market research report 2013*. Enterbrain. (in Japanese).

Japan Online Game Association. (JOGA). http://www.japanonlinegame.org/english/

Japan Social Game Association. (JASGA). http://jasga.or.jp/en/

Kanai, A. (2010). Career transition among working women. [The Japan Institute for Labour Policy and Training.]. *The Japanese Journal of Labour Studies*, *52*(10), 44–53. (in Japanese).

Kohashi, R. (1993). Strategy and organization of Japanese TV game software companies. *Business insight: The journal for deeper insights into business 1*(3), 74–90. (in Japanese).

Kohashi, R. (1997). Software development processes in Japanese TV game software companies. *OIU Journal of International Studies*, *10*(3/4), 81–108. (in Japanese).

Kohashi, R. (1999). Management of development engineers in Japanese video game software companies. *OIU Journal of International Studies*, *12*(4), 1–22. (in Japanese).

Media Create. (2001). *The annual video game industry report in 2001*. (in Japanese).

Media Create. (2002). *The annual video game industry report in 2002*. (in Japanese).

Media Create. (2003). *The annual video game industry report in 2003*. (in Japanese).

Media Create. (2004). *The annual video game industry report in 2004*. (in Japanese).

Media Create. (2005). *The annual video game industry report in 2005*. (in Japanese).

Media Create. (2006). *The annual video game industry report in 2006*. (in Japanese).

Media Create. (2007). *The annual video game industry report in 2007*. (in Japanese).

Media Create. (2008). *The annual video game industry report in 2008*. (in Japanese).

Media Create. (2009). *The annual video game industry report in 2009*. (in Japanese).

Media Create. (2010). *The annual video game industry report in 2010*. (in Japanese).

Media Create. (2011). *The annual video game industry report in 2011*. (in Japanese).

Media Create. (2012). *The annual video game industry report in 2012*. (in Japanese).

Media Create. (2013). *The annual video game industry report in 2013*. (in Japanese).

Ministry of Economy, Trade and Industry (METI). (2006). *Game industry strategy: A vision for the development and the future of the game industry*. (in Japanese).

Shin, K. (2002). *Game development front-line, Samurai was made thus: 660 days war of second production division at the ACQUIRE Corp.* Shinkigensha. (in Japanese).

Shintaku, J., Tanaka, T., & Yanagawa, N. (Eds.). (2005). *Economic analysis of the gaming industry: Strategy and structure of the content industry development*. Toyo Keizai Shinpo Sha. (in Japanese).

TV game museum project (Ed.), (1988). *TV games: Electronic game Encyclopedia*. UPU. (in Japanese).

TV game museum project (Ed.), (1994). *Current of the video games*. Village Center. (in Japanese).

Uemura, M. Hosoi. K., & Nakamura, A. (2013). The life and times of the Nintendo Famicom: The birth of TV games. NTT Publishing. (in Japanese).

KEY TERMS AND DEFINITIONS

Career Transition: In career development theory, "transition" refers to the transition to the next stage from the previous stage. It is assumed that there are problems or events that people encounter that are common in certain age groups, and that people continue to move to the next stage of development while overcoming such problems and life events. "Transition" also refers to a significant turning point in their life, with a focus on the influence of individuals or events such as employment, marriage, childbirth, and changing jobs.

Creativity: In the Japanese gaming industry, a game developer is also called a game creator. "Creativity" is the ability to transcend conventional ideas, rules, customs, relationships, and it is needed to produce new and original meanings for ideas, forms, cultures, and partnerships in the gaming industry. In Japan, a person who has these abilities to create something new is called a game creator.

Diversity: The term "diversity" includes various aspects such as gender, age, nationality, religion, disability, and sexual orientation. It is a term used for all the factors that may produce the difference between individuals and groups. In this paper, the term is employed in discussing diversity from the perspective of the thinking and behavior of Japanese female game developers.

Game Developers: In this paper, "developer" is defined as a general term for creative professionals who take responsibility for the planning, development, and management of games. In particular, it refers to creative professionals such as programmers, graphic artists, planners, directors, and producers.

Generativity: "Generativity" refers to a concern for establishing and guiding the next generation. It is a term coined by Erik Erikson in 1950. The concept is related to telling one's life story. We receive something from the past, we create something out of it, and we pass it on to the future. In this paper, "generativity" is a concept for connecting this generation to the next and to future generations.

Life Story: The life story approach is a qualitative research method that we call the "realism approach" and the "narrative approach." We collect the life stories of many people, assuming that the life story of each individual represents one aspect of objective reality. Through inductive inferences about the accumulated data in terms of the dynamic process of interaction between the storyteller and the listener, we can develop a theoretical model.

Role Model: Japanese female game developers do not have role models to guide them in their career at their studios. Therefore, they may have the feeling that their career perspectives in the present or in the future are unclear. However, they try to be leading role models for young women in the Japanese gaming industry, and to find meaning in their lives. This is one of the key findings in this chapter.

Chapter 7
Women's Participation in the Australian Digital Content Industry

Anitza Geneve
Southbank Institute of Technology, Australia

ABSTRACT

There is a need to understand the phenomenon of women's under-representation in the Australian Digital Content Industry (DCI) workforce. This chapter presents the findings from an Australian case study where both women working in the industry and industry stakeholders were interviewed for their insight into the influences on women's participation. The rich empirical data and findings from the case study are interpreted using the Acts of Agency theory—an original theory by the author of this chapter. As the chapter reveals there are five 'Acts of Agency' (containing 10 agent-driven mechanisms) identified as influencing women's participation. Agent-driven mechanisms recognise the causal effect of people themselves; that is, the role individuals play in their participation.

INTRODUCTION

This chapter discusses women's participation in the Australian Digital Content Industry. As the brief background highlights, women are under-represented in the DCI. There are a broad and complex range of influences on women's participation. The author presents a new and original theoretical approach, titled the *Acts of Agency* theory, as a way to understand these influences. The remainder of the chapter uses the *Acts of Agency* theory to discuss the rich empirical data and findings from a case study examining women's experiences of working in the Australian Digital Content Industry.

BACKGROUND

In 2013, women remain under-represented in the workforce of a number of Australian industries; including those that have been traditionally male-dominated such as mining, construction and utilities (Australian Human Rights Commission, 2013). In industries where women's numbers are more equitable, such as in health care, education and training and retail trade roles, there exists a

DOI: 10.4018/978-1-4666-6142-4.ch007

"stratification" in the number of women in different roles with notably fewer women in management (Australian Human Rights Commission, 2013, p.6). There are at least three reasons why society should foster women's equitable participation. First, there is a national economic benefit. The Grattan Institute reports that if Australia increased female labour force participation to a rate on par with Canada (62.4%) that this would increase Australia's economic growth in the next decade by $25 billion (Australian Human Rights Commission, 2013). Second, organisational innovation is improved with a diverse workforce. Third, there is both a legal and a moral imperative to foster equitable opportunities for individuals regardless of their gender. Equitable participation by women has national, organisational and individual benefits.

Women also remain under-represented in emerging industries. These industries include Information Communication and Technology (ICT), which provides IT services and products such as programming and the Digital Content Industry (DCI) which provides games, website, app and mobile content development. In 2007, women's participation in the Australian games production industry was approximately 10.7% (Australian Bureau of Statistics, 2008). This figure is not dissimilar to international figures reported in 2005 by the International Game Developers Association (IGDA) survey, which surveyed nearly 6500 international games developers and found women's participation rates were approximately 11.5% (Gourdin, 2005). Women are not only under-represented in the DCI workforce, they also face horizontal and vertical occupational segregation with few women involved in technical roles. As Roan & Whitehouse (2007) found, although there were "relatively high numbers of women in 'web/multimedia' jobs" in the Australian DCI, many of these appeared to be "primarily clerical jobs", and "women were rarely found in the more directly technical roles of computer games

design" (p. 31). Haines (2004) identified a similar segregation exists for women working in the UK games industry, where women comprised only 2% of programmers, 3% of audio, 5% of games designers, 8% of production staff, and 9% of artists. More research is needed to understand the under-representation of women in the DCI and the role segregation they experience.

There is a significant body of previous research which has identified a plethora of influences on women's participation in the ICT industry; the ICT industry has many commonalities with the DCI. The influences include culture, which encompasses: general attitudes or values regarding women (Trauth, Quesenberry, & Yeo, 2005); a woman's cultural background (Trauth, Quesenberry, & Huang, 2008); and the organisational culture in which a woman finds herself (Webb & Young, 2005). Organisational culture characteristics, such as the dominant male culture in IT organisations (von Hellens, Nielsen, & Trauth, 2001) and masculinised workplaces (Griffiths, Moore, & Richardson, 2007), can leave women feeling as though they are in the gendered minority. However, identifying and understanding these influences presents a complex challenge for researchers. Indeed, McGrath-Cohoon and Aspray (2006) recognise that the issue of women's equitable participation in Information Technology (IT) is so "complex" that it makes "it difficult to know how to go about reaching a gender balance" (p.viii).

In contrast to the ICT context, there are few empirical studies specifically investigating women's participation in the DCI. In the United Kingdom there are two notable studies; Gill (2002) who focused on new media and Prescott and Bogg (2010) who focused on games development. In Australia, key research papers include Swanson and Wise's (1996) findings (from a national survey of the patterns of training, skills, income and employment of women working in the multimedia industries), which noted that although the industry area was "still" a male-dominated industry, "women stand to gain from their participation in this expanding sector" (p. 3). A decade later, Roan and White-house's (2007) study of DCI organisations in Queensland, Australia, identified that women remain under-represented in multimedia and in the emerging areas of game production. There is both a need for further empirical research and also an approach with which to understand the influences on women's participation which leads to their under-representation in the Australian DCI.

The Acts of Agency Approach

Developed by Geneve (2013) (as a part of a PhD dissertation) the *Acts of Agency* theory offers a new approach with which to understand the influences on women's participation in the Australian DCI. The theory is concerned with understanding the participation of individuals within social contexts. The foundation of the theory lies in a combination of human agency theory and the ontological stance of critical realism. Human agency is a theoretical perspective that recognises an individual's capacity for free will or action, where such human capacity is linked to structural aspects. Gender-related research has recognised the importance of human agency, where women's emancipation involves their "individual will and agency" (Connell, 1987, p. 50). Agency theorists such as Giddens and Bandura are sensitive to gender by recognising that women face certain challenges. Giddens (1993) has recognised that the obstacles women face in their careers include employers who discriminate against women, as they believe women will leave the workforce to have babies (p. 245). Similarly, Bandura (2002) recognises that "socialization practices" "undermine their [women's and minorities'] efficacy for technological and scientific careers" (p. 6). The version of Critical Realism stemming from the work of Bhaskar (1986) encourages understanding the world through the recognition of

three different but interrelated strata or domains. The three domains are: 1) a person's experiences (experience domain); 2) the actual events (actual domain) and 3) underpinning mechanisms (real domain). Although neither, human agency theory or critical realism, has been utilised to any extent to understand women's participation, both approaches hold many strengths.

The key impetus of the *Acts of Agency* theory is the recognition of agent-driven mechanisms. When women harness these agent-driven mechanisms, it can result in actions that foster their participation. For example, cultural influences such as gender stereotypes exist; however, women can challenge those influences. Women can become aware of the inaccuracy of those stereotypes and they can also develop skills that dispel the stereotypes. Importantly, women challenge influences individually; that is, one woman may respond in a certain way and another woman in a different way. The *Acts of Agency* theory and the agent-driven mechanisms that it identifies recognises the complex interactions of environmental and individual factors and that this interaction manifests differently for individual women.

The Australian Case Study

An Australian case study conducted during the period 2007-2012 provides an insight into influences on women's participation in the Digital Content Industry. Empirical case study data involved the primary data source of semi-structured interviews with 18 women working in the Australian industry and stakeholders working in the industry. The women worked in a range of roles including web designer, artificial intelligence games programmer, multimedia developer, graphic artist, senior visual games artist and new media producer; within a range of organisations including government agencies, international games companies and local start-ups. Secondary sources of data included media articles and government and industry reports. The case study data is interpreted using the *Acts of Agency* theory (Geneve, 2013), a new theoretical approach which can be applied to understanding an individual's participation in a particular context.

The Australian case study indicates there are five 'acts of agency', which in turn can be further refined to 10 agent-driven mechanisms, women working in the DCI can employ to foster their participation in the Digital Content Industry. The five 'acts of agency' are: 1) enabled, 2) connected, 3) collaborative, 4) creative, and 5) human. The 10 agent-driven mechanisms are: 1) accessing, 2) imagining, 3) doing, 4) belonging, 5) sharing, 6) problem-solving, 7) transforming, 8) emotion, 9) ethical and 10) being. These 'acts of agency' and the mechanisms within the acts are presented as a model of the *Five Acts of Agency (FAA)* (as illustrated in Table 1). The remainder of this chapter analyses the rich empirical data from the Australian case study using the *Five Acts of Agency* identified in Table 1.

The Enabled Act

The 'Enabled Act' includes the agent-driven mechanism of *accessing*. When women access information, technology and people this can foster their participation. Information can include information about the roles within the industry. Technology can include the tools of the industry such as computers and software. People can include industry mentors.

The case study findings suggest that access to information fostered women's participation. Conversely, a lack of information was seen as limiting the participant's choice to enter the industry. Participants noted: *"I don't think it was ever something that I was interested in because I didn't know enough about it but now I know it I don't think there's anything else I'd prefer to do"* (MARY-production assistant/local games start-up). Another participant suggested that the education system had not provided her with adequate information regarding career choices: *"School didn't give us that information. I went to company websites. It's hard to really say definitively girls are being discouraged or whether there's just not enough information..."* (JANE-junior props artist/local games start-up).

The case study findings suggest that access to technology fostered women's participation. Technology resources (such as computers) were important over a woman's lifespan, including; childhood, education and career stages. A lack of access to technology presented women with challenges during their education: *"When I was doing it, it was even harder because hardly anyone had a computer at home, you'd have to go to the lab and wait two hours until there's one free and you're only allowed on for three hours but your lab for that week could take nine hours"* (LOLA-

Table 1. The Five Acts of Agency (FAA) and the 10 underlying agent-driven mechanisms

Five Acts of Agency				
1. Enabled Access to resources such as technology, people, and information	2. Connected The beliefs and motivations of the agent, including self-efficacy	3. Collaborative The social relationships that foster involvement	4. Creative Problem-solving, or the power to transform	5. Human Human-only traits of emotions and ethics
Agent-Driven Mechanisms				
1. Accessing	2. Imagining 3. Doing	4. Belonging 5. Sharing	6. Problem-solving 7. Transforming	8. Emotion 9. Ethical 10. Being

artificial games programmer/international games company). Technology, such as free software, remains integral to the development of skills that may lead to employment: *"It's interesting because there are new ways to get a job... there's free online engines so these kids are actually making them at home"* (PETA senior character artist/international games company).

The case study findings suggest that access to people, such as mentors, fostered women's participation. Participants identified that access to people and networks were integral to women's entry and continuation in the workforce as many positions in the DCI are not widely advertised: *"I didn't think we advertise jobs that widely"* (FINN games designer/international games company). Access is often fostered through social connection based on friendships and professional networks. *"To be honest most people that come in are people that someone already knows"* (FINN). The industry was *"competitive,* and *"unless you're really well networked it's quite difficult to get a leg in"... "you have to find a way to become involved and there are barriers to that because it's not something highly visible"* (BELL web developer/private multimedia studio).

The influence of the mechanism of *accessing* can be further explained by drawing on previous literature. Access to technological resources has been typically noted in the 'digital divide' literature. Women IT professionals cite access to computers while at school as the most prominent reason for their interest in an IT career (Turner, Bernt & Pecora, 2002). Information resources such as industry websites (such as *gamasutra.com*) are seen as valuable with Australian DCI workers and personal introduction as the most important way to enter the industry (Haukka & Brow, 2010). Similarly, research into new media suggests employment is not the traditional job advertisement in the paper, but informal networks (Gill, 2002).

Women in the case study harnessed the agent-driven mechanism of *accessing* in a number of ways. For example, participants employed active information-seeking behaviours; by researching industry relevant websites and job postings on these websites. Access could be supported by other people. For example, participants in the study identified having access to an older brother's or a father's computer as being important. Accessing information also occurred through serendipitous or emergent events, such as accidentally coming across a job opportunity on the internet.

Strategies aiming to foster women's participation must provide access to resources, such as technology (computers and software), information (about the industry, job opportunities) and people (social networks, mentors). These strategies have been identified by the industry, for example the International Games Developers Association offers an online mentorship scheme (IGDA, 2005).

The Connected Act

The 'Connected Act' includes the two agent-driven mechanisms of 1) *imagining* and 2) *doing*. A person's participation can be fostered if they harness the mechanism of imagining (or visualising) their participation, and gain appropriate skills through doing.

The mechanism of *imagining* was evident when participants indicated that being able to imagine or visualise their participation was an influence. There were several environmental influences that constrained women doing this, including the lack of role models and unclear career pathways in the DCI. *"There isn't an image of a hot female programmer out there that people want to emulate or aspire to"* (SUE project co-ordinator/international games company). An article reporting comments by the IGDA Women in Games SIG panel laments *"that young women could not imagine themselves as game designers"* (Chen, 2009). Several participants noted there was a lack of female role models who worked in the industry and also had children: this lead some case study participants to surmise that they would need to leave the DCI when they had children.

The mechanism of *doing* was evident when participants indicated that developing skills required by the industry was an influence. When a participant mastered technical skills, they felt confident in pursuing that career path; that is, they gained a sense of self-efficacy: *"It just came very easy to me. That made me start thinking maybe I can actually go a bit further with this"* (TONI new media producer/Australian government agency).

The influence of the mechanism of *imagining* can be further explained by drawing on previous literature. The agent-driven mechanism of imagining requires women visualise themselves working in the industry. However, negative perceptions of the IT industry and a lack of female role models can discourage young girls from pursuing careers in IT (Beekhuyzen & Clayton, 2004).

Similarly, the influence of the mechanism of *doing* can be further explained by drawing on previous literature. The agent-driven mechanism of doing requires women develop confidence, or self-efficacy, in their industry skills. Self-efficacy is an important aspect of women's capacity when using technology (Betz & Hackett, 1997). Recent literature regarding the ICT industry continues to recognise self-efficacy as an aspect of students' participation and worker's capacity (Kvasny et al., 2011).

Women in the case study harnessed the agent-driven mechanisms of *imagining* and *doing* in a number of ways. This included seeking out role models even when the industry offered few. Participants recognised the need to gain skills through training or work to gain entry into the industry, maintain employment and progress in their careers. Participants found ways to maintain those skills in the light of ever-changing technology (for example, new technology), and personal circumstances (for example, when becoming a parent). One participant who had returned to the workplace after having a child described actions that she took to maintain her skills while also addressing her parental responsibilities, such as ensuring she had software at home when on maternity leave.

Strategies aiming to foster women's participation must promote female role models working in the industry as this may help girls and women imagine their participation. Furthermore, the industry must provide accurate information about working in the industry. 'Open Days' for school children and work experience provide an opportunity to see the industry and gain skills. A participant described how seeing the industry context whilst on a volunteer work placement in a games development company helped her connect to the industry. She said that *"I was being invited... to see what it was like on the inside, that was a huge thing ... you really need that connection"* (RAY assistant producer/local games start-up).

Strategies must also provide women the opportunity to develop skills required of the industry and to continue learning skills in the workplace context. Skill development has been identified in previous strategies aimed at improving participation rates of women in ICT (Tapia & Kvasny, 2004). Parberry, Kazemzadeh and Roden (2006) pointed out that games workers are expected to learn independently, because the industry continues to push the boundaries of what can be done using new computer technology. This may be because disruptive technologies arrive more regularly in the DCI and are rapidly diffused (DCITA, 2005). Being given adequate time and resources to maintain skills can support women's participation.

The Collaborative Act

The 'Collaborative Act' includes the two agent-driven mechanisms of 1) *belonging* and 2) *sharing*. A person's participation can be fostered if they harness the mechanism of having a sense of belonging within the workplace and also in sharing experiences with other agents.

The mechanism of *belonging* was evident when participants suggested that feeling as though they belonged in their work environment was an influence on their participation. Participants valued collaborative and socially orientated work environments, where *"everyone has input"* (LOLA), and it *"feels more just like a group of friend's kind of interaction"* (SUE). The DCI, for the most part, presents a team oriented environment; it is no longer *"a guy programmer playing on his computer coding in his garage"*, but rather *"quite a close knit sort of group"* (AMY multimedia developer/Australian government agency) with teams of *"forty people for one Playstation game"* (JANE). However, the DCI is still a male dominated industry and women often felt they didn't belong within the workplace due to being in the gendered minority; they felt they weren't *"one of the boys"* (JANE). The actions of male colleagues could leave women feeling as though they didn't belong because of their gender: *"It still feels different, like I feel like they're treading around me"* (ELLE web developer/private studio).

The mechanism of *sharing* was evident when participants suggested that being able to share experiences, knowledge and resources with colleagues through social interaction was crucial for women's participation. Sharing was seen as a positive aspect of the work environment and working alone was seen as a negative influence: *"I was it, so there was no-one there to learn from"* (DI senior manager/international games company). One employer noted: *"In a work environment you need people who understand you and you can talk to... you're mates with and you can share things and I think that's what a balanced work environment is"*. Participants recognised the value of learning from mentors: *"I wanted someone to learn from"* (DI). However, there were few mentors, and fewer female mentors.

The influence of *belonging* and *sharing* can be further explained by drawing on previous research regarding women's participation. For example, "extra-curricular socializing" with male colleagues has been identified as being "necessary" for career progression in the ICT industry (Trauth, 2002, p.101). However, women IT programmers noted negatively that too many "discussions took place down the pub" (Moore et al., 2005, p. 16), suggesting that women were often excluded from socialisation opportunities. Secondary data supports the finding that the male majority can constrain women's access to people and consequently career opportunities. *"My personal experience was that work lunches, afternoon golfing, etc. did not include women. That is one place where relationships are solidified, ideas are hatched, promotions are planned, etc."* (Lealea Design, n. d.).

Previous research in the ICT domain suggests it is important that women gain acceptance in the organisation (Trauth, 1999, p. 159). However, an international *Women in Technology* survey identified that 52% of participants stated that they worked in uninviting workplaces where not being heard made them "question whether this is an environment that they wish to stay in" (Eweek, 2007). As Tapia and Kvasny (2004) identified, "If people don't feel important, they're not motivated to stay" (p.88). A sense of inclusion can lead to better performance, greater job satisfaction, heightened commitment, and the increased likelihood of remaining with the current employer and staying in the IT field (Major et al., 2006). However, it is important to note that although environmental characteristics influence women's sense of belonging that individual women also play a role. Roan and Whitehouse's (2007) study revealed, employees "must be able to fit into the culture. A low ego, they must be able to work with others. It's all teamwork" (p. 30). Secondary sources of data, such as a survey of games workers, further supports the importance of fitting into a team, with one respondent suggesting if you can "work well with the team, welcome aboard" (IGDA, 2005). Thus, as Castells (1998) suggested, being able to align one's identity with the organisational culture is a valuable asset.

Women in the case study harnessed the agent-driven mechanism of *belonging* in a number of ways. For example, participants noted that certain clothing signified their gender. To avoid feeling as though they were in the gendered minority, participants did not were skirts but rather the jeans and t-shirt that was seen to be a uniform of the industry. Belonging also manifested through mastering the technical jargon required by colleagues, and sharing interests and leisure pursuits (such as playing computer games). In some cases, a sense of belonging occurred simply due to the length of time colleagues had worked together: *"I've worked with the guys that – who are the artists – for the last three or four projects so it works on a personal level"* (PETA). Some women were very active in fostering collaboration, recognising that their career progression hinged on being perceived as fitting in:

I was really aggressive about wanting to fit into the team [...] to compete with the other juniors that were hired at the same time as me. I know I talked about a collaborative environment but I still like know I'm being measured. So I always went to lunch with the bosses and we talked about work (LOLA).

When women harnessed the agent-mechanism of sharing they shared their knowledge and skills, which in turn enhanced their sense of being a valued member within the workplace. *"There's a lot of reward to be gained from collaborating with people. People ask me questions and I ask them questions about stuff which shares skills and knowledge"* (BELL).

Strategies aiming to foster women's participation must educate DCI workplaces to be aware of cultural practices in the workplace that may isolate

females. Unprofessional male-orientated practices in the workplace, such as meetings conducted in strip clubs, can ostracise women rather than foster a sense of belonging to the organisational 'culture'. To foster a sense of fit, DCI organisations need to clearly promote a professional organisational culture that encourages equitable work practices. Even something that seems a small aspect of workplace culture can have an influence. For example, by having a relaxed dress code, individuals have the flexibility to express their individuality, and women are not forced to conform to gendered norms of wearing dresses and skirts. Similarly, the physical layout of the workplace is an influence. A number of the women interviewed had a preference for open plan style offices, which can be explained by noting that this type of physical structure encourages transparency, collaboration, and sharing of practices as well as space. Fullerton et al., (2008) suggested that the ideal work environment for women is one with open space.

The Creative Act

The 'Creative Act' includes the two agent-driven mechanisms of 1) *problem solving* and 2) *transforming*. A person's participation can be fostered if they have the opportunity to: 1) be creative through problem solving or 2) in transforming entities such as artefacts, ideas and processes.

The case study findings suggest that the Australian DCI industry is strongly associated with creative skills, supporting previous international research which suggests creativity is highly valued in the new media (Gill & Pratt, 2008) and games industry (Deuze et al., 2007). Case study participants indicated that they entered the industry for an opportunity to be creative and had left other industries because the roles were not creative. With reference to the publishing industry a participant comments, *"What I did before I loved because it allowed me to travel but it was boring...The things that I didn't enjoy about it was that it's not a creative industry... that was what I wanted"* (PETA).

The mechanism of *problem-solving* was evident when participants noted that opportunities for problem-solving provided them with intrinsic reward: *"It's not a professional environment at all it's really like getting together with a bunch of friends and solving problems and in that respect it's one of the brilliant environments to be employed in"* (JANE). Problem-solving skills were seen as being integral to certain roles, such as programming. A participant noted *"...programming, I can organise things, and follow patterns and like doing it, it's like solving a puzzle"* (LOLA). DCI workers needed to have a *"fascination with how things kind of work"* (BELL). Problem-solving also manifested in managing other people or clients' needs; for some, it was *"challenging when the client says I want this and you try to make it something that meets their standards I guess that's where the challenge comes from"* (ELLE).

The mechanism of *transforming* was evident when individuals recounted their creative practice, which involved the creation of new ideas, products or processes. *"I like challenging projects that make me think and bring about new ideas, finding new ways to resolve them, improving myself over time"* (AMY).

The influence of problem-solving and transforming can be further explained by drawing on previous research. Agosto, Gasson and Atwood (2008) noted that problem-solving is important to women in ICT- related careers: "most studies of why women avoid IT have demonstrated that females who are making career choices care a lot about 'solving problems' and much less about 'technology'" (p. 205). Women in IT require "challenging workplace projects" (Trauth, 2002, p. 109). IT employees want to learn, sharpen their skills and hone new ones (Tapia and Kvasny, 2004). Studies of IT professionals identified that women rated 'wanting the opportunity to learn new things' more highly than they rated 'salary' and wanting to 'gain more expertise' and not face 'boredom' rated more highly than being 'discriminated against' or 'not fitting in' (Hoonakker, Carayon, Schoepke,

2006).The situation appears similar in the DCI, with a female games industry veteran of 17 years noting that creativity and problem solving are key skills (Blake, 2011).

Women in the Australian case study harnessed the agent-driven mechanism of problem-solving in a number of ways. Participants were motivated to pursue roles that offered them a challenge, one participant stating: *"[...] that's why I like my job... There's something new, a challenge"* (M10). Occupational roles that did not offer participants challenges were seen as unappealing: *"It's challenging, and it's fun, it's creative. I couldn't imagine filing papers and answering phones all day"* (ELLE). Women avoided roles they perceived as being boring. *"People just do the same thing over and over again and then after a while you can't—I don't know. It doesn't work your muscles in terms of your brain muscles, in terms of your challenges, in terms of your problem solving. So I think that's a big problem"* (JILL).

I get bored easily, what I won't be bored easily with would be computers and would be because there's such a variety with multimedia there's always something different to do in it, because you'll always have to learn new things. That will keep me just hanging for a long time. And so that's why I went with multimedia (JILL).

Strategies aiming to foster women's participation must ensure that the industry provides workers an opportunity for creativity. Opportunities for creativity can vary with roles and types of DCI organisations. For example, indie games production organisations were seen, by women in the case study, as being more creative than larger multi-nationals. Larger organisations were seen as being *"really risk adverse and so with the games designs they just won't do anything innovative or exciting"* (LOLA). Although many participants had entered the industry because they perceived it would offer them an opportunity to be creative, many became disillusioned.

There's so many different jobs in this industry, some are creative and some are not. I think I wasn't fulfilling my creative needs quite early on. When I first got into it I was saying I was very passionate about design and I was doing a lot of hours. I felt like I was expressing a lot of creativity in this work. I think that disappeared fairly quickly, having to design within the limitations of corporate. So it just became pretty much just churn work, really. You tried as much as you could to put creativity into it but you're quite limited (JO).

Participant insights support previous research, such as Perrons (2003) who in reference to women's participation in the new media industry in the UK noted "that work in the larger firms was more likely to become formulaic and less challenging" (p. 80). In game development, Deuze et al., (2007) noted the "tensions" that the environment presents workers with when their creative freedom is tempered by financial control (p. 292).

Conversely, the Digital Content Industry must also recognise the demand workers faced in managing on-going challenges of learning new technology: *"I guess one negative would be the learning curve again and again and again"* (DI). Certain roles such as programming were more demanding, more *"taxing because like the technology changes every, I'd say 6 months to a year so you're constantly reading and learning"* (FINN). Others noted that *"after being challenged so hard so long"* (AMY), it could impact their health: *"Sure it's great to be on the cutting edge - it's more creative & challenging - but it's also incredibly tiring and stressful"* (LOLA).

The Human Act

The 'Human Act' recognises human capacities that an individual possesses. A person's participation can be fostered if they harness the mechanisms of 1) *emotion,* 2) *ethics,* and 3) *being.*

The mechanism of *emotion* was evident when case study participants described the different emotional states they had experienced in educa-

tion and workplace contexts, including: boredom, fun, frustration, passion, fear, loneliness, desire, anxiety, anger, guilt, and obsession. For example, one participant was 'pissed off' (interpreted as anger) that a male colleague was earning more than her in essentially a similar role. Another described the 'excitement' of working on a new project: *"I've never worked on a realistic game...I was like this is so exciting..."* (PETA).

The emotion most cited by participants and the stakeholders interviewed was that of passion. Passion was a necessity to work in the industry: *"Like it's really hard to work in a creative industry so they have to be really passionate and if they have that they're going to succeed..."* (TONI). Passion could counter balance influences that constrained women's participation. For example, being passionate about the work they produced could counter the lack of financial rewards the industry offered: *"The money's not there, it's really not there...I think the only reason you would enter games is because you've got a passion for games"* (MARY). However, the passion to produce quality products, along with the guilt of not staying back with peers after hours to produce those quality products, lead to work practices such as working long hours, which in turn challenged ongoing participation. *"It's a cycle in that you know everyone is passionate about in work to put in these hours so then it's expected, and so then it becomes the norm and then everyone else has to put in"* (FINN).

The mechanism of *ethical* was evident when participants suggested that ethics were an influence on their participation. Participants made indirect reference to the social value of their occupational roles. One participant, who worked as an online content editor (POPPY-online content editor\ Australian government agency), enjoyed her role because it facilitated a wide range of people being able to make comments on a blog. Her background had been in journalism and she saw her current role as facilitating aspects of participatory journalism. Similarly, another identified that a positive of the industry was that it sometimes creates products with social value: *"There are projects that are social projects like road safety and things like that, it doesn't always have to be advertising based"* (DI). In contrast, another participant reflected on the appropriateness of the violence in certain games, and noted that her attitude to those games had changed since having her first child: *"I love violence in terms of the games that I play, I enjoy it…But I now have a little boy… and for the first time ever I'm going oh, I don't know about this. I mean it's fleeting … So it's like hmm"* (PETA). The secondary data suggests that social value of occupational roles is important to women:

Anyway, I got disenchanted with tech from a values standpoint… I didn't think what I was doing mattered enough. So, I tried a career change. I went into Psychology […] and got a job in the field where I felt I'd be helping people. Turns out that field seemed even less 'helpful' to people than tech did (Lealea Design, website blog, n.d.).

The mechanism of *being* was less readily evident than other mechanisms. It has a metaphysical aspect and includes the humanness of the individual and traits such as an individual's reflectivity. The most obvious manner by which the mechanism of *being* surfaced was when participants' accounts showed a high level of reflectivity with regard to their own and other people's actions and circumstances. Indeed, in asking participants about their experiences, there was a sense that they were reflecting or realising something for the first time. For example, when asked about their future plans for children and continuing working in the industry, several responded with a long silence; visually, they appeared to be reflecting.

The influence of *emotions, ethics* and *being* can be further explained, to some extent, by drawing on previous research. Emotions such as stress surface in IT professionals as a result of the rapid technological changes characteristic of the industry ICT (Gallivan, 2004) and anxiety may influence women and minorities "more often and more deeply" (Tapia & Kvasny, 2004, p.88). This may

be a result of women facing higher performance pressure because of their increased visibility in the workplace in which they are a minority (Tapia & Kvasny, 2004). Emotions such as fun were seen as encouraging young women into ICT education pathways (Stockdale & Stoney, 2008) and multimedia in turn was identified by school age girls as being more 'fun' than IT (Turner, 2003).

The emotion of passion has been identified in previous research in the DCI context (Gill, 2007; Roan & Whitehouse, 2007; Deuze et al., 2007) and the IT context (Griffiths et al., 2005). Roan & Whitehouse's (2007) study identified passion as being an important employment trait: "The male senior manager maintained that he hired people with a 'passion for games' and 'a passion for programming'" (p.29). Consalvo (2008) proposed "one word" as being used to explain why women worked in the games industry–"passion" (p. 185).

Extant literature does not readily identify that ethics may be an important mechanism, perhaps because as Elliot (2003) recognised there is a similar sociological aversion to ethics, as the "objectivistically driven fear of emotion and passion" (p. 16). The agent-driven mechanism of *ethical* requires further research.

Women in the case study harnessed the agent-driven mechanisms of *emotion, ethics,* and *being* often in indirect ways. The most obvious manner was when they reflected on these aspects. For example, a participant showed a level of reflection about losing her passion for her role and noted she was planning to address the influence. *"I just knew that I don't have the energy and I don't have the passion for that any more. I certainly did but I grew out of it, so I need to get out of it now before I am stuck here, having to learn the next version"* (JO).

Strategies aiming to foster women's participation must promote the industry as being ethical. This can include illuminating the different types of products and practices that exist. For example, serious games such as *Darfur is Dying* have attracted praise for addressing social issues. Studies indicate that young women see other disciplines, such as education or psychology, as leading to careers that are more focused on solving human problems; consequently, they find these fields more attractive in comparison to IT (Agosto et al., 2008). One initiative that has drawn attention to the salience of ethics for IT workers is the *ITMillion* web site (Passion IT, 2011), which asks people to share their reasons for pursuing an ICT-related career. Respondents to the website emphasise that doctors and lawyers 'help people', thus suggesting that these careers are perceived as having societal value. This perspective is consistent with Margolis and Fisher's (2002) research, which indicated that female computer science majors are motivated to help the world, rather than simply learn algorithms. As Fullerton et al., (2008) suggested, a focus on the social value of games could attract women to the industry.

Relational Understanding of Influences

Although each one of the *Five Acts of Agency* has been discussed individually to date, there is a relational aspect between the different acts. As Table 2 illustrates, all *Five Acts of Agency* are evident when explaining the influence on a women's career (in the DCI) of becoming a mother. The case study revealed that women need *access* (Enabled Act) to accurate information to make decisions regarding maternity leave options. Women faced difficulties in relating to the industry as there were no 'working mother' role models in the industry; thus, they could not *imagine* (Connected Act) their continued participation as working mothers. Women's capacity to feel as though they *belonged* (Collaborative Act) in the workplace; that is, to

Table 2. The Five Acts of Agency and strategies for the event of motherhood

Act		Example of Environmental Influence	Possible Strategies for Stakeholders Such as Employers
Enabled	Access	Limited access to adequate information regarding maternity leave constrained participants' informed decisions.	Government and industry must provide career information on maternity leave options as a part of career planning.
Connected	Imagining	A lack of working mother role models left women not imaging their continued participation as a working mother.	Industry to promote images of working mothers; however, also recognise that working mothers need to retain their professional identity.
	Doing	The industry demands constant up skilling. Career breaks may be detrimental to maintaining skills.	Industry to facilitate access to resources that foster skill development when on maternity leave; for example, access to conferences.
Collaborative	Belonging	Cultural practices can leave working mothers feeling as though they are the 'odd ones out' in the workplace setting; particularly if they are only person in the organisation taking maternity leave.	Industry to facilitate communication among working mothers across organisations, so that they can share information and advice.
	Sharing	Workplace practices may leave working mothers feeling as though they are 'out the loop' whilst on maternity leave.	Employers to provide ongoing contact with those on parental leave (e.g., through email); give the opportunity to 'drop by'.
Creative	Problem-Solving	Working mothers face personal changes that may influence their ability to remain creative e.g. time constraints or changing values.	Industry to provide opportunities for creativity; need to recognise the need to be creative does not disappear with motherhood; it continues and may transform into other skills and ideas.
	Transforming		
Human	Emotion	Family friendly workplace practices can minimise emotions such as guilt. Motherhood will place demands on a person's emotions.	Organisations must allow some flexibility in work practices so that women can maintain their passion; workplace culture must not promote a sense of guilt (for example, if parents leave work early for parental purposes).
	Ethical		
	Being		

feel as though they were 'one of the boys' could also be challenged if they were the only team member to take maternity leave. Women's participation whilst on maternity leave was fostered if they could maintain their skills through *doing* (Connected Act). The difficulties women face in balancing work and life commitments could lead to their facing *emotions* (Human Act) of guilt. Such emotion prompted them to reflect on the value of staying in the industry. Thus, the *Five Acts of Agency* and ten agent-driven mechanisms help provide a more holistic understanding of the influence of motherhood. Furthermore, as Table 2 shows strategies can then be considered in a holistic manner.

Similarly, as Table 3 shows, women can draw on more than one agent driven mechanism in response to a particular environmental influence. For example, women require industry skills to participate in the DCI workforce. Developing skills draws on the agent driven mechanism of 'doing' (Connected Act). Developing skills fosters self-efficacy in the individual. In addition, developing industry relevant skills can then foster the agent-driven mechanisms of 'belonging' and 'sharing'(Collaborative Act), as knowing the industry jargon, such as that required for coding and programming, can help women fit into or belong to the workplace and skills can be shared with colleagues.

Table 3. Examples of environmental influences on women's participation in the DCI

Examples of Environmental Influences	Five Acts of Agency and 10 Agent Driven Mechanisms									
	Enabled		Connected	Collaborative		Creative		Human		
	1. Accessing	2. Imagining	3. Doing	4. Belonging	5. Sharing	6. Problem-Solving	7. Transforming	8. Emotion	9. Ethical	10. Being
Access to Computer and Software	●									
Skills Required			●							
Non Gendered Clothing in the Workplace				●						
Availability of Role Models	○	●								
Open Plan Workplace	○				●					
Training e.g. Mastering Jargon			●	○	○					
Playing Computer Games				○	○					
Coding Challenges						●				
Challenging Workplace Projects						●				
Workplace Stress								●		
Social Value of Games									●	
Childcare Responsibilities								●		○

●Key agent driven mechanism involved in responding to environmental influence   ○Other agent driven mechanisms involved

FUTURE RESEARCH DIRECTIONS

The case study findings provide a valuable insight into a wide range of influences; however, it is important to not simply present an endless list of constraints. To do so can make the problem of women's equitable participation almost seem to be an unsolvable phenomenon for the industry and an insurmountable challenge for the women wishing to pursue careers in the DCI. Accordingly, this chapter has not simply provided an insight into what influences women face but an account of how women have overcome constraints or embraced supports. Future research would refine these substantive insights, including greater in-depth consideration of specific influences identified from the empirical data.

Trauth, Quesenberry and Huang (2009) emphasise that when aiming to understand the complex phenomenon of women's participation in ICT, the core challenge lies in developing a theoretical understanding of the phenomenon; there is, they claim, a "challenge of how to theorize gender under representation" (p. 477). The *Acts of Agency* theory provides a fruitful theoretical approach with which to understand women's participation in the Digital Content Industry.

CONCLUSION

In conclusion the *Acts of Agency* theory provides a way to understand women's participation in the Australian DCI and also offers a new way of planning strategies that may foster women's participation. The theory can help explain the stories of participation that women in the Australian DCI have experienced. Highlighting the agent-driven mechanisms women have employed in their participation reveals a complex interaction between an individual and their environment; both are an influence on that individual's participation.

REFERENCES

Agosto, D., Gasson, S., & Atwood, M. (2008). Changing mental models of the IT professions: A theoretical framework. *Journal of Information Technology Education, 7*(1), 205–221.

Australian Bureau of Statistics (ABS). (2008). (Cat. No. 8515.0). *Digital game development services.* Canberra, Australia: ABS. Retrieved 15 Mar 2009 from http://www.abs.gov.au/AUSSTATS/abs@.nsf/Lookup/8515.0Main+Features12006-07?OpenDocument

Australian Human Rights Commission. (2013). *Women in male-dominated industries: A toolkit of strategies.* Retrieved 15 July from http://www.humanrights.gov.au/publications/women-male-dominated-industries-toolkit-strategies-2013

Bandura, A. (2002). Growing primacy of human agency in adaptation and change in the electronic era. *European Psychologist, 7*(1), 2–16. doi:10.1027//1016-9040.7.1.2

Beekhuyzen, J., & Clayton, K. (2004). ICT career perceptions: Not so geeky? In *Proceedings of the 1st International Conference on Research on Women in IT*, Kuala Lumpur, (pp. 28-30).

Betz, N. E., & Hackett, G. (1997). Applications of self-efficacy theory to the career assessment of women. *Journal of Career Assessment, 5*(4), 383–402. doi:10.1177/106907279700500402

Bhaskar, R. (1986). *Scientific realism and human emancipation.* London: Verso.

Blake, K. (2011). A woman in games: A personal perspective, 1993 – 2010. *International Journal of Gender, Science and Technology, 3*(1).

Castells, M. (1998). *The information age: Economy, society and culture. The rise of network society.* Oxford, UK: Blackwell.

Chen, S. (2009, April 15). *Play games to work smarter: Why it is more critical than ever that women play and develop games*. Retrieved 2011, from http://damedev.blogspot.com.au/2009/04/play-games-to-work-smarter-why-it-is.html

Connell, R. W. (1987). *Gender and power: Society, the person and sexual politics*. Sydney, Australia: Allen and Unwin.

Consalvo, M. (2008). Crunched by passion: Women game developers and workplace challenges. In Y. B. Kafai, C. Heeter, J. Denner, & J. Y. Sun (Eds.), *Beyond Barbie and Mortal Kombat* (pp. 177–192). Cambridge, MA: MIT Press.

DCITA. (2005, March). *Australian digital content industry futures plan*. Prepared for DCITA (Department of Communications, Information Technology and the Arts) by the Centre for International Economics. September 19, 2006 from http://www.dcita.gov.au/__data/assets/pdf_file/37474/Appendix_C.2_Australian_digital_content_futures.pdf

Deuze, M., Martin, C., & Allen, C. (2007). The professional identity of gameworkers. *Convergence*, *13*(4), 335–353. doi:10.1177/1354856507081947

Eweek. (2007, May 14). *Report: Techs gender gap widened by uninviting workplace*. Retrieved August 2008, from http://www.eweek.com/c/a/IT-Management/Report-Techs-Gender-Gap-Widened-by-Uninviting-Workplace/

Fullerton, T., Fron, J., Pearce, C., & Morie, J. (2008). Getting girls into the game: Towards a virtuous cycle. In Y. Kafai, C. Heeter, J., Denner, & J. Sun (Eds.), Beyond Barbie and Mortal Kombat: New perspectives on gender and gaming. Cambridge, MA: MIT Press.

Gallivan, M. J. (2004, Summer). Examining IT professionals' adaptation to technological change: The influence of gender and personal attributes. *The Data Base for Advances in Information Systems*. doi:10.1145/1017114.1017119

Geneve, A. (2013). *Women's participation in the Australian Digital Content Industry* (PhD thesis). Queensland University of Technology, Australia.

Giddens, A. (1993). *New rules of sociological method: A positive critique of interpretive sociologies*. New York: Basic Books.

Gill, R. (2002). Cool, creative and egalitarian? Exploring gender in project-based new media work in Europe. *Information Communication and Society*, *5*(1), 70–89. doi:10.1080/13691180110117668

Gill, R., & Pratt, A. (2008). In the social factory? Immaterial labour, precariousness and cultural work. *Theory, Culture & Society*, *25*(7-8), 1–30. doi:10.1177/0263276408097794

Gourdin, A. (2005). *Game developer demographics: An exploration of workforce diversity*. International Game Developers Association. Retrieved 24 Jan 2008 from http://www.igda.org/diversity/IGDA_ DeveloperDemographics_Oct05.pdf

Griffiths, M., Moore, K., Burns, B., & Richardson, H. (2007, Spring.). *The disappearing women: North West ICT project final report*. Funded by the European Social Fund (ESF). Retrieved Feb 2010 from http://usir.salford.ac.uk/9312/1/Griffiths_DW.pdf

Haines, L. (2004). *Why are there so few women in games?* United Kingdom: Research for Media Training North West.

Haukka, S., & Brow, B. (2010, January). *From education to work in Australia's creative digital industries: Comparing the opinions and practices of employers and aspiring creatives* (60Sox Report Vol. 2). Retrieved 19 June 2011 from http://www.apo.org. au/research/education-work-australias-creative-digital-industries

Hoonakker, P. L. T., Carayon, P., & Schoepke, J. (2006). Discrimination and hostility toward women and minorities in the IT workforce. In E. Trauth (Ed.), *Encyclopaedia of gender and information technology* (pp. 207–215). Hersey, PA: Idea Group Inc. doi:10.4018/978-1-59140-815-4.ch033

IGDA. (2005). *Game developer demographics: An exploration of workforce diversity comments on diversity.* Retrieved from http://archives.igda.org/diversity/IGDA_DeveloperDemographics_Oct05.pdf

Kvasny, L. Joshi, K. D., & Trauth, E. M. (2011). The influence of self-efficacy, gender stereotypes and the importance of IT skills on college students' intentions to pursue IT careers. In *Proceedings of the 2011 iConference*, Seattle, WA.

Lealea Design. (n. d.). *Women in tech: Asking the wrong questions.* Retrieved 2011, from http://www.lealea.net/blog/comments/women-in-tech-asking-the-wrong-questions/#ixzz0cRlJSESg

Major, D. A., Davis, D. D., Sanchez-Hucles, J. V., Germano, L. M., & Mann, J. (2006). IT workplace climate for opportunity and inclusion. In E. M. Trauth (Ed.), *Encyclopedia of gender and information technology* (pp. 856–862). Hershey, PA: IGI Global. doi:10.4018/978-1-59140-815-4.ch134

Margolis, J., & Fisher, A. (2002). *Unlocking the clubhouse.* Cambridge, MA: MIT.

McGrath-Coohan, J. M., & Aspray, W. (Eds.). (2006). *Women in information technology: Research on under-representation.* Cambridge, MA: MIT Press.

Moore, A. K., Griffiths, M., & Richardson, H. (2005a). Moving in, moving up, Moving out? A survey of women in ICT. *Information Systems*, 1–28.

Parberry, I., Kazemzadeh, M., & Roden, T. (2006). The art and science of game programming. In *Proceedings of the 37th SIGCSE Technical Symposium on Computer Science Education.* Houston, Texas, USA

Passion, I. T. (2011). *Technology is a great career choice because....* Retrieved 2011, from http://itmillion.com/

Perrons, D. (2003). The new economy and the work-life balance: Conceptual explorations and a case study of new media. *Gender, Work and Organization*, *10*(1), 65–93. doi:10.1111/1468-0432.00004

Prescott, J., & Bogg, J. (2010). The computer games industry: Women's experiences of work role in a male dominated environment. In A. Cater-Steel, & E. Cater (Eds.), *Women in engineering, science and technology: Education and career challenges* (pp. 138–158). Hershey, PA: Engineering Science Reference. doi:10.4018/978-1-61520-657-5.ch007

Roan, A., & Whitehouse, G. (2007). Women, information technology and waves of optimism: Australian evidence on mixed-skill jobs. *New Technology, Work and Employment*, *22*(1), 21–33. doi:10.1111/j.1468-005X.2007.00181.x

Stockdale, R., & Stoney, S. (2008). Generating a gender balance: Making introductory information systems courses a positive experience. *Australasian Journal of Information Systems, 15*(1).

Swanson, G., & Wise, P. (1996). *Digital futures: Women's employment in the multimedia industries.* Canberra, Australia: Commonwealth Government of Australia, Department of Employment, Education, Training and Youth Affairs. Retrieved from http://www.workplace.gov.au/NR/rdonlyres/CC7EFA3F-1E9F-4E77-ADC1%201A97C-884CADB/0/digitalfutures.PDF

Tapia, A., & Kvasny, L. (2004). Recruitment is never enough: Retention of women and minorities in the IT workplace. In *Proceedings of the ACM Conference on Computer Personnel Research: Careers, Culture, and Ethics in a Networked Environment*, Tucson, AZ (pp. 84-91).

Trauth, E. M. (2002). Odd girl out: An individual differences perspective on women in the IT profession. *Information Technology & People*, *15*(2), 98–118. doi:10.1108/09593840210430552

Trauth, E. M., Quesenberry, J., & Huang, H. (2009). Retaining women in the U.S. IT workforce: Theorizing the influence of organizational factors. *European Journal of Information Systems*, *18*(5), 476-497. doi: http://dx.doi.org/10.1057/ejis.2009.31

Trauth, E. M., Quesenberry, J., & Yeo, B. (2005). The influence of environmental context on women in the IT workforce. In *Proceedings of the 2005 ACM SIGMIS CPR Conference on Computer Personnel Research* (pp. 24 – 31). Atlanta, GA: ACM Press.

Trauth, E. M., Quesenberry, J. L., & Huang, H. (2008). A multicultural analysis of factors influencing career choice for women in the information technology workforce. *Journal of Global Information Management*, *16*(4), 1–23. doi:10.4018/jgim.2008100101

Turner, S. V., Bernt, P. W., & Pecora, N. (2002). Why women choose information technology careers: Educational, social and familial influences. In *Proceedings of the Annual Meeting of the American Educational Research Association*, New Orleans, LA.

Turner, T. (2003). Multimedia is much more fun but I still don't want to do IT. In *Proceedings of the 2003 Australian Women in IT Conference*. Retrieved September 19, 2006 from http://www.auswit.org/2003/papers/3-2_Turner.pdf

Webb, P., & Young, J. (2005). Perhaps it's time for a fresh approach to ICT gender research? *Journal of Research and Practice in Information Technology*, *37*(2), 147–160.

ADDITIONAL READING

Archer, M. S., & Bhaskar, R. (Eds.). (1998). *Critical Realism: essential readings. Critical Realism--interventions*. London: Routledge.

Bandura, A. (1989). Human Agency in Social Cognitive Theory. *The American Psychologist*, *44*, 1175–1184. doi:10.1037/0003-066X.44.9.1175 PMID:2782727

Cunningham, S., Cutler, T., Ryan, M., Hearn, G., & Keane, M. (2003). Research and Innovation Systems in the Production of Digital Content and Applications. Content and Applications, Creative Industries Cluster Study Volume III. Commonwealth of Australia (DCITA). Canberra.

Geneve, A., & Ganito, C. (2011). Women and Technology: Five Acts of Acts of Agency. In Araya, D. Breindl, Y, Houghton, T (eds.) Nexus: New Intersections in Internet Research. Peter Lang: USA ISBN 978-1-4331-0970-6 pb.

Giddens, A. (1988). Social Theory Today. In A. Giddens, & J. Turner (Eds.), *Social Theory Today*. Stanford: Stanford University Press.

Griffiths, M., Keogh, C., Moore, K., Richardson, H., & Tattersall, A. (2006). Inclusion through the ages? Gender, ICT workplaces and lifestage experiences. In J. Kendall, & D. Howcroft et al. (Eds.), *Social inclusion: societal and organisational implications for information systems* (pp. 153–168). New York: Springer. doi:10.1007/0-387-34588-4_11

Hayes, E. (2008). Girls, gaming, and trajectories of technological expertise. In Y. B. Kafai, C. Heeter, J. Denner, & J. Sun (Eds.), *Beyond Barbie and Mortal Kombat: New Perspectives on Gender, Games, and Computing*. Boston: MIT Press.

Jeppson, S. (2005). Critical Realism as an Approach to Unfolding Empirical Findings: Thoughts on Fieldwork in South Africa on SMEs and Environment. *The Journal of Transdisciplinary Environmental Studies*, 4(1).

Lang, C. (2007). Twenty-first Century Australian Women and IT: Exercising the power of choice. *Computer Science Education*, 17(3), 215–226. doi:10.1080/08993400701538120

Layder, D. (1998). *Sociological practice: linking theory and social research*. London: Sage.

Lent, R. W., Brown, S. D., & Hackett, G. (1996). Career development from a social cognitive perspective. In D. Brown, & L. Brooks (Eds.), *Career choice and development* (pp. 373–421). San Francisco, CA: Jossey-Bass Inc.

Lewis, P., & Simpson, R. (2007). *Gendering Emotions in Organizations*. Basingstoke: Palgrave.

Macknight, J. (2001). Nerdy image and blokish behaviour drive women away from IT. *Computer Weekly*, March 8.

Morgan, A. J., Quesenberry, J. L., & Trauth, E. M. (2004). Exploring the Importance of Social Networks in the IT Workforce: Experiences with the 'Boy's Club.' *Proceedings of the Americas Conference on Information Systems* (New York, August).

KEY TERMS AND DEFINITIONS

Acts of Agency Theory: A theory concerned with the participation of individuals within social contexts. Developed by Geneve (2013), the foundation of the theory lies in a combination of human agency theory and the ontological stance of critical realism.

Agent-Driven Mechanisms: The abstraction of agent driven mechanisms involves recognising that the agent is doing something–an action, an act– that has a causal effect.

Australian Digital Content Industry (DCI): A term used by the Australian government to describe the industry developing the following products: interactive visual effects and animation (including virtual and augmented reality and 3D elements), interactive multimedia (e.g. websites, CD-ROM's, mobile applications), computer and online games, educational multimedia (e-learning) and interactive digital film & TV production and film & TV post-production content.

Critical Realism: Stemming from the work of Bhaskar (1986), Critical Realism offers an ontological approach which understands the world through the recognition of three different but interrelated strata or domains: 1) a person's experiences (experience domain); 2) the actual events (actual domain) and 3) underpinning mechanisms (real domain).

Human Agency: A theoretical standpoint encompassing sociological theorists such as Anthony Giddens and Albert Bandura. Human Agency theory recognises that individuals have free will and have the capacity to exercise that free will in response to their environmental context.

Mechanisms: Critical Realism views mechanisms as being the underlying (and possibly unobservable) causal tendencies.

Section 3

Future Outlook

Profile 13: Sabine Hahn

Sabine Hahn had been working in the wireless gaming industry in both the United Kingdom and Germany, for 10 years before currently taking a break to focus more on the academic side of gaming.

According to Jesper Juul ("A Casual Revolution", 2010) there are three main types of gamers: returning players, (ex-) hardcore players and the players who discover games casually, I am one of the last group.

I grew up in the former East Germany and until the wall came down in 1989 (I was 14 at the time) I was never really in contact with any kind of gaming console. I do remember that I had a friend whose grandpa (from West Germany) gave her an Atari Commodore and some games including Frogger but can't really remember whether that was shortly before or after '89. However videogames did not play any role in my life until much later.

In my early 20s I moved into a flat-share while studying at university with two young men one of whom owned a PlayStation 2, and gaming rapidly became important. The boys spent most of their spare time together with friends in our living room, playing car racing or snowboarding games, but even though I enjoyed playing, I could not say that I was hooked in anyway. (I clearly had not had the "Pull", according to Jesper Juul)

After finishing university in 2002 I decided to go abroad in order to gain some work experience in another culture, and I was also struggling to find a job at home with my degree in Sociology, Journalism and Cultural Studies. I moved to London in February 2003 and started as an intern with a company that was engaged in various projects in the telecommunication sector, amongst others and they were trying to make some money via mobile content.

Although I'd received other offers as an intern, I chose Telecom One as they were the only company paying interns, but also because they were interesting to me as a technology corporation. The other internships would have been stereotypical female 'Marketing Assistant' roles, and I clearly could not see myself wearing nice dresses and lipstick when going into the office! I should add that since I can remember I spent most of my (spare) time with boys, doing boys' activities and playing with boys' toys – somehow I am more used to being the only girl around rather than working in a female world.

Telecom One offered me a job after 3 months of my internship, however after 6 months with the company they no longer had enough work for me and I was let go. I am still grateful for my first ever job experience and the direction it gave my career. At this time, I had a boyfriend who was working for Gameloft and through our combined experiences; I just knew I wanted to stay in the "wireless gaming arena".

After this first job I applied quite randomly to a South Korean Mobile Games Company called Com2uS with a goal to get a 'proper' job within the wireless gaming industry. I was hired as 'Assistant Manager' and I was the first European employee they'd had! It was an interesting phase, but it ended after one year with, as I would describe it, now, looking back, a cultural misunderstanding. The South Koreans just could not cope with the fact that I was outspoken and quite direct, and I just could not cope with the fact that women should not be as outspoken and direct!

Following Com2us I went to work as Key Account Manager for the London based Macrospace, and although I'd had interviews with some larger companies like THQ and Namco I did not regret joining a smaller company. In the three years I'd been with Macrospace, (who shortly after I joined, were taken over by an American company and rebranded as Glu Mobile,) I developed a 'proper' career, being promoted every few months. I really did enjoy my time with Glu because of the exceptional speed of the business, the exciting and partly glamorous experiences (Glu went on the NASDAQ in 2006) but mainly because I had great bosses and mentors throughout these years, specifically Kristian Segerstrale, whom I still admire for her people management skills.

At the end of 2006 I went back to Germany to open up a German subsidiary for Glu and also for personal reasons. However, after a while I realized that I'd worked too hard for too long and I was feeling a little tired with my career at Glu and I decided (although it wasn't easy for me) to leave when an opportunity at Electronic Arts Germany came along in 2007. In December 2007 I started my new role as Sales & Marketing Director GSAB at EA in Cologne.

Once again, I realized how rare women in this business are. While at Glu, I at least had some other female colleagues, including one counterpart in the sales team. But at EA Germany where I was at director level there was only one other girl in the same situation – out of approximately 10 directors only 2 were girls. I ran a team of 5 guys all of whom I needed to recruit myself, and one lady, all of the recruits were older than me. I truly enjoyed my position an at EA, although it was hard in the beginning to adapt to a huge company since I would say I am more a 'start-up' kind of worker. I enjoy creativity, dynamism, independence and challenges more than a clear set of rules and guidelines.

From May 2009 – August 2010 I was following my 2nd career, I gave birth to my girls (female twins) and stayed at home until they started going to a day nanny when they were about a year old. Although I was fully committed to returning to work, I decided to only work part time (28 hours a week) in order to be able to be with my daughters. Since I was only working part-time I could not go back to my previous Director job and instead I worked as a Senior Business Manager (still in Wireless Games) at EA. However, after 3 interesting years EA and I decided to go our separate ways.

After the last turn in my career I decided to take a break, not only for my career but more importantly for myself. My husband (an Ex-Disney, Ex-Gameloft, Ex-Nokia employee), had recently become an independent consultant, and we decided together that I should pursue something just for myself and it did not take me long to realize my "plan B".

I am currently about to start writing my PhD, which in Germany is quite a substantial project of at least 3 years duration with the aim of becoming a teacher in Games Studies (or worst case scenario become a consultant) one day. Although it's early days with this project I have a passion for my PhD topic: Female careers in the gaming industry. My university background (Sociology, Media and cultural studies) is a great match for the kind of research I am aiming to do. I want to examine why there are so few women in games, how they feel about it and what games organisations have to say about this. Although only just starting to walk on this academic path I do enjoy it as I realize how important this topic is and how exciting times are for Game Studies are right now.

Looking back at my 10 year games industry career so far I have one key question in mind (which is the reason why I am seriously interested in examining the situation from an academic point of view) - "Why are there so few women in games and why does it matter which sex you are?"

To put it in context: at every single event I've ever been too, in most of the meetings I've held, and even sometimes internally, it (almost) always did matter for everyone except me that I was female. I never understood why it needs to be my sex / gender which is subject of discussion instead of my work. Since I could never be the Barbie style female colleague I automatically fulfilled the other cliché of a masculine and tough woman, and one not very likeable! This was just what I got used to and I never really had a problem, but what I still don't understand is why women do not support each other in business (in my experience), and why men often try to out-do female colleagues instead of trying to benefit from the gender diversity. I've never had an issue with my gender and I am clearly not a feminist but I do start to doubt why this business which I still love and admire so much and was my "home" for the past 10 years, is still so male driven although there are millions of arguments to favour work diversity.

So why do I love the games industry so much? It's hard and easy to explain at the same time. The games industry workforce is a very talented crowd with a unique blend of characters. I have been lucky enough to meet some fantastic individuals over the past 10 years and made great friends across the globe, some of whom are still within my close circle. My husband I met very romantically at CeBIT (a German technology fair) at the Siemens booth (when they were still making mobile phones)! In addition the games industry has an extraordinary atmosphere starting with the jeans & trainers "dress-code" which I personally enjoyed very much during those years, the colloquial way people speak together and last but not least the "Work hard, play hard, party hard" attitude which I've experienced in every organisation. However at the same time the games industry is at the forefront of technology and of most economies in modern societies. The revenue level the games industry has reached over the past 10-20 years is more than substantial; games surpass the music and film industries and there are still super exciting projects to be made and meetings to be held etc, etc. It's just been very thrilling and "sexy" to play in the front of house within this industry. I could go on and on but it seems there are plenty of non-tangible aspects, which I can't even try to describe.

Due to my true passion for the industry and perhaps because I love keeping my illusions I am looking forward to still being a part of the gaming industry 20 years from now, but within a truly diverse, more balanced environment. Eventually I hope to turn my very personal experience as being "the only girl in the village" (which isn't too surprising with an estimated 6% women in the industry) into an academic contribution with my PhD project which I hope will help to identify some of the patterns in this industry that need to be changed.

As for the gaming habits – I've never been a 'gamer' myself but outside of my initial gaming experience in my first flat-share described earlier, I would say I became a casual gamer during my years in the industry. I've been addicted to Tetris, Zuma and Bejeweled at times (all on mobile) and of course I developed an understanding of the products since I needed to sell them. Before my children were born we had a PS3 and Wii which I enjoyed playing with occasionally. Although I am never likely to become a hardcore-player, I am, now hooked by the "art-form" of video-games in various ways.

Profile 14: Elizabeth Richardson

Elizabeth Richardson has grown up with gaming and now runs a channel on YouTube that centres around playing and reviewing video games. The channel started in January 2011 and has been growing ever since.

I remember the first game I ever played, I was probably about five or six and I had a vague understanding of moving a little yellow bird through obstacles in order to reach and free his lady friend that had been trapped by a big blue walrus. The game was New Zealand Story and that was the beginning. After that I was forever pulling at my dad's sleeve to show me more games. He eventually built me a low powered desktop computer and filled it with small games like Arkanoid and Tetris, as well as installing Disney's The Jungle Book with its whopping 12 floppy disks for me to play.

I have an older brother who also liked games, and I feel that is one of the main reasons I fell into gaming so easily. I wanted to copy him and play all the games he was playing, even those not suited to my age range. The first console we played together was the PlayStation 2. Before then, I had the Sega Megadrive and PlayStation all to myself, staying up on school nights to complete the campaigns of the playable characters in Tekken 3, and refusing to give up the fight in Streets of Rage.

Growing up, my other interests included the arts. I loved to draw, and sometimes combined this with my gaming. Lara Croft was a favourite subject of mine until the age of about 11 when I became more interested in drawing real people. My connection between games and art ended there temporarily. I still recognised the beauty of games that could be achieved, but I no longer actively participated in combining the two.

At school I dedicated as much time as possible to painting and drawing in the art rooms and when it came to decided my choices for GCSE's, Art was the first on the list, which I also followed through in my A Levels along with History and English. My art tutor was the one that suggested I go onto study Illustration, advice I took by doing a Foundation degree at Wimbledon University of Arts, and then a Bachelor's degree in Illustration at the University of Hertfordshire.

During my time at university, I explored the realms of online gaming. I wasn't fully able to participate without a headset and microphone, but I enjoyed listening to others talk during team games. I noticed I never heard other girls' voices while playing, so it took me a long time to decide whether to engage in chatter when I did get the equipment to use team chat. When I did take the risk and said hello, I noticed an increase in messages asking for my number, or telling me to 'get off your boyfriend's account'. These made me feel very uncomfortable, so I went silent again, though never stopping play.

After a while, I honed the skill of reading people's chatter to know whether or not I could speak without receiving too much attention. This eventually led to me meeting some members of a gaming clan called Dogs of War Gaming, or DoWG for short. I joined the community and was exposed to the good side of gaming. The members there were open and non-judgmental, and they also didn't treat me like something special. I had made a good group of friends to game with and that was all that mattered to me. I was able to engage fully in team games which led to my skill improving and also was no longer subject to the usual comments I received that were either abusive or intrusive to my privacy.

When I left university, I did my best to find part time work to get by as well as illustration work to further my career. I did manage one small job working in a chocolate store, but the contract only lasted a few months. The economy had begun its decline at this point and it was becoming increasingly difficult to find work. In this time I gamed more, as well as finding useful things to do with my time. While watching some videos on YouTube, I discovered a girl making 'Let's Play' videos, recording herself playing through a game and adding her own commentary. I enjoyed watching the whole series as it reminded me of when I used to watch my brother play. Although I wasn't playing the game myself, I got the experience of the game and still felt involved. I decided it was something I would like to try, and so, for Christmas in 2011, I gifted myself with a capture card and a headset to record my own videos.

When I began my YouTube channel, I didn't have any structure or any clue as to what I was doing. I just played games, recorded and had fun. Gradually I began to get more views and comments on my videos, the vast majority of them were positive.

As time went on, I recorded and posted gameplay videos regularly, developing a schedule that my subscriber base became used to and my channel grew steadily in popularity. This eventually led to my channel being partnered by RPM, Maker Studios. Being partnered allowed me to earn revenue through allowing small unobtrusive ads to be overlaid in my videos. This moment marked a point where I felt that what I was doing had some validity, and it was more than just making videos and having fun. I gained some subscribers that commented regularly, and I understood that I was developing a relationship with my viewers akin to a friendship, and this in turn made my videos more entertaining for the regulars.

There was some negative attention aimed at me being a female, comments making out that it was the only reason I was doing so well, but those comments were few and far between and easily ignored. I feel lucky that I have the type of personality that does not get bothered by or retaliate to the kinds of comments I was receiving. I'm not sure I would have had the same gratifying experiences in my gaming life if I'd have let myself be bullied and let them control my pride.

Looking across the YouTube Gaming community, there are some wonderfully strong women that do what they do because they enjoy it and love it. I feel that within this community there is a growing sense of equality and it's becoming easier for women to be accepted into the gaming world if they have an interest in it. I would like to see more women involved in the development process of gaming, as I feel that even this simple version of diversity would add to a richer gaming experience in general.

At the moment my gaming career on YouTube is very new, and though currently I earn very little money from it, I put what I can towards improving and growing it. I feel I can potentially create a living from my channel, but at the moment I am keeping my options open. I would like to use the networking powers I've gained to perhaps turn my art towards gaming again, perhaps in development. I don't think my gender will hold me back, it hasn't so far.

Profile 15: Faye Windsor-Smith

Faye Windsor-Smith joined Codemasters as a Q.A. Tester in 2011 and is currently working as a Monetisation Games Designer for their Southam Digital development team.

I've always loved games but feel like I kind of fell into the industry. I studied English Literature at university more through a love of the subject than any kind of career goal, and this lack of direction probably somewhat prepared me for the global recession which was in full swing when I graduated in 2009. I managed to talk my way into a temporary Christmas job at GAME on sheer nervous adrenaline, where they and I quickly discovered that I have no aptitude for or inclination towards trying to sell people products they aren't already interested in. Once they realised this, my days were clearly numbered, and I moved into a job designing and maintaining a website for a small independent clothing company. Whilst the work was fun and rewarding I've never been particularly interested in fashion, and when a friend mentioned that a nearby games company was hiring testers it sounded too good an opportunity to pass up.

Despite a ravenous appetite for playing games I really had very little idea of how the industry worked, and Quality Assurance was definitely an eye-opener in that respect. I can't say I had a definite career plan at this point and was more interested in gathering information about how games got made rather than gunning for a particular position.

I was initially pretty nervous when I started at Codemasters; it often felt like people were talking in a language I didn't understand... I had no idea what JIRA was (bug-reporting software) or what OOW stood for (out of world), what exactly 'popping' and 'z-fighting' were, or even what qualified a bug for C2 rather than C3 status. Luckily I was working with an amazing team of people, and they were more than willing to help me out or share their knowledge when I needed them to. I tried to be as useful as I could to them, too - my background in English was beneficial regarding this, as there wasn't a whole host of people queuing up to proofread text strings and I was more than happy to nitpick my way through them!

Working in Q.A. involved lots of overtime, but this meant we gathered a lot of holiday, which I mainly spent travelling. It also meant I got to know my colleagues at their rawest; at 11p.m. on bank holiday evenings, scoffing down half-price pizza and energy drinks and staring, bleary-eyed, at the latest build. You'll have to trust me when I say it was more fun than it sounds, and although I may possibly be viewing this through distinctly rose-tinted glasses, I believe that's a testament to the guys and girls I worked with.

The ratio of women in Q.A. is probably slightly higher than in development, but still tended to average out at about one in fifteen. This situation meant that new female members of staff were treated with more than average curiosity, although only a very small minority of staff were in any way disruptive or less than respectful. Occasionally this became a problem, when attention was drawn more too social developments than work. In these cases I can't help but think the women involved were sometimes unfairly negatively affected.

There are a lot of very talented people in Q.A. and many of them are looking for opportunities within development, so it's easy to feel like a lack of games-specific qualifications is a massive disadvantage. I worked hard, but I also seemed to be rather lucky with timing, managing to prove myself useful whilst work was available, and gaining a permanent position after about a year. Around 6 months later a couple of Monetisation Design positions became available in another department within the company. I applied and was pleasantly surprised when I got one.

The second position was filled by another female member of Q.A. Despite being very different in our approaches to the work we were given, I felt that our approaches complemented each other and that we mutually benefited from working together. The company later underwent extensive restructuring, and our two roles went down to one. It's the first time I've knowingly been in head-to-head competition with another woman for a job, and whilst I expect that it's not a common occurrence within the industry, I can only say it was just as horrible as being in competition with a man... except that I felt like people were less able to say I only kept the job because I'm female.

Currently, my job involves working to design iOS game features which fall outside the remit of pure gameplay, including monetisation, acquisition and retention features, and developing game economies. I spend a lot of time using Word and Excel to create documents for the programmers and artists to use when implementing different features of the games. We work using agile development methods, and have daily stand-up meetings which help to co-ordinate everyone on the team – these have also been an invaluable learning experience for someone as new to development as I am. These were, however, really intimidating at first!

I was open about having no previous design experience when applying for the role, but had played enough social browser games to have picked up some key aspects of monetisation design, and have been learning more and more since. I love finding out what people love about games, and I love trying to make games that people will love.

I'm the only girl in my department at present. I don't think this is as intimidating as it perhaps sounds; the vast majority of my friends outside of work are male and I think I'd feel slightly more out of my comfort zone if working with a female majority, if only because I've never really done it before. I've found that some of the guys I work with tend to be slightly less comfortable with the situation, than I am and, at least at first, will talk about toning down their language and warn others against swearing in front of me. It's very courteous, but entirely unnecessary!

On the whole I feel very accepted in my workplace - much more so than in the wider gaming community. It's the little things that can be frustrating; for example, when shopping for games by myself, sales assistants see no problem with asking me if they can help. If I drag my partner in with me, he will immediately become the target of their attention, and I'm left to browse unhindered. I've lost count of the amount of times he's been asked how he feels about my profession when I tell someone new what I do.

Nowadays I play a lot of mobile games, and it feels good to be able to tell friends it's for research, even though they don't usually accept it as a valid excuse! I still make time for console games, although as I get older there seems to be less and less of them and my 'to play' backlog is always growing. I've always favoured RPGs for their strong story elements... and also because my hand-eye co-ordination leaves much to be desired. The first game I ever became totally obsessed with was Final Fantasy VII, and I don't think my tastes have changed a whole lot since, although they have broadened somewhat. My other all-time favourite games include Psypets, a browser-based pet game based on Maslow's Theory of Hierarchy, Creatures 2, an artificial life simulator, Catherine, essentially a puzzle game, and Monkey Island, which needs no introduction I'm sure. I try to balance gaming with reading, partly because I feel it's easy to overspecialise in games to the point where it feels like they're the only form of media available, but mostly because I really enjoy it.

I love games design and have so much still to learn that I'm currently wholly focused on my present position, rather than thinking too much about what comes next. At some point in the future, however, I'd like to be more involved in narrative design, and I currently take every chance I can get to help out with writing tasks within the studio.

I had a conversation with a friend recently about how being in the games industry affects our self-perception. Whilst he said that he felt like his job did not define him, I think I feel a little differently; as someone in a minority, it's easy to see the combination as a pretty solid identity in and of itself. I have to work to make sure that it doesn't become *all* I am. At the same time, conversely, I have to guard against being sexist myself, as without a lot of female friends and colleagues around, it can be easier to accept negative female stereotypes and simply believe myself 'one of the guys' or the exception to the rule… which is as stupid as it is self-important.

Working in the industry has been an overwhelmingly positive experience and I don't think I'll ever want to leave, although I'm worried that at a certain point in my life I'll be seen as a liability for being of a "maternal" age. I hope that doesn't restrict my career opportunities in the future.

Profile 16: Phil Goddard

Phil Goddard is an obsessive compulsive Creative Director with a 14 year career in Digital Media, Casual Games and Virtual Worlds. Phil has designed and led projects for The Cartoon Network, EA Games, Monty Python, Nickelodeon and the BBC, including the casual MMO Game for the 2014 summer blockbuster movie 'Legends of Oz: Dorothy's Return'. Phil now leads a new indie studio in Manchester focusing on a new gaming project, MMA Federation

The topic of women working in video games has never historically been a 'topic' to me, let alone something I should be concerned with. It was probably early in 2013 after reading an article on Gamasutra and then slowly watching the snowball get bigger as more and more people started to voice their opinions on the subject.

Since then I've written a couple of blog posts and tried to passively promote women in games. I say 'passively' because as with any subject of this nature, in my opinion, if you push it too hard, the pendulum could swing the other way and it can be perceived that you are being prejudice towards males.

As fate would have it, 2013 saw me hiring 3 young women as part of a new team I was responsible for building. These weren't the cliché admin jobs, or recruitment, or marketing positions, but 3D Artist and Illustration roles. So now in 2014 I've had a little more experience of working with women in creative roles within video games.

I've been working in digital media and games for 14 years, preferring smaller / indie teams and focusing on the creative side of projects. I've had a variation of job titles including Creative Director, Product VP and Company Director.

Over the past few years I've worked on a variety of different games. My path into games in general was actually less traditional than most, coming from a digital media background, producing small casual games for clients. This then transitioned into Virtual Worlds where I spent over 5 years working with Dubit on their Virtual Worlds Platform, and then in 2012 opted to move again, this time to focus on Tablet and Mobile games.

I'm currently working on a brand new concept, pioneering Real-World Rewards within casual games, and in this instance, within the world of Mixed Martial Arts.

Our current product and our future products will be aimed at the core target audience for the theme of the game. That is to say as a priority we will not try to force a product with a specific theme or culture, towards a demographic that may not be attracted to it. However, with that said, we DO want our products to be widely accessible and to provide content for players of different dispositions and talents.

For example, with our current MMA project, we highly anticipate a core target audience of 18-35 males, but as with the MMA industry at the moment, more and more women are turning to the sport, and coupling this with our tablet / mobile casual game, we may see a rise in female players as time goes on.

Our next project, built on the same mechanics, will be built for an entirely different industry, which will be split equally between male and female users, and probably slightly younger. Our ultimate goal is to produce a variety of products for different demographics, thus leading us to have a diverse team within the studio.

Within the teams I've been part of and helped build I've always tried to promote a non-hierarchical structure, where managers and directors can work freely, openly and on the same level as production staff. Granted, this is a lot easier to do in smaller teams.

Our current studio is relatively new, so the gender ratio is slightly skewed towards male, due to the theme and nature of the project, and my social group of colleagues. At the time of writing this there are 6 of us in the company, with 3 more roles waiting to be filled. Out of the current six we have one female, our Project Manager, but we hope we will have more women in the studio with the fulfilment of the upcoming roles.

In the staff that I recruit, first and foremost, I always look for immediate talent and future potential. I love to see proof of their proactivity and ambition. You can usually see this in final year pieces in University or if they have taken a leap of faith and worked on their own projects. Ambition and proactivity should be nurtured and encouraged.

Looking forward I never really want to see the team getting too large that people don't know one another. If the company starts to get to this kind of size, we will no doubt open a second office and work with two separate teams.

I have never tried to proactively maintain a balance of male and female staff within a studio, however I have always tried to find a healthy balance between ideas, styles, creativity and talent. With this ethos, and particularly in recent years, this has naturally led to more of a healthy balance between men and women in the studio.

At Rivet Studios, 1/3 of the production team were female with a 70/30 split. If you only consider my Creative Team, this was closer to 50/50. Not only that, as much as I admired the entire team, one of the most talented individuals was female.

Taking a step back it's always difficult promoting a certain ethos in an industry or work environment, be it gender, sexual orientation, age, whatever. There's always a taboo subject to tip-toe around. In the UK, we cannot officially state that 'we're hiring the female applicant because she's female'.

However, in my recent experiences, I've actually found that women show more enthusiasm and ambition. They're hungrier in the games industry, as if they have something to prove. They have all the talents of 'the guys' in the studio, but when the work needs to be done, they are not as easily distracted.

So we cannot officially promote policies to simply 'hire more women', however what we can ask applicants is proof of proactivity, ambition, self-motivated projects etc. and I could probably suggest with confidence that the applicants coming out on top would be female, or at the very least an even split.

Having a more balanced studio in terms of gender, I feel, brings a certain maturity to the group. I don't necessarily mean this in terms of experience; I just feel that women tend to be more 'professional' when they need to be. This can be as simple as organising work load, taking notes in a meeting, making sure a discussion stays on topic etc. They still bring the passion, excitement and enthusiasm, but in my experience can control it methodically. Obviously this is a generalisation and I am speaking purely from my own experiences.

In terms of women excelling more than men in the workplace and gravitating towards more senior roles leads me back to their will and desire to achieve more. Personally I haven't worked with women in a studio long enough to see anybody in particular be promoted through the ranks, however there is one individual who I greatly admire for all of the above reasons. The person in question joined our studio at the time as a 3D Artist, leaning more towards the technical side. Very quickly she became involved with other aspects of production, and even later, with us being a small studio, became our Lead QA. She had the ability to wear many hats, and excelled at everything she did. Even though she had natural talent, I also saw the potential in everyone else, it's just for some reason, she found a way to be slightly more focused and professional in her career.

With regard to encouraging more women to work in games I really don't think the 'industry' has to do much other than to stop 'discouraging' it. In my experience there are many who 'say' there are no issues with gender, sexual orientation or age, but in reality there actually are. There still seems to be this inherited lingering feeling that the games industry is an 'all boys' club', at least here in the UK.

I have always worked and been primarily based in the UK, so the majority of my perceptions are with UK studios. However, I spent a large amount of time working in Helsinki and Espoo in Finland. The company I worked with was actually founded by a woman with a background in creative, and although I'm unsure if she promoted a balance in gender equality, the company she built seemed to have a fairly even split in males and females, with females in roles such as design, illustration and research. My experiences of working in Finland in terms of gender equality were very different to that in the UK.

Tracking back and observing the evolution in games, let's suggest the 'video games industry' really starting to get traction in the early 1990s. I myself was fortunate enough to have an Atari 65XE at the age of 11, and my earliest memories of video games were Gauntlet, Centipede, Loadrunner and Bruce Lee. This means there was an industry that was starting to grow that needed a new breed of employee. We saw programmers coming from software development, we saw artists coming from comics and illustration backgrounds; employees from this era didn't COME from games, they PIONEERED it!

Back in 1990, there were not as many women in work, and the women who were working, they almost certainly weren't drawing cartoon characters or programing computer software. So this new breed of game employees in 1990 was probably almost all men, from a male-oriented workforce.

Fast forward 24 years and we now find ourselves in literally the next generation of game industry employees. We're just about at the time now where we will start to see those earlier pioneers beginning to retire or think about retiring as the 'new breed' start to take their place. Of course this has happened naturally over the years; however the people who were in the industry in 1990 will no longer be responsible for holding the torch over the coming years.

Please don't misinterpret what I am saying; I am not suggesting that all men in 1990 who worked in games were against women in the industry, but as with any industry, people 'get used' to things being a certain way, and the majority of us like routine. They didn't set out to have a male dominated workplace, it just 'was'.

Earlier I touched on the subject of 'theme' in a project. In recent years, with the shift or evolution in games is becoming much more widespread i.e. mobile and tablet games, Nintendo Wii etc. there is reason to believe the audience will grow and evolve with it. Indeed we're seeing more women playing games, younger children are exposed to games, games are used in education, and much more. The audience for video games is growing at a rapid rate, so why not the individuals who work in games?

This also leads me on to the types of games the industry is producing at present. Last year I attended just one University Presentation evening, focusing on Game Design and art. Although there were more males than females in the group of about 30 students, the vast majority of portfolios and final year projects I saw were extremely similar. Most projects were oriented around first person shooters, containing some sort of hard-core hero with a big sword or gun! They were talented individuals, but their scope on creating truly unique games, I feel, was floored by the majority of games in the 'mainstream games industry'... the same 'mainstream industry' led by men.

Don't get me wrong, I love my mainstream games as much as anyone else, such as Assassin's Creed, GTA and Gears of War, however in another ten years, when someone asks me what my favourite games are, I'll probably still be referencing Monkey Island and Gauntlet. These games came from an era where there were free thinkers and people looking to pioneer a new generation and industry! These games were produced by a diverse group of people with just one common connection... they loved games!

So to summarise, I feel regardless of gender, sexual orientation, personal preferences and background, it really does not matter who we are in games and who makes up our teams, providing the individuals involved are true to video games, are passionate about what they do and want to push forward to the next chapter and pioneer a new generation of video game veterans.

I was raised to believe that excellence is the best deterrent to racism or sexism. And that's how I operate my life. - Oprah Winfrey

Chapter 8
Professional Socialization in STEM Academia and its Gendered Impact on Creativity and Innovation[1]

Gloria-Sophia Warmuth
Vienna University of Economics and Business, Vienna

Edeltraud Hanappi-Egger
Vienna University of Economics and Business, Vienna

ABSTRACT

The chapter focuses on internal professionalization processes in STEM academia and their impact on creativity and innovation capacity. The discussion looks at how internal structures and value systems in STEM academia are used to shape the professional self-understanding of members. Exemplified by a higher education institution in the field of science, engineering, technology and math we show how gendered exclusion and inclusion is established structurally. Restrictive and rigid professional scripts and role expectations are identified as the main obstacles to greater potentials for creativity and innovation.

INTRODUCTION

The lack of women in the fields of science, technology, engineering and math (STEM) is a persistent phenomenon, and one that provokes widespread discussion. Hence academics as well as practitioners are searching for ways to attract more women into these professions. In particular, it is argued that the creativity and innovation potential of entire sectors suffer from this low gender diversity (see also Hanappi-Egger, 2011).

Science, technology, engineering and math are seen as professional fields requiring both creativity and innovative thinking, which serve not only to drive these particular sectors but also society as a whole. Research on creativity has traditionally focused on individuals and their creative capabilities (Guilford, 1970). Industries with a high demand for creativity and innovation have generally relied on hiring creative staff to achieve their goals. In the meantime more and more studies are looking at the impact of work culture and

DOI: 10.4018/978-1-4666-6142-4.ch008

conditions in attracting, promoting and binding creative individuals and creative thinking (Amabile, 1996; Henry, 2001). Working conditions and organizational structures are now considered to impact the creative capacity of staff. Since creativity is seen as "the production of novel and useful ideas" (Amabile, 1996, p. 1), organizations must foster an environment that permits and indeed encourages thinking and behaviour that is different from the status quo; to some extent creativity necessarily challenges given and accepted ways of doing. Reflecting this line of research, the current chapter attempts to answer the question: How does academia in STEM, use their internal values and norms to mainstream (not to say male-stream) the professional self-understanding of their members, and how does this consequently limit the creative potential of the field?

The chapter is structured as follows: First the topic of professional socialization and its gendered nature is introduced. Second, based on Barley's structuration model of careers, the role of gender scripts in mainstreaming in STEM organizations is examined. This theoretical discussion is followed by a case study conducted at an Austrian higher education institution of STEM. This study will give an in-depth view of an institution, examining both its organizational and professional culture. We identify rigid professional understandings that can produce feelings of unease in some actors, leading to exclusion of those individuals unwilling to play by the rules. Moreover, this example illustrates the incorrect notion that innovation and creativity are strictly and solely embedded in the individual. At the institution in question, structural frameworks that could support a creative surrounding for working teams with diverse ideas are not regarded as driving forces for innovation and creativity. The chapter concludes with lessons learned in how to foster greater diversity and thus space for creativity.

PROFESSIONAL SOCIALIZATION IN STEM ORGANIZATIONS

When new staff members join an organization, they are immediately confronted by its internal structures and value systems. The subsequent process of professional socialization requires them to internalize the particular values, norms and symbols of the work culture (Hanappi-Egger, 2004; Hanappi-Egger & Warmuth, 2010) in order to become an accepted expert in the field. In general, each occupation has its own set of norms, values, characteristics and attitudes that are expected of its members (Schein, 1978). Those not conforming to the professional culture are discarded at an early stage of their career (Dryburgh, 1999), either by exclusion or self-exclusion[2] (see also Hanappi-Egger, 2012a for the example of female IT specialists who abandon their chosen professions). Newcomers who wish to remain in an organization must demonstrate their sense of belongingness to the professional culture and their close identification with it. McIlwee and Robinson (1992) claim that conformity is achieved both through interaction and impression management (which describes the *appearance* of conformity to organizational culture rather than *actual* conformity). It is assumed that people whose personal value systems closely accord with organizational values can more easily adapt than those whose value systems are at variance. To act against one's self-understanding clearly entails costs in terms of energy and effort.

STEM organizations are viewed as having highly specific workplace cultures, particularly in the way that gender-based practices, structures and interactions are integral to their culture (Rhoton, 2011, p. 698). Many scholars have discussed the historically gendered nature of the STEM field (Hanappi-Egger, 2012b), arguing that masculine values are inscribed into STEM and *vice versa* (Wajcman, 2000; Faulkner & Lohan, 2004; Wajcman & McKenzie, 2005). Certainly it is true that science, technology, engineering and math are often associated with masculine values and identities; STEM professionals are required to be objective, rational, competitive, assertive, resolute, unemotional and analytical – attributes more often associated with men and masculinity than with women and femininity (Dryburgh, 1999; Martin, 2003; Sagebiel, 2005; Ihsen, 2008). Furthermore, STEM norms dictate a work ethic of complete dedication to the job at hand to the exclusion of any other (non-work) obligation. This is obviously a demand that can be more practically met by men than women, who today are still more likely to fulfil childrearing and other familial duties than men (Acker, 1990; Bruni, et al. 2004; Hanappi-Egger, 2012a). There exists a range of other customary requirements in STEM jobs: full-time contracts and a willingness to do overtime, workers must stay up-to-date with the work schedule, accept non-flexible work practices, time pressures and a heavy workload (Faulkner, 2009a). Other life concepts and contexts that do not meet these norms are automatically excluded. In particular, women, who must occupy a number of different roles within the family, find it extremely difficult to cope with these workplace norms (Hanappi-Egger, 2011, 2012c).

In addition to such structural barriers, the gendered practices of everyday work within STEM organizations also shape their workplace culture. Faulkner (2009a) has listed some of these exclusive practices: male-bonding; the generic use of 'he'; offensive, sexist humour; a heteronormative and sexualised culture; pressure to conform to particular forms of masculinity; and the influence of powerful male networks. Those who do not feel comfortable in this workplace culture– which can also be true of men– adopt various coping strategies. Dryburgh (1999) argues that adaptation to the workplace culture, internalization of the stipulated professional identity as well as a display of solidarity with others in the profession are all relevant strategies in the process of professionalization. Some women succeed in adapting to defined access rules

and codes by accepting the masculine culture, by ignoring sexist behaviour (Dryburgh, 1999) and avoiding overtly feminine practices (Miller 2004). Yet their biological sex always marks them as the "others", while gender role expectations place extra burdens on their shoulders (Hanappi-Egger, 20012a). Regardless of how hard they try to adapt, professional work in STEM occupations remains a more gender-authentic option for men than for women, as far as numbers (statistical data) and role expectations are concerned (Faulkner, 2009b).

Alongside the exclusion of femininity in STEM, Wajcman also criticizes the way in which the relationship between masculinity and technology is presented: The impression that is given is of one uniform form of masculinity and one specific form of technology. In contrast, she proposes the existence of a range of masculinities as well as different forms of technology (Wajcman, 1994). The most dominant form of masculinity in the STEM discourse is *heteronormative masculinity*, that is based on heterosexuality, while at the same time other forms of masculinity are subordinated (Connell, 2005, Hanappi-Egger, 2011). This ignores the inherent heterogeneity to be found within any group of men, so that all other types of masculinity that do not accord with the dominant picture of a white, heterosexual man are rejected. Accordingly, it can be assumed that men who do not conform to this picture are required to adapt or will be excluded, as is the case with women.

The workplace culture in STEM organizations can be summarized as highly exclusive in terms of gender. Hanappi-Egger (2012b) describes such a culture as *gender blind*, because the gendered substructures of various work and life contexts are overlooked. This highly exclusive culture in STEM organizations leads to the formation of a largely homogeneous staff structure, which is counter-productive to the professed aim of fostering creativity and innovation. In view of the shortage of skilled workers in this field, it is certainly inevitable that change is on the way. Yet whilst the question of gender is clearly of great importance, most organizations still deny that gendered relations are relevant to the workplace. Therefore it is vital that the professional expectations of specific life contexts and concepts be reconsidered. In the following we will attempt to identify how internal organizational structures and value systems in STEM organizations shape the professional self-understanding of their members.

"BELONGING TO": THE DEVELOPMENT OF PROFESSIONAL SCRIPTS IN STEM ORGANIZATIONS

As already discussed, the process of professional socialization acquaints each individual with the expected values, behaviors and patterns of legitimate thought of the organization. This process can be captured by Barley's structuration model of professional scripts (see Fig. 1), where the basic idea is that the institution or organization presents the individual with scripts that link her/him, firstly, to the organization and, secondly, to the wider social world. The model describes how professionals create their self-understanding, as well as how this professional identity is linked to the institutional value systems and structures. These professional scripts (in Barley's model called *career scripts*) constitute a linking mechanism between the individual and the institution.

In Barley's model, professions strive to maintain this structure-agency duality in the workplace context. From an interpretative perspective, Barley highlights the interconnections between structure and action in relation to career scripts, so that, based on this theoretical underpinning, careers are understood to represent a form of script that mediates the connection between the institution and the individual by offering actors "interpretive schemes, resources and norms for fashioning a course through the social world (1989, p. 53)". Professional scripts can be said to "prescribe patterns of legitimate thought" in a particular setting and act as a link or modality between both individual action and social structures (Duberly et al., 2006). Individuals are required to encode the professional structure and understanding of the institution, and then translate it into individual action before enacting it in daily routines, finally constituting it back into organizational structures.

Of course, each professional community will have its own script for individuals to negotiate and use in enacting their professional understanding. According to Barley, individuals do not interpret and act upon professional scripts in a uniform fashion, but may indeed challenge or even transform them as well as simply maintain the status quo (Duberly et al., 2006). As transformation and change are linked to the possession of power, individuals still undergoing the socialization process are assumed to be more willing to follow accepted

Figure 1. Structuration of professional scripts
Source: Adapted from Barley 1989, p. 54

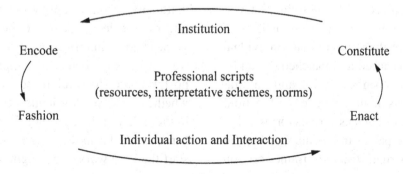

practices rather than actively question and change scripts. More specifically, and for the purposes of this chapter, we propose that individuals who choose a STEM career are constitutionally more likely to accept the current structures, and thus be content to maintain existing institutions, whereas those who are discontented may choose to abandon the profession rather than try to change the system.

In our research setting, professional scripts are considered to be an offered discourse about existing norms, resources and interpretative schemes in a particular community. For professionals just beginning a career in science, engineering, technology or math, such scripts will shape their understanding of what constitutes a career in this field. These professional scripts also indicate the kind of hindrances and burdens that must be overcome in order to become an accepted member of the system. Rather than looking at the micro level of existing personal scripts, this paper focuses on the wider professional understanding and perception that shapes individual action and self-understanding. Moreover, for our purposes it is necessary to analyze those scripts and related hindrances and burdens in terms of *gender* and *diversity sensitivity*. Thus we must identify the degree to which those scripts are gender and diversity neutral. Are they truly (as oft stated) independent of various dimensions of diversity? Are they gender and diversity blind, so that no account is taken of the specific hindrances and barriers which affect certain groups due to their life contexts and demographic characteristics?

In sum, professional scripts are based on a structural framework and culture as well as personal perceptions at the individual level. During the phase of professional socialization, it is essential that the structural and individual levels are well-balanced and matched. It can be assumed that an open structural and cultural framework allows multiple scopes of action, and therefore also embraces various forms of life context and concepts for individuals working in the discipline. A rigid structural framework, on the other hand, reproduces more of the same, as scopes for action are limited and individuals are required to fit in perfectly to her/his social context, or if not, to make the necessary adaptations.

CASE STUDY: PROFESSIONAL SCRIPTS IN STEM ACADEMIA

The theoretical discussion above will now be fleshed out with an in-depth case study of an Austrian higher education institution in the field of science, technology, engineering and math. A single case offers both richness of data and a holistic view of a phenomenon (Yin, 2003). In the case study presented here, various phenomena were analyzed in relation to diversity and STEM. For this book chapter, however, we focus on just one aspect, namely the professionalization process as shaped by the structural framework, values and norms of a discipline. The study sample of individuals within this system was made up, on the one hand, of PhD students in various stages of their doctorate work as well as early post-docs (max. two years after they finished their PhD), employed either as assistant professors or research fellows. The rest of the sample was made up of deans active in supporting early career scientists as well as in translating organizational structural frameworks into their discipline and setting up standards for practice. There was a twofold motivation for focusing on early career scientists: First, higher education institutions in the field of science, engineering, technology and math suffer from a rapidly increasing drop-out rate of female scientists at the highest levels of academic qualification. Second, numerous studies have confirmed the importance of the postgraduate doctoral period in determining whether early career scientists choose to remain in the field of science or not (Wirth et al., 2005; Lind, 2007). From the moment such individuals start the PhD work, they begin to learn the formal and informal rules of the game; they get to know the skills needed to succeed in their new roles (Sallee, 2011). During this initial phase of socialization, they develop an understanding of what it means to be an accepted member of the organization, while at the same time learning what kind a self-understanding is required of a professional scientist.

In contrast to other organizational settings, early career scientists still need to prove their skills, diligence and aptitude during this period via a formal PhD dissertation. Ideally, these processes will give each individual a clear view of whether or not they are fundamentally suited to academic research, so that at the end of this initial phase they can better decide if they wish to pursue a career in science. According to Weideman et al. (2001), early career scientists pass through four stages of socialization: the anticipatory stage, the formal and informal socialization stages and the personal stage. The first of these is the period before entering the organization, during which individuals interact with organization members to learn about the norms, values and attitudes that are related to the new position (Weideman et al., 2001; Tierney & Roads, 1993). After entering the organization, the young scientists pass through stages of both formal and informal socialization. Whereas the former is characterized by expectations that are still somewhat idealized, the latter informal stage is regarded as period when the "individual learns about informal role expectations and tacit assumptions of faculty life" (Sallee, 2011, p. 29). In the final stage the individual internalizes a professional identity, adapting it to her or his disposition (Weideman et al. 2001). While this model posits a concluding fourth stage, other scholars claim that professional socialization is an ongoing process which accompanies an academic career from beginning to end (Tierney & Rhoads, 1993).

During this process of socialization, individuals develop both a scientific identity and a feel-

ing of belonging. According to Golde and Dore (2001), the relationship between advisor and early career scientist, as well as the exchange between colleagues and faculty, help young scientists enjoy smoother trajectories through their graduate time. The success of the integration process will depend on a number of factors: the organizational culture, the cultures of the specific discipline, the faculty and the institute as a whole, as well as that of the individual (Gardner, 2007). Increasingly, reasons for failed socialization processes are identified less at the level of the individual than at the level of organizational structures and cultures (Lovitts, 2001; Golde, 2005).

One argument, which we intend to examine more closely here, is that the selection process is based entirely on objective criteria so that only the most suitable and best qualified individuals choose to remain in science. Although this should certainly be the goal of selection, several studies illustrate that the socialization process is neither gender nor diversity *neutral* (e.g. Beaufays, 2003, 2007; Sallee, 2008, 2011; Solem, 2009) but *blind*. This implies that certain personal factors such as being female or male, being homosexual or heterosexual, being Kenyan or Austrian, could indeed influence the decision to stay in science. Beaufays (2003, 2007), for example, confirms that recognition and attribution processes in science are highly selective. She identifies subtle processes, such as social schemata, that facilitate male scientists to gain influence via anticipated attribution practices. One such scheme is recognized as the understanding of science as a lifestyle more easily embodied by men due to social attributions. Other implicit gendered processes are established by certain norms and values that foster hierarchy and competition, again linked more to the masculine than the feminine gender. Sallee (2011) even claims to detect some differentiation between various forms of masculinity, in which certain masculine forms are favoured over others. Such examples of exclusion mechanisms in academic institutions run the risk of encouraging the self exclusion of scientists, which is then falsely seen as an individual problem (lack of fit) rather than a structural problem. Often those affected will abandon the field because they are made to feel inadequate, not the 'right person' for this kind of job which leads to a considerable waste of creative potential.

METHOD

Regarding methodology, an interpretative and qualitative position was taken. The paper is based on qualitative interviews (Froschauer & Lueger, 2003) and structural data analysis (Lueger 2000). The interviews were conducted in 2011 with 13 early career scientists and four deans from five different faculties and postgraduate schools. The sample group of early career scientists was carefully selected (by means of a pre-interview questionnaire) to ensure a diverse composition in terms of faculty, gender, career aspirations in academia, duration of employment, age as well as familial or other obligations. The open interview design gave participants the opportunity to speak freely, picking up and reflecting on topics they perceived to be relevant. Respondents were invited to review their motivations upon entering the university, to talk about current issues and discuss their future plans and aspirations. The deans were asked to speak about the institutionalized support of early career scientists and typical career paths in their field of study. All interviews were taped and transcribed and, as they were conducted in German, the relevant passages subsequently translated into English.

Structural data analysis is a qualitative method used to investigate the formal and informal characteristics of organizations (Lueger, 2000). In the case at hand, structural data gathering included organizational figures (e.g. from official reports), the formal structure of the organization (e.g. hierarchy), staff information (e.g. age and gender structure, nationalities of the staff) as well as the

mission statement, details of corporate governance and the code of conduct. According to Lueger (2000), the analysis of such data provides important information about organizational norms, values, power distribution and resources, as well as explicit rules of legitimization. Both the interview data and the structural data were analyzed using *Atlas.ti* qualitative data analysis software, which provides tools for both interpretative and qualitative analysis (Gibbs, 2010).

FINDINGS

Context of the Case Study

The analyzed institution is an important player in Austria in the field of science, engineering, technology and math education, with researchers undertaking both basic and applied research. In the Austrian context, the aim of basic research is to investigate fundamental phenomena in order to create knowledge and thereby contribute to the scholarly discourse, whereas applied research is characterized by its strong focus on a specific problem or some industrial application. This is not merely a formal distinction, but is reflected in the organizational culture and the basic understanding of doing science and research. As a result, there is not one consistent professional and career understanding, but rather complex structures split along two basic pathways of professional socialization: one oriented towards basic research and one towards applied science. In the professional practice of the institution investigated in the case study, these are the two competing professional understandings to be described in the following section.

With its 14 postgraduate schools in engineering and natural sciences, the institution aims to guarantee a doctoral education focused on the specific needs of the students. Within the last five years its programs have been adapted to meet the standards set by the Bologna Process. Since then every institute and all teaching staff formally belong to a specific postgraduate school. More than 50% of the overall PhD research is financed either by the global budget of the university or from external funds (like external research grants or cooperative ventures with industrial partners). The sample group for the case study was selected from these funded doctoral students.

Rigid Professional Scripts and Competing Career Scripts

The case study results show the presented professional self-understandings to be highly rigid, leaving little scope for individual action. At the individual level, anticipated professional understandings closely resemble the communicated and practiced professional and organizational image. We identified two academic career scripts for the fields of study at the institution: one for applied research and one for basic research, with substantial differences between the two scripts. Whereas here applied research is linked to the study field of technology and engineering[3], basic research and disciplines are instead related to the natural sciences[4]. For early career scientists this means that the professional structuration of basic and applied science follow different understandings

and logics, each associated with different sets of challenges and hindrances. In the following, these two competing professional scripts, as well as their meaning for early career scientists, will be explained in more detail.

The development of a professional script depends on a number of factors: interpretative schemes, resources, norms and value systems of both professional structures and internal organizational structures. Based on this structure and value framework, early career scientists develop their professional self-understanding at the individual level. Investigation of this interrelation can give insight not only into the structural framework of this professional understanding but also into early career scientists' perception of career options, hindrances, barriers and related gender and diversity specific phenomena. Table 1 illustrates the professional, organizational and personal aspects of this understanding.

The professional structure in basic research is highly competitive and characterized by a global job market. To succeed in this tough arena one has to meet the criteria of excellence, and be willing to compete against others at an international level.

At the level of organizational structures, the dissertation period is seen as the launching pad

Table 1. Professional script in the field of basic research

Basic Research in Natural Science: Professional Script	Interpretative Schemes	Resources	Norms
Professional Structures	• Competition vs. cooperation.	• Global, competitive job market.	• Meeting criteria of excellence.
Organizational Structures	• Dissertation symbolic start of professionalization process – initiation ritual, • Good scientist: nature vs. nurture.	• Excellence. • Maximum flexibility (in time and space). • - Precarious employment status.	• Making sacrifices for science. • Life is science.
Personal Structures	• Good scientist: internal factors: vacation, aptitude. • External factors: good luck/ bad luck, openness and applicability of results. • Structural barriers.	• Maximum flexibility (in time and space). • Precarious employment status. • Support. • Excellence.	• Publication. • Project work. • Practical and scientific relevance of the results.

Source: Own data

of professionalization in science. The process of writing a PhD thesis constitutes a vital period of professional training, and thus a transition towards becoming a real scientist. In stressing the importance of this process, one dean used a drastic metaphor, comparing the dissertation process as transition between "death and life".

A PhD student is no longer a student; the official term is early career scientist. This phase is a transition between life and death – or no, the other way around, between death and life. One needs to promote and support such students but in reality they are working somewhat independently in their thesis (male dean of mathematics).

Picking up on this metaphor, we can perhaps say that the dissertation 'breathes life' into the young scientist. It is a kind of initiation rite through which one must pass in order to become an accepted member of the academic fraternity. To pursue this thought, there exists the strong belief that one should not waste or throw away this gift of a 'donated life'. Thus it comes to seem legitimate that sacrifices must be accepted as part and parcel of the scientific life. In the professional codex of scientists, 'science should be your life'.

Not only must early career scientist strive to obtain a PhD, they must also learn to become 'good' scientists. But what does this mean? The interviewees mentioned a broad continuum of factors constituting good scientific practice, including both natural and nurtured factors. Some argue that becoming a good scientist is largely dependent on vocation and talent:

One needs talent. This is not learnable, or rather it's only learnable to a limited extent, because although, of course, everything can be learned, there comes a certain point when one realizes that the effort is too great – it just becomes a lot of trouble. [...] It is comparable with music. I mean that one can learn how to play the piano, *but you are not going to become a famous pianist if you don't have sufficient talent (male dean of mathematics).*

Others claimed that one becomes a scientist through the process of professional socialization and with sufficient scientific practice. For example, it was stated that in the field of computer science, early career scientists are expected to absorb a great deal of information and skills during their Bachelor's and Master's degree courses. Some interviewees also mentioned commitment, quick thinking and the ability to think abstractly. Skills linked to the dissertation process were communication skills, both oral and written, the ability to defend one's work and knowledge of the craft of publishing. These aspects are described as actively learnable.

But over and above all of these separate attributes and skills, one factor was commonly expressed as a prerequisite to becoming a good scientist: the striving for excellence. One needs to be exceptional, and to possess extraordinary skills, either gained actively during the socialization process or passively through vocational practice or sheer talent, or in combination. Even though the expectations of what is needed to develop those skills differ, there is agreement in the need to be extraordinary. One dean explained his understanding of excellence by pointing out the etymologies of the words *engineer* and *technology:*

Engineer literally means having a talent from above. The term genius is related to this and means: one who has a great deal of this spirit. Consequently, he [the early career scientist] should be able to handle this art skillfully. The word technology originates from the word techné, meaning art. So if he has genius and is able to handle this art, then he becomes a good scientist (male dean of electronics).

This quote combines the two proposed aspects of excellence: On the one hand, the passive aspect, supplied by nature, illustrated by the word genius as someone having brilliant professional aptitude. Moreover, it is seen as a precondition for excellence, and one that is not learnable; either you have it or you do not. On the other hand must be learnt, namely through the art of using one's own excellence in a useful manner. Professional socialization is highly important for this nurtured step.

In contrast to the deans' script, early career scientists not only stress internal factors related to vocation and talent, but also external factors which they feel unable to influence, for example good and bad luck. For early career scientists success is closely linked to concrete results, which are, however, generally quite unpredictable. *Good* results are those that verify the posited hypothesis, are relatively easy to publish and therefore have scientifically and practically greater relevance than *bad* results, which prove the falsity of one's initial hypothesis.

I was lucky as everything has worked out well, more or less; but I think I'm also an exception here. I have a female colleague, for example, who is collaborating with a chemistry company, and it's not working out at all. I guess in chemistry it's not the fault of someone who assigns you to a certain topic, or your acceptance of it; but basically it either works or it doesn't (female early career scientist of chemistry).

Other external factors that early career scientists see as influencing career success, are structural barriers that need to be overcome in the course of their professionalization process. These barriers (as well as resources) are connected to the highly competitive and global market for science jobs. The following two quotes focus on this aspect of a professional script. Whereas the deans' professional script represents the organizational structure of scientific professions at this institution, the early career scientists' perspective on profes-

sionalization represents their personal structure, i.e. their own translations and interpretations of offered and presented professional scripts. One dean summarized the external as well as organizational internal practice as follows:

The PhD course is streamlined towards a scientific career or a highly esteemed position in business. [...] the job market is a global one [in academia], meaning that is really very global. They also know they need to be mobile. It is difficult to appreciate that in the first ten years of their career they will not have a stable job, but will have to apply for vacancies between South Africa, South Korea, Japan and America. But that's how things are (male dean of mathematics).

This quote illustrates the resources one must possess in order to succeed in academia. Early career scientists are expected to be totally flexible in terms of their work schedule and place of work. Moreover, they are required to accept tenuous employment relationships for lengthy periods. The respondent above indicates that this may not be easy for early career scientists, but closes with the statement that those are the rules of the game, which he sees as given and non-negotiable. The impact this structural framework has on early career scientists is expressed in the following quote:

But then sometime I would like to settle somewhere. Many of my colleagues are on the move all the time. One year here as a post doc, two years there, and always just on temporary contracts. In Austria, in Germany or in Switzerland – there is no reasonable chance of getting a job as a post doc. The situation is also quite bad in Italy. It's like three years here, three years there, three years elsewhere. You start to work somewhere, but after one year you need to look for another position, even though you know that you are only going to stay there for another two years. But what happens after that? (female early career scientist of mathematics).

Compared to the sentiments of the first quote, this early career scientist seems to have quite a realistic picture of the situation. She is describing what impact the requirement to offer maximum flexibility means to her, and what she has learnt so far from colleagues. It is clear that she is quite uncertain by this expectation of total flexibility, along with the complete lack of security and inability to make long-term plans.

To sum up, the career script for early career scientist can be described as strict and rigid. The case study shows that most aspects of this career script are incorporated into the scientist's individual scripts. These factors are reflected upon, so that the early career scientists anticipate what this understanding of professionalization means for their life contexts and concepts.

The second script to be outlined in the following is the professional script for scientists working in applied engineering and technology. It differs from the previously described script both in the potential and actual career trajectories, as well as in the general understanding of scientific practice.

The professional script in applied science is characterized by its close links to industry and the private sector, whether in terms of project funding or research projects that are directly carried out within industry and in the private sector. Thus it is clear that understandings of professionalization will differ from the typical idea of a university position in basic research.

According to the deans of applied sciences, the PhD is seen as the highest reasonable educational degree in this professional area. Professorship is more the exception than the rule. During the dissertation period, early career scientists are expected to gain practical experience in project work, and so the dissertation itself is normally closely linked to such projects. Early career scientists usually leave university after obtaining their PhDs or before they have completed their dissertations. The drop-out rate is far higher than in the field of basic research. One of the reasons for this development, it can be assumed, is the rather different professional script embedded in such disciplines. On the one hand, a good job in industry is easy to get, while on the other hand,

Table 2. Professional script in applied science

Applied Engineering and Technology – Professional Script	Interpretative Schemes	Resources	Norms
External Structures		• Close links to industry. • Highly financed. • Hardly any post doc positions.	• Criteria of excellence.
Organizational Structures	• Dissertation as highest educational degree. • Practical experience. • Good scientist: nature vs. nurture.	• Third party/ industry funded research/ cooperation highly relevant during dissertation process. • Many phd positions funded by those cooperations.	• Academic career not the norm. • Career in science closely linked to industry/non-university research/business. • Extraordinary contribution to society.
Personal Structures	• Good scientist: internal factors: vacation, aptitude. • External factors: good luck/ bad luck, openness of results, applicability of results. • Structural barriers.	• Cooperation with industry. • Job in industry more realistic than in academia.	• Publication. • Project work. • Practical and scientific relevance of results.

Source: Own data

it is not viewed as a realistic option to remain in academia after getting one`s PhD. Whereas the connection between a good scientist and excellence is similar to the first script, the structural framework is quite different. This is highlighted by the following two statements from a dean and an early career scientist:

In engineering science, at least in the applied disciplines, it is useful if people first spend time working in the field; and even if they strive for a career at the university, which means becoming a professor, it's best to leave initially after the dissertation (male dean of electronics).

This quote stresses the importance of experience in the field. Furthermore, such outside work is understood as a necessary career move before returning to university (even though a career in science is outside the norm). Thus in order to become a professor, it is important to first leave the academic field in order to achieve some extraordinary, socially-relevant work, after which a return to university seems more legitimate. The university examined in the case study has already initiated tenure track positions for young scientists striving for a university career, yet is finding it difficult to integrate scientists who follow this path, who seem to lack some essential experience (which, of course, is also related to the age of the alumni). The effect this has on the perception of early careers in science is demonstrated by the next statement:

The prospect of a scientific career in Austria is almost zero, while in Germany it is similar, meaning that there are hardly any post doc positions. Hence it is almost impossible to go for an academic career. [...] Typically one could go into industry and return to a university position after a few years in the private economy. Then one gets a professorship. In my opinion this is exactly the origin of the problem which the university faces;

they pick professors from industry, who of course do not value scientific work so much, which is accorded a low status. They think more in terms of the private economy (female early career scientist of construction engineering).

The quote is reminiscent of the first. Thus we could conclude that this early career scientist already knows the rules of the game. Besides describing the situation, she mentions a problem that other early career scientists in this field also experience and confirm in the interviews, namely the disjunction between their expectations when entering the world of science and the actual experience of academic practice. As with early career scientists in basic research, they expect science and research to be the dominant aspect of their work. They are eager to create something new and wish to work intensively on a specific research topic, hoping to be accorded sufficient time to do so. However, what they actually deal with on a daily basis is mostly third-party and industry-financed project work. Their schedules are filled with deadlines, they are under constant time pressures and their scientific output is consequently meager. This situation obviously conflicts with their expectations of research: The strict time framing and the highly deadline-oriented work undermines the creative, unstructured research setting necessary for innovative and productive research.

To conclude, early career scientists of all genders face a number of contradictions when embarking on a career in higher research. The actual research practice can differ from their expectations, causing uncertainty regarding their career paths, or indeed provoking them to drop out of the field entirely. These disciplines also offer highly rigid career paths to early career scientists, in which the choices offered frequently have an either-or aspect, with little room for maneuver.

LESSONS LEARNED: STEM-PROFESSION SCRIPTS AND THEIR IMPACT ON CREATIVITY AND INNOVATION

The two main professional scripts identified above are characterized by strictness and rigidity, both at the organizational and individual level. It can be shown that the organizational value system and professional understanding shape the expectations and self-understandings of early career scientists. In particular, they anticipate structural barriers, trying to match these with their own life contexts. One early career scientist describes the concern of some of his friends as follows:

There is only a limited opportunity to reconcile an academic career with the obligations of family life. I have a lot of friends in various fields of study who claim that they would like to stay in science, but at the same time understand that this would entail them throwing out any private plans. And they are as yet unsure if they are prepared to do so (male early career scientist of informatics).

Thus it is clear that especially for early career scientists with private obligations or family plans, structures that demand absolute flexibility can become an insurmountable barrier. Looking at the gender aspect of the professional scripts, no major disparities could be detected between female and male early career scientists in the way they expressed concerns and uncertainties as well as expectations and anticipations. Of course, this is to be expected when one considers that these early career scientists have already passed through a socialization phase; they have become adapted to codes of conduct and accept the stipulated norms and values. However, the historically-grown expectations, norms and values in STEM match social constructions of masculinity more readily than those of femininity (Hanappi-Egger 2012). Consequently, the professional script for an early

career scientist leans towards masculine connotations, and is consistent with a masculine life context and masculine role expectations. This is the paradox afflicting women in STEM professions, also referred to as double-bind: On the one hand, as already mentioned, female professionals in the STEM field are committed to masculine-coded norms, while at the same time they are equally assigned to socially-constructed norms and role expectations of women (Faulkner, 2007). This has been described by Faulkner (2009b) as the *in/visibility paradox*. In this paradox women are invisible as professionals but visible as women; they are simultaneously required to assimilate to the masculine-connoted culture of the field while retaining their femininity. This causes ambiguity and can lead to exclusion and self-exclusion of those who do not fit the ideal picture of a successful scientist (independent, competitive, single and ambitious). In sum, although both men and women can adapt to such professional career scripts, it is still more authentic and realistic for men (at least in the European cultural context) to reconcile such life concepts while pursuing a career in STEM. Thus it is clear that the process of professional socialization in STEM as well as norms and values embedded in the professional scripts are not gender neutral (Hanappi-Egger, 2012c).

The academic life is very narrowly defined, so that only highly streamlined homogenous groups will be admitted, especially those who are willing and able to adapt to the formal and informal rules of the game and the rigid structural standards of the discipline. This rigid understanding and the strict expectation that an ideal scientist will maintain a high degree of excellence together ensure a very narrow scope of action: either one adapts to the rules or leaves the system. Obviously this serves to weed out diversity, so that the institution will be staffed by a homogenous set of individuals who confirm and perpetuate existing structural framework. Yet this scenario conflicts with the innovation and creativity essential to STEM, characteristics which are stifled by homogeneity and rigid structures that do not permit unstructured, innovative and creative working environments. Strict adherence to these standard scripts lowers the creative and innovative potential of the institution as well as the professional field, and indeed the whole academic field of STEM.

Research into creativity and innovation in organizations and in working groups has revealed the potential force of heterogeneity at the workplace. When people with different genders, ethnical backgrounds and functional or professional backgrounds (and who hold different attitudes and perspectives) come together, then such diversity can serve to increase team creativity and innovation (Cox, 1991; Bassett-Jones, 2005). This positive effect on creativity can be attributed to the exploration and discussion of non-obvious alternatives that result from the input of different points of views, from higher levels of critical analyses as well as broader and richer bases of experiences. Nemeth et al. (2001), for example, argue that dissent in discussion can stimulate more innovative thinking, helping to change attitudes by encouraging individuals to consider the opposing point of view. Obviously this can reduce the risk of groupthink. However, when an organization does not address the issue of diversity whatsoever, then this can lead to the opposite result, namely frictional losses due to misunderstandings, conflict and discrimination (Bassett-Jones, 2005). Roberge and van Dick (2010) assume that some preconditions must be fulfilled in order for diversity to foster higher performance, creativity and innovation in a group setting. Thus it is necessary to consider and address *individual level* mechanisms, such as empathy and self disclosure, as well as *group level* mechanisms, such as communication, group involvement and trust.

Holligsworth (2002) has shown that it is not only personnel structures that influence innovation but also formal organizational structures. He claims that the most successful institutions/universities (in this case, those with the most Noble Prize nominations) have structures that are open to diversity, in particular highly flexible working conditions, sufficient time for research, as well as creative staff whose diverse biographies and career paths are often intertwined. This is consistent with research on innovation in organizations which shows that open organizational structures, a climate of participation as well as cooperation promote creativity and innovation (Woodman et al., 1993; Cosh et al., 2012).

Thus we conclude that in the highly competitive marketplace in which STEM organizations reside, competitive advantage is mostly defined by innovation and creativity. Organizational structures and value systems that address and promote diversity, both within the personnel structure and an open formal organizational structure, will help to foster such creativity. A primary aim should therefore be to open up rigid professional scripts in order to attract more a highly diverse group of individuals.

Turning to the limitations of the study, the specific context of the case restricts any wider generalization of findings beyond the world of academia. Further research is needed to identify professional scripts in other STEM areas. More specifically, it would be of particular interest to duplicate this study with undergraduates and professionals in non-academic STEM workplaces in order to determine similarities and/or differences to the scripts identified here.

CONCLUSION

As the case study has made clear, STEM academia promotes scripts that stipulate the need for creativity as an innate, individual talent. The investigation has provided insight into how the understanding of professionalization is constructed and negotiated by looking at how structures are created and how those rigid structures constrain the scope of action of individuals still in the process of professional socialization.

It can be said that the investigated institution asks for people with an unusually high degree of intellectual accomplishment, dedicated to excellence and self-exploitation. The interviews also revealed a clear demarcation of required traits/capacities: On the one hand, the individual must be naturally talented rather than simply someone whose achievements are down to hard work; on the other hand, the individual must display a strong commitment to the professional value systems, including flexibility, availability and competiveness. To sum up, one has to be a genius operating in a very rigid structural framework. This leads to ambivalence within the actors, causing stress and provoking feelings of frustration and uncertainty.

Such organizational practices conflict with the findings of previous studies on creativity and innovation, which have emphasized the importance of structural context in allowing people to exercise creativity and innovation. In this perspective, creativity is strongly associated with a culture of openness (Amabile 1996), offering space for freedom, and fostering trust and cooperation instead of competition. Therein a healthy work-life balance is seen as one main factor that organizations employ to cultivate the creativity of staff, and thus boost the potential for innovation. Furthermore, Hanappi-Egger (2013) shows how subtle constructions of masculinity in the STEM organizational culture lead to mainstreaming, indeed one can say male-streaming. Again a strict professional script forces individuals (or groups of individuals) to adapt or to leave. As long as this self-understanding of STEM organizations remains unquestioned, the same type of organizational members (namely the same type of professionals) will be attracted and reproduced. Graduates of STEM educational systems are expected to adapt to their institution's understanding of professionalism and excellence, and internalize the according norms and values (see Baer 2011). Such dynamics contribute to the further propagation of the traditional,

and frequently criticized, understanding of the field of technology, which continues to attract the same type of person at the same time as it discards those individuals who hold divergent self-understandings. Yet it is precisely these latter types who are needed if the primary goal is to increase and foster creativity.

REFERENCES

Acker, J. (1990). Hierarchies, jobs, bodies: A theory of gendered organizations. *Gender & Society*, *4*(2), 139–158. doi:10.1177/089124390004002002

Amabile, T. M. (1996). *Creativity in context: Update to the social psychology of creativity*. Boulder, CO: Westview.

Baer, J. (2011). Why teachers should assume creativity is very domain specific. *International Journal of Creativity and Problem Solving*, *21*(2), 57–61.

Barley, S. R. (1989). Careers, identities and institutions. In M. B. Arthur, D. T. Hall, & B. S. Lawrence (Eds.), *The handbook of career theory* (pp. 41–60). Cambridge, UK: Cambridge University Press. doi:10.1017/CBO9780511625459.005

Bassett, J. N. (2005). The paradox of diversity management, creativity and innovation. *Creativity and Innovation Management*, *14*(2), 169–175. doi:10.1111/j.1467-8691.00337.x

Beaufays, S. (2003). *Wie werden Wissenschaftler gemacht? Beobachtungen zur wechselseitigen Konstitution von Geschlecht und Wissenschaft*. Bielefeld, Germany: Transcript.

Beaufays, S. (2007). Alltag und Exzellenz - Konstruktionen von Leistung und Geschlecht in der Förderung wissenschaftlichen Nachwuchses. In R. Dackweiler (Ed.), *Willkommen im Club? Frauen und Männer in Eliten* (pp. 145–165). Münster, Germany: Westfällisches Dampfboot.

Bruni, A., Gherardi, S., & Poggio, B. (2004). Doing gender, doing entrepreneurship: An ethnographic account of intertwined practices. *Gender, Work and Organization, 11*(4), 406–429. doi:10.1111/j.1468-0432.2004.00240.x

Connell, R. (2005). *Masculinities*. Berkeley, CA: University of California Press.

Cosh, A., Fu, X., & Hughes, A. (2012). Organisation structure and innovation performance in different environments. *Small Business Economics, 39*(2), 301–317. doi:10.1007/s11187-010-9304-5

Cox, T. & Blake, S. (1991). Managing cultural diversity: Implications for organizational competitiveness. *The Executive*, 45-56.

Dryburgh, H. (1999). Working hard, play hard: Women and professionalization in engineering – adapting to the culture. *Gender & Society, 13*(5), 664–682. doi:10.1177/089124399013005006

Duberley, J., Cohen, L., & Mallon, M. (2006). Constructing scientific careers: Change, continuity and context. *Organization Studies, 27*(8), 1131–1151. doi:10.1177/0170840606064105

Faulkner, W. (2007). 'Nuts and bolts of people': Gender-troubled engineering identities. *Social Studies of Science, 37*, 331–356. doi:10.1177/0306312706072175

Faulkner, W. (2009a). Doing gender in engineering workplace cultures. I. Observation from the field. *English Studies, 1*(1), 3–18.

Faulkner, W. (2009b). Doing gender in engineering workplace cultures. II. Gender in/authenticity and the in/visibility paradox. *English Studies, 1*(3), 169–189.

Faulkner, W., & Lohan, M. (2004). Masculinities and technologies. Some introductory remarks. *Men and Masculinities, 6*(4), 319–329. doi:10.1177/1097184X03260956

Froschauer, U., & Lueger, M. (2003). *Das qualitative Interview: zur Praxis interpretativer Analyse sozialer Systeme*. Wien: WUV Verlag.

Gardner, S. (2007). "I heard it through the grapevine": Doctoral student socialization in chemistry and history. *The Journal of Higher Education, 54*, 723–740. doi:10.1007/s10734-006-9020-x

Gibbs, G. (2010). *Analyzing qualitative data*. London: The Sage Qualitative Research Kit.

Giddens, A. (1984). *The constitution of society*. Berkeley, CA: University of California Press.

Golde, C. (2005). The role of the department and discipline in doctoral student attrition: Lessons from four departments. *The Journal of Higher Education, 76*(6), 669–700. doi:10.1353/jhe.2005.0039

Golde, C., & Dore, T. (2001). *At cross purposes: What the experiences of today`s doctoral students reveal about doctoral education (Report)*. Philadelphia, PA: The Pew Charitable Trusts.

Guilford, J. P. (1970). Creativity: Retrospect and prospect. *The Journal of Creative Behavior, 4*, 149–168. doi:10.1002/j.2162-6057.1970.tb00856.x

Hanappi-Egger, E. (2011). *The triple m of organizations: Man, management and myth*. Wien, New York: Springer. doi:10.1007/978-3-7091-0556-6

Hanappi-Egger, E. (2012a). "Shall I stay or shall I go"? On the role of diversity management for women's retention in SET professions. *Equality, Diversity and Inclusion. International Journal (Toronto, Ont.), 31*(2), 144–157.

Hanappi-Egger, E. (2012b). Exclusiveness versus inclusiveness in software-development: The triple-loop-learning approach. In R. Pande, & T. van der Weide (Eds.), *Globalization, technology diffusion and gender disparity: Social impacts of ICTs* (pp. 96–109). Hershey, PA: IGI Global. doi:10.4018/978-1-4666-0020-1.ch008

Hanappi-Egger, E. (2012c). Wissenschaftliche Exzellenz: Geschlechtsneutral oder geschlechtsblind. In S. L. Gutierrez-Lobos, & K. Rumpfhuber (Eds.), *Hat wissenschaftliche Leistung ein Geschlecht?* (pp. 15–22). Wien: Facultas.

Hanappi-Egger, E. (2013). Backstage: The organizational gendered agenda in science, engineering and technology professions. *European Journal of Women's Studies, 20*(3), 279–294. doi:10.1177/1350506812456457

Hanappi-Egger, E., & Warmuth, G. S. (2010). Gender-neutral or gender-blind? On the meaning of structural barriers in computer science and engineering. In K. Resetová (Ed.) *CD-Proceedings of the Joint International IGIP-SEFI Conference 2010. Diversity Unifies - Diversity in Engineering Education* (pp. 1153-1153). Brussels, Belgium.

Hollingsworth, R. (2002). *Research organizations and major discoveries in twentieth-century science: A case-study of excellence in biomedical research*. Berlin: Wissenschaftszentrum Berlin für Sozialforschung.

Ihsen, S. (2008). Ingenieurinnen: Frauen in einer Männerdomäne. In R. Becker, & B. Kortendiek (Eds.), *Handbuch der Frauen und Geschlechterforschung. Theorie, Methoden, Empirie* (pp. 791–797). Wiesbaden, Germany: VS Verlag. doi:10.1007/978-3-531-91972-0_96

Lind, I. (2007). Ursachen der Unterrepräsentanz von Wissenschaftlerinnen - Individuelle Entscheidungen oder strukturelle Barrieren? In B. f. B. u. Forschung (Ed.), Exzellenz in Wissenschaft und Forschung -Neue Wege in der Gleichstellungspolitik: Bundesministerium für Bildung und Forschung (pp. 59-86). Köln, Germany.

Lovitts, B. (2001). *Leaving the ivory tower: The causes and consequences of departure from doctoral study*. Lanham, MD: Rowman & Littlefield.

Lueger, M. (2000). *Grundlagen qualitativer Feldforschung*. Wien: WUV Verlag.

MacKenzie, D., & Wajcman, J. (2005). *The social shaping of technology*. Maidenhead, UK: Open University Press.

Martin, P. (2003). "Said and done" versus "saying and doing" gendering practices, practicing gender at work. *Gender & Society, 17*(3), 342–366. doi:10.1177/0891243203017003002

McIlwee, J., & Robinson, G. (1992). *Women in engineering: Gender, power, and workplace culture*. Albany, NY: State University of New York Press.

Miller, G. (2004). Frontier masculinity in the oil industry: The experience of women engineers. *Gender, Work and Organization, 11*(1), 47–73. doi:10.1111/j.1468-0432.2004.00220.x

Nemeth, C., Connell, J., Rogers, J., & Brown, K. (2001). Improving decision making by means of dissent. *Journal of Applied Social Psychology, 31*(1), 48–58. doi:10.1111/j.1559-1816.2001.tb02481.x

Rhoton, L. (2011). Dancing as a gendered barrier – Understanding women scientists' gender practices. *Gender & Society, 25*(6), 696–716. doi:10.1177/0891243211422717

Roberge, M. É., & van Dick, R. (2010). Recognizing the benefits of diversity: When and how does diversity increase group performance? *Human Resource Management Review, 20*(4), 295–308. doi:10.1016/j.hrmr.2009.09.002

Sagebiel, F. (2005). Organisationskultur und Geschlecht in den Ingenieurwissenschaften Europas. *Zeitschrift des Interdisziplinären Zentrums für Frauen und Geschlechterforschung, 22*(30), 48–60.

Sallee, M. W. (2011). Performing masculinity: Considering gender in doctoral student socialization. *The Journal of Higher Education, 82*(2), 187–216. doi:10.1353/jhe.2011.0007

Schein, E. (1978). *Career dynamics. Matching individual and organizational needs*. Reading, MA: Addison-Wesley.

Shore, L. M., Randel, A. E., Chung, B. G., Dean, M. A., Holcombe Erhart, K., & Singh, G. (2011). Inclusion and diversity in work groups: A review and model for future research. *Journal of Management, 37*(4), 1262–1289. doi:10.1177/0149206310385943

Solem, M., Lee, J., & Schlemper, B. (2009). Departmental climate and student experiences in graduate geography programs. *Research in Higher Education, 50,* 268–292. doi:10.1007/s11162-008-9117-4

Tierney, W., & Rhoads, R. (1993). Enhancing promotion, tenure and beyond: Faculty socialization as a cultural process. ASHE-ERIC Higher Education Report, 93(6). Washington, DC.: The George Washington University.

Wajcman, J. (1994). *Technik und Geschlecht. Die feministische Technikdebatte.* Frankfurt, Germany: Campus Verlag.

Wajcman, J. (2000). Reflections on gender and technology studies: In what state is the art? *Social Studies of Science, 30*(3), 447–464. doi:10.1177/030631200030003005

Weidman, J., Twale, D., & Stein, E. (2001). Socialization of graduate and professional students in higher education: A perilous passage? ASHE-ERIC Higher Education Report 28(3). San Francisco: Jossey-Bass.

Wirth, W., Matthes, J., Mögerle, U., & Prommer, E. (2005). Traumberuf oder Verlegenheits-lösung? Einstiegsmotivation und Arbeitssituation des wissenschaftlichen Nachwuchses in Kommunikationswissenschaft und Medienwissenschaft. *Publizistik, 50*(3), 320–343. doi:10.1007/s11616-005-0135-3

Woodman, R., Sawyer, J., & Griffin, R. (1993). Toward a theory of organizational creativity. *Academy of Management Review, 18*(2), 293–321.

Yin, R. K. (2003). *Case study research. Design and methods.* Thousand Oaks, CA: Sage Publication.

ADDITIONAL READING

Baer, M. (2012). Putting creativity to work: The implementation of ceative ideas in organizations. *Academy of Management Journal, 55*(5), 1102–1119. doi:10.5465/amj.2009.0470

Fotaki, M. (2013). No woman is like a man (in academia): The masculine symbolic order and the unwanted female body. *Organization Studies, 34*(9), 1251–1275. doi:10.1177/0170840613483658

Frank Fox, M. (2010). Women and men faculty in academic science and engineering: Social-organizational indicators and implications. *The American Behavioral Scientist, 53*(7), 997–1012. doi:10.1177/0002764209356234

Gunz, H., Evans, M., & Jalland, M. (2000). Career boundaries in a 'boundaryless' world. In M. Peiperl, R. Arthur, R. Goffee, & T. Morris (Eds.), *Career frontiers: New conceptions of working lives* (pp. 24–53). Oxford, England: Oxford University Press.

Hatmaker, D. M. (2013). Engineering identity: Gender and professional identity negotiation among women engineers. *Gender, Work and Organization, 20*(4), 382–396. doi:10.1111/j.1468-0432.2012.00589.x

Jehn, K. A., Northcraft, G. B., & Neale, M. A. (1999). Why differences make a difference: A field study of diversity, conflict and performance in workgroups. *Administrative Science Quarterly, 44*(4), 741–763. doi:10.2307/2667054

Kantola, J. (2008). 'Why do all the women disappear?' Gendering processes in a political science department. *Gender, Work and Organization, 15*(2), 202–225. doi:10.1111/j.1468-0432.2007.00376.x

Koall, I. (2011). Managing complexity: using ambivalence and contingency to support diversity in organizations. *Equality, Diversity and Inclusion. International Journal (Toronto, Ont.), 30*(7), 572–588.

Rodan, S., & Galunic, C. (2004). More than network structure: How knowledge heterogeneity influences managerial performance and innovativeness. *Strategic Management Journal*, *25*(6), 541–562. doi:10.1002/smj.398

Sawyer, R. K. (2006). *Explaining creativity the science of human innovation*. Oxford, England: Oxford University Press.

KEY TERMS AND DEFINITIONS

Creativity: The ability to transform and transcend existing ideas, methods and patterns to create new and significant ideas, methods, concepts, etc.

Exclusion: The state whereby individuals or groups do not enjoy equal access to resources, opportunities and support.

Gender: The social construction of femininity and masculinity.

Innovation: The process of creating something new from existing concepts applied in a novel way or from an entirely new conceptual basis.

Professional scripts: A term referring to offered discourses about existing norms, resources and interpretative schemes in a particular workplace community. Such scripts shape the individual understanding of what constitutes a career in a specific field.

Professional socialization: The process of internalizing particular values, norms and symbols of the work culture.

STEM: Abbreviation for the fields of Science, Technology, Engineering and Math.

ENDNOTES

[1] This chapter is based on an early draft of a presentation entitled "From idealism to realism – career scripts as mechanisms of exclusion in the experiences of doctoral candidates?" at the Postgraduate Supervision Conference 2013 in Stellenbosch, South Africa. The authors thank the stream participants for valuable feedback.

[2] Inclusion and exclusion in social and professional settings can be described along the dimensions of *belongingness* and *uniqueness*. Whereas inclusion is characterized by a high feeling of belongingness and a high value placed on individual uniqueness, exclusion describes the feeling of low belongingness as well as a low value placed on individual uniqueness (Shore et al., 2011). Self-exclusion can be the result of such a process, where the individual decides to abandon an exclusive, unwelcoming professional and/or social setting.

[3] The investigated institution offers technology and engineering doctorates in, for example, electrical engineering, informatics, machine construction and process engineering.

[4] Here natural sciences are understood to encompass chemistry, math and physics as well as life sciences.

Chapter 9
Lessons from the STEM Sector

Vachon M.C. Pugh
Electronic Arts, USA

ABSTRACT

The purpose of this chapter is to examine possible causes such as lack of interest, lack of skill/ability, and anticipated work/family conflict (WFC), in addition to analyzing successful recruitment tactics that have brought more women into various other male dominated fields in an attempt to solve this problem. Results of the literature review show that the main contributing factors for the lack of women within the sector are lack of confidence in skills and abilities, lack of female industry role models, and lack of available mentorship and community outreach programs for interested women. This chapter takes this information into consideration and makes possible suggestions for the industry on how to remedy this problem.

STEM AND THE VIDEO GAME INDUSTRY

The video game industry combines a variety of disciplines to make up its collective whole. It involves both Science, Technology, Engineering, and Math (STEM) disciplines such as programming, animation, audio engineering, and motion capture in addition to non-STEM related disciplines such as art, design, and production; therefore literature from both STEM and non-STEM career disciplines could be effectively applied to the industry. It is important to remember that it is necessary to examine both aspects of the industry in order to benefit it as a whole, because not all STEM methods may be applied to non-STEM disciplines, and vice versa. Therefore what works for one may not work for another, and thus both avenues

must be taken into consideration. The purpose of the following sections is to analyze successful recruitment methods for STEM and non-STEM related fields, and utilize that information in tailoring recruitment methods towards bringing more women into the game industry.

STEM RELATED STUDIES

Method

This study will be a qualitative one. No new data will be recorded or gathered; instead a thorough analysis of prior successful recruitment programs of other STEM and non-STEM disciplines will be conducted, and the results will be applied to the video game industry. This is the most appro-

DOI: 10.4018/978-1-4666-6142-4.ch009

priate method because there have already been successful programs that have been implemented in other disciplines, and instead of developing an entirely new recruitment system for the video game industry that has not been tested yet, generating a practical application of already existing programs would be more appropriate.

Article I

The first article under discussion was written by Pamela Cantrell and Jacque Ewing-Taylor (2009), and deals with the University of Nevada, Reno and how they started a program in 2003 called the K-12 Engineering Education Programs, or KEEP, in order to interest more students into pursuing careers in the STEM fields. By allowing high school juniors and seniors a chance to attend seminars led by professionals in STEM careers, they were able to interest more students, particularly women, into pursuing careers in the STEM fields and becoming more confident about their career choices. The purpose of the study was to answer three different questions. The first question was whether or not the seminars had an impact on the career choices of the students involved. The second question was to determine whether the students could connect the information they received from the seminars to things they were learning in their classes. Finally, the third question was to determine whether grade level or gender differences had an impact on the students' career interests or their ability to relate the information to what they knew from school (Cantrell & Ewing-Taylor, 2009).

Summary

To summarize the main findings of this study, the results showed that female students were less likely to change their minds about their career choices once they were already set on one, and that senior level students were more likely to bridge connections between the information they gained at the

seminars and things they were learning in school (Cantrell & Ewing-Taylor, 2009). Results also showed that attending seminars led by industry professionals did increase female interest in those fields (Cantrell & Ewing-Taylor, 2009). According to the researchers, this was consistent with other literature that found female students and senior students were more stable in their career choices (Cantrell & Ewing-Taylor, 2009). In other words, the results of this study directly supported the results of prior studies as well, and provided the researchers with clear answers to the questions they intended to solve.

Significance

The significance of this article is that it shows that by the time females to get to high school, if they are already set on a career path then it is unlikely they will change their minds even when exposed to various STEM related careers. It also shows that female interest can be increased through exposure to industry professionals as well. This supports the claim that in order to bring more women into the game industry, it is imperative that the career possibilities are exposed to them at a younger age; meaning before they reach high school and are already set on a career path. However, it is important to also remember that this does not take into account the number of students who change their career paths once in college, but this idea will be revisited later in this paper.

Article II

The next article in this section is by T. Carter Gilmer (2007) and deals specifically with women and minorities in STEM fields. It implies that women and minorities make up only a tiny fraction of STEM graduates and are thus highly underrepresented in STEM fields. In order to encourage more women and minorities to pursue STEM careers and help enable them to become highly skilled professionals, Bowling Green State

University (BGSU) created an undergraduate program called Academic Investment in Math and Science, or AIMS, in 2001. The program was created not only to increase the skill level of STEM graduates, but to also give women and minorities an equal chance to excel in STEM fields. This is an interesting article, because it supports the idea that more women could become interested in and highly successful in STEM fields if they receive the right guidance.

Summary

The results of this program found a positive correlation between how well the students performed in the summer classes and their GPA from their first semester. The GPA's of the AIMS students were compared to the control groups, and were found to be higher. The difference in achievement was visible after the first semester, and continued throughout the program. The study showed that a student's first semester is a good indication of how they will perform for the rest of their program. It also showed that students who did not perform as well in their math or science classes the first semester had a higher tendency to switch careers away from STEM areas. Overall, participants in the AIMS program performed better than students who were not exposed to the program (Gilmer, 2007).

Analysis

To further analyze the findings of the study, it showed that by having a support program in place to aid students in their success throughout their undergraduate career, it enabled the student to perform better academically and stay on their STEM career path choices. Without this program, students would have been more likely to change their minds about their majors along the way after being discouraged by a failed math or science class. When students become discouraged, they feel they should change their path because the doubt their ability to be successful. Therefore, it is important for STEM students to have the necessary support in place in order for them to succeed.

Significance

The significance of this study to the game industry lies in the support system for females that have chosen to pursue a STEM related career path. For example, females who have chosen to pursue careers in programming, animation, or audio engineering can benefit from having a support system in place in order to help them get through tough classes and stay focused, which in turn helps ensure that they successfully graduate with the necessary skills needed for the job industry. There are also several schools which offer video game related majors who could aid their female students in being more successful by providing them with the necessary support they need to achieve success. Support groups could also help women feel more confident in their skills and would make them less likely to switch majors, as was found in this study. Therefore, this is another idea that could help in the effort to bring more women into the industry.

Article III

The next article in this section was written by Lisa Tsui (2009), and deals with strategies for recruiting females in to male dominated programs. The article deals directly with mechanical engineering, a field which is also largely male dominated, similar to the software and audio engineering areas of the video game industry. The study consisted of a series of interviews and focus groups from staff members of six different mechanical engineering programs across the U.S. The programs were chosen based off of the data collected by the National Science Foundation's national study on women in engineering. A total of 110 interviews and 25 focus groups were conducted across all six sites (Tsui, 2009).

Analysis

Tsui's study found three key points. The first was that marketing and recruitment needs to be more focused towards females (Tsui, 2009). By adjusting the way that information is presented to females in addition to the content that is found most appealing to them, their interest could be improved substantially. The second point is that community outreach is directly linked to recruitment, specifically K-12 outreach (Tsui, 2009). This directly supports the idea that recruitment for the game industry needs to start at an earlier age instead of waiting until females are already set in their career paths. The third and final key point is that undergraduates play a large role in the effectiveness of community outreach (Tsui, 2009). This is key because prospective students value the opinions of other students who are already in the program because they can relate more to younger students than adults in the same field, and use those opinions to help make their own decisions (Tsui, 2009).

Significance

The significance of this to the video game industry again lies in the fact that the engineering fields of the industry are similar to engineering fields outside of the industry, in the fact they are largely male dominated. The key points from this study support the idea that recruitment and exposure to the industry needs to be done at an earlier age, and suggests a new idea that having undergraduate students in those fields could help the younger females identify with them more, which would in turn increase their interest in joining the industry. These concepts will be applied later in this paper when possible recruitment methods are proposed.

NON-STEM RELATED STUDIES

Article I

The first article in this section is by Jody Kasper (2006) and deals with recruiting women into the Police field. While law enforcement is not directly related to the video game industry, it is also another industry which suffers from a lack of women employees, and is similar to the video game industry in that respect. The article gives several suggestions for recruiting women that can be applied to any industry, and not just the law enforcement field.

Analysis

The first idea suggested in this article is that diverse recruitment teams are necessary to recruit professionals into the field, and that it is important for these teams to reflect the type of people they are trying to recruit (Kasper, 2006, p. 1). This allows potential candidates the opportunity to identify with the recruiters. Kasper also suggests that "One of the barriers that prevents women from considering a job as a police officer is the absence of female role models and mentors working in police positions" (Kasper, 2006, p. 1). This also supports the idea that it is necessary to have women already in the industry speak out to other women and assist by mentoring women who are thinking about joining the industry, in addition to men in the industry who are also supportive of the idea of bringing more women into the game industry. Since the industry is male dominated, having men speak out about the need for more women in the industry could possibly help women feel more comfortable about working in the field. Closely related to this idea are the suggestions for more females in recruitment materials and both male and female mentors, which again support the key points of this chapter.

The next idea is that the company's website should have a special section for women who are interested in applying, since the internet is the primary tool people use to gather information (Kasper, 2006). This can be applied to the video game industry in the way that game companies can include a section like this on the careers page of their websites, which could also possibly attract more women applicants.

The last idea in this article that could be applied to the game industry is the suggestion to keep sexism out of the workplace (Kasper, 2006). While this should be common practice regardless of industry, given the issues in the industry of the hypersexualization of female characters, in addition to the environment of the game industry, this might be the most difficult to enforce. However, in a perfect situation this would be easily attainable, when in truth it is not; it is more likely that this could be enforced on paper, but overlooked as just another risk that "goes along with the territory".

Significance

The significance of this article to the video game industry is that it provides many useful suggestions for recruiting women that can be applied not only to the video game industry but to other industries as well. It stresses the importance of tailoring marketing to females, keeping sexism out of the workplace, utilizing diverse recruitment teams, and having a special area on the website for female applicants. All of these suggestions will be taken into consideration when developing the recruitment strategies that will be the take-away from this chapter.

Article II

The next article in this section is written by Laura Putsche, Debbie Storrs, Alicia E. Lewis, and Jennifer Haylett (2008) on the development of mentoring programs for undergraduate women. The program was developed in order to "improve

the educational climate for female undergraduate students" (Putsche et al., 2008, p. 1). The program consisted of a team of researchers who worked together with the Women's Center to develop a mentoring team for the undergraduates, and data was recorded on mentees who participated on whether or not they returned to the university and continued along in the program. The program was also developed using the feminist and networking models, which stress the encouragement of mutual collaboration and community involvement between mentors and mentees.

Analysis

The results of the mentoring program were that 83% of the mentees that participated and 90% of the mentors who chose not to leave the university, chose to stay in the program. This shows a high success rate of the program, to the effect that only three mentees were dissatisfied with the program. This suggests that mentoring programs are valued by female students who participate in them, and could be helpful to female students pursuing degrees in video game related fields.

RESULTS OF LITERATURE REVIEW

After reviewing these five articles, there are several trends amongst them that can be tied in with the possible causes for the lack of women in the game industry that were presented earlier and also with the proposed solutions that will be presented later. To start with, Cantrell & Ewing-Taylor's study showed a possible trend that more women were interested in STEM careers after attending seminars led by industry professionals, though they also suggested that waiting until students were at the high school level was too late (2009). Tsui also suggested that community outreach for students K-12 could also help increase female interest in STEM fields, especially since younger students are more easily influenced by the opinions of older students already studying in those fields (2009). When combined together, these articles support the idea that if students were exposed to industry professionals at a younger age or even other college students who are already studying STEM related career paths, and then female interest in various STEM careers could possibly be increased. If female interest was indeed increased through the use of Tsui and Cantrell & Ewing's methods, then the issue of lack of interest that was mentioned by Weinburgh (1995) and Baker & Leary (1995) in Blickenstaff's paper (2005) could be combated.

In the study by Gilmer, the trend shown was that women (at the university level) were more likely to stick to their STEM career choices, perform better academically, and feel more confident in their skills and abilities when there was a mentorship and support program in place at their university (2007). If the cause of the lack of women in the industry is due to a lack of confidence in their skills and abilities, as both Hawkes & Spade (1998) and Rinn et al. (2008) suggested, then a mentorship and support program like the one Gilmer (2007) proved to be successful in increasing their confidence could be the answer to that problem as well. Gilmer's program could even possibly be employed on the K-12 level, using freshman level college students already enrolled in similar programs. Tsui (2009) also stressed that the manner of which information is presented, and whether or not the type of information that women consider to be important is what is being presented, plays a big part in whether interest is increased as well. If students are more receptive to the opinions of other students, and are more likely to have increased interest when exposed to others already in the industry or career path, then it only makes sense that developing a mentorship and support program for students of all levels could be beneficial in solving the problem of the lack of women in STEM careers. Again, since the video game industry is closely related to STEM, these proposed methods could be directly applied to it as well.

The main idea stressed by Kasper is that recruitment teams need to reflect the target demographic they are trying to attract (2006). Again, this idea can be supported by Tsui's suggestion that marketing and recruitment need to be directly targeted towards women, and that students are more likely to be influenced by other students who already have experience or are currently pursuing careers in specific fields (2009). For example, both ideas could be combined to construct a recruitment team of female students and industry professionals to recruit other women into the game industry. Another interesting fact is that even though Tsui (2009) dealt with STEM and Kasper (2006) with non-STEM careers, they are still mutually beneficial to each other. This type of interchangeability is critical when attempting to relate methods back to the gaming industry, since it encompasses both sides of the coin as well. Kasper also suggested that the absence of female role models in law enforcement played a large part in the lack of female interest in joining the field (2006). This further supports Blickenstaff's claim that the lack of female role models in STEM plays a large part in the lack of women in STEM related fields (2005). Again, both a STEM related article and a non-STEM related article can be directly related to each other. In relation to the video game industry, this can be applied by having female industry professionals do community outreach in their areas, in order to attract more women into their fields.

Finally, in the article by Putsche et al., the main trend was that the institution of mentorship programs aided in the retention of undergraduate women in their chosen career paths (2008). Again, this study supported the same idea as Gilmer (2007); that the use of mentorship programs could positively impact the number of women continuing on their STEM career paths, and since Putsche et al. (2008) was related to both STEM and non- STEM as well, again this can coincide greatly with the video game industry.

There are several main things to understand from the information gathered from this literature. First, is that both STEM and non-STEM related literature can be easily combined and related to the video game industry. This is apparent in the literature from both areas providing such similar results. Second, the need for women who are currently in the industry to reach out to their communities is dire, and has the potential to greatly influence other women into joining the video game industry. Third, mentorship programs are a necessity, and should be available to women of all education levels, starting as early as primary school. The information this literature provided will be of great use when developing possible applications to the video game industry.

TAKE-AWAY MESSAGES

Proposed Application of Findings to the Video Game Industry

The information in this chapter can be applied to the video game industry in a number of ways in order to increase the number of women it has. For the purpose of take-away messages form the findings, four areas will be focused on; recruitment programs, marketing tactics, mentoring programs, and social games as a possible recruitment avenue. The possible causes of the lack of women in the industry will also be taken into consideration when making suggestions for the industry. It is also important to remember that while each one of these ideas could be successfully used individually, in order to achieve the full benefit, they should be used in conjunction with one another.

Recruitment Programs

Recruitment programs have been shown to have a positive effect on increasing numbers when conducted correctly. The information contained in this chapter provides several helpful tips to in-

crease the success of recruitment programs. When creating a recruitment program, it is important to take into consideration the age demographic of the intended audience. For example, if the goal is to interest more women into pursuing careers in the game industry, research has shown that it is more effective to start introducing females to the idea at an earlier age. Therefore, starting from middle school or late elementary school would be the best idea, since children are more influenced at a younger age.

It is also important to make sure that the recruitment team is comprised of a similar makeup to the intended recruits. For example, if the goal is to interest more females into pursuing careers in the game industry, then it would only make sense for the team to include other females who are already in related undergraduate fields, as younger females are more likely to identify with recruiters around their age group than the older, more seasoned veterans. In the same manner, if the goal is to attract women who already have careers in video game related fields, then it would be helpful to have women in those same fields who are already in the industry be part of the recruitment team, since women are more likely to take into consideration the opinions of other women when making their own decisions. It would also be beneficial when creating recruitment groups for elementary and middle school level if the group included high school or freshman level college students who had already chosen to pursue careers in the video game industry, or were already enrolled in video game related courses at school. The benefit of tailoring the group composition to include other students is to utilize Tsui's idea that children are influenced more by the opinions of other students (2009). This is not to say that the recruitment teams should only be comprised of women, because it is important that there are men included who are supportive of the idea as well, since they are the majority of the industry, and this could help women feel more accepted by the industry and its environment.

Marketing Tactics

The next suggestion is the need for more female oriented marketing. This again stems from Tsui's suggestion that women value different things than men do when making career choices (2009). Again, a big thing to consider when creating marketing tactics is to show women in the industry in the marketing medium, whatever that might be. Another suggestion is the integration of more family friendly practices (FFP's) in the industry, and using those to market to women. However, the success of that idea hinges on the industry's decision to adopt more FFP's, and only time will tell whether or not that will happen. It is also useful to know that the implementation of FFP's in the game industry will not only benefit women who are interested in joining the industry, but would also benefit men in the industry with families as well.

Again, a common thing to keep in consideration when deciding upon marketing tactics is the intended target demographic. Marketing strategies for different age groups also need to be tailored accordingly. For example, the marketing strategy for high school students who have not yet made their college career choices would be completely different from the marketing strategy tailored towards women already in relevant careers that could be also used for the video game industry.

Mentoring Programs

The last suggestion of this chapter is that mentoring programs should be developed for undergraduate women pursuing video game related degrees at the schools that offer them. The benefit of this is the retention of the undergraduates who start in video game industry related programs, but then change their minds or switch majors when they start having difficulties. If there were a mentoring program in place to help these students through their difficult times, they might be more likely to successfully finish their degrees and join the video game industry. Again, just as in the other two areas,

it is important to have women as mentors so that the students can easily identify with them, and not feel intimidated by a largely male presence.

Since mentoring programs seem to be one of the major contributing factors in female retention among college level students, this can be seen as one of the most influential ways of solving the problem of the lack of women in the game industry. To tie it in with the rest of the literature, again the mentors would need to consist of men and women already in the game industry for the college level demographic, and would most likely need to consist of college students for the high school level demographic. The importance of having both male and female role models as mentors could greatly increase other females' confidence in their skills and abilities (which as previous literature states, seems to be a large contributing factor in women choosing other career paths than STEM related fields), which would make them more likely to succeed in their career paths. By having someone to look up to, women would have a more realistic idea of what to expect in the game industry; and the mentors could help coach their mentees throughout all stages or their careers. It is also important to have male role models to reach out to women as well, since they are the majority. Having men who are already in the industry reach out to women as well can help show women that their presence is both needed and wanted, and could possibly help women overcome some of their qualms about joining the industry.

Social Games

While the social games route has not been discussed in detail in this chapter, the recent surge in the independent and social gaming community is worth noting. In both Game Developer Salary Surveys reviewed in a previous chapter (Sheffield & Fleming, 2010; Sheffield & Newman, 2011), they have included a new section on the indie game community. While no gender breakdown for these areas was included, the information did report that the average annual salary was up across the board for all departments, putting it at $55,493 for 2010 (Sheffield & Newman, 2011). Social games are also becoming increasingly popular, especially amongst women. In 2010, Women 2.0, a group of women dedicated to helping more female entrepreneurs get started in technology ventures, conducted a panel called Social Gaming 101. On this panel were several founders and CEO's of various successful social gaming ventures who talked about their journeys into social gaming. Their goal was to enlighten women about social games, and inspire them to start their own social gaming and technology ventures on their own (Women2.org, 2010). Groups like Women 2.0 are the key to helping solve the issue of the lack of women in the game industry, because they are full of not only female role models that can share their knowledge to other women and are willing to help them become successful in the game industry, but also male role models as well. Again, the need for mentorship programs and community outreach groups such as Women 2.0 is crucial if the industry wants to interest more women into joining it.

CONCLUSION

This chapter has attempted to shed some light on the issue of the lack of women in the video game industry. It has examined several different recruitment tactics used in other STEM fields that have successfully been used to increase the number of women in those fields. The main thing that was learned is that through a combination of different tactics from a variety of disciplines can be applied to the video game industry due to the fact that there are many disciplines that the industry combines in order to make it a collective whole. Mentorship and community outreach are definitely things that could make the greatest impact on the situation at hand, because the lack of female role models and industry professionals

to look up to negatively impacts the situation as well. Therefore the greatest thing that was learned through this chapter is the need for all fellow women in the industry to reach out to each other and join together in bringing more women into the industry.

FUTURE QUESTIONS/RESEARCH

There are several things that could stand to be further researched on this topic, such as more research into the number of females currently enrolled in video game related degrees, along with possibly tracking these women throughout their degree programs until they get out in the industry. The booming social games avenue is also worth exploring further, and could possibly be a more desirable area of the video game industry for some women. Finally, the development of a mentorship and community outreach program on either a state or national level needs to be developed, and the success measured over a several year period. In the event that this topic is revisited again on the doctoral level, the implementation of this type of program and its measured success would be the focus of that research. In conclusion, there are several things that still need to be addressed before this problem is solved, but at least now there is a place to start.

REFERENCES

Blickenstaff, J. (2005). Women and science careers: Leaky pipeline or gender filter? *Gender and Education, 17*(4), 369–386. doi:10.1080/09540250500145072

Cantrell, P., & Ewing-Taylor, J. (2009). Exploring STEM career options through collaborative high school seminars. *Journal of Engineering Education, 98*(3), 295–303. doi:10.1002/j.2168-9830.2009.tb01026.x

Gilmer, T. (2007). An understanding of the improved grades, retention and graduation rates of STEM majors at the Academic Investment in Math and Science (AIMS) program of Bowling Green State University (BGSU). *Journal of STEM Education: Innovations and Research, 8*(1/2), 11–21.

Hawks, B., & Spade, J. Z. (1998). Women and men engineering students: Anticipation of family and work roles. *Journal of Engineering Education, 87*(3), 249–256. doi:10.1002/j.2168-9830.1998. tb00351.x

Kasper, J. (2006). *Proven steps for recruiting women.* Retrieved November 12, 2010 from http:// www.hendonpub.com/resources/articlearchive/ details.aspx?ID=965

Putsche, L., Storrs, D., Lewis, A., & Haylett, J. (2008). The development of a mentoring program for university undergraduate women. *Cambridge Journal of Education, 38*(4), 513–528. doi:10.1080/03057640802482322

Rinn, A., McQueen, K., Clark, G., & Rumsey, J. (2008). Gender differences in gifted adolescents' math/verbal self-concepts and math/verbal achievement: implications for the STEM fields. *Journal for the Education of the Gifted, 32*(1), 34–53.

Sheffield, B., & Fleming, J. (2010). Ninth annual game developer salary survey. *Game Developer Magazine, 17*(4), 7–13.

Sheffield, B., & Newman, R. (2011). Tenth annual game developer salary survey. *Game Developer Magazine, 18*(4), 7–13.

Tsui, L. (2009). Recruiting females into male dominated programs: Effective strategies and approaches. *Journal of College Admission, 203*, 8–13.

ADDITIONAL READING

Beede, D.N., Julian, T.A., Langdon, D., McKittrick, G., Khan, B., & Doms, M.E. (2011) Women in STEM: A gender gap to innovation. *Economics and Statistics Administration Issue Brief 4(11).*

Burke, R. J. (2007). 1. Women and minorities in STEM: a primer. Women and Minorities in Science, Technology, Engineering, and Mathematics: Upping the Numbers, 1.

Chesler, N. C., & Chesler, M. A. (2002). Gender-Informed Mentoring Strategies for Women Engineering Scholars: On Establishing a Caring Community. *Journal of Engineering Education, 91*(1), 49–55. doi:10.1002/j.2168-9830.2002. tb00672.x

Cohoon, J. M. (2001). Toward improving female retention in the computer science major. *Communications of the ACM, 44*(5), 108–114. doi:10.1145/374308.374367

Espinosa, L. L. (2011). Pipelines and pathways: Women of color in undergraduate STEM majors and the college experiences that contribute to persistence. *Harvard Educational Review, 81*(2), 209–241.

Fassinger, R. E., & Asay, P. A. (2006). Career counseling for women in science, technology, engineering, and mathematics (STEM) fields. Handbook of career counseling for women, 2.

Glass, C., & Minnotte, K. L. (2010). Recruiting and hiring women in STEM fields. *Journal of Diversity in Higher Education, 3*(4), 218.

Griffith, A. L. (2010). Persistence of women and minorities in STEM field majors: Is it the school that matters? *Economics of Education Review, 29*(6), 911–922. doi:10.1016/j.econedurev.2010.06.010

Johnson, D. R. (2011). Women of color in science, technology, engineering, and mathematics (STEM). *New Directions for Institutional Research*, (152): 75–85. doi:10.1002/ir.410

Kahveci, A., Southerland, S. A., & Gilmer, P. J. (2006). Retaining Undergraduate Women in Science, Mathematics, and Engineering. *Journal of College Science Teaching*, *36*(3), 34–38.

McNeely, C. L., & Vlaicu, S. (2010). Exploring institutional hiring trends of women in the US STEM professoriate. *Review of Policy Research*, *27*(6), 781–793. doi:10.1111/j.1541-1338.2010.00471.x

Milgram, D. (2011). How to Recruit Women and Girls to the Science, Technology, Engineering, and Math (STEM) Classroom. *Technology and Engineering Teacher*, *71*(3), 4–11.

Noe, R. A. (1988). Women and mentoring: A review and research agenda. *Academy of Management Review*, *13*(1), 65–78.

Perna, L. W., Gasman, M., Gary, S., Lundy-Wagner, V., & Drezner, N. D. (2010). Identifying strategies for increasing degree attainment in STEM: Lessons from minority-serving institutions. *New Directions for Institutional Research*, (148): 41–51. doi:10.1002/ir.360

Stout, J. G., Dasgupta, N., Hunsinger, M., & McManus, M. A. (2011). STEMing the tide: using ingroup experts to inoculate women's self-concept in science, technology, engineering, and mathematics (STEM). *Journal of Personality and Social Psychology*, *100*(2), 255. doi:10.1037/a0021385 PMID:21142376

Szelényi, K., & Inkelas, K. K. (2011). The Role of Living–Learning Programs in Women's Plans to Attend Graduate School in STEM Fields. *Research in Higher Education*, *52*(4), 349–369. doi:10.1007/s11162-010-9197-9

Thompson, C., Beauvais, L., & Lyness, K. (1999). When work-family benefits are not enough: The influence of work-family culture on benefit utilization, organizational attachment, and work-family conflict. *Journal of Vocational Behavior*, *54*(3), 392–415. doi:10.1006/jvbe.1998.1681

Xu, Y. J. (2008). Gender disparity in STEM disciplines: A study of faculty attrition and turnover intentions. *Research in Higher Education*, *49*(7), 607–624. doi:10.1007/s11162-008-9097-4

KEY TERMS AND DEFINITIONS

Family Friendly Practices (FFP): Various programs put in place by the employer in an attempt to help employees balance work and family roles—such as mental health programs, maternity/paternity leave, and childcare options.

Game Industry: An entertainment industry that focuses on the software development of video games.

Gender: The state of being male or female (typically used with reference to social and cultural differences rather than biological ones).

Mentor: An experienced and trusted adviser.

Mentorship: A personal developmental relationship in which a more experienced or more knowledgeable person helps to guide a less experienced or less knowledgeable person.

Social Games: A type of online game that is played through social networks, and typically features multiplayer and asynchronous gameplay mechanics.

STEM: An acronym referring to careers in the fields of science, technology, engineering or math.

Chapter 10
A Framework for Addressing Gender Imbalance in the Game Industry through Outreach

Monica M. McGill
Bradley University, USA

Adrienne Decker
Rochester Institute of Technology, USA

Amber Settle
DePaul University, USA

ABSTRACT

Though the lack of diversity in the game industry workforce has received a great deal of attention recently, few initiatives have been implemented to address it. In particular, gender composition in the game industry workforce and among students studying games at post-secondary institutions is highly imbalanced, with an approximate 9 to 1 ratio of male to female students. This chapter considers three key aspects: 1) the current demographics of the game industry, 2) the effects of gender imbalance on the game industry and one of its current pipelines, and 3) a potential framework to address the imbalance. The proposed outreach strategy is informed by a discussion of established frameworks for initiating change in related fields. The chapter concludes with suggestions for future research to address the gender imbalance in the game industry and its pipeline.

INTRODUCTION

There is a lack of diversity in the game industry workforce, and it is has been acknowledged as a serious problem for the game industry, among both AAA companies and independent developers (Contestabile, 2012; Serviss, 2013; Sinclair, 2013). Recently Ben Serviss (2013), an American independent games developer, made a call for something different than the straight white males that have typically dominated the game industry, adding another voice to a growing number calling for a more diverse set of individuals developing digital games (Contestabile, 2012; IGDA, 2005; Ligman, 2013; Sinclair, 2013). Diversity in the workforce has been considered a quality of life issue by the International Game Developers Association (IGDA), which has conducted industry

DOI: 10.4018/978-1-4666-6142-4.ch010

surveys on the topic (IGDA 2005, Margolis et al., 2012). Recent activity, such as heated exchanges on industry social media sites, has indicated that this topic is being widely discussed, with workforce diversity and representation in games being considered one of the top five trends of the game industry in 2012 (Graft, 2012; Isaacson, 2012; Plunkett, 2012). One of the most egregious areas of diversity imbalance remains gender, with little change in this area in the past ten years.

This lack of diversity leads to a number of questions regarding the game industry's gender imbalance. How do we attract and cultivate diverse talent? How do we retain the diverse talent in our degree and training programs once we have them? How do we ensure that individuals have the opportunities to grow within the industry and effect the kind of change that more and more people agree needs to happen? How do we make some in the industry understand what an important issue diversity is? All of these questions beg another: Where do we begin?

As those questions indicate, the path to creating more diversity in the game industry is not straightforward and there will be many points of entry for those wishing to explore and address this issue. There are three key questions this chapter investigates:

- What is the current state of gender imbalance in the game industry and its pipelines?
- Why is the issue of gender imbalance important in the game industry?
- What are ways in which this issue can be addressed?

The goal of this chapter is to provide a framework for future research and outreach initiatives to bring more women into the industry. A discussion of established frameworks for initiating change in related fields informs the development of the framework for addressing the imbalance in the game industry.

BACKGROUND

Depending on the reader's perspective, diversity may be viewed as an issue of fairness or of moral obligation, or even for some, not an issue at all. Less subjective and open to debate, however, is that a diverse workforce can create broader market shares and increased revenues (Barrington & Troske, 2001, Contestabile, 2012). The demographics of the game industry, demographics of students and faculty at post-secondary institutions, effects of gender imbalance, and successful outreach initiatives are components that must be considered in any research evaluating diversity and its importance within a field. Since the digital game industry is relatively new compared to other related fields such as art or STEM (science, technology, engineering, and mathematics) fields, we provide results of related research and activities for comparison and analogy when data for the game industry is unavailable.

Game Industry Demographics

Over the last decade there has been an increased awareness of the lack of diversity in the game industry, culminating in the recent identification by a prominent industry association site as one of the top five topics in the game industry (Graft, 2012). The game industry has recently faced repeated criticism for sexist policies, culture, and practices, with the Twitter hashtag #1reasonwhy becoming associated with multiple stories of gender discrimination in the industry (Haines, 2004; Isaacson, 2012; Plunkett, 2012). Concern about the lack of a diverse workforce prompted the IGDA to examine workforce diversity, conducting two full-scale industry surveys on the topic since 2005 (IGDA, 2005; IGDA, 2011) as well as a 2008-2009 Quality of Life Survey (Legault & Weststar, 2012). While the IGDA surveys included questions on a multitude of demographic categories, including age, ethnicity, education, compensation, sexual orientation, and disability status, we focus here on the results for gender.

In the 2005 IGDA survey, 66% of the 4,006 counted responses were from the United States, 18% from Canada, 12% from the United Kingdom, and 4% from Australia (IGDA, 2005, p. 7). Among these, 11.5% identified as female and 88.5% identified as male (IGDA, 2005, p. 12). This figure is supported by the 2002 Skillset Census in the United Kingdom, which found that women comprised only 16% of the game workforce and an independent study conducted in 2004, which found that women comprised only 17% of the game workforce (Haines, 2004).

Of the 3,362 respondents to the IGDA Quality of Life survey, 86% were male and 14% were female (Legault & Weststar 2012, p. 11). Though this is higher than previous surveys, it cannot necessarily be used to conclude that higher numbers of women are entering the field as it may be the case that more females responded (Legault & Weststar, 2012, p. 11). In contrast, the results of the 2010 TIGA-Hewitt Games Software Developers' Salary Survey in the United Kingdom found that women comprise just 6.6% of the workforce (Gamasutra, 2010).

Despite a very small difference in years in industry, survey data also revealed that women earn on average $9,000 a year less (IGDA, 2005, p. 13-14). When gender representation was considered by job title, the highest female representation was found in operations/information technology/human resources with 46% of the workforce (IGDA, 2005, p. 13). Writing, marketing/PR/sales, and production were 30%, 25%, and 21% female respectively. Females held only 13% of quality assurance positions. Females comprised 12%, 11%, 10%, 10%, and 5% of executive, visual arts, design, audio, and programming roles, respectively.

Diversity in Game Degree Programs

Increasingly the game industry considers universities as a viable pipeline for potential employees. Thus, examining diversity among students is critical in understanding the demographics of potential future employees (Gamasutra, 2010; Hall, 2012; Skillset, 2013). As part of researching the pipeline for the game industry, we created the Game Industry Employee Pipeline Survey. Many of these questions were taken directly from the 2005 IGDA survey "Game Developer Demographics: An Exploration of Workforce Diversity" and the 2011 IGDA Industry Survey with permission (IGDA, 2005; Margolis et. al, 2012; McGill, Settle and Decker, 2013a; 2013b). The survey consisted of demographic questions, including gender, ethnicity, religious preferences, sexual orientation preferences, political views, and disabilities.

Though the current trend among undergraduate institutions is that female attendance exceeds male attendance (Camp, 2012; Fuller, 2010), results indicated that there is nearly a nine to one ratio of men to women studying game design and development. This is further supported by the fact that only 10 percent of students studying games in the United Kingdom are female (Gamasutra, 2010). These figures are in line with the 2005 IGDA Diversity survey of game industry employees, which showed the same lack of diversity, though it is slightly more than reported in the United Kingdom, where only 5% of students in game degree programs were found to be female (Haines, 2004). It is also nearly identical to the ratio of men to women studying computing (CRA, 2012).

Though gender composition within the student demographic is a crucial data point, another data point is the gender of women in faculty positions in the game degree programs. Previous studies have shown that there is a positive relationship between the retention of female students in their first year of studies and their percentage of math and science courses taught by female faculty (Bettinger and Long, 2005; Neumark and Gardecki, 1998; Robst et. al, 1998), though results of whether there is a clear impact in disciplines where female students are a minority are mixed (Bettinger and Long, 2005). Despite these mixed results, faculty gender data for top-ranked post-secondary institutions in the United States should be defined.

Since 2010, the Princeton Review, a private source of nationally-ranked academic institutions, has ranked the top undergraduate and graduate game design programs at U.S. post-secondary four-year institutions. In 2012, the list of undergraduate schools was divided into 15 ranked schools and 15 honorable mentions. As shown in Table 1, twelve of the ranked schools and eight of the honorable mention schools had websites with a faculty directory that contained names and photographs. Of the schools that provided this information, a total of 42 of the 160 were women, or 26.2% (Princeton Review, 2013).

Effects of Gender Imbalance in the Game Industry

According to a 2012 report by Forbes, workforce diversity has great bearing on competitiveness in industry (Forbes, 2012). Companies with a diverse workforce typically do not have lower rates of productivity than companies with less diverse workforces and, in some cases, have higher rates of productivity (Barrington & Troske, 2001). Global interest in diversity is strongly evidenced by the focus of the 2012 World Economic Forum's Global Agenda Council on Competitiveness, in which one of the two issues emphasized was "[s]tructural and institutional reforms to overcome barriers to competitiveness," with a focus on diversity (Murphy, 2012).

Lynne Featherstone MP, UK Minister of Equalities, directly addressed this when she remarked that "...some companies 'risk being uncompetitive' if they did not address the gender imbalance in the games industry." (Gamustra, 2010, p. 1). This risk is due to the fact that in many countries women are now nearly equal players and consumers of games. For example, in the U.S., females comprise 45% of gamers and women 18 or older represent a significantly greater portion of the game-playing population (31%) than boys age 17 or younger (19%) (Entertainment Software Association, 2013). Women in the U.S. also comprise 46% of game purchasers (Entertainment Software Association, 2013). Given that women are an increasing target audience for games, it seems logical to include female team members in the development process (Contestabile, 2012). For example, eight of the 20 top selling computer games of 2012 are variants of the Sims (Entertainment Software Association 2013, p. 9), the first version of which had a development team consisting of 40% women (Parfitt, 2010).

Little research has been conducted on the effects of gender imbalance on the game industry, though a review of related fields provides critical insight. Many of the positions in the game industry are highly technical and are considered to be under the umbrella of the STEM fields. A recent report by the United Kingdom Resource Centre (UKRC) places a monetary value on the effect of gender imbalance in STEM positions, stating that the "The UK economy loses billions of pounds when qualified women scientists, technologists and engineers work below their level of qualification, are unemployed or economically inactive" (Kirkup, Zalevski, Maruyama and Batool, 2010, p. 7).

Table 1. Gender of full-time faculty at the top-ranked game degree programs in the United States

U.S. Undergraduate Game Degree Programs	Full-Time Faculty					
	Institutions	Men		Women		Total
		#	%	#	%	
Top 15	12	70	74.5	24	25.5	94
Honorable Mentions	8	48	72.8	18	27.2	66
Top 15 & Honorable Mentions	20	118	73.8	42	26.2	160

A primary reason for this is the deficit of skilled STEM employees despite the recent economic downturn, with 43% of STEM employers in the United Kingdom reporting problems recruiting qualified employees and 52% expecting problems within the next three years (UKRC, 2012, p. 1). An increase of women in STEM fields could help fill this widening gap. However, despite recent efforts to fill these positions, there remains a lack of women employees in STEM fields across Europe, with the European average of women in these fields established at 17% (UKRC, 2012, p.1) This reflects national trends in the United States, where a lack of women in STEM fields continues to be a problem in the science and engineering (S&E) workforce, with the 2012 S&E Indicators reporting that women constitute only 38% of the S&E field in 2008 (National Science Board, 2012).

In the more narrowly-focused technology field, women in the United States make up 25% of computer and information scientists, and from 1993 to 2008 women's share of computer and mathematical scientist positions dropped from 31 to 26% (National Science Board, 2012). Although computing began as a field in which female programmers were the norm, gender parity does not currently exist in technology-focused fields (Abbate, 2012). Concern about inclusion is not limited to computer science, as women are underrepresented in information technology (IT) positions. In 1991, women filled 36% of IT jobs, but by 2008 this number had fallen to 25% (Trauth, 2012). This deficit will continue to exist in the short-term, since it is larger than the current pool of female undergraduate students studying IT (National Science Board, 2012; UKRC, 2012; Vesgo, 2005).

The effects of gender disparity trickle down into society and have been recognized in research evaluating the social return on investment of outreach and mentoring efforts for under- and unemployed women with STEM training (UKRC, 2010). Through this training women felt less isolated, more confident, and more work ready, resulting in women applying for more science, engineering, and technology (SET) related jobs, gaining employment, and/or getting a higher level position. This resulted in more disposable income for the women and an increase in tax revenue from increased salaries. Employers noted that they gained an employee who is more motivated and can "hit the ground running" (UKRC, 2010).

Addressing gender diversity in the game industry pipeline is important for those interested in improving gender parity in the games industry since the 2005 IGDA survey found that over 80% of the workforce had a university-level education or higher, with 64.3% possessing a college or university degree, 14.4% a Masters degree, and 1.7% a Ph.D. (IGDA, 2005, p. 20). As game degree programs in tertiary institutions grow and mature, it is more likely that employees will be recruited from this pipeline due to its need for a specialized workforce (IGDA, 2005, p. 20). Improving gender balance in the pipeline, then, is paramount in changing the current workforce imbalance.

Gender parity has been shown to result in different questions being asked as technology is researched and developed, producing products and services with a broader reach (Camp, 2012). A 2007 study with a 2012 follow-up study by the National Center for Women in IT, for example, found that IT patents issued to mixed-gender teams were more frequently cited than similar IT patents earned by all male or all female teams (Ashcraft & Breitzman, 2007; Ashcraft & Breitzman, 2012). Part of the explanation of this pattern is that mixed-sex teams tended to be larger and that patents by larger teams are more influential. Athena SWAN, a United Kingdom organization that promotes and encourages women in science, refers to this succinctly in its underlying beliefs of its charter, stating that "science cannot reach its full potential unless it can benefit from the talents of the whole population, and until women and men can benefit equally from the opportunities it affords." (Athena SWAN, 2012)

Both in the United States and the United Kingdom, a gender wage gap continues to exist, with working women earning only 82.2% of men's median weekly earnings in the United States and 87.4% in the United Kingdom (Hegewisch, Williams & Harbin, 2012; Kirkup et al., 2010). Reasons are complex, with some noting that it is due to devaluation of work done by women and gender segregation of jobs related to women's roles as mothers (England, 2005; Reskin, 1988). Examining all of the factors that contribute to gender inequality in various occupations and countries is beyond the scope of this chapter, but gender imbalance in the game industry is not unique and represents a specific instance of the broader STEM phenomenon.

Long-established cultural norms have an impact on individual career choices and both effect companies' global diversity efforts (Forbes, 2012; Natale, 2002). In a 2002 study, Natale (2002) explored eight hypotheses related to cultural norms and found that "...careers in the computer industry are truly affected by a male-oriented gaming culture" and that "...computer games are leading to the imbalance of gender in the computer industry." (Natale, 2002, p. 29) The CEO of TIGA, the trade association representing the games industry in the United Kingdom, noted that "...if the games industry was to recruit a more diverse workforce then more girls in schools and women in colleges and universities should be supported and encouraged to study courses relevant to the industry." (Gamasutra, 2010, p. 1) The association notes that the video game industry would like to recruit more women, but first an effort needs to be made to "...encourage more women to both study courses relevant to the games industry and to highlight the career opportunities that exist in the sector." (Gamasutra, 2010, p. 1).

Both the games industry and its pipeline suffer from a lack of diversity, with a gender imbalance that is particularly troubling. There is evidence that a diverse workforce has an impact on the type of games produced and the market share of those games, making improved diversity a sound business decision. Therefore there is a need for initiatives such as outreach programs to recruit and retain more underrepresented groups, especially women, in the games industry and its pipeline.

Outreach Initiatives

Outreach programs offer one way of addressing the gender diversity imbalance. Outreach programs come in many forms. Some are conducted through individual institutions or organizations such as universities, schools, or clubs. Some outreach programs are implemented at the institution level but are overseen by a larger organization, such as the National Center for Women & Information Technology (NCWIT, 2013). Outreach programs across disciplines have common elements, such as a focus on building a sense of community, but the specific content of the program is dependent on the field for which the outreach program has been developed. And the way in which outreach is conducted is culturally and geographically dependent in some cases, with different approaches applied in different countries.

Though there are currently no similar organized efforts to recruit students to study games at post-secondary institutions in the United Kingdom or United States, there are efforts in related fields to provide potential for efficacy of such efforts. Recruiting students, especially female students, is of particular interest in the broader STEM fields, since there is a strong relationship between degree specialization and employment field for workers in STEM areas (National Science Board, 2012, pp. 16-17). Recruiting and retaining a higher percentage of female undergraduates in the STEM fields has been shown to improve the workforce situation (Camp, 2012).

Outreach initiatives have been established to engage students more deeply in aspects of a specific discipline and to inform younger girls about careers in the STEM fields. Several of these efforts involve summer camps designed to create interest and foster understanding of concepts so participants leave with a deeper appreciation of how STEM fits into their lives. Many of these efforts focus on urban, rural or international communities where exposure to these topics can be lacking (Birinci Konur, Şeyihoğlu, Sezen, & Tekbiyik, 2011; Carroll, Smith & Castori, 2009; Foster & Shiel-Rolle, 2011; Miranda & Hermann, 2010). Still others have looked to increase the gender diversity in engineering disciplines by focusing camp experiences and outreach towards girls in middle and high schools (Dave et al., 2010; Zywno, Gilbride & Gudz, 2000).

With respect to computing, games are considered by many outreach organizers to be a good motivator for fostering interest in further study. Therefore, many computing outreach activities use games as their focus (Denault, Kienzle & Vybihal, 2008; Javidi & Shayban, 2008; Maxim, Grosky & Baugh, 2007). Several programs target increased participation by women specifically through summer and academic year programs (Burge, Gannod, Doyle & Davis, 2013; Pivkina, Pontelli, Jensen & Haebe, 2009, Wang, Tang, Zhang & Cukierman, 2012). Other outreach efforts aimed at attracting girls to computing disciplines exist as extensions of corporate outreach efforts (DigiGirlz) or as national outreach efforts supported by educational organizations (Dot Diva) or non-profit organizations (Girls Who Code) (Girls Who Code, 2013; Rowland, 2010; WGBH Educational Foundation, 2010).

Some outreach initiatives use a blend of topics to motivate their students. Davis, Greene-White, Ferdinand & Santangelo (2008) use the creation of digital art as the hook to attract students into computing. This approach could also be useful in recruiting for game students. Wigal, Alp, Mc-Cullough, Smullen & Winters (2002) describe a summer camp for middle school girls that blends engineering with computing and space and extends the activities into the school year.

Outreach efforts for broadening participation in computing became a national initiative in the United States with the National Science Foundation's Broadening Participation in Computing (BPC) awards (National Science Foundation, 2009). Two examples of successful efforts that arose from the BPC awards are Georgia Computes! and the STARS Alliance (Bruckman et al., 2009; Dahlberg, Barnes, Buch & Rorrer, 2011). Georgia Computes! presents workshops and camps to both students and faculty in summer and academic year, serving approximately 1600 students and 200 teachers in the 2007-08 academic year (Bruckman et al., 2009). The STARS (Students and Technology in Academia, Research, and Service) Alliance is a national network of twenty colleges and universities that partner with various community organizations for outreach. Aside from curriculum development efforts and workshops, STARS uses the university students to shape and lead the outreach projects (Dahlberg et al., 2011; Doran, Boyce, Finkelstein & Barnes, 2012).

In the United Kingdom, the Computing at School Working Group (CAS) is a grass-roots organization that has worked to promote the teaching of computing at the pre-secondary level (CAS, 2013). The organization has supported Information, Communication and Technology (ICT) and computing teachers by providing them with teaching material, local gatherings, and newsletters, and it has also advocated for computing as a subject at the national level. The group has devised a computing curriculum which describes in concrete terms what such a program would entail at the school level. Partly as a result of their advocacy, computer science is now a part of the English Baccalaureate, enabling students to have increased opportunities to study computing (Coughlan, 2013). This is a significant development since the CAS leadership has argued that computing should be a key part of every child's education, much like English, maths, science, languages, and humanities.

Evaluation of these programs shows a positive result on participants, particularly areas that measure attitudes, efficacy, and affinity before and after the outreach experiences. Participants feel they have better understanding, more affinity, and more interest in the field. However, the UKRC report states "The impact of programmes based on games and activities to demonstrate what STEM careers are about has yet to be shown. Much of the recent research finds that demonstrating the range of actual jobs available is more effective in actually attracting girls and other groups into these careers, combined with inspirational and good quality teaching (Aspire Facts & Fiction/ Institute of Physics)." (UKRC, 2012, p. 1) While currently being widely used, it appears that the effectiveness of some of these outreach programs is in need of further study.

Work at broadening participation in STEM fields is not restricted to the U.S. or the UK. Two programs, Go Girl, Go for IT and Technology Takes You Anywhere (TTYA), have targeted girls in primary and secondary schools in Australia (Craig et al, 2013). These programs have been evaluated and been shown to be effective at engaging girls, and a framework for how to produce an effective outreach experience has been developed (Craig et al, 2013).

Women are underrepresented in the game industry and remain underrepresented in post-secondary institutions, one of the viable paths to learn the skills necessary to be successful in the industry. Given that the game industry's economic concerns and the fact that major corporations have shown economic benefits of workforce diversity, astute leaders in the game industry have acknowledged the need for improving diversity in their workforce and have even taken some steps to improve it. As shown in previous outreach activities directed solely to computing and STEM fields, outreach activities can be beneficial in increasing affinity of participants toward the discipline and could provide a pathway for students into more in-depth study.

ADDRESSING GENDER IMBALANCE: A FRAMEWORK FOR A MORE INCLUSIVE INDUSTRY

The data presented in the previous section supports the conclusion that women are underrepresented in the games industry and that outreach programs may help address the imbalance. What now needs to be addressed is the ways in which gender diversity in the pipeline can be improved. This section reviews existing efforts for addressing gender imbalance. The review informs the development of a proposed framework to address gender imbalance in the games industry.

While the games industry as a whole includes many jobs that do not fall under the STEM umbrella, including many positions that fall within creative areas, the gender balance in development teams is the most skewed (IGDA, 2005) and the skills needed by workers in those positions are closely aligned with STEM disciplines.

What now needs to be addressed is the ways in which gender diversity in the pipeline can be improved. To do this, we review existing efforts to improve the gender balance in various disciplines and use them to inform a framework to address gender imbalance in the games industry.

Existing Frameworks for Addressing Gender Imbalance

Improving the gender balance in the game design and development discipline is not a new idea, and Haines (2004) has developed a framework specific to the game industry. Her framework is comprised of recommendations for improving gender imbalance and is based on three key points: make technology and games interesting, make the industry more visible to girls, and make the industry more welcoming to women. To make games more interesting to women, she suggests that the industry design more games that women and girls love to play as a first step in attracting girls. She suggests including rudimentary design and study of games in primary and secondary school curriculum and developing more initiatives that increase game development skills and enthusiasm among females.

Haines suggests making the industry more visible to girls by informing them of the opportunities the industry offers, encouraging companies to work with local schools and universities, and having women role models attend schools, careers fairs, universities and games events. Haines addresses the idea of making the industry more welcoming to women, with her findings similar to previous findings that reported that women believe there is a need for "…more women in the industry, and in order to do so [the industry] will need to eliminate "boys only" practices such as "Booth Bimbos"." (IGDA, 2005, p. 13) To this end, she suggests widening recruitment efforts to hire more qualified women via non-traditional networks, managing the industry practice of crunch time more effectively, encouraging a creative, egalitarian atmosphere, and offering networking and mentoring to women in the industry.

The game industry is not the first to attempt to address workforce gender imbalance. In the related field of computing, there are a couple of frameworks of interest, including from CAS in the United Kingdom and from Computer Science Teachers Association (CSTA) in the United States. In a recent keynote speech in July 2013, Simon Peyton-Jones outlined five steps CAS used to initiate change in the United Kingdom: identify the mission, articulate and explain the mission, engage the community, engage the policy makers, and conduct the ground war by initiating the process (Jones, 2013). CAS members note that its grassroots and flat structure are critical to its success. Efforts include the creation of model curriculum, influencing policymakers through lobbying efforts, primary and secondary teacher training, and the creation of networking and learning opportunities for teachers (Brown et al., 2013.)

The CSTA model suggest three primary pillars to increase diversity in computing, including the dispelling of myths about the role of women and minorities in technology in order to recruit diverse students, establishing partnerships with primary and secondary teachers, and establishing partnerships across various sectors (Simard, Stephenson and Kosaraju, 2010). The CSTA model for system change includes the engagement of various stakeholders, including academia, government, industry, teachers, and supporting organizations (Figure 1). The model calls for industry to provide access to cutting-edge technology, role models, financial support, and more. It calls on academia and government to develop standards, provide role models, perform further research on success factors, and encourage student participation in the classroom. Primary and secondary computing teachers are called on to field test and refine curriculum/technology in their respective classrooms.

In the U.S. additional frameworks exist, including one for broadening participation through scalable game design, which builds on the Fluency with Information Technology (FIT) framework defined by National Academy of Sciences (Repenning & Ioannidou, 2008). This framework deemphasizes programming and emphasizes collaborative and design tasks related to information technology. Similarly, the STARS Alliance model encourages school hubs and student-led regional engagement for broadening participation (Dahlberg et al., 2011).

In addition to the related field of computing, STEM outreach initiatives also rely on several preconceived frameworks. The National Science Foundation in the United States has made a concerted effort to broaden participation in STEM fields (National Science Foundation, 2008). Their framework for action centers on internal methods for improving opportunities for underrepresented researchers, including raising awareness and outreach activities. More specifically, these include coordinating efforts to engage all people from all types of institutions and regions of the country, increasing the diversity of experts who review STEM proposals, raising awareness internally to

Figure 1. The CSTA model for creating cross-sector partnerships to enhance primary and secondary computer science education in the United States. © 2010 Computer Science Teachers Association. Used with permission.

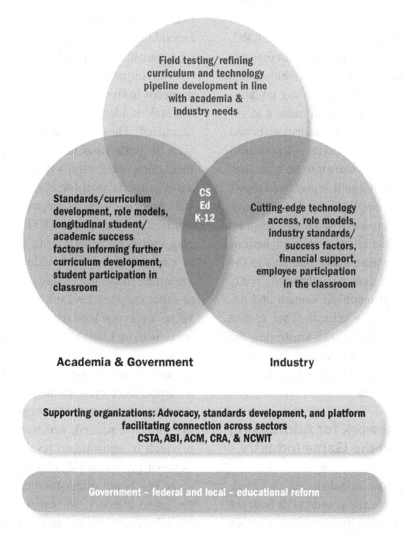

inform staff of workforce development issues and mitigating implicit bias in the review process, and raising awareness externally via a publicly accessible web page with related information. These efforts come with criteria for measuring their effectiveness and reporting on these practices.

Interest in a broader workforce extends beyond the National Science Foundation, and the U.S. Department of Defense has developed a framework for creating a diverse, highly-skilled workforce that will be achieved through four basic goals, inspiring the nation, developing the talent, attracting this talent into their recruitment pool, and delivering a set of programs to achieve this (Department of Defense, 2009). The National Aeronautics and Space Administration (NASA) in the US created their own framework, called the Innovative Conceptual Engineering Design (ICED), based on 37 years of research in practice and four years of piloting the program (Camarda, 2012). Their outreach program provides an eight-step model from selecting an "epic" challenge, selecting the participating key schools to serves as challenge hubs, advertising the challenge, and selecting subject matter experts to serve as coaches and mentors.

In the United Kingdom, the UKRC (UKRC, 2010) recommends several initiatives for increasing women's participation in STEM fields based on evidence-based practices, including collaborating with other organizations to make a larger impact. Using social media to inform girls and their relatives, particularly parents, of possibilities in the field has been shown to be effective, particularly when the information presented shows viable paths towards employment. The initiative also emphasizes role models, since girls respond to female role models along with explanations of the various, authentic careers available in the field. Demonstrating that the industry is ready and willing to accept qualified women and underrepresented groups is critical. This speaks directly to industry culture. Demonstrating the merits (including financial) of studying games, particularly in primary and secondary schools, should be fully described.

Proposed Framework for Addressing the Imbalance in the Game Industry

Addressing the gender imbalance in the game industry will take time and resources at both the micro and macro levels, similar to the summary of frameworks provided in Table 2. We propose a comprehensive framework to address this imbalance, described in detail in Table 3. The framework relies on previously established frameworks as discussed above, previous research, and the community at large, including professionals in the game industry, educators in secondary and tertiary institutions, parents, and other interested individuals. The framework shares many aspects of initiatives found in computing and STEM disciplines: it involves a broad set of stakeholder to ensure that plans produced are useful and effective for various groups; the framework suggests that

a small group of individuals will shepherd the plans through the various stages to ensure that momentum is not lost; and the development of plans involves subject-matter experts, which is crucial for maintaining quality in the individuals who remain in the pipeline.

The initiative described in the framework proceeds in five stages. In the first stage the various stakeholders necessary for the initiative are identified. These include first-line stakeholders such as trade associations and game development companies, who will directly benefit from a more diverse workforce, as well as second-line stakeholders, such as organizations in related fields like computing and STEM disciplines who may indirectly benefit from a more diverse set of students in the game industry pipeline. Also important in the initial stage is the identification of other stakeholders, since an initiative that involves everyone who may have a contribution to make is more likely to be successful. The second stage of the initiative identifies best practices in creating and retaining a more diverse pool of students. Here clear information from outreach activities conducted in computing and STEM disciplines is needed, which may require further research to consolidate results from individual outreach programs. Also important at this second stage is a better understanding of the culture in the game industry, so that it can be contrasted with the culture found in computing and STEM fields and the lessons learned from previous outreach activities adapted. In the third stage a comprehensive plan for increasing diversity in the game development industry is formulated. Both long-term and short-term interventions need to be devised, and all the various stakeholders need to provide input to ensure that the plans meets their needs and also draws upon the best practices from outreach activities in other disciplines. In the fourth stage, the plans devised in the previous stage are implemented. The plans will be implemented in a variety of institutions, including elementary, secondary, and tertiary educational instutions, game development companies, and as necessary, governmental institutions. The results of the efforts will be evaluated in the last stage of the initiative, with the effectiveness of the plan reported in academic, industry, and government conferences and meetings.

It should be noted that this is an early concept of the framework, and as such it is both subject to change and it proposes initial steps at an abstract level. In order to be effective, an outreach initiative needs to have the buy-in of all the various stakeholders. This buy-in is typically only achieved by active participation of multiple groups in the development of the framework, and the next steps in this research will involve broader participation to allow for appropriate refinement.

FUTURE RESEARCH DIRECTIONS

This proposed framework and the accompanying background research is a first step in creating an initiative to address gender imbalance in the games industry. We propose this framework to spark serious dialogue about approaches best suited for this industry. If any widespread initiative is to be successful, however, academic researchers cannot control the process. As previous models have shown, alliances that include industry, government, academics, and primary and secondary school teachers are necessary to ground and successfully motivate this endeavor.

To propel this issue forward, we propose stakeholders who see value in such an initiative create an active counsel with experienced leader-

Table 2. Summary of foundational objectives found in frameworks used in outreach initiatives for improving workforce diversity

	Haines	CAS	CSTA	STARS Alliance	FIT	NSF	DoD	ICED (NASA)	UKRC
Create more games that appeal to females	X								
Career Awareness	X			X			X		X
Make industry more welcoming to women	X						X		
Networking Opportunities (Hubs, social media, etc.)		X		X				X	
Create repository of initiatives		X	X	X		X	X		
Curriculum change	X	X	X	X	X	X		X	
Primary/ Secondary partners	X	X	X	X	X			X	
University partners		X	X	X				X	
Primary/ Secondary teacher training		X	X						
Workshops, sessions, challenges	X	X	X	X				X	X
Role models	X			X					X
Academic/ Industry Alliances	X	X	X	X			X		
Influence Policy Makers		X							

Table 3. Proposed framework for improving the gender imbalance in the game industry

Vision: Craft a well-formulated, comprehensive outreach program for addressing the gender imbalance in the entertainment and serious game industry		
Mission: To ensure that the game industry workforce is as diverse as the audience for the products and services created, which will allow optimal creative and innovative practices		
Stage	**Description**	**Preliminary Steps**
Identify and engage stakeholders	Engage the game communities and related fields to determine who might be interested in creating a more diverse talent pool.	• Identify and engage first-line stakeholders, such as trade associations and game companies, who will directly benefit from a more diverse pool. • Identify and engage second-line stakeholders, such as associations in related fields like computing, STEM, and art/sound communities, who may benefit indirectly from a more diverse pool. • Identify and engage other stakeholders (academia, others interested in expanding opportunities for women).
Identify best practices in creating and retaining a more diverse talent pool	Thoroughly research outreach activities in related fields to determine the most effective ways to increase and sustain a diverse talent pool within the game industry.	• Research effectiveness of STEM, computing, and art outreach initiatives. • Research and report on cultural practices within the game industry, focusing on best practices for retaining employees from underrepresented groups. • Make this research widely available to all stakeholders.
Create a comprehensive plan for increasing diversity	Create a plan that includes both long- and short-term initiatives for reaching out to the wider community, including educators, game industry professionals, and government officials.	• Bring stakeholders together to create a plan that meets their needs and that draws upon best practices from previous outreach plans. This includes a vision, a mission, a strategic plan, and a strong case for the benefits of implementing the plan. • Create awareness of the plan to the broader community through media and stakeholders.
Implement plans	Engaged stakeholders will promote, support, and implement various parts of the plan that align with their specific interests. Plans will focus on effective recruitment and retention policies at various institutions including schools, universities, and game companies.	• Implement plans as needed in pre-secondary educational institutions. • Implement plans as needed in tertiary institutions as needed. • Implement plans as needed in companies involved in the game industry. • Implement plans as needed in various governmental institutions.
Report on the effectiveness of efforts	Report on the effectiveness of the plan, including individual pieces and the plan as a whole. Develop new approaches based on results of initial interventions.	• Disseminate research results at relevant academic conferences and journals. • Distribute and promote press releases. • Present information and results at industry conferences and meetings. • Present information and results to relevant governmental organizations.

ship in similar efforts. In addition to considering, critiquing, and revising the proposed framework, clear objectives for each of the areas and steps for creating systematic change need to be created. These areas and steps will depend greatly on the intersection between the interests and resources of the various stakeholders.

Organizing special tracks at conferences or hosting a working group for addressing the gender imbalance at a conference attended by all stakeholders could facilitate further discussion regarding suitable frameworks. The presentation of other viewpoints on how to approach the issue could lead to revisions of this framework and identification of industry, academic, and governmental stakeholders ready to participate in such an initiative and work on the next steps. The commitment of these leaders would be crucial to ensure that initial enthusiasm is not lost as the difficult work of modifying the pipeline and culture of the game industry proceeds.

CONCLUSION

The current game industry employee pipeline appears to be no more diverse than the games industry, with a dearth of women in the game design and development fields. As previously mentioned, the IGDA found that women comprise between 5% and 11% of the game art, design, sound, and programming fields (IGDA, 2005). Unfortunately, this is similar to what has been found in the game industry pipeline (McGill et al., 2013a, 2013b), indicating that the trend for games to be developed by a vast majority of men will most likely continue in the near future unless efforts are made to address this issue.

Though there are no formal efforts underway to actively engage more women in the game industry, we can turn to similar initiatives and draw upon their successes. For example, with a nine-to-one ratio of men to women studying game design and development the gender imbalance is nearly identical to the ratio of men to women studying computing (CRA, 2012). The computing field, along with other STEM fields, has struggled with the issue of gender imbalance for many years, and outreach programs have been one way to create and foster interest from minorities, including women. Because of the perception that games are a draw for a variety of students, some of these programs have a games focus to their activities, although most programs do not explicitly recruit students for the games industry. These previous and ongoing initiatives have been extensive, including programs for children in grade school, high school students, and undergraduates. As a whole, these outreach programs report an improvement in attitudes, efficacy, and affinity for the varied disciplines as a result of the interventions. Whether the outreach activities for improving diversity throughout the past decade and beyond have resulted in a higher percentage of female employees in the respective fields is not definitely known, the message sent is clear. There is a strong interest in diversifying the respective industries and their pipelines.

Given that the gender balance in the games industry is at least as skewed as in the computing field, it is surprising that the game industry and educators have not yet done the same. Those interested in improving the gender balance in the game industry must take similar steps to begin to balance gender in the game industry and its pipeline and to make it clear to girls and women that they are welcome in the field.

Until purposeful action is taken to change the gender imbalance, the game industry will continue to face criticism and condemnation from those within as well as those outside of the industry. This chapter has identified various sources of such criticism and concern. Since this issue appears to only be receiving more and more discussion and debate, the chapter addresses the benefits of outreach programs in related fields and proposes a framework for tackling this issue. The framework provides a well-researched approach based on various other similar large-scale outreach initiatives in related fields. It is meant to serve as a starting point for a serious, outcome-based discussion for stakeholders who want to see the gender imbalance issue in the game industry addressed. As such, the framework is a living document that can be altered to meet the desires and available resources of these stakeholders.

REFERENCES

Abbate, J. (2012). *Recoding gender: Women's changing participation in computing.* Cambridge, MA: The MIT Press.

Ashcraft, C., & Breitzman, A. (2012). *Who invents IT? Women's participation in information technology patenting (2012 update).* Boulder, CO: NCWIT.

Athena, S. W. A. N. (2012). *The charter.* Retrieved from http://www.athenaswan.org.uk/content/charter

Barrington, L., & Troske, K. (2001). *Workforce diversity and productivity: An analysis of employer-employee matched data.* Retrieved from http://gatton.uky.edu/Faculty/troske/working_pap/barrington_troske.pdf

Bettinger, E. P., & Long, B. T. (2005). Do faculty serve as role models? The impact of instructor gender on female students. The American Economic Review, 95(2), 152–157. doi:10.1257/000282805774670149

Birinci Konur, K., Şeyihoğlu, A., Sezen, G., & Tekbiyik, A. (2011). Evaluation of a science camp: Enjoyable discovery of mysterious world. Educational Sciences: Theory and Practice, 11(3), 1602–1607.

Brown, N. C. C., Kölling, M., Crick, T., Jones, S., Humphreys, S., & Sentence, S. (2013.) Bringing computer science back into schools: Lessons from the UK. In *Proceedings of the 44th ACM Technical Symposium on Computer Science Education(SIGCSE '13)* (pp. 269-274). New York: ACM.

Bruckman, A., Biggers, M., Ericson, B., McKlin, T., Dimond, J., DiSalvo, B., et al. (2009). Georgia computes!: Improving the computing education pipeline. In *Proceedings from SIGCSE '09: The 40th ACM Technical Symposium on Computer Science Education.* Chattanooga, TN: ACM.

Burge, J. E., Gannod, G. C., Doyle, M., & Davis, K. C. (2013). Girls on the go: A CS summer camp to attract and inspire female high school students. In *Proceedings from SIGCSE '13: The 44th ACM Technical Symposium on Computer Science Education.* Denver, CO: ACM.

Camarda, C. (2012). *A new strategy for stem education and innovative engineering problem solving.* Retrieved from http://web.mit.edu/sydneydo/www/ICED2012App/A%20New%20Strategy%20for%20Stem%20Education%20and%20Innovative%20Engineering%20Problem%20Solving%20rev%207.pdf

Camp, T. (2012). Computing, we have a problem.... ACM Inroads, 3(4), 34–40. doi:10.1145/2381083.2381097

Carroll, B., Smith, A., & Castori, P. (2009). *The Exploratorium's XTech program: Engaging STEM experiences for middle-school youth summative evaluation report.* Retrieved from http://informalscience.org/images/evaluation/2009-09_Rpt_XTECH-SummRpt-final-1019-2009.pdf

Computing at School (CAS). (2013). *Computing for the next generation.* Retrieved from http://www.computingatschool.org.uk/

Computing Research Association. (2012). *CRA Taulbee survey.* Retrieved from http://cra.org/resources/taulbee/

Contestabile, G. B. (2012, December 12). *Diversity in the game industry: It's just good business.* Retrieved from http://www.edge-online.com/features/diversity-in-the-game-industry-its-just-good-business/

Coughlan, S. (2013, February 4). *Computer science part of English Baccalaureate.* Retrieved from http://www.bbc.co.uk/news/education-21261442

Craig, A., Coldwell-Neilson, J., & Beekhuyzen, J. (2013). Are ICT interventions for girls a special case? In *Proceedings from SIGCSE '13: The 44th ACM Technical Symposium on Computer Science Education.* Denver, CO: ACM.

Dahlberg, T., Barnes, T., Buch, K., & Rorrer, A. (2011). The STARS Alliance: Viable strategies for broadening participation in computing. ACM Transactions in Computing Education, 11(3). doi:10.1145/2037276.2037282

Dave, V., Blasko, D., Holliday-Darr, K., Kremer, J. T., Edwards, R., Ford, M., et al. (2010). Re-enJEANeering STEM education: Math options summer camp. Journal of Technology Studies, 36(1), 35–45.

Davis, K. C., Greene-White, L., Ferdinand, T., & Santangelo, M. (2008). Digital arts for computing outreach. In *Proceedings from 38th ASEE/IEEE Frontiers in Educations Conference.* Saratoga Springs, NY: IEEE.

Denault, A., Kienzle, J., & Vybihal, J. (2008). Be a computer scientist for a week: The McGill Game Programming Guru summer camp. In *Proceedings from 38th ASEE/IEEE Frontiers in Educations Conference.* Saratoga Springs, NY: IEEE.

Department of Defense. (2009). *Stem education and outreach strategic plan.* Retrieved from http://www.ngcproject.org/sites/default/files/DoD-wide%20STEM%20Education%20and%20Outreach%20Strategic%20Plan%20-%202010%20-%202014.pdf

Doran, K., Boyce, A., Finkelstein, S., & Barnes, T. (2012). Outreach for improved student performance: A game design and development curriculum. In *Proceedings from ITiCSE '12: Proceedings of the ACM Conference on Innovation and Technology in Computer Science Education.* Haifa, Israel: ACM.

England, P. (2005). Gender inequality in labor markets: The role of motherhood and segregation. Social Politics, 12(2), 264–288. doi:10.1093/sp/jxi014

Entertainment Software Association. (2013). *Essential facts about the computer and video game industry.* Retrieved from http://www.theesa.com/facts/pdfs/ESA_EF_2013.pdf

Forbes. (2012). *Diversity & inclusion: Unlocking global potential.* Retrieved from http://www.dpiap.org/resources/pdf/global_diversity_rankings_2012_12_03_20.pdf

Foster, J. S., & Shiel-Rolle, N. (2011). Building scientific literacy through summer science camps: A strategy for design, implementation and assessment. Science Education International, 22(2), 85–98.

Fuller, A. (2010, January 26). Female undergraduates continue to outnumber men, but gap holds steady. *The Chronicle of Higher Education.* Retrieved from http://chronicle.com/article/Female-Undergraduates-Continue/63726/

Gamasutra. (2010). *TIGA comments on gender imbalance in the games industry.* Retrieved from http://www.gamasutra.com/view/pressreleases/60966/TIGA_comments_on_gender_imbalance_in_the_gamesindustry.php

Graft, K. (2012). *The 5 trends that defined the game industry in 2012.* Retrieved from http://www.gamasutra.com/view/news/182954/The_5_trends_that_defined_the_game_industry_in_2012.php#.UMn3em_Ad8E

Haines, L. (2004). *Why are there so few women in games?* Retrieved from http://www.equalworks.info/resources/contentfiles/537.pdf

Hall, L. (2012). *Game industry jobs: Ten tips for graduates.* Retrieved from http://www.edge-online.com/get-into-games/game-industry-jobs-ten-tips-graduates/

Hegewisch, A., Williams, C., & Harbin, V. (2012). *The gender wage gap by occupation.* Retrieved from http://www.iwpr.org/publications/pubs/the-gender-wage-gap-by-occupation-1

International Game Developers Association (IGDA). (2005). *Game developer demographics: An exploration of workforce diversity.* Retrieved from http://www.igda.org/game-developer-demographics-report

International Game Developers Association (IGDA). (2011). *Game industry survey 2011.* Retrieved from https://www.surveymonkey.com/s/IGDA2011

Isaacson, B. (2012, November 29). *#1 Reason Why reveals sexism rampant in the gaming industry.* Retrieved from http://www.huffingtonpost.com/2012/11/29/1reasonwhy-reveals-sexism-gaming-industry_n_2205204.html

Javidi, G., & Sheybani, E. (2008). Digispired: Digital inspiration for interactive game design and programming. Journal of Computing Sciences in Colleges, 24(3), 144–150.

Jones, S., Hernandez, A., Ortiz, P., Aldana, G., Conrad, P., & Franklin, D. (2010). eVoices: A website supporting outreach by attracting target groups to computer science through culturally relevant themes. Journal of Computing Sciences in Colleges, 25(4), 134–140.

Jones, S. P. (2013). *Computing at school.* Presentation at Innovation the 18th Annual Conference on Innovation and Technology in Computer Science Education, University of Kent, Canterbury, UK.

Kirkup, G., Zalevski, A., Maruyama, T., & Batool, I. (2010). *Women and men in science, engineering and technology: The UK statistics guide 2010.* Retrieved from http://www.theukrc.org/files/useruploads/files/final_sept_15th_15.42_ukrc_statistics_guide_2010.pdf

Legault, M. J., & Weststar, J. (2012). *More than the numbers: Independent analysis of the IGDA 2009 quality of life survey.* Retrieved from http://gameqol.org/wp-content/uploads/2012/12/Quality%20of%20Life%20in%20the%20Videogame%20Industry%20-%202009%20IGDA%20Survey%20Analysis.pdf

Ligman, K. (2013, April 19). *Centipede creator sees lack of diversity in the game industry.* Retrieved from http://www.gamasutra.com/view/news/190878/

Margolis, J., Ryoo, J. J., Sandoval, C. D. M., Lee, C., Goode, J., & Chapman, G. (2012). Beyond access: Broadening participation in high school computer science. ACM Inroads, 3(4), 72–78. doi:10.1145/2381083.2381102

Maxim, B. R., Grosky, W. I., & Baugh, J. P. (2007). Work in progress – Introducing information technology through game design. In *Proceedings from 37th ASEE/IEEE Frontiers in Educations Conference.* Milwaukee, WI: IEEE.

McGill, M. M., Settle, A., & Decker, A. (2013). Demographics of undergraduates studying games in the United States: A comparison of computer science students and the general population. Computer Science Education, 23(2), 158–185. doi:10.1080/08993408.2013.769319

McGill, M. M., Settle, A., & Decker, A. (2013). Demographics of undergraduate students in game degree programs in the United States and United Kingdom. In *Proceedings of the 14th Annual Conference on Information Technology Education (SIGITE 2013).* Orlando, FL: ACM.

Miranda, R. J., & Hermann, R. S. (2010). A critical analysis of faculty-developed urban K-12 science outreach Programs. Perspectives on Urban Education, 7(1), 109–114.

Murphy, K. X. (2012, November 16). *Keeping focused on the global competitiveness agenda* [Blog post]. Retrieved http://forumblog.org/2012/11/keeping-focused-on-the-global-competitiveness-agenda/

Natale, M. J. (2002). The effect of a male-oriented computer gaming culture on careers in the computer industry. ACM SIGCAS Computers and Society Newsletter, 32(2), 24–31. doi:10.1145/566522.566526

National Center for Women & Information Technology. (2013). http://www.ncwit.org

National Science Board. (2012). Science and engineering labor force: Demographics of the S&E workforce. In *Science and Engineering Indicators 2012* (Chapter 3 Section 4). Retrieved from http://www.nsf.gov/statistics/seind12/c3/c3s4.htm

National Science Foundation. (2008). *Broadening participation at the national science foundation: A framework for action.* Retrieved from http://www.nsf.gov/od/broadeningparticipation/nsf_frameworkforaction_0808.pdf

National Science Foundation. (2009). *Broadening participation in computing (BPC).* Retrieved from http://www.nsf.gov/funding/pgm_summ.jsp?pims_id=13510

Neumark, D., & Gardecki, R. (1998). Women helping women? Role model and mentoring effects on female Ph.D. students in economics. The Journal of Human Resources, 33(1), 220–246. doi:10.2307/146320

Parfitt, B. (2010, October 4). *Interview: The Sims, the market for computer & video games.* Retrieved from http://www.mcvuk.com/news/read/interview-the-sims/01837

Pivkina, I., Pontelli, E., Jensen, R., & Haebe, J. (2009). Young women in computing: Lessons learned from an educational & outreach program. In *Proceedings from SIGCSE '09: The 40th ACM Technical Symposium on Computer Science Education.* Chattanooga, TN: ACM.

Plunkett, L. (2012, November 27). *Here's a devastating account of the crap women in the games business have to deal with. In 2012.* Retrieved from http://kotaku.com/5963528/heres-a-devastating-account-of-the-crap-women-in-the-games-business-have-to-deal-with-in-2012

Princeton Review. (2013). *Top undergraduate schools for video game design.* Retrieved from http://www.princetonreview.com/top-undergraduate-schools-for-video-game-design.aspx

Repenning, A., & Ioannidou, A. (2008). Broadening participation through scalable game design. SIGCSE Bulletin, 40(1), 305–309. doi:10.1145/1352322.1352242

Reskin, B. F. (1988). Bringing the men back in: Sex differentiation and the devaluation of women's work. Gender & Society, 2(1), 58–81. doi:10.1177/089124388002001005

Robst, R., Keil, J., & Russo, D. (1998). The effect of gender composition of faculty on student retention. Economics of Education Review, 17(4), 429–439. doi:10.1016/S0272-7757(97)00049-6

Rowland, S. (2010). Getting' digi with it: Microsoft helps young girls shape future careers. IEEE Women in Engineering Magazine, 4(1), 28–29. doi:10.1109/MWIE.2010.936181

Serviss, B. (2013, August 8). *Beyond the straight white dude: Why a more diverse game industry benefits all.* Retrieved from http://www.dashjump.com/beyond-straight-white-dude-diversity/

Simard, C., Stephenson, C., & Kosaraju, D. (2010). *Addressing core equity issues in K-12 computer science education: Identifying barriers and sharing strategies.* Retrieved from http://csta.acm.org/Communications/sub/DocsPresentationFiles/ABI-CSTAEquityFinal.pdf

Sinclair, B. (2013, March 27). *Diversity means dollars.* Retrieved from http://www.gamesindustry.biz/articles/2013-03-27-pushing-diversity-to-pull-in-money

Skillset. (2013). *Skills & training for the games industry.* Retrieved from http://www.creativeskillset.org/games/qualifications/article_2769_1.asp

Trauth, E.M. (2012). Are there enough seats for women at the IT table?. *ACM Inroads, 3*(4).

United Kingdom Resource Center (UKRC). (2010). *Social return on investment.* Retrieved from http://www.theukrc.org/files/useruploads/files/ukrc_sroi_assured_report_apr_2010.pdf

United Kingdom Resource Centre (UKRC). (2012). *Engaging girls in science, technology, engineering, and maths: What works?* Retrieved from http://www.theukrc.org/files/useruploads/files/resources/wise_report_july_2012_bae_systems_what_works_summary.pdf

Vegso, J. (2005, May). Interest in CS as a major drops among incoming freshman. Computing Research News, 17(3).

Wang, C. Q., Tang, C., Zhang, L., & Cukierman, D. (2012). Try/CATCH - a CS outreach event organized by female university students for female high school students: a positive experience for all the parts involved. In *Proceedings from WCCCE '12: The Seventeenth Western Canadian Conference on Computing Education.* Vancouver, BC, Canada: ACM.

WGBH Educational Foundation. (2010). *Dot diva.* Retrieved from http://www.dotdiva.org/

Wigal, C. M., Alp, N., McCullough, C., Smullen, S., & Winters, K. (2002). ACES: Introducing girls to and building interest in engineering and computer science careers. In *Proceedings from 32nd ASEFJ/IEEE Frontiers in Education Conference.* Boston, MA: IEEE.

Zywno, M. S., Gilbride, K. A., & Gudz, N. (2000). Innovative outreach programs to attract and retain women in undergraduate engineering programs. Global Journal of Engineering Education, 4(3), 293–302.

ADDITIONAL READING

Alvarado, C., Dodds, Z., & Libeskind-Hadas, R. (2012). Increasing women's participation in computing at Harvey Mudd College. ACM Inroads, 3(4), 55–64. doi:10.1145/2381083.2381100

Chinn, D., & VanDeGrift, T. (2008). Gender and Diversity in Hiring Software Professionals: What do Students say? Proceedings from ICER '08: The 4th Annual International Computing Education Research Workshop. Sydney, Australia: ACM.

Coder, L., Rosenbloom, J. L., Ash, R. A., & Dupont, B. R. (2009). Economic and Business Dimensions: Increasing Gender Diversity in the IT Workforce. Communications of the ACM, 52(5), 25–27. doi:10.1145/1506409.1506417

Crutchfield, O. S. L., Harrison, C. D., Haas, G., Garcia, D. D., Humphreys, S. M., Lewis, C. M., & Khooshabeh, P. (2011). Berkeley Foundation for Opportunities in Information Technology: A Decade of Broadening Participation. *Transactions on Computing Education*, 11:3, Article 15.

Educate to Innovate. (2013). The White House. Retrieved August 20, 2013 from http://www.whitehouse.gov/issues/education/k-12/educate-innovate

Guzdial, M., Ericson, B. J., McKlin, T., & Engelman, S. (2012). A Statewide Survey on Computing Education Pathways and Influences: Factors in Broadening Participation in Computing. Proceedings from ICER '12: The 9th Annual International Computing Education Research Workshop. Auckland, New Zealand: ACM.

Ladner, R. E., & Litzler, E. (2012). The Need to Balance Innovation and Implementation in Broadening Participation. Communications of the ACM, 55(9), 36–38. doi:10.1145/2330667.2330679

Lang, C., & Kosaraju, D. (2012). Continental drift. ACM Inroads, 3(4), 65–71. doi:10.1145/2381083.2381101

Margolis, J., & Fischer, A. (2002). Unlocking the Clubhouse: Women in Computing. MIT Press.

Peckham, J., Harlow, L. L., Stuart, D. A., Silver, B., Mederer, H., & Stephensen, P. D. (2007). Broadening Participation in Computing: Issues and Challenges. Proceedings from ITiCSE '07: The 12th Annual SIGCSE Conference on Innovation and Technology in Computer Science Education. Dundee, Scotland, UK: ACM.

Settle, A., McGill, M. M., & Decker, A. (2013). Diversity in the Game Industry: Is Outreach the Solution? Proceedings of the 14th Annual Conference on Information Technology Education (SIGITE 2013), Orlando, FL: ACM.

Warr, P. (2013) Valve unveils Pipeline, a resource for teens eyeing up the gaming industry. Gaming, July 15, 2013. Retrieved from http://www.wired.co.uk/news/archive/2013-07/15/valve-pipeline-website

Webb, D. C., Repenning, A., & Koh, K. H. (2012). Toward an Emergent Theory of Broadening Participation in Computer Science Education. Proceedings from SIGCSE '12: The 43rd ACM Technical Symposium on Computer Science Education. Raleigh, NC: ACM.

KEY TERMS AND DEFINITIONS

Broadening Participation: Working to ensure that the population represented in a group is diverse and more accurately representative of the broader population, typically done by formulating and implementing appropriate outreach programs.

Computing: Fields involving the design, development, and direct utilization of computer systems, including computer science, information technology, information systems, information sciences, computer engineering, and software engineering.

Diverse: Being composed of multiple, distinct groups of individuals, ideally representative of the wider population from which the group is drawn. Relevant demographic characteristics may include sex, age, race, ethnic group, disability status, and sexual orientation.

Game Degree Programs: Refers to university-level courses and majors or programs in games, such as Game Design, Computer Game Technology, Game Development, etc.

Game Industry: Companies involved in the design, development, and testing of hardware, software, and peripherals for electronic games.

Game Industry Pipeline: Sources of new hires for companies involved in the game industry. For companies that tend to hire college-educated employees this means tertiary institutions such as community colleges, four-year colleges, and universities.

Outreach: Policies, programs, or other interventions that target populations underrepresented or underserved by existing institutions or programs in order to improve the recruitment and/or retention of the underserved populations.

STEM: The science, technology, engineering, and mathematics disciplines, which typically includes the computing field.

Chapter 11
Female Game Workers, Career Development, and Aspirations

Julie Prescott
University of Bolton, UK

Jan Bogg
University of Liverpool, UK

ABSTRACT

Understanding the career factors that influence women's career aspirations in male-dominated occupations is important for increasing women's progression within these occupations. This chapter assesses the impact of career influencers on career aspirations of women working in the male-dominated computer games industry. An online questionnaire obtained international data from 450 women working in the computer games industry. A structural equation model was employed to investigate the influencers. Findings suggest that to increase women's career development and career aspirations within the computer games industry, self-efficacy, attitudes towards career barriers, work-life balance attitudes, person-environment fit and job satisfaction are crucial.

INTRODUCTION

Within the workforce men and women are segregated into certain occupations, industries and levels. Although women are increasing in the workforce, some jobs are defined as women's jobs and others as men's (horizontal segregation). There is also segregation in the form of working in the lower levels (vertical segregation) within sectors and organisations. Gendered occupational segregation persists in many societies including the USA, Canada, Australia, Europe and the UK despite legislation to counter this. This is evi-

denced through the newer technology industry of computer games development (Prescott & Bogg, 2013). The computer games industry falls within the Science, Engineering and Technology (SET) sector. The computer games industry is, however, a relatively new industry or approximately four decades, compared to some of the more established industries within the sector such as engineering. Although women are increasingly becoming gamers, especially more casual gamers their representation as game workers in all aspects of the game development process is limited and they are still on the periphery of the game culture and

DOI: 10.4018/978-1-4666-6142-4.ch011

industry (Prescott & Bogg, 2014). According to Skillset (2009) women represent just 4% of the UK's computer games industries workforce, a reduction from 12% in 2008. Similar figures have been reported in America (Gourdin, 2005), and Canada (Dyer-Whitheford & Sharman, 2005). Highlighting the need for research into this area in order to understand why this might be the case. There have been a number of reasons put forward as to why women are under represented within the computer games industry. For instance, the lack of flexible working hours, and the long hours culture associated with the industry (Prescott & Bogg, 2010; Consalvo, 2008; Deuze et al, 2007; Haines, 2004; Krotoski, 2004). It can therefore be seen that there are a number of workforce issues associated with the computer games industry especially for the developmental areas of computer games development such as design, production, writing and programming. According to Consalvo (2008), what the games industry needs is to not only increase its diversity, but also change the organisational structures in order to maintain a more diverse workforce. It is therefore important not only to understand why women do not enter or remain within male-dominated industries such as computer games, but also to gain an understanding of women who are working in male-dominated industries.

BACKGROUND

Career Aspirations and Career Development

According to Mayrhofer et. al. (2005):

Career aspirations reflect the strength of an individual's intention to be active in a particular career field. They consist of a cluster of needs, motives and behavioural intentions that individuals articulate with respect to different career fields (p40).

Mayrhofer et al (2005) suggest that career aspirations are a form of self-selection since individual's self-select success in a field dependent on personal strengths and weaknesses. Therefore, career aspirations are particularly important to consider for women in male-dominated occupations since the environment and how individuals feel and are made to feel within that environment can determine the extent of their career aspirations. Social Cognitive Career Theory (SCCT), purported by Lent, Brown and Hackett (1994) developed from Bandura's 1986 social cognitive theory, highlights how career preferences are influenced by self-beliefs, including gender role beliefs and perceived social structures. Since its development, SCCT has been a dominant theory in understanding women's career choice. For instance, research has linked women's perceived barriers as negatively impacting on the career development of women (Lindley, 2005; Swanson & Woitke, 1997).

Career aspirations are important to consider when looking at women's advancement and career development (Mayrhofer et al, 2005). Career aspirations are influenced by many factors including gender, socioeconomic status, race, parent's occupation, educational level and expectations (Domenico & Jones, 2006). Women and men tend to use different kinds of measures for assessing their own career success. Men tend to use more objective measures such as level and salary, whereas women tend to use more subjective measures including satisfaction with their work and non-work lives, which also includes opportunities for advancement and work-life balance (Powell and Butterfield, 2003). Career success can be either subjective or objective (Ng et al, 2005). Objective career success is usually externally measured through things such as highest level attained, highest salary earned, and professional honours. Subjective career successes, on the other hand, are typically attitudes, emotions, or perceptions of how the individual feels about their accomplishments, which previous researchers have measured via job satisfaction, organisational commitment, and professional identity (Feldman & Ng, 2007).

Women face a variety of barriers within the labour market in terms of career progression and advancement. Key issues in the literature include limited networking opportunities, limited access to mentors and role models, limited flexibility and child care provision, general discrimination, gender segregation of the workforce and higher values placed on masculine attributes. (i.e. Swanson & Woitke, 1997; Arfken, Bellar, & Helms, 2004; McCathy, 2004; Allen, 2005). All of these issues impact upon career development opportunities and reducing wellbeing for women (Perrewe & Nelson, 2004). These issues are particularly prevalent for women working in male-dominated industries, especially those working in the science, engineering and technology (SET) sector (Prescott & Bogg, 2012).

Key Career Constructs: Person-Environment Fit, Job Satisfaction and Self-Efficacy

The current study includes a number of psychological constructs that are deemed important to career development and career aspirations. Readers may not be familiar with these constructs and so it is important to discuss these constructs and how they may relate to women's careers.

Person-Environment Fit

Person-environment fit refers to how much an individual matches or fits the environment in which they work. Theoretically, environments will recruit and retain people whose characteristics are congruent to the working environment and people will prefer and persist in environments that are congruent with their vocational personalities. Person-environment fit positively influences job

satisfaction and organizational commitment and negatively relates to turnover (O'Reilly et al., 1991).

There is a distinction between employees' perceptions of person-job fit and person-organisation fit. Lauver and Kristof-Brown (2001) put forward that person-environment fit is defined as the match between the abilities of a person and the demands of a job, or the needs of a person and what the job provides. In contrast, person-organisation fit refers to how an individual matches an organisation's values, beliefs and goals. The authors developed a five-item scale in order to measure perceived person-job fit and a three-item scale to measure perceived person-organisation fit. Person-environment fit has been shown to relate to individual differences such as self-efficacy. Self-efficacy theory suggests that people will be attracted to jobs and organisations based on the extent to which they believe they can succeed. Therefore, individuals with higher self-efficacy will be more likely to value their subjective perceptions of fit, more heavily when judging attraction to an organisation, than individuals with lower self-efficacy (Bandura, 1986).

Self-Efficacy

The key concept in the theory, self-efficacy was defined by Bandura (1986) as, 'people's judgements of their capabilities to organise and execute courses of action required to attain designated types of performances' (p. 391). Central to Banduras self-efficacy theory is the focus on expectancies for success. Bandura distinguished between two types of expectancy beliefs: outcome expectations, which are beliefs that certain behaviours will lead to certain outcomes, and efficacy expectations, which are the beliefs about whether one can effectively perform the behaviours necessary for the outcome. Changes in self-efficacy beliefs will lead to changes in occupational interests (Lent et.

al., 1994). Self-efficacy is important to women's career development. According to Betz and Hackett (1981), 'there exist significant and consistent sex differences in self-efficacy with regards to traditional and non-traditional occupations' (p. 407). Some suggest that high self-efficacy can have a circular or reciprocal effect, in that, high self-efficacy facilitates performance and successful performance nurtures self-efficacy (Gist and Mitchell, 1992). Self-efficacy predicts actual performance in a broad range of settings and so raising self-efficacy can have practical consequences for the productivity of individuals in organisations. Once in a job negative beliefs about your abilities may reduce the willingness to take risks, and reduce the desire to be visible, both of which can hinder career progression (Heliman, 1983). Hence it can be seen from this brief overview of the literature how self-efficacy is important in the workplace for both men and women.

Job Satisfaction

Locke (1976) defined job satisfaction as, 'a pleasurable or positive emotional state resulting from an appraisal of one's job or job experiences' (cited in Ilies & Judge 2004, p. 1300). More simply, job satisfaction is the degree to which individuals like their job (Spector, 1985). There are a variety of facets within the construct of job satisfaction. These involve employees' feelings toward different dimensions of their work role and work environment i.e. satisfaction with pay, promotion, co-workers or organisational structure. Satisfaction with one's job or organisation is related to factors such as the job role, the working environment and identifying with organisational goals and objectives. Recently, Weiss (2002) defined job satisfaction as, 'positive (or negative) evaluation judgement one makes about one's job or job situation' (cited in Brief and Weiss, 2002, p. 283).

Understanding the job satisfaction of employees is an important organisational goal. Many organisational outcomes such as productivity and efficiency are related to employees' levels of job satisfaction (Ellinger et. al., 2002). When employees are dissatisfied at work, they are less committed and will often look for opportunities to leave the organisation (Perryman 2004; Gorden & Denisi, 1995). For instance, Shields and Ward (2001) found that job satisfaction was the single most important determinant of intention to quit among NHS nurses. Those who reported being very dissatisfied with their job were 65% more likely to report an intention to quit than those who reported being satisfied (p. 679).

Theoretical Background: Social Cognitive Career Theory (SCCT)

SCCT is a highly utilised theory and framework for much research on career choice and development and a dominant theory in understanding women's career choice. For instance, the extent women perceive barriers as impacting their career development has been positively related to their outcome expectations (Lindley, 2005). According to Lindley, women may idealise male-dominated careers that they view implausible due to gender related barriers. Lindley goes on to suggest that future research should consider the impact barriers have on career choice and the distinction between internal and external barriers and barriers of specific fields. Self-efficacy for coping with barriers may also be an important consideration, since how an individual copes may determine if an individual will attempt to, and succeed in overcoming perceived barriers to career development. Cunningham, Doherty and Gregg (2007) used SCCT theory to look at the under-representation of women in coaching. The results of the American study, that collected data from 66 assistant coaches from numerous sports fields, found that men had greater coaching self-efficacy, anticipated more positive outcomes associated with being a head coach, and possessed greater interest and more intention in becoming head coach than women did.

SCCT has also been shown as a useful theory in assessing women's perceived career barriers (Swanson & Woitke, 1997). Perceived barriers are important to SCCT and occupational choice. Even if an individual has high self-efficacy for a career, positive outcome expectations and interest, they may still avoid that career if they perceive considerable barriers to attaining it (Brown & Lent, 1996). SCCT research has often focused on maths and science disciplines due to the under-representation of women (and ethnic minorities) in these fields and the suggestion that self-efficacy intervention may eliminate this under-representation (Betz & Schifano, 2000). Fouad, Smith and Zao (2002) looked at extending SCCT across academic domains by successfully applying the model to students across a number of academic disciplines: art, social science, maths/science and English, highlighting the theories applicability to a range of disciplines.

SCCT is a dynamic theory concerned with situation-specific aspects of people and their environments. This differs from trait like theories such as that proposed by Holland (1973) who suggests attributes remain fairly constant. SCCT requires domain-specific measures, which in the case of the current study, is the workplace/career. The theory focuses on the connection of self-efficacy, outcome expectations, personal goals, interests and environmental factors that influence an individual's career choice. SCCT is concerned with dynamic and situation-specific aspects of people (e.g. self-views, future expectations) and their environment (Lent & Brown, 2006). SCCT has five core constructs:

1. Self-efficacy, meaning 'people's judgments of their capabilities to organize and execute courses of action required to attain designated types of performance' (Bandura, 1986 cited in Lent & Brown, 2006 p. 15);
2. Outcome expectations, including anticipated social (benefits to family), material (financial gain) and self-evaluative (self-approval) (Bandura, 1986, cited in Lent & Brown, 2006);
3. Goals, referring to activity and performance goals (Lent & Brown, 2006);

4. Interests, covering the likes, dislikes and indifferences people have with different activities (Lent & Brown, 2006); and
5. Contextual supports and barriers, which can be actual or perceived (Lent & Brown, 2006).

According to Lent and Brown (2006) there are four basic outcomes of SCCT: academic or vocational interest, choice content, performance outcomes and satisfaction outcomes. They suggest that SCCT can be used to relate to other criteria but it may be inappropriate to frame the study as a test of SCCT hypotheses. They suggest that:

This is not to deny that there may be valuable opportunities to extend SCCT to a new domain or dependent variable of interest, in such cases, the objective may more accurately be portrayed as examining the theory's range of applicability rather than testing the validity of its formal hypotheses per se (Lent and Brown, 2006, p. 22).

Research Questions and Aims

This study looked at women working in the games industry; primarily working in the production of games via an online questionnaire, investigating the career aspirations, motivations and attitudes of women within the industry. The studies main aim was to develop a model of career influences using Structural Equation Modelling (SEM) as a statistical technique and SCCT as a theoretical framework.

The current study aims to expand the usage and applicability of SCCT, to determine if the theory is a useful framework for examining career aspirations once an individual has embarked on a career path. Career aspirations have the potential to fit within SCCT theory by expanding the theory to look specifically at career development. Typically SCCT is used to look at the career choice or academic choice of predominantly student populations. It has also been used to illustrate why women do not choose certain disciplines of study and hence career. This study intends to extend SCCT to look at its usage as a career development theory for female game workers already in a career. The study is unique in that it will see how SCCT may be used for people already in careers to evaluate aspirations, and satisfaction. In addition, the study also proposes to extend the traditional SCCT model in developing a model of career influences. The study aims to develop a model of career influences, examining the range, usage and applicability of SCCT. The study will also help to advance our understanding of women working in the relatively new industry of computer games.

METHOD

Sample and Procedure

The study design is cross-sectional. The sample inclusion criterion was women currently working in the computer games industry. The sample was purposive, in that, women needed to be working in the computer games industry. The study aimed to get an International sample but due to the questionnaire only being in English it was inevitable that the majority of participants would be from Western-English speaking countries. The study was quantitative in nature and involved an online survey which was available at www.survey.bris. ac.uk/breakingbarriers/games (a hard copy of the questionnaire was also available on request). For all formats of the questionnaire anonymity and confidentiality was assured. The study was advertised and the questionnaire link was available on numerous game websites and social network sites. Internet hypertext weblinks to the study were placed on prominent national and international computer games websites such as www.women-gamers.com, www.womeningamesinternational. com, www.gamesnet.com and www.gamejournal. org. Game industry related groups on the social network sites of Facebook and Linkedin were also utilised to advertise the study and online questionnaire. Electronic and paper mail shots were distributed to games companies throughout the UK, Other parts of Europe, Canada and America. The questionnaire was online from 1st September 2008 until 28th February 2009.

The online questionnaire obtained demographic data (i.e. role, age, etc.) and work related measures on 450 women. The data was generated through 450 participants, consisting of female game workers with the majority, 42% (N 189) worked in the USA and 30% worked in the UK (N 134), who occupy varying professional identities and grades within the industry. The female participants varied a wide range of roles within the industry for example 15% (N 66) were artists and animators, 14% (N 62) were designers, 13% (N 58) were producers and 13% (N 57) were executives. The positions with the fewest participants included writers (2.4%, N 11), engineers (2.4%, N 11), and audio/sound engineers (1.1%, N 5). Participants also varied by grade with surprisingly 56% (N 250) considering themselves as being in a senior role. 28% (N 127) viewed themselves in a middle level role and 16% (N 72) at junior level. The majority of participants in the study worked full time (88%, N 397), the majority 84% (N 380) where from a white ethnic background, 69% (N 312) were aged 35 or under, 35% (N 159) were single, whilst 59% (N 168) were married or lived with a partner and 79% (N 357) of the women had no children.

A questionnaire was developed using a combination of new and existing measures. The questionnaire consisted of eleven sub-sections. Section one sought personal and professional biographical information as discussed above and the remaining sections included the study measures deemed important to women's careers and the fitting with the SCCT framework. These measures will now be discussed in detail.

Measures

Occupational Self-Efficacy. The short version of the occupational self-efficacy scale developed by Rigotti, Schyns and Mohr (2008). The scale consists of six items measured on a six-point Likert scale, ranging from 1 (not at all) to 6 (completely true) and resulting in a total self-efficacy score (α=0.85). Scale ranges from 6-36 with scores between 6-18 considered low self-efficacy, 19-24 medium and 24-36 high self-efficacy.

Work-Life Balance (WLB). Is measured by four observed variables: I am happy with my WLB, the number of hours I work affects my personal relationships, the number of hours I work does not affect my personal health (reverse score) and my colleagues approve when I need to leave work because of outside commitments. A six-point Likert scale, ranging from 1 'very strongly disagree' to 6 'very strongly agree' was used to measure the extent to which participants agreed/disagreed with the statements.

Career Barriers. Is measured by four observed variables: I think the glass ceiling exists (reverse measure), equal opportunities legislation means there are no barriers to women in employment, women are well represented in my profession and women are well represented in my organisation measured the latent variable. Measured on a six point Likert scale, ranging from 1 'very strongly disagree' to 6 'very strongly agree'.

Job Satisfaction. Measured via the job and organisational satisfaction scale of the Pressure Management Index (Williams & Cooper 1998). The scale consists of twelve items, divided into two subscales. Job satisfaction measures how satisfied participants are with the type of work they do (α=0.89). Organisation satisfaction measures how satisfied participants are with the way the organisation is structured and the way it works (α=0.83). The questionnaire is a Likert scale ranging from 1= 'very strongly disagree', to 6= 'very strongly agree'. Higher scores indicate more

satisfaction. Scale ranges from 12-72 with higher scores indicate a greater level of satisfaction.

Person-Environment Fit. Scale developed by Lauver and Kristof-Brown (2001). The scale consists of eight items, measured on a seven point Likert response scale, ranging from 1 'very strongly disagree' to 7 'very strongly agree'. The scale is divided into two subscales, person-job fit (α=0.79), measures how well an individual perceives they match their job and person organisation fit (α=0.83), which measures how well an individual perceives they match with a single organisation in a single industry. Scale ranges from 8-56 with higher scores indicating more fit.

Career Aspirations (Aspirations). Is measured by three observed variables; promotion is important to me, I intend to climb the career ladder and I am prepared to make personal sacrifices in order to do so and to be recognised in my field is important to me. Participants were asked to indicate the extent they agree/disagree with statements on career progression and promotion, measured on a six point Likert scale, ranging from 1 'very strongly disagree' to 6 'very strongly agree'.

Data Analysis

Data was analysed using the statistics package SPSS version 15 and the structural equation model (SEM) was applied using AMOS version 6. Data were screened for outliers and nonnormality.

Results

Descriptive statistics and correlations between all the measures are reported in Table 1.

Multivariate normality assumptions were met, maximum-likelihood estimation was used, and scaling metrics for the latent variables were fixed be setting factor variances (reference variables) to 1. Model fit was assessed using the x^2 test statistic. However, due to the lack of guidance x^2 index provides in determining the extent to which the model fits the data we rely on other indexes

Table 1. Correlations, means, and standard deviations

	1	2	3	4	5	6	7	8	9	10	11	12	13	14	15	16	M	SD
1 WLB-happy with my WLB																	3.87	1.101
2 WLB-hours affects my personal relationships	.636**																3.68	1.245
3 WLB- hours affect my health	-.455**	-.519**															3.53	1.165
4 WLB-colleagues approve	.424**	.300**	-.233**														3.70	1.107
5 Self-efficacy	-.104*	-.072	.028	-.063													28.86	4.776
6 Job Fit	-.062	-.057	.042	-.063	.707**												29.30	4.742
7 Organisational Fit	-.051	-.025	.018	-.050	.363**	.421**											16.13	3.690
8 Aspirations-promotion is important to me	-.008	-.004	.039	-.012	.183**	.175**	-.041										4.46	1.118
9 Aspirations-I intend to climb the career ladder and I am prepared to make personal sacrifices in order to do so	-.017	.009	.050	-.046	.186**	.184**	.089	.592**									3.76	1.297
10 Aspirations-to be recognised in my field is important to me	-.086	-.057	.058	-.134**	.090	.069	.048	.368**	.344**								4.65	.955
11 Job Satisfaction	.015	.064	-.045	.003	.414**	.430**	.518**	.001	.093*	.022							26.53	5.015
12 Organisational Satisfaction	.096*	.091	-.089	.024	.284**	.264**	.562**	-.085	.090	-.042	.657**						23.60	5.736
13 Satisfaction	.064	.086	-.075	.016	.378**	.375**	.595**	-.049	.100*	-.013	.897**	.922**					50.12	9.791
14 Career Barriers-glass ceiling	-.035	.029	.008	.004	-.089	-.092	-.183*	.076	-.005	.048	-.200**	-.218**	-.230**				2.93	1.238
15 Career Barriers-equal opps	-.025	.017	.026	-.002	.043	.013	.077	-.060	.007	-.008	.098*	.129**	.126**	-.279**			3.29	1.471
16 Career Barriers-represented in profession	-.015	-.016	.038	-.095*	.029	.103*	.011	.063	.018	.123**	.046	-.010	.018	.167**	-.058		2.21	1.002
17 Career Barriers-represented in organisation	-.033	-.024	.033	-.036	.070	.067	.167**	-.026	.021	-.001	.169**	.224**	.218**	-.521**	.448**	-.213**	2.88	1.272

Note: WLB=work-life balance, M=mean, SD = standard deviation, *p=.05, **p=.01

Figure 1. Model fit

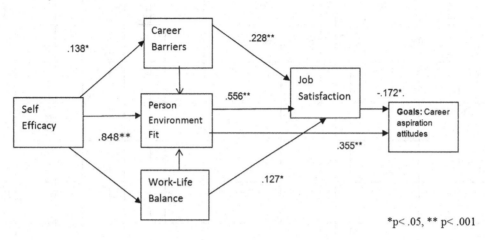

*p< .05, ** p< .001

of fit; the goodness-of-fit (GFI), Tucker–Lewis (TLI), and comparative-fit (CFI) indexes, and the root mean square error of approximation (RMSEA) (Byrne, 2001). As the x^2 test statistic is sensitive to sample size (the more participants, the higher the value), it has been recommended that it be used with caution (Medsker, Williams, & Holahan, 1994), and to consider an x^2 value 2 to 3 times greater than the degrees of freedom (DF) is viewed acceptable (Carmines & McIver, 1981). Modification indexes were also examined to assess possible improvement to the fit of the models being tested (Byrne, 2001). Values for the GFI (goodness of fit index), TLI (Tucker Lewis index), and CFI (comparative fit index) range from 0 to 1; with estimates of .9 or above indicating an acceptable measure of fit (Byrne, 2001). The RMSEA (Root mean square error of approximation index) has a lower boundary of zero, with values of less than .08 indicating an acceptable error of approximation (Byrne, 2001).

Acceptable fit was found ($x^2$426.64, 182 DF, 2.34 x^2/DF), figure 1 shows the model. Values for the GFI (.915), TLI (.916), and CFI (.927) are all above .9 indicating an acceptable measure of fit and the RMSEA (.055) has a value of less than .08 indicating an acceptable error of approximation.

The model contains the following variables; 53 variables, 21 of which are observed variables, 32 unobserved variables, 27 exogenous variables and 26 endogenous variables. The Observed, endogenous variables; SelfE1, SelfE2, SelfE3, SelfE4, SelfE5, SelfE6, WL2, WL1, WLB3_REV, WL7, ORGFIT, JOBFIT, Barriers2, BARRIERS1_REV, Barriers5, Barriers6, ORGSAT, JOBSAT, CP2, CP1 and CP5. Unobserved, endogenous variables; Fit, Satisfaction, Aspirations, WLB, Barriers, Unobserved, exogenous variables; Self Efficacy, e1, e2, e3, e4, e5, e6, e7, e8, e9, e10, e11, e12, e13, e14, e15, e16, e17, e18, e19, e20, e21, res1, res2, res3, res4 and res5.

Table 2 shows the un-standardized coefficients (estimate), its standard error (S.E.), the critical ratio (C.R.) and the probability value associated with the null hypothesis that the test is zero (P) for the study model (see figure 1). Each un-standardized coefficient represents the amount of change in the dependent variable for each one unit of change in the variable preceding it.

DISCUSSION

The research has a number of interesting findings. Due to the fact that the study design includes a number of different psychological constructs, the discussion section has been split to discuss the constructs individually to discuss how they relate to each of the other constructs in the model as well as the model overall.

Table 2. Maximum likelihood estimate: Regression weights

Variables	Estimate	S E	CR	P
Career Barriers: Self Efficacy	.075	.034	2.200	**
Work-life balance: Self Efficacy	-.121	.062	-1.936	.053
Person Environment Fit: Self Efficacy	4.411	.282	15.638	***
Person Environment Fit: Work-life balance	.004	.198	.021	.983
Person Environment Fit: Career Barriers	-.030	.434	-.070	.944
Job Satisfaction: Career Barriers	.698	.210	3.330	***
Job Satisfaction: Person Environment Fit	.178	.021	8.376	***
Job Satisfaction: Work-life balance	.191	.075	2.557	**
Career Aspirations: Person Environment Fit	.078	.018	4.450	***
Career Aspirations: Job Satisfaction	-.119	.053	-2.249	**

*p<.05, **p<.01, ***p<.001.

Occupational Self-Efficacy. Occupational self-efficacy had a significant positive effect on attitudes towards career barriers in that; higher occupational self-efficacy resulted in awareness of, or acknowledgement of career barriers towards women's careers (.138, p<.05). This suggests that having more efficacy or competence enables women to overcome any barriers they face. Occupational self-efficacy had a significant positive effect on person-environment fit (.848, p<.001); higher occupational self-efficacy resulted in higher person-environment fit. Higher efficacy resulted in a stronger feeling of fitting in. This supports Bandura's (1986) assertions that people will be attracted to jobs and organisations based on the extent to which they believe they can succeed. Therefore, individuals with higher self-efficacy will be more likely to value their subjective perceptions of fit more heavily when judging attraction to an organisation than individuals with lower self-efficacy (Bandura, 1986). However, occupational self-efficacy was not significant to attitudes towards work-life balance. This finding suggests that competence had no effect on how participants felt towards their work-life balance, either positively or negatively. Findings emphasise the importance of self-efficacy in the workplace.

Career Barriers. Attitudes towards career barriers did not significantly affect person-environment fit. This is a surprising finding as it was

expected that attitudes towards women's career barriers would affect their workplace congruence. It was expected that a more positive attitude would result in more fit/congruence, however this was not the case and there was no relationship either positive or negative. Attitudes towards work-life balance issues did not have a significant effect on person-environment fit as expected. Again, this is a surprising finding that suggests fit and congruence with the working environment and job whatever the work-life balance situation.

Work-Life Balance. Work-life balance issues were significantly related to satisfaction (.127, p<.05), with a positive attitude towards work-life balance linked to higher satisfaction at work. This implies that gaining a suitable work-life balance is important to satisfaction at work for women in the games industry. Indeed, Scandura and Lankau (1997) found the ability to combine family and work-life was particularly important to the job satisfaction of female employees. Balancing work and life is important to today's workforce (Blyton & Jenkins, 2007).

Person-Environment Fit. Person-environment fit was significantly related to satisfaction at work (.556, p<.001); higher fit or congruence resulted in higher satisfaction, supporting previous findings (O'Reilly et al, 1991). Person-environment fit was significantly related to career aspirations (.355, p<.001); congruence with the working environment leads to greater career aspirations. Previous research has found opportunities for career advancement as an important determinant of job satisfaction (Shields and Ward, 2001), which these findings tend to support. Female game workers attitudes towards career barriers were significantly related to satisfaction (.228, p<.001). Awareness of women's career barriers resulted in higher satisfaction. This might suggest that career barriers can be overcome, or it may be due to the specific barriers women encounter in the workplace (Swanson and Woitke, 1997).

Job Satisfaction. Satisfaction at work was significantly related to career aspirations (-.172, p<.05). However the relationship was a negative one in that when satisfaction goes up, aspirations go down. This could mean that being satisfied with your job is more important than career aspirations for women in this industry. Person-environment fit was significantly related to career aspirations (.355, p<.001); congruence with the working environment leads to greater career aspirations. Therefore, although person-environment fit is important to satisfaction, fit is more important to career aspirations than satisfaction. It seems that career fit or congruence leads to wanting, or indeed having more positive/higher career aspirations.

The study model posited that career aspirations arise and are influenced by internal and external career factors. The results suggest that each of these factors influence career aspirations in differing degrees. To increase women's career development and career aspirations, self-efficacy, attitudes towards career barriers, work-life balance attitudes, person-environment fit and job satisfaction are all important factors to be considered. Paying attention to various career related factors especially those related to supports and barriers may be a fruitful area of future focus.

Attitudes towards career barriers and work-life balance issues were significantly related to satisfaction within the model no matter the role, yet these were not significant to person-environment fit. The findings add to the literature on satisfaction at work since satisfaction at work is therefore influenced by the outside work influences of both work-life balance issues and attitudes towards career barriers. The influence and relationship of outside work influences is an area of job satisfaction viewed as needing research (Blyton & Jenkins, 2007). Although further research is needed, the findings do suggest a preliminary relationship. It seems person-environment fit is influenced by self-efficacy and person-environment fit influences satisfaction and aspirations. Whereas, satisfaction is influenced by person-environment fit, attitudes towards career barriers, work-life balance issues and it negatively influences career aspirations. Unlike the findings of previous research, satisfaction did not increase aspirations. This provides useful theoretical findings to career development researchers since findings reveal person-environment fit proved more influential. This may also be an important finding for the computer games industry as it highlights the importance of fitting into your role and working environment, as important for the career aspirations of women working within the industry.

LIMITATIONS AND FUTURE DIRECTION

The findings of this study are limited by the fact that the participants are self-selected and there is no way of knowing the number of women who did not take part in the study and the reasons they did not take part. Research in this area would be strengthened from a sample of women with a more diverse demographic. For instance, the model may differ on a sample of women with different demographics, such as women with children. What is interesting from the demographical information of the participants in the current study is that the majority of participants had no children. With a larger sample the number of women with children in the sample may be increased as it may be interesting to see if motherhood status impacts significantly on the career factors specifically and the model overall.

Another limitation in terms of the demographics of the sample is that the majority of participants worked in the USA and the UK. This is perhaps due to the sampling strategy employed in the study, however a more varied sample in terms of the where the participants worked. This would include a larger sample from other Westernised countries such as Canada and Australia as well a larger sample from Non-Westernised countries including across Europe, South America and Japan. Countries aside from the USA and the UK have large gamer populations and the perspective of women working in game development within these countries is paramount to gaining a greater understanding of the issues involved for women working in the computer games industry. There may also be differences between women working in the games industry that are producing different games such as serious games and commercial games or games developed for different platforms such as console or mobile phone games.

It would also be useful to see if the career influences model is applicable to men in the games industry and across the ICT sector. It is also possible that the relationships suggested by the model may change overtime. Therefore, the model needs to be cross-validated. Additionally a replication of the study is needed in order to strengthen not just the model, but also the usage and applicability of a SCCT framework for similar future research. This could be achieved through applying the model to women in the wider ICT industry or other industries both male and female dominated in order to see if the same career factors influence the aspirational attitudes of women in different work domains.

Lent et al. (2000) suggest that individuals with strong coping efficacy may be more likely to persist in their goal attainment than individuals who believe they are less efficacious in dealing with obstacles or accessing resources in helping them to cope. This would be of particular benefit in light of the current findings, especially since it may have been the efficiency of the women that

perhaps enabled them to overcome any career barriers perceived. One possible way forward would be to develop a model over two or more time stages in a career. The research area would also be strengthened by the use of longitudinal methods to provide useful information on the career progression of women within the games industry. Indeed, research might highlight the strategies women adopt in order to adapt or fit into male-dominated work environments. According to Brown and Lent (1996) even people with high self-efficacy might avoid a career if they perceive considerable barriers to attaining it. Perhaps women in the current study did not perceive any barriers before entering the career, but this may alter the longer they are in it.

CONCLUSION

Using SCCT as a framework, the current study was able to develop a career model of influences towards aspirations using structural equation modelling (SEM). The model that best fits the data in the current study shows how SCCT can be utilised as a framework for understanding the career aspirations of women already in a career. The main concepts of SCCT self-efficacy, environmental factors, outcome expectations, and goals are included in the model. SCCT is a situation specific theory that focuses on the connection between the concepts influencing an individual's career choice or, in this study, career advancement and development. In line with theoretical expectations, the results of this study suggest that a combination of external and internal factors can be used in models of career factors to predict women's career development and aspirations. Future research should continue to refine these relationships to further enhance our understanding of the effects of career factors on women's aspirations in male-dominated occupations. Enhancing knowledge of women's career aspirations may help contribute to progressing the working environment to be more inclusive and female friendly which should help industries such as the computer games industry attract and retain more female workers in more diverse roles across the industry. Increasing knowledge in this area may also ultimately lead to helping eradicate gendered occupational segregation and the detrimental effects and implications it has on women's working and non-working lives.

REFERENCES

Allen, I. (2005). Women doctors and their careers: What now? *British Medical Journal, 331*(September), 569–572. doi:10.1136/bmj.331.7516.569 PMID:16150771

Arfken, D. E., Bellar, S. L., & Helms, M. H. (2004). The ultimate glass ceiling revisited: The presence of women on corporate boards. *Journal of Business Ethics, 50*, 177–186. doi:10.1023/B:BUSI.0000022125.95758.98

Bandura, A. (1986). *Social foundations of thought and action: A social cognitive theory.* Englewood Cliffs, NJ: Prentice Hall.

Betz, N. E., & Hackett, G. (1981). Applications of self-efficacy theory to the career assessment of women. *Journal of Career Assessment, 5*(4), 383–402. doi:10.1177/106907279700500402

Betz, N. E., & Schifano, R. S. (2000). Evaluation of an intervention to increase realistic self-efficacy and interests in college women. *Journal of Vocational Behavior, 56*(1), 35–52. doi:10.1006/jvbe.1999.1690

Blyton, P., & Jenkins, J. (2007). *Key concepts in work.* London: Sage. doi:10.4135/9781446215814

Brief, A. P., & Weiss, H. M. (2002). Organizational behavior: Affect in the workplace. *Annual Review of Psychology, 53*, 279–307. doi:10.1146/annurev.psych.53.100901.135156 PMID:11752487

Brown, S. D., & Lent, R. W. (1996). A social cognitive framework for career choice counseling. *The Career Development Quarterly, 44*, 354–366. doi:10.1002/j.2161-0045.1996.tb00451.x

Brown, S. G., & Barbosa, G. (2001). Nothing is going to stop me now: Obstacles perceived by low-income women as they become self-sufficient. *Public Health Nursing (Boston, Mass.), 18*, 364–372. doi:10.1046/j.1525-1446.2001.00364.x PMID:11559420

Byrne, B. M. (2001). *Structural equation modelling with AMOS: Basic concepts, applications and programming.* Mahwah, NJ: Lawrence Erlbaum Associates.

Carmines, E. G., & McIver, P. J. (1981). Analyzing models with unobserved variables: Analysis of covariance structures. In G. W. Bohrnstedt, & E. F. Borgatta (Eds.), *Social measurement: Current issues* (pp. 65–115). Beverly Hills, CA: Sage Publications.

Consalvo, M. (2008). Crunched by passion: Women game developers and workplace challenges. In H. Kafai, Denner & Sun (Ed.), Beyond Barbie and Mortal Kombat: New perspectives on gender and gaming (pp. 177-192). Cambridge, MA: The MIT Press.

Cunningham, G. B., Doherty, A. J., & Gregg, M. J. (2007). Using social cognitive career theory to understand head coaching intentions among assistant coaches of women's teams. *Sex Roles, 56*, 365–372. doi:10.1007/s11199-006-9175-z

Deuze, M., Martin, C. B., & Alen, C. (2007). The professional identity of gameworkers. *Convergence: The International Journal of Research into New Media Technologies, 13*(4), 335–353. doi:10.1177/1354856507081947

Domenico, D. M., & Jones, K. H. (2006). Career aspirations of women in the 20th Century. *Journal of Career and Technical Education, 22*(2), 1–7.

Dyer-Whitheford, N., & Sharman, Z. (2005). The political economy of Canada's video and computer game industry. *Canadian Journal of Communication*, *20*, 187–210.

Ellinger, A. D., Ellinger, A. E., Yang, B., & Howton, S. W. (2002). The relationship between the learning organization concept and firms' financial performance: An empirical assessment. *Human Resource Development Quarterly*, *13*, 5–21. doi:10.1002/hrdq.1010

Feldman, D. C., & Ng, T. W. H. (2007). Careers: Mobility, embeddedness, and success. *Journal of Management*, *33*(3), 350–377. doi:10.1177/0149206307300815

Fouad, N. A., Smith, P. L., & Zao, K. E. (2002). Across academic domains: Extensions of the social cognitive career model. *Journal of Counseling Psychology*, *49*(2), 164–171. doi:10.1037/0022-0167.49.2.164

Gist, M. E., & Mitchell, T. R. (1992). Self-efficacy: A theoretical analysis of its determinants and malleability. *Academy of Management Review*, *17*, 183–211.

Gordon, M., & Denisi, A. (1995). A re-examination of the relationship between union membership and job satisfaction. *Industrial & Labor Relations Review*, *48*, 222–236. doi:10.2307/2524484

Gourdin, A. (2005). *Game developers demographics: An exploration of workforce diversity*. International Game Developers Association. Retrieved from http://archives.igda.org/diversity/IGDA_DeveloperDemographics_Oct05.pdf

Graner Ray, S. (2004). *Gender inclusive game design: Expanding the market*. Hingham, MA: Charles River Media Inc.

Haines, L. (2004). Why are there so few women in games?. *Research for Media Training North West, September*.

Heilman, M. E. (1983). Sex bias in work settings: The lack of fit model. *Research in Organizational Behavior*, *5*, 269–298.

Holland, J. L. (1973). *Making vocational choice: A theory of careers*. Englewood Cliffs, NJ: Prentice-Hall.

Ilies, R., & Judge, T. A. (2004). An experience-sampling measure of job satisfaction and its relationships with affectivity, mood at work, job beliefs, and general job satisfaction. *European Journal of Work and Organizational Psychology*, *13*(3), 367–389. doi:10.1080/13594320444000137

Krotoski, A. (2004). *Chicks and joysticks: An exploration of women and gaming* (Entertainment and Leisure Software Publishers Association White paper).

Lauver, K., & Kristof-Brown, A. (2001). Distinguishing between employees' perceptions of person-job and person-organization fit. *Journal of Vocational Behavior*, *59*, 454–470. doi:10.1006/jvbe.2001.1807

Lent, R. W., & Brown, S. D. (2006). On conceptualizing and assessing social cognitive constructs in career research: A measurement guide. *Journal of Career Assessment*, *14*(1), 12–35. doi:10.1177/1069072705281364

Lent, R. W., Brown, S. D., Brenner, B., Chopra, S. B., Davis, T., Talleyrand, R., & Suthakaran, V. (2001). The role of contextual supports and barriers in the choice of math/science educational options: A test of social cognitive hypotheses. *Journal of Counseling Psychology*, *48*(4), 474–483. doi:10.1037/0022-0167.48.4.474

Lent, R. W., Brown, S. D., & Hackett, G. (1994). Toward a unifying social cognitive theory of career and academic interest, choice and performance. *Journal of Vocational Behavior*, *45*, 79–122. doi:10.1006/jvbe.1994.1027

Lent, R. W., Brown, S. D., & Hackett, G. (2000). Contextual supports and barriers to career choice: A social cognitive analysis. *Journal of Counseling Psychology*, *47*(1), 36–49. doi:10.1037/0022-0167.47.1.36

Lindley, L. D. (2005). Perceived barriers to career development in the context of social cognitive career theory. *Journal of Career Assessment*, *13*(3), 271–287. doi:10.1177/1069072705274953

Mayrhofer, W., Steyrer, J., Meyer, M., Strunk, G., Schiffinger, M., & Iellatchitch, A. (2005). Graduates career aspirations and individual characteristics. *Human Resource Management Journal*, *15*(1), 38–56. doi:10.1111/j.1748-8583.2005.tb00139.x

McCarthy, M. (2004). *Girlfriends in high places: How women's networks are changing the workplace*. New York: Demos.

Medsker, G., Williams, L., & Holahan, P. (1994). A review of current practices for evaluating causal models in organizational behavior and human resources management research. *Journal of Management*, *20*(2), 439–464. doi:10.1016/0149-2063(94)90022-1

Ng, T. W. H., Eby, L. T., Sorensen, K. L., & Feldman, D. C. (2005). Predictors of objective and subjective career success: A meta analysis. *Personnel Psychology*, *58*, 367–408. doi:10.1111/j.1744-6570.2005.00515.x

O'Reilly, C. A., Chatman, J., & Caldwell, D. F. (1991). People and organizational culture: A profile comparison approach assessing person-organization fit. *Academy of Management Review*, *34*(3), 487–516. doi:10.2307/256404

Perrewe, P. L., & Nelson, D. L. (2004). Gender and career success: The facilitative role of political skill. *Organizational Dynamics*, *33*(4), 366–378. doi:10.1016/j.orgdyn.2004.09.004

Perryman, R. D. (2004). Healthy attitudes: Quality of working life in the London NHS, 2000-2002 (Report by The National Health Service, UK).

Powell, G. N., & Butterfield, D. A. (2003). Gender, gender identity, and aspirations to top management. *Women in Management Review*, *18*(1/2), 88–96. doi:10.1108/09649420310462361

Prescott, J., & Bogg, J. (2010). The computer games industry: Women's experiences of work role in a male dominated environment. In A. Cater-Steel, & E. Cater (Eds.), *Women in engineering, science and technology: Education and career challenges* (pp. 138–152). Hershey, PA: IGI Global. doi:10.4018/978-1-61520-657-5.ch007

Prescott, J., & Bogg, J. (2013). *Gendered occupational differences in science, engineering, and technology careers*. Hershey, PA: IGI Global.

Prescott, J., & Bogg, J. (2014). *Gender divide and the computer gaming industry*. Hershey, PA: IGI Global.

Rigotti, T., Schyns, B., & Mohr, G. (2008). A short version of the occupational self-efficacy scale: Structural and construct validity across five countries. *Journal of Career Assessment*, *16*(2), 238–255. doi:10.1177/1069072707305763

Shields, M. A., & Ward, M. (2001). Improving nurse retention in the National Health Service in England: The impact of job satisfaction on intentions to quit. *Journal of Health Economics*, *20*, 677–701. doi:10.1016/S0167-6296(01)00092-3 PMID:11558644

Skillset. (2009). 2009 employment census: The results of the seventh census of the creative media industries December 2009. In The Sector Skills Council for Creative Media (Ed.), *The Sector Skills Council for Creative Media*.

Spector, P. E. (1985). Measurement of human service staff satisfaction: Development of the job satisfaction survey 1. *American Journal of Community Psychology*, *13*(6), 693–713. doi:10.1007/BF00929796 PMID:4083275

Swanson, J. L., & Woitke, M. B. (1997). Theory into practice in career assessment for women: Assessment and interventions regarding perceived career barriers. *Journal of Career Assessment*, *5*, 443–462. doi:10.1177/106907279700500405

Taylor, T. L. (2003). Multiple pleasures: Women and online gaming. *Convergence*, *9*(1), 21–46. doi:10.1177/135485650300900103

Williams, S., & Cooper, C. L. (1998). Measuring occupational stress: Development of the pressure management indicator. *Journal of Occupational Health Psychology*, *3*(4), 306–321. doi:10.1037/1076-8998.3.4.306 PMID:9805279

ADDITIONAL READING

Bain, O., & Cummings, W. (2000). Academe's glass ceiling: societal, professional-organizational, & institutional barriers to the career advancement of academic Women. *Comparative Education Review*, *44*(4), 493–514. doi:10.1086/447631

Bajo, L. M., & Dickson, M. W. (2002). Perceptions of organisational culture and women's advancement in organisations: A cross-cultural examination. *Sex Roles*, *45*, 399–414. doi:10.1023/A:1014365716222

Bandura, A., & Locke, E. A. (2003). Negative Self-Efficacy and Goal Effects Revisited. *The Journal of Applied Psychology*, *88*(1), 87–99. doi:10.1037/0021-9010.88.1.87 PMID:12675397

Betz, N. E. (2007). Career self-efficacy recent research and emerging directions. *Journal of Career Assessment*, *15*(4), 403–422. doi:10.1177/1069072707305759

Betz, N. E., Borgen, F. H., & Harmon, L. W. (2006). Vocational confidence and personality in the prediction of occupational group membership. *Journal of Career Assessment*, *14*(1), 36–55. doi:10.1177/1069072705282434

Betz, N. E., & Hackett, G. (1997). Applications of self-efficacy theory to the career assessment of women. *Journal of Career Assessment*, *5*(4), 383–402. doi:10.1177/106907279700500402

Brief, A. P., & Weiss, H. M. (2002). Organizational behavior: affect in the workplace. *Annual Review of Psychology*, *53*, 279–307. doi:10.1146/annurev.psych.53.100901.135156 PMID:11752487

Britton, D. M. (2000). The epistemology of the gendered organization. *Gender & Society*, *14*(3), 418–434. doi:10.1177/089124300014003004

Britton, D. M., & Logan, L. (2008). Gendered organizations: progress and prospects. *Social Compass*, *2*(1), 107–121. doi:10.1111/j.1751-9020.2007.00071.x

Burke, R. J., & McKeen, C. A. (1994). *Carer development among managerial and professional women. Women in management: current research issues*. M. Davidson, & Burke, R. London: Paul Chapman Publishing.

Cable, D. M., & DeRue, D. S. (2002). The convergent & discriminant validity of subjective fit perceptions. *The Journal of Applied Psychology*, *87*, 1–17. doi:10.1037/0021-9010.87.5.875 PMID:12395812

Cable, D. M., & Judge, T. A. (1996). Person-organization fit, job choice decisions, and organizational entry. *Organizational Behavior and Human Decision Processes*, *67*, 294–311. doi:10.1006/obhd.1996.0081

Correll, S. J. (2004). Constraints into preferences: gender, status and emerging career aspirations. *American Sociological Review*, *69*, 93–133. doi:10.1177/000312240406900106

Eccles, J. (1994). Understanding women's educational & occupational choices. *Psychology of Women Quarterly*, *18*, 585–609. doi:10.1111/j.1471-6402.1994.tb01049.x

Eccles, J. S. (1987). Gender roles and women's achievement-related decisions. *Psychology of Women Quarterly*, *11*, 135–172. doi:10.1111/j.1471-6402.1987.tb00781.x

Ehrhart, K. H., & Ziegert, J. C. (2005). Why are individuals attracted to organizations? *Journal of Management*, *31*(6), 901–919. doi:10.1177/0149206305279759

Farmer, H. S. (1985). Model of career & achievement motivation for women & men. *Journal of Counseling Psychology*, *32*(3), 363–390. doi:10.1037/0022-0167.32.3.363

Farmer, H. S. (1997). Women's motivation related to mastery, career salience and career aspirations: a multivariate model focusing on the effects of sex role socialization. *Journal of Career Assessment*, *5*(2), 355–381. doi:10.1177/106907279700500401

Farmer, H. S., & Chung, Y. B. (1995). Variables related to career commitment, mastery motivation, and level of career aspirations among college students. *Journal of Career Development*, *21*(4), 265–278. doi:10.1177/089484539502100401

Kottke, J. L., & Agars, M. D. (2005). Understanding the processes that facilitate and hinder efforts to advance women in organizations. *Career Development International*, *10*(3), 190–202. doi:10.1108/13620430510598319

Lent, R. W., & Brown, S. D. (2006). On conceptualizing and assessing social cognitive constructs in career research: a measurement guide. *Journal of Career Assessment*, *14*(1), 12–35. doi:10.1177/1069072705281364

Lent, R. W., Brown, S. D., Schmidt, J., Brenner, B., Lyons, H., & Treistman, D. (2003). Relation of contextual supports & barriers to choice behaviour in engineering majors: test of alternative social cognitive models. *Journal of Counseling Psychology*, *50*(4), 458–465. doi:10.1037/0022-0167.50.4.458

Lent, R. W., Sheu, H.-B., Gloster, C. S., & Wilkins, G. (2010). Longitudinal test of the social cognitive model of choice in engineering students at historically Black universities. *Journal of Vocational Behavior*, *76*, 387–394. doi:10.1016/j.jvb.2009.09.002

Lent, R. W., Singley, D., Sheu, H.-B., Schmidt, J. A., & Schmidt, L. C. (2007). Relation of social-cognitive factors to academic satisfaction in engineering students. *Journal of Career Assessment*, *15*(1), 87–97. doi:10.1177/1069072706294518

O'Neil, D. A., & Bilimoria, D. (2005). Women's career development phases idealism, endurance & reinvention. *Career Development International*, *10*(3), 168–189. doi:10.1108/13620430510598300

Srsic, C. S., & Walsh, W. B. (2001). Person-environment congruence & career self-efficacy. *Journal of Career Assessment*, *9*(2), 203–213. doi:10.1177/106907270100900207

KEY TERMS AND DEFINITIONS

Career Aspirations: The desire to progress through jobs to achieve a better job position.

Career Development: Progression through jobs which results in more responsibility and income than the previous position.

Job Satisfaction: The satisfaction level an individual has with their current job position.

Male Dominated Occupations: Occupations and industries that are viewed as being traditionally male. Where the majority of the workforce within that occupation or industry is male.

Occupational Self-Efficacy: The belief an individual has that they can do a certain job role.

Person-Environment Fit: Congruence between the personality and type of person an individual is and the job role they are in.

Final Thoughts and Concluding Comments

Recent developments and technological advances have significantly impacted gaming in the areas of who plays games and where they play them. Firstly, the Internet and the emergence of online multi-players means that gamers do not need a gaming console but can play games through a PC, as well as allowing gamers to play against one another and collaborate in team games with players around the world. Secondly the emergence of wireless platforms, enables players to play games on mobile phones (smartphones) and other handheld gaming devices. As a major entertainment and leisure activity for adults and children globally, the computer games industry is an important industry in the contemporary media landscape. According to Galarneau (2014) the top 10 gaming trends are:

1. Women are playing more and more games, and so is the older generation.
2. Gaming families and friend networks are the norm.
3. Revenue from games and game context is up and on par with the movie industry.
4. Games are going more and more mobile.
5. Casual, casino, mobile and social games are becoming as popular as other PC and console games.
6. Free to play business models have redefined the marketplace.
7. Video game violence is more of a problem for the media than for gamers or their families.
8. Variety is the spice of life- there are over fourteen different genres of games to choose from.
9. Asia is still the hotbed for gaming- the gaming landscape in Asia is dominated by social games.
10. The only thing that is ever guaranteed is more change- many regions such as Africa, the Middle East, Central America and South Asia have limited online access to the Internet but more and more people in these geographical areas are getting online.

Many of these issues in the top ten trends are discussed within this book, however the list is worth mentioning as it reiterates the point that this is an important industry as discussed briefly in the preface. Gendered occupational segregation is an issue across the globe. Women are underrepresented in a number of careers especially careers within the STEM (Science, Technology, Engineering and Mathematics careers). Throughout the chapters included within this book it is evident that women's underrepresentation within

DOI: 10.4018/978-1-4666-6142-4.chcon

the computer games industry is a pertinent issue. As stated in the preface this books guiding message comes from the perspective that there is a need for women to be involved in the production of computer games and all forms of technology development, at all levels. When considering who develops and produces computer games as well as the content of games, one influences the other. In that, the content of games influences who is interested in playing computer games, which influences who desires to work in the industry, which in turn influences the content of the games, all based on gender assumptions (Prescott & Bogg, 2014). What is particularly encouraging about the chapters within this book is that the chapters included in this edition highlight the vast array of research that is being conducted which is focussing on the issue of underrepresentation of women in STEM subjects and particularly the computer games industry. What is of particular interest and particularly exciting is that research into women's underrepresentation in the computer games industry is taking place across the globe including in Japan, Australia, the USA, UK and in Europe. As highlighted in the preface, there are three geographic gaming markets and game developing areas: North America, Europe and Japan, with distinct differences between the Western (American and Europe) and Eastern (Japanese) markets and developing strategies (Johns, 2006; Consalvo, 2006). Therefore this global view is important to highlight as this enables researchers to understand the similarities and differences that exists within this industry for female developers across the globe.

The chapters in this edition have been divided into three sections which perhaps leads us to consider three main areas for consideration when investigating the gender divide in the computer games and digital media industries. The first section considers education and gaming with research looking at how games can both reinforce and also challenge gender stereotypes in girls. It also considers the link between playing games and

developing an interest in studying computer science, and games development, and research which investigates the experiences of females currently studying a computer games undergraduate degree and how their background and experiences on the course as well as their views of the games industry.

The chapters within section two are critical to this book as they give the women in the industry a voice and provide readers with an insight into their lived experiences. What is particularly interesting and a major contribution of this book is that it has chapters from women in different parts of the world. As acknowledged throughout this edition, women working in the computer games industry are an understudied, under researched area, resulting in a lack of knowledge about the experiences of females working within the industry. Section two adds to the literature in the area and adds to our understanding of women working in male dominated work environments and industries. The final section, section three, has four chapters which look at the future outlook for women within the industry and considers research which has looked at women in the STEM sector. These chapters provide readers with an understanding of the underrepresentation of women in the sector and how this sector may be beneficial to the gaming industry.

GUIDING MESSAGE OF THE RESEARCH

In this section of the conclusion we would like to consider the main findings and conclusions from each of the individual chapters included in this edition and how they add to the literature and our understanding of women's underrepresentation in developing computer games and involvement within the industry. In chapter one King and Douai conclude from their historical look at games and games for girls as well as their in-depth study of Webkinz World that there is perhaps a complicated relationship between gender and gaming. They argue that on the one hand gendered stereotypes can be transcended by games and games can increase girls' engagement and interest with technology. Conversely, games such as Webkinz World can also reinforce feminine stereotypes in girls. Through a look at the historical context of games, the authors also illustrate how games are cultural text and how through these cultural text, children learn social norms and establish identities through play. When discussing their findings in relation to the gender divide in computer games they recognize the improvements in the representation of females in computer games and importantly recognize that despite the female underrepresentation within the industry, the important work those female developers that have broken into this male domain and are working in the industry have made in order to 'challenge[d] the industry's stereotypical treatment of females'. This chapter highlights the importance of increasing female games into the overall gaming culture in order to challenge and change the demographics of the gaming market and games industry, increasing the diversity of those that make games and for whom.

In chapter two, Denner, Ortiz and Werner's findings show that among student gamers who are taking an introductory computer programming class, there is great variation in how and why they game. Interestingly, their findings suggest that certain practices, motivations and types of gaming are associated with a greater interest in pursuing the study of computer science. The authors found a number of differences and similarities between the genders. For instance, despite previous research suggesting women play fewer games than men, many of the female participants in this study played as frequently as their male counterparts. However, findings revealed that females tended to be motivated by the challenge found in solving puzzle games, whereas men were motivated by the challenge in action games. Both genders were also motivated by story. Interestingly, the study found that many of the female participants hid their game play, viewing it as less socially

acceptable for females to play. This is interesting as the study did not find frequency of play as an important predictor of interest in computer science, but rather the extent to which the participant identifies as a gamer.

Findings revealed that the females who played a wide range of game genres, enjoyed playing games for fun, relaxation and social interaction, were more likely to say they wanted to study computer science. Those that wanted to study computer science were also more likely to be interested in the structure and mechanics of the game rather than just playing the game and they were found to be less likely to only play casual games. This chapter enhances our understanding of the potential link in getting more females interested in studying computer science through playing computer games. Game play has often been associated with one potential avenue in increasing female participation in ICT (information, communication and technology) careers including the computer games industry; this chapter provides further insight into this potential link.

In chapter three, Elliot and Prescott found some interesting findings from their small sample of female gaming students. This chapter provides an interesting insight into the experiences of the females on the course, as well as their views of entering (or at least potentially entering) the male dominated computer games industry. The female students interviewed choose to study games because they enjoyed playing games. Despite all four participants experiencing the course positively, there was some apprehension expressed about going into the industry. Interestingly it seems that the male dominated working environment may be off-putting to women, even women studying and interested in going into this area of work. The main 'off-putting' themes to emerge were the long hours culture and potential sexism within the industry.

It is somewhat difficult to draw similarities between the three chapters within this section since although the focus is education the age of the participants in the chapters is quite different.

However from this educational section, despite the fact that the three chapters are investigating very different aspects of educational factors, it is apparent from all of these chapters that game play is important in developing a potential interest in computer games and developing the skills required.

In chapter four, author Pugh considered the gender breakdown of the industry by role from a review of previous research. The chapter examined the gender breakdown of each department, explored the relationship between STEM and the games industry. The chapter suggests more research is needed to uncover the reason for the underrepresentation of women in the industry especially in the areas of; lack of interest, work-family conflict, and the social stigmas of the industry.

Chapter five by Prescott and Bogg focuses on the experiences of women currently working in developmental roles within the games industry. From the interviews with seven female developers, the study finds a number of reoccurring issues relating to the working environment and working practices in the industry. In particular, work life balance issues and the long hours culture are viewed specifically as issues for women within the industry. Overt instances of discrimination and sexism experienced by some of the women in the study highlights the barriers women may face within this and other male dominated industries. These experiences may indeed contribute to the finding from the study that the women tended to view themselves as different from other women and that it takes a certain type of female to be able to work in this working environment. 'Tomboy' was a word frequently used to describe women in the industry, as was having a thick skin and not being very feminine.

Despite the participants in this study all being in a developmental role within the industry, they did feel that women were more likely to work in non-developmental roles in areas traditionally viewed as female roles/jobs such as human resources, marketing and administration rather than in developmental roles. Even within the developmental

roles there appears to be the view that women are more likely to work as artists and thus a more female role than in other more traditionally male roles within the industry such as coding, design and producing. Although this chapter highlights barriers women in the industry experience, it does also illustrate the many benefits the women gain from working in the industry. The benefits include the monetary gains and the fact that the women all enjoyed working in a challenging, creative and constantly developing industry. Many of the women in the study had worked in it for over a decade and viewed it as changing positively in part due to the increasing number of female gamers and more females entering the industry.

Chapter six by Fujihara investigates the under researched and relatively unknown, especially for Western audiences, viewpoint of Japanese female game developers and their experiences and career paths. This fascinating chapter highlights the issue faced by female game developers working in an industry quite separate from the Western computer games industry. The study of twenty-one one-to-one interviews with female game developers, who have worked in the industry for at least five years, provides a unique insight into their careers. The study found that past gamer experience had enabled the female participants to develop an interest and skills which led to their careers in the industry. The study aimed to understand the career progression of female game developers but found there was no typical career pattern but rather there appears to be various individual styles of career progression.

As with the study on UK game developers by Prescott and Bogg in this edition it was found that Japanese female game developers enjoy their jobs, while continuing to develop their skills and careers. Again, similar to UK findings, Fujihara found that the Japanese women do not conform to feminine stereotypes. The women in the study with children found work life balance an issue, with adaptions needing to be made in their working life and environment, and there was also the recognition of the impact children may have on their career progression within the industry. Fujihara's research provides a positive outlook for Japanese female game developers suggesting that 'they have the ability to alter their work situation, and evaluate and manage it if needed'. As mentioned by Pugh, mentoring was again an important issue for the women in this study. Fujihara found that the women aimed to be role models and mentors in their workplace because there are so few female developers in the Japanese gaming industry.

Chapter seven is a study of Australian female game developers and women working in other digital media industries by Geneve. This chapter used the Acts of Agency theory as a way to understand female participation in this industry in Australia. According to Geneve the theory helps explain the stories of participation that women in the Australian industry have experienced. The chapter provides an insight into the Acts of Agency theory and also the experiences of women within the industries involved in the study. The study suggests that a complex interaction between an individual and their environment is at play, positing that both are an influence on an individual's participation. This section provides women a voice from research with participants working in the games industry in the UK, USA, Japan and Australia. This research is vital for understanding the experiences of women in the industry. Although the chapters within this section all take a slightly different theoretical and/ or methodological approach to the subject, it is apparent that many of the issues are similar across the countries. Indeed the underrepresentation of women within this industry is evident through the research studied and reported in these chapters.

The chapters within section three highlight how we can gain lessons and ideas from the established STEM sector. For instance chapter ten suggests taking advantage of the successful outreach programs and initiatives within the STEM sector to further develop the diversity and gender imbal-ance within the computer games industry. Chapter eight by Warmuth and Hanappi-Egger investigated through interviews with STEM academics how professionalization is constructed and negotiated. The study looked at how structures are created and how these structures impact peoples creativity and innovation. With good work life balance essential in cultivating creativity in employers. This chapter and other research on STEM academics could help further our understanding of gender in the games industry and academia. Chapter nine by Pugh focused on how lessons from research investigating the underrepresentation of women working in the STEM sector can be applied to both understanding the underrepresentation of women working in the computer games industry and how this understanding can potentially provide ways forward for the computer games industry. Pugh concludes that the games industry would benefit from looking at tactics from many disciplines that make up the games industry in order to find solutions. More female role models within the industry was highlighted as a specific factor that would attract and encourage more women into the industry.

Chapter ten by McGill, Decker and Settle considers the success and benefits of outreach programs in enhancing and increasing diversity within the STEM sector and consider how similar initiatives are the way forward in enhancing the diversity in the computer games industry. From their research they suggest that purposeful action is needed in order to change the gender imbalance within the games industry. The final chapter, chapter eleven by Prescott and Bogg uses the theoretical framework of SCCT (Social Cognitive Career Theory) to investigate the career influences and motivations of an international sample of female game workers. The study found that in line with theoretical expectations, a combination of external and internal factors can be used in models of career factors to predict women's career development and aspirations.

THEMES AND COMMONALITIES FROM THE PROFILES

We thought it would be interesting and informative to collate some themes and commonalities from the profile insights included in the book. It was deemed informative to consider the views of the female (and one male) profiler included in this edition. The profiles inform the reader of the experiences and points of view of women working in the industry in a variety of roles and for differing lengths of time. The vast array of experiences is therefore deemed worthy of further consideration, pulling prominent themes from the profiles. Many of the themes within the profiles are discussed throughout the chapters of the book; in particular the issue of work life balance and the different skills women bring to the industry. The profiles also highlight that the women enjoy working in games, emphasizing and supporting a major premise of the book- that more women should be involved in the industry, especially in developmental roles.

The profiles cover 15 women from Sweden, Germany, US, Canada and the UK, and also includes a single male perspective of women working within games. The women are involved in varying capacities within the games industry e.g. game design, QA, production, art, code, lecturing, recruitment, sales, and span a wide range of experiences from entry level/graduate to Director. The approximate age rage of the profiles is from early 20s to mid 40s (although not all gave their age), and of the 15 women profiled only four highlighted they had children/family.

Starting a Career in the Games Industry

The majority of the women, especially the women with more years in the industry, 'fell' into the industry with no previous career aims of working in games,

'My friend was a games artist at Psygnosis. I visited the studio with him and I saw a potential new creative job, in an exciting, fun and cutting edge industry where artists could possibly have a secure job with a salary, pension and even the much-fabled end-of-game bonuses. I wanted to be part of all of that. I met some of the women on my friend's team and was unaware, still, that as women in games they were relatively rare' (Jo Daly).

'On a fall evening in 1989, after my weekly Dungeons and Dragons game had ended for the night, the players were packing up their dice and books when the guy who was the newest addition to the group approached me. "You know, my company has an opening for a writer," he said, "and with all the writing you've been doing for this weekly game, I think you'd be a natural. Want me to take your resume in?" A week later I had my interview at Origin Systems, with Warren Specter. I had my offer later that day. So I gave my notice at my job with the American Diabetes Association and two weeks later I started as a "writer" on the Ultima games at Origin Systems' (Sheri Graner Ray).

'I've always loved games but feel like I kind of fell into the industry. I studied English Literature at university more through a love of the subject than any kind of career goal, and this lack of direction probably somewhat prepared me for the global recession which was in full swing when I graduated in 2009. I managed to talk my way into a temporary Christmas job at GAME on sheer nervous adrenaline, where they and I quickly discovered that I have no aptitude for or inclination towards trying to sell people products they aren't already interested in. Once they realised this, my days were clearly numbered, and I moved into a job designing and maintaining a website for a small independent clothing company. Whilst the work was fun and rewarding I've never been particularly interested in fashion, and when a friend mentioned that a nearby games company was hiring testers it sounded too good an opportunity to pass up' (Faye Windsor-Smith).

The women tended to play games, even if they did not play them so much as adults, most had played games as a child. However, as one female notes, as a child a career in games did not seem a viable one,

'I grew up playing games from 'Orc Attack' on the Atari 600 in the early 80s, where loading games from the cassette deck took an age, to the handheld Donkey Kong on Nintendo Game and Watch following through to the Sega Mega Drive console at the turn of the '90s. Many hours were spent chasing rings in Sonic the Hedgehog or casting spells in Mickey Mouse World of Illusion. I spent so much time playing Sonic the Hedgehog trying to beat Dr Robotnik I used to catch rings in my sleep! Games were never a vocation I considered growing up, and I imagine that ultimately this was because I had no idea of how you would go about getting work in the industry' (Julie McGurren).

The younger profilers tended to have a different approach and perspective to gaining a career in games, this is mainly due to the increase in games related degree programs available as a catalyst into the industry. For instance,

'As I progressed through school and then sixth form, I prioritised Art and IT as subjects. The fine art course at my school focused on teaching traditional skills like painting and ceramics, but in my personal work I ventured more into digital art and got my first graphics tablet on my 16th birthday. When I reached the end of sixth form and started looking at universities, I thought more seriously about getting into games as a career. I was surprised to find that there were courses perfectly tailored to this and I applied to a few, but after attending various open days the one that really stood out was the Computer Games Design course at the University of Wales, Newport' (Hannah Payne).

Shockingly, one of the female profilers experienced barriers in the form of the sexist attitude of a lecture when enquiring about games courses,

'While in England, I decided I would like to stay and complete a degree there instead of going back to Sweden. I went to an open day at Staffordshire University thinking I would do CGI and Animatronics or Robotics. However, while talking to someone about the Robotics course and realising I found programming the most interesting, they kindly suggested I should go and check out the Games Programming or Software Engineering courses. So off I went to go to the Games Programming talk, where I was met by a lecturer (who later taught me), who immediately believed my boyfriend was the one interested in the course, and started talking to him. Once he realised it was me applying he said "This is a course with a lot of advanced maths and stuff, maybe you should check out Games Design downstairs". Quite demoralised and shot down, I left and decided to go to the games design talk, which did absolutely nothing for me. I remember thinking "I don't want to re-skin a bin lid to look like a pizza; I want to make it behave like a pizza". So, partly because I wanted to prove that lecturer wrong, and partly because the advanced maths that he had mentioned excited me, I decided to apply for the Games Programming course at Staffordshire University' (Anna Ljungberg).

Working in the Industry: Benefits and the Skills Women Bring

Although it appears that the women either fell into a career in games or went through a more structured and planned route through game courses, once in the industry the females all enjoy working in the industry. For instance one profiler although at the beginning of her career recognises the benefits of working in the industry,

'I'm still at the start of my career, but it's a career that is rewarding, both financially and emotionally. I work alongside like-minded people in a stimulating environment, and my work is something I truly feel passionate about. I love working as a games programmer, and firmly believe that choosing a career in the games industry was the best decision that I could have made. I hope that I will be a good role model for others looking for a rewarding and challenging career in the games industry' (Elinor Townsend).

A number of profilers referenced that being a women is advantageous in trying to get a job in the games industry as their CV stands out,

'When applying for roles in the games industry it may even be suggested that being female might be an advantage. In an endless sea of male applicants the occasional female is certainly noticeable and possibly even memorable. Some men that I have worked with in games have suggested they prefer having a mixed gender team to create a less testosterone filled working environment and add a little social balance and decorum. I have certainly noticed a little flurry of excitement amongst some of the male team members when it becomes known that a new woman is being interviewed or is starting work on a team' (Jo Daly).

'It was an interview at the Liverpool based Bizarre Creations in Feb 1999 that led me to my first job. I was aware of the company and their products as I had been playing their F1 games on the Sony PlayStation. I had a small portfolio of 3D work alongside my traditional artwork and knowledge of the built environment gained during my undergrad degree. At this point, a job within games as an artist was attainable, even with minimal 3D experience. Games courses were few and far between and most artists came into the industry via a variety of backgrounds some with no 2D or 3D skills just a strong traditional art portfolio that illustrated a creative ability. I do believe when my CV landed on the desk at Bizarre it probably attracted attention as I was female and very much a rarity in the late 90s, I like to think the BMX comment probably helped too! I was thrilled to be given the opportunity to join a successful team and my games career began as a 3D artist making content for Metropolis Street Racer (MSR) on the Sega Dreamcast' (Julie McGurren).

Another theme mentioned was the different skills females bring to the industry and the games they make and how this is a benefit to the industry,

'I don't feel that being a woman in the games industry is a barrier to advancing my career; in fact I believe that it may well be an advantage as the industry becomes more accepting of females who are aiming to start a career in games. The studio I work for actively encourages and seeks out female employees, and aims to someday have a 50/50 split between men and women. Rivet believes that in order to make fun games that will appeal to all audiences, it's important to reflect that demographic in the work place' (Carrie Warwick).

'During my time at Bizarre I was heavily involved in the recruitment of artists and C.Vs were few and far between from female applicants. In my experience, introducing females into the workplace often changes the dynamic of a group; it introduces new ways of thinking and throws different opinions into the mix' (Julie McGurren).

It was noted that females within the industry, whilst bringing a number of additional qualities to the industry, may feel they have to work harder in order to prove themselves,

'I've actually found that women show more enthusiasm and ambition. They're hungrier in the games industry, as if they have something to prove. They have all the talents of 'the guys' in the studio, but when the work needs to be done, they are not as easily distracted. So we cannot officially promote policies to simply 'hire more women', however what we can ask applicants is proof of proactivity, ambition, self-motivated projects etc. and I could probably suggest with confidence that the applicants coming out on top would be female, or at the very least an even split. Having a more balanced studio in terms of gender, I feel, brings a certain maturity to the group. I don't necessarily mean this in terms of experience; I just feel that women tend to be more 'professional' when they need to be. This can be as simple as organising work load, taking notes in a meeting, making sure a discussion stays on topic etc. They still bring the passion, excitement and enthusiasm, but in my experience can control it methodically' (Phil Goddard).

Whereas one profiler observed that women tend to climb the career ladder within games quicker than their male counterparts,

'Of those women that had been employed at Bizarre, I would say generally they gravitated to the top of the pile and became leads and seniors more quickly than their male counterparts. I would also note that the same is also true within Codemasters with a number of the key art lead positions held by females during my time with the company' (Julie McGurren).

The Issue of Work Life Balance and Having Children

As mentioned previously, a theme evident throughout many of the chapters within this book is the issue of work life balance. Not surprisingly, work life balance was a theme in a number of the profiles. Especially when considering children;

'Working in the industry has been an overwhelmingly positive experience and I don't think I'll ever want to leave, although I'm worried that at a certain point in my life I'll be seen as a liability for being of a "maternal" age. I hope that doesn't restrict my career opportunities in the future' (Faye Windsor-Smith).

One resolution of the difficulty in maintaining a work life balance by a number of the profilers was to continue their career in games through teaching games, rather than working directly in the industry,

'I was also keen to see what job I could do that might improve my work/life balance. Games development does tend to involve very long working hours during crunch and few holidays and after many years of that lifestyle I was keen to see where else I might use my skills' (Jo Daly).

'I'll be turning 40 this year and I can feel that the young start-up companies are weary of hiring a 40 year old mom because they wonder if I'm

to be able to work the 60 hour work weeks like I did 10 years ago. As a veteran in the industry, my position translates to a high salary and with today's current economy and fast paced consumer market it's become more difficult for me to compete with all the young and eager new graduates. Production budgets are tight, team sizes are small and everyone is looking to make the next Angry Birds. Currently, I'm taking some time off from the industry and teaching at Vancouver Film School part time which is affording me the opportunity to spend more time with my family and allowing me to plan out the next stage of my career, while the industry reboots itself' (Lindsey Williamson Christy).

'After the last turn in my career I decided to take a break, not only for my career but more importantly for myself. My husband (an Ex-Disney, Ex-Gameloft, Ex-Nokia employee), had recently become an independent consultant, and we decided together that I should pursue something just for myself and it did not take me long to realize my "plan B".I am currently about to start writing my PhD, which in Germany is quite a substantial project of at least 3 years duration with the aim of becoming a teacher in Games Studies (or worst case scenario become a consultant) one day. Although it's early days with this project I have a passion for my PhD topic: Female careers in the gaming industry. My university background (Sociology, Media and cultural studies) is a great match for the kind of research I am aiming to do. I want to examine why there are so few women in games, how they feel about it and what games organisations have to say about this. Although only just starting to walk on this academic path I do enjoy it as I realize how important this topic is and how exciting times are for Game Studies are right now' (Sabine Hahn) .

One profiler recognised the difficulties of having children and working in the industry, but despite the difficulties felt that having children made her more creative and patient in the workplace,

'I am now 29 years old and live in Woking, whilst working in London. I have a partner who also works in the games industry and we have a 1 year old son. This is one of the reasons I had to leave Headstrong once, and I stayed at home with my son for 5 months before I went back to work. My son now stays with a child-minder whilst I am at work. Working while having children makes a bit of a difference. I can't always do overtime because I need to get back home to my son, and weekend work (which is quite rare anyway) is not an option. I also have to save my holidays in case he gets ill. One thing I have noticed, since having my son is that children make you even more creative. Children need entertainment or distractions and I have had to be quite creative with the things I have had around me to entertain him. I have found this has actually made me even more creative at work where I tackle problems in ways that I wouldn't have done before. I also feel that I have more patience now, both when it comes to dealing with issues and people' (Joy Dey).

The Importance of Role Models and the Encouragement of Females into the Industry

We hope this book will provide encouragement of females and a more diverse workforce into the industry. Being role models and encouraging more females into the industry, another theme mentioned within a number of the chapters within this book, was also important to a number of the profilers,

'I am a member of the Women in Games Jobs network, and have attended the yearly Women in Games conference twice, now. I don't believe that women in this industry are any more special or need more attention than women in any other industry, or males for that matter, but I do think it is important to encourage diversity. The amount of women in the industry should be the amount of women wanting to get into the industry, which is quite significantly lower than the amount of men wanting to have a career in games. I am not part of the network because I feel the need to identify myself with other people in the same situation, but instead to encourage and be a role model to younger girls finding an interest in technology and especially games' (Anna Ljungberg).

'We visit schools and colleges to encourage new students to our courses. In some cases these are all girl schools. My experience so far has been that by the time they are leaving school, if students aren't already bought in to the idea of a career in games, it's probably already too late. We need to stimulate interest far earlier in their school subject choices. There is a current trend to encourage more girls to participate in STEM subjects. Hopefully this will result in us seeing more females on our games courses and in the industry itself. The recent huge rise of female gamers playing casual games may also have an impact. A large number of these gamers are mothers. If they can be encouraged to recognise themselves as gamers then there may be a chance that this will result in there being less of a 'geeky boy' image attached to the perception of a 'gamer'. This may in turn encourage their daughters to see playing computer games as an acceptable pastime for girls and eventually bring more females into the industry itself' (Jo Daly).

'I never had a role model or someone I looked up to and wanted to become career wise, but I do believe the fact that my parents always encouraged me to do what I found interesting and did not push me into any field of study or activity, made the career choice a lot easier as I only had to decide what I wanted to do. Therefore, I do think it is important to give the same encouragement to young girls out there, who may not have the same courage and backing from their friends and family, and may require that extra push or piece of friendly advice to jump in there and follow their dreams' (Anna Ljungberg).

Diversity and the Type of Game Made

The type of game made was viewed as possibly being influential in the diversity of the game making workforce involved,

'The number of women working at Ninja Theory is greater compared to that at Bizarre Creations and a lot of other game studios, not just in the art department, but in the programming, production and design departments too. I believe that one reason for this could be due to the style of games that are made at Ninja Theory which are very creative and usually fantasy/story driven. Whilst studying for my master's degree, I completed an assignment based on women in the games industry. I came across many theories as to the type of video games women prefer to play and why, many of which I thought to be totally untrue and outdated. One theory which I do believe that could be true on this subject is that in general, women prefer to play games which are story and character driven. These two features are quite prominent in recent Ninja Theory games. (This theory is not taking into account mobile gaming). If these types of games are more attractive to play, then they are also more attractive to make, encouraging more women to apply to the company' (Dianne Botham).

'The stereo types of Booth babes and hyper sexualized images of women never really played into my career at Radical, we just didn't make those types of games. I can say now however that ageism is an issue for me and feels to be a limiting factor' (Lindsey Williamson Christy).

'Our next project, built on the same mechanics, will be built for an entirely different industry, which will be split equally between male and female users, and probably slightly younger. Our ultimate goal is to produce a variety of products for different demographics, thus leading us to have a diverse team within the studio' (Phil Goddard).

'In recent years, with the shift or evolution in games is becoming much more widespread i.e. mobile and tablet games, Nintendo Wii etc. there is reason to believe the audience will grow and evolve with it. Indeed we're seeing more women playing games, younger children are exposed to games, games are used in education, and much

more. The audience for video games is growing at a rapid rate, so why not the individuals who work in games?' (Phil Goddard).

Masculine/Tomboy Identity

Many of the women mentioned having a masculine or tomboy image, again a theme highlighted in a number of chapters within the book,

'Being a girl at a company focused on creating racing games is quite an experience, there are very few girls in the whole company, making the queues to the toilets very short, but the atmosphere very male dominated. During my whole life I have always had more male friends than female, mostly due to my interests being geared towards technology. Even at school I used to be out playing in the mud and climbing trees with mostly boys. Therefore I find the situation quite natural and I believe the people around me do too, as I have never felt like my gender has changed peoples opinion about me or that it has in any way affected my job' (Anna Ljungberg).

'I never really faced sexism in the games industry, possibly because I never allowed myself to be a victim. My team was always 95% male, I was always in a position of authority and I always felt respected. I've always been a tomboy, I swear like a trucker and used to be able to keep up with the boys, and so fitting in with the guys was never an issue for me' (Lindsey Williamson Christy).

'I have never thought about my gender being any kind of issue in this industry. I grew up with two brothers and my mum was a single mother so I spent a lot of time with my brothers. I used to go everywhere with them so I ended up doing a lot of boy stuff as a kid. We played football, video games and climbed anything that could be climbed. I have always found it easier to become friends with boys than with girls, mainly because of my interests. I was never into fashion, makeup and other, what were considered girl interests, and because of this I usually ended up being the only girl in some classes in school that we were allowed to choose ourselves. The same was also true during my University studies. I have always felt like I was equal to the boys and there was no special treatment (either positive or negative) towards me because I am a girl' (Joy Dey).

'Although I'd received other offers as an intern, I chose Telecom One as they were the only company paying interns, but also because they were interesting to me as a technology corporation. The other internships would have been stereotypical female 'Marketing Assistant' roles, and I clearly could not see myself wearing nice dresses and lipstick when going into the office! I should add that since I can remember I spent most of my (spare) time with boys, doing boys' activities and playing with boys' toys – somehow I am more used to being the only girl around rather than working in a female world' (Sabine Hahn).

Career Progression

Interestingly for one profiler in particular, career progression was not as important as being creative and making the games,

'I am very critical of my own work and I am always striving to improve my skills and learn new and faster techniques. I do welcome promotion but only if I am still allowed to be creative on a daily basis. My career goals have not altered much during my time in the games industry. My main goal is to be creative and be the best artist that I can be' (Dianne Botham).

For others, being female was not an issue for 'getting on' in the industry,

'I have never felt my progression has been impeded because I am female, and I believe some of my progression has been enhanced because of it, for example my move into art management. I enjoy the working environment and don't feel awkward as a female working within a predominantly male workplace. Being one of the only females within a team can feel quite special and interestingly I have

found myself wary of new female employees, it can feel like you are being usurped when others join the group and I may have missed opportunities to bond with other female staff because of this' (Julie McGurren).

Gender Divide and the Wider Gaming Community

On the whole the female profilers enjoyed their careers and felt accepted within the workplace. However some had experienced barriers and felt unaccepted in the wider gaming community,

'On the whole I feel very accepted in my workplace - much more so than in the wider gaming community. It's the little things that can be frustrating; for example, when shopping for games by myself, sales assistants see no problem with asking me if they can help. If I drag my partner in with me, he will immediately become the target of their attention, and I'm left to browse unhindered. I've lost count of the amount of times he's been asked how he feels about my profession when I tell someone new what I do' (Faye Windsor-Smith).

Within the wider gaming community this profiler was treated differently for being a woman,

'During my time at university, I explored the realms of online gaming. I wasn't fully able to participate without a headset and microphone, but I enjoyed listening to others talk during team games. I noticed I never heard other girls' voices while playing, so it took me a long time to decide whether to engage in chatter when I did get the equipment to use team chat. When I did take the risk and said hello, I noticed an increase in messages asking for my number, or telling me to 'get off your boyfriend's account'. These made me feel very uncomfortable, so I went silent again, though never stopping play. After a while, I honed the skill of reading people's chatter to know whether or not I could speak without receiving too much attention' (Elizabeth Richardson).

Working in the Industry: Enjoyment and a Positive Outlook

As mentioned at the beginning of this section, it is evident from the profiles that the women who submitted profiles enjoyed their jobs and enjoyed working in the industry, here are just a few examples from the profilers,

'I believe the fact that I have no idea where the past few months have gone is testament to how much I'm enjoying working in the games industry. It's such a massively different experience to my past jobs in retail and customer service, and it's wonderful to see something that you've put so much time and hard work into be published and enjoyed by other people. As is always the case with any job, there are some days where it's stressful and I think to myself 'am I really cut out for this?', but then the payoff when you create something that people love is well worth the stress' (Carrie Warwick) .

My work hasn't changed how I feel about games as a hobby, and I still play them often. I feel incredibly lucky to be doing what I'm doing and my experience of the industry so far has been a very positive one. I'm hoping this will be the case for many years to come (Hannah Payne).

'I don't believe you need to be a gamer to work in games you just need to be passionate about what you do, for me I was passionate about my art and this led me to a career in games. I don't play games like I used to and as my role has changed so has my passion. Whilst my output is less tangible in a production role I am driven by the thrill of working within a team to deliver games played my people across the globe and ultimately that's what gets me out of bed' (Julie McGurren).

'I was open about having no previous design experience when applying for the role, but had played enough social browser games to have picked up some key aspects of monetisation design, and have been learning more and more since. I love finding out what people love about games, and I love trying to make games that people will love' (Faye Windsor-Smith).

'Due to my true passion for the industry and perhaps because I love keeping my illusions I am looking forward to still being a part of the gaming industry 20 years from now, but within a truly diverse, more balanced environment. Eventually I hope to turn my very personal experience as being "the only girl in the village" (which isn't too surprising with an estimated 6% women in the industry) into an academic contribution with my PhD project which I hope will help to identify some of the patterns in this industry that need to be changed' (Sabine Hahn).

We would like to end this section on the profiles and what are, to us, some of the main messages and themes from them with two positive outlook quotes, which we hope encourage females to consider a career in games,

'I can wholeheartedly say that the games industry in an extremely worthwhile endeavor for women to undertake, especially if they are dedicated professionals with a clear understanding of the competitive marketplace, the blue chip level of knowledge required to excel, and a preparedness to learn, experience and gain from their peers and managers. The games industry, like other entertainment sectors, is a "people" business, meaning it is very much about the relationships that are developed and maintained. It's also an environment of both vibrant camaraderie and encouraged self-learning when it comes to the actual craft of making games. Ask, and you will learn. Game developers are interested in sharing their knowledge, and most prefer to see their colleagues reaching for a higher level of achievement. Given the team nature of game production, the entire group benefits as a whole, the more capable, enthusiastic and committed their peers are about the production process' (Fiona Cherbak).

'Looking across the YouTube Gaming community, there are some wonderfully strong women that do what they do because they enjoy it and love it. I feel that within this community there is a growing sense of equality and it's becoming easier for women to be accepted into the gaming world if they have an interest in it. I would like to see more women involved in the development process of gaming, as I feel that even this simple version of diversity would add to a richer gaming experience in general' (Elizabeth Richardson).

THE WAY FORWARD: FUTURE RESEARCH QUESTIONS

It would appear that strategies for addressing the problems women face within the games industry need to come from a variety of standpoints and perspectives. In order to devise better solutions we need a richer knowledge of the complex, multifaceted issues in order to help gain successful solutions. Due to the number of issues involved we have considered areas for future research under the four broad themes of; educational factors, STEM related factors, gamers and workforce issues. Next to each area of future research is the chapter number or numbers where the issues are discussed.

Rather than merely highlighting limitations, we hope this book has encouraged possibilities and future research directions with some areas for suggestion below.

Educational Factors

- Understand how children learn gender roles through playing online games and in virtual worlds (chapter 1).
- Investigate how children use games and virtual worlds to develop identities both on and offline (chapter 1).
- Understand the wider motivations of play and how they link to an interest in studying computer science. (chapter 2).
- How game play preferences and game genres relate to an interest in computer science and other technology fields. (chapter 2).

- Gain a further understanding of women studying for game related degrees (chapter 5).

STEM Related Factors

- Employ and further develop outreach programs and initiatives that have proved successful in the STEM sector for the computer games industry (chapter 10).
- Learn from the STEM sector and the research on women working in that sector (chapter 4 and 8).

Gamers

- Understand female gamers who embrace the gamer identity (chapter 2).
- Investigate the social games sector of the industry and uncover if more women would be interested in working in the industry due to these games (chapter 9).
- Investigate gender based discrimination and barriers in the wider gaming community, an issue brought up in a number of the individual profiles.

Workforce Issues

- Deeper understanding of how the masculine identity of the industry may discourage females entering the industry (chapter 9).
- Do male dominated industries attract a certain type of woman or do women have to adapt to its masculine culture? (chapter 4 and 5).
- Evaluate the effect of long hours and crunch time has on both women and men in the industry (chapter 4, 5 and 11).
- Investigate the possible psychological and physical health implications associated with the long hours working model.

- Evaluate women who work flexibly and the impact this is having on their careers (chapter 4 and 5).
- The development of a mentorship and community outreach programs and measure it's outputs over a several year period. (chapter 9).
- Understand what attracts women to work in the games industry and other male dominated industries (chapter 2, 3 and 11).
- Encourage women and girls to enter the games industry workforce, especially in core content creation roles (chapter 2, 3, 4, 5, 6, 7, 8, 10 and 11).
- Understanding of the effects of career factors on women's aspirations in male-dominated occupations (chapter 6, 8 and 11).
- Consider how women have overcome constraints or embraced supports. Future research would refine these substantive insights, including greater in-depth consideration of specific influences identified from the empirical data (chapter 7).
- Investigate the women who plan to leave the sector and why (chapter 5).
- Future research may consider gaining the views of women who have left the industry in order to gain a fuller insight into why women leave the industry (chapter 5).
- It might be valuable to understand the experiences of women who are senior members of women in games organisations such as WIGI (Women in Games International) as well as the executive women in games organisations (chapter 4, 7 and 11).
- More research about career development among female Japanese game developers and developers, both male and female in other countries (chapter 6).
- Research on countries not included in this book i.e. South Korea, China and more European countries.

- From the profiles, the type of game made and the platform it is played was viewed as perhaps being influential in the diversity of the game making workforce, more research is needed into this.

A COMMON GROUND: FUTURE POSSIBILITIES

As we stated in the preface, the overall objective of this book is to present a collection of recent empirical studies and theoretical work related to the careers of women working in the computer games industry and digital media. The book has brought together current International research investigating underrepresentation in gaming and digital media industries. In particular, the book includes research looking at the experience of workers working in this male dominated environment; including the personal and professional barriers of working in this industry including viewpoints from female industry workers. We hope this book represents a valuable snapshot of the current state of the field with the aim of bringing together a wide range of perspectives in the area and sparks more debates and future research questions.

This book has hopefully provided a valuable contribution, adding to the literature on women working in male dominated industries, the new industries of digital media and women's underrepresentation in the wider SET and ICT sectors. We hope this book provides readers with a valuable contribution as it highlights the personal experiences of women who currently work in this new technological industry and male dominated work environment. Not only does the research within this book focus on the experiences of women working in the sector but it also considers research investigating the role of education, socialisation and play can have on influencing females potential interest and participation in the industry, as well as considering how the STEM sector can impact the gaming and digital media industries.

The research and writings within the chapters of this book are from researchers and authors from a number of different backgrounds and academic disciplines. For instances we have chapters written by academics of the field of psychology, computer science, education, games and media, digital design, IT and interactive media. There are also chapters by one female who works in the industry but has recently conducted academic research in the area. Throughout this book and the issues discussed it is clear that there is the need for more research in order to both understand the issues more fully and in order to further develop and implement possible solutions. We hope this book provides readers with an interesting outlook of the issues and encourage a multidisciplinary approach to considering the underrepresentation of women in the computer games industry.

Male dominated occupations and industries adhere to the male model of working evidenced throughout a number of chapters, and the profiles within this book. The male model of working makes entry into certain occupations unappealing to women and career advancement difficult. A number of barriers are prevalent within the literature, including lack of access to networks, mentors and a lack of flexible working (Prescott & Bogg, 2012). Initiatives such as access to mentoring and networking opportunities can help women progress. Women remain underrepresented in a number of industries, investigating their career aspirations and career development is important. Gaining an understanding of women in male dominated occupations and industries will be beneficial in attracting other women, as well as highlighting potential careers for future generations of women. We hope this book goes some way into helping the computer games industry be viewed as a viable career to future generations of females. Table 1 highlights key recommendations for developing

Table 1. Key recommendations for developing workplace diversity

Key Recommendations
Enable Career Progression   Increase training opportunities for Continuing Professional Development, encourage female role models and mentors within the industry
Promote Flexible Working Practices   Ensure those who take this option are not excluded from career opportunities
Enhance the Profile of working in games   Promote the industry as a viable career for women

Challenge
    Increase role models for women, ethnic minorities, and disabled workers
    Challenge perceptions of stereotypical organisational cultures and views of 'fit in to succeed'

Adapt   Attract a more diverse workforce by challenging the image that the games industry is for males only
Recruit   Highlight the variety of roles and skills required within the industry.
Encourage   Ensure diversity is encouraged and practiced in the workplace

Enable Diversity as a 'good business' model
    Challenge stereotypes and the male model of working i.e Long hours culture as the norm
    Lack of diversity has an impact on the contribution of women i.e. the type of computer games developed, the type of children who identify with certain careers

Table 2. Key industry issues and recommendations

Industry Issues	
The Gender Divide	The image of technology needs to change to incorporate a female view. Eradicate gender based stereotypes such as the image that computers and computer games are for 'boys only'. There is a need for more female role models to encourage female students to pursue education and careers in computing and computer gaming. The increasing use of technology is making technology more inclusive. However, major gender differences exist to the detriment of females. More is required to reduce this gendered gap especially with regard to confidence and self-efficacy. Increase girls/women's self-efficacy and self esteem in male dominated disciplines and environments by making them more female inclusive This fast moving industry needs to take into account the skill needs of it employers. This is especially important in retaining a female workforce. Provide more support for female students to engage with computing and technology. Female game workers should be encouraged to remain after maternity leave and given the support to update or regain their skills needed for their role. There is a need to reduce the gender digital divide through education initiatives that focus on getting girls to the same confidence level with ICT as boys. Initiatives need to be more widely available and include a number of digital technologies used in everyday lives in order to help reduce this gap. Girls/women should be equally encouraged to engage with technology.
Impact of Females Working in the Industry	The industry like the wider ICT and SET sector needs to eradicate the image of being a male domain in order to attract a more gender diverse workforce. The industry needs to consider ways in how to reduce the effects of the working practices in order to both attract and retain a more diverse workforce. Promote initiatives such as flexible working. For retention ask women workers what they need. Reduce where possible the expectation of long hours as the 'norm' or regular occurrence. The computer games industry could benefit from highlighting the various roles and skills required in the industry as well as the various backgrounds, both educational and occupational, that people who enter the industry come from. Women who are in the industry especially those in core content creation roles could act as role models for girls considering a career within the industry. More females playing games could potentially increase the number of females interested in making games. More female game developers have the potential in making the industry and the games developed attract a more diverse audience. Female game developers increase the potential impact of the industry. There is a need for greater gender neutral game design. Research on women working in the games industry is sparse. More research is needed to consider the barriers and drivers of women in this male dominated industry. Encourage the workforce to have a work life balance. Have transparency in pay and promotional structures. Help plug the leaky pipeline through developing retention strategies such those related to work life balance issues. Support women in senior positions through mentoring and networking opportunities. Encourage women to apply for management/senior positions Support female mentees for promotion into senior roles. Promote gender equality in the workplace at all levels from recruitment to retention.
Recruitment	Training of selection group members to avoid unconscious bias. Ensure women are represented in adequate numbers on promotion, job, prize committees etc. Check for implicit bias in criteria for awards and nominations and research assessment type RAE exercises. Remove barriers to women being recruited to and remaining in the organisation. Foster a supportive work environment that appeals to women's values and work styles. Highlight the diversity of roles and skills required within the games industry. Highlight the benefits of working in this industry such monetary benefits; it is viewed as fun work and part of both the knowledge and creative industries. Highlight the benefits of working in a creative, interesting and rewarding industry. Review current policies relating to hours of work and flexible working practices.

continued on following page

Table 2. Continued

Industry Issues	
Career Motivation	Recognise the contribution women can make in publication in the leading scientific journals is particularly useful for career progression. Make the environment one that fosters motivation regardless of gender.
Retention	Remove barriers to women being recruited to and remaining in the organisation. Organisational level issues, to be addressed by management, for change to occur and encourage women to remain in the industry. Increase flexible working practices. Identify the barriers and opportunities for job satisfaction. Encourage the uptake of flexible working practices. Employ strategies to help reduce the long hours culture. Make long hours and crunch time a rarity rather than the norm. Develop staff in project management skills in order to help reduce the long hours needed as deadlines approach. Encourage the workforce to be more accepting to the needs of women with children and other caring responsibilities.

Prescott & Bogg (2014)

workplace diversity which has been adapted from Prescott and Bogg's (2012) focus on women in the SET/STEM sector to reflect key recommendations for developing workplace diversity specifically within the computer games industry.

The main premise of this book has been to consider recent empirical research in the area of female underrepresentation in the computer games industry, understand the issues and help future research in the area ask more questions in order to find viable solutions. Although women are increasingly becoming gamers, playing more games and more often, it is apparent that female are not anywhere near being equally represented in the computer games industries workforce. Therefore, men are still designing games for both males and females with little input from a female perspective. With the massive growth of the global gaming audience and the advances in technology as well as creative possibilities, the games industry offers a wide range of interesting career opportunities. However these opportunities are currently appealing more to males than females. Despite legislation over the past 40 years, gender disparities in certain occupations remain. It appears that a number of issues run throughout the industry which contribute to the underrepresentation of women. Factors such as the long hour's culture associated with the industry, the lack of flexible working available, the lack of females, especially

females with families within the industry and thus the lack of role models, as well as the image of the industry as masculine, contributes to the low representation of women. However it may not just be workforce issues at play resulting in the low representation of women within the industry. As the research within this edition has illustrated, educational factors can play a part and an important place/stage at which to begin gaining female interest and skill. Although the focus of this book was computer games and other digital media industries, we have included two chapters which have focused specifically on the STEM sector as an established sector in which the computer games industry may take some guidance. Indeed this is a message Prescott and Bogg (2012) have previously highlighted since many of the issues in the newer technology based industries such as computer games have many of the same issues. Researchers have been particularly interested in the lack of women in computing and information and communication technology (ICT) careers for which the computer games industry fall under the umbrella of.

For the wider ICT sector, the geeky image and the unsocial nature of computer related work are barriers to women's participation. Overt sexism and discrimination is not as evident within the sector, however our research findings suggest it can still exist. It appears that gender segregation persists in new industries, as well as the older more established ones such as science, engineering and finance (Prescott and Bogg, 2012). What is apparent from the computer games industry is that gendered occupational segregation exists, and persists in this relatively new industry and the culture does not generally appeal to or support women in the workplace. Like the more established science, engineering and technology sector (SET), this new industry has many of the same issues including the long hour's culture, inflexible working practices and a lack of women with children in the industry. Women in the industry tend to be concentrated within the more traditional less technical roles, which are the non-content creation roles such as human resources, marketing and administration roles. Therefore when discussing underrepresentation of women within the industry, one must be aware that it is not just increasing women in the industry as a whole that is important, but also increasing women's participation in all areas and occupations, within the industry, in order for true gender equity. Table 2 has key industry issues and recommendations adapted from Prescott and Bogg (2014).

REFERENCES

Consalvo, M. (2006). Console video games & global corporations: Creating a hybrid culture. *New Media & Society*, *8*(1), 117–137.

Galarneau, L. (2014). *2014 global gaming stats: Who's playing what, and why?* Retrieved January, 2014, from http://www.bigfishgames.com/blog/2014-global-gaming-stats-whos-playing-what-and-why

Johns, J. (2006). Video games production networks: Value capture, power relations & embeddedness. *Journal of Economic Geography*, *6*(2), 151–180.

Prescott, J., & Bogg, J. (2012). *Gendered occupational differences in science, engineering, and technology careers*. Hershey, PA: IGI Global.

Prescott, J., & Bogg, J. (2014). *Gender divide and the computer gaming industry*. Hershey, PA: IGI Global.

ONLINE RESOURCES

We have provided a list of online resources which readers my find useful in gaining further information on the issues of women and computer games, the wider ICT sector and STEM sector. The list is not complete, it will hopefully be a good starting guide for those interested in gaining further information and wanting to become more involved.

Computer Games Sites for Women/Girls

The following is a list of online resources that specifically looks at girls/women and computer games.

Computer Club 4 Girls

http://www.cc4g.net/
 Computer Clubs for Girls (CC4G) is a new kind of club full of interesting things to do. It's exclusively for 10 to 13 year old girls.

Girl Gamers

http://girlgamers.co.uk/about/
 GirlGamers.co.uk is a dedicated girl gaming site. So if you're female and you love playing video games, then you've come to the right place.

Frag Dolls

http://www.fragdolls.com/us/
 The Frag Dolls are a group of girl gamers whose site includes their individual blogs, a forum, and a calendar of events, including opportunities to play against one or more of the

Mary Margaret

Mary-Margaret.com
 http://www.mary-margaret.com/Public/Home/index.cfm The Mary-Margaret Network encompasses a diverse clientele in the games, electronic media, and entertainment industries. We place outstanding candidates - from individual contributors to C-level executives - in positions in every department: from art to engineering, production to sales, and graphics to operations. Since 1996, our focus on superior service to employers and candidates has earned us an unsurpassed reputation for recruitment services and career management.

IGDA Women in Games Development

http://archives.igda.org/women/
 Extensive list of resources and links at the International Game Developers Association 'Women in Games Development' Special Interest Group.

Thumbbandits

http://thumbbandits.com/
Thumb Bandits is a Gaming Community for both male and female gamers, however the site is heavily slanted towards Women Gamers, the Games Industry Re Women Gamers, Female Gaming within Academia and many interest pieces on / about women.

Women Gamers.com

http://www.womengamers.com/
Because women do play! A website aimed at women who play computer games.

WIGI

http://www.womeningamesinternational.org/
Women in Games International works to promote the inclusion and advancement of women in the global games industry. We believe diversifying the game development, media, academic and publishing workplace results in not only a more equitable space, but better products. Women In Games International advocates for issues important to both women and men in the game development industry, including a better work/life balance and healthy working conditions.

Computer Games Sites for Gay Gamers

Gay Namer Net

http://gaygamer.net/

The Gay Gamer

http://www.thegaygamer.com/

Computer Games Sites for Older Gamers

The Older Gamers. com

http://www.theoldergamers.com/

Mature Gamer

http://www.maturegamer.co.uk/

Mature video gamer.com

http://www.maturevideogamer.co.uk/

The Older Gamer.com Forum

A forum for gamers aged over 25
    http://www.theoldergamers.com/forum/

Serious Games

There is an abundance of serious games on the market today, here are some useful website.

Games for Change

    http://www.gamesforchange.org/

Persuasive Games

    http://www.persuasivegames.com/

Mission to Learn

    http://www.missiontolearn.com/2009/09/more-learning-games-for-change/

Epistemic Games

    http://epistemicgames.org/eg/

ICT Related Resources

Anita Borg Institute

http://www.anitaborg.org
    California-based organization, whose mission is to increase the impact of women on technology and to increase the positive impact of technology on women's lives. Formerly called the Institute for Women and Technology, it now bears the name of its distinguished founder, Anita Borg. The site includes information about its initiatives and links to related sites.

Association for Women in Computing

http://www.awc-hq.org
    Information about the AWC, links to local chapters and related sites.

BCS Women's Forum

http://www.bcs.org/category/8630

This website from the British Computing Society focuses on issues concerning women's participation in information technology. The aim is to stimulate "dialogue and discussion about the policies and practices in IT and using them to make IT a place that is inclusive." The site offers profiles of women in IT, statistics and research, annotated links to related groups and organizations, and the opportunity to participate in online discussion forums.

Binary Girl

http://www.binarygirl.com

This web site, "where girls and technology click," aims to "share knowledge with those interested in learning more about technology through an interactive community of women."

Computer Girl

http://www.computergirl.us/

Started by Stanford undergraduate Amy Wu, the Computer Girl site is designed "to bridge the gap between young women in high school and the computer world." It offers abundant resources: web sites, articles, role models, statistics, job categories, summer camp listings, and more. It also provides a place where students can ask questions about the field of computer science [e.g., the job market, salaries, finding mentors, scholarships, work/life balance, etc.].

Center for Women and Information Technology

http://www.umbc.edu/cwit/

Established to encourage women's and girls' greater involvement with information technology, the Center offers many resources on its web site, including extensive news coverage of women and IT, announcements of relevant conferences and calls for papers, a bibliography of books about women and IT, a huge collection of web-based syllabi for women- and gender-related courses, Internet resources dealing with women and IT, and more.

Committee on the Status of Women in Computing Research (CRA-W)

http://cra-w.org/

Site includes a number of useful annotated links to sites/events/statistics of particular interest to women interested in computer science.

Cyber Grrl

www.cybergrrl.com

A site for women interested in technology with the slogan: 'inspiring, informing and celebrating women'

Digital Sisters

http://www.digital-sistas.org

Digital Sisters has been created "to promote and provide technology education and enrichment for young girls and women of color." The web site provides information about relevant events, news, educational resources, reports and statistics, and links to related sites.

Dot Diva

www.dotdiva.org

A site for women with the philosophy that computing can make a better world.

Exploring Gender and Technology

http://www.gse.harvard.edu/~wit/exploring/index.htm

"This site presents current research, perspectives, and innovative approaches to the gender gap in technology collected from secondary research." It offers statistics, case studies, a video, online discussion, an annotated bibliography, and annotated links for educators and for girls.

Girl Geeks

http://www.girlgeeks.org/

GirlGeeks aims to encourage women to develop their careers in technology.

Girl Geek Dinners

http://girlgeekdinners.com/

Hold local events to bring women together to educate each other over dinner. A number of girl geek organizations exist through the world including Canada, USA, Australia, Japan, Indian and throughout Europe.

Girly Geekdom

http://girlygeekdom.com/

'GirlyGeekdom hopes to bring fun, exciting and inspirational content along with relevant news and information from the Science, Technology and Engineering industry'.

Girl Start

http://www.girlstart.org/

Girlstart is a non-profit organization created to empower girls to excel in math, science, and technology. Resources, information and games available on the website.

Girltech

http://www.girlstech.douglass.rutgers.edu/

Girlstech explains and demonstrates a framework to evaluate electronic resources (web sites, CD-ROMs, and games) for girls and young women to encourage and increase their involvement in the sciences and technology.

Girl Tech

http://www.girltech.com/

Girl Tech's mission is to enhance girls' lives and foster their use of technology by bringing to market technology-enhanced lifestyle electronics just for girls ages 8-12. These products are designed with girls' play preferences in mind, addressing issues that are important to them such as privacy and communication.

Interactive Selection

http://www.interactiveselection.com/women.asp

Interactive selection support WiG (women in games) and look to recruit women in the games industry. They have a specific site for women- http://www.womeningamesjobs.com/

Rapunsel

http://www.rapunsel.org/

"Realtime, applied programming for under-represented students' early literacy (RAPUNSEL) is Rapunsel is single-player dance game designed to teach computer programming to 10-12 year olds. The project was started with the goal of empowering young girls to learn programming as a way of addressing the critical shortage of women in technology related careers and degree programs. By giving players the opportunity to explore coding through scaffolded challenges in a playful world, we hope to empower young people to learn about computer science. It is a cross platform, downladable game created in the Torque game engine".

The National Center for Women and IT

www.ncwit.org/

The NCWIT works to increase diversity in IT and computing. NCWIT believes that greater diversity will create a larger and more competitive workforce, and will foster the design of technology that is as broad and innovative as the population it serves. NCWIT focuses on improving diversity across the entire spectrum: K-12 through college education, and on to academic, corporate and entrepreneurial careers.

Web Grrls

http://www.webgrrls.com

Webgrrls is an online and offline networking organization of professional women focusing on propelling our careers and businesses forward by *leveraging the power of women*, *technology*, and *tools* that help us succeed. For over 15 years Webgrrls has been at the forefront of the women's movement online. We're an online and offline networking organization of professional women focusing on propelling our careers and businesses forward by *leveraging the power of women*, *technology*, and *tools* that help us succeed.

Whyville

http://www.whyville.net/top/gates.html

Whyville is an imaginative web site that aims to help elementary, middle, and high school students (boys and girls) understand and enjoy science. It differs from most science education sites in its use of avatars, games, computer simulation and modelling, a Whyville newspaper, and interactivity among Whyville participants.

Women and Girls Tech Up

http://www.techup.org/index.html

Online zine grew out of an 18-month private collaborative online meeting of 16 small organizations for women and girls. To encourage women and girls - and the organizations which serve them - to use technology to share ideas, opinions, support, creativity and political action. The project was co-sponsored by The Women's Foundation and The Electronic Frontier Foundation, and funded by Pacific Bell.

Women in Tech

http://www.womenintech.com/

A Hawaii-based organization that seeks to improve the "economic quality of life for women by encouraging them into higher-paying technology occupations." Women in Technology has developed a number of initiatives to achieve this goal, some aimed at middle- and high school students, others at college students and women in the workforce. The web site includes information about all the initiatives, along with resource articles, scholarship information, a calendar of events, and extensive links to related sites.

Women in Technology

http://www.womenintechnology.co.uk/

At womenintechnology.co.uk we are committed to increasing the number of women working and achieving in the UK's technology profession. We provide a complete recruitment service, offer a dedicated online IT job board, regularly host networking events, run personal development and career orientated training courses and provide in-depth information about key matters affecting the IT industry and the people who work within it.

Zoey's Room - A Tech Know Community for Girls

http://www.zoeysroom.com/

"Zoey's room is an online community for girls ages 10-14, a place where girls can go to explore math, science and technology in a fun, safe and creative environment." Zoey's room offers an online collaborative community, a chance to communicate with Zoey in her chat room, Fab Female role model online chats, a place to showcase girls' creative work, and hands on challenges that lead to big prizes such as digital cameras.

SET/STEM Related Resources

Association for Women in Mathematics

http://www.awm-math.org/index.html

In addition to information about AWM membership, the site offers announcements of current grants, lectures, workshops, projects, and prizes, as well as extensive links to related sites.

AWIS: Association for Women in Science

http://www.awis.org

Among the resources on the AWIS web site are information about awards, scholarships, statistics, job openings, book reviews, profiles of outstanding women in science, a searchable registry of women in science, links to related sites, and more.

BCS Women's Forum

http://www.bcs.org/category/8630

This website from the British Computing Society focuses on issues concerning women's participation in information technology. The aim is to stimulate "dialogue and discussion about the policies and practices in IT and using them to make IT a place that is inclusive." The site offers profiles of women in IT, statistics and research, annotated links to related groups and organizations, and the opportunity to participate in online discussion forums.

Black Women in Mathematics

http://www.math.buffalo.edu/mad/wmad0.html

This site, created and maintained by mathematics professor Scott W. Williams, provides a history of Black women in mathematics, biographies of Black female mathematicians, relevant articles, and links to related sites.

Braincake

http://www.braincake.org/default.aspx

Aimed at middle school girls, this web site promotes math and science by creating an online community where girls can interact with their peers about current science topics, solve science mysteries, and discuss careers with young women scientists and engineers. The site offers chat rooms, games, contests with cash prizes, mentoring programs, scholarship resources, and more.

Central European Centre for Women and Youth in Science

http://www.cec-wys.org/html/

The Centre aims to promote, mobilize, and network women and youth in science in Central Europe, to raise awareness of the importance of including a gender dimension in scientific research, to prepare young researchers to advance in their careers, to encourage policy developments at the national level concerning women in science, and more. Among the Centre's many initiatives is an interdisciplinary database of women scientists from Central Europe. The site also includes relevant news, statistics, information arranged by country, links to related sites, and more.

Committee on the Status of Women in Astronomy

http://www.aas.org/cswa/

The website of the American Astronomical Society's Committee on the Status of Women in Astronomy contains a searchable database of women in astronomy, copies of CSWA periodicals, statistics concerning women in astronomy, links to related web sites, and more.

Committee on Women in Science and Engineering

http://sites.nationalacademies.org/PGA/cwsem/index.htm

The Committee on Women in Science, Engineering, and Medicine (CWSEM) is a standing committee of the National Research Council (NRC). Its mandate is to coordinate, monitor, and advocate action to increase the participation of women in science, engineering, and medicine. Established in 1990 as CWSE, the committee expanded its scope in 2007 to include medicine.

Engineer Girl

http://www.engineergirl.org/

The Engineer Girl website is part of the NAE's Celebration of Women in Engineering project. This project tries to bring national attention to the opportunity that engineering represents to all people at any age, but particularly to women and girls. The site includes information about what engineers do, great achievements in engineering, career facts, puzzles and games, the opportunity to ask questions of engineers, and links to related sites. Sponsored by the National Academy of Engineering.

eGFI

http://egfi-k12.org/about/

eGFI is proudly brought to you by the American Society for Engineering Education (ASEE). We are committed to promoting and enhancing efforts to improve K-12 STEM and engineering education.

Expanding Your Horizons Network

http://www.expandingyourhorizons.org/

The mission of the Network is the promotion of the continuing development in mathematics and science of all people, with a particular emphasis on the needs of women and girls. The primary goal is to increase the participation, retention, and advancement of girls and women in mathematics, science, technology and engineering through the Expanding Your Horizons in Science and Mathematics (EYH conferences).

Engineer Your Life

http://www.engineeryourlife.org/

This site describes itself as "a guide to engineering for high school girls." It includes photos and videos of young women who are engineers as well as information about what engineering is, why it is important, attractive careers in engineering, and how to prepare to become an engineer. The site also includes sections for counselors and parents and for engineers.)

European Platform of Women Scientists

http://www.epws.org/

An organization formed "to build a structural link between women scientists and research policy makers. The aim is to introduce a new key strategic actor into the research policy debate by making the voice of women scientists heard." The site offers relevant news, position papers, official publications on women in science, and links to European Union institutions involved in the decision-making process.

Fairer Science

http://www.fairerscience.org

Funded by the National Science Foundation, Fairer Science offers current information and presentations about women in science, technology, engineering, and mathematics that can be of use to policy makers, educators, and parents.

Female Nobel Prize Laureates

http://www.nobelprizes.com/nobel/women.html

Information about all the women who have won the Nobel Prize.

GEMS: Girls Excelling in Math and Science

http://www.gemsclub.org/index.html

The GEMS club has been in existence since 1994 to expose 5th and 6th grade girls to the fun and wonder of math, science, and technology. The web site offers information about the club's activities and history, instructions for starting a similar club, tips for adults, and links to related sites for girls.

Institute for Women's Policy Research

http://www.iwpr.org/

The sites mission statement reads: The Institute for Women's Policy Research conducts rigorous research and disseminates its findings to address the needs of women, promote public dialog, and strengthen families, communities, and societies.

It is the leading think tank in the U.S. focusing primarily on domestic women's issues. Founded in 1987, IWPR's reports and other informational resources have informed policies and programs across the U.S., in each of its key program areas:

Employment, Education, and Economic Change: Employment and Job Quality, Economic Status of Women in the States, Pay Equity and Discrimination, Access to Higher Education, Unemployment and the Economy.

Democracy and Society: The Status of Women and Girls, Immigration and Religion, Women in Unions, Women's Political Participation.

Poverty, Welfare, and Income Security: Retirement and Social Security, Poverty, Katrina and the Gulf Coast, Welfare Reform.

Work and Family: Early Care and Education, Family Leave and Paid Sick Days, Workplace Flexibility.

Health and Safety: Women's access to health insurance, costs and benefits of preventative health services for women, costs of domestic violence.

MentorNet

http://mentornet.net/

MentorNet is the award-winning nonprofit e-mentoring network that addresses the retention and success of those in engineering, science and mathematics, particularly but not exclusively women and other under-represented groups. Founded in 1997, MentorNet provides highly motivated protégés from many of the world's top colleges and universities with positive, one-on-one, email-based mentoring relationships with mentors from industry and academia. In addition, the MentorNet Community provides opportunities to connect with others from around the world who are interested in diversifying engineering and science.

National Science Foundation

http://www.nsf.gov/

Get news, information, funding opportunities, publications and statistics from this American based organization.

Sally Ride Science

http://www.sallyridescience.com/index.shtml

Founded by former astronaut Sally Ride, Sally Ride Science is an organization whose mission is "to increase the number of girls who are technically literate and who have the foundation they need to go on in science, math, or engineering." The web site, intended for parents, teachers, and girls, provides information about why such efforts are needed and activities and resources designed to achieve this mission.

The Association for Women Geoscientists

http://www.awg.org

The Association for Women Geoscientists exists to promote the professional development of its members, to provide geoscience outreach to girls, and to encourage women to become geoscientists.

The National Association of Women in Construction

http://www.nawic.co.uk/

The NAWIC encourages women to pursue, establish and sustain successful careers in the Construction Industry. The NAWIC is an international, non-profit, voluntary organisation run by professional women working either directly in the Construction Industry or for businesses who provide services to the Construction Industry. The association aims to promote the positives in the Construction Industry as a whole and to highlight the fantastic work carried out by professionals working in the Construction Industry. We organise regular events in each of the regions focusing on: networking, education, site visits and skills.

Women in Architecture

http://www.diversecity-architects.com/WIA/wia.htm

Women In Architecture aims to provide a forum for people to meet, share experiences and jointly lobby for better conditions and opportunities for women. We aim to raise the profile of women within the profession and represent their views.

Women in Banking and Finance

http://www.wibf.org.uk/

Women in banking and finance (Wibf) based in London, is a non-profit making leading professional organisation committed to empowering its members in the banking and finance industry to realise their full potential.

Women in Construction Action Network

http://www.wicnet.org.uk/index.php

The Action Network is providing valuable access to training that will help to facilitate 'job readiness' and proactively encourage network opportunities for women working in the construction industry in the North West of England. It will also provide a valuable source of information for those women wishing to find out more about entering the industry.

Women and Manual Trades

http://www.wamt.org/

The UK's national organisation for tradeswomen and women training in the trades. WAMT has been championing tradeswomen in the UK for 30 years through campaigning and training, and is the only membership organisation specifically for tradeswomen.

The Association of Women In Property

http://www.womeninproperty.org.uk/

Women in property is a national organisation that seeks to enhance the profile of women in the construction and property sector, both by providing a dynamic forum for women in these professions and by encouraging and nurturing aspiring talent.

Women in Mathematics

http://camel.math.ca/Women/

Sponsored by the Canadian Mathematical Society, this site contains information and links of interest to women in mathematics and to those contemplating careers in mathematics.

Women in Science, Technology, Engineering, and Mathematics ON THE AIR!

http://www.womeninscience.org/

This site describes itself as "an audio resource for young girls, young women, parents, middle and high school teachers, college professors, guidance counsellors, . . . and anyone interested in learning more about the past, present, and future role of women in science and technology education, fields, and careers."

Women of NASA

http://women.nasa.gov/?utm_source=SSTI+Weekly+Digest&utm_campaign=d91152c2f0-Digest_for_the_Week_of_March_16_2011&utm_medium=email

Site designed to encourage more young women to pursue careers in science, math, and technology. Includes profiles of female scientists, ideas for integrating the site's information into the curriculum, an annotated bibliography of books related to gender equity in math and science, and more.

Women Who Walk Through Time

http://www.agiweb.org/pubs/pubdetail.html?item=300165

Women Who Walk Through Time—a site about women in the Earth Sciences with special features for young girls. Includes information about a video that encourages girls and young women to consider a career in the earth sciences and career information. "Women Who Walk Through Time demonstrates the challenges which inspire geoscientists and why they enjoy their work".

Gender and Diversities Institute

http://www2.edc.org/gdi/

An institute "dedicated to improving the well-being of individuals and communities, especially women and girls, through innovative, gender-healthy approaches to life-long learning."

256

Related References

To continue our tradition of advancing information science and technology research, we have compiled a list of recommended IGI Global readings. These references will provide additional information and guidance to further enrich your knowledge and assist you with your own research and future publications.

Abrams, S. S. (2010). The dynamics of video gaming: Influences affecting game play and learning. In P. Zemliansky, & D. Wilcox (Eds.), *Design and implementation of educational games: Theoretical and practical perspectives* (pp. 78–91). Hershey, PA: Information Science Reference. doi:10.4018/978-1-61520-781-7.ch006

Achtenhagen, L., & Johannisson, B. (2013). Games in entrepreneurship education to support the crafting of an entrepreneurial mindset. In S. de Freitas, M. Ott, M. Popescu, & I. Stanescu (Eds.), *New pedagogical approaches in game enhanced learning: Curriculum integration* (pp. 20–37). Hershey, PA: Information Science Reference. doi:10.4018/978-1-4666-3950-8.ch002

Akcaoglu, M. (2013). Using MMORPGs in classrooms: Stories vs. teachers as sources of motivation. In Y. Baek, & N. Whitton (Eds.), *Cases on digital game-based learning: Methods, models, and strategies* (pp. 15–24). Hershey, PA: Information Science Reference.

Al-Jenaibi, B. (2011). Gender issues in the diversity and practice of public relations in the UAE case study of P.R. male managers and female P.R. practitioners. *International Journal of E-Politics*, 2(3), 35–56. doi:10.4018/jep.2011070104

Albert, L. J., Hill, T. R., & Venkatsubramanyan, S. (2011). Effects of perceiver/target gender and social networking presence on web-based impression formation. *International Journal of E-Politics*, 2(2), 55–73. doi:10.4018/jep.2011040104

Albert, L. J., Hill, T. R., & Venkatsubramanyan, S. (2012). Gender differences in social networking presence effects on web-based impression formation. In C. Romm Livermore (Ed.), *Gender and social computing: Interactions, differences and relationships* (pp. 200–220). Hershey, PA: Information Science Publishing.

Albuquerque, O., & Moreira, G. G. (2011). The contribution of videogames to anti-social attitudes and behaviours amongst youngsters. In M. Cruz-Cunha, V. Varvalho, & P. Tavares (Eds.), *Business, technological, and social dimensions of computer games: Multidisciplinary developments* (pp. 237–251). Hershey, PA: Information Science Reference. doi:10.4018/978-1-60960-567-4.ch015

Aldrich, C., & DiPietro, J. C. (2011). An overview of gaming terminology: Chapters I – LXXVI. In I. Management Association (Ed.), Gaming and simulations: Concepts, methodologies, tools and applications (pp. 24-44). Hershey, PA: Information Science Reference. doi: doi:10.4018/978-1-60960-195-9.ch102

Alkhattabi, M., Neagu, D., & Cullen, A. (2012). User perceptions of information quality in e-learning systems: A gender and cultural perspective. In R. Pande, & T. Van der Weide (Eds.), *Globalization, technology diffusion and gender disparity: Social impacts of ICTs* (pp. 138–145). Hershey, PA: Information Science Reference. doi:10.4018/978-1-4666-0020-1.ch012

Anagnostou, K. (2011). How has the internet evolved the videogame medium? In M. Cruz-Cunha, V. Varvalho, & P. Tavares (Eds.), *Business, technological, and social dimensions of computer games: Multidisciplinary developments* (pp. 448–462). Hershey, PA: Information Science Reference. doi:10.4018/978-1-60960-567-4.ch027

Anderson, B. (2010). MMORPGs in support of learning: Current trends and future uses. In R. Van Eck (Ed.), *Gaming and cognition: Theories and practice from the learning sciences* (pp. 55–81). Hershey, PA: Information Science Reference. doi:10.4018/978-1-61520-717-6.ch003

Appiah, O., & Elias, T. (2011). Race-specific advertising on commercial websites: Effects of ethnically ambiguous computer generated characters in a digital world. In M. Eastin, T. Daugherty, & N. Burns (Eds.), *Handbook of research on digital media and advertising: User generated content consumption* (pp. 161–179). Hershey, PA: Information Science Reference.

Arroyo-Palacios, J., & Romano, D. M. (2010). Bio-affective computer interface for game interaction. *International Journal of Gaming and Computer-Mediated Simulations*, 2(4), 16–32. doi:10.4018/jgcms.2010100102

Asbell-Clarke, J., Edwards, T., Rowe, E., Larsen, J., Sylvan, E., & Hewitt, J. (2012). Martian boneyards: Scientific inquiry in an MMO game. *International Journal of Game-Based Learning*, 2(1), 52–76. doi:10.4018/ijgbl.2012010104

Bachvarova, Y., & Bocconi, S. (2014). Games and social networks. In T. Connolly, T. Hainey, E. Boyle, G. Baxter, & P. Moreno-Ger (Eds.), *Psychology, pedagogy, and assessment in serious games* (pp. 204–219). Hershey, PA: Information Science Reference.

Balachandar, A., & Gurusamy, R. (2012). Conflict segments of women employees of IT sector in India: Its relevance with the demographic profile. *International Journal of Human Capital and Information Technology Professionals*, 3(1), 42–53. doi:10.4018/jhcitp.2012010104

Balzac, S. R. (2010). Reality from fantasy: Using predictive scenarios to explore ethical dilemmas. In K. Schrier, & D. Gibson (Eds.), *Ethics and game design: Teaching values through play* (pp. 291–310). Hershey, PA: Information Science Reference. doi:10.4018/978-1-61520-845-6.ch018

Baranowski, T., O'Connor, T., Hughes, S., Beltran, A., Baranowski, J., & Nicklas, T. … Buday, R. (2013). Smart phone video game simulation of parent-child interaction: learning skills for effective vegetable parenting. In S. Arnab, I. Dunwell, & K. Debattista (Eds.), Serious games for healthcare: Applications and implications (pp. 247-264). Hershey, PA: Medical Information Science Reference. doi: doi:10.4018/978-1-4666-1903-6.ch012

Barlow, M. (2011). Game led HCI improvements. In M. Cruz-Cunha, V. Varvalho, & P. Tavares (Eds.), *Business, technological, and social dimensions of computer games: Multidisciplinary developments* (pp. 126–145). Hershey, PA: Information Science Reference. doi:10.4018/978-1-60960-567-4.ch009

Bates, M. (2013). The ur-real sonorous envelope: Bridge between the corporeal and the online technoself. In R. Luppicini (Ed.), *Handbook of research on technoself: Identity in a technological society* (pp. 272–292). Hershey, PA: Information Science Reference.

Belfo, F. (2011). Business process management in the computer games industry. In M. Cruz-Cunha, V. Varvalho, & P. Tavares (Eds.), *Business, technological, and social dimensions of computer games: Multidisciplinary developments* (pp. 383–400). Hershey, PA: Information Science Reference. doi:10.4018/978-1-60960-567-4.ch023

Ben, E. R. (2012). Gendering professionalism in the internationalization of information work. In R. Pande, & T. Van der Weide (Eds.), *Globalization, technology diffusion and gender disparity: Social impacts of ICTs* (pp. 51–69). Hershey, PA: Information Science Reference. doi:10.4018/978-1-4666-0020-1.ch005

Berzsenyi, C. (2014). Writing to meet your match: Rhetoric and self-presentation for four online daters. In H. Lim, & F. Sudweeks (Eds.), *Innovative methods and technologies for electronic discourse analysis* (pp. 210–234). Hershey, PA: Information Science Reference.

Bevc, T. (2010). Models of politics and society in video games. In P. Zemliansky, & D. Wilcox (Eds.), *Design and implementation of educational games: Theoretical and practical perspectives* (pp. 47–64). Hershey, PA: Information Science Reference. doi:10.4018/978-1-61520-781-7.ch004

Bhatnagar, K. (2013). Supply chain management and the other half. In I. Association (Ed.), *Supply chain management: Concepts, methodologies, tools, and applications* (pp. 106–120). Hershey, PA: Business Science Reference.

Bishop, J. (2010). Increasing capital revenue in social networking communities: Building social and economic relationships through avatars and characters. In S. Dasgupta (Ed.), *Social computing: Concepts, methodologies, tools, and applications* (pp. 1987–2004). Hershey, PA: Information Science Reference. doi:10.4018/978-1-60960-100-3.ch509

Bishop, J. (2011). Increasing capital revenue in social networking communities: Building social and economic relationships through avatars and characters. In I. Management Association (Ed.), Virtual communities: Concepts, methodologies, tools and applications (pp. 1720-1737). Hershey, PA: Information Science Reference. doi: doi:10.4018/978-1-60960-100-3.ch509

Bishop, J. (2013). The psychology of trolling and lurking: The role of defriending and gamification for increasing participation in online communities using seductive narratives. In J. Bishop (Ed.), *Examining the concepts, issues, and implications of internet trolling* (pp. 106–123). Hershey, PA: Information Science Reference. doi:10.4018/978-1-4666-2803-8.ch009

Black, E. W., Ferdig, R. E., DiPietro, J. C., Liu, F., & Whalen, B. (2011). Visual analyses of the creation of avatars. In R. Ferdig (Ed.), *Discoveries in gaming and computer-mediated simulations: New interdisciplinary applications* (pp. 284–300). Hershey, PA: Information Science Reference. doi:10.4018/978-1-60960-565-0.ch016

Blasko, D. G., Lum, H. C., White, M. M., & Drabik, H. B. (2014). Individual differences in the enjoyment and effectiveness of serious games. In T. Connolly, T. Hainey, E. Boyle, G. Baxter, & P. Moreno-Ger (Eds.), *Psychology, pedagogy, and assessment in serious games* (pp. 153–174). Hershey, PA: Information Science Reference.

Blomqvist, M. (2010). Absent women: Research on gender relations in IT education mediated by Swedish newspapers. In S. Booth, S. Goodman, & G. Kirkup (Eds.), *Gender issues in learning and working with information technology: Social constructs and cultural contexts* (pp. 133–149). Hershey, PA: Information Science Reference. doi:10.4018/978-1-61520-813-5.ch008

Boa-Ventura, A. (2012). Virtual worlds and behavioral change: Overcoming time/ space constraints and exploring anonymity to overcome social stigma in the case of substance abuse. In N. Zagalo, L. Morgado, & A. Boa-Ventura (Eds.), *Virtual worlds and metaverse platforms: New communication and identity paradigms* (pp. 271–286). Hershey, PA: Information Science Reference.

Boivie, I. (2010). Women, men and programming: Knowledge, metaphors and masculinity. In S. Booth, S. Goodman, & G. Kirkup (Eds.), *Gender issues in learning and working with information technology: Social constructs and cultural contexts* (pp. 1–24). Hershey, PA: Information Science Reference. doi:10.4018/978-1-61520-813-5.ch001

Booth, S., & Wigforss, E. (2010). Approaching higher education: A life-world story of home-places, work-places and learn-places. In S. Booth, S. Goodman, & G. Kirkup (Eds.), *Gender issues in learning and working with information technology: Social constructs and cultural contexts* (pp. 173–191). Hershey, PA: Information Science Reference. doi:10.4018/978-1-61520-813-5.ch010

Braun, P. (2011). Advancing women in the digital economy: eLearning opportunities for meta-competency skilling. In I. Management Association (Ed.), Global business: Concepts, methodologies, tools and applications (pp. 1978-1990). Hershey, PA: Business Science Reference. doi: doi:10.4018/978-1-60960-587-2.ch708

Bryant, J. A., & Drell, J. (2010). Family fun and fostering values. In K. Schrier, & D. Gibson (Eds.), *Ethics and game design: Teaching values through play* (pp. 167–180). Hershey, PA: Information Science Reference. doi:10.4018/978-1-61520-845-6.ch011

Buraphadeja, V., & Dawson, K. (2011). Exploring personal myths from the Sims. In I. Management Association (Ed.), Gaming and simulations: Concepts, methodologies, tools and applications (pp. 1750-1762). Hershey, PA: Information Science Reference. doi: doi:10.4018/978-1-60960-195-9.ch705

Byrd, M. Y. (2012). Critical race theory: A framework for examining social identity diversity of Black women in positions of leadership. In C. Scott, & M. Byrd (Eds.), *Handbook of research on workforce diversity in a global society: Technologies and concepts* (pp. 426–439). Hershey, PA: Business Science Reference. doi:10.4018/978-1-4666-1812-1.ch025

Carneiro, M. G. (2011). Artificial intelligence in games evolution. In M. Cruz-Cunha, V. Varvalho, & P. Tavares (Eds.), *Business, technological, and social dimensions of computer games: Multidisciplinary developments* (pp. 98–114). Hershey, PA: Information Science Reference. doi:10.4018/978-1-60960-567-4.ch007

Chandra, S., Gruber, T., & Lowrie, A. (2012). Service recovery encounters in the classroom: Exploring the attributes of professors desired by male and female students. *International Journal of Technology and Educational Marketing*, *2*(2), 1–19. doi:10.4018/ijtem.2012070101

Chandra, S., Gruber, T., & Lowrie, A. (2013). Service recovery encounters in the classroom: Exploring the attributes of professors desired by male and female students. In P. Tripathi, & S. Mukerji (Eds.), *Marketing strategies for higher education institutions: Technological considerations and practices* (pp. 219–239). Hershey, PA: Business Science Reference.

Chen, K., Chen, J. V., & Ross, W. H. (2010). Antecedents of online game dependency: The implications of multimedia realism and uses and gratifications theory. *Journal of Database Management*, *21*(2), 69–99. doi:10.4018/jdm.2010040104

Chen, K., Chen, J. V., & Ross, W. H. (2012). Antecedents of online game dependency: The implications of multimedia realism and uses and gratifications theory. In K. Siau (Ed.), *Cross-disciplinary models and applications of database management: Advancing approaches* (pp. 176–208). Hershey, PA: Information Science Reference.

259

Chiu, M. (2013). Gaps between valuing and purchasing green-technology products: Product and gender differences. *International Journal of Technology and Human Interaction, 8*(3), 54–68. doi:10.4018/jthi.2012070106

Cicchirillo, V. (2010). Online gaming: Demographics, motivations, and information processing. In M. Eastin, T. Daugherty, & N. Burns (Eds.), *Handbook of research on digital media and advertising: User generated content consumption* (pp. 456–479). Hershey, PA: Information Science Reference. doi:10.4018/978-1-60566-792-8.ch023

Concha, A. S. (2012). Filipino cyborg sexualities, chatroom masculinities, self-ascribed identities, ephemeral selves. In R. Pande, & T. Van der Weide (Eds.), *Globalization, technology diffusion and gender disparity: Social impacts of ICTs* (pp. 211–224). Hershey, PA: Information Science Reference. doi:10.4018/978-1-4666-0020-1.ch018

Conger, S. (2011). Web 2.0, virtual worlds, and real ethical issues. In I. Management Association (Ed.), Virtual communities: Concepts, methodologies, tools and applications (pp. 226-238). Hershey, PA: Information Science Reference. doi: doi:10.4018/978-1-60960-100-3.ch117

Costin, Y. (2012). Adopting ICT in the mompreneurs business: A strategy for growth? In C. Romm Livermore (Ed.), *Gender and social computing: Interactions, differences and relationships* (pp. 17–34). Hershey, PA: Information Science Publishing.

Costin, Y. (2013). Adopting ICT in the mompreneurs business: A strategy for growth? In I. Association (Ed.), *Small and medium enterprises: Concepts, methodologies, tools, and applications* (pp. 322–339). Hershey, PA: Business Science Reference.

Coverdale, T. S., & Wilbon, A. D. (2013). The impact of in-group membership on e-loyalty of women online shoppers: An application of the social identity approach to website design. *International Journal of E-Adoption, 5*(1), 17–36. doi:10.4018/jea.2013010102

Cox, A. D., Eno, C. A., & Guadagno, R. E. (2012). Beauty in the background: A content analysis of females in interactive digital games. *International Journal of Interactive Communication Systems and Technologies, 2*(2), 49–62. doi:10.4018/ijicst.2012070104

Cozza, M. (2010). Gender and technology: Mind the gap! In A. Hallin, & T. Karrbom-Gustavsson (Eds.), *Organizational communication and sustainable development: ICTs for mobility* (pp. 256–274). Hershey, PA: Information Science Reference.

Cramer, J., & Crocco, M. S. (2010). Women and technology, upon reflection: Linking global women's issues to the digital gender divide in urban social studies education. In J. Yamamoto, J. Kush, R. Lombard, & C. Hertzog (Eds.), *Technology implementation and teacher education: Reflective models* (pp. 184–202). Hershey, PA: Information Science Reference. doi:10.4018/978-1-61520-897-5.ch011

Deale, D. F., Key, S. S., Regina, M., & Pastore, R. (2012). Women and gaming. *International Journal of Gaming and Computer-Mediated Simulations, 4*(1), 86–89. doi:10.4018/jgcms.2012010105

Devyatkov, V., & Alfimtsev, A. (2011). Human-computer interaction in games using computer vision techniques. In M. Cruz-Cunha, V. Varvalho, & P. Tavares (Eds.), *Business, technological, and social dimensions of computer games: Multidisciplinary developments* (pp. 146–167). Hershey, PA: Information Science Reference. doi:10.4018/978-1-60960-567-4.ch010

Dhar-Bhattacharjee, S., & Takruri-Rizk, H. (2011). Gender segregation and ICT: An Indo-British comparison. *International Journal of E-Politics*, *2*(1), 45–67. doi:10.4018/jep.2011010104

Driouchi, A. (2013). Women empowerment and ICTs in developing economies. In *ICTs for health, education, and socioeconomic policies: Regional cases* (pp. 146–164). Hershey, PA: Information Science Reference. doi:10.4018/978-1-4666-3643-9.ch007

Dubbels, B. (2013). Gamification, serious games, ludic simulation, and other contentious categories. *International Journal of Gaming and Computer-Mediated Simulations*, *5*(2), 1–19. doi:10.4018/jgcms.2013040101

Duin, H., Hauge, J. B., Hunecker, F., & Thoben, K. (2011). Application of serious games in industrial contexts. In M. Cruz-Cunha, V. Varvalho, & P. Tavares (Eds.), *Business, technological, and social dimensions of computer games: Multidisciplinary developments* (pp. 331–347). Hershey, PA: Information Science Reference. doi:10.4018/978-1-60960-567-4.ch020

Dunn, R. A. (2013). Identity theories and technology. In R. Luppicini (Ed.), *Handbook of research on technoself: Identity in a technological society* (pp. 26–44). Hershey, PA: Information Science Reference.

Durbin, S. (2010). SET women and careers: A case study of senior female scientists in the UK. In A. Cater-Steel, & E. Cater (Eds.), *Women in engineering, science and technology: Education and career challenges* (pp. 232–254). Hershey, PA: Engineering Science Reference. doi:10.4018/978-1-61520-657-5.ch011

Ellcessor, E., & Duncan, S. C. (2011). Forming the guild: Star power and rethinking projective identity in affinity spaces. *International Journal of Game-Based Learning*, *1*(2), 82–95. doi:10.4018/ijgbl.2011040106

Elwell, M. G. (2011). Questing for standards: Role playing games in second life. In M. Cruz-Cunha, V. Varvalho, & P. Tavares (Eds.), *Business, technological, and social dimensions of computer games: Multidisciplinary developments* (pp. 81–97). Hershey, PA: Information Science Reference. doi:10.4018/978-1-60960-567-4.ch006

Erdör, M. (2012). Developments in e-entrepreneurship in Turkey and a case study of a startup company founded by a woman entrepreneur. *International Journal of E-Entrepreneurship and Innovation*, *3*(4), 47–52. doi:10.4018/jeei.2012100104

Ertl, B., Helling, K., & Kikis-Papadakis, K. (2012). The impact of gender in ICT usage, education and career: Comparisons between Greece and Germany. In C. Romm Livermore (Ed.), *Gender and social computing: Interactions, differences and relationships* (pp. 98–119). Hershey, PA: Information Science Publishing.

Essid, J. (2011). Playing in a new key, in a new world: Virtual worlds, millennial writers, and 3D composition. In A. Cheney, & R. Sanders (Eds.), *Teaching and learning in 3D immersive worlds: Pedagogical models and constructivist approaches* (pp. 169–184). Hershey, PA: Information Science Reference. doi:10.4018/978-1-60960-517-9.ch010

Eveleth, D. M., & Eveleth, A. B. (2010). Team identification, team performance and leader-member exchange relationships in virtual groups: Findings from massive multi-player online role play games. *International Journal of Virtual Communities and Social Networking*, *2*(1), 52–66. doi:10.4018/jvcsn.2010010104

Falcão, T. (2012). Structures of agency in virtual worlds: Fictional worlds and the shaping of an in-game social conduct. In N. Zagalo, L. Morgado, & A. Boa-Ventura (Eds.), *Virtual worlds and metaverse platforms: New communication and identity paradigms* (pp. 192–205). Hershey, PA: Information Science Reference.

Farmer, L. S. (2011). Gaming in adult education. In V. Wang (Ed.), *Encyclopedia of information communication technologies and adult education integration* (pp. 687–706). Hershey, PA: Information Science Reference.

Farmer, L. S. (2011). Gender impact on adult education. In V. Wang (Ed.), *Encyclopedia of information communication technologies and adult education integration* (pp. 377–395). Hershey, PA: Information Science Reference.

Farmer, L. S., & Murphy, N. G. (2010). eGaming and girls: Optimizing use in school libraries. In R. Van Eck (Ed.), *Interdisciplinary models and tools for serious games: Emerging concepts and future directions* (pp. 306–332). Hershey, PA: Information Science Reference. doi: doi:10.4018/978-1-61520-719-0.ch013

Fatma, S. (2013). ICT in Arab education: Issues and challenges. In F. Albadri (Ed.), *Information systems applications in the Arab education sector* (pp. 136–147). Hershey, PA: Information Science Reference.

Feinberg, J. R., Schewe, A. H., Moore, C. D., & Wood, K. R. (2013). Puttering, tinkering, building, and making: A constructionist approach to online instructional simulation games. In R. Hartshorne, T. Heafner, & T. Petty (Eds.), *Teacher education programs and online learning tools: Innovations in teacher preparation* (pp. 417–436). Hershey, PA: Information Science Reference.

Felicia, P., & Pitt, I. (2011). Harnessing the emotional potential of video games. In I. Association (Ed.), *Instructional design: Concepts, methodologies, tools and applications* (pp. 1282–1299). Hershey, PA: Information Science Reference. doi:10.4018/978-1-60960-503-2.ch511

Ferri, G. (2013). Rhetorics, simulations and games: The ludic and satirical discourse of molleindustria. *International Journal of Gaming and Computer-Mediated Simulations*, 5(1), 32–49. doi:10.4018/jgcms.2013010103

Fitz-Walter, Z., Tjondronegoro, D., & Wyeth, P. (2013). Gamifying Everyday activities using mobile sensing. In D. Tjondronegoro (Ed.), *Tools for mobile multimedia programming and development* (pp. 98–114). Hershey, PA: Information Science Reference.

Fogel, G. K., & Lewis, L. F. (2012). Target marketing and ethics: Brand advertising and marketing campaigns. In E. Carayannis (Ed.), *Sustainable policy applications for social ecology and development* (pp. 214–231). Hershey, PA: Information Science Reference. doi:10.4018/978-1-4666-1586-1.ch016

Forman, A. E., Baker, P. M., Pater, J., & Smith, K. (2011). Beautiful to me: Identity, disability, and gender in virtual environments. *International Journal of E-Politics*, 2(2), 1–17. doi:10.4018/jep.2011040101

Forman, A. E., Baker, P. M., Pater, J., & Smith, K. (2012). The not so level playing field: Disability identity and gender representation in second life. In C. Romm Livermore (Ed.), *Gender and social computing: Interactions, differences and relationships* (pp. 144–161). Hershey, PA: Information Science Publishing.

Fox, J., & Ahn, S. J. (2013). Avatars: Portraying, exploring, and changing online and offline identities. In R. Luppicini (Ed.), *Handbook of research on technoself: Identity in a technological society* (pp. 255–271). Hershey, PA: Information Science Reference.

Freier, N. G., & Saulnier, E. T. (2011). The new backyard: Social and moral development in virtual worlds. In K. Schrier, & D. Gibson (Eds.), *Designing games for ethics: Models, techniques and frameworks* (pp. 179–192). Hershey, PA: Information Science Reference.

Friedman, A., Hartshorne, R., & VanFossen, P. (2010). Exploring guild participation in MMOR-PGs and civic leadership. In Y. Baek (Ed.), *Gaming for classroom-based learning: Digital role playing as a motivator of study* (pp. 176–204). Hershey, PA: Information Science Reference. doi:10.4018/978-1-61520-713-8.ch011

Gabriels, K., Bauwens, J., & Verstrynge, K. (2012). Second life, second morality? In N. Zagalo, L. Morgado, & A. Boa-Ventura (Eds.), *Virtual worlds and metaverse platforms: New communication and identity paradigms* (pp. 306–320). Hershey, PA: Information Science Reference.

García-Gómez, A. (2013). Technoself-presentation on social networks: A gender-based approach. In R. Luppicini (Ed.), *Handbook of research on technoself: Identity in a technological society* (pp. 382–398). Hershey, PA: Information Science Reference.

Ghosh, A. (2012). Leveraging sexual orientation workforce diversity through identity deployment. In C. Scott, & M. Byrd (Eds.), *Handbook of research on workforce diversity in a global society: Technologies and concepts* (pp. 403–424). Hershey, PA: Business Science Reference. doi:10.4018/978-1-4666-1812-1.ch024

Ghuman, D., & Griffiths, M. (2012). A cross-genre study of online gaming: Player demographics, motivation for play, and social interactions among players. *International Journal of Cyber Behavior, Psychology and Learning, 2*(1), 13–29. doi:10.4018/ijcbpl.2012010102

Gilbert, S. (2010). Ethics at play: Patterns of ethical thinking among young online gamers. In K. Schrier, & D. Gibson (Eds.), *Ethics and game design: Teaching values through play* (pp. 151–166). Hershey, PA: Information Science Reference. doi:10.4018/978-1-61520-845-6.ch010

Goeke, R. J., Hogue, M., & Faley, R. H. (2010). The impact of gender and experience on the strength of the relationships between perceived data warehouse flexibility, ease-of-use, and usefulness. *Information Resources Management Journal, 23*(2), 1–19. doi:10.4018/irmj.2010040101

Gomes, T., & Carvalho, A. A. (2011). The pedagogical potential of MMOG: An exploratory study including four games and their players. In M. Cruz-Cunha, V. Varvalho, & P. Tavares (Eds.), *Computer games as educational and management tools: Uses and approaches* (pp. 103–121). Hershey, PA: Information Science Reference. doi:10.4018/978-1-60960-569-8.ch007

Gómez, M. C., García, A. V., Llorente, A. M., Dávila, P. A., & Sepúlveda, P. Z. (2013). Gender violence experiences of urban adult indigenous women: Case study. In F. García-Peñalvo (Ed.), *Multiculturalism in technology-based education: Case studies on ICT-supported approaches* (pp. 79–99). Hershey, PA: Information Science Reference.

Griffiths, M., Hussain, Z., Grüsser, S. M., Thalemann, R., Cole, H., Davies, M. N., & Chappell, D. (2011). Social interactions in online gaming. *International Journal of Game-Based Learning, 1*(4), 20–36. doi:10.4018/ijgbl.2011100103

Griffiths, M., Hussain, Z., Grüsser, S. M., Thalemann, R., Cole, H., Davies, M. N., & Chappell, D. (2013). Social interactions in online gaming. In P. Felicia (Ed.), *Developments in current game-based learning design and deployment* (pp. 74–90). Hershey, PA: Information Science Reference.

Griffiths, M., & Richardson, H. (2010). Against all odds, from all-girls schools to all-boys workplaces: Women's unsuspecting trajectory into the UK ICT sector. In S. Booth, S. Goodman, & G. Kirkup (Eds.), *Gender issues in learning and working with information technology: Social constructs and cultural contexts* (pp. 99–112). Hershey, PA: Information Science Reference. doi:10.4018/978-1-61520-813-5.ch006

Grimes, G., & Bartolacci, M. (2010). Second life: A virtual world platform for profiling online behavior for network and information security education? An initial investigation. *International Journal of Interdisciplinary Telecommunications and Networking, 2*(4), 60–64. doi:10.4018/jitn.2010100105

Gulz, A., & Haake, M. (2010). Challenging gender stereotypes using virtual pedagogical characters. In S. Booth, S. Goodman, & G. Kirkup (Eds.), *Gender issues in learning and working with information technology: Social constructs and cultural contexts* (pp. 113–132). Hershey, PA: Information Science Reference. doi:10.4018/978-1-61520-813-5.ch007

Gunraj, A., Ruiz, S., & York, A. (2011). Power to the people: Anti-oppressive game design. In K. Schrier, & D. Gibson (Eds.), *Designing games for ethics: Models, techniques and frameworks* (pp. 253–274). Hershey, PA: Information Science Reference.

Gupta, M., Jin, S., Sanders, G. L., Sherman, B. A., & Simha, A. (2012). Getting real about virtual worlds: A review. *International Journal of Virtual Communities and Social Networking, 4*(3), 1–46. doi:10.4018/jvcsn.2012070101

Guth, J., & Wright, F. (2010). "We don't have the key to the executive washroom": Women's perceptions and experiences of promotion in academia. In A. Cater-Steel, & E. Cater (Eds.), *Women in engineering, science and technology: Education and career challenges* (pp. 159–182). Hershey, PA: Engineering Science Reference. doi:10.4018/978-1-61520-657-5.ch008

Guthrie, R. A., Soe, L., & Yakura, E. K. (2011). Support structures for women in information technology careers. *International Journal of E-Politics, 2*(1), 30–44. doi:10.4018/jep.2011010103

Gwee, S., San Chee, Y., & Tan, E. M. (2011). The role of gender in mobile game-based learning. *International Journal of Mobile and Blended Learning, 3*(4), 19–37. doi:10.4018/jmbl.2011100102

Gwee, S., San Chee, Y., & Tan, E. M. (2013). The role of gender in mobile game-based learning. In D. Parsons (Ed.), *Innovations in mobile educational technologies and applications* (pp. 254–271). Hershey, PA: Information Science Reference.

Hackbarth, G., Dow, K. E., Wang, H., & Johnson, W. R. (2010). Changing attitudes toward women IT managers. *International Journal of Information Systems and Social Change, 1*(3), 28–44. doi:10.4018/jissc.2010070103

Hackbarth, G., Dow, K. E., Wang, H., & Johnson, W. R. (2012). Changing attitudes toward women IT managers. In J. Wang (Ed.), *Societal impacts on information systems development and applications* (pp. 114–129). Hershey, PA: Information Science Reference. doi:10.4018/978-1-4666-0927-3.ch008

Halder, D., & Jaishankar, K. (2012). Cyber laws for preventing cyber crimes against women in Canada. In *Cyber crime and the victimization of women: Laws, rights and regulations* (pp. 82–94). Hershey, PA: Information Science Reference.

Halder, D., & Jaishankar, K. (2012). Cyber space regulations for protecting women in UK. In *Cyber crime and the victimization of women: Laws, rights and regulations* (pp. 95–104). Hershey, PA: Information Science Reference.

Halder, D., & Jaishankar, K. (2012). Definition, typology and patterns of victimization. In *Cyber crime and the victimization of women: Laws, rights and regulations* (pp. 12–39). Hershey, PA: Information Science Reference.

Halder, D., & Jaishankar, K. (2012). Etiology, motives, and crime hubs. In *Cyber crime and the victimization of women: Laws, rights and regulations* (pp. 40–54). Hershey, PA: Information Science Reference.

Halder, D., & Jaishankar, K. (2012). Introduction. In *Cyber crime and the victimization of women: Laws, rights and regulations* (pp. 1–11). Hershey, PA: Information Science Reference.

Halder, D., & Jaishankar, K. (2012). Legal treatment of cyber crimes against women in USA. In *Cyber crime and the victimization of women: Laws, rights and regulations* (pp. 69–81). Hershey, PA: Information Science Reference.

Halder, D., & Jaishankar, K. (2012). Women's rights in the cyber space and the related duties. In *Cyber crime and the victimization of women: Laws, rights and regulations* (pp. 55–68). Hershey, PA: Information Science Reference.

Hamari, J., & Järvinen, A. (2011). Building customer relationship through game mechanics in social games. In M. Cruz-Cunha, V. Varvalho, & P. Tavares (Eds.), *Business, technological, and social dimensions of computer games: Multidisciplinary developments* (pp. 348–365). Hershey, PA: Information Science Reference. doi:10.4018/978-1-60960-567-4.ch021

Hartshorne, R., VanFossen, P. J., & Friedman, A. (2012). MMORPG roles, civic participation and leadership among generation Y. *International Journal of Gaming and Computer-Mediated Simulations*, *4*(1), 55–67. doi:10.4018/jgcms.2012010103

Harwood, T. (2012). Emergence of gamified commerce: Turning virtual to real. *Journal of Electronic Commerce in Organizations*, *10*(2), 16–39. doi:10.4018/jeco.2012040102

Heeter, C., Lee, Y., Magerko, B., & Medler, B. (2011). Impacts of forced serious game play on vulnerable subgroups. *International Journal of Gaming and Computer-Mediated Simulations*, *3*(3), 34–53. doi:10.4018/jgcms.2011070103

Heeter, C., Lee, Y., Magerko, B., & Medler, B. (2013). Impacts of forced serious game play on vulnerable subgroups. In R. Ferdig (Ed.), *Design, utilization, and analysis of simulations and game-based educational worlds* (pp. 158–176). Hershey, PA: Information Science Reference. doi:10.4018/978-1-4666-4018-4.ch010

Heeter, C., Magerko, B., Medler, B., & Fitzgerald, J. (2011). Game design and the challenge-avoiding, self-validator player type. In R. Ferdig (Ed.), *Discoveries in gaming and computer-mediated simulations: New interdisciplinary applications* (pp. 49–63). Hershey, PA: Information Science Reference. doi:10.4018/978-1-60960-565-0.ch004

Heeter, C., Sarkar, C. D., Palmer-Scott, B., & Zhang, S. (2012). Engineering sociability: Friendship drive, visibility, and social connection in anonymous co-located local wi-fi multiplayer online gaming. *International Journal of Gaming and Computer-Mediated Simulations*, *4*(2), 1–18. doi:10.4018/jgcms.2012040101

Heider, D., & Massanari, A. L. (2010). Friendship, closeness and disclosure in second life. *International Journal of Gaming and Computer-Mediated Simulations*, *2*(3), 61–74. doi:10.4018/jgcms.2010070104

Heitmann, M., & Tidten, K. (2011). New business models for the computer gaming industry: Selling an adventure. In M. Cruz-Cunha, V. Varvalho, & P. Tavares (Eds.), *Business, technological, and social dimensions of computer games: Multidisciplinary developments* (pp. 401–415). Hershey, PA: Information Science Reference. doi:10.4018/978-1-60960-567-4.ch024

Heo, M., & Spradley-Myrick, L. M. (2012). Girls and computers - Yes we can!: A case study on improving female computer confidence and decreasing gender inequity in computer science with an informal, female learning community. In I. Management Association (Ed.), Computer engineering: Concepts, methodologies, tools and applications (pp. 1126-1143). Hershey, PA: Engineering Science Reference. doi: doi:10.4018/978-1-61350-456-7.ch504

Hewahi, N. M., & Baraka, A. M. (2012). Emotion recognition model based on facial expressions, ethnicity and gender using backpropagation neural network. *International Journal of Technology Diffusion, 3*(1), 33–43. doi:10.4018/jtd.2012010104

Hewett, S. (2011). Using video games to improve literacy levels of males. In I. Association (Ed.), *Instructional design: Concepts, methodologies, tools and applications* (pp. 192–206). Hershey, PA: Information Science Reference. doi:10.4018/978-1-60960-503-2.ch115

Hicks, D. (2014). Technology, gender, and professional identity. In *Technology and professional identity of librarians: The making of the cybrarian* (pp. 128–147). Hershey, PA: Information Science Reference.

Hobbs, R., & Rowe, J. (2011). Creative remixing and digital learning: Developing an online media literacy learning tool for girls. In I. Management Association (Ed.), Gaming and simulations: Concepts, methodologies, tools and applications (pp. 971-978). Hershey, PA: Information Science Reference. doi: doi:10.4018/978-1-60960-195-9.ch405

Hoffman, E. (2010). Sideways into truth: Kierkegaard, Philistines, and why we love sex and violence. In K. Schrier, & D. Gibson (Eds.), *Ethics and game design: Teaching values through play* (pp. 109–124). Hershey, PA: Information Science Reference. doi:10.4018/978-1-61520-845-6.ch008

Hoffmann, E. M. (2010). Women in computer science in Afghanistan. In S. Booth, S. Goodman, & G. Kirkup (Eds.), *Gender issues in learning and working with information technology: Social constructs and cultural contexts* (pp. 48–63). Hershey, PA: Information Science Reference. doi:10.4018/978-1-61520-813-5.ch003

Hsu, C. (2010). Exploring the player flow experience in e-game playing. *International Journal of Technology and Human Interaction, 6*(2), 47–64. doi:10.4018/jthi.2010040104

Huang, J., & Aaltio, I. (2010). Social interaction technologies: A case study of Guanxi and women managers' careers in information technology in China. In T. Dumova, & R. Fiordo (Eds.), *Handbook of research on social interaction technologies and collaboration software: Concepts and trends* (pp. 257–269). Hershey, PA: Information Science Reference.

Hughes, G. (2010). Queen bees, workers and drones: Gender performance in virtual learning groups. In S. Booth, S. Goodman, & G. Kirkup (Eds.), *Gender issues in learning and working with information technology: Social constructs and cultural contexts* (pp. 244–254). Hershey, PA: Information Science Reference. doi:10.4018/978-1-61520-813-5.ch014

Igun, S. E. (2010). Gender and national information and communication technology (ICT) policies in Africa. In E. Adomi (Ed.), *Handbook of research on information communication technology policy: Trends, issues and advancements* (pp. 208–221). Hershey, PA: Information Science Reference. doi:10.4018/978-1-61520-847-0.ch013

Igun, S. E. (2013). Gender and national information and communication technology (ICT) policies in Africa. In B. Maumbe, & J. Okello (Eds.), *Technology, sustainability, and rural development in Africa* (pp. 284–297). Hershey, PA: Information Science Reference. doi:10.4018/978-1-4666-3607-1.ch018

Ikolo, V. E. (2010). Gender digital divide and national ICT policies in Africa. In E. Adomi (Ed.), *Handbook of research on information communication technology policy: Trends, issues and advancements* (pp. 222–242). Hershey, PA: Information Science Reference. doi:10.4018/978-1-61520-847-0.ch014

Ikolo, V. E. (2013). Gender digital divide and national ICT policies in Africa. In I. Association (Ed.), *Digital literacy: Concepts, methodologies, tools, and applications* (pp. 812–832). Hershey, PA: Information Science Reference.

Ionescu, A. (2012). ICTs and gender-based rights. *International Journal of Information Communication Technologies and Human Development, 4*(2), 33–49. doi:10.4018/jicthd.2012040103

Ionescu, A. (2013). Cyber identity: Our alter-ego? In R. Luppicini (Ed.), *Handbook of research on technoself: Identity in a technological society* (pp. 189–203). Hershey, PA: Information Science Reference.

Ionescu, A. (2013). ICTs and gender-based rights. In J. Lannon, & E. Halpin (Eds.), *Human rights and information communication technologies: Trends and consequences of use* (pp. 214–234). Hershey, PA: Information Science Reference.

Irving, C. J., & English, L. M. (2011). Women, information and communication technologies, and lifelong learning. In V. Wang (Ed.), *Encyclopedia of information communication technologies and adult education integration* (pp. 360–376). Hershey, PA: Information Science Reference.

Jarmon, L. (2010). Homo virtualis: Virtual worlds, learning, and an ecology of embodied interaction. *International Journal of Virtual and Personal Learning Environments, 1*(1), 38–56. doi:10.4018/jvple.2010091704

Jayasingh, S., & Eze, U. C. (2012). Analyzing the intention to use mobile coupon and the moderating effects of price consciousness and gender. *International Journal of E-Business Research, 8*(1), 54–75. doi:10.4018/jebr.2012010104

Jenson, J., & de, C. S. (2010). Gender and digital gameplay: Theories, oversights, accidents, and surprises. In D. Kaufman & L. Sauvé (Eds.), *Educational gameplay and simulation environments: Case studies and lessons learned* (pp. 96-105). Hershey, PA: Information Science Reference. doi:10.4018/978-1-61520-731-2.ch006

Johnson, R. D. (2011). Gender differences in e-learning: Communication, social presence, and learning outcomes. *Journal of Organizational and End User Computing, 23*(1), 79–94. doi:10.4018/joeuc.2011010105

Johnson, V. (2012). The gender divide: Attitudinal issues inhibiting access. In R. Pande, & T. Van der Weide (Eds.), *Globalization, technology diffusion and gender disparity: Social impacts of ICTs* (pp. 110–119). Hershey, PA: Information Science Reference. doi:10.4018/978-1-4666-0020-1.ch009

Jyothi, P. (2012). Challenges faced by women: BPO sector. In R. Pande, & T. Van der Weide (Eds.), *Globalization, technology diffusion and gender disparity: Social impacts of ICTs* (pp. 147–155). Hershey, PA: Information Science Reference. doi:10.4018/978-1-4666-0020-1.ch013

Kafai, Y. B., Fields, D., & Searle, K. A. (2010). Multi-modal investigations of relationship play in virtual worlds. *International Journal of Gaming and Computer-Mediated Simulations, 2*(1), 40–48. doi:10.4018/jgcms.2010010104

Kallay, J. (2010). Rethinking genre in computer games: How narrative psychology connects game and story. In R. Van Eck (Ed.), *Interdisciplinary models and tools for serious games: Emerging concepts and future directions* (pp. 30–49). Hershey, PA: Information Science Reference. doi:10.4018/978-1-61520-719-0.ch002

Kallergi, A., & Verbeek, F. J. (2014). Playful interfaces for scientific image data: A case for storytelling. In K. Blashki, & P. Isaias (Eds.), *Emerging research and trends in interactivity and the human-computer interface* (pp. 471–489). Hershey, PA: Information Science Reference.

Karl, K., Peluchette, J., & Schlagel, C. (2010). A cross-cultural examination of student attitudes and gender differences in Facebook profile content. *International Journal of Virtual Communities and Social Networking, 2*(2), 11–31. doi:10.4018/jvcsn.2010040102

Kaul, A., & Kulkarni, V. (2010). Gender and politeness in Indian emails. In R. Taiwo (Ed.), *Handbook of research on discourse behavior and digital communication: Language structures and social interaction* (pp. 389–410). Hershey, PA: Information Science Reference. doi:10.4018/978-1-61520-773-2.ch025

Ke, F., Yildirim, N., & Enfield, J. (2012). Exploring the design of game enjoyment through the perspectives of novice game developers. *International Journal of Gaming and Computer-Mediated Simulations, 4*(4), 45–63. doi:10.4018/jgcms.2012100104

King, E. (2013). Possibility spaces: Using the Sims 2 as a sandbox to explore possible selves with at-risk teenage males. In P. Felicia (Ed.), *Developments in current game-based learning design and deployment* (pp. 169–187). Hershey, PA: Information Science Reference.

Kirkup, G. (2010). Gendered knowledge production in universities in a web 2.0 world. In S. Booth, S. Goodman, & G. Kirkup (Eds.), *Gender issues in learning and working with information technology: Social constructs and cultural contexts* (pp. 231–243). Hershey, PA: Information Science Reference. doi:10.4018/978-1-61520-813-5.ch013

Kirkup, G., Schmitz, S., Kotkamp, E., Rommes, E., & Hiltunen, A. (2010). Towards a feminist manifesto for e-learning: Principles to inform practices. In S. Booth, S. Goodman, & G. Kirkup (Eds.), *Gender issues in learning and working with information technology: Social constructs and cultural contexts* (pp. 255–274). Hershey, PA: Information Science Reference. doi:10.4018/978-1-61520-813-5.ch015

Koh, E., Liu, N., & Lim, J. (2012). Gender and anonymity in virtual teams: An exploratory study. In C. Romm Livermore (Ed.), *Gender and social computing: Interactions, differences and relationships* (pp. 1–16). Hershey, PA: Information Science Publishing.

Kongmee, I., Strachan, R., Pickard, A., & Montgomery, C. (2012). A case study of using online communities and virtual environment in massively multiplayer role playing games (MMORPGs) as a learning and teaching tool for second language learners. *International Journal of Virtual and Personal Learning Environments, 3*(4), 1–15. doi:10.4018/jvple.2012100101

Koo, G., & Seider, S. (2010). Video games for prosocial learning. In K. Schrier, & D. Gibson (Eds.), *Ethics and game design: Teaching values through play* (pp. 16–33). Hershey, PA: Information Science Reference. doi:10.4018/978-1-61520-845-6.ch002

Kumari, B. R. (2012). Gender, culture, and ICT use. In R. Pande, & T. Van der Weide (Eds.), *Globalization, technology diffusion and gender disparity: Social impacts of ICTs* (pp. 36–50). Hershey, PA: Information Science Reference. doi:10.4018/978-1-4666-0020-1.ch004

Kwok, N. W., & Khoo, A. (2011). Gamers' motivations and problematic gaming: An exploratory study of gamers in World of Warcraft. *International Journal of Cyber Behavior, Psychology and Learning, 1*(3), 34–49. doi:10.4018/ijcbpl.2011070103

Kwok, N. W., & Khoo, A. (2013). Gamers' motivations and problematic gaming: An exploratory study of gamers in World of Warcraft. In R. Zheng (Ed.), *Evolving psychological and educational perspectives on cyber behavior* (pp. 64–81). Hershey, PA: Information Science Reference.

Lamoreaux, K., & Varghese, D. (2012). Deliberate leadership: Women in IT. In I. Management Association (Ed.), Computer engineering: Concepts, methodologies, tools and applications (pp. 1381-1402). Hershey, PA: Engineering Science Reference. doi: doi:10.4018/978-1-61350-456-7.ch601

Lankoski, P., Johansson, A., Karlsson, B., Björk, S., & Dell'Acqua, P. (2011). AI design for believable characters via gameplay design patterns. In M. Cruz-Cunha, V. Varvalho, & P. Tavares (Eds.), *Business, technological, and social dimensions of computer games: Multidisciplinary developments* (pp. 15–31). Hershey, PA: Information Science Reference. doi:10.4018/978-1-60960-567-4.ch002

Laosethakul, K., Leingpibul, T., & Coe, T. (2010). Investigation into gender perception toward computing: A comparison between the U.S. and India. *International Journal of Information and Communication Technology Education, 6*(4), 23–37. doi:10.4018/jicte.2010100103

Laosethakul, K., Leingpibul, T., & Coe, T. (2012). Investigation into gender perception toward computing: A comparison between the U.S. and India. In L. Tomei (Ed.), *Advancing education with information communication technologies: Facilitating new trends* (pp. 305–319). Hershey, PA: Information Science Reference.

Lawrence, H. R. (2013). Women's roles: Do they exist in a technological workforce? In S. Wang, & T. Hartsell (Eds.), *Technology integration and foundations for effective leadership* (pp. 57–69). Hershey, PA: Information Science Reference.

Lin, T., Wu, Z., Tang, N., & Wu, S. (2013). Exploring the effects of display characteristics on presence and emotional responses of game players. *International Journal of Technology and Human Interaction, 9*(1), 50–63. doi:10.4018/jthi.2013010104

Linares, K., Subrahmanyam, K., Cheng, R., & Guan, S. A. (2011). A second life within second life: Are Virtual world users creating new selves and new lives? *International Journal of Cyber Behavior, Psychology and Learning, 1*(3), 50–71. doi:10.4018/ijcbpl.2011070104

Linares, K., Subrahmanyam, K., Cheng, R., & Guan, S. A. (2013). A second life within second life: Are virtual world users creating new selves and new lives? In R. Zheng (Ed.), *Evolving psychological and educational perspectives on cyber behavior* (pp. 205–228). Hershey, PA: Information Science Reference.

Livermore, C. R., & Somers, T. M. (2011). Gender, power, and edating. *International Journal of E-Politics, 2*(2), 74–88. doi:10.4018/jep.2011040105

Lorentz, P. (2012). Is there a virtual socialization by acting virtual identities? Case study: The Sims. In N. Zagalo, L. Morgado, & A. Boa-Ventura (Eds.), *Virtual worlds and metaverse platforms: New communication and identity paradigms* (pp. 206–218). Hershey, PA: Information Science Reference.

Losh, S. C. (2013). American digital divides: Generation, education, gender, and ethnicity in American digital divides. In I. Association (Ed.), *Digital literacy: Concepts, methodologies, tools, and applications* (pp. 932–958). Hershey, PA: Information Science Reference.

Ludi, S. (2012). Educational robotics and broadening participation in STEM for underrepresented student groups. In B. Barker, G. Nugent, N. Grandgenett, & V. Adamchuk (Eds.), *Robots in K-12 education: A new technology for learning* (pp. 343–361). Hershey, PA: Information Science Reference. doi:10.4018/978-1-4666-0182-6.ch017

Lund, K., Lochrie, M., & Coulton, P. (2012). Designing scalable location based games that encourage emergent behaviour. *International Journal of Ambient Computing and Intelligence*, *4*(4), 1–20. doi:10.4018/jaci.2012100101

Ma, M., & Oikonomou, A. (2010). Network architectures and data management for massively multiplayer online games. *International Journal of Grid and High Performance Computing*, *2*(4), 40–50. doi:10.4018/jghpc.2010100104

Macgregor, R., Hyland, P. N., & Harvey, C. (2012). The effect of gender on associations between driving forces to adopt ICT and benefits derived from that adoption in medical practices in Australia. In C. Romm Livermore (Ed.), *Gender and social computing: Interactions, differences and relationships* (pp. 120–142). Hershey, PA: Information Science Publishing.

Macgregor, R., Hyland, P. N., & Harvey, C. (2013). The effect of gender on associations between driving forces to adopt ICT and benefits derived from that adoption in medical practices in Australia. In I. Association (Ed.), *Small and medium enterprises: Concepts, methodologies, tools, and applications* (pp. 1186–1207). Hershey, PA: Business Science Reference.

MacGregor, R. C., Hyland, P. N., & Harvie, C. (2011). The effect of gender on perceived benefits of and drivers for ICT adoption in Australian medical practices. *International Journal of E-Politics*, *2*(1), 68–85. doi:10.4018/jep.2011010105

Maguire, K. C. (2011). Is it a boy or a girl? Anonymity and gender in computer-mediated interactions. In I. Management Association (Ed.), Virtual communities: Concepts, methodologies, tools and applications (pp. 1590-1610). Hershey, PA: Information Science Reference. doi: doi:10.4018/978-1-60960-100-3.ch501

Mano, R. S. (2013). Gender effects on managerial communication and work performance. *International Journal of Cyber Behavior, Psychology and Learning*, *3*(2), 34–46. doi:10.4018/ijcbpl.2013040103

Manuel, A. (2010). The career challenge of the gendered academic research culture: Can internet technologies make a difference? In A. Cater-Steel, & E. Cater (Eds.), *Women in engineering, science and technology: Education and career challenges* (pp. 255–279). Hershey, PA: Engineering Science Reference. doi:10.4018/978-1-61520-657-5.ch012

Marache-Francisco, C., & Brangier, E. (2014). The gamification experience: UXD with a gamification background. In K. Blashki, & P. Isaias (Eds.), *Emerging research and trends in interactivity and the human-computer interface* (pp. 205–223). Hershey, PA: Information Science Reference.

Marciano, A. (2011). The role of internet newsgroups in the coming-out process of gay male youth: An Israeli case study. In E. Dunkels, G. Franberg, & C. Hallgren (Eds.), *Youth culture and net culture: Online social practices* (pp. 222–241). Hershey, PA: Information Science Reference.

Maree, D. J., & Maree, M. (2010). Factors contributing to the success of women working in science, engineering and technology (SET) careers. In A. Cater-Steel, & E. Cater (Eds.), *Women in engineering, science and technology: Education and career challenges* (pp. 183–210). Hershey, PA: Engineering Science Reference. doi:10.4018/978-1-61520-657-5.ch009

Martin, S. (2012). Exploring identity and citizenship in a virtual world. *International Journal of Virtual and Personal Learning Environments*, *3*(4), 53–70. doi:10.4018/jvple.2012100105

Martins, H. F. (2012). The use of a business simulation game in a management course. In M. Cruz-Cunha (Ed.), *Handbook of research on serious games as educational, business and research tools* (pp. 693–707). Hershey, PA: Information Science Reference. doi:10.4018/978-1-4666-0149-9.ch035

Masrom, M., & Ismail, Z. (2010). Women access to computers and internet: A Malaysian perspective. In A. Cater-Steel, & E. Cater (Eds.), *Women in engineering, science and technology: Education and career challenges* (pp. 211–231). Hershey, PA: Engineering Science Reference. doi:10.4018/978-1-61520-657-5.ch010

Mattingly, D. J. (2012). Indian women working in call centers: Sites of resistance? In R. Pande, & T. Van der Weide (Eds.), *Globalization, technology diffusion and gender disparity: Social impacts of ICTs* (pp. 156–168). Hershey, PA: Information Science Reference. doi:10.4018/978-1-4666-0020-1.ch014

McDaniel, R., & Fiore, S. M. (2010). Applied ethics game design: Some practical guidelines. In K. Schrier, & D. Gibson (Eds.), *Ethics and game design: Teaching values through play* (pp. 236–254). Hershey, PA: Information Science Reference. doi:10.4018/978-1-61520-845-6.ch015

McDonald, J., Loch, B., & Cater-Steel, A. (2010). Go WEST - Supporting women in engineering, science and technology: An Australian higher education case study. In A. Cater-Steel, & E. Cater (Eds.), *Women in engineering, science and technology: Education and career challenges* (pp. 118–136). Hershey, PA: Engineering Science Reference. doi:10.4018/978-1-61520-657-5.ch006

McKinnell Jacobson, C. (2011). Virtual worlds and the 3-D internet. In I. Management Association (Ed.), Virtual communities: Concepts, methodologies, tools and applications (pp. 1855-1879). Hershey, PA: Information Science Reference. doi: doi:10.4018/978-1-60960-100-3.ch520

McLean, L., & Griffiths, M. D. (2013). Gamers' attitudes towards victims of crime: An interview study using vignettes. *International Journal of Cyber Behavior, Psychology and Learning*, *3*(2), 13–33. doi:10.4018/ijcbpl.2013040102

Mellström, U. (2010). New gender relations in the transforming IT-industry of Malaysia. In S. Booth, S. Goodman, & G. Kirkup (Eds.), *Gender issues in learning and working with information technology: Social constructs and cultural contexts* (pp. 25–47). Hershey, PA: Information Science Reference. doi:10.4018/978-1-61520-813-5.ch002

Mena, R. J. (2014). The quest for a massively multiplayer online game that teaches physics. In T. Connolly, T. Hainey, E. Boyle, G. Baxter, & P. Moreno-Ger (Eds.), *Psychology, pedagogy, and assessment in serious games* (pp. 292–316). Hershey, PA: Information Science Reference.

Mendes, R. (2010). Glass ceilings in Portugal? An analysis of the gender wage gap using a quantile regression approach. *International Journal of Human Capital and Information Technology Professionals*, *1*(2), 1–18. doi:10.4018/jhcitp.2010040101

Miller, K. B. (2013). Gaming as a woman: Gender difference issues in video games and learning. In S. D'Agustino (Ed.), *Immersive environments, augmented realities, and virtual worlds: Assessing future trends in education* (pp. 106–122). Hershey, PA: Information Science Reference.

Milolidakis, G., Kimble, C., & Grenier, C. (2011). A practice-based analysis of social interaction in a massively multiplayer online gaming environment. In M. Cruz-Cunha, V. Varvalho, & P. Tavares (Eds.), *Business, technological, and social dimensions of computer games: Multidisciplinary developments* (pp. 32–48). Hershey, PA: Information Science Reference. doi:10.4018/978-1-60960-567-4.ch003

Mitgutsch, K. (2011). Playful learning experiences: Meaningful learning patterns in players' biographies. *International Journal of Gaming and Computer-Mediated Simulations, 3*(3), 54–68. doi:10.4018/jgcms.2011070104

Modesto, F. A. (2012). Virtual worlds innovation with open wonderland. In M. Cruz-Cunha (Ed.), *Handbook of research on serious games as educational, business and research tools* (pp. 250–268). Hershey, PA: Information Science Reference. doi:10.4018/978-1-4666-0149-9.ch013

Mora-García, A. M., & Merelo-Guervós, J. J. (2012). Evolving bots' ai in Unreal. In A. Kumar, J. Etheredge, & A. Boudreaux (Eds.), *Algorithmic and architectural gaming design: Implementation and development* (pp. 134–157). Hershey, PA: Information Science Reference. doi:10.4018/978-1-4666-1634-9.ch007

Moro, M. M., Weber, T., & Freitas, C. M. (2012). Women in Brazilian CS research community: The state-of-the-art. In I. Management Association (Ed.), Computer engineering: Concepts, methodologies, tools and applications (pp. 1824-1839). Hershey, PA: Engineering Science Reference. doi:doi:10.4018/978-1-61350-456-7.ch801

Mörtberg, C., & Elovaara, P. (2010). Attaching people and technology: Between E and government. In S. Booth, S. Goodman, & G. Kirkup (Eds.), *Gender issues in learning and working with information technology: Social constructs and cultural contexts* (pp. 83–98). Hershey, PA: Information Science Reference. doi:10.4018/978-1-61520-813-5.ch005

Mosca, I. (2013). From fiction to reality and back: Ontology of ludic simulations. *International Journal of Gaming and Computer-Mediated Simulations, 5*(1), 13–31. doi:10.4018/jgcms.2013010102

Moseley, A. (2012). An alternate reality for education? Lessons to be learned from online immersive games. *International Journal of Game-Based Learning, 2*(3), 32–50. doi:10.4018/ijgbl.2012070103

Moseley, A. (2014). A case for integration: Assessment and games. In T. Connolly, T. Hainey, E. Boyle, G. Baxter, & P. Moreno-Ger (Eds.), *Psychology, pedagogy, and assessment in serious games* (pp. 342–356). Hershey, PA: Information Science Reference.

Murphy, J., & Zagal, J. (2011). Videogames and the ethics of care. *International Journal of Gaming and Computer-Mediated Simulations, 3*(3), 69–81. doi:10.4018/jgcms.2011070105

Mutaza, S., & Sami, L. K. (2012). Gender aspects in the use of ICT in information centres. In R. Pande, & T. Van der Weide (Eds.), *Globalization, technology diffusion and gender disparity: Social impacts of ICTs* (pp. 129–137). Hershey, PA: Information Science Reference. doi:10.4018/978-1-4666-0020-1.ch011

Nezlek, G., & DeHondt, G. (2011). Gender wage differentials in information systems: 1991 – 2008 a quantitative analysis. *International Journal of Social and Organizational Dynamics in IT, 1*(1), 13–29. doi:10.4018/ijsodit.2011010102

Nezlek, G., & DeHondt, G. (2013). Gender wage differentials in information systems: 1991 – 2008 a quantitative analysis. In B. Medlin (Ed.), *Integrations of technology utilization and social dynamics in organizations* (pp. 31–47). Hershey, PA: Information Science Reference.

Ng, E. M. (2011). Exploring the gender differences of student teachers when using an educational game to learn programming concepts. In P. Felicia (Ed.), *Handbook of research on improving learning and motivation through educational games: Multidisciplinary approaches* (pp. 550–566). Hershey, PA: Information Science Reference. doi:10.4018/978-1-60960-495-0.ch026

Nikolaos, P. (2013). A conceptual "cybernetic" methodology for organizing and managing the e-learning process through [D-] CIVEs: The case of "second life". In P. Renna (Ed.), Production and manufacturing system management: Coordination approaches and multi-site planning (pp. 242-277). Hershey, PA: Engineering Science Reference. doi:doi:10.4018/978-1-4666-2098-8.ch013

Nitsche, M. (2012). The players' dimension: From virtual to physical. In N. Zagalo, L. Morgado, & A. Boa-Ventura (Eds.), *Virtual worlds and metaverse platforms: New communication and identity paradigms* (pp. 181–191). Hershey, PA: Information Science Reference.

Nordlinger, J. (2010). Virtual ethics: Ethics and massively multiplayer online games. In K. Schrier, & D. Gibson (Eds.), *Ethics and game design: Teaching values through play* (pp. 102–108). Hershey, PA: Information Science Reference. doi:10.4018/978-1-61520-845-6.ch007

Nsibirano, R., Kabonesa, C., & Madanda, A. (2012). Gender symbolism and technology uptake: A literature review. In R. Pande, & T. Van der Weide (Eds.), *Globalization, technology diffusion and gender disparity: Social impacts of ICTs* (pp. 120–127). Hershey, PA: Information Science Reference. doi:10.4018/978-1-4666-0020-1.ch010

Okafor, C., & Amalu, R. (2012). Motivational patterns and the performance of entrepreneurs: An empirical study of women entrepreneurs in south-west Nigeria. *International Journal of Applied Behavioral Economics*, *1*(1), 29–40. doi:doi:10.4018/ijabe.2012010103

Okdie, B. M., Guadagno, R. E., Petrova, P. K., & Shreves, W. B. (2013). Social influence online: A tale of gender differences in the effectiveness of authority cues. *International Journal of Interactive Communication Systems and Technologies*, *3*(1), 20–31. doi:10.4018/ijicst.2013010102

Ortiz, J. A. (2011). Knowing the game: A review of videogames and entertainment software in the United States - Trends and future research opportunities. In M. Cruz-Cunha, V. Varvalho, & P. Tavares (Eds.), *Business, technological, and social dimensions of computer games: Multidisciplinary developments* (pp. 293–311). Hershey, PA: Information Science Reference. doi:10.4018/978-1-60960-567-4.ch018

Ortiz de Gortari, A. B., Aronsson, K., & Griffiths, M. (2011). Game transfer phenomena in video game playing: A qualitative interview study. *International Journal of Cyber Behavior, Psychology and Learning*, *1*(3), 15–33. doi:10.4018/ijcbpl.2011070102

Orvalho, V. C., & Orvalho, J. (2011). Character animation: Past, present and future. In M. Cruz-Cunha, V. Varvalho, & P. Tavares (Eds.), *Business, technological, and social dimensions of computer games: Multidisciplinary developments* (pp. 49–64). Hershey, PA: Information Science Reference. doi:10.4018/978-1-60960-567-4.ch004

Özdemir, E. (2012). Gender and e-marketing: The role of gender differences in online purchasing behaviors. In C. Romm Livermore (Ed.), *Gender and social computing: Interactions, differences and relationships* (pp. 72–86). Hershey, PA: Information Science Publishing. doi:10.4018/978-1-4666-1598-4.ch044

Pande, R. (2012). Gender gaps and information and communication technology: A case study of India. In R. Pande, & T. Van der Weide (Eds.), *Globalization, technology diffusion and gender disparity: Social impacts of ICTs* (pp. 277–291). Hershey, PA: Information Science Reference. doi:10.4018/978-1-4666-0020-1.ch022

Pande, R. (2013). Gender gaps and information and communication technology: A case study of India. In I. Association (Ed.), *Digital literacy: Concepts, methodologies, tools, and applications* (pp. 1425–1439). Hershey, PA: Information Science Reference.

Pannicke, D., Repschläger, J., & Zarnekow, R. (2011). Business opportunities in social virtual worlds. In M. Cruz-Cunha, V. Varvalho, & P. Tavares (Eds.), *Business, technological, and social dimensions of computer games: Multidisciplinary developments* (pp. 432–447). Hershey, PA: Information Science Reference. doi:10.4018/978-1-60960-567-4.ch026

Parker, J. R., & Becker, K. (2013). The simulation-game controversy: What is a ludic simulation? *International Journal of Gaming and Computer-Mediated Simulations*, 5(1), 1–12. doi:10.4018/jgcms.2013010101

Phelps, D. (2010). What videogames have to teach us about screenworld and the humanistic ethos. In K. Schrier, & D. Gibson (Eds.), *Ethics and game design: Teaching values through play* (pp. 125–149). Hershey, PA: Information Science Reference. doi:10.4018/978-1-61520-845-6.ch009

Poggi, A. (2011). Enhancing online games with agents. In M. Cruz-Cunha, V. Varvalho, & P. Tavares (Eds.), *Business, technological, and social dimensions of computer games: Multidisciplinary developments* (pp. 65–80). Hershey, PA: Information Science Reference. doi:10.4018/978-1-60960-567-4.ch005

Pole, A. (2012). Would Elizabeth Cady Stanton blog?: Women bloggers, politics, and political participation. In C. Romm Livermore (Ed.), *Gender and social computing: Interactions, differences and relationships* (pp. 183–199). Hershey, PA: Information Science Publishing.

Poster, W. R. (2012). The case of the U.S. mother / cyberspy / undercover Iraqi militant: Or, how global women have been incorporated in the technological war on terror. In R. Pande, & T. Van der Weide (Eds.), *Globalization, technology diffusion and gender disparity: Social impacts of ICTs* (pp. 247–260). Hershey, PA: Information Science Reference. doi:10.4018/978-1-4666-0020-1.ch020

Pragnell, C., & Gatzidis, C. (2012). Addiction in World of Warcraft: A virtual ethnography study. In H. Yang, & S. Yuen (Eds.), *Handbook of research on practices and outcomes in virtual worlds and environments* (pp. 54–74). Hershey, PA: Information Science Publishing.

Prakash, N. (2012). ICT and women empowerment in a rural setting in India. In R. Pande, & T. Van der Weide (Eds.), *Globalization, technology diffusion and gender disparity: Social impacts of ICTs* (pp. 15–24). Hershey, PA: Information Science Reference. doi:10.4018/978-1-4666-0020-1.ch002

Prescott, J., & Bogg, J. (2010). The computer games industry: Women's experiences of work role in a male dominated environment. In A. Cater-Steel, & E. Cater (Eds.), *Women in engineering, science and technology: Education and career challenges* (pp. 138–158). Hershey, PA: Engineering Science Reference. doi:10.4018/978-1-61520-657-5.ch007

Prescott, J., & Bogg, J. (2013). Career development, occupational choice, and organizational culture: Societal expectations, constraints, and embedded practices. In *Gendered occupational differences in science, engineering, and technology careers* (pp. 136–165). Hershey, PA: Information Science Reference.

Prescott, J., & Bogg, J. (2013). Career promoters: A gender divide. In *Gendered occupational differences in science, engineering, and technology careers* (pp. 216–238). Hershey, PA: Information Science Reference.

Prescott, J., & Bogg, J. (2013). Engendered workplace segregation: Work is still essentially a male domain. In *Gendered occupational differences in science, engineering, and technology careers* (pp. 1–25). Hershey, PA: Information Science Reference.

Prescott, J., & Bogg, J. (2013). Final thoughts and concluding comments. In *Gendered occupational differences in science, engineering, and technology careers* (pp. 239–263). Hershey, PA: Information Science Reference.

Prescott, J., & Bogg, J. (2013). Male dominated industries: Jobs for the boys. In *Gendered occupational differences in science, engineering, and technology careers* (pp. 26–63). Hershey, PA: Information Science Reference.

Prescott, J., & Bogg, J. (2013). Progression aspirations and leadership. In *Gendered occupational differences in science, engineering, and technology careers* (pp. 192–215). Hershey, PA: Information Science Reference.

Prescott, J., & Bogg, J. (2013). Self, career, and gender issues: A complex interplay of internal/external factors. In *Gendered occupational differences in science, engineering, and technology careers* (pp. 79–111). Hershey, PA: Information Science Reference.

Prescott, J., & Bogg, J. (2013). Stereotype, attitudes, and identity: Gendered expectations and behaviors. In *Gendered occupational differences in science, engineering, and technology careers* (pp. 112–135). Hershey, PA: Information Science Reference.

Prescott, J., & Bogg, J. (2013). The computer games industry: New industry, same old issues. In *Gendered occupational differences in science, engineering, and technology careers* (pp. 64–77). Hershey, PA: Information Science Reference.

Prescott, J., & Bogg, J. (2013). Work life balance issues: The choice, or women's lack of it. In *Gendered occupational differences in science, engineering, and technology careers* (pp. 167–191). Hershey, PA: Information Science Reference.

Preston, J. A., Chastine, J., O'Donnell, C., Tseng, T., & MacIntyre, B. (2012). Game jams: Community, motivations, and learning among jammers. *International Journal of Game-Based Learning, 2*(3), 51–70. doi:10.4018/ijgbl.2012070104

Quan, J. J., Dattero, R., Galup, S. D., & Dhariwal, K. (2011). The determinants of information technology wages. *International Journal of Human Capital and Information Technology Professionals, 2*(1), 48–65. doi:10.4018/jhcitp.2011010104

Quesenberry, J. L. (2012). Re-examining the career anchor model: An investigation of career values and motivations among women in the information technology profession. In R. Pande, & T. Van der Weide (Eds.), *Globalization, technology diffusion and gender disparity: Social impacts of ICTs* (pp. 169–183). Hershey, PA: Information Science Reference. doi:10.4018/978-1-4666-0020-1.ch015

Quick, J. M., Atkinson, R. K., & Lin, L. (2012). Empirical taxonomies of gameplay enjoyment: Personality and video game preference. *International Journal of Game-Based Learning, 2*(3), 11–31. doi:10.4018/ijgbl.2012070102

Quick, J. M., Atkinson, R. K., & Lin, L. (2012). The gameplay enjoyment model. *International Journal of Gaming and Computer-Mediated Simulations, 4*(4), 64–80. doi:10.4018/jgcms.2012100105

Raditloaneng, W. (2012). Gender equality as a development factor in the application of ICT for agro-forestry. In R. Lekoko, & L. Semali (Eds.), *Cases on developing countries and ICT integration: Rural community development* (pp. 123–133). Hershey, PA: Information Science Reference.

Rafi, M. S. (2010). The sociolinguistics of SMS ways to identify gender boundaries. In R. Taiwo (Ed.), *Handbook of research on discourse behavior and digital communication: Language structures and social interaction* (pp. 104–111). Hershey, PA: Information Science Reference. doi:10.4018/978-1-61520-773-2.ch006

Rajesh, M. N. (2012). Virtual tourism as a new form of oppression against women. In R. Pande, & T. Van der Weide (Eds.), *Globalization, technology diffusion and gender disparity: Social impacts of ICTs* (pp. 200–209). Hershey, PA: Information Science Reference. doi:10.4018/978-1-4666-0020-1.ch017

Rambo, K., & Liu, K. (2011). Culture-sensitive virtual e-commerce design with reference to female consumers in Saudi Arabia. In B. Ciaramitaro (Ed.), *Virtual worlds and e-commerce: Technologies and applications for building customer relationships* (pp. 267–289). Hershey, PA: Business Science Reference.

Ratan, R. (2013). Self-presence, explicated: Body, emotion, and identity extension into the virtual self. In R. Luppicini (Ed.), *Handbook of research on technoself: Identity in a technological society* (pp. 322–336). Hershey, PA: Information Science Reference.

Reimann, D. (2012). Shaping interactive media with the sewing machine: Smart textile as an artistic context to engage girls in technology and engineering education. In I. Management Association (Ed.), Computer engineering: Concepts, methodologies, tools and applications (pp. 1342-1351). Hershey, PA: Engineering Science Reference. doi:doi:10.4018/978-1-61350-456-7.ch517

Reiners, T., & Wood, L. C. (2013). Immersive virtual environments to facilitate authentic education in logistics and supply chain management. In Y. Kats (Ed.), *Learning management systems and instructional design: Best practices in online education* (pp. 323–343). Hershey, PA: Information Science Reference. doi:10.4018/978-1-4666-3930-0.ch017

Rensfeldt, A. B., & Riomar, S. (2010). Gendered distance education spaces: "Keeping women in place"? In S. Booth, S. Goodman, & G. Kirkup (Eds.), *Gender issues in learning and working with information technology: Social constructs and cultural contexts* (pp. 192–208). Hershey, PA: Information Science Reference. doi:10.4018/978-1-61520-813-5.ch011

Resmi, A. T., & Kamalanabhan, T. J. (2013). Confirmatory factor analysis and alternate test models for impression management in SMEs: A gender based study. *International Journal of Information Systems and Supply Chain Management*, 6(2), 72–87. doi:10.4018/jisscm.2013040106

Rhima, T. E. (2010). Gender and ICT policy. In E. Adomi (Ed.), *Frameworks for ICT policy: Government, social and legal issues* (pp. 164–181). Hershey, PA: Information Science Reference. doi:10.4018/978-1-61692-012-8.ch011

Rodrigues, R. G., Pinheiro, P. G., & Barbosa, J. (2012). Online playability: The social dimension to the virtual world. In M. Cruz-Cunha (Ed.), *Handbook of research on serious games as educational, business and research tools* (pp. 391–421). Hershey, PA: Information Science Reference. doi:10.4018/978-1-4666-0149-9.ch021

Romm-Livermore, C., Somers, T. M., Setzekorn, K., & King, A. L. (2012). How e-daters behave online: Theory and empirical observations. In C. Romm Livermore (Ed.), *Gender and social computing: Interactions, differences and relationships* (pp. 236–256). Hershey, PA: Information Science Publishing.

Rommes, E. (2010). Heteronormativity revisited: Adolescents' educational choices, sexuality and soaps. In S. Booth, S. Goodman, & G. Kirkup (Eds.), *Gender issues in learning and working with information technology: Social constructs and cultural contexts* (pp. 150–172). Hershey, PA: Information Science Reference. doi:10.4018/978-1-61520-813-5.ch009

Rosas, O. V., & Dhen, G. (2012). One self to rule them all: A critical discourse analysis of French-speaking players' identity construction in World of Warcraft. In N. Zagalo, L. Morgado, & A. Boa-Ventura (Eds.), *Virtual worlds and metaverse platforms: New communication and identity paradigms* (pp. 337–366). Hershey, PA: Information Science Reference.

Rose, L. (2012). Social networks, online technologies, and virtual learning: (Re)structuring oppression and hierarchies in academia. In N. Ekekwe, & N. Islam (Eds.), *Disruptive technologies, innovation and global redesign: Emerging implications* (pp. 266–279). Hershey, PA: Information Science Reference. doi:10.4018/978-1-4666-0134-5.ch014

Rowan, L., & Bigum, C. (2011). Reassembling the problem of the under-representation of girls in IT courses. In A. Tatnall (Ed.), *Actor-network theory and technology innovation: Advancements and new concepts* (pp. 208–222). Hershey, PA: Information Science Reference.

Russo, M. R., & Bryan, V. C. (2013). Technology, the 21st century workforce, and the construct of social justice. In V. Wang (Ed.), *Handbook of research on technologies for improving the 21st century workforce: Tools for lifelong learning* (pp. 56–75). Hershey, PA: Information Science Publishing.

Saadé, R. G., Kira, D., & Otrakji, C. A. (2012). Gender differences in interface type task analysis. *International Journal of Information Systems and Social Change*, *3*(2), 1–23. doi:10.4018/jissc.2012040101

Sadowska, N. M. (2010). Commerce and gender: Generating interactive spaces for female online user. In T. Dumova, & R. Fiordo (Eds.), *Handbook of research on social interaction technologies and collaboration software: Concepts and trends* (pp. 245–256). Hershey, PA: Information Science Reference.

Salminen-Karlsson, M. (2010). Computer courses in adult education in a gender perspective. In S. Booth, S. Goodman, & G. Kirkup (Eds.), *Gender issues in learning and working with information technology: Social constructs and cultural contexts* (pp. 209–230). Hershey, PA: Information Science Reference. doi:10.4018/978-1-61520-813-5.ch012

San Chee, Y., Gwee, S., & Tan, E. M. (2011). Learning to become citizens by enacting governorship in the statecraft curriculum: An evaluation of learning outcomes. *International Journal of Gaming and Computer-Mediated Simulations*, *3*(2), 1–27. doi:10.4018/jgcms.2011040101

Sánchez-Apellániz, M., Núñez, M., & Charlo-Molina, M. J. (2012). Women and globalization. In C. Wankel, & S. Malleck (Eds.), *Ethical models and applications of globalization: Cultural, socio-political and economic perspectives* (pp. 119–140). Hershey, PA: Business Science Reference.

Sappleton, N. (2011). Overcoming the segregation/stereotyping dilemma: Computer mediated communication for business women and professionals. *International Journal of E-Politics*, *2*(2), 18–36. doi:10.4018/jep.2011040102

Sappleton, N. (2012). Overcoming the segregation/stereotyping dilemma: Computer mediated communication for business women and professionals. In C. Romm Livermore (Ed.), *Gender and social computing: Interactions, differences and relationships* (pp. 162–182). Hershey, PA: Information Science Publishing.

Sauvé, L., Villardier, L., & Probst, W. (2010). Online multiplayer games: A powerful tool for learning communication and teamwork. In D. Kaufman, & L. Sauvé (Eds.), *Educational gameplay and simulation environments: Case studies and lessons learned* (pp. 175–194). Hershey, PA: Information Science Reference. doi:10.4018/978-1-61520-731-2.ch012

Sawyer, B. (2011). Research essay: What will serious games of the future look like? *International Journal of Gaming and Computer-Mediated Simulations*, *3*(3), 82–90. doi:10.4018/jgcms.2011070106

Schulz, H. M., & Eastin, M. S. (2010). An opportunity for in-game ad placement: The history of the video game industry interpreted through the meaning lifecycle. In M. Eastin, T. Daugherty, & N. Burns (Eds.), *Handbook of research on digital media and advertising: User generated content consumption* (pp. 480–490). Hershey, PA: Information Science Reference. doi:10.4018/978-1-60566-792-8.ch024

Sedehi, H., & Baleani, F. (2012). Business interactive game business interactive game (BIG): An innovative game to support enterprise management training. In M. Cruz-Cunha (Ed.), *Handbook of research on serious games as educational, business and research tools* (pp. 859–872). Hershey, PA: Information Science Reference. doi:10.4018/978-1-4666-0149-9.ch044

Sefyrin, J. (2010). "For me it doesn't matter where I put my information": Enactments of agency, mutual learning, and gender in IT design. In S. Booth, S. Goodman, & G. Kirkup (Eds.), *Gender issues in learning and working with information technology: Social constructs and cultural contexts* (pp. 65–82). Hershey, PA: Information Science Reference. doi:10.4018/978-1-61520-813-5.ch004

Sell, A., de Reuver, M., Walden, P., & Carlsson, C. (2012). Context, gender and intended use of mobile messaging, entertainment and social media services. *International Journal of Systems and Service-Oriented Engineering*, *3*(1), 1–15. doi:10.4018/jssoe.2012010101

Seth, N., & Patnayakuni, R. (2012). Online matrimonial sites and the transformation of arranged marriage in India. In C. Romm Livermore (Ed.), *Gender and social computing: Interactions, differences and relationships* (pp. 272–295). Hershey, PA: Information Science Publishing.

Sevo, R., & Chubin, D. E. (2010). Bias literacy: A review of concepts in research on gender discrimination and the U.S. context. In A. Cater-Steel, & E. Cater (Eds.), *Women in engineering, science and technology: Education and career challenges* (pp. 21–54). Hershey, PA: Engineering Science Reference. doi:10.4018/978-1-61520-657-5.ch002

Shaw, A. (2011). Toward an ethic of representation: Ethics and the representation of marginalized groups in videogames. In K. Schrier, & D. Gibson (Eds.), *Designing games for ethics: Models, techniques and frameworks* (pp. 159–177). Hershey, PA: Information Science Reference.

Shin, N., Norris, C., & Soloway, E. (2011). Mobile gaming environment: Learning and motivational effects. In P. Felicia (Ed.), *Handbook of research on improving learning and motivation through educational games: Multidisciplinary approaches* (pp. 467–481). Hershey, PA: Information Science Reference. doi:10.4018/978-1-60960-495-0.ch022

Shirk, S., Arreola, V., Wobig, C., & Russell, K. (2012). Girls' e-mentoring in science, engineering, and technology based at the University of Illinois at Chicago women in science and engineering (WISE) program. In I. Management Association (Ed.), Computer engineering: concepts, methodologies, tools and applications (pp. 1144-1163). Hershey, PA: Engineering Science Reference. doi:doi:10.4018/978-1-61350-456-7.ch505

Sicart, M. (2010). Values between systems: Designing ethical gameplay. In K. Schrier, & D. Gibson (Eds.), *Ethics and game design: Teaching values through play* (pp. 1–15). Hershey, PA: Information Science Reference. doi:10.4018/978-1-61520-845-6.ch001

Simão de Vasconcellos, M., & Soares de Araújo, I. (2013). Massively multiplayer online role playing games for health communication in Brazil. In K. Bredl, & W. Bösche (Eds.), *Serious games and virtual worlds in education, professional development, and healthcare* (pp. 294–312). Hershey, PA: Information Science Reference. doi:10.4018/978-1-4666-3673-6.ch018

Simkins, D. (2010). Playing with ethics: Experiencing new ways of being in RPGs. In K. Schrier, & D. Gibson (Eds.), *Ethics and game design: Teaching values through play* (pp. 69–84). Hershey, PA: Information Science Reference. doi:10.4018/978-1-61520-845-6.ch005

Stacey, P., & Nandhakumar, J. (2011). Emotional journeys in game design teams. In M. Cruz-Cunha, V. Varvalho, & P. Tavares (Eds.), *Business, technological, and social dimensions of computer games: Multidisciplinary developments* (pp. 220–236). Hershey, PA: Information Science Reference. doi:10.4018/978-1-60960-567-4.ch014

Staines, D. (2010). Videogames and moral pedagogy: A neo-Kohlbergian approach. In K. Schrier, & D. Gibson (Eds.), *Ethics and game design: Teaching values through play* (pp. 35–51). Hershey, PA: Information Science Reference. doi:10.4018/978-1-61520-845-6.ch003

Starosky, P., & Pereira, M. D. (2013). Role-playing game as a pedagogical proposition for story co-construction: A Brazilian experience with deaf individuals in an educational context. In C. Gonzalez (Ed.), *Student usability in educational software and games: Improving experiences* (pp. 274–292). Hershey, PA: Information Science Reference.

Steinkuehler, C., & Johnson, B. Z. (2011). Computational literacy in online games: The social life of mods. In R. Ferdig (Ed.), *Discoveries in gaming and computer-mediated simulations: New interdisciplinary applications* (pp. 218–231). Hershey, PA: Information Science Reference. doi:10.4018/978-1-60960-565-0.ch012

Surgevil, O., & Özbilgin, M. F. (2012). Women in information communication technologies. In C. Romm Livermore (Ed.), *Gender and social computing: Interactions, differences and relationships* (pp. 87–97). Hershey, PA: Information Science Publishing.

Švelch, J. (2010). The good, the bad, and the player: The challenges to moral engagement in single-player avatar-based video games. In K. Schrier, & D. Gibson (Eds.), *Ethics and game design: Teaching values through play* (pp. 52–68). Hershey, PA: Information Science Reference. doi:10.4018/978-1-61520-845-6.ch004

Swain, C. (2011). Culturally responsive games and simulations. In I. Management Association (Ed.), Gaming and simulations: Concepts, methodologies, tools and applications (pp. 1298-1312). Hershey, PA: Information Science Reference. doi: doi:10.4018/978-1-60960-195-9.ch504

Swim, J., & Barker, L. (2012). Pathways into a gendered occupation: Brazilian women in IT. *International Journal of Social and Organizational Dynamics in IT*, 2(4), 34–51. doi:10.4018/ijsodit.2012100103

Takruri-Rizk, H., Sappleton, N., & Dhar-Bhattacharjee, S. (2010). Progression of UK women engineers: Aids and hurdles. In A. Cater-Steel, & E. Cater (Eds.), *Women in engineering, science and technology: Education and career challenges* (pp. 280–300). Hershey, PA: Engineering Science Reference. doi:10.4018/978-1-61520-657-5.ch013

Tan, S., Baxa, J., & Spackman, M. P. (2010). Effects of built-in audio versus unrelated background music on performance in an adventure role-playing game. *International Journal of Gaming and Computer-Mediated Simulations*, 2(3), 1–23. doi:10.4018/jgcms.2010070101

Tara, S., & Ilavarasan, P. V. (2012). Western work worlds and altering approaches to marriage: An empirical study of women employees of call centers in India. In R. Pande, & T. Van der Weide (Eds.), *Globalization, technology diffusion and gender disparity: Social impacts of ICTs* (pp. 262–276). Hershey, PA: Information Science Reference. doi:10.4018/978-1-4666-0020-1.ch021

Teixeira, P. M., Félix, M. J., & Tavares, P. (2012). Playing with design: The universality of design in game development. In M. Cruz-Cunha (Ed.), *Handbook of research on serious games as educational, business and research tools* (pp. 217–231). Hershey, PA: Information Science Reference. doi:10.4018/978-1-4666-0149-9.ch011

Teng, C., Jeng, S., Chang, H. K., & Wu, S. (2012). Who plays games online? The relationship between gamer personality and online game use. *International Journal of E-Business Research*, 8(4), 1–14. doi:10.4018/jebr.2012100101

Terry, A., & Gomez, R. (2012). Gender and public access ICT. In R. Gomez (Ed.), *Libraries, telecentres, cybercafes and public access to ICT: International comparisons* (pp. 51–64). Hershey, PA: Information Science Publishing.

Thacker, S., & Griffiths, M. D. (2012). An exploratory study of trolling in online video gaming. *International Journal of Cyber Behavior, Psychology and Learning*, 2(4), 17–33. doi:10.4018/ijcbpl.2012100102

Thomas, D. I., & Vlacic, L. B. (2011). Human and virtual beings as equal collaborative partners in computer games. In M. Cruz-Cunha, V. Varvalho, & P. Tavares (Eds.), *Computer games as educational and management tools: Uses and approaches* (pp. 23–51). Hershey, PA: Information Science Reference. doi:10.4018/978-1-60960-569-8.ch003

Toprac, P., & Abdel-Meguid, A. (2011). Causing fear, suspense, and anxiety using sound design in computer games. In M. Grimshaw (Ed.), *Game sound technology and player interaction: Concepts and developments* (pp. 176–191). Hershey, PA: Information Science Reference.

Tran, B. (2012). Gendered technology-based organizations: A view of the glass cliff through the window of the glass ceiling. In D. Jemielniak, & A. Marks (Eds.), *Managing dynamic technology-oriented businesses: High-tech organizations and workplaces* (pp. 253–272). Hershey, PA: Business Science Reference. doi:10.4018/978-1-4666-1836-7.ch015

Tran, B. (2014). Rhetoric of play: Utilizing the gamer factor in selecting and training employees. In T. Connolly, T. Hainey, E. Boyle, G. Baxter, & P. Moreno-Ger (Eds.), *Psychology, pedagogy, and assessment in serious games* (pp. 175–203). Hershey, PA: Information Science Reference.

Trauth, E. M., Quesenberry, J. L., & Huang, H. (2010). Factors influencing career choice for women in the global information technology workforce. In M. Hunter, & F. Tan (Eds.), *Technological advancement in developed and developing countries: Discoveries in global information management* (pp. 23–48). Hershey, PA: Information Science Reference.

Trepte, S., Reinecke, L., & Behr, K. (2011). Playing myself or playing to win? Gamers' strategies of avatar creation in terms of gender and sex. In R. Ferdig (Ed.), *Discoveries in gaming and computer-mediated simulations: New interdisciplinary applications* (pp. 329–352). Hershey, PA: Information Science Reference. doi:10.4018/978-1-60960-565-0.ch019

Tu, C., Yen, C., & Blocher, M. (2011). A study of the relationship between gender and online social presence. *International Journal of Online Pedagogy and Course Design*, *1*(3), 33–49. doi:10.4018/ijopcd.2011070103

Tyagi, A. (2011). Virtual reality and identity crisis—: Implications for individuals and organizations. In K. Malik, & P. Choudhary (Eds.), *Business organizations and collaborative web: Practices, strategies and patterns* (pp. 202–218). Hershey, PA: Information Science Reference. doi:10.4018/978-1-60960-581-0.ch013

Umarov, I., & Mozgovoy, M. (2012). Believable and effective AI agents in virtual worlds: Current state and future perspectives. *International Journal of Gaming and Computer-Mediated Simulations*, *4*(2), 37–59. doi:10.4018/jgcms.2012040103

Ursyn, A. (2014). Challenges in game design. In *Computational solutions for knowledge, art, and entertainment: Information exchange beyond text* (pp. 413–428). Hershey, PA: Information Science Reference.

Uzun, L., Ekin, M. T., & Kartal, E. (2013). The opinions and attitudes of the foreign language learners and teachers related to the traditional and digital games: Age and gender differences. *International Journal of Game-Based Learning*, *3*(2), 91–111. doi:10.4018/ijgbl.2013040106

van de Laar, B., Reuderink, B., Bos, D. P., & Heylen, D. (2010). Evaluating user experience of actual and imagined movement in BCI gaming. *International Journal of Gaming and Computer-Mediated Simulations*, *2*(4), 33–47. doi:10.4018/jgcms.2010100103

van der Weide, T. (2012). A digital (r)evolution to the information age. In R. Pande, & T. Van der Weide (Eds.), *Globalization, technology diffusion and gender disparity: Social impacts of ICTs* (pp. 1–14). Hershey, PA: Information Science Reference. doi:10.4018/978-1-4666-0020-1.ch001

Velazquez, M. (2013). "Come fly with us": Playing with girlhood in the world of pixie hollow. In Y. Baek, & N. Whitton (Eds.), *Cases on digital game-based learning: Methods, models, and strategies* (pp. 1–14). Hershey, PA: Information Science Reference.

Veltri, N. F., Webb, H. W., & Papp, R. (2010). GETSMART: An academic-industry partnership to encourage female participation in science, technology, engineering and math careers. In A. Cater-Steel, & E. Cater (Eds.), *Women in engineering, science and technology: Education and career challenges* (pp. 56–77). Hershey, PA: Engineering Science Reference. doi:10.4018/978-1-61520-657-5.ch003

Vikaros, L., & Degand, D. (2010). Moral development through social narratives and game design. In K. Schrier, & D. Gibson (Eds.), *Ethics and game design: Teaching values through play* (pp. 197–215). Hershey, PA: Information Science Reference. doi:10.4018/978-1-61520-845-6.ch013

Voulgari, I., & Komis, V. (2011). Collaborative learning in massively multiplayer online games: A review of social, cognitive and motivational perspectives. In P. Felicia (Ed.), *Handbook of research on improving learning and motivation through educational games: Multidisciplinary approaches* (pp. 370–394). Hershey, PA: Information Science Reference. doi:10.4018/978-1-60960-495-0.ch018

Wakunuma-Zojer, K. J. (2012). Gender and ICT policy for development and empowerment: A critique of a national ICT policy. In I. Management Association (Ed.), Regional development: Concepts, methodologies, tools, and applications (pp. 1005-1027). Hershey, PA: Information Science Reference. doi: doi:10.4018/978-1-4666-0882-5.ch510

Wallgren, L. G., Leijon, S., & Andersson, K. M. (2013). IT managers' narratives on subordinates' motivation at work: A case study. In A. Mesquita (Ed.), *User perception and influencing factors of technology in everyday life* (pp. 282–297). Hershey, PA: Information Science Reference.

Weber, R., & Shaw, P. (2009). Player types and quality perceptions: A social cognitive theory based model to predict video game playing. *International Journal of Gaming and Computer-Mediated Simulations, 1*(1), 66–89. doi:10.4018/jgcms.2009010105

Wei, Z., & Kramarae, C. (2012). Women, big ideas, and social networking technologies: Hidden assumptions. In R. Pande, & T. Van der Weide (Eds.), *Globalization, technology diffusion and gender disparity: Social impacts of ICTs* (pp. 70–82). Hershey, PA: Information Science Reference. doi:10.4018/978-1-4666-0020-1.ch006

Weiss, A., & Tettegah, S. (2012). World of race war: Race and learning in World of Warcraft. *International Journal of Gaming and Computer-Mediated Simulations, 4*(4), 33–44. doi:10.4018/jgcms.2012100103

White, G. (2010). Increasing the numbers of women in science. In A. Cater-Steel, & E. Cater (Eds.), *Women in engineering, science and technology: Education and career challenges* (pp. 78–95). Hershey, PA: Engineering Science Reference. doi:10.4018/978-1-61520-657-5.ch004

White, M. M. (2012). Designing tutorial modalities and strategies for digital games: Lessons from education. *International Journal of Game-Based Learning, 2*(2), 13–34. doi:10.4018/ijgbl.2012040102

Winter, A. (2010). The smart women – Smart state strategy: A policy on women's participation in science, engineering and technology in Queensland, Australia. In A. Cater-Steel, & E. Cater (Eds.), *Women in engineering, science and technology: Education and career challenges* (pp. 1–20). Hershey, PA: Engineering Science Reference. doi:10.4018/978-1-61520-657-5.ch001

Wolfenstein, M. (2013). Digital structures and the future of online leadership. In S. D'Agustino (Ed.), *Immersive environments, augmented realities, and virtual worlds: Assessing future trends in education* (pp. 257–279). Hershey, PA: Information Science Reference. doi:10.4018/978-1-4666-4502-8.ch096

Woodfield, R. (2012). Gender and employability patterns amongst UK ICT graduates: Investigating the leaky pipeline. In R. Pande, & T. Van der Weide (Eds.), *Globalization, technology diffusion and gender disparity: Social impacts of ICTs* (pp. 184–199). Hershey, PA: Information Science Reference. doi:10.4018/978-1-4666-0020-1.ch016

Yakura, E. K., Soe, L., & Guthrie, R. (2012). Women in IT careers: Investigating support for women in the information technology workforce. In C. Romm Livermore (Ed.), *Gender and social computing: Interactions, differences and relationships* (pp. 35–49). Hershey, PA: Information Science Publishing.

York, A. M., & Nordengren, F. R. (2013). E-learning and web 2.0 case study: The role of gender in contemporary models of health care leadership. In H. Yang, & S. Wang (Eds.), *Cases on formal and informal e-learning environments: Opportunities and practices* (pp. 292–313). Hershey, PA: Information Science Reference.

Yost, E., Handley, D. M., Cotten, S. R., & Winstead, V. (2010). Understanding the links between mentoring and self-efficacy in the new generation of women STEM scholars. In A. Cater-Steel, & E. Cater (Eds.), *Women in engineering, science and technology: Education and career challenges* (pp. 97–117). Hershey, PA: Engineering Science Reference. doi:10.4018/978-1-61520-657-5.ch005

Youngs, G. (2012). Globalization, information and communication technologies, and women's lives. In R. Pande, & T. Van der Weide (Eds.), *Globalization, technology diffusion and gender disparity: Social impacts of ICTs* (pp. 25–34). Hershey, PA: Information Science Reference. doi:10.4018/978-1-4666-0020-1.ch003

Zhang, S., Jiang, H., & Carroll, J. M. (2010). Social identity in Facebook community life. *International Journal of Virtual Communities and Social Networking*, *2*(4), 64–76. doi:10.4018/jvcsn.2010100105

Zhao, Y., Wang, W., & Zhu, Y. (2010). Antecedents of the closeness of human-avatar relationships in a virtual world. *Journal of Database Management*, *21*(2), 41–68. doi:10.4018/jdm.2010040103

Zutshi, A., & Creed, A. (2010). ICT and gender issues in the higher education of entrepreneurs. *International Journal of E-Entrepreneurship and Innovation*, *1*(1), 42–59. doi:10.4018/jeei.2010010103

Compilation of References

Abbate, J. (2012). Recoding gender: Women's changing participation in computing. Cambridge, MA: The MIT Press.

Acker, J. (1990). Hierarchies, jobs, bodies: A theory of gendered organizations. *Gender & Society, 4*(2), 139–158. doi:10.1177/089124390004002002

Agosto, D., Gasson, S., & Atwood, M. (2008). Changing mental models of the IT professions: A theoretical framework. *Journal of Information Technology Education, 7*(1), 205–221.

Allen, I. (2005). Women doctors and their careers: What now? *British Medical Journal, 331*(September), 569–572. doi:10.1136/bmj.331.7516.569 PMID:16150771

Alvermann, D. E., & Hagood, M. C. (2000). Critical media literacy: Research, theory, and practice in new times. *The Journal of Educational Research, 93*(3), 193–205. doi:10.1080/00220670009598707

Amabile, T. M. (1996). *Creativity in context: Update to the social psychology of creativity*. Boulder, CO: Westview.

Angelo, J. (2004). *New study reveals that women over 40 who play online games spend more time playing than male or teenage gamers*. Business Wire.

Arfken, D. E., Bellar, S. L., & Helms, M. H. (2004). The ultimate glass ceiling revisited: The presence of women on corporate boards. *Journal of Business Ethics, 50*, 177–186. doi:10.1023/B:BUSI.0000022125.95758.98

Ashcraft, C., & Breitzman, A. (2012). Who invents IT? Women's participation in information technology patenting (2012 update). Boulder, CO: NCWIT.

Ashcraft, C., & Blithe, S. (2010). *Women in IT: The facts*. National Center for Women & Information Technology.

Athena, S. W. A. N. (2012). *The charter*. Retrieved from http://www.athenaswan.org.uk/content/charter

Auerbach, C. F., & Silverstein, L. B. (2003). *Qualitative data: An introduction to coding and analysis*. New York: NYU Press.

Australian Bureau of Statistics (ABS). (2008). (Cat. No. 8515.0). *Digital game development services*. Canberra, Australia: ABS. Retrieved 15 Mar 2009 from http://www.abs.gov.au/AUSSTATS/abs@.nsf/Lookup/8515.0Main+Features12006-07?OpenDocument

Australian Human Rights Commission. (2013). *Women in male-dominated industries: A toolkit of strategies*. Retrieved 15 July from http://www.humanrights.gov.au/publications/women-male-dominated-industries-toolkit-strategies-2013

Babcock, L., & Laschever, S. (2009). *Women don't ask: Negotiation and the gender divide*. Princeton, NJ: Princeton University Press.

Baer, J. (2011). Why teachers should assume creativity is very domain specific. *International Journal of Creativity and Problem Solving, 21*(2), 57–61.

Bandura, A. (1994). Self-efficacy. In V. S. Ramachaudran (Ed.), *Encyclopedia of human behavior* (Vol. 4, pp. 71-81). New York: Academic Press. (Reprinted in H. Friedman [Ed.], *Encyclopedia of mental health*. San Diego: Academic Press, 1998). Retrieved from http://www.uky.edu/~eushe2/Bandura/BanEncy.html

Bandura, A. (1986). *Social foundations of thought and action: A social cognitive theory*. Englewood Cliffs, NJ: Prentice Hall.

Bandura, A. (2002). Growing primacy of human agency in adaptation and change in the electronic era. *European Psychologist*, 7(1), 2–16. doi:10.1027//1016-9040.7.1.2

Barley, S. R. (1989). Careers, identities and institutions. In M. B. Arthur, D. T. Hall, & B. S. Lawrence (Eds.), *The handbook of career theory* (pp. 41–60). Cambridge, UK: Cambridge University Press. doi:10.1017/CBO9780511625459.005

Barrington, L., & Troske, K. (2001). *Workforce diversity and productivity: An analysis of employer-employee matched data*. Retrieved from http://gatton.uky.edu/Faculty/troske/working_pap/barrington_troske.pdf

Bartol, K. M., & Aspray, W. (2006). The transition of women from the academic world to the IT workplace: A review of the relevant research. In J. M. Cohoon, & W. Aspray (Eds.), *Women and information technology: Research on underrepresentation* (pp. 377–419). Cambridge, MA: MIT Press. doi:10.7551/mitpress/9780262033459.003.0013

Bassett, J. N. (2005). The paradox of diversity management, creativity and innovation. *Creativity and Innovation Management*, 14(2), 169–175. doi:10.1111/j.1467-8691.00337.x

Beasley, B., & Standley, T. C. (2002). Shirts vs. skins: Clothing as an indicator of gender role stereotyping in video games. *Mass Communication & Society*, 5(3), 279–293. doi:10.1207/S15327825MCS0503_3

Beaufays, S. (2003). *Wie werden Wissenschaftler gemacht? Beobachtungen zur wechselseitigen Konstitution von Geschlecht und Wissenschaft*. Bielefeld, Germany: Transcript.

Beaufays, S. (2007). Alltag und Exzellenz - Konstruktionen von Leistung und Geschlecht in der Förderung wissenschaftlichen Nachwuchses. In R. Dackweiler (Ed.), *Willkommen im Club? Frauen und Männer in Eliten* (pp. 145–165). Münster, Germany: Westfälisches Dampfboot.

Beavis, C. (2005). Pretty good for a girl: Gender, identity and computer games. In *Proceedings of DiGRA 2005 Conference: Changing Views – Worlds in Play*.

BECTA. (2008). *How do boys and girls differ in their use of ICT?* (Research report). *BECTA, Coventry*. Retrieved from http://www.vital.ac.uk/community/file.php/872/gender_ict_briefing.pdf

Beekhuyzen, J., & Clayton, K. (2004). ICT career perceptions: Not so geeky? In *Proceedings of the 1st International Conference on Research on Women in IT*, Kuala Lumpur, (pp. 28-30).

Behm-Morawitz, E., & Mastro, D. (2009). The effects of the sexualization of female video game characters on gender stereotyping and female self-concept. *Sex Roles*, 61, 808–823. doi:10.1007/s11199-009-9683-8

Bergman, L. R., Magnusson, D., & El-Khouri, B. M. (2003). *Studying individual development in an interindividual context: A person-oriented approach*. Mahwah, NJ: Erlbaum.

Bettinger, E. P., & Long, B. T. (2005). Do faculty serve as role models? The impact of instructor gender on female students. The American Economic Review, 95(2), 152–157. doi:10.1257/000282805774670149

Betz, N. E., & Hackett, G. (1997). Applications of self-efficacy theory to the career assessment of women. *Journal of Career Assessment*, 5(4), 383–402. doi:10.1177/106907279700500402

Betz, N. E., & Schifano, R. S. (2000). Evaluation of an intervention to increase realistic self-efficacy and interests in college women. *Journal of Vocational Behavior*, 56(1), 35–52. doi:10.1006/jvbe.1999.1690

Beyer, S., & Haller, S. (2006). Gender differences and intragender differences in Computer Science students: Are female CS majors more similar to male CS majors or female nonmajors? *Journal of Women and Minorities in Science and Engineering*, 12(4), 337–365. doi:10.1615/JWomenMinorScienEng.v12.i4.50

Beyer, S., Rynes, K., Perrault, J., Hay, K., & Haller, S. (2003). Gender differences in computer science students. *ACM SIGCSE Bulletin*, 35(1), 49–53. doi:10.1145/792548.611930

Bhaskar, R. (1986). *Scientific realism and human emancipation*. London: Verso.

Birinci Konur, K., Şeyihoğlu, A., Sezen, G., & Tekbiyik, A. (2011). Evaluation of a science camp: Enjoyable discovery of mysterious world. Educational Sciences: Theory and Practice, 11(3), 1602–1607.

Black, R. W., & Reich, S. M. (2013). A sociocultural approach to exploring virtual worlds. In G. Merchant, J. Gillen, J. Marsh, & J. Davies (Eds.), *Virtual literacies: Interactive spaces for children and young people*. New York: Routledge.

Blake, K. (2011). A woman in games: A personal perspective, 1993 – 2010. *International Journal of Gender, Science and Technology, 3*(1).

Blickenstaff, J. (2005). Women and science careers: Leaky pipeline or gender filter? *Gender and Education, 17*(4), 369–386. doi:10.1080/09540250500145072

Blyton, P., & Jenkins, J. (2007). *Key concepts in work.* London: Sage. doi:10.4135/9781446215814

Bonanno, P., & Kommers, P. A. M. (2008). Exploring the influence of gender & gaming competence on attitudes towards using instructional games. *British Journal of Educational Technology, 39*(1), 97–109.

Bouça, M. (2012). Angry birds, uncommitted players. In *Proceedings of DiGRA Nordic 2012 Conference: Local and Global – Games in Culture and Society.*

Bourhis, A., & Mekkaoui, R. (2010). Beyond work-family balance: Are family-friendly organizations more attractive? *Relations Industrielles. Industrial Relations, 65*(1), 98–117. doi:10.7202/039529ar

Brathwaite, B. (2010, March 24). *Women in games from famine to Facebook.* Retrieved from http://www.huffingtonpost.com/brenda-brathwaite/women-in-games-from-famin_b_510928.html

Braun, V., & Clarke, V. (2006). Using thematic analysis in psychology. *Qualitative Research in Psychology, 3*(2), 77–101. doi:10.1191/1478088706qp063oa

Brief, A. P., & Weiss, H. M. (2002). Organizational behavior: Affect in the workplace. *Annual Review of Psychology, 53*, 279–307. doi:10.1146/annurev.psych.53.100901.135156 PMID:11752487

British Academy of Film and Television Arts. (2012). *The BAFTA career pathways survey: Career pathways in film, television and games: A report published by the British Academy of Film and Television Arts.* Retrieved from http://static.bafta.org/files/career-survey-booklet-v8-online-1569.pdf

Briton, D. (2010). The virtual expanses of Canadian popular culture. In B. Beaty, D. Briton, G. Filax, & R. Sullivan (Eds.), *How Canadians communicate III: Contexts of Canadian popular culture* (pp. 319–352). Edmonton, Canada: Athabasca University Press.

Brown, N. C. C., Kölling, M., Crick, T., Jones, S., Humphreys, S., & Sentence, S. (2013.) Bringing computer science back into schools: Lessons from the UK. In *Proceedings of the 44th ACM Technical Symposium on Computer Science Education(SIGCSE '13)* (pp. 269-274). New York: ACM.

Brown, S. D., & Lent, R. W. (1996). A social cognitive framework for career choice counseling. *The Career Development Quarterly, 44*, 354–366. doi:10.1002/j.2161-0045.1996.tb00451.x

Brown, S. G., & Barbosa, G. (2001). Nothing is going to stop me now: Obstacles perceived by low-income women as they become self-sufficient. *Public Health Nursing (Boston, Mass.), 18*, 364–372. doi:10.1046/j.1525-1446.2001.00364.x PMID:11559420

Bruckman, A., Biggers, M., Ericson, B., McKlin, T., Dimond, J., DiSalvo, B., et al. (2009). Georgia computes!: Improving the computing education pipeline. In *Proceedings from SIGCSE '09: The 40th ACM Technical Symposium on Computer Science Education.* Chattanooga, TN: ACM.

Bruni, A., Gherardi, S., & Poggio, B. (2004). Doing gender, doing entrepreneurship: An ethnographic account of intertwined practices. *Gender, Work and Organization, 11*(4), 406–429. doi:10.1111/j.1468-0432.2004.00240.x

Bryce, J., & Rutter, J. (2003). Gender dynamics and the social and spatial organization of computer gaming. *Leisure Studies, 22*, 1–15. doi:10.1080/02614360306571

Burge, J. E., Gannod, G. C., Doyle, M., & Davis, K. C. (2013). Girls on the go: A CS summer camp to attract and inspire female high school students. In *Proceedings from SIGCSE '13: The 44th ACM Technical Symposium on Computer Science Education.* Denver, CO: ACM.

Byrne, B. M. (2001). *Structural equation modelling with AMOS: Basic concepts, applications and programming.* Mahwah, NJ: Lawrence Erlbaum Associates.

Camarda, C. (2012). *A new strategy for stem education and innovative engineering problem solving.* Retrieved from http://web.mit.edu/sydneydo/www/ICED2012App/A%20 New%20Strategy%20for%20Stem%20Education%20 and%20Innovative%20Engineering%20Problem%20 Solving%20rev%207.pdf

Camp, T. (2012). Computing, we have a problem…. ACM Inroads, 3(4), 34–40. doi:10.1145/2381083.2381097 doi:10.1145/2381083.2381097

Campbell, S. M., & Collaer, M. L. (2009). Stereotype threat and gender differences in performance on a novel visuospatial task. *Psychology of Women Quarterly, 33*(4), 437–444. doi:10.1111/j.1471-6402.2009.01521.x

Cantrell, P., & Ewing-Taylor, J. (2009). Exploring STEM career options through collaborative high school seminars. *Journal of Engineering Education, 98*(3), 295–303. doi:10.1002/j.2168-9830.2009.tb01026.x

Carmines, E. G., & McIver, P. J. (1981). Analyzing models with unobserved variables: Analysis of covariance structures. In G. W. Bohrnstedt, & E. F. Borgatta (Eds.), *Social measurement: Current issues* (pp. 65–115). Beverly Hills, CA: Sage Publications.

Carrington, V., & Hodgetts, K. (2010). Literacy-lite in *BarbieGirls™. British Journal of Sociology of Education, 31*(6), 671–682. doi:10.1080/01425692.2010.515109

Carroll, B., Smith, A., & Castori, P. (2009). *The Exploratorium's XTech program: Engaging STEM experiences for middle-school youth summative evaluation report.* Retrieved from http://informalscience.org/images/evaluation/2009-09_Rpt_XTECH-SummRpt-final-1019-2009. pdf

Carter, L. (2006). Why students with an apparent aptitude for computer science don't choose to major in computer science. *ACM SIGCSE Bulletin, 38*(1), 27–31. doi:10.1145/1124706.1121352

Cassell, J., & Jenkins, H. (1998). Chess for girls? Feminism and computer games. In J. Cassell, & H. Jenkins (Eds.), *From Barbie to Mortal Kombat: Gender and computer games* (pp. 2–45). Cambridge, MA: MIT Press.

Castells, M. (1998). *The information age: Economy, society and culture. The rise of network society.* Oxford, UK: Blackwell.

Cejka, M. A., & Eagly, A. H. (1999). Gender-stereotypic images of occupations correspond to the sex segregation of employment. *Personality and Social Psychology Bulletin, 25*(4), 413–423.

Chen, S. (2009, April 15). *Play games to work smarter: Why it is more critical than ever that women play and develop games.* Retrieved 2011, from http://damedev. blogspot.com.au/2009/04/play-games-to-work-smarter-why-it-is.html

Chen, M. (1986). Gender and computers: The beneficial effects of experience on attitudes. *Journal of Educational Computing Research, 2*, 265–282. doi:10.2190/WDRY-9K0F-VCP6-JCCD

Chess, S. (2011). A 36-24-36 cerebrum: Productivity, gender, and video game advertising. *Critical Studies in Media Communication, 28*(3), 230–252. doi:10.1080/1 5295036.2010.515234

Cinamon, R. (2006). Anticipated work-family conflict: Effects of gender, self-efficacy, and family background. *The Career Development Quarterly, 54*(3), 202–215. doi:10.1002/j.2161-0045.2006.tb00152.x

Computer and video games. (n. d.). *Science Daily.* Retrieved from http://www.sciencedaily.com/articles/c/computer_and_video_games.htm

Computer Entertainment Supplier's Association (CESA). (2013). *2012 CESA games white paper.*

Computing at School (CAS). (2013). *Computing for the next generation.* Retrieved from http://www.computingatschool.org.uk/

Computing Research Association. (2012). *CRA Taulbee survey.* Retrieved from http://cra.org/resources/taulbee/

Connell, R. (2005). *Masculinities.* Berkeley, CA: University of California Press.

Connell, R. W. (1987). *Gender and power: Society, the person and sexual politics.* Sydney, Australia: Allen and Unwin.

Consalvo, M. (2008). Crunched by passion: Women game developers & workplace challenges. In H. Kafai, Denner & Sun (Ed.), Beyond Barbie & Mortal Kombat: New perspectives on gender & gaming (pp. 177-192). Cambridge, MA: The MIT Press.

Consalvo, M. (2008). Crunched by passion: Women game developers and workplace challenges. In H. Kafai, Denner & Sun (Ed.), Beyond Barbie and Mortal Kombat: New perspectives on gender and gaming (pp. 177-192). Cambridge, MA: The MIT Press.

Consalvo, M. (2006). Console video games & global corporations: Creating a hybrid culture. *New Media & Society, 8*(1), 117–137.

Consalvo, M. (2008). Crunched by passion: Women game developers and workplace challenges. In Y. B. Kafai, C. Heeter, J. Denner, & J. Y. Sun (Eds.), *Beyond Barbie and Mortal Kombat* (pp. 177–192). Cambridge, MA: MIT Press.

Contestabile, G. B. (2012, December 12). *Diversity in the game industry: It's just good business.* Retrieved from http://www.edge-online.com/features/diversity-in-the-game-industry-its-just-good-business/

Cosh, A., Fu, X., & Hughes, A. (2012). Organisation structure and innovation performance in different environments. *Small Business Economics, 39*(2), 301–317. doi:10.1007/s11187-010-9304-5

Coughlan, S. (2013, February 4). *Computer science part of English Baccalaureate.* Retrieved from http://www.bbc.co.uk/news/education-21261442

Cox, T. & Blake, S. (1991). Managing cultural diversity: Implications for organizational competitiveness. *The Executive,* 45-56.

Cragg, A., Taylor, C., & Toombs, B. (2007). *Video games: Research to improve understanding of what players enjoy about video games, and to explain their preferences for particular games.* London: British Board of Film Classification.

Craig, A., Coldwell-Neilson, J., & Beekhuyzen, J. (2013). Are ICT interventions for girls a special case? In *Proceedings from SIGCSE '13: The 44th ACM Technical Symposium on Computer Science Education.* Denver, CO: ACM.

Craig, K. M., & Rand, K. A. (1998). The perceptually privileged group member: Consequences of solo status for African Americans and Whites in task groups. *Small Group Research, 29,* 339–358. doi:10.1177/1046496498293003

Crocker, J., & McGraw, K. M. (1984). What's good for the goose is not good for the gander: Solo status as an obstacle to occupational achievement for males and females. *The American Behavioral Scientist, 27*(3), 357–369. doi:10.1177/000276484027003007

Crossley, R. (2010). *Female count of UK dev workforce 'falls to 4%'.* Retrieved January 27, 2010 from http://www.develop-online.net/news/35806/Female-count-of-UK-dev-workforce-falls-to-4

Cunningham, G. B., Doherty, A. J., & Gregg, M. J. (2007). Using social cognitive career theory to understand head coaching intentions among assistant coaches of women's teams. *Sex Roles, 56,* 365–372. doi:10.1007/s11199-006-9175-z

CVG. (2013) *GTA V global retail sales top $800 million in one day.* Retrieved from http://www.computerandvideogames.com/430009/gta-v-global-retail-sales-top-800-million-in-one-day/

Dahlberg, T., Barnes, T., Buch, K., & Rorrer, A. (2011). The STARS Alliance: Viable strategies for broadening participation in computing. ACM Transactions in Computing Education, 11(3). doi:10.1145/2037276.2037282

Dar-Nimrod, I., & Heine, S. J. (2006). Exposure to scientific theories affects women's math performance. *Science, 314,* 435. doi:10.1126/science.1131100 PMID:17053140

Dave, V., Blasko, D., Holliday-Darr, K., Kremer, J. T., Edwards, R., Ford, M., et al. (2010). Re-enJEANeering STEM education: Math options summer camp. Journal of Technology Studies, 36(1), 35–45.

Davis, K. C., Greene-White, L., Ferdinand, T., & Santangelo, M. (2008). Digital arts for computing outreach. In *Proceedings from 38th ASEE/IEEE Frontiers in Educations Conference.* Saratoga Springs, NY: IEEE.

DCITA. (2005, March). *Australian digital content industry futures plan.* Prepared for DCITA (Department of Communications, Information Technology and the Arts) by the Centre for International Economics. September 19, 2006 from http://www.dcita.gov.au/__data/assets/pdf_file/37474/Appendix_C.2_Australian_digital_content_futures.pdf de Castell, S., Jenson, J., & Taylor, N. (2007). Digital games for education: When meanings play. In *Situated Play, Proceedings of DiGRA 2007 Conference*.

Denault, A., Kienzle, J., & Vybihal, J. (2008). Be a computer scientist for a week: The McGill Game Programming Guru summer camp. In *Proceedings from 38th ASEE/ IEEE Frontiers in Educations Conference*. Saratoga Springs, NY: IEEE.

Denner, J., Bean, S., & Werner, L. (2005). Girls creating games: Challenging existing assumptions about game content. In *Proceedings of DiGRA 2005 Conference: Changing Views – Worlds in Play*.

Denner, J., & Bean, S. (2006). Girls, games, and intrepid exploration on the computer. In E. M. Trauth (Ed.), *Encyclopedia of gender and information technology* (pp. 727–732). Hershey, PA: Idea Group Reference. doi:10.4018/978-1-59140-815-4.ch113

Denner, J., & Campe, S. (2008). What games made by girls can tell us. In Y. B. Kafai, C. Heeter, J. Denner, & J. Y. Sun (Eds.), *Beyond Barbie & Mortal Kombat: New perspectives on gender & gaming* (pp. 129–144). Cambridge, MA: The MIT Press.

Denner, J., Ortiz, E., Campe, S., & Werner, L. (in press). Beyond stereotypes of gender and gaming: Video games made by middle school students. In H. Agius, & M. Angelides (Eds.), *Handbook of digital games*. New York: Institute of Electrical and Electronic Engineers. doi:10.1002/9781118796443.ch25

Denner, J., Werner, L., O'Connor, L., & Glassman, J. (Manuscript submitted for publication). Community college men and women: A test of three widely held beliefs about who persists in computer science. *Community College Review*.

Department for Education. (2013). *Consultation on the order for replacing the subject of ICT with computing government response (Report)*. Crown.

Department of Defense. (2009). *Stem education and outreach strategic plan*. Retrieved from http://www.ngcproject.org/sites/default/files/DoD-wide%20STEM%20Education%20and%20Outreach%20Strategic%20Plan%20-%202010%20-%202014.pdf

Deuze, M., Martin, C. B., & Alen, C. (2007). The professional identity of gameworkers. *Convergence: The International Journal of Research into New Media Technologies*, *13*(4), 335–353. doi:10.1177/1354856507081947

DFC. (2004). *DFC intelligence releases new market forecasts for video game industry*. Retrieved from http://www.dfcint.com/news/prsep222004.html

Dietz, T. L. (1998). An examination of violence and gender role portrayals in video games: Implications for gender socialization and aggressive behavior. *Sex Roles*, *38*(5/6), 425–442. doi:10.1023/A:1018709905920

Dill, K. E., & Thill, K. P. (2007). Video game characters and the socialization of gender roles: Young people's perceptions mirror sexist media depictions. *Sex Roles*, *57*(11/12), 851–864. doi:10.1007/s11199-007-9278-1

DiSalvo, A., Crowley, K., & Norwood, R. (2008). Learning in context: Digital games and young black men. *Games and Culture*, *3*(2), 131. doi:10.1177/1555412008314130

Domenico, D. M., & Jones, K. H. (2006). Career aspirations of women in the 20th Century. *Journal of Career and Technical Education*, *22*(2), 1–7.

Doran, K., Boyce, A., Finkelstein, S., & Barnes, T. (2012). Outreach for improved student performance: A game design and development curriculum. In *Proceedings from ITiCSE '12: Proceedings of the ACM Conference on Innovation and Technology in Computer Science Education*. Haifa, Israel: ACM.

Dryburgh, H. (1999). Working hard, play hard: Women and professionalization in engineering – adapting to the culture. *Gender & Society*, *13*(5), 664–682. doi:10.1177/089124399013005006

Duberley, J., Cohen, L., & Mallon, M. (2006). Constructing scientific careers: Change, continuity and context. *Organization Studies*, *27*(8), 1131–1151. doi:10.1177/0170840606064105

Dukes, T. (2010). *Female role in gaming industry grows*. Retrieved September 23, 2010 from http://scienceinthetriangle.org/2010/09/female-role-in-gaming-industry-grows/

Dyer-Whitheford, N., & Sharman, Z. (2005). The political economy of Canada's video and computer game industry. *Canadian Journal of Communication*, *20*, 187–210.

Eagly, A. H. (1987). *Sex differences in social behavior: A social role interpretations*. Hillsdale, NJ: Erlbaum.

Eagly, A. H., & Carli, L. L. (2003). The female leadership advantage: An evaluation of the evidence. *The Leadership Quarterly, 14*, 807–834.

Eatough, V., & Smith, J. A. (2007). Interpretative phenomenological analysis. In C. Willig, & W. Stainton Rogers (Eds.), *Handbook of qualitative psychology* (pp. 179–194). London: Sage.

Eckert, P., & McConnell-Ginet, S. (2003). *Language and gender*. New York: Cambridge University Press. doi:10.1017/CBO9780511791147

Eisenberg, R. (1998). Girl games: Adventures in lip gloss. *Gamasutra*. Retrieved from www.gamasutra.com/view/feature/3252/girl_games_adventures_in_lip_gloss.php

Ellinger, A. D., Ellinger, A. E., Yang, B., & Howton, S. W. (2002). The relationship between the learning organization concept and firms' financial performance: An empirical assessment. *Human Resource Development Quarterly, 13*, 5–21. doi:10.1002/hrdq.1010

England, P. (2005). Gender inequality in labor markets: The role of motherhood and segregation. Social Politics, 12(2), 264–288. doi:10.1093/sp/jxi014

Entertainment Games, I. G. N. (2010). *SMU graduate program shows women's interest in video game development careers on the rise* [Press Release]. Retrieved January 27, 2011 from http://games.ign.com/articles/106/1068196p1.html

Entertainment Software Association. (2013). *2013 sales, demographics, and usage data*. Retrieved from http://www.theesa.com/facts/pdfs/ESA_EF_2013.pdf

Entertainment Software Association. (2013). *Essential facts about the computer and video game industry*. Retrieved from http://www.theesa.com/facts/pdfs/ESA_EF_2013.pdf

ESA. (2011). *Essential facts about games & violence*. Entertainment Software Association. Retrieved from http://www.theesa.com/facts/pdfs/ESA_EF_About_Games_&_Violence.pdf

ESA. (2011a). *Video games & the economy*. Retrieved from http://www.theesa.com/gamesindailylife/economy.pdf

ESA. (2011b). Essential facts about the computer & video game industry. Entertainment Software Industry. Retrieved from www.theESA.com

ESA. (2012). *Essential facts about the computer & video game industry 2012 sales, demographic & usage data*. Entertainment Software Association.

Eweek. (2007, May 14). *Report: Techs gender gap widened by uninviting workplace*. Retrieved August 2008, from http://www.eweek.com/c/a/IT-Management/Report-Techs-Gender-Gap-Widened-by-Uninviting-Workplace/

Faulkner, W. (2007). 'Nuts and bolts of people': Gender-troubled engineering identities. *Social Studies of Science, 37*, 331–356. doi:10.1177/0306312706072175

Faulkner, W. (2009a). Doing gender in engineering workplace cultures. I. Observation from the field. *English Studies, 1*(1), 3–18.

Faulkner, W. (2009b). Doing gender in engineering workplace cultures. II. Gender in/authenticity and the in/visibility paradox. *English Studies, 1*(3), 169–189.

Faulkner, W., & Lohan, M. (2004). Masculinities and technologies. Some introductory remarks. *Men and Masculinities, 6*(4), 319–329. doi:10.1177/1097184X03260956

Feldman, D. C., & Ng, T. W. H. (2007). Careers: Mobility, embeddedness, and success. *Journal of Management, 33*(3), 350–377. doi:10.1177/0149206307300815

Feng, J., Spence, I., & Pratt, J. (2007). Playing an action video game reduces gender differences in spatial cognition. *Psychological Science, 18*(10), 850–855. doi:10.1111/j.1467-9280.2007.01990.x PMID:17894600

Forbes. (2012). *Diversity & inclusion: Unlocking global potential*. Retrieved from http://www.dpiap.org/resources/pdf/global_diversity_rankings_2012_12_03_20.pdf

Foster, J. S., & Shiel-Rolle, N. (2011). Building scientific literacy through summer science camps: A strategy for design, implementation and assessment. Science Education International, 22(2), 85–98.

Fouad, N. A., Smith, P. L., & Zao, K. E. (2002). Across academic domains: Extensions of the social cognitive career model. *Journal of Counseling Psychology, 49*(2), 164–171. doi:10.1037/0022-0167.49.2.164

Frenkel, K. A. (1990). Women and computing. *Communications of the ACM, 33*(11), 34–46. doi:10.1145/92755.92756

Froschauer, U., & Lueger, M. (2003). *Das qualitative Interview: zur Praxis interpretativer Analyse sozialer Systeme*. Wien: WUV Verlag.

Fuegen, K., & Biernat, M. (2002). Re-examining the effects of solo status for women and men. *Personality and Social Psychology Bulletin, 28*(7), 913–925. doi:10.1177/014616720202800705

Fujihara, M. (2009). Career development of producer in the Japanese gaming industry. *Journal of career design studies, 5*, 5–21.

Fujihara, M. (2010). Issues of career development and career awareness among Japanese game developers. *Research Report on the Application of Advanced Technology in Digital Content Creation*, 253–300. Digital Content Association Japan. (In Japanese).

Fuller, A. (2010, January 26). Female undergraduates continue to outnumber men, but gap holds steady. *The Chronicle of Higher Education*. Retrieved from http://chronicle.com/article/Female-Undergraduates-Continue/63726/

Fullerton, T., Fron, J., Pearce, C., & Morie, J. (2008). Getting girls into the game: Towards a virtuous cycle. In Y. Kafai, C. Heeter, J., Denner, & J. Sun (Eds.), Beyond Barbie and Mortal Kombat: New perspectives on gender and gaming. Cambridge, MA: MIT Press.

Fullerton, T., Fron, J., Pearce, C., & Morie, J. (2008). Getting girls into the game: Toward a virtuous cycle. In Y. Kafai, C. Heeter, J. Denner, & J. Sun (Eds.), *Beyond Barbie and Mortal Kombat: New perspectives on gender and gaming* (pp. 161–176). Cambridge, MA: MIT Press.

Galarneau, L. (2014). *2014 global gaming stats: Who's playing what, and why?* Retrieved January, 2014, from http://www.bigfishgames.com/blog/2014-global-gaming-stats-whos-playing-what-and-why

Gallivan, M. J. (2004, Summer). Examining IT professionals' adaptation to technological change: The influence of gender and personal attributes. *The Data Base for Advances in Information Systems*. doi:10.1145/1017114.1017119

Gamasutra. (2010). *TIGA comments on gender imbalance in the games industry*. Retrieved from http://www.gamasutra.com/view/pressreleases/60966/TIGA_comments_on_gender_imbalance_in_the_gamesindustry.php

Gansmo, H. J., Nordli, H., & Sorensen, K. H. (2003). The gender game. A study of Nigerian computer game designers. In C. MacKeogh, & P. Preston (Eds.), *Strategies of inclusion: Gender & the information society. Experiences from private & voluntary sector initiatives* (pp. 139–159). Trondheim, Norway: NTNU.

Gardner, S. (2007). "I heard it through the grapevine": Doctoral student socialization in chemistry and history. *The Journal of Higher Education, 54*, 723–740. doi:10.1007/s10734-006-9020-x

Gee, J. P. (2007). *Good video games and good learning*. New York: Peter Lang.

Geneve, A. (2013). *Women's participation in the Australian Digital Content Industry* (PhD thesis). Queensland University of Technology, Australia.

Geneve, A. A. (2013). *Women's participation in the Australian digital content industry* (PhD thesis). Queensland University of Technology, Australia. Retrieved from http://eprints.qut.edu.au/60898/1/Anitza_Geneve_Thesis.pdf

Geneve, A., Christie, R. J., & Nelson, K. J. (2009). Women's participation in the Australian digital content industry: Initial case study findings. In K. Prpić, L. Oliveira, & S. Hemlin (Eds.), Women in science & technology (pp. 139-161). Zagreb, Croatia: Institute of Social Research-Zagreb Sociology of Science and Technology Network of ESA (European Sociological Association).

Geneve, A., Nelson, K. J., & Christie, R. J. (2008). *Passion, women and the games industry: Influences on women's participation in the Australian Digital Content Industry*. Paper presented at Women in Games, Warwick, UK.

Gibbs, G. (2010). *Analyzing qualitative data*. London: The Sage Qualitative Research Kit.

Gibbs, S. (2013). Computer self-efficacy-Is there a gender gap in tertiary level introductory computing classes? *Journal of Applied Computing and Information Technology, 17*(1).

Giddens, A. (1984). *The constitution of society*. Berkeley, CA: University of California Press.

Giddens, A. (1993). *New rules of sociological method: A positive critique of interpretive sociologies*. New York: Basic Books.

Gill, R. (2002). Cool, creative and egalitarian? Exploring gender in project-based new media work in Europe. *Information Communication and Society*, 5(1), 70–89. doi:10.1080/13691180110117668

Gill, R., & Pratt, A. (2008). In the social factory? Immaterial labour, precariousness and cultural work. *Theory, Culture & Society*, 25(7-8), 1–30. doi:10.1177/0263276408097794

Gilmer, T. (2007). An understanding of the improved grades, retention and graduation rates of STEM majors at the Academic Investment in Math and Science (AIMS) program of Bowling Green State University (BGSU). *Journal of STEM Education: Innovations and Research*, 8(1/2), 11–21.

Gist, M. E., & Mitchell, T. R. (1992). Self-efficacy: A theoretical analysis of its determinants and malleability. *Academy of Management Review*, 17, 183–211.

Golde, C. (2005). The role of the department and discipline in doctoral student attrition: Lessons from four departments. *The Journal of Higher Education*, 76(6), 669–700. doi:10.1353/jhe.2005.0039

Golde, C., & Dore, T. (2001). *At cross purposes: What the experiences of today`s doctoral students reveal about doctoral education (Report)*. Philadelphia, PA: The Pew Charitable Trusts.

Good, C., Aronson, J., & Harder, J. A. (2008). Problems in the pipeline: Stereotype threat and women's achievement in high-level math courses. *Journal of Applied Developmental Psychology*, 29(1), 17–28. doi:10.1016/j.appdev.2007.10.004

Gordon, M., & Denisi, A. (1995). A re-examination of the relationship between union membership and job satisfaction. *Industrial & Labor Relations Review*, 48, 222–236. doi:10.2307/2524484

Gottfredson, L. S. (1981). Circumscription and compromise: A development theory of aspirations. *Journal of Counseling Psychology*, 28(6), 545–579.

Gourdin, A. (2005). *Game developer demographics: An exploration of workforce diversity*. International Game Developers Association. Retrieved 24 Jan 2008 from http://www.igda.org/diversity/IGDA_ DeveloperDemographics_Oct05.pdf

Graft, K. (2012). *The 5 trends that defined the game industry in 2012*. Retrieved from http://www.gamasutra.com/view/news/182954/The_5_trends_that_defined_the_game_industry_in_2012.php#.UMn3em_Ad8E

Graner Ray, S. (2004). *Gender inclusive game design: Expanding the market*. Hingham, MA: Charles River Media Inc.

Granic, I., Lobel, A., & Engels, C. M. E. (2013). The benefits of playing video games. *The American Psychologist*. doi:10.1037/a0034857 PMID:24295515

Gras-Velazquez, A., Joyce, A., & Derby, M. (2008). Women and ICT: Why are girls still not attracted to ICT studies? *European Schoolnet, Brussels*. Retrieved from http://blog.eun.org/insightblog/upload/women_and_ICT_FINAL.pdf

Griffiths, M., Moore, K., Burns, B., & Richardson, H. (2007, Spring.). *The disappearing women: North West ICT project final report*. Funded by the European Social Fund (ESF). Retrieved Feb 2010 from http://usir.salford.ac.uk/9312/1/Griffiths_DW.pdf

Guilford, J. P. (1970). Creativity: Retrospect and prospect. *The Journal of Creative Behavior*, 4, 149–168. doi:10.1002/j.2162-6057.1970.tb00856.x

Haines, L. (2004). Why are there so few women in games? [Report]. *Media Training North West*. Retrieved from http://archives.igda.org/women/MTNW_Women-in-Games_Sep04.pdf

Hall, L. (2012). *Game industry jobs: Ten tips for graduates*. Retrieved from http://www.edge-online.com/get-into-games/game-industry-jobs-ten-tips-graduates/

Hanappi-Egger, E., & Warmuth, G. S. (2010). Gender-neutral or gender-blind? On the meaning of structural barriers in computer science and engineering. In K. Resetová (Ed.) *CD-Proceedings of the Joint International IGIP-SEFI Conference 2010. Diversity Unifies - Diversity in Engineering Education* (pp. 1153-1153). Brussels, Belgium.

Hanappi-Egger, E. (2011). *The triple m of organizations: Man, management and myth.* Wien, New York: Springer. doi:10.1007/978-3-7091-0556-6

Hanappi-Egger, E. (2012a). "Shall I stay or shall I go"? On the role of diversity management for women's retention in SET professions. *Equality, Diversity and Inclusion. International Journal (Toronto, Ont.), 31*(2), 144–157.

Hanappi-Egger, E. (2012b). Exclusiveness versus inclusiveness in software-development: The triple-loop-learning approach. In R. Pande, & T. van der Weide (Eds.), *Globalization, technology diffusion and gender disparity: Social impacts of ICTs* (pp. 96–109). Hershey, PA: IGI Global. doi:10.4018/978-1-4666-0020-1.ch008

Hanappi-Egger, E. (2012c). Wissenschaftliche Exzellenz: Geschlechtsneutral oder geschlechtsblind. In S. L. Gutierrez-Lobos, & K. Rumpfhuber (Eds.), *Hat wissenschaftliche Leistung ein Geschlecht?* (pp. 15–22). Wien: Facultas.

Hanappi-Egger, E. (2013). Backstage: The organizational gendered agenda in science, engineering and technology professions. *European Journal of Women's Studies, 20*(3), 279–294. doi:10.1177/1350506812456457

Hare-Mustin, R. T., & Marecek, J. (1988). The meaning of difference: Gender theory, postmodernism, and psychology. *The American Psychologist, 43*(6), 455–464. doi:10.1037/0003-066X.43.6.455

Hartmann, T., & Klimmt, C. (2006). Gender and computer games: Exploring females' dislikes. *Journal of Computer-Mediated Communication, 11*(4), 910–931. doi:10.1111/j.1083-6101.2006.00301.x

Harvey, A. (2011). Architectures of participation in digital play: Social norms, gender, and youth gameplay. *Information Communication and Society, 14*(3), 303–319. doi:10.1080/1369118X.2010.542821

Hatmaker, T. (2010). *The (gender) trouble with video game avatars.* Retrieved from http://www.autostraddle.com/the-gender-trouble-with-avatars-56108/

Haukka, S., & Brow, B. (2010, January). *From education to work in Australia's creative digital industries: Comparing the opinions and practices of employers and aspiring creatives* (60Sox Report Vol. 2). Retrieved 19 June 2011 from http://www.apo.org. au/research/education-work-australias-creative-digital-industries

Hawks, B., & Spade, J. Z. (1998). *Women and men engineering students: Anticipation of family and work roles. Journal of Engineering Education, 87*(3), 249-256. Retrieved May 24, 2011 from http://www.jee.org/1998/july/570.pdf

Hawks, B., & Spade, J. Z. (1998). Women and men engineering students: Anticipation of family and work roles. *Journal of Engineering Education, 87*(3), 249–256. doi:10.1002/j.2168-9830.1998.tb00351.x

Hayes, E. (2005). Women, videogaming, and learning: Beyond stereotypes. *TechTrends, 49*(5), 23–28. doi:10.1007/BF02763686

Heeter, C., Egidio, R., Mishra, P., Winn, B., & Winn, J. (2009). Alien games: Do girls prefer games designed by girls? *Games and Culture, 4*(1), 74–100. doi:10.1177/1555412008325481

Hegewisch, A., Williams, C., & Harbin, V. (2012). *The gender wage gap by occupation.* Retrieved from http://www.iwpr.org/publications/pubs/the-gender-wage-gap-by-occupation-1

Heilman, M. E. (1983). Sex bias in work settings: The lack of fit model. *Research in Organizational Behavior, 5*, 269–298.

Heilman, M. E., & Okimoto, T. G. (2007). Why are women penalized for success at male tasks?: The implied communality deficit. *The Journal of Applied Psychology, 92*, 81–92. PMID:17227153

Heilman, M. E., Wallen, A. S., Fuchs, D., & Tamkins, M. M. (2004). Penalties for success: Reactions to women who succeed at male gender-typed tasks. *The Journal of Applied Psychology, 89*, 416–427. PMID:15161402

Hess, R. D., & Miura, I. T. (1985). Gender differences in enrolment in computer camps and classes. *Sex Roles, 13*(3-4), 193–203. doi:10.1007/BF00287910

Hoffman, B., & Nadelson, L. (2010). Motivational engagement and video gaming: A mixed methods study. *Educational Technology Research and Development*, 58(3), 245–270. doi:10.1007/s11423-009-9134-9

Holland, J. L. (1973). *Making vocational choice: A theory of careers*. Englewood Cliffs, NJ: Prentice-Hall.

Hollingsworth, R. (2002). *Research organizations and major discoveries in twentieth-century science: A case study of excellence in biomedical research*. Berlin: Wissenschaftszentrum Berlin für Sozialforschung.

Hoonakker, P. L. T., Carayon, P., & Schoepke, J. (2006). Discrimination and hostility toward women and minorities in the IT workforce. In E. Trauth (Ed.), *Encyclopaedia of gender and information technology* (pp. 207–215). Hersey, PA: Idea Group Inc. doi:10.4018/978-1-59140-815-4.ch033

Huizinga, J. (1955). *Homo Ludens: A study of the play element in culture*. Boston: Beacon Press.

IGDA. (2005). *Game developer demographics: An exploration of workforce diversity comments on diversity*. Retrieved from http://archives.igda.org/diversity/IGDA_DeveloperDemographics_Oct05.pdf

Ihsen, S. (2008). Ingenieurinnen: Frauen in einer Männerdomäne. In R. Becker, & B. Kortendiek (Eds.), *Handbuch der Frauen und Geschlechterforschung. Theorie, Methoden, Empirie* (pp. 791–797). Wiesbaden, Germany: VS Verlag. doi:10.1007/978-3-531-91972-0_96

Ilies, R., & Judge, T. A. (2004). An experience-sampling measure of job satisfaction and its relationships with affectivity, mood at work, job beliefs, and general job satisfaction. *European Journal of Work and Organizational Psychology*, 13(3), 367–389. doi:10.1080/13594320444000137

Innstrand, S. T., Langballe, E. M., Falkum, E., Espnes, G. A., & Aasland, O. G. (2009). Gender-specific perceptions of four dimensions of the work/family interaction. *Journal of Career Assessment*, 17(4), 402–416. doi:10.1177/1069072709334238

Insights, F. (2012). *Diversity & inclusion: Unlocking global potential*. Retrieved from.http://images.forbes.com/forbesinsights/StudyPDFs/global_diversity_rankings_2012.pdf

Interactive Selection. (2013). *Interactive promotes women in games development*. Retrieved from http://www.interactiveselection.com/women.asp

International Game Developers Association (IGDA). (2005). *Game developer demographics: An exploration of workforce diversity*. Retrieved from http://www.igda.org/game-developer-demographics-report

International Game Developers Association (IGDA). (2011). *Game industry survey 2011*. Retrieved from https://www.surveymonkey.com/s/IGDA2011

Isaacson, B. (2012, November 29). *#1 Reason Why reveals sexism rampant in the gaming industry*. Retrieved from http://www.huffingtonpost.com/2012/11/29/1reasonwhy-reveals-sexism-gaming-industry_n_2205204.html

Javidi, G., & Sheybani, E. (2008). Digispired: Digital inspiration for interactive game design and programming. Journal of Computing Sciences in Colleges, 24(3), 144–150.

Jenkins, H. (2001). *From Barbie to Mortal Kombat: Further reflections*. Retrieved from http://culturalpolicy.uchicago.edu/papers/2001-video-games/jenkins.html

Jenkins, H., & Cassell, J. (2008). From quake grrls to desperate housewives: A decade of gender and computer games. In Y. Kafai, C. Heeter, J. Denner, & J. Sun (Eds.), *Beyond Barbie and Mortal Kombat: New perspectives on gender and computer games* (pp. 5–20). Cambridge, MA: MIT Press.

Jenson, J., & de Castell, S. (2008). Theorizing gender and digital gameplay: Oversights, accidents, and surprises. *Eludamos: Journal for Computer Game Culture*, 2(1), 15–25.

Johns, J. (2006). Video games production networks: Value capture, power relations & embeddedness. *Journal of Economic Geography*, 6(2), 151–180. doi:10.1093/jeg/lbi001

Jones, S. P. (2013). *Computing at school*. Presentation at Innovation the 18th Annual Conference on Innovation and Technology in Computer Science Education, University of Kent, Canterbury, UK.

Jones, S., Hernandez, A., Ortiz, P., Aldana, G., Conrad, P., & Franklin, D. (2010). eVoices: A website supporting outreach by attracting target groups to computer science through culturally relevant themes. Journal of Computing Sciences in Colleges, 25(4), 134–140.

Juul, J. (2012). *A casual revolution: Reinventing video games and their players.* Cambridge, MA: MIT Press.

Kafai, Y. B., Heeter, C., Denner, J., & Sun, J. Y. (2008). *Preface: Pink, purple, casual, or mainstream games: Moving beyond the gender divide. Beyond Barbie and Mortal Combat: New perspectives on gender and gaming.* London: The MIT Press.

Kafai, Y., Heeter, C., Denner, J., & Sun, J. (Eds.). (2008). *Beyond Barbie and Mortal Kombat: New perspectives on gender and gaming.* Cambridge, MA: MIT Press.

Kannankutty, N. (2008). *Unemployment rate of U.S. scientists and engineers drops to record low 2.5% in 2006.* Retrieved January 9, 2011 from http://www.nsf.gov/statistics/infbrief/nsf08305/

Kasper, J. (2006). *Proven steps for recruiting women.* Retrieved November 12, 2010 from http://www.hendon-pub.com/resources/articlearchive/details.aspx?ID=965

Kawakami, C., White, J. B., & Langer, E. J. (2000). Mindful and masculine: Freeing women leaders from the constraints of gender roles. *The Journal of Social Issues, 56*(1), 49–63.

Keller, J. (2002). Blatant stereotype threat and women's math performance: Self-handicapping as a strategic means to cope with obtrusive negative performance expectations. *Sex Roles, 47*(3/4), 193–198. doi:10.1023/A:1021003307511

Kell, H. J., Lubinski, D., Benbow, C. P., & Steiger, J. H. (2013). Creativity and technical innovation. *Psychological Science, 24*(9), 1831–1836. doi:10.1177/0956797613478615 PMID:23846718

Khine, M. S. (2011). *Learning to play: Exploring the future of education with video games.* New York: Peter Lang.

Kinzie, M. B., & Joseph, D. R. (2008). Gender differences in game activity preferences of middle school children: implications for educational game design. *Educational Technology Research and Development, 56*(5-6), 643–663. doi:10.1007/s11423-007-9076-z

Kirkup, G., Zalevski, A., Maruyama, T., & Batool, I. (2010). *Women and men in science, engineering and technology: The UK statistics guide 2010.* Retrieved from http://www.theukrc.org/files/useruploads/files/final_sept_15th_15.42_ukrc_statistics_guide_2010.pdf

Kline, S., Dyer-Witheford, N., & de Peuter, G. (2003). *Digital play: The interaction of technology, culture & marketing.* Montreal, Canada: McGill-Queen's University Press.

Kohashi, R. (1996). *Household gaming industry in Japan: Organizational structure and the process* (Doctoral thesis). Graduate School of Business Administration, Kobe University, Japan.

Krotoski, A. (2004). *Chicks and joysticks: An exploration of women and gaming* (Entertainment and Leisure Software Publishers Association White paper).

Krotoski, A. 2004. *White paper: Chicks and joysticks.* London: Entertainment & Leisure Software Publishers Association (ELSPA).

Kvasny, L. Joshi, K. D., & Trauth, E. M. (2011). The influence of self-efficacy, gender stereotypes and the importance of IT skills on college students' intentions to pursue IT careers. In *Proceedings of the 2011 iConference*, Seattle, WA.

Laurel, B. (2008). Notes from the utopian entrepreneur. In Y. Kafai, C. Heeter, J. Denner, & J. Sun (Eds.), *Beyond Barbie and Mortal Kombat: New perspectives on gender and gaming* (pp. 21–32). Cambridge, MA: MIT Press.

Lauver, K., & Kristof-Brown, A. (2001). Distinguishing between employees' perceptions of person-job and person-organization fit. *Journal of Vocational Behavior, 59*, 454–470. doi:10.1006/jvbe.2001.1807

Lealea Design. (n. d.). *Women in tech: Asking the wrong questions.* Retrieved 2011, from http://www.lealea.net/blog/comments/women-in-tech-asking-the-wrong-questions/#ixzz0cRlJSESg

Legault, M. J., & Weststar, J. (2012). *More than the numbers: Independent analysis of the IGDA 2009 quality of life survey.* Retrieved from http://gameqol.org/wp-content/uploads/2012/12/Quality%20of%20Life%20in%20the%20Videogame%20Industry%20-%202009%20IGDA%20Survey%20Analysis.pdf

Lenhart, A., Jones, S., & Macgill, A. (2008). Adults and video games. *Pew Internet and Family Life Project.* Retrieved on December 9, 2011 from http://www.pewinternet.org/Reports/2008/Adults-and-Video-Games.aspx

Lent, R. W., & Brown, S. D. (2006). On conceptualizing and assessing social cognitive constructs in career research: A measurement guide. *Journal of Career Assessment, 14*(1), 12–35. doi:10.1177/1069072705281364

Lent, R. W., Brown, S. D., Brenner, B., Chopra, S. B., Davis, T., Talleyrand, R., & Suthakaran, V. (2001). The role of contextual supports and barriers in the choice of math/science educational options: A test of social cognitive hypotheses. *Journal of Counseling Psychology, 48*(4), 474–483. doi:10.1037/0022-0167.48.4.474

Lent, R. W., Brown, S. D., & Hackett, G. (1994). Toward a unifying social cognitive theory of career and academic interest, choice and performance. *Journal of Vocational Behavior, 45*, 79–122. doi:10.1006/jvbe.1994.1027

Lent, R. W., Brown, S. D., & Hackett, G. (2000). Contextual supports and barriers to career choice: A social cognitive analysis. *Journal of Counseling Psychology, 47*(1), 36–49. doi:10.1037/0022-0167.47.1.36

Ligman, K. (2013, April 19). *Centipede creator sees lack of diversity in the game industry.* Retrieved from http://www.gamasutra.com/view/news/190878/

Lind, I. (2007). Ursachen der Unterrepräsentanz von Wissenschaftlerinnen - Individuelle Entscheidungen oder strukturelle Barrieren? In B. f. B. u. Forschung (Ed.), Exzellenz in Wissenschaft und Forschung -Neue Wege in der Gleichstellungspolitik: Bundesministerium für Bildung und Forschung (pp. 59-86). Köln, Germany.

Lindley, L. D. (2005). Perceived barriers to career development in the context of social cognitive career theory. *Journal of Career Assessment, 13*(3), 271–287. doi:10.1177/1069072705274953

Livingstone, I., & Hope, A. (2011). *Next gen: Transforming the UK into the world's leading talent hub for the video games and visual effects industries.* London: NESTA.

Lovitts, B. (2001). *Leaving the ivory tower: The causes and consequences of departure from doctoral study.* Lanham, MD: Rowman & Littlefield.

Lucas, K., & Sherry, J. L. (2004). Sex differences in video game play: A communication-based explanation. *Communication Research, 31*(5), 499–525. doi:10.1177/0093650204267930

Lueger, M. (2000). *Grundlagen qualitativer Feldforschung.* Wien: WUV Verlag.

Lynn, K. M., Raphael, C., Olefsky, K., & Bachen, C. M. (2003). Bridging the gender gap in computing: an integrative approach to content design for girls. *Journal of Educational Computing Research, 28*(2), 143–162. doi:10.2190/79HP-RVE7-3A9N-FV8C

MacKenzie, D., & Wajcman, J. (2005). *The social shaping of technology.* Maidenhead, UK: Open University Press.

Mai, P. (2010). *The highest & lowest grossing video game-based movies.* Retrieved from http://blogs.ocweekly.com/heardmentality/2010/07/hollywoods_lowest_grossing_vid.php

Major, D. A., Davis, D. D., Sanchez-Hucles, J. V., Germano, L. M., & Mann, J. (2006). IT workplace climate for opportunity and inclusion. In E. M. Trauth (Ed.), *Encyclopedia of gender and information technology* (pp. 856–862). Hershey, PA: IGI Global. doi:10.4018/978-1-59140-815-4.ch134

Margolis, J., Ryoo, J. J., Sandoval, C. D. M., Lee, C., Goode, J., & Chapman, G. (2012). Beyond access: Broadening participation in high school computer science. ACM Inroads, 3(4), 72–78. doi:10.1145/2381083.2381102

Margolis, J., & Fisher, A. (2002). *Unlocking the clubhouse: Women in computing.* Cambridge, MA: The MIT Press.

Marsh, J. (2010). Young children's play in online virtual worlds. *Journal of Early Childhood Research, 8*(1), 23–39. doi:10.1177/1476718X09345406

Martin, C., Eisenbud, L., & Rose, H. (1995). Children's gender-based reasoning about toys. *Child Development, 66*, 1453–1471. doi:10.2307/1131657 PMID:7555224

Martin, P. (2003). "Said and done" versus "saying and doing" gendering practices, practicing gender at work. *Gender & Society, 17*(3), 342–366. doi:10.1177/0891243203017003002

Marx, D. M., Ko, S. J., & Friedman, R. A. (2009). The 'Obama effect': How salient role model reduces race-based performance differences. *Journal of Experimental Social Psychology, 45*, 953–956. doi:10.1016/j.jesp.2009.03.012

Maxim, B. R., Grosky, W. I., & Baugh, J. P. (2007). Work in progress – Introducing information technology through game design. In *Proceedings from 37th ASEE/IEEE Frontiers in Educations Conference*. Milwaukee, WI: IEEE.

Mayrhofer, W., Steyrer, J., Meyer, M., Strunk, G., Schiffinger, M., & Iellatchitch, A. (2005). Graduates career aspirations and individual characteristics. *Human Resource Management Journal, 15*(1), 38–56. doi:10.1111/j.1748-8583.2005.tb00139.x

McCarthy, M. (2004). *Girlfriends in high places: How women's networks are changing the workplace*. New York: Demos.

McGill, M. M., Settle, A., & Decker, A. (2013). Demographics of undergraduates studying games in the United States: A comparison of computer science students and the general population. Computer Science Education, 23(2), 158–185. doi:10.1080/08993408.2013.769319

McGrath-Coohan, J. M., & Aspray, W. (Eds.). (2006). *Women in information technology: Research on underrepresentation*. Cambridge, MA: MIT Press.

McIlwee, J., & Robinson, G. (1992). *Women in engineering: Gender, power, and workplace culture*. Albany, NY: State University of New York Press.

McIntyre, R. B., Paulon, R. M., & Lord, C. G. (2003). Alleviating women's mathematics stereotype threat through salience of group achievements. *Journal of Experimental Social Psychology, 39*, 83–90. doi:10.1016/S0022-1031(02)00513-9

MCV. (2008). *Salary survey*. Retrieved from http://www.mcvuk.com/news/29399/Industry-salary-survey

MCV. (2014). *Recruitment special: Industry salary survey*. Retrieved from http://www.mcvuk.com/news/read/recruitment-special-industry-salary-survey

Medsker, G., Williams, L., & Holahan, P. (1994). A review of current practices for evaluating causal models in organizational behavior and human resources management research. *Journal of Management, 20*(2), 439–464. doi:10.1016/0149-2063(94)90022-1

Mercier, E. M., Barron, B., & O'Connor, K. M. (2006). Images of self & others as computer users: The role of gender & experience. *Journal of Computer Assisted Learning, 22*(5), 335–348. doi:10.1111/j.1365-2729.2006.00182.x

Miller, P. (2012). *Eleventh annual game developer salary survey*. Retrieved August 13, 2013 from http://twvideo01.ubm-us.net/o1/vault/GD_Mag_Archives/GDM_April_2012.pdf

Miller, P. (2013). *Twelfth annual game developer salary survey*. Retrieved August 13, 2013 from http://twvideo01.ubm-us.net/o1/vault/GD_Mag_Archives/GDM_April_2013.pdf

Miller, G. (2004). Frontier masculinity in the oil industry: The experience of women engineers. *Gender, Work and Organization, 11*(1), 47–73. doi:10.1111/j.1468-0432.2004.00220.x

Milliszewska, I., & Moore, A. (2010). Encouraging girls to consider a career in ICT: A review of strategies. *Journal of Information Technology Education, 9*, 143–166.

Miranda, R. J., & Hermann, R. S. (2010). A critical analysis of faculty-developed urban K-12 science outreach Programs. Perspectives on Urban Education, 7(1), 109–114.

Moore, A. K., Griffiths, M., & Richardson, H. (2005a). Moving in, moving up, Moving out? A survey of women in ICT. *Information Systems*, 1–28.

Murphy, K. X. (2012, November 16). *Keeping focused on the global competitiveness agenda* [Blog post]. Retrieved http://forumblog.org/2012/11/keeping-focused-on-the-global-competitiveness-agenda/

Murray, J. (2012). Pupils need to understand computers, not just how to use them. *The Guardian*. Retrieved January 12, 2012, from http://www.guardian.co.uk/education/2012/jan/09/computer-studies-in-schools

Natale, M. J. (2002). The effect of a male-oriented computer gaming culture on careers in the computer industry. *Computers & Society, 32*(2), 24–31. doi:10.1145/566522.566526

National Center for Women & Information Technology. (2013). http://www.ncwit.org

National Science Board. (2012). Science and engineering labor force: Demographics of the S&E workforce. In *Science and Engineering Indicators 2012* (Chapter 3 Section 4). Retrieved from http://www.nsf.gov/statistics/seind12/c3/c3s4.htm

National Science Foundation. (2008). *Broadening participation at the national science foundation: A framework for action*. Retrieved from http://www.nsf.gov/od/broadeningparticipation/nsf_frameworkforaction_0808.pdf

National Science Foundation. (2009). *Broadening participation in computing (BPC)*. Retrieved from http://www.nsf.gov/funding/pgm_summ.jsp?pims_id=13510

National Science Foundation. (2013). *Women, minorities, and persons with disabilities in science and engineering: 2013*. Retrieved December 3, 2013 from http://www.nsf.gov/statistics/wmpd/2013/pdf/nsf13304_full.pdf

Nemeth, C., Connell, J., Rogers, J., & Brown, K. (2001). Improving decision making by means of dissent. *Journal of Applied Social Psychology*, *31*(1), 48–58. doi:10.1111/j.1559-1816.2001.tb02481.x

Neumark, D., & Gardecki, R. (1998). Women helping women? Role model and mentoring effects on female Ph.D. students in economics. The Journal of Human Resources, 33(1), 220–246. doi:10.2307/146320 Ng, T. W. H., Eby, L. T., Sorensen, K. L., & Feldman, D. C. (2005). Predictors of objective and subjective career success: A meta analysis. *Personnel Psychology*, *58*, 367–408. doi:10.1111/j.1744-6570.2005.00515.x

Ogan, C., Robinson, J. C., Ahuja, M., & Herring, S. C. (2006). Gender differences among students in computer science and applied information technology. In J. M. Cohoon, & W. Aspray (Eds.), *Women and information technology: Research on underrepresentation* (pp. 279–300). Cambridge, MA: The MIT Press. doi:10.7551/mitpress/9780262033459.003.0009

Ogletree, S. M., & Drake, R. (2007). College students' video game participation and perceptions: Gender differences and implication. *Sex Roles*, *56*, 537–542. doi:10.1007/s11199-007-9193-5

Olson, C. K. (2010). Children's motivations for video game play in the context of normal development. *Review of General Psychology*, *12*(2), 180–187. doi:10.1037/a0018984

O'Reilly, C. A., Chatman, J., & Caldwell, D. F. (1991). People and organizational culture: A profile comparison approach assessing person-organization fit. *Academy of Management Review*, *34*(3), 487–516. doi:10.2307/256404

Oswald, D. L. (2008). Gender stereotypes and women's reports of liking and ability in traditionally masculine and feminine occupations. *Psychology of Women Quarterly*, *32*(2), 196–203. doi:10.1111/j.1471-6402.2008.00424.x

Oswald, D. L., & Lindstedt, K. (2006). The content and function of gender self-stereotypes: An exploratory investigation. *Sex Roles*, *54*, 447–458. doi:10.1007/s11199-006-9026-y

Oxford Economics. (2008). *The economic contribution of the UK games industry: Final report*. Retrieved from http://www.oef.com/FREE/PDFS/GAMESIMPACT.PDF

Parberry, I., Kazemzadeh, M., & Roden, T. (2006). The art and science of game programming. In *Proceedings of the 37th SIGCSE Technical Symposium on Computer Science Education*. Houston, Texas, USA

Parfitt, B. (2010, October 4). *Interview: The Sims, the market for computer & video games*. Retrieved from http://www.mcvuk.com/news/read/interview-the-sims/01837

Passion, I. T. (2011). *Technology is a great career choice because….* Retrieved 2011, from http://itmillion.com/

Pearce, C., Fullerton, T., Fron, J., & Ford Morie, J. (2007). Sustainable play: Toward a new games movement for the digital age. *Games and Culture*, *2*, 261–278. doi:10.1177/1555412007304420

Pelletier, C. (2008). Gaming in context: How young people construct their gendered identities in playing and making games. In Y. Kafai, C. Heeter, J. Denner, & J. Sun (Eds.), *Beyond Barbie and Mortal Kombat: New perspectives on gender and gaming* (pp. 145–159). Cambridge, MA: MIT Press.

Perrewe, P. L., & Nelson, D. L. (2004). Gender and career success: The facilitative role of political skill. *Organizational Dynamics*, *33*(4), 366–378. doi:10.1016/j.orgdyn.2004.09.004

Perrons, D. (2003). The new economy and the work-life balance: Conceptual explorations and a case study of new media. *Gender, Work and Organization, 10*(1), 65–93. doi:10.1111/1468-0432.00004

Perryman, R. D. (2004). Healthy attitudes: Quality of working life in the London NHS, 2000-2002 (Report by The National Health Service, UK).

PISA. (2006). *Science competencies for tomorrow's world. The programme for international student assessment.* OECD. Retrieved from http://www.oecd.org/dataoecd/15/13/39725224.pdf

Pivkina, I., Pontelli, E., Jensen, R., & Haebe, J. (2009). Young women in computing: Lessons learned from an educational & outreach program. In *Proceedings from SIGCSE '09: The 40th ACM Technical Symposium on Computer Science Education.* Chattanooga, TN: ACM.

Plunkett, L. (2012, November 27). *Here's a devastating account of the crap women in the games business have to deal with. In 2012.* Retrieved from http://kotaku.com/5963528/heres-a-devastating-account-of-the-crap-women-in-the-games-business-have-to-deal-with-in-2012

Powell, G. N., & Butterfield, D. A. (2003). Gender, gender identity, and aspirations to top management. *Women in Management Review, 18*(1/2), 88–96. doi:10.1108/09649420310462361

Pratt, M. (2007). *Computer game industry looks to women for fresh insights.* Retrieved September 23, 2010 from http://www.computerworld.com/s/article/293317/Computer_game_industry_looks_to_women_for_fresh_insights

Prensky, M. (2002). *What kids learn that's positive from playing video games.* Retrieved from http://www.paaco.org/ArticlesBooksCourses/What_Kids_Learn_That_s_POSITIVE_from_Playing_Video_Games.html

Prescott, J., & Bogg, J. (2010). The computer games industry: Women's experiences of work role in a male dominated environment. In A. Cater-Steel, & E. Cater (Eds.), *Women in engineering, science & technology: Education & career challenges* (pp. 138–158). Hershey, PA: IGI Global. doi:10.4018/978-1-61520-657-5.ch007

Prescott, J., & Bogg, J. (2011). Segregation in a male dominated industry: Women working in the computer games industry. *International Journal of Gender. Science and Technology, 3*(1), 205–227.

Prescott, J., & Bogg, J. (2012). *Gendered occupational differences in science, engineering, & technology careers.* Hershey, PA: IGI Global. doi:10.4018/978-1-4666-2107-7

Prescott, J., & Bogg, J. (2013). *Gendered occupational differences in science, engineering, and technology careers.* Hershey, PA: IGI Global.

Prescott, J., & Bogg, J. (2013). *The gendered digital divide and the computer games industry.* Hershey, PA: IGI Global. doi:10.4018/978-1-4666-4534-9

Prescott, J., & Bogg, J. (2014). *Gender divide and the computer gaming industry.* Hershey, PA: IGI Global.

Princeton Review. (2013). *Top undergraduate schools for video game design.* Retrieved from http://www.princetonreview.com/top-undergraduate-schools-for-video-game-design.aspx

Putsche, L., Storrs, D., Lewis, A., & Haylett, J. (2008). The development of a mentoring program for university undergraduate women. *Cambridge Journal of Education, 38*(4), 513–528. doi:10.1080/03057640802482322

Repenning, A., & Ioannidou, A. (2008). Broadening participation through scalable game design. SIGCSE Bulletin, 40(1), 305–309. doi:10.1145/1352322.1352242

Reskin, B. F. (1988). Bringing the men back in: Sex differentiation and the devaluation of women's work. Gender & Society, 2(1), 58–81. doi:10.1177/089124388002001005

Rhoton, L. (2011). Dancing as a gendered barrier – Understanding women scientists' gender practices. *Gender & Society, 25*(6), 696–716. doi:10.1177/0891243211422717

Rigotti, T., Schyns, B., & Mohr, G. (2008). A short version of the occupational self-efficacy scale: Structural and construct validity across five countries. *Journal of Career Assessment, 16*(2), 238–255. doi:10.1177/1069072707305763

Rinn, A., McQueen, K., Clark, G., & Rumsey, J. (2008). Gender differences in gifted adolescents' math/verbal self- concepts and math/verbal achievement: implications for the STEM fields. *Journal for the Education of the Gifted, 32*(1), 34–53.

Roan, A., & Whitehouse, G. (2007). Women, information technology and waves of optimism: Australian evidence on mixed-skill jobs. *New Technology, Work and Employment, 22*(1), 21–33. doi:10.1111/j.1468-005X.2007.00181.x

Roberge, M. É., & van Dick, R. (2010). Recognizing the benefits of diversity: When and how does diversity increase group performance? *Human Resource Management Review, 20*(4), 295–308. doi:10.1016/j.hrmr.2009.09.002

Roberts, E. S., Kassianidou, M., & Irani, L. (2002). Encouraging women in computer science. *ACM SIGCSE Bulletin, 34*(2), 84–88. doi:10.1145/543812.543837

Robst, R., Keil, J., & Russo, D. (1998). The effect of gender composition of faculty on student retention. Economics of Education Review, 17(4), 429–439. doi:10.1016/S0272-7757(97)00049-6

Rockstar Spouse. (2010). *Wives of Rockstar San Diego employees have collected themselves.* Retrieved January 27, 2011 from http://www.gamasutra.com/blogs/RockstarSpouse/20100107/4032/Wives_of_Rockstar_San_Diego_employees_have_collected_themselves.php

Rowland, S. (2010). Getting' digi with it: Microsoft helps young girls shape future careers. IEEE Women in Engineering Magazine, 4(1), 28–29. doi:10.1109/MWIE.2010.936181

Royse, P., Lee, J., Undrahbuyan, B., Hopson, M., & Consalvo, M. (2007). Women and games: Technologies of the gendered self. *New Media & Society, 9*(4), 555–576. doi:10.1177/1461444807080322

Sackrowitz, M., & Parelius, A. (1996). An unlevel playing field: Women in the introductory computer science courses. *SIGCSE '96 Proceedings of the Twenty-Seventh SIGCSE Technical Symposium on Computer Science Education, 28*(1), 37-41.

Sagebiel, F. (2005). Organisationskultur und Geschlecht in den Ingenieurwissenschaften Europas. *Zeitschrift des Interdisziplinären Zentrums für Frauen und Geschlechterforschung, 22*(30), 48–60.

Sakurai, A. (2005). To interpret the interview text. In A. Sakurai, A., & T. Kobayashi T. (Eds.), Life story interview: Introduction to qualitative research (pp. 129–-183). Tokyo: Serica Shobo.

Sallee, M. W. (2011). Performing masculinity: Considering gender in doctoral student socialization. *The Journal of Higher Education, 82*(2), 187–216. doi:10.1353/jhe.2011.0007

Sambandam, R. (2003). Cluster analysis gets complicated. *Marketing Research, 15*(1), 16–21.

Sapp, J. (2010). *IGDA: Regarding overtime concerns at Rockstar San Diego.* Retrieved January 27, 2011 from http://www.igda.org/igda-regarding-overtime-concerns-rockstar-san-diego

Schein, E. (1978). *Career dynamics. Matching individual and organizational needs.* Reading, MA: Addison-Wesley.

Schlossberg, N. K. (2000). *Overwhelmed: Coping with life's ups and downs.* Lanham, MD: Lexington Books.

Schmader, T. (2002). Gender identification moderates stereotype threat effects on women's math performance. *Journal of Experimental Social Psychology, 38,* 194–201. doi:10.1006/jesp.2001.1500

Schott, G., & Horrell, K. (2000). Girl gamers & their relationship with the gaming culture. *Convergence: The International Journal of Research into New Media Technologies, 6*(4), 36–53. doi:10.1177/135485650000600404

Scragg, G., & Smith, J. (1998). A study of barriers to women in undergraduate computer science. *ACM SIGCSE Bulletin, 30*(1), 82–86.

Sector Skills Council for Creative Media. (2012). *2012 creative skillset employment census of the creative media industries* [Data File]. Retrieved August 14, 2013 from http://courses.creativeskillset.org/assets/0000/2819/Census_report_6.pdf

Sekaquaptewa, D., & Thompson, M. (2002). The differential effects of solo status on members of high- and low-status groups. *Personality and Social Psychology Bulletin, 28*(5), 694–707. doi:10.1177/0146167202288013

Sekaquaptewa, D., & Thompson, M. (2003). Solo status, stereotype threat, and performance expectancies: Their effects on women's performance. *Journal of Experimental Social Psychology*, *39*, 68–74. doi:10.1016/S0022-1031(02)00508-5

Serviss, B. (2013, August 8). *Beyond the straight white dude: Why a more diverse game industry benefits all.* Retrieved from http://www.dashjump.com/beyond-straight-white-dude-diversity/

Shaw, A. (2010). What is video game culture?: Cultural studies and game studies. *Games and Culture*, *5*(4), 403–424.

Sheffield, B., & Fleming, J. (2010). Ninth annual game developer salary survey. *Game Developer Magazine*, *17*(4), 7–13.

Sheffield, B., & Newman, R. (2011). Tenth annual game developer salary survey. *Game Developer Magazine*, *18*(4), 7–13.

Sheperd, J. (2012). ICT lessons in schools are 'highly unsatisfactory', says Royal Society. *The Guardian.* Retrieved January 12, 2012, from http://www.guardian.co.uk/education/2012/jan/13/ict-lessons-uk-schools-unsatisfactory

Sherry, J. L., Lucas, K., Greenberg, B. S., & Lachlan, K. (2006). Video game uses and gratifications as predictors of use and game preference. In P. Vorderer, & J. Bryant (Eds.), *Playing video games: Motives, responses, and consequences* (pp. 213–224). Mahwah, NJ: Erlbaum.

Shields, M. A., & Ward, M. (2001). Improving nurse retention in the National Health Service in England: The impact of job satisfaction on intentions to quit. *Journal of Health Economics*, *20*, 677–701. doi:10.1016/S0167-6296(01)00092-3 PMID:11558644

Shintaku, J. (2000). Development of the software market by venture-capital company. In *Economic analysis of the gaming industry: Strategy and structure of the content industry development* (pp. 97–115). Tokyo: Toyo Keizai Shinpo Sha. (In Japanese)

Shore, L. M., Randel, A. E., Chung, B. G., Dean, M. A., Holcombe Erhart, K., & Singh, G. (2011). Inclusion and diversity in work groups: A review and model for future research. *Journal of Management*, *37*(4), 1262–1289. doi:10.1177/0149206310385943

Simard, C., Stephenson, C., & Kosaraju, D. (2010). *Addressing core equity issues in K-12 computer science education: Identifying barriers and sharing strategies.* Retrieved from http://csta.acm.org/Communications/sub/DocsPresentationFiles/ABI-CSTAEquityFinal.pdf

Sinclair, B. (2013, March 27). *Diversity means dollars.* Retrieved from http://www.gamesindustry.biz/articles/2013-03-27-pushing-diversity-to-pull-in-money

Skillset. (2009). *2009 employment census: The results of the seventh census of the Creative Media Industries December 2010.* The Sector Skills Council for Creative Media.

Skillset. (2011). Computer games sector: Labour market intelligence digest. *The Sector Skills Council for Creative Media.* Retrieved from http://www.creativeskillset.org/uploads/pdf/asset_16891.pdf?4

Skillset. (2013). *Skills & training for the games industry.* Retrieved from http://www.creativeskillset.org/games/qualifications/article_2769_1.asp

Smith, P. K. (2013). *The encyclopedia on early childhood development.* Retrieved from http://www.child-encyclopedia.com/pages/PDF/play.pdf

Smithers, R. (2011). *Should we collect vouchers to fund equipment for schools?* The Guardian Mortarboard Blog. Retrieved 19 March, 2014 from http://www.theguardian.com/education/mortarboard/2011/feb/16/should-we-collect-school-vouchers

Solem, M., Lee, J., & Schlemper, B. (2009). Departmental climate and student experiences in graduate geography programs. *Research in Higher Education*, *50*, 268–292. doi:10.1007/s11162-008-9117-4

Spector, P. E. (1985). Measurement of human service staff satisfaction: Development of the job satisfaction survey 1. *American Journal of Community Psychology*, *13*(6), 693–713. doi:10.1007/BF00929796 PMID:4083275

Spouse, E. A. (2004). *EA: The human story.* Retrieved January 27, 2011 from http://ea-spouse.livejournal.com/274.html

Statistics Canada. (2013a). 2011 national household survey: Education in Canada: Attainment, field of and location of study. *The Daily*. Released June 26, 2013. Retrieved from http://www.statcan.gc.ca/daily-quotidien/130626/dq130626a-eng.pdf

Statistics Canada. (2013b). Public postsecondary enrolments and graduates, 2010/2011. *The Daily*. Released January 23, 2013. Retrieved from http://www.statcan.gc.ca/daily-quotidien/130123/dq130123a-eng.pdf

Steele, C. M., & Aronson, J. (1995). Stereotype threat and the intellectual test of African Americans performance. *Journal of Personality and Social Psychology, 69*(5), 797–811. doi:10.1037/0022-3514.69.5.797 PMID:7473032

Steele, J. R., & Ambady, N. (2006). Math is hard! The effect of gender priming on women's attitudes. *Journal of Experimental Social Psychology, 42*, 428–436. doi:10.1016/j.jesp.2005.06.003

Steele, J., James, J. B., & Barnett, R. C. (2002). Learning in a man's world: Examining the perceptions of undergraduate women in male-dominated academic areas. *Psychology of Women Quarterly, 26*, 46–50. doi:10.1111/1471-6402.00042

Stockdale, R., & Stoney, S. (2008). Generating a gender balance: Making introductory information systems courses a positive experience. *Australasian Journal of Information Systems, 15*(1).

Swanson, G., & Wise, P. (1996). *Digital futures: Women's employment in the multimedia industries.* Canberra, Australia: Commonwealth Government of Australia, Department of Employment, Education, Training and Youth Affairs. Retrieved from http://www.workplace.gov.au/NR/rdonlyres/CC7EFA3F-1E9F-4E77-ADC1%201A97C884CADB/0/digitalfutures.PDF

Swanson, J. L., & Woitke, M. B. (1997). Theory into practice in career assessment for women: Assessment and interventions regarding perceived career barriers. *Journal of Career Assessment, 5*, 443–462. doi:10.1177/106907279700500405

Sweetser, P., Wyeth, P., McMahon, N., & Johnson, D. (2013). Female game developers wanted: Low pay, long hours, inflexible work environments. In *Proceedings of the Games Innovation Conference (IGIC), 2013 IEEE International.* doi: 10.1109/IGIC.2013.6659142

Tajfel, H., & Turner, J. C. (1986). The social identity theory of intergroup behaviour. In S. Worchel, & W. G. Austin (Eds.), *Psychology of intergroup relations* (2nd ed., pp. 7–24). Chicago: Nelson-Hall.

Tanaka, T. (2000a). *A demonstration of network externalities between hardware and software. Economic analysis of the gaming industry: Strategy and structure of the content industry development* (pp. 41–94). Tokyo: Toyo Keizai Shinpo Sha. (In Japanese)

Tanaka, T. (2000b). *The background and concentration into big companies. Economic analysis of the gaming industry: Strategy and structure of the content industry development* (pp. 117–143). Tokyo: Toyo Keizai Shinpo Sha. (In Japanese)

Tapia, A., & Kvasny, L. (2004). Recruitment is never enough: Retention of women and minorities in the IT workplace. In *Proceedings of the ACM Conference on Computer Personnel Research: Careers, Culture, and Ethics in a Networked Environment*, Tucson, AZ (pp. 84-91).

Taylor, C. A., Lord, C. G., McIntyre, R. B., & Paulson, R. M. (2011). The Hillary Clinton effect: When the same role model inspires or fails to inspire improved performance under stereotype threat. *Group Processes & Intergroup Relations, 14*(4), 447–459. doi:10.1177/1368430210382680

Taylor, N., Jenson, J., & de Castell, S. (2009). Cheerleaders/booth babes/ Halo hoes: Pro-graming, gender and jobs for the boys. *Digital Creativity, 20*(4), 239–252. doi:10.1080/14626260903290323

Taylor, T. L. (2003). Multiple pleasures: Women and online gaming. *Convergence, 9*(1), 21–46. doi:10.1177/135485650300900103

Terlecki, M. S., & Newcombe, N. S. (2005). How important is the digital divide? The relation of computer and videogame usage to gender differences in mental rotation ability. *Sex Roles, 53*(5-6), 433–441. doi:10.1007/s11199-005-6765-0

Thornham, H. (2008). It's a boy thing. *Feminist Media Studies, 8*, 127–142. doi:10.1080/14680770801980505

Tierney, W., & Rhoads, R. (1993). Enhancing promotion, tenure and beyond: Faculty socialization as a cultural process. ASHE-ERIC Higher Education Report, 93(6). Washington, DC.: The George Washington University.

Tillberg, H. K., & Cohoon, J. M. (2005). Attracting women to the CS major. *Frontiers: A Journal of Women Studies, 26*(1), 126-140.

Tong, S. (2008). *Women in the game industry.* Retrieved September 23, 2010 from http://www.gamespot.com/news/6197045.html?tag=result,title,0

Trauth, E. M., Quesenberry, J., & Huang, H. (2009). Retaining women in the U.S. IT workforce: Theorizing the influence of organizational factors. *European Journal of Information Systems, 18*(5), 476-497. doi: http://dx.doi.org/10.1057/ejis.2009.31

Trauth, E. M., Quesenberry, J., & Yeo, B. (2005). The influence of environmental context on women in the IT workforce. In *Proceedings of the 2005 ACM SIGMIS CPR Conference on Computer Personnel Research* (pp. 24 – 31). Atlanta, GA: ACM Press.

Trauth, E.M. (2012). Are there enough seats for women at the IT table?. *ACM Inroads, 3*(4).

Trauth, E. M. (2002). Odd girl out: An individual differences perspective on women in the IT profession. *Information Technology & People, 15*(2), 98–118. doi:10.1108/09593840210430552

Trauth, E. M., Quesenberry, J. L., & Huang, H. (2008). A multicultural analysis of factors influencing career choice for women in the information technology workforce. *Journal of Global Information Management, 16*(4), 1–23. doi:10.4018/jgim.2008100101

Traylor, S. (2013). *Tween virtual worlds by the numbers.* 360Blog. Retrieved December 9, 2013, from http://www.360kid.com/blog/2013/08/

Traylor, S. (2012, November). Inside the World of Webkinz: An interview with creative director Karl Borst. *Children's. Technology Review,* 6–8.

Tsui, L. (2009). Recruiting females into male dominated programs: Effective strategies and approaches. *Journal of College Admission, 203,* 8–13.

Turner, S. V., Bernt, P. W., & Pecora, N. (2002). Why women choose information technology careers: Educational, social and familial influences. In *Proceedings of the Annual Meeting of the American Educational Research Association,* New Orleans, LA.

Turner, T. (2003). Multimedia is much more fun but I still don't want to do IT. In *Proceedings of the 2003 Australian Women in IT Conference.* Retrieved September 19, 2006 from http://www.auswit.org/2003/papers/3-2_Turner.pdf

Turner, J. C., Hogg, M. A., Oakes, P. J., Reicher, P. J., & Wetherall, M. S. (1987). *Rediscovering the social group: A self-categorization.* Oxford, UK: Blackwell.

UCAS Communications and Public Affairs. (2013). *2013 cycle applicant figures – June deadline* [Report]. UCAS Communications and Public Affairs.

UKRC. (2008). *Women's underrepresentation in SET in the UK: Key facts.* UK Resource Centre for Women in Science, Engineering and Technology. Retrieved January 2, 2008, from http://www.theukrc.org/resources/key-facts-and-figures/underrepresentation

UNESCO. (2005). *Towards knowledge societies: UNESCO world report.* United Nations Educational, Scientific and Cultural Organization. Retrieved February 1, 2012, from. http://unesdoc.unesco.org/images/0014/001418/141843e.pdf

United Kingdom Resource Center (UKRC). (2010). *Social return on investment.* Retrieved from http://www.theukrc.org/files/useruploads/files/ukrc_sroi_assured_report_apr_2010.pdf

United Kingdom Resource Centre (UKRC). (2012). *Engaging girls in science, technology, engineering, and maths: What works?* Retrieved from http://www.theukrc.org/files/useruploads/files/resources/wise_report_july_2012_bae_systems_what_works_summary.pdf

United Nations. (1989). *Convention on the rights of the child.* Retrieved from https://treaties.un.org/doc/Publication/UNTS/Volume%201577/v1577.pdf

Valenduc, G., et al. (2004). *Widening women's work in information and communication technology, European Commission.* Retrieved from http://www.ftu-namur.org/fichiers/D12-print.pdf

Valenduc, G., Vendramin, P., Guffens, C., Ponzellini, A., Lebano, A., & D'ouville, L. et al. (2004). *Widening women's work in information and communication technology.* Namur, Belgium: European Commission.

Van Looy, J., Courtois, C., & Vermeulen, L. (2010). *Why girls play video games: A gender-comparative study into the motivations for and attitudes towards playing video games*. Paper presented at the Future Reality of Gaming (FROG) conference, Vienna.

Vancouver Film School (VFS). (2010). *The game industry now & in the future 2010: Industry facts, trends & outlook*. Vancouver Film School.

Vegso, J. (2005, May). Interest in CS as a major drops among incoming freshman. Computing Research News, 17(3).

Wai, J., Lubinski, D., Benbow, C. P., & Steiger, J. H. (2010). Accomplishment in science, technology, engineering, and mathematics (STEM) and its relation to STEM educational dose: A 25-year longitudinal study. *Journal of Educational Psychology, 102*, 860–871. doi:10.1037/a0019454

Wajcman, J. (1994). *Technik und Geschlecht. Die feministische Technikdebatte*. Frankfurt, Germany: Campus Verlag.

Wajcman, J. (2000). Reflections on gender and technology studies: In what state is the art? *Social Studies of Science, 30*(3), 447–464. doi:10.1177/030631200030003005

Walkerdine, V. (2007). *Children, gender, video games: Toward a relational approach to multimedia*. New York: Palgrave Macmillan. doi:10.1057/9780230235373

Wallop, H. (2009, Dec. 26). Video games bigger than film. *The Daily Telegraph*. [Online.] Retrieved January 4, 2009 from http://www.telegraph.co.uk/technology/video-games/6852383/Video-games-bigger-than-film.html

Wang, C. Q., Tang, C., Zhang, L., & Cukierman, D. (2012). Try/CATCH - a CS outreach event organized by female university students for female high school students: a positive experience for all the parts involved. In *Proceedings from WCCCE '12: The Seventeenth Western Canadian Conference on Computing Education*. Vancouver, BC, Canada: ACM.

Webb, P., & Young, J. (2005). Perhaps it's time for a fresh approach to ICT gender research? *Journal of Research and Practice in Information Technology, 37*(2), 147–160.

Webkinz. (2013). *Frequently asked questions: For parents*. Retrieved December 9, 2013, from http://www.webkinz.com/faq/j.html#6

Weidman, J., Twale, D., & Stein, E. (2001). Socialization of graduate and professional students in higher education: A perilous passage? ASHE-ERIC Higher Education Report 28(3). San Francisco: Jossey-Bass.

WGBH Educational Foundation. (2010). *Dot diva*. Retrieved from http://www.dotdiva.org/

White, J. B. (2008). Fail or flourish? Cognitive appraisal moderates the effect of solo status on performance. *Personality and Social Psychology Bulletin, 34*(9), 1171–1184. doi:10.1177/0146167208318404 PMID:18678859

Wigal, C. M., Alp, N., McCullough, C., Smullen, S., & Winters, K. (2002). ACES: Introducing girls to and building interest in engineering and computer science careers. In *Proceedings from 32nd ASEFJ/IEEE Frontiers in Education Conference*. Boston, MA: IEEE.

Willemson, T. M. (2002). Gender typing of the successful manager - A stereotype reconsidered. *Sex Roles, 46*, 385–391.

Williams, D., Consalvo, M., Caplan, S., & Yee, N. (2009). Looking for gender: Gender roles and behaviors among online gamers. *The Journal of Communication, 59*(4), 700–725. doi:10.1111/j.1460-2466.2009.01453.x

Williams, S., & Cooper, C. L. (1998). Measuring occupational stress: Development of the pressure management indicator. *Journal of Occupational Health Psychology, 3*(4), 306–321. doi:10.1037/1076-8998.3.4.306 PMID:9805279

Winn, J., & Heeter, C. (2009). Gaming, gender, and time: Who makes time to play? *Sex Roles, 61*, 1–13. doi:10.1007/s11199-009-9595-7

Wirth, W., Matthes, J., Mögerle, U., & Prommer, E. (2005). Traumberuf oder Verlegenheits-lösung? Einstiegsmotivation und Arbeitssituation des wissenschaftlichen Nachwuchses in Kommuni-kationswissenschaft und Medienwissenschaft. *Publizistik, 50*(3), 320–343. doi:10.1007/s11616-005-0135-3

Wohlwend, K. E., Vander Zanden, S., Husbye, N. E., & Kuby, C. R. (2011). Navigating discourses in place in the World of Webkinz. *Journal of Early Childhood Literacy*, *11*(2), 141–163. doi:10.1177/1468798411401862

Women in Games Jobs Network. (2013). *About women in games jobs*. Retrieved from http://www.womeningames-jobs.com/?page_id=2

Woodman, R., Sawyer, J., & Griffin, R. (1993). Toward a theory of organizational creativity. *Academy of Management Review*, *18*(2), 293–321.

Yee, N. (2006). Motivations for play in online games. *Cyberpsychology & Behavior*, *9*(6), 772–775. doi:10.1089/cpb.2006.9.772 PMID:17201605

Yee, N. (2008). Maps of digital desires: Exploring the topography of gender and play in online games. In Y. Kafai, C. Heeter, J. Denner, & J. Sun (Eds.), *Beyond Barbie and Mortal Kombat: New perspectives on gender and gaming* (pp. 82–96). Cambridge, MA: MIT Press.

Yin, R. K. (2003). *Case study research. Design and methods*. Thousand Oaks, CA: Sage Publication.

Yoder, J. D. (1994). Looking beyond numbers: The effects of gender status, job prestige, and occupational gender-typing on tokenism processes. *Social Psychology Quarterly*, *57*(2), 150–159. doi:10.2307/2786708

Yonekura, S., & Ikuine, F. (2005). Japanese game software industry: Trap of series strategy. *Hitotsubashi Business Review*, *53*(3), 52–69.

Zywno, M. S., Gilbride, K. A., & Gudz, N. (2000). Innovative outreach programs to attract and retain women in undergraduate engineering programs. Global Journal of Engineering Education, 4(3), 293–302.

About the Contributors

Julie Prescott (CPsychol, PhD, MA, BSc, AFHEA) is a Lecturer in Psychology at The University of Bolton, UK. Julie has a research career spanning over ten years in academic and public sector environments. Julie's background is in psychology and women's studies; she has a particular interest in women's careers, especially in terms of barriers and drivers, occupational segregation, and the experiences of women working in male dominated occupations/industries, in particular the computer games industry. Julie has co-authored two books published by IGI Global 'Gendered Occupational Differences in Science, Engineering, and Technology Careers' and 'Gender Divide and the Computer Gaming Industry'.

Julie Elizabeth McGurren (BA, MSc) has worked in the UK games industry since 1999 where following studying a Masters in Computer Graphics at Teesside University she joined the Liverpool based games company Bizarre Creations. After working as an artist on Metropolis Street Racer and PGR1/2 she moved in an art management role on PGR3 and continued to work in this position on PGR4 and BLUR. These games have sold millions of copies across the globe and are rated highly amongst critics and gamers alike. After Bizarre closed in 2011 she moved to Codemasters and has worked as an Art Producer on DIRT Showdown and GRID2, the sequel to the critically acclaimed and BAFTA awarding winning GRID. She continues to work at Codemasters as an Art Producer on an unannounced title.

* * *

Jan Bogg (BA, M.Sc, Ph.D, C. Psych, FHEA) is a senior lecturer in the Faculty of Health and Life Sciences, at the University of Liverpool, UK. Her Breaking Barriers research addresses career progression, barriers and drivers for women in science and equity and diversity issues in the workplace. Jan is an organizational psychologist, her research focuses on workforce issues, leadership and gender in the workplace; she is a member of the United Kingdom Athena Swan Steering Committee, The Athena SWAN Charter (http://www.athenaswan.org.uk) recognises commitment to advancing women's careers in science, technology, engineering, maths and medicine (STEMM).

Adrienne Decker, PhD is an assistant professor at Rochester Institute of Technology's School of Interactive Games and Media and a member of the RIT Laboratory for Media, Arts, Games, Interaction and Creativity (MAGIC). Her research interests involve using games and other motivating examples for teaching computing concepts as well as development of better tools and methodologies for teaching computing in the first year of university education. She is also interested in efforts to broaden participation in computing, gaming, and other related disciplines. Her work has led to a focus on development and assessment of interventions in the educational process. Most recently, she has begun explorations in the area of development and assessment of educational and learning games.

Jill Denner is Senior Research Scientist at ETR (Education, Training, Research), a non-profit organization in California. She does applied research, with a focus on increasing the number of women and Latino/a students in computer science and information technology. Her current focus is on how middle school students learn while creating computer games, the role of peers and families in children's educational pathways, and increasing diversity in community college computer science classes. Dr. Denner has been a Principal Investigator (PI) on several NSF grants, published numerous peer-reviewed articles, and co-edited two books: Beyond Barbie and Mortal Kombat: New Perspectives on Gender and Gaming, published by MIT Press in 2008, and Latina Girls: Voices of Adolescent Strength in the U.S., published by NYU Press in 2006. Dr. Denner has a PhD in Developmental Psychology from Teachers College, Columbia University.

Aziz Douai (Ph.D. in Mass Communications, Pennsylvania State University) is an Assistant Professor of Communication at the University of Ontario Institute of Technology, Canada. His research focuses on new media and activism, Arab media and democracy, global media and international conflict, among other areas of international communications. He is the co-editor of *New media influence on social and political change in Africa* (IGI-Global, 2013), and the Managing Editor of the *American Communication Journal*. In addition to contributing to several books, Dr. Douai's other publications have appeared in the *Journal of International Communication, Global Media Journal, First Monday, Journal of Arab & Muslim Media Research, Arab Reform Bulletin, International Communication Research Journal, The Westminster Papers in Communication and Culture*, and *Journal of Computer Mediated Communication*.

Lauren Elliott is a third year undergraduate student at the University of Bolton, studying psychology with a keen interest in Cyberpsychology, in particular online gaming. She is due to graduate in July 2014 and hopes to eventually pursue a career in research as well as obtaining her masters and PhD.

Masahito Fujihara is a Lecturer in School of Network and Information at Senshu University, and a Visiting Researcher in Interfaculty Initiative in Information Studies at the University of Tokyo. His research interests and publications are in the areas of career development of Japanese game developers.

Anitza Geneve (PhD, MPC, BA, AssocDegAppSc, GradDipAdultVocEd.) is Head of Department in the School of Digital Design and IT, at the Southbank Institute of Technology, Brisbane, Australia. Anitza has worked in the digital content industry as a developer and industry trainer. She has over 15 years' experience teaching digital media-related content at vocational and university level in both Australia and the UK. Her research interest lies in the participation of minority groups in the digital content industry workforce in Australia. She actively promotes the digital content industry as a career option for women.

Edeltraud Hanappi-Egger is from her educational background a computer scientist and an experienced researcher and head of interdisciplinary teams. Since 2002 she is full professor for "gender and diversity in organizations" at WU. She was at various national and international research institutions guest researcher (e.g. 2011 at LSE) and her work was awarded several times. Prof. Hanappi-Egger is an expert on organization studies and gender topics, and as such she is in great demand as reviewer in international conferences and journals as well as a member of national and international advisory boards and juries. Her research focus is on management myths, feminist economics, gender and diversity management in organizations. Edeltraud Hanappi-Egger has published more than 250 articles, books and book chapters on gender and diversity, organization studies and diversity management.

Alyson E. King, Ph.D., is an Assistant Professor in the Faculty of Social Science & Humanities at the University of Ontario Institute of Technology (UOIT). She conducts interdisciplinary research in multiliteracies, higher education, and gender history. Recent research and publications include: graphic novels and multiliteracies, autoethnographic narratives by university students, literacies and the knowledge economy, literacies and mental health issues, women and higher education, and oral history interviews about the founding of UOIT. She teaches in the Community Development and Policy Studies program.

Monica M. McGill is an Assistant Professor at Bradley University in the Department of Interactive Media, where she serves as the Game Design Lead. She holds a B.S. in computer science and mathematics, an M.S. in computer science, and an Ed.D. in Curriculum and Instruction. Her research includes serious games, with a particular interest in games for health and motivational design. Additional research areas include diversity in the game industry, skills required by the game industry, and educational research in computer science. She facilitates the design and development of games by integrated teams of undergraduate students and is the producer for two upcoming serious games, one for Type II Diabetic patients and the other for wastewater treatment.

Eloy Ortiz has been a Research Associate at Education, Training, Research (ETR) since 2006, where he plans, develops, and coordinates evaluation and data collection activities in a variety of settings. Mr. Ortiz has served as the research coordinator for three National Science Foundation funded projects focused on improving female and minority middle school students' interest in computer science and STEM coursework focusing on Latino populations. Mr. Ortiz holds a Bachelor of Arts in Psychology from the University of California at Santa Cruz and a Masters of Urban and Regional Planning from the University of California at Irvine. His previous professional experience includes positions working in education, public health and community-focused nonprofit organizations.

Vachon Pugh, M.S. is a Development Manager for the Madden gameplay team at Electronic Arts, Tiburon in Orlando, FL. Vachon received her BS in Game Software Development from Westwood College, and also holds a Master's Degree in Game Design and Production from Full Sail University. Her master's thesis focused on methods to increase the number of women in the game industry, a topic which she still continues to research. She also is an active member of the Diversity and Inclusion Guild for Electronic Arts, and participates in lectures surrounding increasing the diversity of the game industry.

Amber Settle is a Vincent de Paul Associate Professor in the School of Computing at DePaul University and has been on the full-time faculty since September 1996. She earned a B.S. in mathematics and a B.A. in German from the University of Arizona, and a M.S. and Ph.D. in computer science from the University of Chicago. Her research interests include information technology and computer science education and theoretical computer science. She has served on the Advisory Board for the ACM Special Interest Group for Computer Science Education (SIGCSE) since 2010. Recently Dr. Settle has been involved in the organization of the Conference on Innovation and Technology in Computer Science Education (ITiCSE) and the Conference on Information Technology Education (SIGITE). She is a member of the Editorial Advisory Board for ACM Inroads.

Gloria Warmuth is research associate and doctoral candidate at the Department of Management, Gender and Diversity Management Group, Vienna University of Economics and Business (WU). Gloria Warmuth studied Business Administration at the Vienna University of Economics and Business and the Copenhagen Business School (CBS). In addition she holds a master's degree in Mediation and Conflict Resolution. The main focus of her research is diversity in organizations, gendered organizations and gender and diversity in SET (science, engineering and technology) field and research. Moreover, she lectures on basic topics of gender and diversity and strategic diversity management.

Linda Werner (PhD) is an Adjunct Professor and Lecturer of Computer Science at the Jack Baskin School of Engineering at the University of California, Santa Cruz. Dr. Werner has extensive experience as an educator and researcher in both K-12 and higher education. She has published research on effective pair programming practices to aide in the retention of female students and on computational thinking. Dr. Werner's research areas include software engineering, computer science education, children and computer game creation, testing, increasing diversity in the computer science field, and social issues. Dr. Werner is affiliated with the UCSC Center for Games and Playable Media and with the Center for Information Technology in the Interest of Society.

Index

A

Acts of Agency Theory 125, 127-128, 138, 142, 227
Agent-Driven Mechanisms 125, 127-130, 132, 135, 137-138, 142
Australian Digital Content Industry (DCI) 125, 142

B

Broadening Participation 192-194, 205

C

Career Aspirations 46-47, 162, 206-208, 210, 212, 215-217, 222, 238
Career Development 110-113, 115, 119-120, 124, 206-211, 216-217, 222, 227, 238
Career Transition 113, 118, 124
Children 2-3, 5-6, 8-12, 16-17, 20, 37, 40-42, 46, 48, 87-88, 94-95, 103-104, 113, 115, 117-119, 130, 135, 181, 199, 211, 216, 223, 225-228, 231-233, 241
Community College 22, 29, 35
Computer Games 1-4, 6, 8, 11-12, 16, 19, 21-23, 29, 35-37, 39-41, 44, 55, 92-95, 97-99, 103-105, 126, 132, 189, 191, 206-207, 211, 216-218, 223-227, 229, 232, 237-238, 240-243
Computer Science 18-19, 21-24, 30-32, 35, 40-41, 48, 83, 136, 164, 190, 192, 194-195, 205, 224-225, 238, 245, 247
Creativity 8, 11, 20, 30, 111, 118, 124, 132-134, 156-158, 168-170, 174, 227, 248
Critical Realism 127, 142
Crunch Time 37, 87, 91, 94, 104, 115, 194

D

Diverse 37, 39-40, 55, 83, 94, 110-111, 120, 126, 157, 162, 169, 178-179, 186-187, 189, 191, 194-196, 199, 205, 207, 216, 218, 232-233, 235, 242
Diversity 31, 48, 83, 93, 99, 111, 124, 156-157, 160-161, 163, 168-169, 186-194, 196, 199, 207, 225, 227, 232, 236, 240, 247

E

Education 23, 36-41, 55, 113, 117-118, 125, 128, 134, 136, 156-157, 160, 162, 176, 181, 187, 190, 192, 195, 224-225, 233, 237-238, 246-248, 251, 253-254
Educational Goals 18-19, 22, 24, 35
Exclusion 156-158, 161-162, 168, 174

F

Family Friendly Practices (FFP) 91, 185
Feminism 3-4, 17
Flexible Working 36-37, 87, 93-94, 104, 109, 169, 207, 238, 240

G

Game Degree Programs 188, 190, 205
Game Developers 4, 87, 97, 105, 110-120, 124, 126, 186, 226-227, 235, 242
Gendered Occupational Segregation 37, 41, 55, 93, 105, 109, 206, 218, 223, 241
Generativity 120, 124

H

Human Agency 127, 142

I

Innovation 30, 126, 156-158, 168-170, 174, 227

J

Job Satisfaction 131, 206, 208-209, 212, 215-216, 222

L

Life Story 113, 124
Long Hours 36-37, 45-46, 48, 55, 87-88, 94, 103-105, 109, 134, 207, 225-226

M

Male Dominated 20, 36-38, 44, 48, 55, 82, 87, 92-94, 97, 99, 101, 103, 105, 131, 175, 177-178, 222, 224-226, 233, 237-238
Mechanisms 125, 127-130, 132, 134-135, 137-138, 142, 161, 169
Mentor 110, 117, 185
Mentorship 129, 175, 180-181, 183, 185
Motivation 19-24, 26-30, 32, 35, 40, 160

O

Occupational Self-Efficacy 212, 215, 222
Outreach 175, 178-180, 183, 186-187, 190-197, 199, 205, 227, 253

P

Person-Environment Fit 206, 208, 212, 215-216, 222
Professional scripts 156, 159-160, 163, 165, 168-169, 174
Professional socialization 156-157, 159-162, 164-165, 168-169, 174

R

Recruitment 23, 37, 41, 55, 175-176, 178-181, 183, 194-195, 205, 228, 230, 242, 248
Role Model 38, 124, 230, 232, 249

S

Social Games 120, 181-183, 185
STEM 7, 37, 41, 55, 83, 86-88, 91, 93, 156-160, 168-170, 174-177, 179-183, 185, 187, 189-194, 196, 199, 205, 223-224, 226-227, 232, 236, 238, 240, 242, 249, 251
Stereotypes 1-3, 5, 7, 10, 12, 17, 37-39, 41, 95, 119, 127, 224-226
Stereotype Threat 38-39

W

Work and Family 86, 91, 117, 185
Work Life Balance 48, 92, 103, 105, 109, 226-228, 231